THE ARNOLD HISTORY OF EUROPE

The Arnold History of Europe

This new series explores European history, from the last years of the Roman Empire to the end of the twentieth century. Each volume tackles a broad sweep of history, not invariably sticking to conventional periodizations, and asks bold questions of its material. The series aims to make sense of periods and eras, across countries and cultures, but without trying to homogenize everything.

Published volumes include:

The Transformation of Europe 1300–1600
by David Nicholas

Europe 1600–1789
by Anthony F. Upton

Volumes covering the following periods are in preparation:

1789–2000
by James F. McMillan

1000–1300
by Eddie Coleman

300–1000
by Guy Halsall

EUROPE 1600–1789

ANTHONY F. UPTON

Emeritus Professor of Modern History,
University of St Andrews

A member of the Hodder Headline Group
LONDON

Distributed in the United States of America by
Oxford University Press Inc., New York

First published in Great Britain in 2001 by
Arnold, a member of the Hodder Headline Group,
338 Euston Road, London NW1 3BH

http://www.arnoldpublishers.com

Distributed in the United States of America by
Oxford University Press Inc.,
198 Madison Avenue, New York, NY10016

British Library Cataloguing in Publication Data
A catalogue record for this book is available from the British Library

Library of Congress Cataloging-in-Publication Data
A catalog record for this book is available from the Library of Congress

ISBN 0 340 66337 5 (hb)
ISBN 0 340 66338 3 (pb)

2 3 4 5 6 7 8 9 10

Typeset in 10/12 Sabon by Saxon Graphics Ltd, Derby
Printed in India by Replika Press Pvt. Ltd.

What do you think about this book? Or any other Arnold title?
Please send your comments to feedback.arnold@hodder.co.uk

Contents

Maps

Preface

This book is a general history of Europe, which essentially offers the reader a narrative. The author is convinced that narrative should be the basic form of history writing, and should tell a story. This book attempts to show how the Europe of 1600 developed into the Europe of 1789, and suggests ways of understanding why it developed as it did. The scope of the narrative has to be partial and selective. It is inherent in the study of history that the final truth about what happened in past time cannot be recovered: too much evidence is lost. On the other hand, the labours of historians constantly uncover new evidence, or suggest new ways of looking at existing interpretations, which is what makes historical study a dynamic and rewarding pursuit. The publishers, quite rightly, have set a maximum length for the book. Because of this it is not possible for the narrative to cover all the relevant episodes within its chronological span, except by reducing the account to a level of superficiality that would deny it a claim to serious attention. Some drastic exclusions have had to be made. It was decided not to include the domestic history of the Ottoman empire, even though substantial numbers of Europeans were subjects or servants of the Sultan. It was also decided that although the American Revolution had a far-reaching impact on European developments it was not possible to include an account of it. Among other casualties of exclusion are the often interesting histories of some of Europe's smaller entities that can legitimately be regarded as marginal to the main narrative. One obvious casualty is the Venetian republic, still a significant commercial and imperial power in 1600 which then developed into a playground for the entertainment of Europe's nobilities during the eighteenth century.

The basic concept behind this narrative is that Europe in 1600 had been seriously destabilized by a series of events that had shaken centuries' old certainties. There had been marked economic development, driven by demographic expansion and fuelled in part by wealth brought back from the Americas, which had enriched some, but also combined inflation with falling real earnings, and the disruption of traditional trades and manufactures. Parallel with this there had been major culture shocks, whose impact was enormously increased by the revolutionary introduction of printing. The Renaissance had recovered access to aspects of classical civilization which had, for example, undermined the acceptance of Aristotle as the supreme thinker of the ancient world, and disrupted an education system built on this assumption. The geographical discoveries themselves had demonstrated in concrete fashion that the material world was not as people had imagined it to be, and held out promise of further new discoveries to come. But most destabilizing of all had been the Protestant Reformation that had shattered the religious unity of European society. It had created a religious pluralism which was almost universally unacceptable, since the existence of religious uniformity was the force that had bound all Europe's communities together and guaranteed their common identity as members of Christendom.

The story line of the book is how the Europeans of 1600, alarmed and disoriented by the unprecedented developments of the previous 150 years, set about rebuilding stability and certainty in their society. After a last desperate attempt to recover religious unity by force had failed, and the peace settlements of Westphalia in 1648 formally accepted that religious pluralism was irreversible, Europe's ruling elites increasingly looked for security to the development of the modern secular state, in which a strong central government, sustained by a professional bureaucracy and a standing military establishment could provide the security which the churches could no longer guarantee. By 1789 there was much evidence of how the evolving European state system had created new levels of internal order and strengthened the grip of the ruling elites, most of them noble landlords, over all aspects of society. They had also provided the political and military resources that had enabled Europeans to assert their hegemony worldwide and were steadily enlarging the boundaries of direct European control, by incorporating Russia and its expanding empire into the European community, and pushing the Ottoman empire back from the Black Sea and the borders of Austria into Asia Minor and the southern Balkans.

But behind the facade of growing political security, major disruptive forces were apparent and the narrative draws attention to these. First, around 1740, the long demographic and economic stagnation began to dissolve, and Europe entered the phase of material expansion that has continued ever since. Central to this process was the rise of the capitalist market economy, with Great Britain in the lead. By 1789 the British economy was so powerful that it could shrug off the loss of the American colonies and continue its advance towards world hegemony regardless – the industrial revolution was under way and the world would be changed for ever. The second was a negative force arising from a failure of European civilization to develop. It had from its early origins always been a predatory, militarist culture whose ruling class, the landed nobilities, rested their claim to superiority on their role as warriors. The governments of the emerging European states had the maximizing of their military potential as their first priority; and they were, as they had always been, militarist states locked into an unending and destructive power game. When Europeans were not asserting their military capacity on outsiders, like the Ottomans, they turned it against their neighbours. It was still as true in 1789 as it had always been that intermittent, internecine warfare was the norm in European society, and the rare periods of prolonged peace were breathing spaces in which the participants prepared for the next round of conflict. Finally, the Reformation had done more than disrupt religious uniformity, it had paralysed the systems of thought control that had required all intellectual activity to be consistent with religious orthodoxy. In the seventeenth century the scientific movement had broken free and asserted the right of the scientist to follow the evidence wherever it led, regardless of whether it was consistent with the Word of God in Scripture. In the eighteenth century the Enlightenment thinkers were laying the foundations for the uninhibited materialism and utilitarianism that is the basis of our contemporary civilization. In the face of these forces of change, the apparent stability of the old order in Europe in 1789 proved to be an illusion.

It is usual to end a preface with acknowledgements to those who have contributed to the work. In this case it would be invidious to single out individuals. The book arises from more than 40 years of interaction by the author with academic colleagues, librarians and archivists, and not least successive generations of undergraduate students of history. They all deserve thanks for their contributions, though of course the end result is wholly the responsibility of the author.

I

THE END OF AN ERA

1

The European World of the Seventeenth Century

The study of history is based on a contradiction or paradox. The past can only be understood at all because over time basic human nature does not change. The men and women of 1600 were not essentially different from ourselves in their basic needs and desires, so that we can intuitively understand what drives their behaviour at one level. On the other hand, their lives were totally different from ours because of the very different physical and mental environments in which they lived. That is the significance of the terminal date for this volume, although it is obviously artificial to make one specific year the date when one era ended and a new one began. But the convulsions that swept Europe in consequence of the French Revolution created a deep discontinuity with a traditional way of life that had prevailed with little basic structural change through the medieval period. It is necessary to set the scene by giving some account of the physical and mental parameters that controlled the lives of early modern Europeans if the reader is to be able to make sense of what they did.

In a geographical sense the Europe of 1600 had much the same contours as it has today, but it can be divided into three zones which in important respects had been developing along different lines. The old hegemonic core of Europe had been developed in the Mediterranean area, roughly corresponding with the European part of the Roman empire. Its most advanced area, the leader in culture, trade and industry, had been Italy. But during the sixteenth century it was apparent that the lead was moving, away from a declining Mediterranean basin, north and west towards the Atlantic coast. This process can be illustrated by the Portuguese opening of the sea route to India and the Orient, which diverted this lucrative, external trade from Mediterranean ports like Venice to first Lisbon, then Antwerp, and then around 1600 to Amsterdam. The effect had been compounded by a second consequence of expanded oceanic enterprise, the European discovery of the Americas. The characteristic feature of this development was that, unlike the Orient, where there were powerful empires at levels of development

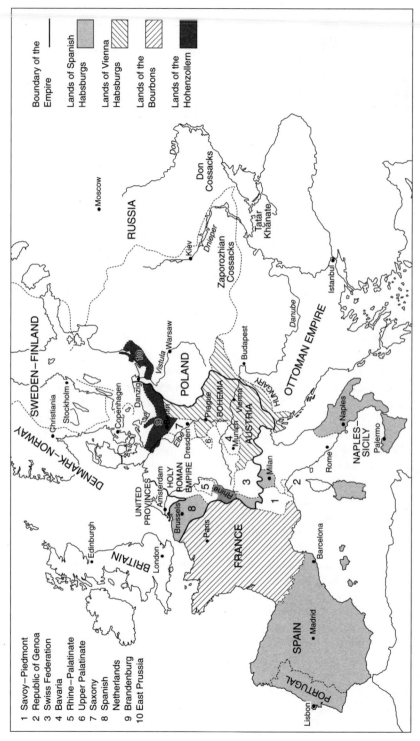

Legend:
- Boundary of the Empire
- Lands of Spanish Habsburgs
- Lands of Vienna Habsburgs
- Lands of the Bourbons
- Lands of the Hohenzollern

1 Savoy–Piedmont
2 Republic of Genoa
3 Swiss Federation
4 Bavaria
5 Rhine–Palatinate
6 Upper Palatinate
7 Saxony
8 Spanish Netherlands
9 Brandenburg
10 East Prussia

Map 1.1 Europe in 1600

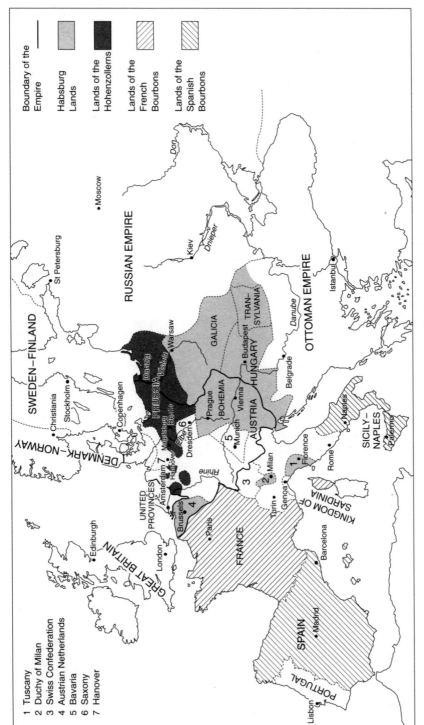

Boundary of the Empire

Habsburg Lands

Lands of the Hohenzollerns

Lands of the French Bourbons

Lands of the Spanish Bourbons

1 Tuscany
2 Duchy of Milan
3 Swiss Confederation
4 Austrian Netherlands
5 Bavaria
6 Saxony
7 Hanover

GREAT BRITAIN

Edinburgh

London

DENMARK–NORWAY

SWEDEN–FINLAND

Christiania

Stockholm

Copenhagen

St Petersburg

RUSSIAN EMPIRE

Moscow

Kiev

Dnieper

Don

UNITED PROVINCES

Amsterdam

Brussels

Hanover

Magdeburg

PRUSSIA

Berlin

Elbe

Dresden

Danzig

Vistula

Warsaw

Paris

FRANCE

Rhine

Munich

Prague

BOHEMIA

Vienna

AUSTRIA

Budapest

HUNGARY

GALICIA

TRAN-SYLVANIA

Danube

Belgrade

OTTOMAN EMPIRE

Istanbul

Turin

Genoa

Milan

Florence

Rome

Naples

KINGDOM OF SARDINIA

SICILY–NAPLES

Palermo

SPAIN

Madrid

Barcelona

PORTUGAL

Lisbon

Map 1.2 Europe in 1795

comparable with Europe, with whom it was possible to make commercial treaties to regulate the trade, there were no such potential trading partners in the Americas. If the Europeans wanted to develop and exploit the resources of America, they would have to, and did, establish colonies of settlement. The kingdom of Castile, whose ruler had patronized the original voyages of Columbus, claimed the exclusive right to develop these new lands, and sought to monopolize all trade with them through the port of Seville. In 1600 this monopoly was still substantially intact, protected by the power of the Spanish monarchy which was the dominant power of western and Mediterranean Europe in 1600. The main impact on the European world had been the discovery of vast reserves of silver in Mexico and Peru. The steadily rising shipment of the silver to Europe in the annual silver fleets was the basis for Spanish political dominance, and one major component of the price inflation that had occurred throughout Europe in the sixteenth century. Thus, through necessity rather than design, Europe by 1600 had established an overseas, colonial extension which in turn reinforced the significance of its western seaboard.

The third zone lay to the east. It was oriented on the Baltic Sea and comprised the Scandinavian kingdoms of Denmark and Sweden, the great medieval Polish kingdom, and beyond that the realm of the tsar, or grand prince of Moscow. This was, and had long been, in commercial contact with the European heartland, but pursued its own political agenda, largely independent of the rest of Europe. However, in the case of Muscovy, there was the barrier of religious difference. Moscow was now the last independent polity professing the Orthodox version of Christianity. Rulers and people had formed their identity round the concept of Moscow as the Third Rome, the divinely appointed guardian of the true faith. There was a cultural iron curtain that separated Muscovy from all the rest of Europe. In the sixteenth century Muscovy was pursuing its own expansionist policies, pushing its southern borders south-east into the steppe country and down the Volga towards the Caspian Sea, and was beginning the eastward drive into Siberia, which by 1652 brought Russian pioneers to the Pacific coast. Finally, on its south-eastern boundaries, Europe came up against another impenetrable cultural and political boundary in the Ottoman empire. Here Europe's boundaries had contracted, since the Ottomans had completed their conquest of the Balkans and most of Hungary by the 1520s. The Christian populations of this region, mostly Orthodox, though largely left in place by the Ottomans as a tolerated alien community, had been lost to European culture. By 1600 the border with the Ottomans had been stabilized, but constituted an uneasy frontier zone, attractive to adventurers, oppressed peasants and bandits, who were both a menace, but also a protective cordon for the settled communities. The border zone, between the limits of Polish and Muscovite settlement and the Black Sea, had on the one side the Tartar khans of the Crimea, nominally Ottoman subjects, who combined trading with raiding for slaves and booty, and outlaw communities of Cossacks, who sometimes fought them, and occasionally joined them, in marauding expeditions. Here the borders of Europe petered out in the arid wilderness.

Once historians move from geography to the human society that lived in Europe they have to ask questions that cannot be answered with any certainty, for reliable data is hard to come by. There are two problems: that the facts are often beyond recovery, and that they tend to be locally based. As will be stressed throughout this study, early modern Europe was highly decentralized, making it dangerous to build general assertions on the back of incomplete evidence. Modern demographic historians can do wonders with the evidence, using sophisticated projections, or reconstitutions of populations, but the results have to be provisional.[1] Very broadly, the impression is that after an undoubted surge in European population during the sixteenth century, levels stabilized or even fell towards mid-century, and were showing some modest recovery at its end. Suggested totals give the population in 1600 as 80 million, falling to 74 million in 1650, and rising back to 83 million by 1700. But the shifts were unevenly spread. Scandinavia, England and the Netherlands were increasing throughout, and ended up with a population increase over the century of about 25 per cent. France and the Mediterranean area ended with a stable population after a mid-century decline, except that the population of Spain fell about 16 per cent. In Germany the Thirty Years War left the population reduced by about a third, and by 1700 it was still some 12 per cent below the 1600 level.

It is at least agreed that overall the population increase came to an end and was recovering rather slowly by the end of the century. There is no such agreement about what the mechanisms of change were. Historians have identified preventive checks: for example, that communities were able to limit population growth to available resources by shifting the age of marriage. In England, France and the Netherlands there are studies to suggest that people married only when they could establish an independent household, so that the age of marriage was high, and since in most areas studied illegitimate births were consistently low, birth rates fell. If the community suffered demographic setback by famine or disease, the marriage age fell and generally the losses were made good quite quickly, after which population stabilized again. The other preventive check was migration: significant numbers went overseas, to America or, in the United Provinces, enlisted in the East Indies trade. Probably it was internal migrations that moved populations around, usually to escape religious persecution or war. The diaspora of the French Huguenots after 1685 was an example of this. But there are convincing reasons for arguing that positive checks were most important: famine, disease and war. Local famines arising from crop failure – usually two successive harvest failures sufficed – were endemic in Europe, except in the Netherlands and England where they disappeared during the century. But since these were local, their impact was limited. The damage was done by periodic general crop failures over most of Europe: these occurred, for example, in 1648–9, 1660–1 and the persistent dearth period of the mid-1690s. Crop failure was then compounded by epidemic disease, though how far this in turn was triggered by famine is vigorously debated.[2] Whatever the cause, epidemics – bubonic plague was the most deadly, but typhus, smallpox and malaria were also major killers – are a dramatic feature of the century. Plague struck northern France three times between 1616 and 1660, killing about 10 per cent of the population each time. The northern Italian epidemic of 1630–1 killed 22 per cent and a similar visitation in southern Italy in 1654 killed 24 per cent. It is probably safe to conclude that the combination of famine and epidemic was a major and very effective population check in seventeenth-century Europe.

It can be agreed that whatever the population was, the overwhelming majority lived in the countryside and engaged in agriculture. It was also the case that, with a few exceptions, agriculture mirrored the stagnation of population growth in the seventeenth century. It is very difficult to make generalizations about what happened because the pattern of farming practices was extremely complex: for instance, a study of English farming in the period identified tens of different farming regimes being followed, each of which had its own history, some prospering, others in difficulties. The same was true all over Europe: in France four basic regional patterns existed. About a third of the rural population lived on the plains of northern France in peasant communes dedicated to cereal production. In Brittany and on the Atlantic coast another quarter pursued a more varied regime; the land was wooded and more pasture was available. Although the soils were often poor, the variety of resources seems to have given a reliable, if basic, subsistence to the peasant. The Mediterranean zone, where another third lived, had a more varied regime, supplementing cereal production with vineyards and olive groves, and using irrigated terraces and hill pastures. This regime, too, largely operated by share cropping, gave a poor but reliable subsistence, with patches of prosperity: for example, vineyards, if carefully managed, could yield a decent subsistence to a peasant family. Finally, about 15 per cent of the population lived in the hills of the central and alpine regions, where some pastoral farming and forest crafts were combined with regular migratory labour to other regions. But, as in England, a more detailed analysis of these regional patterns breaks down into a complex patchwork of agrarian regimes.

The agrarian sector had experienced a phase of expansion in the sixteenth century, boosted by the monetary inflation which saw cereal prices rise absolutely, and in relation to other farm produce. For example, in Spier between 1520 and 1620 the price of rye increased 15 times, wheat 13 times, but meat only six times. This had encouraged investment in cereal production, of which one of the most significant examples was the development of the Baltic grain trade. Production was organized by Dutch capital and commercial skills, and the grain exported in Dutch ships to Amsterdam and from there distributed to the areas of grain deficit in southern Europe. This encouraged the 'second serfdom', the large-scale demesne production of grain for the market by exploiting peasant labour services, which became the dominant agrarian pattern in eastern Germany, Poland and Russia. This boom in cereal production suffered a drastic reversal in the first half of the seventeenth century in most European countries. The timing and severity of regional crises varied. In Castile, after the severe epidemics of the 1590s, there were nearly four decades of falling production of the order of 30–50 per cent. In northern Italy the demographic disaster of 1630–1 triggered a comparable fall in output. The French cereal slump occurred in the 1630–60 period with production losses of 20–40 per cent, while it is not possible to specify the full extent of the destruction wrought on German production in the Thirty Years War. Once more, the expert historians are engaged in lively discussion of the causes of the first agrarian depression.[3] But the real cause was probably the pressures on the small peasant producer, which are poorly documented but combined a deadly mix of manpower shortage and indebtedness arising from famine and epidemics, landlord pressures to increase their share of output as it fell and, probably worst of all, the ratcheting up of the demands for state taxes to cope with the costs of war. The most dramatic example of that process was in France, where the taille, the basic direct tax, which fell on the village commune collectively, was increased 300 per cent between 1620 and 1640, triggering the series of major peasant revolts that characterized those decades. Whatever the combination of causes, the fact is clear that European agriculture went from boom to bust in the first half of the century. In principle the decline could have been mitigated by changes in farming practice, leading to higher productivity. The techniques were known, and worked where they were used in the two economies that offered exceptions to the general pattern of decline, the Netherlands and England. The basic solution was to convert cereal monoculture to mixed farming, increasing the animal herds and the added manure that this provided. Instead of taking fields out of production every third year to recover productivity, crops like turnips or clover were sown, which could feed livestock and enrich the soil. It was not lack of technical skills that was strangling farming, but other socio-economic factors.

This was illustrated by the second round of depression that struck agriculture over most of Europe, a severe and prolonged decline in agricultural prices, which set in in the 1650s and persisted for some 70 years thereafter. There was an adjustment of relativities when cereal prices fell much further than prices for pastoral farm produce, but again this did not prevent the new depression affecting most of Europe. This could, in theory, have helped to change farming practices and introduce capitalist, market-oriented farming. Yet with the exception of England this did not happen. The continuing depression, combined with a continuing period of dearth and disease, hit the small peasant farmer hardest. In times of dearth he had to sell or eat his livestock, or go into debt for basic foodstuffs or to buy seed for a new harvest. As peasant indebtedness increased, the lenders had the opportunity to foreclose on peasant farms, which in turn facilitated the development of large consolidated farming units, which could be rented out to farmers producing for the market.

Various factors hindered such development. Governments, who rightly saw the peasant farmer as the core of their tax base, intervened to prevent their dispossession. This happened most obviously in western Germany, where rulers prevented landlords from taking advantage of the post-war reconstruction by insisting on the reinstatement of the peasant commune, with security of tenure and fixed rents and dues. Further east, in Brandenburg, the ruler intervened to maintain the peasant base of farming by preventing landlords intensifying the exploitative possibilities of enlarging their demesnes and working them by increased labour services. This was to the landlords' advantage in the end: the peasants, though legally serfs, were prosperous enough to be able to perform their labour services with their own tools and plough teams, and often the serfs themselves hired substitute labourers to fulfil their obligations. The advantage can be seen by comparison with what happened further east, in Poland and Russia, where peasants were not protected from landlord exploitation. As the Baltic grain trade declined after 1660 and the profitability of demesne farming fell, eastern European landlords tried to compensate by increasing their demands on the peasantry for labour services. This was self-defeating in the longer run: forced labour is inherently inefficient, and the growing impoverishment of the peasants led to the loss of their draught animals, plough teams and carts, so landlords were often driven in the end to use wage labour as well. Their one relief was to use their legislative powers to establish and exploit monopoly rights to distilling.

However, the new depression also undermined Dutch farming, which had been a model of progressive and profitable agriculture. The basic factors here were the combination of falling market prices with the renewal of large-scale warfare involving the United Provinces after 1672, which eventually raised taxation levels on agriculture sixfold. As farming became increasingly unprofitable, the wealthy burgher investors, whose capital had sustained the earlier prosperity, sold out and transferred their investments to urban properties and state and government loans. The agricultural sector of the Dutch economy went into prolonged decline. In England, a trend towards the impoverishment of the small peasant farmer and the development of large consolidated farms rented to tenants did create a rise in productivity. Despite the falling market prices after 1660, these developments transformed England into a significant food-exporting country and finally ended the threat of famine, even when harvests were poor. English gentleman landlords were willing to invest in farming improvements and to help their tenants over difficult times by adjusting rents. They usually resided in the country and took a personal interest in farming their lands: they were not absentee investors. More importantly, the English landlords had strong political influence through their representation in parliament and their control of local administration in their county communities. By controlling taxation they could keep rural taxation at relatively low levels, while locally they controlled the process of assessment and collection. But they could also use their legislative muscle in parliament to protect their interests by establishing export subsidies for corn after 1660. Finally, they were in no danger of government intervention to control the economic forces that were driving the small peasant farmer into giving up his holding and being reduced to the status of cottager and wage labourer, a process that was already more advanced in England than anywhere outside the serf agriculture of the east.

The enduring agrarian depression that struck Europe early in the seventeenth century and remained dominant into the eighteenth constitutes one of the main parameters of the history of the period. Farming was the economic basis for the whole society, and while it remained depressed and, over wide areas, pressed down to a precarious subsistence level, the possibilities for any new phase of general economic and material advance were limited. Since the possibilities of creating significant new sources of wealth were so few, society directed its efforts to repartitioning the meagre productive surpluses that were being generated, which is the polite way of saying that the ruling elites were motivated both to intensify the levels of exploitation of the labouring majority, so brutally evident in the eastern serf-agriculture zone, more subtly exemplified in the quiet elimination of the English peasant farmer, and to enter a fierce struggle within their own ranks over sharing out the proceeds.

The urban sector had a vital role in European society, although most Europeans lived in the countryside by farming. It was an area set apart, symbolized by the existence of a town wall, within which different rules and values from those of the rural society operated. While there were still a handful of sovereign cities – Venice, which still ranked as a major power, was the best known – most cities acknowledged an overlord of some kind from whom at some historic point the city had received its founding charter. This was true of the Imperial Free Cities of the Empire, like Augsburg, Nüremburg and Hamburg, which enjoyed a very real autonomy; or perhaps the most powerful city in seventeenth-century Europe, Amsterdam, which had some nominal subordination to the Holland States, but could in fact often behave as though it were the sovereign not only of the province of Holland but of the whole United Provinces. On a slightly lesser scale, the trading city of Danzig, though subject to the king of Poland, acted for most of the time independently of crown authority. But these star performers were not typical of the European urban sector, for the average urban settlement was small, and its influence did not extend much beyond the rural hinterland which it served. Still, the city wall, the city charter of privileges and liberties, the fact that almost everywhere in Europe the citizens were legally recognized as a separate Estate of Burghers, with exclusive privileges, emphasized that the urban sector existed to provide specialist services, largely unavailable outside the city walls.

The most basic privilege was the right to hold markets. And since the rural populace needed to go into town to sell their surplus products, it was a

convenient place for the provision of specialist services not readily available
in the villages. Manufacturing was still, in 1600, largely carried on in towns,
usually under the control and supervision of craft guilds, which should have
guaranteed stability of prices and quality. Although the countryside could
manufacture some of the artefacts it needed, for more sophisticated products and services it was necessary to go to town. Textiles and leather, food-
processing trades like brewing, and building trades were found in towns.
Towns were usually disproportionately well endowed with ecclesiastical
institutions including schools, were more likely to have specialist medical
doctors and, since they were often the seats of the local law courts, might
have resident lawyers. Most could offer some kind of financial services,
money-lending and banking. For one of the distinguishing features of urban
society was that it was largely monetarized and market-oriented. It was the
point at which the largely natural economy of the countryside engaged with
the world of commerce and trade. Some towns were centres of government,
the seats of provincial governors and royal tax-collectors, perhaps with a
royal castle and garrison.

The urban sector had shared in the sixteenth-century boom and its economic expansion, and in 1600 the main axis of the urban economy was
formed by the Italian and German trading cities, which took the produce of
the Mediterranean and distributed it throughout Europe, and also took in
the primary produce of eastern Europe. Germany and east-central Europe,
which they serviced, contained almost a third of Europe's population. This
whole trading area was disrupted by the outbreak of the Thirty Years War.
In 1622 there was a spate of currency devaluations, and a rapid shrinkage of
trade and manufacture set in as the war prolonged itself. This was compounded by the demographic crises after 1630, the crisis in agriculture and
loss of rural spending power, combined with the rocketing demands of war
for government taxes and the subventions demanded at gun point by the
armies of all the combatants in the areas in which they operated. The economic disaster was then made worse by the marked fall in imports of
American silver in the 1630s and 1640s. The causes are still vigorously
debated,[4] but the effects were clear enough in the falling American demand
for European manufactures, to say nothing of the impact on the capacity of
the Spanish crown to maintain its war effort.

The impact can be measured in terms of declining populations and commercial activity, marked in Italian cities and in southern Germany, where
established textile trades shrank drastically, and in the case of the south
German cities permanently. But the disruption of war and epidemics cannot
wholly account for the changes in manufacturing that occurred, like the
drastic collapse of urban industry in Spain, where established textile centres
like Toledo, Cordoba and Segovia had lost up to 50–70 per cent of population and output by 1650. Some historians see them as the victims of successful competition from a switch, particularly in north-west Europe, from
guild-regulated production in the chartered towns to the putting-out system

of manufacture, in which urban capitalists took the raw materials out into the villages, where there was abundance of cheap labour, desperate for a chance to make supplementary cash income, which made up the cloth on low piece rates. In the case of textiles, this also involved a lowering of quality of the produce, but this seems to have been possible because of one of the earliest instances of a response to consumer-led demand, which produced the 'new draperies'. The long-established acceptance of heavy-weight woollen garments, which had the virtue of durability, was replaced by a preference for lighter and more varied and colourful fabrics, made from cheaper wool, often mixed with other fibres. They seemed to originate in Flanders, and the Netherlands revolt caused many Protestant craftsmen to seek refuge in England and the United Provinces, bringing their new techniques with them. Dutch and English merchants then distributed the cloth through Spain where they captured the American trade from local producers, and into France and Italy, where they captured the Mediterranean markets. The competition was crippled by its adherence to guild controls, and the refusal of guilds to modify either their product or their traditional use of costly skilled manpower. This process of de-skilling manufacture and putting out the work to unorganized rural labour has been labelled by historians proto-industrialization. In its beginnings it did not necessarily involve taking the work into the countryside. The Flemish refugees who brought the 'new draperies' into England revitalized old guild-regulated textile towns like Colchester and Norwich, which had gone into decline, pursuing their new methods in an urban context. There was a more dramatic illustration of this in the Dutch city of Leiden. Here the traditional industry which had almost disappeared by the 1580s was dramatically revived by the influx of Flemish refugees, making Leiden the biggest textile manufacturer in Europe by 1650.

But in fact the future of European manufacture proved to lie in the countryside, for the migration of manufacturing spread rapidly after 1650. Relocation in the countryside revived the textile industry of northern France, and was taken up in Italy and applied to other branches of manufacture like linen weaving, and in northern Italy the production of silk. It could also be applied to the metal trades. Naturally the declining towns, and sometimes governments, seeking to prop up their urban sectors and disturbed at the lack of controls in the new production methods, sought to obstruct the process. In some areas they succeeded: for example, in the serf-agriculture zone of eastern Europe the landlords levied dues on their serfs for permission to engage in manufacture, or sought to control the supply of raw materials themselves, and in succeeding negated the development by making the process uncompetitive.

However, the move to the countryside could not be stopped. A new factor from 1650, as population stabilized or fell, was that wages began a slow recovery, while at the same time textile prices went into decline. It was this process that caused textile production in Leiden to fall by two-thirds between 1650 and 1700, and destroyed the linen-weaving trade in Haarlem in the same period. In Amiens, in the 1690s, the wages paid to craftsmen under the guild system were three times as high as wages in the rural hinterland, and the weaving trades moved out of the city. This major economic shift may well have been the salvation of many hard-pressed peasant communities. The cash earnings from manufacturing work enabled them to survive in spite of the growing weight of taxes which they had to carry. However, in many areas the urban sector managed to survive the shift. An urban situation was still advantageous for trades that required skilled labour, like many of the finishing processes in textile manufacture, and the resilience of the north Italian cities, most of which found ways of adapting to economic changes, enabled them to find a new role in the manufacture of luxury goods and the development of service industries for the elites. It is apparent that Venice, which seemed to be facing a disastrous decline in its traditional export trades after 1600, managed to find new specialisms, conserve its highly skilled and tightly organized labour force, and remain economically viable into the eighteenth century. The older assertion that after the demographic catastrophes of the 1630s and 1650s the Italian cities sank into irreversible decline has been revealed as an exaggeration.

Present knowledge of the fortunes of the European economy after 1600 clearly leaves large areas about which little is known with any certainty. But the overall impression that a previous period of economic growth came to a halt, or was even reversed in some areas, so that the material basis – the production of wealth on which all other developments ultimately depended – was at best stagnant, meant that changes generally represented a redistribution of assets rather than the creation of new ones. The century was labelled by one of its recent historians the 'iron century', because its lack of growth meant in the end that the minorities who ruled society had to find any extra resources they needed for their various enterprises by reducing the share allotted to the labouring majority. Whether it was the eastern European serfs, whose impoverishment paid for the development of demesne farming for the market, or the struggling French peasantry in the face of inexorably rising levels of taxation, or the native Americans in Mexico and Peru whose forced labour produced the bullion inflows, the basic process was the same. And since the margins that remained to be squeezed from a stagnant population were limited, the general recession set real limits to the possibility of change.

It is well known that men do not live by bread alone, and historians now recognize the role of mentalities in shaping the development of societies. In this area it is possible to argue that the behaviour of seventeenth-century Europeans – and it has been no different in any other place or epoch – was constrained by what they believed or knew about their world. Before men can set about changing their world they need to believe that change is legitimate, desirable and possible. The major obstacle to understanding this period for modern students of history is that twenty-first-century Europeans take continuing change for the better as axiomatic, and make it an organizing principle of their culture. It can be said, naturally as a broad generalization, that most Europeans in 1600 did not share this view, and regarded change, mutability, interference with a traditional order of things which they believed had stood unchanged for centuries, and expected to continue unchanged into an indefinite future, were evils to be avoided. This arose basically because if these seventeenth-century Europeans had been asked who they were, insofar as they would have understand such a question, they would have answered that they were Christians, and if they wanted a word to identify their culture they would have been likely to have chosen Christendom. This was what defined the place of Europe in the world: Europeans were the chosen people who espoused the one true faith, for most of them the religion developed from Latin Christianity. Obviously a similar belief in reverse defined the Orthodox Christians of the east, equally confident that they were the chosen people, the guardians of the same true faith. In principle, the two broad Christian communities recognized one another as springing from a common root, categorizing the other faith as schismatic. In practice, they ignored one another, except on the borders where their faiths met and to some extent intermingled. There the usual relationship was intermittent warfare; whenever land changed hands, the new possessors would set about converting or confessionally cleansing their gains.

It was therefore crucial that Christianity, like all the major monotheistic belief systems, claimed an exclusive possession of religious truth, and that therefore outside the church there was no salvation to eternal life; on the contrary, there was the doom of eternal damnation. The church could not, therefore, tolerate any dissent, since anything that deviated from orthodox belief was by definition false and led to judgement. Nor could it ever change, for God had revealed the true faith from the beginning, and the ground rules were enshrined in Scripture, which was the literal Word of God. That said, it is impossible for the historian to pontificate about the actual religious belief system of ordinary Europeans – we know what the church said they ought to believe, but we have no way of discovering the real extent of their understanding and acceptance of those teachings. Clergymen, and they nearly always were clergymen, who investigated the religious knowledge of their flocks, always emerged horrified by the ignorance and misconceptions that they found, and the humanist critiques by figures like Erasmus, and after him the polemics of Protestant assailants of the established church order, could make powerful propaganda out of this deplorable reality.

It would be naive to suppose that all, or most early modern Europeans had successfully internalized the essentials of their faith. But they knew that they were Christian and set apart from all other believers, and if they confronted dissenters, would enthusiastically participate in extirpating them. The revocation of the Edict of Nantes by Louis XIV in 1685 and the subsequent elimination of the Huguenots in France was one action enthusiastically supported by the 95 per cent of Louis's subjects who were Catholic. It is reasonable, therefore, to make the assumption that early modern Europeans accepted the official Christian belief that applied in their community, remembering that since the church usually monopolized education in these societies, and that regular church attendance by everyone was required by law, their beliefs should have been constantly boosted. The known facts that large numbers were highly irregular in their attendance, and that many preferred to spend their sabbath rest in the ale house rather than the church, only tell us that human nature does not change in that respect. The point is that the only belief system to which they had access was that propagated by their established church. They were never offered a choice of beliefs, and since most were uneducated and illiterate they had no realistic possibilities of critically evaluating what they were offered. Individuals could scoff and blaspheme, as many are recorded doing, but their own internal world picture remained the only one they had ever encountered.

Christianity is a historic religion; it teaches that God created the world and everything in it as part of a planned historic scenario and actively presides over everything that happens in it, intervening as necessary by punishments and rewards to prevent mankind from deviating into wickedness: that is, disobedience to the divine will. The whole creation would be transformed at the second coming, when all who had ever lived would face judgement and have their eternal future resolved. The point here is that life in the material world is not an end in itself; rather the world is a stage on which God acts out his predetermined scenario, and, for the individual, life is a time of trial during which he will be tested and judged. This belief system does not encourage the believer to devote his life to the pursuit of material gains: rather the contrary. Believers were in fact liable to be selfish and worldly, as men always have been, but they knew that this was wrong. Market forces definitely did not rule in the world of 1600; God did. As one historian remarked of the seventeenth century, the Scarlet Woman was more real than economic man. This was reinforced by a further basic teaching of the church, that all mankind was involved in the original sin of Adam, so that all human beings were born with an innate tendency to wickedness. Left to themselves all men are hopeless sinners and can only be redeemed by the intervention of God's grace. The church existed to enable men to benefit from the gift of grace, but to help it do so, God had also instituted secular power on earth, vested in kings, magistrates and priests in an ordered hierarchy of authority, often called the 'great chain of being'. This authority rested on divine right: God's omnipotence was devolved to his chosen deputies on earth, and through them it was devolved further to the ground level, to the patriarchal head of a household of family and servants, which was the basic building block of society.

It was the religious duty of everyone, whatever their position in the hierarchy, to render unquestioning obedience to their divinely ordained superiors and impose it on those entrusted to their charge. Without this control, the innate wickedness of fallen man would result in general anarchy and insecurity. This repressive system was a precondition for any kind of orderly life on earth. As an English official homily asserted, without this seamless system of subordination and discipline, no man would be able to travel the roads unrobbed, nobody could sleep secure in their beds at night.

It has also long been realized that the official Christian culture had been superimposed over the centuries on older, pre-Christian systems of belief. It is at this point that hard evidence becomes very scarce. Yet both Christianity and the older folk cultures were a response to the same basic human need for some kind of reassurance and comfort in a world filled with dangerous powers which were beyond human control. Harvest failure leading to famine, epidemic disease, fire and flood, the destruction wrought by war, were the work of superhuman powers. In the absence of practical measures of defence, human societies had always fallen back on magical powers of various kinds which might be effective in averting danger. Christianity, which like all religions incorporates a sophisticated and partly rationalized form of magic, could easily coexist with other magic beliefs in fearful minds. So the Europeans had an extensive range of magic beliefs and practices, served by an array of practitioners. For the elites the dominant belief system was astrology, taken very seriously indeed. There was nothing incongruous in the Emperor Rudolf employing, as he did, the eminent mathematician and astronomer Johannes Kepler as his court astrologer, nor in the fact that the scientist sincerely believed in the importance of his astrological studies. At the grassroots level, the common folk resorted to the cult of saints, believed in the powers of magicians and witches, danced round bonfires and may-poles, and consulted local wise women, people reputedly gifted with second sight, and followed a spectrum of magic formulae to cure sick animals, iden-tify future marriage partners, and locate lost or stolen property.

A manifestation of the widespread belief in the supernatural which has caught the attention of historians is the European witch hysteria, which was at its peak between the 1570s and 1680. Some in the elite who promoted witch persecutions may have done so with the idea of reinforcing their own social control, but most believed in it as fervently as the most ignorant labourer. It was accepted that some men and women deliberately sold themselves to Satan, had the power to fly through the air to attend satanic rituals, most of which parodied orthodox Christian ceremonies, and were endowed by Satan with power to inflict harm on anyone who offended them. Famous intellectuals, including King James VI and I in Britain, or the internationally famous lawyer and political theorist Jean Bodin, publicly and vehemently asserted the reality of witchcraft and the need to exterminate its practitioners. Mercifully, out-breaks of witch persecution were intermittent and localized, but by the end, when a changing intellectual climate persuaded the ruling elites that such irra-tional beliefs were unseemly and false, and they actively intervened to prevent further proceedings, thousands of innocents had been accused, most of them convicted, and many subjected to judicial torture, mainly to elicit names of accomplices. It is plausible that over the period about 100,000 accusations were initiated and some tens of thousands of these executed. Their fates are a testimony to the basic fears and insecurities that permeated the culture.[5]

The problem with assessing mentalities is that in the last resort nobody knows what makes particular men and women act the way they do. It is only possible to build on what was said and written at the time, to observe what seem to be the typical responses of early modern people to their world, and to deduce that if their minds really did move as indicated, this would tend to reinforce some patterns of behaviour and discourage others. This culture reinforced acceptance and conformity; both formal religious belief and experience and folk wisdom worked together to this end. It was clear enough that men were only very partially in control of their own destinies, so that they were always the victims of fear and uncertainty. Official religion told them that the world was the way it was because God had so ordained it, and it would continue unchanged until the final convulsion intimated by the Old Testament prophets and the Book of Revelation. Patient acceptance of whatever the divine will turned out to be was the obvious policy to follow, a submission very much recommended by the church. In the end it was to be accepted that God moved in mysterious ways that were beyond mere human understanding. Beyond this it was equally sensible to conform to what was decreed by lawful authority, for that too had the stamp of divine approbation: all authority was of God, and not to be questioned.

Christianity stood for an authoritarian world which had no place for the concept of loyal opposition. Making representations was allowed – to God directly by prayer, to secular authority through the humble petition – on the clear understanding that the subsequent ruling was final. But at least this structure of authority, sanctioned by God, offered something firm to cling to. Such attitudes created a basic conservatism: in a world where uncertainty reigned, it was safest to follow the wisdom of the ancestors and the ancient traditions and customs of the community, hence the reverence shown at all levels for the force of precedent as the safest guide to present action. It was easier to follow custom, or the rulings of lawful authority: this avoided the danger of having to make decisions, and placed responsibility for the outcome elsewhere. It can be shown repeatedly that early modern people, though willing to be consulted, were shy of accepting the responsibility of decision, except where their own immediate group interests were concerned, which usually meant seeking to evade or modify the latest demand from above for additional taxation or services, or seeking to prevent some other group in the society winning an advantage over them.

The deep-rooted conservatism of the early modern mentality is almost certainly related to the absence of any alternative system of thought. Below the higher levels of the educated elites, the monolithic teachings of religious orthodoxy were unchallenged or, if challenged, exposed the challenger to accusations of heresy or subversion, and the elites usually found it easy to mobilize popular feeling against the alleged disturbers of the divine order. This gave these societies, in some respects so vulnerable to upset, an underlying security.

It is significant that when there were requests for change from below, they tended to be regressive. Men sought relief or improvement by what they conceived as the restoration of a traditional order that had been improperly altered. An extreme example of this can be found in the polemics of the Leveller radicals in the English Revolution, who claimed to seek the overthrow of the 'Norman yoke' introduced by William the Conqueror. Their conception of a brave new world was to reinstate Saxon liberty, which of course was entirely mythical. This is in the end why mentalities are important. If the prevailing mentality teaches that there is no realistic alternative to the world as it is, it becomes impossible to advocate, with any plausibility, policies of radical change. That was why, in this respect, the Europe of 1600, though exposed to some traumatic experiences during the seventeenth century, was still basically unchanged in essentials by 1700 or even by 1789. Another way of comprehending this phenomenon is to recognize that basically, for most of Europe's inhabitants, these were not politicized, but consensus societies. The basis of political activity is the making of choices between different solutions to problems. In a consensus society this need does not usually arise, for the kinds of problems that occurred were familiar to all, as were the accepted remedies. If the price of bread rose in times of dearth, everyone knew the reason was that an anti-social conspiracy of merchants was deliberately withholding supplies from the markets to maximize their profits. The remedy was for the authorities to intervene in the markets and enforce a fair price, and, if they could, expose and punish the delinquent dealers. The concept of a just price for commodities was deeply ingrained in everyone's thinking and all that was needed was to enforce it. If the authorities failed to act, then repeated examples show that the community would act in their place, and grain rioting would ensue. But the aim of the rioters would be to enforce custom and precedent, not to challenge or change the system.

Thus, over a broad spectrum of public affairs, there was no necessity to analyse and discuss what needed to be done; to every problem there were answers based on what had always been done before. If the traditional solutions were not working, then it must be that somewhere in the system there was a malevolent conspiracy of self-interested persons, who put personal interest above the common welfare. The best-known example of this arises in times of rebellion. Since it was a fundamental rule in all circumstances that the orders of lawful authority must be obeyed, resistance to a sovereign ruler was unacceptable. The humble petition was the only legitimate channel for a subject to question the decision of a superior. Yet rebellion and resistance to legitimate rulers did occur, so how were they to be justified? The standard response was that the ruler was being deliberately misled by 'evil councillors' and the remedy was to remove them. Then all would be well. It is possible to see this concept at work in an extreme form in the English Revolution, when parliament actually fought a prolonged civil war against Charles I, who nobody questioned for a moment was the divinely appointed king, on the grounds that he had been captured by an evil clique of papists and adventurers. The aim of the parliamentary armies was to rescue him, and when this was done, and the conspirators eliminated, the crisis would be resolved. When, in the course of the war, the radical MP Henry Marten suggested that Charles be deposed, the outraged members immediately silenced him and sent him to the Tower. That was the rationale for the repeated parliamentary demand that the king choose councillors in whom parliament could have confidence, which meant allowing the two Houses to approve his choice of advisers. This, as the king was not slow to point out, was an outrageous breach of the traditional constitution, in effect a proposed seizure of the sovereign power by the two Houses, but it would have been impossible for them to concede this openly. Their position seems absurd to the modern observer, but there were no other terms in which they could have explained to a profoundly apolitical public opinion why they appeared to be flouting the most basic of all rules of their society, and reassure them that in reality they were still operating within the traditional conventions.

It is interesting to observe how these societies handled the one area of public policy-making that was politicized, namely what today is called foreign policy – the relations between sovereign rulers. In this field too there were conventions and traditions, but there was no final authority with powers of adjudication except God himself, and war between sovereign princes was conceptualized as a process of appeal to the Almighty, who delivered judgement through the outcome. But in the process real choices had to made: whether, where and when to attack, what alliances to make, what terms to settle for. Early modern Europeans put this kind of policy-making into a special category: 'matters of state', which only sovereigns and their chosen advisers were competent to handle. The community at large, even its elite elements, was excluded unless the sovereign chose to consult. In 1621, James VI and I was genuinely outraged when his House of Commons presumed to offer him advice on how he should conduct his international policy without being asked. He denounced it as unheard-of behaviour. Most contemporaries would probably have agreed, and also agreed with the view expressed by the Estate of the Clergy in the Swedish Diet in 1680, when invited to comment on the king's conduct of foreign affairs, that they lacked the necessary knowledge and competence to judge such matters of high policy, and remitted everything to the king's own gracious judgement. Foreign policy was the one area where the exclusive elite groups who were involved in policy-making could argue, and organize and intrigue around policies. Otherwise, in a consensus society the 'political' questions were not what policy aims should be pursued, for on that there was general agreement, but which person, or group of persons, should be entrusted, under the sovereign, to carry them out.

The structures of society

Thomas Hobbes is one of the first 'modern' political theorists. The frontispiece of his master work, Leviathan, published in 1651, reflected his conception of the state. It is an image of a dominant, crowned figure, but made up of a mass of individual men and women who have put themselves under a sovereign power, so that they can pursue their individual satisfactions under its protection. It represents a society constructed to serve the interests of the individual. That was not a common contemporary view of society, and Hobbes's work was considered scandalous. A popular work on politics in the England of the seventeenth century was Sir Robert Filmer's Patriarcha. This argued that society had grown naturally from the sons of Adam, who as the first father had been invested by God with absolute authority over his wife and children. All lawful authority was patriarchal and hereditary by divine right, and sovereign rulers were the fathers of their subjects, exercising the original parental authority over them. Filmer argued that any theory of authority based on consent was flawed, since not only was there no historical record of any such act of consent, but the consent of any group of individuals could not logically bind their unborn descendants, so the consent would need to be renewed with each generation, which was absurd.[6]

Filmer was more acceptable to seventeenth-century European minds than Hobbes, because his society was an organic growth, not an artefact. Europeans' view of society was anthropomorphic: it was 'the body politic' composed of head and members, who were the inhabitants working together under the direction of the head for the welfare of the whole body. If the members did not obey the directions of the head, the whole body would sicken and might perish. The almost universally accepted idea of a society of Estates, each with its distinctive function, expressed this concept. Society was based on collectives, not on individuals. People were classified not by who they were, but by the collective to which they belonged, and they were expected to conform to the rules laid down for their particular group. This kind of thinking left little room for any concept of individual liberty or equality. It was true that all men were equal in the sight of God, and at the Judgement Day would get their deserts irrespective of earthly rank or status. But, in the material world, rights were distributed most unequally, according to social function.

Each collective was governed by rules specific to its members. This is why the word 'liberty' carried a meaning almost the opposite of its modern connotation. An early modern liberty is a right pertaining to some specific group, which is denied to all others. It is justified as necessary if the group is to perform its social function. Thus noblemen might have exclusive right to own certain categories of land; the clergy were commonly exempted from public taxation or the obligation to military service; the burghers might have monopoly rights to hold markets or participate in specified commercial or industrial activity. Generally, the early modern state in 1600 was a loose confederation of largely self-governing collectives, all of whom acknowledged obedience to the same sovereign power to which they owed a duty of unquestioning obedience.

It was very unusual for anyone to refuse the direct order of their sovereign. But it was very common indeed to submit a humble petition, declaring the recipient's eagerness to comply with the demand, but pointing out all sorts of practical difficulties which compliance would involve. This would generally open a negotiation that would result in a compromise. An alternative mechanism was to profess obedience in public, but take no action locally to give effect to it, in the well-founded confidence that they would probably get away with it. The possibility of enforcement was partly a matter of size. A compact city-republic like Venice, or a small principality like many in Italy and the Empire, could enforce its decrees much more easily than a kingdom like France, which in 1600 was largely a 'geographical expression', being a heterogeneous collection of territories built up over centuries by the French kings, each with its own law and customs. The sheer size of the kingdom made close central supervision almost impossible, given the resources available to an early modern ruler. In England, where the statute laws passed by parliament were held to be binding through the whole kingdom, a survey by the government of Charles I in the 1630s into the application of the Poor Law of 1601, supposedly uniform everywhere, revealed how local communities picked and chose the bits they found useful and ignored the rest.

In the European societies of 1600, the sovereign power was usually exercised by a single person, ruling by hereditary succession, that is by divine right. There could be collective sovereigns, as in the United Provinces, where the States General were sovereign, but this was rare. There were still elective monarchies, the greatest being the Holy Roman Empire, though tradition had reserved the office of Emperor for the Habsburg dynasty. But the possibility of electing an outsider existed. The extreme case of elective monarchy was the kingdom of Poland, where the king was elected at a mass meeting of the whole nobility, a process open to every kind of chicanery and manipulation. Still, Poland generally adhered to the dynastic principle in choosing its kings, as did other elective monarchies like Denmark, Bohemia and Hungary. An elected ruler was weaker than a hereditary ruler in two obvious respects. He was often required to grant a charter of privileges on election, and since most elected monarchs wished to keep the crown in their family, they also had to bargain to secure the succession. That was why the Habsburg Emperors always tried to get their heir elected King of the Romans during their lifetime, since then his subsequent election was automatic. That said, the powers of a sovereign by election were no different from those of a hereditary sovereign, for all lawful authority was derived directly or indirectly from God, and the duty of the subject to obey without question was the same as it was even in the few republican systems of government.

Therefore, most European societies in 1600 were ruled by a personal monarch who held the sovereign powers as a personal benefice. The monarch had three main functions, first and most important in theory being to uphold and defend the true Christian religion and defend the liberties of the church and its clergy. The second was to organize the defence and security of his territories against external enemies and lead his subjects in war. The third was to uphold the laws and customs of his territories and to provide impartial justice for all his subjects. It was almost universally held that, in performing these duties, the prince should seek the advice of his subjects. The willingness to take advice was a defining characteristic of the good prince, and it has been noted that one of the rare grounds justifying resistance to the prince was that he had been taking advice from 'evil councillors'. Although it was generally held to be a princely prerogative to be free to choose his advisers, the machinery for advising the prince was institutionalized in some communities. In England parliament, the meeting of king, Lords and Commons, was often understood as being the 'great council of the realm'. In France the king was expected to consult the members of the high courts of the realm, the *parlements*, over proposed legislation, which could not take effect legally until the relevant *parlement* had registered it. In Scandinavia there were Councils of State, whose advice the prince was expected to hear on matters of state; in Poland there was a statutory Crown Council of leading ecclesiastics, landed magnates and great officers of the realm, elected at each Diet, whose advice to the king was mandatory on him. In Castile a system of councils, staffed by university-educated nobles, had been developed to consider proposals submitted by the king, to which they replied with formal written recommendations. But none of this altered the basic position that the final decision-making power rested with the monarch.

It followed that the true centre of government was the royal court, where the ruler resided, usually with an entourage of formal officeholders – leading ecclesiastical and secular magnates, who sometimes had a formal legal right of access to the ruler – and his chosen personal companions. Here the ruler governed his realm in much the same way as a landed magnate organized his estates. There was some sort of council of advisers, which might be formal or informal, or might even be replaced by a personal chief minister to whom a ruler devolved much of his responsibility, in which case the chief minister would need his own personal council of advisers. Formal judicial business, arising from the ruler's position as the final judge, was usually devolved to professional judges for resolution, always reserving the ultimate right to appeal to the sovereign in person. This followed the pattern in private feudal estate administration, in which the seigneurial courts were usually presided over by professional lawyers. At the level of the royal court secular administration needed a secretariat to process the documentation, and the head of this branch was often the Chancellor. The secretaries were working professionals and would come from relatively modest social backgrounds. As executive officers they should have played no direct role in decision-making, but in fact, because they controlled the paper work and kept the archives, and they organized the agendas of the councils they serviced, and above all as men whose work gave them immediate knowledge of the most secret matters of state, the secretaries had the potential to be a major power in government.

Finally, a princely government, like a private estate, had to have a department of finance, which managed and audited the receipts and expenditures. All rulers had a treasurer, who was usually recognized as a senior officer of state, and presided over the public finances. It is impossible to generalize about the types of financial administration that existed by 1600. Some were centuries-old, sophisticated institutions, like the English Exchequer, with a recognized legal status. Some financial administrations were informal, rejigged from reign to reign to suit the individual requirements of successive rulers. But as a general rule it can be said that a unified, central financial control hardly existed anywhere. New *ad hoc* bodies appeared constantly, if some new revenue source was opened, and most rulers had some kind of privy purse: a personal fund under their direct control. It followed that effective financial budgeting was almost impossible and rarely attempted. No ruler of a principality of any size knew exactly what his annual revenues were, nor could he form any reliable estimate of what expenditures were likely to be. Consequently, policies were planned in almost total disregard of where the funding was to come from. Financial ignorance and irresponsibility was one of the weakest points of early modern government.

Any close examination of the working of early modern government, compared with modern administration, reveals first of all how small the central administration was. The number of paid servants of even a major ruler, including the domestic servants of the court, was extremely small, and most of these were working in the judiciary. It is a matter of fierce debate among historians how far bureaucratic administration existed at all by 1600, in the sense of administration by trained, career professionals, following established routines and keeping comprehensive records.[7] In general, an office was a benefice held for life, sometimes hereditary and very often purchased, and it could be traded like any other property. Salaries were usually low or nominal, and also unreliably paid. On top of this the officeholder had to meet the expenses of hiring subordinate staff and running an office. Most officers of government were financed by those with whom they were dealing, who paid recognized scales of fees for services rendered, and in addition usually offered gratuities as well. The officers could also extort, embezzle and accept outright bribes, which was illegal, but the risks of detection and prosecution were minimal. They enjoyed perquisites, like the practice of revenue collectors delaying making returns of their money, often for months, during which time they could invest the balances for private gain. Indeed it was not unknown for them to lend the ruler his own tax revenues at high rates of interest. All this arose not because early modern Europeans were exceptionally venal or dishonest, but because no regime of that period could have afforded to run a properly salaried administration.

It is now perhaps easier to see why the European societies of 1600 were loose confederations. Below the level of the royal court, government depended on the work of self-regulating collectives, whose distinguishing characteristic was their self-financing character. They were not dependent on funding from the central government for their operations, so they were truly autonomous. It is clear that under this system there could be no question of government by central command; whatever the theoretical entitlement of the ruler to be obeyed, he simply lacked the machinery to make it a reality. These were governments that had no permanent security forces, or other comparable means of coercion, which modern governments take for granted. They could not have afforded them either. The paradox was that, despite the widespread acceptance of the divine right of rulers, the system actually worked by negotiation between rulers and ruled, the basis of which was the broad consensus over the aims of government – to uphold and secure the status quo against every kind of subversive threat. Given that, government by coercion was unnecessary.

That leaves the question of why such a highly devolved system did not collapse in disorder or total ineffectiveness. The answer lies in the extent of the devolution. The mosaic of self-governing collectives, each of which was supposed to have a well-defined role in the working of the society as a whole as members of the body politic, were in fact in a condition of endless rivalry and competition for relative advantage. This was the opening the central regime needed. If we ask how an apparently weak central government could none the less drive through increasing tax demands, the answer is the disunity of the potential opposition. This can be illustrated from the history of the Swedish Diet. When faced with new tax demands, the four Estates did not form a common taxpayers' front to resist the demand; they engaged in furious intra-Estate disputes about the relative share of the different Estates. This was a universal condition; in fact the collectives were in endless dispute over relativities of all sorts – demarcation disputes about who does what. If the society was to function, there had to be an umpire who could be assumed to be impartial, and that was the monarch. The collectives were in competition for the royal favour. The main tool, apart from ideological indoctrination into the duty of obedience, by which central government could exert influence over the collectives, was patronage. The sovereign ruler had the undisputed power to distribute or withhold facilities which his subjects ardently desired. He could grant offices and privileges, confer titles of nobility, issue new charters to corporations, intervene in judicial process to help or hinder litigation, and in the last resort could call a case for personal resolution and grant pardons. He could license all kinds of commercial activities, confer monopoly rights, vary taxation demands, grant immunities from billeting and conscription, grant lands and annuities to those who earned his favour. Patronage was the oil that enabled the machinery of government to function, and was the essential link between central government and the government of the local communities. The apparently chaotic structure of fiercely autonomous units was held together by chains of patronage, emanating in the last instance from the ruler himself. Patronage could be devolved to his local agents in the communities, who could use it to boost their own personal standing and ability to get things done. It is apparent from the record that the exploitation of patronage called for political skills on the part of the ruler. The aim was to get the right level of distribution; the danger was the creation of excluded groups by concentrating patronage distribution too narrowly, which could create dangerous internal discontents.

In an agrarian culture the most important groups with which rulers had to deal were the landlords who constituted the nobilities and gentries in almost all European societies. In some parts feudal jurisdictions were prevalent, which meant that the ruler had only an indirect power of government over his tenants and serfs. Feudal power had been in decline in some parts of Europe, but was very much a reality in others. The grandees of Spain, who had been encouraged to colonize the lands won back from the Muslims, had built up extensive holdings and exercised an almost sovereign authority over their territories. It was only with their cooperation that the crown could levy taxation or recruit soldiers in their areas. A more extreme case was found in Poland, where the powers of the noble landlords were legally entrenched. There was a mix of great magnate families, whose revenues exceeded those of the king himself, and who built up vertical clientage networks among the lesser nobility, who had to be negotiated with almost as sovereign powers. In the Habsburg lands of central Europe – Bohemia, Austria, Hungary – the landlords had their authority over their tenants reinforced by their control of provincial Diets, which had broad jurisdiction over the collection and assessment of taxation and the administration of justice and maintenance of order. Here government was unworkable without the cooperation of the Diets, which had to be negotiated with rather than commanded. The same was true in Brandenburg, where by 1600 the Electors, in return for financial support, had allowed the *kreis* nobles to take charge of their districts. Even in areas where, formally at least, rulers had retained control of the agencies of provincial government, their possibilities of exercising that control directly were limited. For example, the French kings had the power to appoint the provincial governor, who in the king's name was responsible for the military administration of his province, and could command the local garrisons and castles. In effect the king's choice of governor was restricted to the senior landowning families in the province, who alone had the resources and the personal status in the local community to exercise effective control. As a result these powerful royal offices became the hereditary property of the dominant magnate family. Their cooperation had to be negotiated and rewarded through royal patronage. In England, where the crown had an impressive machinery of control of county government through its power to nominate lords lieutenant, sheriffs and commissions of the peace, and to dismiss them at will, in reality if the appointees were to be able to exercise their responsibilities effectively, they had to be selected from the leading landed families, who had the necessary connections and standing in their communities; so that from some points of view, English county government can be seen as quasi-independent, with established local power structures that central government had to respect.

In spite of the enormous variety of styles and organization found among the local communities in Europe, there was a basic common pattern. The landlords tended to organize themselves collectively around a small nucleus of leading families, whose heads negotiated the terms of collaboration with the ruler and his administration on behalf of the collective, and distributed the rewards from the crown. The system was oligarchic throughout, the members of the collectives ranked in an accepted order of status, in a way typified by the prevalent English system, of a small group of elite families, often members of peerage, who had direct contacts at court and engaged in public service at the national level; a larger group of the more wealthy local families, who held the key local offices and controlled the county militia and the quarter sessions; and the much larger remnant of lesser, but recognized gentry whose power and influence did not extend beyond their own parish.[8] However, this always left the possibility of central management playing a part through the endless internal power struggles within the local communities, which could be decisively influenced by the exercise of crown patronage. This system implies that normal patterns of government in the Europe of 1600 were built on the partnership of rulers with the communities of noble landlords to exploit the productive resources of the peasants and labourers under their jurisdiction.

If the partnership of monarchs and their nobilities was the main foundation of early modern government, it was not the whole story. All rulers had also to come to terms with the church in their realms, whatever its confessional identity might be. One reason was that in most of Catholic Europe, but also in England with its idiosyncratic Anglican church structure, the churches were major landlords themselves, who had to be included in the process of governing rural societies. But the churches were also part of the patronage system, since the monarchs usually had a significant share of patronage in the church and could use this to gratify the ambitions of ruling families, or to put their clients into the key administrative positions in the church hierarchy. This was necessary because the churches controlled wide areas of government. In general the clergy monopolized the contemporary education systems and administered much of what would now be called the social services – poor relief, basic medical services and hospitals – at its own expense. Further, the churches still had wide jurisdiction, through their own tribunals, over the discipline of the clergy themselves, and usually the laity too, in respect of such matters as matrimony, moral conduct, slander and inheritance. They also performed vital media functions, being the main channel for communicating and explaining public policy to the common people. There were also parts of Europe where, in rural communities, the local priest was one of the very few literate persons, and would be looked to by the community to articulate its grievances to the rulers, to write their petitions, and to carry them to the appropriate authority.

This meant that the role of the church was not just the cure of souls, though that was always its chief function, but was also an essential part of the machinery of government. In principle, churches claimed a wide area of autonomy – the liberties of the church – which should have excluded interference by lay authority over church affairs. In practice, the secular powers, from the sovereign rulers down, had always sought to maximize their control, and had largely succeeded. Churches tended to have vocal critics: not heretics, but anti-clerical laymen, who would criticize the ways in which the churches used their wealth, and from time to time, when relations became strained, would voice demands for the expropriation of church property and its conversion to more productive uses. In the Protestant Reformation, some of these programmes had been realized. Throughout the ages there had also been tension between the churches and the sovereign rulers, who aspired to extend their control over their clergy, and could not resist the urge to infringe the tax exemptions which the clergy had traditionally enjoyed. By 1600, in Protestant Europe, secular rulers had established some form of lay supremacy over their churches. Those in Catholic Europe continued their campaigns to reduce the autonomy of the clergy by bullying, and here the existence of anti-clericalism was a useful tactical aid. The monarch could make it clear to his clergy that it was his authority alone that could keep their lay critics at bay. Or the ruler could use his direct relations with the pope to negotiate concordats extending his control in return for promises of continuing protection. The kings of France and Spain had been particularly successful in this way. The king of Spain received regular permission from the popes to levy extra taxes on the Spanish clergy and these were naturally resisted. But the grants were expressed in terms of a percentage of clerical revenues, and to determine the monetary equivalents, and to activate the process of assessment and collection, the crown had to negotiate with the Assembly of the Clergy of Castile, a body consisting of the elected delegates of the dioceses. Evidence shows that the process was time-consuming, and that despite the Assembly's regular claims that they would be ruined, they repeatedly succeeded in talking down the final sum and maintaining it at a tolerable level. The Assembly itself was manipulated by the delegates of the wealthiest dioceses, so that the assessments bore more heavily on the poorer ones. This illustrates a near universal feature of the early modern representative systems: that they were manipulated by a minority of their more affluent constituents at the expense of the rest. It also shows how the rulers of Castile, even at the peak of their power, and with the support of the pope, could not command their clergy, but had to negotiate.[9]

The relations of central governments with the urban sector followed the same pattern. Here the government was usually looking for financial assistance, taxes or loans, but in general urban oligarchies were easier to deal with, because they rightly felt themselves threatened by current developments: economically by the rising trend towards rural manufacturing, and in central and eastern Europe in particular, the drive by the landed nobility to establish competitive enterprises, worked by serf labour on their demesnes. Only the authority of the sovereign ruler could offer some protection. There was also the tendency, particularly marked in the Mediterranean area, for the nobility to seek residence in the chartered towns and take control of the municipalities at the expense of genuine burghers. Large cities with growing financial and commercial power could bargain with rulers on level terms. London virtually monopolized the credit-raising facilities of the kingdom, as did Paris, whose municipality was actually entrusted with the management of the crown's funded, permanent debt: the *rentes de l'hôtel de ville*. But small market towns needed repeated support from rulers to reinforce their chartered rights and protect their guild systems from erosion.

The urban sector also displayed the tendency to oligarchic control, and the assumption of effective authority by an elite of their more affluent citizens. By 1600 it was becoming more common to formalize this by abandoning elections in favour of cooption as the basis for renewing the council. The reasons for this development seem to grow from a spreading disillusion with representative systems and the harsh reality that holding local office was expensive. In the Castilian Assembly of the Clergy, delegates had to travel to the meetings and pay for subsistence, and their dioceses were obliged to refund expenses. Over time the poorer dioceses simply declined to send delegates. Similarly, participation in urban government involved expense, particularly when it came to holding local offices, of both time and money, and an urban citizen, struggling to keep his business going, could not afford either. The trend is observable at the lowest levels in parish councils, which were part of most contemporary ecclesiastical systems, where their standing executive committees, under whatever title they appeared, like the vestry in England or the *sexmän* in Sweden, followed the trend to cooption or automatic reselection. The process also operated at the highest levels of society. For example, by 1600 the old Castilian *cortes*, which had once included the usual three Estates, had shrunk to a meeting of the proctors of 18 cities, and as the century developed gradually ceased to meet altogether, not because it was suppressed by an absolutist crown, but because both sides found it cheaper and easier to negotiate taxation directly at local level. In the Swedish Diet all the commoner Estates – Clergy, Burghers and Peasants – saved expense by constituencies sharing a common delegate, while in many parts of Europe, in Brandenburg and the Habsburg lands, for example, 'committee diets', where the full Diet committed its authority to a select group of members, had a tendency to make full meetings of the Estates redundant. And under full serfdom in Russia, in the peasant commune, made up of meetings of the heads of families, which had an essential role in managing the working of the village, a few of the more affluent village families tended to monopolize the leading positions.

The general tendency to consolidate oligarchy and concentrate decision-making in early modern Europe was the result of different tendencies working in parallel. The basic factor is that the society was still so relatively poor that the consumable surpluses which it generated did not suffice to carry the cost of using professional administrators and executive officials. Devolved self-administration was imposed by necessity. But the same factor meant that the poorer majority could not afford to participate, except marginally, in the administration of their communities. Power gravitated naturally into the hands of the more affluent, more personally enterprising, more literate members, tending to produce stable oligarchies under which many roles became hereditary. There were therefore strong pragmatic reasons for this development, which was also reinforced by the dominant mentality which accepted hierarchy and status as a part of the God-given order of life, and subordination to lawful superiors, on the principle of patriarchal authority.

Forces of change

The importance of mentalities is always critical to the understanding of history. The human mind, like human vision, is geared to perceiving the expected. Our brains do not take in what our eyes see, but interpret it in the light of what is 'normal'. This is no doubt economical, but does lead to the phenomenon of men 'not seeing what is before their eyes' or being 'unable to believe' what they see. It has been suggested that one fundamental difference between the Europe of 1600 and today is that we take for granted the idea of progress: that not only do things constantly change, but overall most change is for the better. The men of 1600 had an opposite belief, based on their religious ideology and reinforced by experience, that the world they had was the only one available, and would not change before Doomsday. Further, since it was God's plan that his creation would persist unchanged to its ending, the changes that did occur reflected the activity of evil-minded persons who, for their own selfish advantage, were acting in disregard of the divine will. This is reflected in the language of English criminal indictments which assert that the accused, 'not having the fear of God before his eyes' pursued his or her criminal activity.

The central importance of the mentality is how it prevents men getting a realistic appreciation of what is happening and encourages them to employ false explanations. For example, in the late fourteenth century, a Parisian mathematician, Nicolas d'Orême, produced a powerful argument in favour of a heliocentric universe, asserting that observable astronomical phenomena could be more easily interpreted on the basis that the Earth was in orbit round the Sun. In fact he more or less anticipated the arguments of Copernicus some 200 years later. Yet at the time Orême's hypothesis had no impact. It is true that, since printing had not then been introduced, very few people had any possibility of reading his argument. But the important factor was mentality. In 1300 the European educated world had it on two authorities, Scripture and their current scientific paradigms based on Aristotle, that the Earth was fixed and motionless at the centre of the universe. Orême knew this too – he added a note that of course his hypothesis was only an intellectual game, for the truth was known to all. Because of his mentality, he could see, but could not believe what he saw.

The background to the European world of 1600 was that, over the previous century and a half, it had experienced, and was trying to come to terms with, a whole series of disturbing novelties. There were the economic shifts already discussed. The first was the increase in population, which was driving up food prices and rents, driving down real wages and producing the novel phenomenon of structural unemployment, with its dreaded exemplar, the bands of able-bodied vagrants who either demanded poor relief, or helped themselves, bringing crime and disorder to settled communities. At this point mentality kicked in with an unreal interpretation. Since the real causes of the change were not perceived, it seemed obvious at the time that if able-bodied men and women were not working, it must be their own fault, and they were choosing the vagrant life as preferable to honest labour. The remedy was obvious and universally adopted: the vagrants must be rounded up, confined in workhouses if necessary, and compelled to work. It was the same with the parallel factor of currency inflation caused by the massive increase in bullion stocks through American imports. There were individuals at the time who worked out the relationship between prices and the supply of money, but they had little impact, any more than did the dissenting voices arguing that current witch beliefs were fantasy. It was clear that the rise in prices was the result of market manipulation by evil-minded hoarders and speculators, and the answer was strict regulation of markets and the prosecution of the profiteers. The manifest failure of these common-sense remedies left men baffled, fearful and insecure. Another chain of novelties, with enormous potential power to destabilize the prevailing culture, was the beginning of the scientific movement, though it must be said that, by 1600, its impact on the public consciousness was very limited. In the background were two developments: one was what historians call the Renaissance – the widening of intellectual horizons through the recovery of whole areas of classical literature and thought which demonstrated the pluralism of classical culture. Aristotle was not the universal authority of the ancient world; there was a whole range of alternative wisdom to explore.

The impact of Renaissance ideas was exponentially increased by the adoption of printing, which revolutionized public access to ideas, at least among the literate sector of society.[10] The printed book not only facilitated the spread of ideas, it undermined the systems of thought control. Now any literate person could receive information and ideas direct from the source and draw his own conclusions. Copernicus had published his *De Revolutionibus* in 1542 and only a handful of specialists took note of it. But they were stimulated to explore the issues raised by Copernicus; in particular scholars like the eccentric Danish nobleman Tycho Brahe and his gifted assistant, the German Johannes Kepler, set about a programme of observations of the heavens and the collection of data, and in Italy the mathematician and physicist Galileo developed a systematic questioning of Aristotelian concepts of the laws of motion. The net effect by 1600 was to develop, with the aid of printing, a European academic community increasingly persuaded that the whole Aristotelian model of how the cosmos was structured needed to be re-evaluated by testing it against the results of systematic observation. One of the main underpinnings of the traditional mentality, hitherto accepted as axiomatic, was under threat. The extent of the danger was only slowly realized, but a major stimulus was a novel move by Galileo to popularize his ideas with a broad literate public. Hitherto academics had almost always published their work in Latin, in a format unintelligible even to educated laymen. Galileo was possessed by a missionary fervour to communicate, and in 1609 published his *Siderial Messenger* in Italian, making capital out of his work with the improved telescopes that had become available, inviting readers to try them and look for themselves, and they would see phenomena that, according to Aristotle, should not be. The Moon was not a perfect disc: its surface was rough; neither was the Sun: it had sunspot activity, and this came and went, though the Sun was in the heavenly sector where there was no change or mutability. One of his most disturbing observations was the discovery of the moons of Jupiter, clearly orbiting the planet, another impossibility in traditional learning, and telescopic observation showed that the number of the stars was much greater than had been known, suggesting that God's universe was vastly bigger than had been imagined. Galileo was issuing a public challenge to the academic establishment, which was also a clerical establishment for the most part, and since he was a convinced Copernican, the issue of possible discrepancy between secular learning and the teachings of Scripture at last came out into the open. Galileo met the issue head on in his *Letter to the Grand Duchess Christina*, which was published in 1616, and asserted that lay science and theology represented different branches of knowledge and operated by different conventions. And just as the scientists must not presume to meddle in matters of faith and doctrine, the theologians must respect the autonomy of secular learning, and if that produced results that appeared to contradict Scripture, but were based on evidential proof, then Scripture must be interpreted to fit the discoveries of science. There could not have been a more dangerous challenge to the Christian hegemony that provided the intellectual foundation of European culture, or to the authority of the religious establishment.

Its potential was further revealed through a rather different source, the writings of Francis Bacon, who combined a long political career in England, which reached its peak when he became Lord Chancellor in 1621, with a lifelong dedication to learning. And though Bacon published much of his work in Latin, he also was a popularizer writing in English, including his major polemic, *The Advancement of Learning*. Bacon was a lay dilettante in science, he was never a committed Copernican, but he was convinced that systematic observational research into the natural world, to be organized as a broad collective endeavour, could expose the workings of the material universe, and by the use of such knowledge men would acquire the possibility of changing their natural environment. Bacon was very much a man of the ruling elites, and he too could see the potential for confrontation between the work of the scientists and the teachings of dogmatic religion. Therefore, he, like Galileo, but more tactfully, suggested that the spheres of religious and secular knowledge would have to be explored separately, and the primacy of religion was of course beyond question. But Bacon was one of the first converts to the modern ideology of progress: that through investment in research and applied knowledge, men could better their material conditions of life. He argued that already unplanned discovery had produced the mariner's compass and gunpowder, as well as printing, resulting in striking material advances. The potential results of organized research were almost unlimited. Bacon's exalted social status ensured him a respectful hearing, though he made no immediate breakthrough. But the Baconian idea was to become an essential component of the intellectual revolution of seventeenth-century Europe, which in turn became one of the foundations of our own secular culture of materialism and progress.

The immediate effects of Baconian thinking on the Europe of 1600 pale into insignificance by comparison with the havoc wrought to traditional systems by the Protestant Reformation, which until the 1570s had seemed poised to triumph over the whole of Latin Christian society, though the Orthodox world remained sealed off from its influence. At its peak, Protestantism had overrun three-quarters of the Empire, penetrated the eastern border zones in Poland, Bohemia and Hungary, was deeply entrenched in the Netherlands and dominant in Scandinavia, taken over in England and Scotland, and was penetrating France. It was only in Italy and Iberia that its spread had been firmly repulsed. The Reformation was a many-faceted phenomenon, and it is not difficult to discern how material interests, most obviously the possibility of secularizing ecclesiastical properties, were involved in its spread. Yet it is facile to see the movement as secular greed operating behind a facade of religious piety. There were hard-faced exploiters who could see how the Protestant work ethic – abolition of an excessive number of religious holidays, emphasis on the need for internalized self-discipline, a marginally more relaxed attitude to usury – might work in their interests. But there were equally hard-faced business communities who firmly rejected the Protestant ideology: the great trading republics of Venice and Genoa and the economically more advanced regions of France around Paris remained highly resistant throughout, as did the capitalists of Lyon and Marseille. It was in the less-developed parts of the Mediterranean zone that the Huguenots took root.

It is worth emphasizing that the Reformation was a religious movement, which aspired to raise the quality of spiritual life in the church everywhere. It is also worth emphasizing that it was an elitist movement generated within the ruling sector of society, and where it succeeded it had to be imposed on a hostile or indifferent majority. The accompanying phenomena of mass popular participation did occur, but they were ephemeral, and the result of agitation by an activist minority, which was indeed the basic characteristic of both the Reformation and the Counter-Reformation. The feeling that the religious life was in need of renewal, that the existing religious practices were being reduced to mechanical rituals, and that there was widespread scandal and corruption within the clergy had swept the European communities intermittently throughout the medieval period. It had found expression in the fifteenth century in Christian humanism, exemplified by men like Thomas More and Erasmus above all, and in the so-called 'new devotion' movement which spread in the Netherlands. The evidence is that laymen were looking for a more involved role in the church, and that activists, primarily in urban society, were resorting to self-help movements, the most prominent and widespread being the formation in parishes of lay fraternities or guilds, which often hired their own chaplains and organized their own religious lives. This activity is evidence of a genuine need for reform, but it generated no demand for secession from the Church of Rome.

It is clear that initially Martin Luther had not contemplated schism; that developed when his open defiance of the authority of both the pope and the Emperor occurred in a political context where immediate and successful repression proved impossible. Once schism was a fact, confrontation and conflict were unavoidable. Christianity was an exclusive faith, a unique religious truth outside of which there was no salvation. The long-term acceptance of religious pluralism was unthinkable. For a subject who asserted a right to choose a different religious faith from that of his lawful superior struck at the root of the system of authority on which the continuing existence of an orderly society depended. Luther was rejecting the great chain of being, denying his role in the body politic by claiming a right to decide for himself whether to obey lawful commands. And in disobeying the powers ordained of God, who were his deputies on earth, he was defying the Divinity. And there was no doubt that God would visit his punishments on any community that tolerated schism and heresy. Everywhere the authorities sought to suppress religious dissidence if they could, in the certainty that this was essential if they were to retain effective powers of government, and that in doing so they were carrying out their most basic religious obligations. Yet, from the opposite point of view, the dissident subject saw himself as authorized by God to resist the commands of an ungodly or heretic ruler. It was fortunate that the realities of living in these societies helped to mitigate the potentially destructive power of religious pluralism. It was repeatedly shown in practice that the ordinary folk, conditioned to obedience to authority, would usually continue to submit. Some dissidents would offer open defiance and risk the consequences, like the 300 victims of the Marian persecution in England, most of them humble commoners, but that was unusual. Others would emigrate, but most would simply stay in their communities and conform. That made it easier to tackle the activist minorities who would not.

The situation was complicated because it was apparent from the beginning that the existence of religious difference could be exploited for secular political ends. This was demonstrated in the continuing dynastic power struggles between the Valois kings of France and their Habsburg rivals. Although both professed Catholicism, the French kings could not forgo the advantages to be gained by supporting Protestant dissidents in the Empire and the Netherlands. It became a standing tactic all over Europe to seek to exploit religious dissidence for political ends. The Reformation inevitably intensified the power-political struggles over territory and status. Problems which could have been resolved by bargaining and compromise had a religious–ideological component introduced into them, which could not be compromised. These confessional conflicts could be resolved only by the definitive defeat of the opponent, and since that was usually unattainable, the only resort, when the combatants were exhausted, was to conclude uneasy truces.

The greatest of these was the Peace of Augsburg of 1555 to settle the religious conflicts within the the Empire. This had the basic assumption written in to it that it was a provisional arrangement until such time as the religious differences had been resolved and religious uniformity restored. The permanent existence of religious pluralism remained unthinkable. But to prevent continuing conflict, it introduced the principle that every territorial lord in the Empire had the right to decide the confessional status of his dominions, and the subjects must either conform or move to another, sympathetic territory with their property. There was thus no question of legalizing religious toleration. The Imperial Free Cities did not enjoy the same rights as the territorial rulers; there provisions were made to safeguard the continued right of a minority confession to worship freely. On top of that there was the Ecclesiastical Reservation concerning the religious principalities. Thus Augsburg did not bring religious peace or stability to the Empire, since both confessions sought to bend its provisions in their own favour. The only places where at least a temporary, working toleration could be established were those where the central government was too weak to impose conformity. This was to be found in Poland, Bohemia, Hungary, the Swiss Confederation and the United Provinces.

There was a further complication, which had emerged at a very early stage of the Reformation, that the demand for reform was not confined to that developed by Luther. The Protestant movement quickly developed a more radical wing whose programmes were as unacceptable to the Lutherans as they were to the Catholics. Some of these elements clearly derived from heretical sects that had managed an underground existence, like the Lollards in England, who felt able to come out when the grip of the Roman Church was weakened. A startling example of extremism, which was preserved as a dreadful warning in the memory of established religions of any confession, were the Anabaptists. They seized control of the city of Münster and established an egalitarian, communist society, until the forces of order crushed them. The dreadful mythology that developed about Münster became a powerful propaganda weapon against all demands for religious reform. The Anabaptists remained everywhere an outlawed sect. But there was also a respectable radicalism that did not involve social revolution, and by 1600 this had become a powerful, international competitor to Lutheranism. Its most creative spiritual leader had been the French theologian, Jean Calvin, and his followers had consolidated control of the Swiss city-state of Geneva, which became the headquarters of a third major confession, the Calvinists. By 1600 the Calvinists were at the cutting edge of the Protestant Reformation and the Protestant movement was irrevocably split. The Lutherans regarded Calvinists as a greater threat than Rome. The emergence of the Calvinists was a further blow to any hopes that the Peace of Augsburg could be the basis for a religious settlement, since the Calvinists were not recognized in the Peace, and had no legal status in the Empire.

While the Protestants were dissipating their energies in internecine disputes over doctrine, the Catholics began their recovery. In any straight contest between Catholicism and Protestantism for the allegiance of the masses, the Catholics had significant advantages. Leaving aside the inertial force of tradition, Catholicism, for most lay people, was a more user-friendly faith. The Catholic Church, accepting the incurable sinfulness of fallen man, did not expect the laity to lead fully Christian lives. The church acted as mediator between the sinners and God; in a sense the clergy lived properly Christian lives on behalf of the lay majority. Both the visible church on earth, and the invisible community of the saints in heaven, served to purvey divine forgiveness of sins to the repentant on easy terms, some of which, like the scandalous abuse of the sale of indulgences, which had sparked Luther's protest, degenerated into crude commercialism. But the religion and its rituals, redolent with the kind of magic that was deeply rooted in popular culture, were aimed at the emotions rather than the intellect, and were something the common layman could respond to. Further, the church could accept a low level of active participation from the laity, because the church had had no serious competitor. Such deviants as did appear were usually quickly and efficiently repressed. The widespread popular criticism, which expressed itself through the endemic anti-clericalism in lay society, did not challenge the church's doctrines, nor its claim to universality. The old religion had a captive clientele.

Protestantism was an altogether more demanding religion. It swept away the mediatory function of the church by proclaiming the priesthood of all believers. It denounced magic elements, like the doctrine of the mass; it abolished visual and sensual aids, images and music, processions and drama, because Protestantism was a religion of the word. It drew its authority from the Word of God in Scripture; the role of its clergy was educational, to point out to their flock how God expected them to live. God had provided in

Scripture an exclusive rule-book for this purpose. But the responsibility lay on the individual to order his life accordingly. Ideally he should be literate himself, and the Scriptures were translated into the vernacular so that he could inform himself from the source. Not only did the Protestant Church offer no magic short cuts to salvation, but by its addiction to the incomprehensible doctrine of predestination it could offer no assurance that even if a man lived by the book he would find salvation. That depended on God's free gift of grace, which was not conferred for meritorious action, for fallen men were incapable of that, but on an arbitrary distribution made on principles that no human mind could fathom.

It took the leadership of the Roman Church some time to grasp the seriousness of the Protestant challenge, first to organize their defences, and then go on the offensive to recover their lost adherents. The first task had been the remit of the Council of Trent, which finalized its conclusions in 1563. The Tridentine reforms were based on the realization that the church had lost its monopoly position and would have to engage in continuous competition for adherents. This meant that the passive acceptance of the laity was no longer sufficient; they too would have to be educated to make a personal commitment to an active religious life, and Trent tackled this first by defining what the Catholic belief was, and then attacking the abuses that had made the old religion so vulnerable to Protestant criticism. They must re-educate and re-organize their own clergy and administrative structures so that they could service and maintain an active and committed church membership.

For the second task of recovering their lost adherents, they were presented with a highly effective new fighting force, the Order of Jesus. This was a task force of educated and disciplined clergy, under the direct orders of the pope, who would lead the attack. The Jesuits were far from popular within their own church. The established clergy saw them as dangerous rivals, a praetorian guard intent on concentrating all power in their own hands. But there was no denying their success. They understood that the Protestants were correct in the emphasis they put on education, but they also grasped the importance of concentrating on the education of the ruling elites, from kings downwards. The Jesuits had remarkable success in winning appointments as royal confessors, a role with great potential power, and even more success with the education they offered in the new Jesuit colleges, offering a reformed and relevant education suited to the nobility and gentry. They aimed to get their pupils into the key positions in society. But the common people were not neglected. The Jesuits were a preaching order which made a science of evangelization through the spoken and written word. The fact that they were autonomous, working outside the ordinary structures of diocese and parish, gave them the liberty to professionalize their work. One of the first Jesuit triumphs was Bavaria, where the Jesuits, working closely with the dukes from the 1570s, turned back a threatened penetration by Lutherans and made Bavarian society the bastion of unwavering Catholicism in Germany that endured into modern times.

They moved on to do the same in much more difficult conditions in the southern Netherlands, which had been won back for Catholicism by 1600, and were active throughout central and eastern Europe. In Poland, which also became in time a bastion of the Catholic faith, the excellence of their colleges attracted non-Catholic noblemen to send their sons for education. It would be wrong to give the whole credit for the Catholic recovery to the Jesuits – other preaching orders developed and joined in the evangelization movement – but it was the Jesuits who perceived the essential change of strategy that was needed: that the task of the Roman Church was not to recover populations temporarily estranged, but to treat Protestant Europe as a mission field, where the church would have to rebuild its following from the ground up.

2

The First European War

The prelude

Christian Europe had always been a militarist culture. Its most prestigious social elite, the nobilities, defined themselves as a warrior class. War was the 'sport of kings', who in the intervals between slaughtering their fellow men filled in much of their time in the hunting and slaughter of animals. War was the natural state of affairs. The historian Sir G. Clark wrote: 'war was not a mere succession of occurrences, but an institution, a regular and settled mode of action, for which provision was made throughout the ordering of social life ... European civilization in the seventeenth century was a military civilization.' In Francis Bacon's essay *Of the true greatness of kingdoms and estates*, he took the permanence of warfare as a natural human condition. He declared, 'But above all, for empires and greatness, it importeth most, that a nation do profess arms as their principal honour, study, and occupation'; indeed he asserted that frequent warfare was necessary to the health of the community: 'no body can be healthful without exercise, neither natural body nor politic: and certainly to a kingdom or estate, a just and honourable war is the true exercise'.[1]

It was therefore inevitable that, given the general climate of insecurity and fear in 1600, there would be a resort to war to solve the problems that arose. This was the message of Justus Lipsius, one of the writers who most influenced the thinking of the ruling elites in 1600. His teachings, labelled 'neo-stoicism' by historians, had identified the current European crisis in his *Politicorum libri sex* as one of threatened disintegration. The historical model he used, for any lasting restoration of civil peace and order, was the Roman empire. That had rested on the subjection of the civilized world to one supreme ruler, backed up by a military force capable of putting down both external and internal challenges. Lipsius placed his hopes, naturally enough, on the rulers of Spain, considered the European super-power of the age. The current of apocalyptic thinking was intensified by the religious forces released by the Reformation. Religious teaching was the principal medium from which most people acquired their world-view and it was, almost universally, couched in the language of war and conflict. God's creation was the stage for endless warfare between the forces of light and the forces of darkness. Christians were in a struggle with Satan and the agents of the Antichrist, whose identity could be selected to suit the current circumstances.[2] In the words of the preachers and pamphleteers, the political conflicts of the day were assimilated into this endless cosmic struggle. Most people were not even trying to analyse the real causes of conflict in their society. They were predisposed towards conspiracy theories. Protestants, who saw themselves as God's chosen people, readily saw events as the work of an unending popish plot, masterminded in Rome and carried out by the Jesuits, to destroy true religion. The Catholic world had the mirror image of this kind of thinking. There was a Calvinist plot, directed from Geneva, unceasingly working to overthrow the true Church of Rome.

But international relations were also driven by dynastic politics. The rulers of Europe were engaged in a permanent struggle for prestige and status, and the assets needed to maintain them: territory, subjects, financial resources. This gave Thomas Hobbes the model he needed to describe his view of the original state of nature, which preceded the development of political societies. It would be: 'that condition which is called war and such a war as is of every man against every man ... In such condition there is, worst of all, continual fear and danger of violent death, and the life of man solitary, poor, nasty, brutish and short.'

To those who asserted that no such state of nature had ever existed, Hobbes pointed to the contemporary state of international relations, where no ruler could avoid involvement in the unending armed competition for relative advantage. The dynastic principle, with its inbuilt drive towards competitive enhancement of power, was the dominant motivating force in international relations. For example, confessional conflict, however bitter, could not be pursued unless secular princes were willing to give their support. That also meant that confessional conflict would in practice be inextricably entwined with the secular interests of the protagonist princes. The centrality of dynasticism in international relations involved a further strain on the system, for it gave a decisive importance to the genetic lottery, a factor not subject to control or predictability. Dynastic fecundity was basic to ensuring family survival and facilitated enlargement by matrimony; dynastic sterility could lead to the extinction of ruling lines, which nearly always resulted in embittered succession disputes. Indeed it will be noted in the period covered in this volume how many of the major European conflicts were labelled wars of succession. There was the further complication that the personality of ruling princes was a major factor in their relations. It mattered crucially whether a ruler was intelligent or stupid, healthy or sick, aggressive or passive, diligent or idle. That was why a royal minority posed serious problems of how to organize a regency regime without unleashing a destructive internal power struggle. In the case of the Bourbon rulers of France, each of the three regencies in this period were periods of dangerous political instability, the first two causing civil wars. The problem was the fundamental principle that hereditary succession was by divine right, directly expressing God's will, and that no human agency could interfere with its outcomes. The horrendous damage this could cause is best seen in the last Habsburg king of Spain. Charles II was physically and mentally feeble and also sterile. Although any reasonable observer could see the damage his possession of the throne of Spain was causing, the obvious solution, to depose and replace him, was unthinkable.

There were thinkers and publicists who dreamed up plans for a general pacification of Europe, though it must be said they usually supposed that once the Christian principalities stopped fighting one another they would all join in a crusading war against Islam. Nobody took that kind of thing seriously. The only reliable force, other than accidents, like the death of a leading participant, that was capable of ending hostilities for more than brief truces was sheer attrition – the participants could no longer find the resources to carry on. Europe was entering such a phase in 1600. In 1598 Henry IV of France concluded the Peace of Vervins with Spain, and issued the Edict of Nantes, guaranteeing the rights of the Huguenots on generous terms, and ending for the moment nearly 40 years of confessional conflict. He then entered, with his chief minister the duke of Sully, on a period of reform and recuperation. The ongoing hostilities between England and Spain were also wound up after the accession of James VI of Scotland to the English throne. The last Spanish effort to support the Catholic rebellion against English rule in Ireland had failed, and was followed soon afterwards by the negotiated end of the uprising. It had become clear that neither belligerent had the capacity to inflict decisive damage on the other and the continuance of hostilities had become pointless. The peace was concluded in 1604.

That left the ongoing hostilities between the Spanish monarchy and its former provinces, the seven United Provinces of the Netherlands. Here, on the one hand, the Spanish crown had achieved substantial success in winning back the loyalty of the southern Netherlands, and was running a successful Counter-Reformation to consolidate its control. But serious efforts to re-conquer the lost provinces north of the river barrier had been abandoned. The military initiative had passed to the rebel provinces both on land and sea, but the failure of the last major land campaign to save the Protestant port city of Ostend from Spanish siege, and the withdrawal of the principal foreign allies of the rebellion, France and England, had led to a powerful peace party developing in the key province of Holland demanding a negotiated settlement. This was opposed to the end by the prince of Orange, for whom the war was his career opportunity as Captain General. Holland had a powerful leader in the Grand Pensionary, Oldenbarneveldt, and was stimulated by awareness that a great economic leap forward was developing, as their established dominance of the maritime carrying trades was augmented by the new 'rich trades' to the East and West Indies, and by the capital and skills brought northwards by the Protestant *émigrés* from the south. The resources tied up in a futile war effort could be better used. Once

Spain showed willingness to accept a cessation on terms favourable to the United Provinces, it was hard to resist and in 1609 a truce was agreed until the year 1621. That ended formal hostilities between rulers in western Europe. On the eastern frontiers, the intermittent war between the Vienna Habsburgs and the Ottomans was concluded by the Peace of Vasvar in 1606, another example of combatants abandoning a deadlocked struggle. The republic of Venice maintained a running naval struggle with the Ottomans over her remaining trading posts in the eastern Mediterranean, but this remained their separate dispute; the rest of Europe was not involved. On the northern periphery there was an ongoing and complex power struggle involving Denmark, Sweden, Poland and Russia over the control of the eastern Baltic, but that too was a separate conflict detached from the mainstream of European power politics.

The temporary cessation of hostilities achieved by 1609 was recognized on all sides as vulnerable, for it had postponed, not settled, the outstanding issues. This was apparent in France, where the Edict of Nantes was bitterly resented by the Catholic majority. It was even more apparent in the Empire, where the Augsburg settlement of 1555 was under constant threat. Both sides had systematically cheated: while the Protestants were in the ascendancy they had continued to secularize Catholic bishoprics within their territories; when the Counter-Reformation began to assert itself, there was a growing determination to reverse this process. The coupling of religious enthusiasm with the chance of territorial gain was a lethal combination giving real substance to the confessional disputes. It can be seen in the case of the Wittelsbach dukes of Bavaria, who having engineered one of the most successful Counter-Reformations in their own dominions, became the leading domestic champions of counter-reform in the Empire. They were also traditionally outstanding in their ability to place cadet members of the dynasty into ecclesiastical benefices in the Empire, and thus had a most direct interest in preserving these from Protestant encroachment, and in possibly winning back those already lost.

There were other factors which made the situation increasingly unstable. First, as confessional confrontation hardened, the ruling institutions of the Empire, the imperial Diet and the imperial Chamber Court, through which solutions should have been negotiated, ceased to function. The Diet did meet on occasion but was deadlocked, as was the Court, while the Protestants declined to recognize the Emperor's own prerogative tribunal, the Aulic Council. Thus neither legislation nor litigation was possible. That left resort to force, which increasingly happened. In a series of disputes over the interpretation of the ecclesiastical reservation as it applied to imperial cities, the threat of force was increasing until it climaxed over Donauwörth in 1606, where the Protestants were unable to prevent Maximilian of Bavaria putting a garrison into the city, divided by confessional dispute, and forcibly re-catholicizing it. Against this background, when the Diet met in 1608, the Calvinists, led by the Elector Palatine, walked out, and the full Diet effectively ceased to function until after 1648. The next step was logical: the Protestant princes and cities of the Empire formed a military alliance for mutual protection, the Protestant Union, and began to canvass support from anti-Habsburg foreign powers. It was an indication of the complexities of the problem that one of their possible patrons was the Catholic king of France, always interested in what might weaken his Habsburg rivals. The obvious riposte followed when Maximilian established a Catholic League, thus formally dividing the Empire into two armed camps.

A further complication in a situation that called for skilled political management was a simultaneous failure of leadership in the principal European powers: this was the genetic lottery at work. In Spain, the leading principality, the able Philip II had been succeeded in 1598 by Philip III, a man plagued by uncertain health, and temperamentally disinclined to work on administration. He established a tradition in Spain of devolving authority to a favourite, publicly recognized as the *valido*, whose power was built on his control of direct access to the sovereign and hence of all major political decision-making. Philip's choice fell on the duke of Lerma, an amiable nonentity whose aim in office seemed to focus on the enrichment of himself and his family at public expense. The seat of government moved from the monastic ambience of the Escorial to the amenities of the fast-growing capital city, Madrid, where a splendid, free-spending court was established. The professional and relatively low-status public servants of Philip II were removed and the noble elite, the grandee families, were allowed to occupy public offices from which they had been previously excluded. Administrative effectiveness declined, patronage, cronyism and outright corruption spread. The result was that an opportunity, created by the ending of large-scale warfare, to reform and strengthen the institutions of the kingdom, was squandered.

The power of Spain depended on its incomparable royal revenues, swollen by the yearly influx of American bullion. This steady cash-flow provided the basis for raising credits, year by year, mainly from the bankers of Genoa, who had financed the war effort on a scale none of Spain's competitors could match. But it was a powerful reason for concluding the Truce that there was a realization in ruling circles that even Spain's resources were overloaded. The reality was that the domestic revenues too had been systematically hypothecated as security for loans, in the form of *juros* – fixed interest annuities – the general European device for raising revenue from the propertied classes who were largely tax-exempt. The repeated 'bankruptcies' of the Spanish crown, which were in fact suspensions of interest payments on government obligations, were evidence of the growing overload on the system. The pause in general warfare, which lasted until 1618, was an opportunity for all kinds of reform, and one school of commentators had ideas how that might be done. The Lerma regime clearly wasted it, indeed the financial problem was probably exacerbated by the introduction of a copper coinage, the *vellon*, which was a covert debasement, harmful for the economy and undermining confidence in public credit, though in the short term it brought easy relief to a cash-strapped regime. One obvious consequence was that the Lerma govenment lacked the means to fund foreign-policy initiatives, or prepare a strategy for the crisis that everyone knew must come.

But the position of the junior branch of the Habsburgs was no better. Theoretically, as holders of the imperial crown, they should have been the focus of policy-making in the European crisis. Genetics struck again: the reigning emperor in 1600, Rudolf, was probably clinically insane, obsessed with astrology, magic and patronage of the arts. He, or his advisers, did have a strategy, which was to use the Counter-Reformation as the lever to rebuild the imperial authority, both in the Empire and in their hereditary lands, Bohemia, the Austrian duchies and the rump of Christian Hungary. All of them were heavily penetrated by religious dissidence, which meant that the local Estates, who had a major voice in the government of all these territories, were dominated by Protestants. Rudolf was childless and his heir presumptive was the Archduke Matthias, who was anxious to exert some control over his brother's eccentricities, which he could only do by cultivating the support of his Estates, and joining them in their demands for the formal establishment of religious toleration in his dominions. This was the force that produced the formal *Letter of Majesty* issued for Bohemia in 1609, which guaranteed non-discrimination, and several more informal promises promoted by Matthias to other provinces. But Matthias was a weak and indecisive character. On his eventual accession as Emperor in 1612, he came under increasing pressures from Catholic activists to prepare for confrontation, and, with his chief minister Cardinal Khlesl, adhered to the strategy of seeking to strengthen his grip in the hereditary lands by rebuilding the position of the Catholic Church, but for the present seeking to avoid open confrontation in the Empire. This naturally motivated the militants in both camps to step up the pressures. These further intensified since the heir to the childless Matthias was the Archduke Ferdinand of Styria, who had made himself notorious by his forceful reconversion of his duchy from Protestantism to Catholicism, facing his subjects with the choice of conformity or exile and then following up with a vigorous educational programme directed by the Jesuits. Ferdinand was one of the early Catholic rulers to fall wholly under Jesuit influence and was a genuine and sincere convert to militant counter-reform. The threat posed by Ferdinand inspired attempts to orchestrate a common front of Protestants between the provincial Estates of the hereditary lands, the Protestant Union and some foreign backers, but they proved hopelessly divided about how far they were prepared to prosecute their resistance. In 1617 even the Bohemian Estates voted to recognize Ferdinand as heir apparent, though everyone knew of his bitter opposition to the *Letter of Majesty*. He could not be elected to the Bohemian crown while Matthias still lived.

The situation was further complicated by the position of the French monarchy. After nearly a decade of peaceful inactivity, Henry IV was showing signs of restlessness, perhaps alarmed at how the Truce might free the hands of the Spanish monarchy, perhaps merely anxious to resume his pursuit of military reputation. Whatever his motives, in 1610 he deliberately resolved to re-open the dynastic contest with the Habsburgs, with the southern Netherlands as his objective. He was assassinated in Paris on the eve of departing for the war, which therefore failed to materialize. France now faced a prolonged regency for the child Louis XIII, and the regency, as was customary in France, was vested in his mother, Marie de Medici. She was a woman of low political intelligence and a foreigner, and unable to exercise the authority of the crown effectively. So now there was another weak and divided government in charge of a major power. For a time it looked as though France might regress to the weakness of the wars of religion. Counter-Reformation militants, the *dévot* faction, saw an opportunity to strike back at the Edict of Nantes. Huguenot militants urged their aristocratic leaders to organize resistance, and a period of threatened rebellion and insincere compromises set in. This made effective French intervention in the European situation unfeasible.

It is possible to see in the surviving documentary evidence of correspondence, and the flood of printed polemic of the time, that Europe was drifting towards a general armed confrontation, and there was a prevalant neo-stoic resignation to this, since all could agree that the current religious pluralism must be ended and the Christian consensus on which the whole culture was built reinstated. The precariousness of the current truce was illustrated in 1614, when a commonplace succession dispute in the Empire over the Rhine duchies of Cleves and Jülich came to a head. They had a strategic position close to the borders of the United Provinces, which could be important for the expected future war. There were two plausible claimants, one Protestant, the other Catholic. It was impossible for the problem to be solved by the normal means, for such disputes fell within the prerogative of the Emperor and he was clearly a partisan. But in spite of considerable military preparations on both sides, the confrontation did not come in 1614; both sides hesitated and the obvious fudge of a partition was agreed.

The thinking of the rulers and their advisers seems to have focused on the ending of the Truce in 1621, when a final decision between war and peace must be made. The evidence suggested it would be war. The Lerma government had no coherent strategy. The local, nominally autonomous administration in Brussels was divided: its civilian members tended to urge avoidance of war. But there was a powerful lobby among military men and diplomats, particularly the royal viceroys in Naples and Milan and the ambassadors at the imperial court, who urged that they faced an international Protestant conspiracy, and it must be met by force. They pointed out how the conflict in the Netherlands and that in the Empire interlocked. One factor that has now been established arose from the position of Spain's military strike force, the army of Flanders, the only professional standing army in Europe.

Because Spain had lost control of the seas to the Dutch, this had to be sustained overland. Its organizing base was in the Spanish-ruled duchy of

Milan, which was convenient for assembling the recruits and supplies contracted for by the asientos with the crown's Genoese bankers. These then
had to be passed overland, across the Alpine passes and down the Rhine
valley. Some of the key Swiss passes were controlled by Protestant cantons,
like the Valtelline pass, and then the route ran close to French territory for
much of its length, and by the lands of the militant and Calvinist Elector
Palatine. It was seen as vulnerable, and could be strengthened by reassertion
of the authority of the Habsburg emperors and the support of the Catholic
princes, particularly Maximilian of Bavaria. It is common that when an
imperial power has weak government at the centre, its agents out in the field
tend to take their own policy initiatives. They encouraged potential allies
like Ferdinand of Styria and Maximilian with proffers of Spanish subsidies
to pursue their hard-line Catholicizing policies. While in Brussels the two
Spinola brothers, one a major international banker, the other the professional commander of the army of Flanders, canvassed the advantages to be
gained by a Spanish seizure of the Rhine Palatinate, preferably prior to the
expiry of the Truce. Furthermore, the war party managed to negotiate a
family compact between the Madrid and Vienna Habsburgs in 1617 for
cooperation in Germany, and eventually a commitment by the Emperor to
involve the Empire in the war with the United Provinces.[3]

Another factor that pointed in the direction of war in 1621 was the
feeling in Madrid that the Truce had favoured the United Provinces. There
was substance in the belief: there had been a surge of economic growth in
every direction after 1609, making the United Provinces the leading commercial and financial power in Europe. This contrasted with the feelings that
Spain was stagnating economically, which was also true, and that something
would have to be done to reassert her status as the leading world power. In
debates within the Spanish government, there was a preoccupation with this
problem of reputation. Zuñiga, a leading member and a level-headed professional, would stress its importance: 'In my view a monarchy that has lost its
reputation, even if it has lost no territory, is a sky without light, a sun
without rays, a body without a soul.' If in 1621 Spain agreed to prolong the
Truce on the existing terms, the world would see it as a confession of weakness. He knew, and most accepted, that the United Provinces could not be
recovered by conquest. But before agreeing to a long-term settlement they
must be compelled to make concessions over such issues as the treatment of
Catholics in the republic, the continued closure of the Scheldt, and their
commercial intrusions into the colonial trades.

But there had been a hardening of attitudes on the other side.
Oldenbarneveldt, with the support of the majority of the commercial oligarchs who controlled the province of Holland, was in favour of extending
the Truce. The prince of Orange was not. He had acquiesced in the Truce,
but was seeking to form a coalition among those who opposed it. One powerful lobby was the immigrants from the south, looking in part for revenge,
in part for new economic openings, both domestically, where their prospects

were often blocked by the established oligarchies, and in the Spanish and Portuguese empires. He could expect the support of the nobility of the inland provinces, who found career opportunity in the army, and where some communities could make a living out of servicing garrisons and fortifications. He could find support in Zeeland, where privateering had flourished. And chance gave another powerful constituency.

Almost simultaneously with the conclusion of the Truce a major controversy broke out in the Calvinist Reformed Church around the revisionist writings of a Leiden professor, Arminius. These proposed relaxations of the strict Calvinist position on salvation and predestination, suggesting that salvation might be open to most believers, and that the sacraments and good works might have a role in achieving it. He went further, to suggest that Catholics were to be considered fellow Christians burdened with erroneous beliefs, not as the agents of Antichrist. Finally Arminius' programme, set out in a public *Remonstrance* in 1609, was strongly Erastian in supporting the ultimate superiority of the civil magistrates over the church. The revisionist movement got a positive response in Holland, and with Oldenbarneveldt. In a debate before the Holland provincial Estates the orthodox faction, under the leadership of a rival professor, Gomarus, fiercely denounced the revisionists as closet papists, and published their *Counter-remonstrance*. The ensuing controversy divided opinion throughout the United Provinces and spread to the international Calvinist movement. Prince Maurice, the stadholder, did not declare open support for the counter-remonstrants but they looked to him for encouragement in their confrontations with Oldenbarneveldt and the Holland regents. By 1617, when counter-remonstrant demonstrations threatened regent control in Amsterdam and the Hague, the stadholder declined to sanction intervention by the army to restore order. The Holland States then asserted their own control over the Holland contingents in the army and were denounced by Maurice for 'an affront to the true Reformed religion and our person'. He demanded the calling of an international synod to resolve the issues, known to history as the Synod of Dordrecht, which drafted a new declaration of faith denouncing the Arminians. Those who would not conform would be expelled. The stadholder was then empowered by the Estates General to secure the common good, and launched a general purge, arresting Oldenbarneveldt, who was later subjected to a show trial and executed. Under cover of the general purge which followed the synod, Maurice was able to restructure the urban regencies and install his own men in the key public positions, so that as the end of the Truce approached he was in charge of policy.

It is unclear whether Maurice was determined to renew the war whatever happened. There are indications that the Truce might have been prolonged on the existing terms, but any of the concessions being demanded by Spain were out of the question. The victory of the militant faction at the synod put the Dutch Reformed Church at the head of the international Calvinist movement. This suited Maurice's strategy of exploiting conditions in the Empire to divert the centre of hostilities away from the territory of the United

Provinces, and encouragement and modest subsidies were made available to the Protestant Union and the subsequent Protestant resistance against the Habsburgs. In the end, in 1621, once it was clear that the United Provinces would make no further concessions to buy an extension of the Truce, the government in Madrid allowed it to expire and accepted renewal of the war. The prestige of the monarchy had to be upheld.

The European war 1618–1648: the Habsburg phase

The outbreak of the war, like that of most wars, resulted from a mix of calculation and accident. A militant faction in the Protestant Union, led by Christian of Anhalt, had long considered how to end the Habsburg tenure of the imperial throne. The Emperor was chosen by the College of Electors, three secular princes, all Protestant, and three ecclesiastical Electors and the decision rested with the seventh elector, the king of Bohemia, who was a

Map 2.1 The Thirty Years War

Habsburg. Since the Bohemian crown was elective, and Bohemia was pre-dominantly a Protestant society, it would be possible to secure a Protestant king, who in turn would secure a Protestant majority in the College of Electors. The obstacles in the way of realizing this scenario were multiple. The first was tradition. The Habsburgs had held the imperial crown for cen-turies by 1600, and been undisputed kings of Bohemia since 1526. There was a deep-seated reluctance to contemplate challenging their customary rights. This can be seen in the action of the Bohemian Estates in 1617 in rec-ognizing Ferdinand of Styria as heir, in spite of the absence of guarantees on continuing religious toleration. Then there was division: the Protestant Electors were divided. The most influential, the Lutheran John George of Saxony, was a traditionalist and strongly opposed to Calvinist militancy. Nor was Bohemia a consolidated kingdom. It consisted of the four linked provinces, each with its own laws and Estates, of Bohemia, Moravia, Silesia and Lusatia. As always in the devolved European societies of the period, for most people, most of the time, the interests of their province took prece-dence over the joint interests of the kingdom as a whole. But as the Bohemian Estates met in May 1618, they could not ignore the cumulative evidence that Matthias was actively using the Catholic minority, through crown patronage, to reinforce crown authority, and that, after him, Ferdinand certainly intended to promote Counter-Reformation policies, and the fears were enough, temporarily, to unite all the provinces behind a policy of prevention.

This was the background to one of the best-known incidents in European history, the defenestration of Prague, when a group of militant Protestant councillors threw the two most prominent Catholics, whom they identified as 'evil councillors' poisoning the ruler's mind, out of a high window, though fortunately they landed on the castle dunghill and survived. But this excited enough tension for the Protestant councillors to persuade the Estates to set up a provisional government for Bohemia, the Directory, then to raise an army and appeal to foreign powers to come to their assistance. Evidence sug-gests that Ferdinand and his militant advisers decided to meet the challenge head on. Negotiation continued with the Bohemians, but the death of Matthias in March 1619 precipitated a rebel renunciation of their alle-giance. By August 1619, the Bohemian Estates and the Directory had full control of the kingdom, were suppressing the Catholic loyalists, and had enacted a revised constitution, vesting sovereign authority in the Estates and guaranteeing religious toleration. Finally they elected a new king, Frederick, the Calvinist Elector Palatine.

Events showed that the Bohemian revolt had been a mistake. The support the rebels had looked for from the Protestant community did not materi-alize. In the Empire the Protestant Union gave only reluctant endorsement, and its most prominent member, the Elector of Saxony, stood aside, once he was assured of a reward – the acquisition of the province of Lusatia. As a result, Ferdinand was elected Emperor in 1619 without opposition in the electoral college. Among the foreign powers, only the prince of Orange promised assistance, since this distraction in the Empire, diverting Habsburg resources, was just what he had wanted in view of the coming end of the Truce. The rebels had hoped that they would be supported by Protestant-dominated Estates in other parts of the Habsburg dominions. This happened in a disjointed way. The Hungarian rebel Bethlen Gabor and the Estates of Lower Austria also joined in, but it proved impossible to consolidate these movements into an effective military alliance.

Even so, at first Ferdinand's position looked weak, since he lacked the means to raise forces to suppress the rebels. With the institutions of the Empire paralysed, and his own Estates in rebellion, he could not raise taxes. When the Madrid government realized what had happened, it did not hesitate to order intervention. The Council of Finance told Lerma in August 1618 that there were no spare funds to support an intervention, but even Philip III was roused to action and ordered that 'the Council of Finance must find a way. Germany cannot simply be lost.' A small force financed by credits raised in Italy by the local viceroy was sent to Bohemia. But much more decisive was the order to implement Spinola's plans, by moving Spanish troops from the Netherlands into the Palatinate, which was done in 1620, immensely improving the security of the Spanish Road and depriving Frederick of his home base. Then Ferdinand, helped by promises of Spanish funding, recruited Maximilian of Bavaria and the army of the Catholic League to his cause. Maximilian had aims of his own, partly driven by a wish to diminish Spanish influence in the Empire, and to prevent a successful Ferdinand acquiring the power to rebuild the imperial authority in the Empire at the expense of the territorial princes. Ferdinand too had no wish to become a helpless client of Madrid, and made his own private deal with Maximilian to outlaw Frederick and deprive him of his lands and electoral title. The title and the lands of the Upper Palatinate would be his reward, while the transfer of the title would guarantee Catholic control of the electoral college. Maximilian and the Catholic League he directed then mobilized their forces under the command of a competent military professional, Count Tilly.

In 1620, while Spinola secured the Palatinate, Tilly's army succeeded in defeating the forces of the rebel Austrian Estates and then participated in the decisive battle outside Prague at the White Mountain in August. Frederick and the rebel leaders did not try to prolong resistance in Bohemia, but fled into exile. This exposed the basic weakness of the Bohemian rebellion. Frederick had proved an inept ruler, and his aggressive Calvinism had offended the largely Lutheran nobility and burghers. But the revolt was undermined by the narrowness of its support inside Bohemia. The Estates were entirely controlled by the nobility: they had been urged by radicals to widen their power base by making concessions to the burghers and peasants but had refused to do so. The bulk of the Bohemian population remained passive. There was nothing to prevent the restored Habsburg authorities executing such rebel leaders as came into their hands, after show trials in 1621, and moving towards a strengthened royal power on the basis of a restored Catholic Church and a purged nobility and burghers, placing the kingdom in safe Catholic–loyalist hands.

At this point the crisis in the Empire should have been resolved. There was a residual Protestant resistance, led by Christian of Anhalt, sustained by the forces of a mercenary contractor, Count Mansfeld. They were so short of funding that Mansfeld could do little more than keep the field by living off whatever unfortunate corner of Germany he could occupy.

There had been a change of government in Madrid when Philip III died in 1621. His successor, Philip IV, was a more active monarch, but retained the system of government through *privado*, installing his tutor and mentor, who is known to the history books as the Count-Duke of Olivares. He was a favourite of a different class from Lerma: no less avid to accumulate worldly goods, he was also a dedicated politician bent on reform within the kingdom and the recovery of Spain's international hegemony. Olivares, with the unswerving support of his sovereign, directed Spanish policies until the disasters of the 1640s. As he saw it, the Protestant threat to Germany posed by the Bohemian revolt was now removed, and there should be a negotiated settlement in the Empire, which would then join Spain in prosecuting the war on the United Provinces. To secure this, he wanted a repentant Frederick reinstated as Elector Palatine.

What ensued demonstrated how a war, once started, gains a momentum of its own. Ferdinand had raised and maintained his principal force, the army of the Catholic League, by promising the rank of Elector and territorial gains to Maximilian. In 1623, as Emperor, Ferdinand tried to implement his agreements, with the consent of the other Electors. At a meeting of the Electors at Regensburg, held early in 1623, Ferdinand found a general refusal to recognize the transfer of Frederick's electoral title or to consider giving a grant of taxation. Though he compromised by decreeing that Maximilian's tenure of the electoral title was only for his own lifetime, the meeting was deadlocked and the Protestant princes walked out. Instead, Ferdinand had to pay further bribes to Maximilian, allowing him to assume control of his province of Upper Austria to support his army.

In spite of this, Ferdinand was able to use his military superiority to strengthen his position in the Empire, and this was augmented by a change of emphasis in the policy of Olivares. During 1625, the army of Flanders won its last major military success against the United Provinces by a successful siege of the fortress of Breda. If military success could be seconded by economic pressures, the United Provinces might be forced to settle on favourable terms. Already the revival of Habsburg power in Germany enabled Olivares to blockade the Dutch river trade into central Europe. Now Olivares conceived a plan for pressing on into Protestant north Germany, with a view to establishing Habsburg naval power in the Baltic and stopping the vital Dutch carrying trade there. At this point both camps were reinforced. In 1627 the king of Denmark, Christian IV, took up the Protestant cause. He was an ambitious ruler endowed with a significant private income from the tolls levied on shipping passing through into the Baltic. He was also a prince of the Empire with a territorial interest in the major secularized bishoprics of the north-west. On the other side, the Emperor, seeking to free himself from his dependence on the Catholic League army, found the means to raise a new army of his own. Albrecht Wallenstein was a Bohemian nobleman who had done well out of the resettlement of Bohemia in the wake of the rebellion. Assisted by his Dutch Calvinist bankers, he built up a vast landed estate, whose resources were developed to provide supplies for a large contract army. He began by offering the Emperor a force of 50,000 mercenaries on advantageous cash terms and was accepted. When Christian IV entered the conflict, Ferdinand encouraged Wallenstein to increase his force to 140,000, and, together with the League army under Tilly, he met and defeated Christian at the battle of the Lutter in 1627, and then went on to overrun north Germany and penetrate into Jutland. As reward, Wallenstein acquired further large estates in Mecklenburg which he absorbed into his economic complex for the support of his army. He too began to take an interest in establishing a naval presence in the Baltic and in 1628 he besieged the port of Stralsund. Here he was defeated by the intervention of the king of Sweden, Gustav Adolf, who saw a Habsburg naval presence in the Baltic as a direct challenge to the security of his kingdom.

In spite of this check, the Emperor was now in a position to consolidate his control of the north, depite the resentment of Maximilian and the League at the expansion of Wallenstein's power, and the threat that eventually the Emperor might use Wallenstein to impose his authority on the territorial princes and destroy their autonomy in the Empire. In 1629 Ferdinand and his advisers launched a major new initiative in the Edict of Restitution. This ordered the surrender of all ecclesiastical properties that had been secularized in defiance of the Augsburg settlement of 1555. These were then available for rewarding Ferdinand's supporters at the expense of the Protestant principalities. Wallenstein was ordered to use his troops to execute the decree. He further consolidated the victory by allowing Christian IV to disengage from the conflict on favourable terms. At this point it seemed Ferdinand would establish a restructured Empire, under firm central control, with Wallenstein and his army as its executive arm. This prospect alarmed both the Protestant princes and the Catholic League, and the territorial princes joined in pressing Ferdinand to dismiss Wallenstein and disband his army. Ferdinand had incentives to comply, the most important simply being the danger represented by Wallenstein's accumulated military and economic power, and the well-founded fear that he was pursuing an agenda of his own. Another was the pull of dynastic interest. Olivares had extended his operations into northern Italy to frustrate a bid by Richelieu to install a French client prince in the strategic duchy of Mantua. He expected

Ferdinand, who as Emperor claimed feudal jurisdiction in northern Italy, to assist, which he did, causing an open confrontation with Wallenstein, when he was ordered to detach forces for service in Italy. Ferdinand was also under renewed pressure from Madrid to use his regained authority to declare war on the United Provinces, to which Wallenstein was also opposed.

In 1630 the Emperor called a meeting of territorial princes of the Empire at Regensburg, and asked them to elect his son King of the Romans and thus secure the imperial succession. He also asked for confirmation of the Edict of Restitution and for a declaration of war on the United Provinces. The leading Protestant princes absented themselves, while the Catholic princes, led by Maximilian, refused any concessions until Wallenstein was dismissed and military command in the Empire returned to the Catholic League. The Emperor incautiously accepted the conditions and, in October 1630, Wallenstein was dismissed, upon which the princes, having got what they wanted, declined to agree to any of Ferdinand's requests.

The Swedish intervention

Gustav Adolf succeeded to the Swedish throne in 1611 and inherited wars with all his neighbours: Denmark, Russia and Poland. In 1613 he had negotiated his way out of the Danish war, which had gone badly for Sweden, at the price of an enormous cash ransom for Sweden's only Atlantic port, Älvsborg. He fared better in Russia, which had nearly collapsed in the anarchy of the 'time of troubles' between 1600 and 1613, and he was able to conclude a satisfactory peace at Stolbova in 1617, which extended his eastern borders right round the Gulf of Finland, pushing the Russians back from direct access to the Baltic. The struggle with Poland was more intractable, because King Sigismund III of Poland maintained his claim to the Swedish crown. Gustav had been little interested in the Bohemian revolt and remained focused on Poland, attacking and seizing the major trading port of Riga in 1621, and when this failed to persuade Sigismund to abandon his claims, he pushed on to occupy the whole province of Livonia. He had been solicited after 1624 to lead an intervention in Germany, but was outbid by Christian IV and turned his attention back to Poland. From 1626 he was engaged in a doubtful campaign to extend Swedish control over the ports of Polish Prussia, not only to keep up the pressure on Sigismund, but also to use control of the ports to levy tolls on shipping using them. But in 1628 the victories of Tilly and Wallenstein in north Germany, and awareness of Habsburg plans to establish a naval presence in the Baltic, decided the king that his kingdom's security demanded that these plans be stopped.

By early 1628 he told his Council he intended to intervene in the German war, and had in fact joined Denmark in lifting Wallenstein's siege of Stralsund, then retaining the city by installing a garrison, his first German base. He could not act further while the Polish war continued, but he secured the agreement of the Swedish Estates for an intervention in 1629. This became possible when Richelieu negotiated a truce with Poland for six years, leaving Sweden the right to collect the Prussian port tolls while it lasted. Even so Gustav Adolf needed extra funding to intervene in Germany. He appreciated that for a small, impoverished kingdom like Sweden any prolonged war must be made to pay for itself, either by financial subsidy from allies, or revenue extorted from conquered territories.[4] In June 1630 the king landed at Peenemünde, claiming limited objectives: to secure north Germany and its littoral from Habsburg expansionism and secure Sweden's position in the Baltic. He was not welcomed by the German Protestant princes, who had taken advantage of the disbanding of Wallenstein's army and the diversion of the Habsburg war effort into northern Italy to try and reconstruct a united Protestant front in the Empire: one of their main aims was to put an end to foreign intervention. Gustav had to impose himself first on the duke of Pomerania, to secure an extended coastal base, and then force the Elector of Brandenburg into alliance. Early in 1631 Gustav concluded a subsidy agreement with France.

The imperialist forces, under Tilly, spent the first half of 1631 besieging the city of Magdeburg, from which they could expect to extort a substantial contribution to the upkeep of the army. Gustav had promised to relieve the city, but the need to collect resources held him back. Magdeburg fell and, unusually for this type of war, was stormed, sacked and burned to the ground. The disaster was almost certainly unintended, as all belligerents knew that a captured city was a valuable economic resource and a devastated city was useless. Tilly himself acknowledged this, and also realized it was a propaganda gift to the Protestants. He told Maximilian: 'Our danger has no end, for the Protestant Estates will without doubt only be strengthened in their hatred by this.' They were. The desperate Tilly, still looking for supplies, finally moved on Saxony, where John George, the Elector, had been standing out against a Swedish alliance, but the threat of occupation at last drove him into acceptance. In November 1631, Gustav moved to confront the League army, and at the battle of Breitenfeld won the first decisive Protestant victory of the war. Tilly's army was destroyed. The king of Sweden became the Protestant hero and marched his troops down into the Catholic south as far as Bavaria, plundering and exacting contributions. Breitenfeld was as important psychologically as militarily, because it broke the cycle of imperialist successes, but it coincided with other factors damaging to the Habsburg position.

The most important was the growing activism of Louis XIII and Richelieu, pursuing a policy of wearing down Spanish resources by indirect interventions, like the subsidy to Gustav, or inducements to Maximilian to withdraw from the war and accept French protection. There was also Richelieu's successful diversion into northern Italy. Here a vigorous but small-scale military campaign by French forces inflicted a major blow against Habsburg power, enabling Richelieu to close the Alpine passes in the crucial winter of 1631–2. He took advantage of Habsburg disarray to install French garrisons in Lorraine, securing control of a major border area, and setting up a new threat to the Spanish Road. Richelieu could do this because, in 1630, following the long siege of La Rochelle, the threat of Huguenot rebellion, which had paralysed French policy-making, was settled. The Huguenots were disarmed but assured of continuing, though controlled, religious toleration. Richelieu's aim was to weaken the Habsburgs while sparing France the burdens of open warfare.

At the same time the structural weaknesses in the position of the Spanish monarchy were being exposed. On a wave of optimism created by the capture of Breda in 1625 and the successful repulse of a Dutch expedition to seize the Portuguese sugar colony of Brazil, Olivares had extended his commitments by accepting the French challenge in northern Italy. This may be seen as the last straw in the process of overextension, which is the nemesis of all aspiring superpowers. The truth was brutally revealed in 1628 by the Dutch destruction of that year's treasure fleet, which at a stroke shattered the basis of Spain's war finance for the year. Although the total loss of a fleet was a rare occurrence, it coincided with a serious decline in American silver output, apparently due to production problems in America and a tendency for more bullion to be consumed in the colonies. The fall was stabilized after the 1650s, but it hit the Spanish war effort at its most difficult stage. It caused a turnround in the Netherlands campaigns: in 1629 the Spanish went on to the defensive, while Frederick Henry, the new stadholder, persuaded the Estates General to expand the army and took the offensive, capturing s'Hertogenbosch and Wesel, a major strategic gain. The government in Madrid, under heavy pressure from Brussels, now offered to negotiate a new truce. From then on there were continuing negotiations for a settlement, accompanied by new offensive operations, which in 1632 brought the capture of Maastricht, and a modest, but steady, penetration by the Dutch army into the northern border regions of Flanders and Brabant. Frederick Henry, a pragmatic politician, was not averse to a negotiated settlement, but on his own terms. Political opinion in the United Provinces hardened, as an economic recession that had affected parts of the economy on the renewal of hostilities lifted in the 1630s, and the Dutch economic domination of Europe surged ahead.

Within the Empire the winter of 1631–2 was a desperate time for Ferdinand, with his only army wrecked and his Spanish paymasters desperately seeking to fend off bankruptcy. In his hour of need he reluctantly appealed to Wallenstein to raise a new army. It is not known exactly what the terms of the agreement were, but they probably gave Wallenstein broad autonomy over how his army was used. The record shows that Wallenstein was not eager to engage in battle with the Swedes, though the very existence of the new force put an end to the unopposed rampage through the Catholic south. Gustav now stated Sweden's terms for a settlement: full restoration of the Protestant position in the Empire, to be protected by a new institution, a *corpus evangelicorum*, with power to secure the settlement. Sweden would need compensation for her expenses, and as security would take control of the whole Baltic coast.

In November 1632 Wallenstein linked up with the remnants of Tilly's army and Gustav attacked their combined force at Lützen. The battle was indecisive though Wallenstein retreated, but most importantly Gustav Adolf was killed, leaving Sweden to his daughter Christina and the prospect of a long regency. The government, in effect, came into the hands of Gustav's Chancellor and long-term confidant, Axel Oxenstierna, who had the incomparable advantage as political leader that he was not a sovereign prince with dynastic interests to pursue, and could take an unusually pragmatic and realist view of politics. He had of course the corresponding weakness that, not being a sovereign prince, he lacked status and authority in dealing with princes – in the first instance in holding together the alliance that Gustav had established. Oxenstierna, one of the few really great political managers of the seventeenth century, pursued a consistent policy of seeking an end to Sweden's participation, but only on terms that would secure her international position.

The year 1633 was dominated by the enigma of Wallenstein. His intentions, if he had any consistent strategy, have remained obscure, but it is fair to assume he wanted to use his army to secure for himself a permanent princely status, perhaps as king of Bohemia, and that Ferdinand, his employer, had good reason to be alarmed. His army was notably inactive; it was also showing signs of strain, part of its resource base having been seized or devastated by Gustav's depredations, and there are signs that he had problems holding the allegiance of his officers.[5] By the end of the year, Madrid was calling for his elimination and Ferdinand agreed. Wallenstein was dismissed, arrested by a group of dissident officers and murdered. His army was fused with that of the Catholic League under the command of the Emperor's son and heir, the Archduke Ferdinand.

Spain was now prepared for another effort to seize the initiative, assembling a new army in northern Italy, which would march up the Spanish Road and restore the military situation both in the Empire and the Netherlands. In 1634 the march began, and the army encountered the Swedish forces and their mercenary ally, Bernard of Saxe-Weimar, at the battle of Nördlingen, winning a convincing victory This transformed the situation. It opened the way for John George to pursue his agenda of a negotiated peace in the Empire, to be followed by an end to external interference in its affairs. Ferdinand was now prepared to compromise on the confessional front. The result was the Peace of Prague, concluded in 1635 and open to all members of the Empire. The religious position was to be stabilized around the status quo of 1627, and the Edict of Restitution formally suspended. This legally recognized the Habsburg conversion of Bohemia, but otherwise re-established the old confessional divide. However, the Peace did concede wider executive powers to the Emperor, who would have the sole right to maintain armed forces in the Empire, so all princely armies and all separatist alliances must disband, including the Catholic League. Only three princes of importance refused to agree: the Elector Palatine and the rulers of Hesse-Cassel and Brunswick-Lüneberg.

The disaster at Nördlingen had threatened to disintegrate the Protestant front, which Oxenstierna had constructed as the League of Heilbronn. As its resources shrank and allies defected, even the core Swedish troops began to mutiny. Finally the danger of a renewed collapse of the anti-Habsburg alliance compelled a reluctant Richelieu and Louis XIII to intervene openly with a declaration of war on Spain and the Empire. France entered into alliance with the United Provinces for joint operations against the Spanish Netherlands. Richelieu also made new treaties with Oxenstierna and his German allies, Sweden was acknowledged as an equal ally with Louis XIII, and the two powers would jointly guarantee any eventual peace settlement. They would also pursue a common war effort, with France providing subsidies and military assistance. In return France would be entitled to extend her borders to the Rhine from Breisach to Strasbourg.

The last phase of the German war

With the Peace of Prague and the formal entry of Louis XIII into the war, the character of the conflict had shifted. It had not lost its confessional dimension, despite the oddity of the leader of the Protestant side being the Most Catholic king of France with a cardinal as his first minister. But religion was definitely subordinated to the traditional secular concerns of struggle for territory and assets between sovereign rulers. The last major independent mercenary contractor, Bernard of Saxe-Weimar, died in 1639 and his troops were taken into the service of the French king. Henceforth, the armies involved were the official forces of sovereign states. Oxenstierna had temporarily lost control of the Swedish army in 1641, when its commander Baner died, and the Swedish army, left without a commander or pay, threatened to enlist in French service. Oxenstierna regained control by sending out a new commander, Torstensson, with reinforcements and money from Sweden. He not only brought the army back under control, but launched it on a new round of striking military victories, reinstating the impression of Swedish invincibility in the field.

The result of the French intervention was disappointing in a military sense. No major strategist emerged on the French side and resources were spread thinly round several separate war fronts. It was also apparent that at first the French armies suffered from lack of recent military experience. They failed to achieve any decisive success until 1643, when Condé's rather overrated victory at Rocroi over part of the veteran army of Flanders caught the contemporary imagination. Formal negotiations for a general peace in the Empire were set up in 1641 between France, Sweden and the Emperor. The conflict between Spain and the United Provinces was the subject of separate negotiation, while there were no serious proposals for settling the dynastic struggle between France and Spain.

The formal framework for the peace negotiation was that of an imperial Diet, with the Catholic representatives, including the French, meeting in Münster and the Protestants, including Sweden, in Osnabrück. There was a direct correlation between progress made and the military and political fortunes of the participants. Rocroi seems to have convinced Ferdinand to take the negotiation seriously; even so, his senior negotiator and confidant, Trautmansdorff, did not arrive until late in 1645. Before that there had been a major problem over the status of the German territorial princes in the proceedings. The Emperor would have wished to negotiate in the name of the Empire as a whole, but after embittered wrangling it was conceded that the territorial princes would participate as sovereign rulers. Things eased once the republic of Venice was accepted as the neutral mediator. The Venetians had long-established professional diplomatic experience and their mediator at the congress played a vital role in forcing progress.

The settlement which emerged in the autumn of 1648, known collectively as the Peace of Westphalia, consisted of two main groups of agreements, the one concerned with the future status of the Holy Roman Empire, the other with the interests of the foreign powers that had been engaged in the conflict. Within the Empire the starting point for the religious settlement was to set the confessional position of the year 1624 as the norm. In future, even if the sovereign changed his confessional allegiance, it would not change the religious status of his territory. That meant that the Edict of Restitution was revoked. There was in future to be confessional parity in the Empire. The Calvinists were not formally recognized as a third confession, but regarded as a variant of the Protestant Augsburg Confession and entitled to the same rights as the Lutherans. In cases where ecclesiastical principalities had been secularized by 1624, their Protestant administrators could take their seats in the imperial Diet. In accordance with the principle of parity, the Diet itself would divide into two sections whenever a matter related to religion arose, which meant almost any issue of substance, and both would have to agree before any resolution could pass: that is, both parties had a right of veto over imperial legislation. The imperial prerogatives covering the raising of armed forces or the levying of taxation were exercised with the consent of the Diet. The same principle of parity was applied to the imperial Chamber Court. The net effect was to make any alteration to the status quo set out in the treaties virtually impossible unless total consensus prevailed.

There were further provisions regulating the status of the imperial power. For the imperial election the pre-1618 system was reinstated and the Elector Palatine was restored to his Rhenish lands and his electorate. To accommodate Maximilian, a new electorate was created for him and his heirs, and he retained the lands of the Upper Palatinate granted in 1623. To balance this, the three Protestant Electors were jointly to exercise an additional electoral vote, sustaining the principle of parity. The Emperor had to concede the recognition of the principle of *Landeshoheit* – the right of the territorial princes to unfettered sovereignty over their territories – including the right to raise troops and engage in diplomatic relations with foreign powers, with the sole proviso that these could not be used against the Emperor. This left the Emperor with important prerogatives: all the members of the Empire were still subject to imperial laws and in disputed cases the Emperor remained the final court of appeal. This was particularly important in cases of dynastic inheritance: if there was no clear successor, the Emperor could dispose of the territory, and in every case of succession, whether disputed or not, a prince of the Empire had to seek formal investment from the Emperor as his feudal overlord. He also retained the exclusive power to grant titles of nobility within the Empire. Even so, there was now no legal way in which the Emperor could remodel the Empire as a unitary state. It was destined to remain a loose federal union, with most powers devolved, including the exercise of military powers, which for the Empire as whole were devolved to the ten 'circles' into which the Empire was divided, where the participating rulers would decide how to implement the levy of imperial troops and taxation. The treaty also clarified the status of the Swiss Confederation, which ceased to be part of the Empire, but acquired its internationally recognized status as permanently neutral. So far as the Empire was concerned, 30 years of embittered political and religious turmoil was resolved by seeking to turn the clock back. Where this was not possible, as with Maximilian's electoral title, then compensatory adjustments were made to restore a similitude of the original power structure. However, there was one conspicuous exception written into the treaties, respecting the hereditary territories of the Habsburgs, which were specifically exempted from the application of the 1624 norm. The Swedish negotiators held out for some time for full restitution of Bohemia, but in the end abandoned it in order to secure their own immediate political objectives. The Habsburgs remained free to maintain and extend the confessional cleansing of Bohemia and the Austrian duchies.

The Westphalia settlement is usually taken, with good reason, as symbolic of a significant shift in European thinking about the basis of their society, and this is embodied in the religious provisions which tacitly accepted a permanent state of religious pluralism in the Empire, which in turn undermined the wider concept of a monolithic culture which had no place for deviance. In the Empire, at least, the individual now had a right to choose his religion, provided he fitted into one of the recognized confessions, and, if he felt the need, to transfer, with his property, into another territory that suited him better. It pointed the way to the development of a more open society.

The other part of the Westphalia settlement regulated the relations between the Empire and the foreign participants in its wars. The Swedish position had not changed over the years, in part because Oxenstierna remained in control of policy, even after 1644 when Queen Christina was

declared of age and assumed the government. Sweden required two provisions as the price for ending hostilities: 'satisfaction' and 'security'. The first
meant the payment of her war costs, in effect the price of withdrawing and
disbanding her armies. This was to be settled by the Empire collectively. The
process took most of the three years after 1648, but worked remarkably
smoothly. Clearly the Germans, or their rulers, thought that getting rid of
the Swedes was worth every penny they could extort from their taxpayers;
and perhaps the common folk thought so too, since they had been bearing
the burden of sustaining the armies during the fighting. Security meant territorial safeguards against threats to Sweden's security interests in the Baltic.
From the first, Gustav Adolf had sought this in his control of the duchy of
Pomerania, which had been under permanent Swedish occupation. The
problem was that the last native duke had died childless during the war and
the Hohenzollern Electors of Brandenburg, whose territories adjoined the
duchy, had a plausible claim to the succession. The solution, facilitated by
French mediation, was to divide the duchy at the line of the river Oder, with
Brandenburg taking the eastern share and Sweden the western, including the
trading city of Stettin. The Elector was compensated with valuable secularized lands elsewhere, including the reversion of the city of Magdeburg, and
the Swedes with the secularized bishoprics of Bremen, though not the free
city of that name, and Werden. This left Sweden solidly entrenched along the
entire southern coast of the Baltic from the Elbe to the Gulf of Finland,
except for the break represented by eastern Pomerania, and the Prussian
duchies, which were dependencies of the Polish crown. These territories
were from one point of view a defensive zone, from another jumping-off
points for armed interventions in Germany. This would enable Sweden to
exercise the responsibilities of her elevation to the rank of a major European
power, confirmed in her status as joint guarantor, with the king of France, of
the integrity of the settlement. The possession of the territories also made the
king or queen of Sweden a prince of the Empire, with right of participation
in the Diet, which further enhanced Sweden's possibilities of intervention in
German affairs.

France had a comparable interest in borderlands of the Empire as part of
her rulers' standing dynastic rivalry with the Habsburgs. It had been the
policy of Richelieu and his successor, Cardinal Mazarin, to strengthen the
French position by getting possession of key crossing points, usually fortified
towns which controlled river crossings or strategic mountain passes. Even
before entering the war, Richelieu had taken advantage of the chaos in the
Empire to infiltrate French garrisons into key places in the duchy of Lorraine,
a part of the Empire. The question of Lorraine, however, was not touched on
in the treaties. But on France entering the war it became a war aim, written
into the alliance treaties with Sweden and her German Protestant allies, to
secure for the French king strategic territories in what is now called Alsace,
but was then an inextricable mosaic of territories and feudal jurisdictions
which were part of the Empire. The Emperor was prepared, as the price of

settlement, to make concessions; on the other hand, the German princes at Westphalia were resistant to formally ceding imperial lands to the French king. So, as was and is usual in international treaties, the issue was fudged. The Emperor ceded to the king of France his personal rights and jurisdictions in imperial lands on the west bank of the Rhine. What this implied was then written into the treaty in obscure, and partially contradictory, formulae, to evade saying outright that the sovereignty over the territories had been transferred. What was made clear was that the French rights did not confer on the king the status of prince of the Empire, and hence he did not acquire a seat in the imperial Diet.

The pacification of 1648 also included the ending of the struggle between Spain and the United Provinces, embodied in the separate treaty of Münster. When France entered the war after 1635, it had been one of the aims of Richelieu's policy to intervene in the Netherlands campaign, in the hope that joint operations by France and the United Provinces would drive the Spaniards out of the southern Netherlands, which could then be partitioned. This attractive strategic plan failed to produce results, mainly because of the faltering performance of the French armies, though the United Provinces was making slow, if modest, gains of territory in its annual campaigns. As the war dragged on, there was a growing movement in the United Provinces for a negotiated peace which, after a brief interval of hope following the battle of Nördlingen in 1634, was also increasingly desired by the governments in Madrid and Brussels. One reason for the change of mood, partly stimulated by the conduct of the French as allies, was the realization among the leaders of the United Provinces that France might be an uncomfortable neighbour, and their interests better served by leaving a weak buffer state to the south under Spanish sovereignty. By 1646, Frederick Henry came round to the view that the war should not be prolonged; hostilities virtually ended and the treaty was negotiated. It was entirely in favour of the United Provinces, giving unequivocal recognition of their sovereignty and reopening Spain to Dutch trade, retaining the closure of the Scheldt and rejecting Spain's pretentions to act as protector of the Catholic community in the republic. The Dutch also rejected any restraints being put on their trading in the Americas. The outcome is a standing monument to the reality that although war was the principal preoccupation of European society, it was by any standard massively inefficient. The Spanish monarchy, disposing of the most powerful military machine in the world, had waged some 80 years of warfare to subdue the rebel United Provinces and had failed completely. The same conclusion follows from the war in central Europe. This had been a case of the superimposition of different levels of conflict, the religious drive to reinstate confessional unity from the Counter-reformation and Calvinist camps, and the Habsburg political drive to create a strong central executive in the Empire. None of these objectives had been achieved after 30 years of armed conflict. The Empire would remain a loose federation, incapable of exerting collective political power on its own behalf in the

European political arena. It created a power vacuum in the heart of Europe, facilitating a permanent state of political instability.

This leaves a question which has been the subject of one of the longest-running historiographical debates, which began during the war itself, about the effect of the war on central European society and economy.[6] The assertion that the war devastated central Europe, caused massive depopulation, destroyed large parts of the infrastructure, ruined its trade and commerce, so that it took more than a century before the region even recovered the levels of material well-being attained by 1618, while the rest of Europe had forged ahead, became entrenched in European thinking. The flood of atrocity propaganda, such as the Collot prints of the disasters of war, which even today often illustrate history books on the period, and the German picaresque novel by Grimmelhausen, *Simplicissimus*, which came to be quoted as a conclusive authority on the unique destructiveness of this conflict, built up the image. It later became a useful tool for German nationalist publicity to explain the relatively late emergence of national self-consciousness and self-assertion.

In the twentieth century there has been active revisionism, aimed at reducing this scenario to reality. The problem is that the solid information available is so thin, and much of it of suspect integrity, that the construction of reliable statistics needed to underpin any realistic interpretation is almost impossible. For example, systematic population data does not exist. Substantial populations do seem to get lost, but whether they really died or migrated, which certainly happened on a large scale – perhaps 200,000 Bohemian dissidents eventually settled elsewhere – cannot be determined. Most contemporary accounts were compiled by the clergy, who had a propagandist interest in describing the horrors inflicted by their confessional enemies, and much supposed economic data comes from communities seeking to emphasize the destruction caused by the war as grounds for the lowering of their taxes and services. Magdeburg, the supreme horror story, may have lost up to 90 per cent of its population after the sack of 1631, but within a decade or two it was once more a substantial urban community. It can be shown that war damage was not spread evenly through the region: there were lucky areas, like the north-west, which saw relatively little campaigning, and here the city of Hamburg seems to have done well out of the war, and showed impressive growth in the war years. Other areas, like much of Bohemia or the Rhine valley, that were campaigned over repeatedly, almost certainly did suffer long-lasting damage. It is likely that the war, by impoverishing the urban and rural populations of the area east of Elbe, was a factor in the 'second serfdom' that developed there during the century, mainly because of the burdens of debt it forced on peasant farmers and the towns. On the other hand the city of Leipzig, often the focus of military operations and sometimes occupied by hostile forces, appears to have survived reasonably well, and certainly its great trade fairs continued to take place.

If population is taken as the best general indicator, since it was relatively easier to study, there are serious estimates that range from Steinberg's assertion that there was no absolute population decline between 1600 and 1650, to assertions that two-thirds of the population was lost. It is probably safe to work on the assumption that 30 years of continual campaigning, with its physical damage, and above all the armies' demands for contributions for their subsistence wherever they went, would have had negative effects on economic development. Manpower was the most important input into the early modern economy. If, as Rabb suggested, an overall reduction of population in central Europe of 30–40 per cent is plausible, that would go far to explain the relative backwardness of the German economy over the century after 1650. But in one sense it does not matter whether the catastrophic image of the war is true or not. For what is indisputable is that among the elites who decided Europe's affairs it was widely believed that the war had been uniquely destructive, and it was necessary to ensure that nothing like it could happen again. It encouraged their belief that in future reason, not passion, should be the basis of public policy, and that security required the maintenance of strong governments, powerful enough to control events.

A Franco-Spanish coda

In 1648, Spain had ended the war with the United Provinces and liquidated her commitments in the Empire. On the other hand, since 1640, the government faced a new internal front within Iberia, when first Catalonia and then Portugal launched separatist rebellions, both of which had attracted support from the French. Olivares had retired in 1642 and no new *privado* was appointed. Philip IV intended to rule in person henceforth, but displayed no talent for the role of war leader. There was no strategic plan, only a blind adherence to the most basic dynastic principle: that a ruler had an absolute duty to preserve his inheritance, improve it if he could, but certainly pass it on undiminished to his successors. In 1647 there had been another state bankruptcy, and in 1653 yet another. It was clear that the government's financial resources were stretched to breaking point, yet the king and his advisers were determined to fight on against the Bourbons. In France, Richelieu had died in 1642, followed by Louis XIII, and the regency for the child Louis XIV was in the hands of the queen-mother, herself a Habsburg, and Richelieu's successor, Cardinal Mazarin, was also a foreigner. The French revenue system too was clearly close to breakdown by 1648, and the regency government lacked the power that had come from the combination of Louis XIII and Richelieu.

Mazarin was a gifted and experienced diplomatist, and to him the Peace of Westphalia opened up the prospect that France, in single combat with a palpably weakened Spanish monarchy, could expect to extract further gains from pursuing the war. He was blown off course by the round of rebellions and civil wars known as the Fronde. They were fuelled by discontents at the seemingly endless rise of taxation, which by 1648 was encroaching on the rights and privileges of the elites as well as the common people. The legal oligarchy of the *parlements* voiced the growing popular protests, but Mazarin had ignored their remonstrances. In 1648 the *parlement* of Paris in effect went on strike in protest at the government's alleged illegalities and found massive popular support from the populace of Paris. They also created the opening for discontented aristocratic factions, headed by members of the royal family like the king's uncle, the duke of Orléans, and the prince of Condé to declare support and demand the dismissal of Mazarin. The *parlementaires*, who were not happy with their aristocratic allies, were detached by Mazarin, who offered to implement their programme of reforms. That only exacerbated the rebellious magnates, who launched a civil war against the cardinal. Thus the French government was paralysed from 1648 until 1653 by political disruption, which gave Spain a breathing space and an opportunity to intervene in the French unrest. When Mazarin succeeded in dividing his aristocratic enemies by skilled use of patronage, and the revolt collapsed in 1653, Condé, the victor of Rocroi, entered the service of Philip IV and became one of his leading generals.

But Mazarin could resume serious military operations against Spain. Basically he was relying on attrition, reckoning, probably correctly, that the resources of the French crown would outlast those of the Spanish. He could also be encouraged by the evidence of growing military competence in the French armies, such as another striking victory over the army of Flanders at Lens in 1648. The French were finding effective military leaders, like Turenne, one of the most gifted generals of the century. The French strategy was to concentrate on keeping alive the rebellions in Catalonia and Portugal, while pressing forward on the frontiers with the Spanish Netherlands, which Mazarin identified as the main objective. He wrote:

> The acquisition of the Spanish Netherlands would give the city of Paris an impregnable rampart, and it could then truly be called the heart of France ... so much blood and money would be well-spent if ... the provinces were annexed to the crown of France.

The Spanish, in spite of their deteriorating finances, maintained a surprisingly strong resistance, but then suffered a further blow from the entry on to the international stage of the English republic. Driven by the prolonged civil strife of the 1640s, the English had at last developed world-class armed forces, and having finished fighting domestic enemies, had in 1652–4 waged an impressive naval war on the United Provinces for colonies and trade. With this over, the government of Oliver Cromwell considered who to fight next, and the choice seemed to be intervention in the ongoing Franco-Spanish conflict. Cromwell decided to target Spain and launched the completely unprovoked assault on Spain's Caribbean possessions that resulted in the capture of Jamaica. It also enabled the English navy to capture or destroy two successive Spanish bullion fleets, so that no American bullion reached

Spain in 1657–8, a deadly blow to her ability to carry on. Mazarin then made the obvious move of entering into alliance with England, and in 1658 an English army joined the French in a successful attack on Dunkirk, in which the Spanish relieving army was destroyed at the battle of the Dunes, where the new professionalism of the English army was demonstrated for the first time on the continent.

At this point both Mazarin and Philip IV seem to have concluded that further pursuit of the war was either impractical or even counter-productive. Philip was now prepared to compromise to the extent of buying off the French with marginal territorial concessions on the Netherlands borders and the Pyrenees, though with the clear intention of continuing his war to reconquer Portugal, assisted by a worthless French promise of non-intervention. Mazarin may have been becoming aware of the intolerable strain building up on the crown's financial resources, was perhaps more aware of his own approaching end, and may have wished to crown his career with some permanent achievement. The Treaty of the Pyrenees of 1659 was meant to settle all outstanding issues between the two crowns, and was secured by a marriage alliance between Louis XIV and the Spanish infanta.

The wars of the northern periphery

While most of western and central Europe had been plunged in warfare, there had been a parallel period of belligerency in the northern and eastern periphery of Europe. This was fed by two long-running power struggles: between the crowns of Denmark and Sweden for primacy in the Baltic Sea, and by the drive of the crown and magnates of the Polish–Lithuanian commonwealth to colonize to the east, partly at the expense of Russia, which was an obvious prey for its neighbours during the anarchy of its 'time of troubles'. This ended with the recognition of the Romanov family as tsars in 1613, but it took time for the Russian autocracy to rebuild its domestic authority, so that it remained a temptation to the predators. In the empty and politically unorganized steppes of the Ukraine, a lawless frontier zone, Polish magnates aspired to gain control. The two centres of conflict, the Swedish–Danish and the Polish–Russian, were interlinked by the dynastic adventures of the Swedish Vasa rulers, which had resulted in a family feud. The Vasa kings of Poland, who had converted to Catholicism, claimed to be the rightful heirs to the Swedish throne in place of the Lutheran Vasa kings of Sweden.

In the early years of the seventeenth century, the conflicts in the Baltic area seemed to be detached from events elsewhere in Europe and they could be regarded as local wars between the Baltic powers. In the eastern end, Sweden had been exploiting Russian weakness to push out her frontier, a process finally brought to a conclusion by the Treaty of Stolbova in 1617. At the western end, the disturbing factor was the restless ambition of Christian

IV of Denmark, sitting on the accumulated surpluses of his Sound toll revenues, and looking to use these to increase his power and reputation. Christian's first venture, an attack on Sweden in 1611, was checked by a lack of support from the Danish Council, which was controlled by a noble oligarchy, combined with intervention from the United Provinces and England to secure a peace. This showed that the Baltic was of concern to Europe as a whole, and to the Dutch in particular, because of the importance of the grain trade through Danzig and the Sound. This was obviously at risk while hostilities continued. Further, the Sound tolls were a major factor in the trade and there was understandable reluctance to see Christian extend his power.

When the Bohemian revolt set off war in the Empire in 1618, both the Scandinavian monarchs were interested: Christian was in any case a prince of the Empire with a strong interest in secularized church lands, though Gustav Adolf and Oxenstierna were still inclined to give priority to their unresolved conflict with Poland. So in the attempts to construct a Protestant coalition of the 1620s to include the Scandinavian monarchies, it was Christian, with his much stronger direct interests, who agreed to intervene in 1626. It was only after he came to grief that Gustav Adolf intervened in Germany, and the 1628 rescue of Stralsund was the first instalment. He could not go further until the Polish conflict was wound up, and this problem was solved by the intervention of Richelieu, who in 1629 negotiated the truce of Altmark between Sweden and Poland for six years. At this point the two conflicts, in the Baltic and in the Empire, had come together.

The Emperor did his best to restart the Swedish–Polish war, but the Poles became embroiled in renewed hostilities with Russia. Although Poland had failed in its attempt to exploit the anarchy in Russia by putting its own candidate on the Russian throne, it had made substantial territorial gains at Russian expense, capturing Smolensk in 1611 and taking most of White Russia in the peace of 1618. In 1632, after the death of Sigismund III and in the interregnum before the election of his son Ladislas IV, the Russians, with some encouragement from Sweden, had attempted to recapture Smolensk and failed. In 1634 they made peace with Poland, which left the new king with the options of renewing the contest with Sweden when the truce expired in 1635 or concentrating on further eastward penetration into the Ukraine. The reluctance of the Polish nobility to support the dynastic claims of Ladislas, and the willingness of the weakened Swedish government in 1635 to buy off a Polish intervention by surrendering the Prussian port tolls, enabled Richelieu to negotiate a renewal of the Polish truce at Stuhmsdorf. For a brief interval the wars in the Baltic were suspended, leaving Sweden free to concentrate on recovering its position in the Empire.

It was Christian IV of Denmark who opened the next phase in 1643. He had been casting around for means to recover his losses since 1629, raising the Sound tolls and trying to get control of Hamburg and the tolls on the river Elbe, and by 1643 he was openly seeking to build a new coalition of

Denmark, Poland, Russia and the Emperor against Sweden. This was pre-vented by a swift pre-emptive strike by the Swedish army in Germany into Jutland. The Emperor sent help to the Danes, but the decisive moment came when the United Provinces sent its fleet into the Baltic to assist the Swedes. Christian was forced into another humiliating peace at Brömsebro in 1645. He had to cede three Norwegian frontier provinces to Sweden and give Swedish shipping exemption from the Sound tolls, while the Dutch, the English and the French took advantage of his weakness to force reductions on their shipping too. As a result, the revenue from the tolls fell by more than half. Brömsebro is generally taken as signalling that pre-eminence in the Baltic had now passed from Denmark to Sweden, though the role of the United Provinces in bringing it about was a reminder that naval domination was ultimately under Dutch control. The Danish interlude had once more connected the Baltic conflicts with the struggle in the Empire, and the Westphalia settlements made a further contribution through the territorial gains made by Sweden.

The ending of hostilities in 1648 soon revealed a harsh truth about the balance of European power. The exalted status which Sweden had acquired as guarantor of the treaties could not be sustained out of her own limited resources. While the immediate costs of demobilization and readjustment to peacetime conditions could be met out of the indemnities and the resources of the newly acquired provinces, these would not meet the long-term costs of keeping a military establishment able to ensure the security of the realm. For the price of Sweden's military adventures was to be surrounded by resentful and vengeful neighbours. Denmark, Russia, Poland, Brandenburg and the Emperor himself all nursed legitimate grievances over their treatment by the Swedish crown. There was no doubt of their readiness to seize any sign of Swedish weakness to seek revenge. The truth was that Sweden, since the death of Gustav Adolf, or certainly since the disaster at Nördlingen in 1634, had been a hired mercenary. Her swollen military machine was sustained by foreign subsidies and the continuing exploitation of occupied territories in Germany. In 1648 both these resources were cut off.

In 1652 the Swedish Diet debated the situation, and the majority agreed that it was necessary for the kingdom's security to maintain a high level of military preparedness. The situation in Poland was at that point very unstable. The drive of colonizing Polish landlords into the Ukraine had alienated the resident Cossack populations, threatening to reduce them to serfdom, in addition to which there was a confessional confrontation between the aggressively Catholic Polish colonizers and a population that was either Uniate or Russian Orthodox. The opening created by the death of Ladislas IV in 1648, with an ensuing interregnum, and the appearance of a capable charismatic leader among the Cossacks, Bogdan Khmelnitsky, led to a massive rising of the common folk against the Polish overlords. With the support of the Crimean Tartars, the Cossack forces annihilated the Polish armies, slaughtered landlords and Jews, who had often been the landlords' estate managers, and penetrated deep into Poland. The outcome was a clear indication of the hopelessness of early modern peasant revolt. Khmelnitsky's horde had no concept of how they could consolidate their success and form a viable political community. They were and remained an anarchic mob as long as they lacked the kind of organizing skills that only members of the ruling elites could provide. Khmelnitsky was driven in the end to seek legitimation from an established ruler, and offered the allegiance of the Ukrainian Cossack communities to Tsar Alexis, primarily on the religious grounds of their common Orthodox faith. In 1654 Alexis agreed, and thereby got into war with Poland. In that country's state of weakness, the Russians were able to advance and recover Smolensk.

In Sweden there had been a change of ruler. In 1654 Queen Christina abdicated in favour of her cousin who became Charles X Gustav. The new king was a professional soldier and making war was his sole serious interest in life. He lost no time in persuading the Swedish Council to raise the level of military preparedness. For a country with Sweden's limited resources that meant war since, as a member of the Council reminded them, to raise troops and not use them on foreign soil amounted to waging war on yourself. In 1655 Swedish armies moved in on Poland and won astonishing success. Polish resistance collapsed, Warsaw and Cracow were taken. If the Swedish attack had a reasonable objective at first, it had probably been to force the Polish king, John Casimir, to wind up the old dynastic struggle by renouncing his claim to the Swedish crown and recognizing Sweden's possession of Livonia. In addition, there was the possibility of seizing Polish Prussia and its port tolls, thus eliminating the gap in Swedish control of the south Baltic shore between the Vistula and the borders of Livonia. But the extraordinary success of the opening campaign led the king to seek total control of Poland by deposing John Casimir and substituting a Swedish puppet ruler.

The grandiose design, fundamentally impractical in any circumstances, crashed in face of a patriotic rally of the Polish nobility in defence of their king and the Catholic religion. Charles X was faced by a persistent guerrilla war that forced him to disperse his army into garrisons and offered no target on which he could make a decisive assault.

As soon as it was apparent that the Swedish effort was faltering, the enemies closed in. Tsar Alexis invaded Livonia; the Emperor declared war in support of John Casimir; the Elector of Brandenburg, after first supporting the Swedes in return for a promise of sovereignty over East Prussia, which he held as a vassal of the Polish crown, changed sides in return for the same promise from Poland and the prospect of winning the Swedish half of Pomerania. Finally, the new king of Denmark, Frederick III, entered the war in 1657 and invaded Bremen and Werden. This gave Charles X his opportunity to extricate himself from the deadlock in Poland. The main army was switched into a swift counter-attack through Pomerania and into Denmark and invaded Jutland. This was followed up by one of the most spectacular military operations of the century when, in the winter of 1657–8, Charles marched his army over the frozen sea and attacked the island of Zealand, threatening Copenhagen. Frederick III sued for peace and accepted the harsh terms of the Treaty of Roskilde, ceding the province of Skåne and with it Danish control of both sides of the Sound, together with Bornholm and the province of Trondheim in Norway. This brought the Swedish kingdom to its maximum territorial expansion and consolidated its position of primacy over the Baltic.

Roskilde left Poland, Brandenburg and the Emperor to be dealt with, for Tsar Alexis prudently offered a truce to the Swedes. Then, for the second time in this war, Charles X overreached himself. Instead of reviving a difficult campaign in Poland, he resolved to go for a final solution in Denmark and renew the war with a view to its complete incorporation in Sweden. The Swedish army once more closed in on Copenhagen. The outcome was similar to that in Poland: a patriotic rally among the Danes, with the citizens of Copenhagen voluntarily throwing themselves into the defence of the city. The Swedish move also roused the United Provinces, which had no wish to see Sweden controlling both sides of the Sound, and when Charles declined a Dutch plan for a compromise peace, they sent forces to help raise the siege and drive the Swedes out of the Danish islands. What would have happened had Charles X lived is unpredictable. It is certain he had no thought of making peace, but providentially he died suddenly in February 1660. The new regency government in Sweden, for the child king Charles XI, readily accepted a Dutch-sponsored compromise, and Denmark recovered Bornholm and Trondheim.

For the northern war, 1660 was the moment when all the belligerents became persuaded there was no point in carrying on fighting. After the settlement between Denmark and Sweden, the French helped mediate a settlement of the other conflicts, mainly at the expense of Poland. John Casimir formally renounced his dynastic claim and accepted Sweden's possession of Livonia. Poland also had to agree that the Elector of Brandenburg receive sovereignty over East Prussia. Finally the truce between Russia and Sweden was turned into a peace treaty at Kardis in 1661 on the basis of the status quo. But the Polish–Russian war dragged on until 1667 when a settlement was made giving Russia possession of White Russia and Smolensk, and of the Ukraine up to the Dnieper river, including Kiev.

In some respects these northern wars seem to confirm that the northeastern periphery of Europe was a world of its own, only loosely connected to developments in central and western Europe. Sweden had made a dramatic irruption on to the wider European stage, but by 1660 it was slipping back into the periphery of affairs. Poland was obviously undergoing some kind of critical decline, but this aroused little attention as yet in the west. But there was also some indication that closer integration of the northern fringe was under way. It was notable how the United Provinces had twice intervened at crucial moments: in the conflict of 1643–5 to ensure that Sweden emerged victorious, and in 1658–60 to ensure that its success did not go too far. The Baltic trade, in which the Dutch were the principal bankers, investors and carriers, was too important to tolerate interruption or distortion arising out of the local power struggles.

|3|

The Origins of the Modern State: The Absolutist Route

The military revolution

If Louis XIV ever said, in 1655 'l'état, c'est moi', he was only uttering a truism. The concept of the state as an impersonal institution, separate from the ruler who presided over it, was a novelty in early modern thought. When he did say, on his deathbed in 1715, 'I am departing, but the state will remain for ever', he showed that the concept of the state as autonomous, and the ruler as only its chief officeholder, was taking root. The development of the modern concept of the state was one of the most important changes in the history of European government, and it took off after 1600. From beginning to end the driving force behind the development had been war. The historian D. H. Pennington summed up the basic position when he wrote:

> Wars came more and more to be fought only by states: and states became more and more institutions for fighting wars ... So long as the military structure within a state was a major part of the political establishment, there had to be a potential conflict. Standing armies required standing enemies.

There is now an extensive literature, and considerable disagreement, about the 'military revolution' in early modern Europe.[1] It is agreed, however, that some significant changes in military technology, with a knock-on effect on the use and organization of armies, did take place. They began in the Netherlands, where the Spanish armies, the most formidable fighting machine in Europe, were based on the *tercio* which in battle formed a column of disciplined soldiers, perhaps 15 men wide and 60 deep, whose weight and momentum would break the hostile line, after which the cavalry could go in and slaughter the scattered enemy troops. By the 1590s the Dutch army led by Prince Maurice was experimenting with tactics to defeat the Spanish columns. The idea is generally credited to his reading of Roman treatizes on war describing the linear formations of Roman armies. The new tactic was to draw up his men in thin lines, no more than ten deep, with a preponderance of musketeers and pikemen to ward off cavalry, and to repel enemy attack by fire power. The formation enabled the organization of volley firing which, given the short range and inaccuracy of contemporary firearms, was the most effective way to use them.

Then Gustav Adolf introduced Maurice's tactics into the Swedish army, with some modifications. He thinned out the lines even further, down to four or five ranks, and reinforced their fire power by introducing new types of lighter cannon, which could be manhandled on the battlefield and placed among the infantry formations. He also changed the cavalry tactics. The custom had been for the horsemen to soften up the opposing infantry by riding up and discharging their pistols or carbines at close range. They only moved in with swords when the enemy had broken. It is generally agreed that given the quality of their firearms, they could do little damage. Gustav Adolf trained his cavalry to use momentum, charging into the enemy in disciplined, tightly packed squadrons, relying on the sword as their principal tool for killing. This tactic demonstrated its worth in his victory at Breitenfeld, where Tilly's army was organized in columns, which were swept away by Swedish fire power. The lesson was learned, and when he faced Wallenstein's army at Lützen in 1632, they were adopting the new formations. But reliance on fire power on the field put a premium on better-trained soldiers, because succ-essful volley firing required the musketeers to master elaborate drills if it was to be effective. The old methods of recruiting an army in the spring and then disbanding it in the autumn became less cost-effective. Once a body of trained men had been formed it paid to keep them permanently. They would form the hard core of an army and be diluted by new recruits raised for each campaign. These changes raised costs. Artillery, muskets and the powder and ammunition they consumed were a heavy charge.

It is also a demonstrable fact that armies were getting larger. In the Netherlands campaigns, a force of 12,000 men was a substantial field army. At Breitenfeld, the Swedish army numbered 30,000 and for the war of 1689–97 Louis XIV had as many as 340,000 men under arms. A contribu-tory factor was the concentration on siege warfare rather than battle. This went back to the sixteenth-century introduction of the new Italian-style for-tifications for cities and fortresses. The system of ramparts and redoubts, sheltered by broad ditches, meant they were generally impossible to take by assault, and prolonged blockade and engineering works were needed to per-suade the enemy to capitulate. While the siege continued, the besiegers in turn needed to construct earthworks of their own to ward off relieving armies. The process demanded large numbers of infantry and pioneers, who all had to be maintained and supplied over long periods. The combined costs of fortifying one's own cities and garrisoning them, and of laying siege to those of the enemy, seriously inflated the costs of war.

In 1600 the standard procedure for raising armies had been the merce-nary contract. The contractor would agree to raise at his own costs the agreed number of troops, but the employer was expected to provide upkeep and at the end of the day repay the contractor's initial outlays. It was usual for the employing rulers to run out of money, and hence they had to authorize the troops to levy contributions in the areas they occupied, and this weakened control by the employer. The contractor had a strong incentive not to imperil his investment by exposing it to the hazard of battle, and was often driven by necessity to look for reasonably undamaged areas where he might be able to extract the contributions he needed. This could mean that whatever strategic plan the employer wanted to pursue could be frustrated by the contractor's need to survive and stay in business.

It is fair to say that in 1600 nearly all the governments of Europe were financially overextended, and perhaps always had been. There were rare exceptions, like Christian IV of Denmark, sustained by the Sound tolls, and Maximilian of Bavaria, whose father had successfully overhauled the finances of the duchy, while the United Provinces were always a special case. Otherwise, even the Spanish monarchy, with its huge bullion resources, was desperately overstretched. The modern state was the end product of the process by which rulers sought to feed their habit of serial belligerency. They had to find greatly enlarged and reliable revenues and access to credit facilities, and build up administrative systems to facilitate this, both to retain their subjects in obedience and to control and manage the forces that they raised.

The crisis of the French monarchy

The French monarchy had the potential to be the most powerful in Europe. Its territories were consolidated in one geographical block and contained a population around 20 million in 1600, probably larger than the territories of the Spanish and and Vienna Habsburgs combined. But in reality seventeenth-century France was a geographical expression: a federation of provinces, each with its own laws and customs and linked only by a common personal allegiance to the king. The peace with Spain in 1598, and the issue of the Edict of Nantes to settle the confessional issue, inaugurated a decade of internal and external peace during which Henry IV's minister the duke of Sully promoted a reform of the royal finances, and may have produced a modest surplus.[2] But Henry IV would have re-opened the dynastic struggle with the Habsburgs in 1610 had he not been assassinated. France then faced the most dangerous of contingencies – a regency for the child Louis XIII, vested in the queen-mother, an unpopular and politically incompetent foreigner. A new round of aristocratic faction fighting began, with the control of the court and its patronage the main aim, but with Huguenot magnates like the dukes of Rohan and Soubise pursuing their own political agenda. The Estates General was summoned in 1614 to resolve the crisis, but could offer no political solutions. Each of the constituent Estates pursued its own sectional interests. They were adept at articulating their

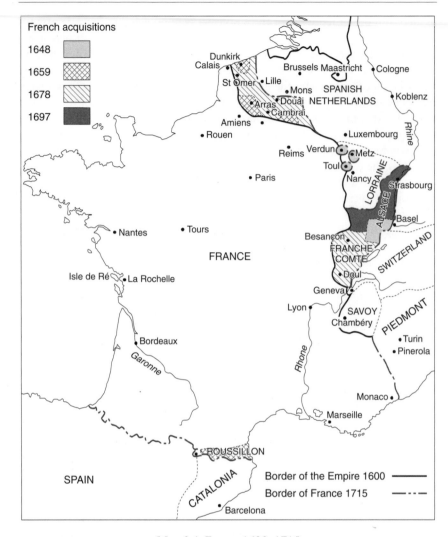

Map 3.1 France 1600–1715

grievances, but no national consensus emerged. The fact that the Estates were not to meet again until 1789 was not because an increasingly absolutist monarchy feared them, but because they were patently politically useless as a means of tackling the monarchy's problems.

In 1620 Louis XIII took his first political initiative and resolved to reduce the bases of Huguenot military strength. He started in the province of Béarn, which was solidly Calvinist, and was forced by military action to re-admit Catholic worship. Success there encouraged an expanding campaign to reduce other Huguenot strongholds, where the feeble resistance exposed internal divisions in the Huguenot community between its aristocratic leaders and the urban communities and clergy, who were willing to settle for legal toleration. It was in this context, in 1624, that the king took Richelieu into the government as first minister. There was no affection between them at first. Louis had doubts about his reliability, but Richelieu quickly established himself as a competent executive. By 1626 the king wrote: 'everything has gone well since you have been [my minister]. My trust in you is complete, and it is true that I have never found anyone whose service has pleased me as much.'

Richelieu was one of the first European statesmen to take public relations seriously. All his life he employed a team of publicists to boost his image, and one fruit was two extensive documents, the so-called *Mémoires*, compiled by his secretariat as an official record of his ministry, and his *Testament politique*, written as guidance for the king. These project the image of a man whose policies are based on reason. 'Reason must be the universal rule and guide: all things are to be done according to reason, without allowing oneself to be swayed by emotion.' He implied that he had a clear programme of domestic reconstruction and a foreign policy based on reducing the Habsburg hegemony in Europe as a necessary basis for a lasting peace. He defined this policy in 1629:

> One's constant aim must be to check the advance of Spain ... France must only think of fortifying herself at home and of opening gates into all the neighbouring states, so as to defend them against Spanish oppression as the occasion arises. We must think of fortifying Metz and, if possible, of reaching out to Strasbourg, so as to gain entry into Germany ... this must be done in the long term, very discreetly and in a manner that is moderate and secret.

This foreshadows his actions down to 1634, when he clearly hoped to weaken Habsburg power indirectly, saving France from the expenses and dangers of open war. It was the disaster to the Protestant cause at Nördlingen that forced him to change policy.

But his priority after 1624 was to reinforce the royal authority within the realm by eliminating the armed defiance of the last major Huguenot fortified city, the port of La Rochelle. It took two years of campaigning and a most obdurate siege before he finally forced its surrender in 1629. In 1630, by the settlement of Alais, he effectively ended the Huguenot threat by combining their total disarmament with a confirmation of the basic Edict of Nantes, assuring the individual Huguenot freedom to practise his religion under the protection of the law. Richelieu's publicity consistently suggests that the next step should have been a serious programme of domestic reforms in the kingdom. It is difficult to be sure how serious he ever was in this. It is conspicuous that during a major attempt to find some consensus on domestic issues, by summoning a Council of Notables in 1627, Richelieu was curiously inactive; nor did he make much effort to promote the few measures that were agreed: that was left to the Chancellor, Marillac. Later, in 1640,

Richelieu produced a radical scheme of tax reforms, though its implementation was to be delayed until after the war. It is perhaps more revealing to
follow his many realistic comments about the prospect of reform in face of
all the vested interests opposed to it. He conceded that most reforming proposals, like ending the sale of offices, were not politically feasible.

It is on record that in 1630 Richelieu advised the king, after the fall of La
Rochelle, to move immediately into an armed incursion into northern Italy
to secure bases from which Spanish communications through the Alps could
be threatened. Marillac, leading a faction of the Catholic *dévot* party at
court including the queen-mother, argued that they should avoid further
hostility with Spain, particularly as it involved alliances with heretics, concentrate on further internal reform, not least programmes for the conversion
of the Huguenots and the strengthening of the Catholic Church, and provide
an opportunity to bring some order to the crown's finances. Richelieu
insisted that the anti-Habsburg programme must be pursued until victory
was achieved, and argued that all projects for internal reforms would have
to wait. The king, who was basically a *dévot* himself by inclination, hesitated. When he fell ill in the summer of 1630, he seems to have promised his
mother he would dismiss Richelieu and reverse policy. The crisis was
resolved in the 'Day of Dupes', when Richelieu's enemies gathered at court
expecting the announcement of his dismissal, only to find the king had
changed his mind and confirmed Richelieu in office.

Richelieu's image-building has so impressed later historians with the idea
that he was essentially a modern statesman, dragging a reluctant community
into a new age, that it is often overlooked how much he himself was constrained by contemporary values. Recently his personal power structure has
been exposed, and in brief it aimed to make of Richelieu a classic overmighty
subject. He ruthlessly gathered round himself a clique of family and clients,
personally bound to himself, and pushed them into all the key positions in
government. In particular the four secretaries of state, who between them
controlled the actual machinery of executive government, were all his
appointees. Enemies were ruthlessly eliminated, and his record is stained by
a number of judicial abuses.[3] He used his position to acquire enormous personal wealth and died the wealthiest man in France. The wealth was used, in
the traditional ways of aristocratic faction politics, to build up a strong
provincial power base around the dukedom he was granted. He reinforced
this by control of the local provincial governorship and strategic marriage
alliances into powerful magnate families. He was well aware that his power
at court could at any time have been destroyed by the action of the king, but
if that happened, he would have a powerful refuge to retire into.

Modern research has enabled historians to make a more realistic assessment of Richelieu's achievement than one based on his own propaganda.[4]
One institution always credited to him is the establishment of the office of
intendant. This was an attempt to get to grips with the extreme devolution of
local power in the kingdom, combined with the entrenched administrative

system of venal officeholding. Most royal officials had purchased their offices for life, and on payment of the levy known as the *paulette*, acquired the right to pass them on to their heirs. This meant that the crown had only limited possibilities of controlling its own servants. The intendant was an agent, nearly always a professional lawyer, holding a direct commission from the king to inspect and if necessary intervene to ensure that the royal policies were being implemented. The decisive step came in 1642 when the intendants were specifically charged with overseeing tax collection. It was an idea with a great future, but in Richelieu's day these outsiders, penetrating the provinces with their commission, came up against the hard fact that compliance in the localities could not be commanded, but had to be negotiated. The intendants undoubtedly did manage to facilitate the collection of taxation and the mobilization of the armies, but in doing so aroused much bitter resentment among the local elites, which after the cardinal's death built up into a dangerous backlash. A more solid achievement was the introduction of specialization into the central secretariat: one of the four secretaries was identified as the secretary for war, who handled relations with the armies, another as foreign minister. Even this had limits. No central minister of the interior developed, since the four secretaries had traditionally divided the kingdom up between them, each taking responsibility for a group of provinces. There were also the efforts to reinforce obedience to royal authority through the kingdom and the much publicized enforcement of the law against duelling, a significant assertion of the principle that nobles were not privileged to take the law into their own hands. The spectacular execution of Montmorency after a provocative defiance of the decree tends to obscure the reality that it was unique, and that in fact the practice of duelling, seen as an inherent right of nobility, continued undisturbed. The campaign to clip the wings of overmighty subjects such as provincial governors, seeking to confine them to their purely military functions and prevent the establishment of local power bases, was ironic in view of Richelieu's own efforts to do exactly that. He had some success in the interior of the kingdom: walled towns had to demolish their fortifications and private noblemen disarm their castles. Yet the outbreak of the Fronde within seven years of Richelieu's death was a spectacular demonstration that magnate power in the provinces was alive and well.

The limits of what could be done can be seen in the army. Here the aim was to create a reliable force under direct royal control. It did become policy that within the kingdom the raising of mercenary contract armies was discontinued. Instead the system used was the state commission army, where noblemen – and they always were nobles – were given a royal commission to raise military units, under regulations laid down by the secretary of war, and under the command of generals appointed by the king. Here the problem was that the crown could not afford to pay them, and in practice those commissioned to raise regiments, the colonels and captains, were expected to provide many of the running costs themselves. To judge by the response, there were plenty of noblemen willing to undertake this for the prestige and, equally important, the patronage that a commission put in their hands. But it also meant that direct central control was difficult to enforce. In 1650, the then secretary for war, Michel Le Tellier, said that the army was 'a republic whose cantons are made up of the corps commanders'. When the time came for open war after 1634, it is to be noted that Richelieu was unable to achieve his projected mobilization of 160,000 men and the actual force raised for 1635 was nearer 70,000. When it came to appointing the army commanders, Richelieu had no option but to accept traditional appointees from the greatest magnate families, many of them no friends of his, starting with the king's brother and heir, Gaston duke of Orléans, and the duke of Bouillon with his brother Turenne.

The real weakness of most of Richelieu's governmental projects was his handling of government finance. It was suggested in his own writings that he did not concern himself directly in financial policy and left that to the Controller, Bullion. But it is true that he had no realistic proposals of his own how to raise the enormous extra revenues required to fund the war. The times were bad. By the mid-1630s, the comparative boom in agriculture that had prevailed since 1600 began to turn to recession; farm prices were falling, and both the peasant taxpayer and his noble landlord faced declining real incomes just when the demands of the crown for taxes were being racheted up to unprecedented levels. One problem was the ingrained aristocratic attitude to money, recognizable at all levels from the king down, that it was for their subordinates to come up with the necessary funding for their projects. Under Richelieu, all attempt at rational financing was dropped. Existing taxes, like the *taille*, were increased, the scope of the *gabelle* widened, and a range of new indirect taxes introduced. When this failed to produce the money, borrowing was pushed to the limits and beyond, and financial chicanery employed to squeeze the venal officers and extract revenue from the normally tax-exempt elites. It has to be said that the crown was never actually bankrupt, but it came close. Things got particularly critical by 1640, after Richelieu had introduced several new taxes – a sales tax and a levy on food, in addition to the pressure to raise income from the taille, which seem to have been counter-productive, since *taille* revenue tended to fall during his ministry. In early 1639 an issue of *rentes* left 600,000 livres unsold. Bullion warned Richelieu: 'Your Excellency has cause to wish for peace urgently. The finances have never been in such a bad state. None of the financiers want to conclude any kind of agreement, and the people will not pay anything.'

Richelieu scarcely needed to be told, for the 1630s had witnessed an extraordinary series of taxpayers' revolts in France. There is considerable debate over the significance of these uprisings,[5] but what they all have in common is outraged protest at the increasing tax burden. A prominent feature was the violence of the rebels against crown officials, the agents of the tax-farmers, who were often lynched, and their offices and dwellings destroyed. A further aggravation was the depredations of unpaid soldiers as they moved round the kingdom.

There had always been sporadic outbreaks of disorder, which were easily contained. But in 1636–7 probably the biggest peasant revolt before 1789 spread through central and southern France: the *croquant* rebellion. Its programme was a broad protest against exploitation by the elites, attacking taxes, feudal dues, tithe and legal charges. Initially the authorities were helpless and Richelieu had to buy the rebels off with promises of relief in 1636. When he reneged in the following year, the revolt was renewed, and now there were signs that in some parts local noblemen were participating. It fell mostly to the provincial governors, combining negotiation with use of force, to restore order. There was then a respite until the next round of peasant unrest on a similar scale in 1643–4. It is notable that the new intendants often found themselves powerless in face of local resistance and non-cooperation by local authorities.

There were parallel revolts in the towns, though the townsfolk rarely linked up with the peasants. The town oligarchies were fearful of admitting the rural insurgents inside their communities. The most dangerous revolt, because it did eventually unite peasants, townsmen and even the local *parlement*, broke out in Normandy in protest against the gabelle in 1639. This revolt had a rudimentary organization, and a supposed chief, Jean Nu-pieds, whose true identity is unknown. The *gabelle* was a grievance that united town and country, and seems to have drawn in many parish clergy and some nobles. In its later stages, the city of Rouen joined the rebels for a time, and the *parlement* did not exert itself to restore order. On this occasion Richelieu, who always called for a hard line against the rebellions, determined to make an example. Regular troops were brought in and swept through the province, looting as they went, imposing punitive billeting on the towns, and summarily executing the rebel leaders they caught. Richelieu wrote to his intendant: 'I urge on you to remember always that one cannot make too severe an example in this case.' This looks like absolutism successfully imposing its will by force. The ambivalent attitude of the *parlement* and other local officeholders particularly angered the government. They threatened to suppress their offices and introduce new officials in their place. Yet within a year this scheme was dropped, and the old officers were reinstated. That was realistic: the truth was that the province was ungovernable without the cooperation of the established elites.

The revolts signalled that the central government, itself driven by the inexorable financial demands of the war, was bearing down too hard on the taxpayers, and was now also infringing the privileges of the normally tax-exempt elites. But none of these uprisings actually threatened the monarchy: on the contrary, rebel manifestos routinely affirm their loyalty to the king and blame their grievances on the misconduct of his officials. They offer no alternative political programme; they want the hated innovations reversed and the traditional status quo restored. Restoration not reformation, much less revolution, is the basis of the rebel demands. Given this conservative mentality, the government in the long run had little to fear. A traditional mixture of negotiation and concessions that could quickly be reversed when the unrest died down could be combined with violent repression, where possible and expedient, which would in the end see the regime survive – it was not as fragile as it was sometimes made to appear. Despite all the short-term violence and disorder, as long as the prevailing consensus mentality held, it could endure.

Richelieu died in 1642 in circumstances that make it clear that no great reformation of government had occurred. His regime had lived by expedients forced on it by circumstances, and the impression given in the *Mémoires* that he was pursuing policies based on clear political principle was some way from reality. At his death the foreign situation, following his unintended entry into open war with the Habsburgs after Nördlingen in 1634, had been a great disappointment. Certainly by 1642 the situation in Germany was steadily moving in his favour, but the main fronts against Spain had yielded no significant military success. He would have wished to negotiate a settlement, but in the absence of results could not find an acceptable basis: the war looked like dragging on indefinitely.

In his *Testament*, Richelieu recommended as his successor Cardinal Mazarin, and urged the king to persevere with the current policies and personnel in government. It seemed that Louis XIII would do this, but he survived Richelieu by less than a year. France was then plunged into a new, prolonged regency for the five-year-old Louis XIV. As normal, the queen-mother, who was a Habsburg herself, and a committed *dévot*, became regent. She had been no friend of Richelieu, but did have good, eventually perhaps intimate, relations with Mazarin, thus ensuring that the Richelieu policies would be continued, though in practice the new regime proved anxious to dissociate itself from its predecessor, claiming Henry IV as its role model.

It is likely that Richelieu's achievement will always give rise to new interpretations. What he wrote can be taken as a vision of a new style of government, embracing the idea of an abstract state, which all, perhaps even rulers, are required to serve. He wrote:

> Harshness towards those who flout the laws and commands of the state is for the public good ... In the matter of state crime, one must close the door on pity, ignore the complaints of the parties concerned and the speeches of the ignorant populace, which sometimes condemns that which is most useful and necessary ... even if conscience can tolerate ... a notable crime going unpunished, reason of state cannot allow it ... what is done for the state is done for God, who is the basis and foundation of it.

This seems clear enough, yet when the offence was caused by someone like the king's brother Gaston, he remained untouchable. Richelieu could be a realist: 'those who work for the king must remember that there is a great difference between ordering what needs to be done, and getting the orders carried out'. But he never discovered any viable way for bridging this gap, which may explain, if not excuse, his resort to political terrorism against those who opposed him on occasion. Yet this was also the man who wrote: 'there can be no successful war that is not just, even if the outcome were good in the eyes of the world, it would still be necessary to render account of it before the tribunal of God'. And he persistently defined his war aims as securing 'a good peace for the whole of Christendom'. Yet he told Louis XIII in 1629 that their priority should be 'to make oneself the most powerful and the most respected monarch in the world'. We cannot know whether he believed what he stated to be the principles on which international relations should be based, but his practice fell somewhat short of them. Despite his later reputation as a constructive statesman, it is possible to argue that, but for him, the carnage in the Empire might have been stopped and the thirty years of war reduced to fifteen, whereas at his death his king was still locked into an increasingly exhausting conflict, with no sign that he had any feasible policies for ending it.

The new Mazarin regime was inherently weaker than that of the iron cardinal. Mazarin was a negotiator by instinct and generally averse to violent confrontations. Further, he was a foreigner of noble, but not exalted birth. The queen-mother was also foreign, but of the bluest of blue blood, and to her credit entirely devoted to the interests of her son, despite her Habsburg origins. But for political advice she was wholly dependent on Mazarin, to the furious resentment of the magnates, particularly those of the blood like Condé and Gaston of Orléans, who felt they were entitled to places of influence around the king. As the war dragged on, punctuated at home by repeated protest revolts from taxpayers, the government was forced to screw up its borrowings from tax-farmers and financiers, and look for ways of extorting contributions from the tax-exempt elites. By 1647 ministers were focused on the legal oligarchy of the *parlements* and the venal officeholders.

Various scams were open to government, like duplicating offices, thereby devaluing them for the holders, to force the existing officeholders to buy them out. Then in 1648 it was time to renew the paulette, the levy charged for continuing rights of inheritance in offices. In January 1648, the president of the *parlement* of Paris, Talon, led a public refusal to register the latest tax decrees, and when Mazarin threatened to overrule the decision by a *lit de justice*, in which the king personally exercised the authority he had delegated to his *parlements*, Talon questioned whether this was legal during a minority. Mazarin and the queen-mother decided to accept the challenge and coerce the *parlement* into submission, arresting its leaders Talon and Molé, and intending to exile the rest to the provinces. But under cover of the lawyers' stance of loyal support for a strong monarchy within the law, other malcontents, particularly among the magnates, sensed an opportunity to displace Mazarin, while the lower orders in the capital began to demonstrate in support. During the ongoing arguments, the *parlement* of

Paris evolved a reform programme. It amounted to a defence of its own corporate interests against crown encroachments, the withdrawal of the intendants, ending the practice of arbitrary imprisonment by *lettres de cachet*, strict investigation into the financial malpractices of financiers and tax-farmers, and a general reduction of the *taille* by a quarter, while in future all proposals to raise taxes must be submitted to the *parlements* for verification. This programme was far from revolutionary and certainly not anti-monarchical. Everyone was conscious of the events across the Channel that would end in regicide and they were horrified. The *parlement* formally condemned the English execution of Charles I, calling those responsible 'wicked men who have violated every law and dipped murderous hands in the blood of that most pious king'.

In August 1648, the common people of Paris rose in arms on the 'day of the barricades' in defence of the *parlement* of Paris, and were soon joined by magnates led by Condé, demanding the dismissal of Mazarin. The court fled the capital, called up troops and attempted to besiege the city. In the end Mazarin split the opposition coalition by a separate deal with the *parlementaires*, conceding to their demands. They then swung their support back behind the regency government, for they had achieved their objective: a strong central executive, based on law and acting in partnership with the *parlements*. The aristocratic magnates launched their own campaign to oust Mazarin and entrench themselves at court. They too wanted a powerful monarchy, but one that shared power with the great noble families. In the ensuing power struggle, the magnates tried to mobilize their provincial power bases, spreading disorder and civil war through the kingdom. It is significant that at no time before the whole movement collapsed in 1653 could a united opposition front be formed. The diverse aspirations of the greater nobles, the *parlementaires* and the venal officeholders, the financiers and the urban bourgeoisie, and the ordinary taxpayer were often mutually inconsistent, and gave no basis for unity among them. On the contrary, each individual province tended to witness its own local power struggles between the interest groups. The one place where, for most of 1652–3, a truly radical movement for political and social reform emerged was in the city of Bordeaux, where for a time a populist regime, based on an elected assembly, defied all the local power brokers, Condé himself, the *parlement* of Bordeaux, the oligarchs of the city corporation, and the agents of the royal government. Towards the end the radicals, known to history as the *Ormée*, even established contact with the Cromwellian republicans. But in the end, the rival elite groups closed ranks against them and the *Ormée* was suppressed.

There were other signs of the weakness of the Fronde, as this episode is known. At one point the court, manoeuvring to undermine the magnates, promised to call an Estates General and during 1651 there were electoral meetings of the provincial nobilities. They proved to have aspirations at odds with the *parlementaires* and officeholders: they wanted an end to the purchase of offices and the reservation of offices to noblemen. They were also at odds with the magnates, for they wanted the power of central government diminished, and the autonomy of the provincial communities restored. One side effect of the breakdown of authority was the end of censorship, releasing a flood of polemical writings, the *Mazarinades*. Their most significant feature was the absence of any coherent political programme of reforms. They wanted Mazarin and other hate figures removed from power, but beyond that they could only call for the restoration of the situation prevailing before increasing central authority began its usurpation of corporate liberties. Acceptance of monarchy by divine right was never questioned, and loyalty to the young Louis XIV common to all. Once the Fronde was reduced to an armed faction fight between the great families, Mazarin, despite two brief periods when he found it expedient to leave the country, negotiated and bargained his way back into power, playing off one opposition group against the other, and when in 1653 Condé took service with the king of Spain, it was all over. The monarchy emerged strengthened, in October 1652 the young king was declared of age, and the government returned to an enthusiastic capital. Mazarin continued to rule and, being a man of diplomacy, quietly undermined the settlement with the *parlements*. The regime of desperate fiscal expedients started up again and the intendants were soon back in action. It had all been for nothing.

At least for the historian the history of the Fronde reveals basic truths about the political structure of *ancien régime* France. It was in reality a deeply divided community, a mosaic of corporate interest groups and provincial immunities, which offered little opening for effective centralization. Mazarin's biographer has remarked: 'that frondeur hostility ... was directed so largely at Mazarin, as the man who allegedly abused the system, rather than the system itself is revealing: no less so is their failure to secure his permanent removal'.

France was a seething mass of competing corporate interest groups on which the early modern monarchy had little prospect of imposing a uniform order, but under the right leadership it could negotiate and manoeuvre the extension of its own authority until a kind of royal hegemony was secured.

Spain

Spain in 1600 was even more a geographical expression than France. In the Iberian Peninsula, the monarchy's heartland, the king ruled three wholly independent kingdoms, Castile, Aragon and Portugal, and of these Castile was a composite kingdom, where Navarre and the Basque provinces had wide autonomy, and the kingdom of Aragon was a composite of Aragon itself, the kingdom of Valencia and the principality of Catalonia. These had their own laws, customs, currencies and administrations. In Italy the king was ruler of three entirely independent countries: Milan, Naples and Sicily. In the north of Europe, Spain still retained the larger, southern part of the

Netherlands, which again was politically quite separate. And beyond all this Castile was ruler of one great oceanic empire in America and the Pacific, and Portugal was ruler of another, including Brazil and a string of trading posts and settlements round Africa, in India and beyond that in the Far East.

In order to impose some kind of coherence of government over such a range of possessions, a sophisticated administrative structure had evolved. Of necessity the local government of the different components was left largely in local hands, supervised by royal viceroys, but these were in turn controlled by the government machinery in Madrid. This consisted of a structure of councils, at the centre of which was the Council of State, with its subordinate Council of War, and a Council of Finance. These were supported by a range of advisory councils for Castile, Aragon, the Indies, Portugal, Italy and Flanders and not least the Inquisition. Ultimate power of decision rested of course with the king, advised by the Council of State. The councils were staffed by qualified, usually university–trained, professional bureaucrats, recruited from the nobilities. The basic procedure was that the king consulted the various secretaries of the councils, drew up their agendas and received a report on each item, which was laid before him for final decision. The decision then went back to the appropriate council for implementation. This apparatus was certainly somewhat slow to produce decisions, but provided the king kept the paper circulating, and dealt with it promptly, it worked quite well.

The Spanish king, unlike most contemporary rulers, was served by a professional bureaucracy. Its main weakness was that, except in the cases of the Indies and the Inquisition, the councils did not have their own local administrative agents on the ground. The implementation of their orders had to be negotiated with the local elites such as the urban and judicial oligarchies, or the feudal landlords. The crown had long been raising funds by selling grants of jurisdiction to the nobility, by selling offices of all kinds, and by farming revenues. The net effect was that the impressive professional administration of the councils in Madrid had to work with a local administration that was substantially privatized. It has been argued that the real power in the Spanish monarchy was largely devolved to the *pueblo*, the basic social unit of Spanish society, nearly always controlled by an oligarchy of the wealthiest property-owners. It depended on these people whether taxes were collected, or recruits mobilized, or royal commands enforced. They also made up the delegations to the local Estates that still functioned in most parts of the king's dominions, and almost everywhere had power of consent over direct taxation, and a voice at least in legislation. Finally, in parts of Castile and most of Aragon, there were grandees, feudal landlords with large followings of clients and tenants, who still had the means of raising substantial military forces. Although for some time they had not seriously challenged the royal authority, they had not yet abandoned old traditions of private feuding and banditry.

The key to Spanish power, which sustained this complex structure, was the crown revenues. In the peninsula, this meant the revenues from Castile.

It was accepted by Madrid that Portuguese revenues were retained for that kingdom, mainly to sustain the defence of its empire. Aragon yielded only a marginal net revenue to the centre after covering its own local expenses. And in Castile taxation had to be negotiated with the *cortes* of Castile, a body composed of two delegates from the 18 principal cities. The *cortes* were usually amenable to continuing their grants of taxation, but these had to be negotiated, and were nearly always appropriated by the *cortes* to specific purposes, and further they were assessed and collected by officials appointed by and answerable to the *cortes*. But the king also enjoyed substantial cash revenue from the empire. The Netherlands were a net drain on revenue while the war lasted, but the Italian possessions made substantial contributions from their taxes, and the American colonies contributed the crown's bullion revenues, the core of which were the annual shipments of silver. In 1600 the American silver made up between 20 and 25 per cent of total crown revenue. Beyond this the crown, with the assistance of the pope, was able to levy regular and quite heavy taxes on the income of the church, though this too had to be negotiated.

The whole financial structure, impressive though it was by comparison with the resources available to Spain's rivals, was under severe strain. One factor was the wave of epidemics in the 1590s which caused a lasting drop in population – a loss of about 10 per cent and hence a shrinkage of the tax base. The burdens on the survivors drove increasing numbers of peasant farmers off the land. Spanish landowners were *rentiers*, usually urban-based, living off the rents and feudal dues of their tenants. Since most of the property-owners were tax-exempt, the whole tax burden fell on the peasantry, who also had heavy tithe payments to the church. The commentators who were allowed free publication in Spain, the *arbitristas*, identified the problem. Cellerigo wrote in 1600: 'the peasant who works in the field has to support himself, his lord, the clergy, the money lender and all others who batten on him'. Figures from New Castile suggest farmers were paying out half their gross income in rent, feudal dues, tithe and taxes. The main indicator of overload in the system was the dependence of the regime on credit. This was raised in two main forms: one short-term, the *asiento*, was a contract to advance credit in anticipation of revenue. The best known of these are the *asientos* in anticipation of the arrival of the American silver each year, when mainly Genoese bankers advanced the cash needed to sustain the war effort. The other form were *juros*: annuities at guaranteed rates of interest, secured on specific branches of the revenue. This meant that most of each year's revenue was pledged in advance, and the amount left for free disposal severely limited. In fact the Spanish regime ran a permanent budget deficit, and had to relieve it by expedients, like the policy inaugurated in 1607 of issuing copper currency. This brought substantial short-term profit to the crown, but in the longer term fuelled inflation and discouraged enterprise. The other was to declare a 'bankruptcy', which usually meant suspending or reducing the rate of interest on the *juros*. This could ease an immediate cash-flow crisis, but with later damage to the crown's credit.

Philip III, who succeeded in 1598, was disinclined to undertake the work of government, and introduced the appointment of an official *privado*, a favourite commissioned to oversee administration on his behalf. The first of these, the duke of Lerma, was also disinclined to labour at the chores of administration, except in so far as it promoted his personal power and wealth and that of his family. In fact the administration bore up quite well, and the councils attended to routine government business. What was lacking was active strategic planning at the centre. This was the more serious since the Truce in the Netherlands in 1609 created an opening to undertake structural reform of the finances and consider future policy. The outcome was drift: there was general acceptance that when the Truce expired the war would have to be resumed. Apart from the blow the Truce represented for the prestige of the monarchy, it was very much working in favour of the Dutch, who were using it to penetrate both the Spanish and Portuguese parts of the empire.

The one major policy achievement of the Lerma years was the expulsion of the *moriscos*,[6] the nominally converted Moorish peasants and artisans, who had stayed on after the Christian re-conquest. They were viewed adversely from two points of view: they could be a security risk in Aragon, where they were most numerous, and their very existence was a slur on a Christian monarchy. The decision to deport them coincided with the conclusion of the Truce, and in part may have been a move to divert attention from it. The actual operations were efficiently carried through. By 1614 some 275,000 had gone, although perhaps another 10,000 managed to evade deportation. It was an immensely popular policy, except with some Aragonese landowners, whose tenants they had been, and their creditors. In Castile where *moriscos* were few it probably made little economic difference, but it certainly set back farming in Aragon, where resettlement of the empty farms was a slow process. It is an exaggeration to see the expulsion as a disaster for the weakening Iberian economy, but the overall impact on production must have been negative. Yet very few contemporaries would have thought this important in comparison with the confessional cleansing of the peninsula, which would certainly earn them divine favour.

Thus the opportunity offered by the brief pause in hostilities was squandered, in that there was lively public discussion of how the declining economy might be revived, but no action. In the absence of control from the top, the other characteristic of the period was how Spain's men in the field, the viceroys and ambassadors, were pursuing their own political agendas, effectively committing the monarchy to intervene in the Empire in support of the Vienna Habsburgs, thus ensuring that when the Truce expired the ensuing conflict would be on a much wider scale. It would be untrue to say the monarchy drifted aimlessly into renewal of hostilities. There was debate, with a vocal faction urging renewal of the Truce, which lost out to those who saw the honour and reputation of the monarchy as at stake, and those who were convinced that the Truce was weakening Spain economically while strengthening the Dutch. It was this which led to the decision that unless new and more favourable terms could be secured, it was best to let it run out.

Philip III died at the critical moment of decision in 1621. His successor Philip IV was inexperienced and unsure of himself, and took as his *valido* his former tutor and confidant Olivares. Olivares had qualities that were not commonly found at the top of the Spanish elite. He much resembled his great rival Richelieu. He was totally absorbed in the power to get things done. Elliott has remarked on 'the obsessive determination which they both displayed to be the absolute masters of themselves and the world'. Yet both prided themselves on their rationalism, realism and pragmatism. On foreign policy Olivares was a traditionalist. He told the new king in 1621 that he was:

> the greatest monarch in the world, in kingdoms and possessions ... Almost all the kings and princes of Europe are jealous of your great-ness. You are the main defence and support of the Catholic religion: for this reason you have renewed the war with the Dutch and other enemies of the church who are their allies: and your principal obliga-tion is to defend yourself and attack them.

Olivares' commitment to traditional foreign policies, giving priority to upholding the primacy that the kings of Spain had established in world affairs, did much to ensure the failure of his other policy interest – domestic reforms that would restore and strengthen the ability of the kingdoms to sustain the international pretentions of the monarchy.

The new reign saw a broad movement for internal reform, though it is significant that most programmes started with moral reform, suppression of excess consumption and luxury, a drive to clean up public life from the per-vasive corruption that flourished at all levels, and a thorough overhaul of the whole structure of public finance and taxation. In 1622 the Council of State set up a *Junta Grande de Reformacion*. It produced a comprehensive reform package, which was circulated around the ruling elites and the *cortes*, and in 1623 debated there. It at once appeared that while there was general support for reforms in principle, there were powerful vested interests which were opposed to almost any specific suggestion. In face of this, Olivares aban-doned his programme and it was shelved in return for traditional grants of supply. Although talk of reform continued, it is fair to say that no significant domestic reform was ever implemented.

But Olivares repeatedly showed that he did have modernizing aspirations for a far-reaching reform of the monarchy. These were partly outlined in the 'Great Memorial' presented to the king in 1624. It starts with an apocalyptic warning: 'the present state of these kingdoms is, for our sins, quite possibly the worst that has ever been known'. He outlined a long-term strategy to create a unified kingdom embracing the whole peninsula. As set out in a further memorandum to the king in 1625 it asserted:

> The most important thing in your Majesty's monarchy is for you to become king of Spain ... to secretly plan and work to reduce these kingdoms of which Spain is composed to the style and laws of Castile, with no difference whatsoever. And if your Majesty achieves this, you will be the most powerful prince in the world.

This appears to the modern observer a well-conceived project of rationalization, but Olivares knew – and that is why it was to be kept secret – that in his world it would be utterly unacceptable, every one of the vested interests threatened by it would do their utmost to frustrate it.

What Olivares did attempt was a first stage, a plan known as the 'Union of Arms'. This would commit all the component parts of the monarchy, including the empire, to grant permanent support for a local military force. This was based on the perception that the current arrangements threw a quite disproportionate burden on Castile. As an inducement to the other provinces they could be offered the possibility of admission to employments at present reserved for Castilians and even some access to the American empire. The plan laid down precise quotas of men and equipment which each province would provide. It met with universal hostility. Although it was claimed in 1626 that the Union of Arms had been accepted, since most of the provinces were reluctant to reject it outright, in fact the most that could be achieved were local compromises that fell far short of the original concept. It is possible to follow other radical proposals for reform, like the plan of 1627 for redeeming the debased *vellon* currency, which were all rendered futile by local opposition. This was as prevalent in the council bureaucracies as it was in the cortes or among other local elites. Olivares increasingly tried to bypass bureaucratic obstructions by setting up special *juntas* to deal with problems. But their plans met the same obstructions, as Elliott noted: 'over ambitious schemes, shortage of funds, the opposition of vested interests, a resistance to innovation – all these inhibited the *Junta de Poblacion*'s attempts to promote economic recovery in the Castile of the 1620s'.

The war, which had seemed to develop favourably down to 1627, took a disastrous turn for the worse in 1628 when the Dutch captured the treasure fleet and no American bullion reached Spain. No immediate collapse followed, but from then on Olivares had to struggle to keep the war effort going, using ever more desperate fiscal expedients. A background factor was the serious decline in the American trades that set in from the 1620s.[7] The figures suggest that between 1623 and 1650 the decline in traffic between Spain and the Americas was of the order of 50 per cent. Further, within that trade, by 1650 two-thirds of the shipping involved was foreign, as were the outward cargoes, mainly textiles and hardware manufactured in France or the United Provinces. Then the crown, desperate for funds, increasingly began to confiscate the private returns of bullion, issuing *juros* in compensation. Naturally the shipments tended to diminish and contraband trade flourished. Even so, for most of the 1630s, it proved possible to maintain a reasonably steady flow of supply to the main theatre of operations in the Netherlands, an average of 4.5 million ducats a year.

With the French entry into the war in 1635, new fronts opened up, particularly on the borders of Catalonia. It was necessary to raise fresh forces within the peninsula, and the principles of the Union of Arms were resurrected. They again provoked a very hostile response. First there was an attempt to involve Portugal in the local defence of the peninsula. In 1634 a new Castilian viceroy had been sent to Lisbon, and the regime tried to get Portuguese agreement to a regular contribution to defence costs. In 1637 there was an outbreak of tax rioting in Portugal, which was successfully repressed, but the underlying tensions were growing, and some among the Portuguese ruling elite began to consider plans to throw off the dynastic link with Spain and restore independence under the Braganza dynasty. The more immediate danger arose from the necessity to defend Catalonia. The province of Catalonia which had unusually strong provincial privileges, and whose interests were directed mainly into the Mediterranean, had always been reluctant to contribute to the policies of the monarchy. There was a record of attempts under Olivares to get contributions for the war, but Catalonia stood out in its absolute rejection of the Union of Arms scheme. It seemed obvious to Olivares that the war with France, and the threat of invasion, offered an opportunity to break down Catalonian provincialism. What happened, when the French did invade after 1637, was a whole new series of disputes over admitting royal troops, making financial contributions, billeting and supplying the armies. Olivares displayed his usual inability to follow a consistent strategy, either to persuade by concession, or use the troops to coerce, which naturally destroyed his credibility with the Catalans, who finally, in 1640, broke into open rebellion, murdered the viceroy in Barcelona, renounced their allegiance and decided to seek the protection of the king of France. Olivares was utterly taken aback and persisted in believing the Catalans could be managed by concessions.

The disaster was then compounded by the revolt of Portugal against Castilian interference, and attempts to make Portuguese revenues contribute to the general war effort. Olivares had further angered the Portuguese because, since 1627, he had been negotiating with the Portuguese Jewish community, nominally converted, which had a dominant role in commerce there, to participate in the *asientos* for Castilian revenue. The pay-off was to strengthen their legal rights in Portugal, such as protecting them from the Inquisition, something utterly repugnant to all Portuguese opinion, and not well received in Castile either. By early 1640 the Portuguese elites, the nobility, the church and the burghers were in a state of near revolt. When Olivares, ignoring Portuguese sentiment, demanded military service from the nobility to assist in the re-conquest of Catalonia, there was a coup in Lisbon. The Spanish viceroy and councillors were expelled and John of

Braganza proclaimed king. Now, in addition to all the other burdens of war, there were two internal fronts inside the peninsula, because the idea of letting Portugal go never arose. It seems clear that by this point Olivares had lost control of policy. He swung wildly from optimism to pessimism, making repeated misjudgements of events. In 1640 he told the king: 'In many centuries there cannot have been a more unlucky year than the present one ... I propose peace and more peace ... We must certainly pray God to give us a general peace, which even if it is not good, or even average, would be better than the most advantageous war.'

Yet he seems to have had no idea how this might be achieved. In 1643 the king reluctantly let him retire, and his enemies at court were able to come back into power. But they had no constructive ideas either, the war continued and the government staggered from one expedient to another. The *vellon* currency was devalued in 1642, revalued in 1651, devalued in 1652; there were state 'bankruptcies' in 1647, 1653 and 1662. This was a society that repeatedly demonstrated that it was incapable of adaptation. The king asked the *cortes*, in 1655, to devise a restructuring of the taxes and find 'a universal means which would yield the same, yet would fall on those with personal fortunes, and not on the poor beggar, the labourer, the artisan and other people who can only suppport themselves by their labour'. The *cortes* was quite unable to suggest anything. Instead it continued the existing taxes and authorized the sale of a new batch of offices, one result of which would be to expand further the numbers of the tax-exempt.

Spain seems to be the extreme case of a society that lived by war, yet was incapable of adapting to the new levels of expenditure which it demanded. There was no lack of ideas about how things might be restructured: the *arbitristas* had them in abundance; Olivares had them in the domestic field; there were even a few realistic ideas about the foreign policy of the dynasty. In 1635 the count of Hermanes submitted a memorandum proposing that Flanders be given up and Milan neutralized, leaving the monarchy to concentrate on defence of Iberia, Naples and Sicily and the American empire. He seems to have been ignored. There could not be a better illustration of the sheer entrenched conservatism of these early modern societies. If there were to be radical change, it would have to be enforced from the top, and this would demand will and perseverance from the only source of unchallengeable authority: the divinely appointed monarch. And genetics ensured that the Habsburgs of Madrid could not produce such a ruler.

4

The Origins of the Modern
State: Alternative Routes

The British Isles

Britain, like Spain or France, was a geographical expression not a political
community. Like Spain, it contained three kingdoms, England, Scotland and
Ireland, which in 1603 on the death of Queen Elizabeth were brought
together under a single ruler, James VI of Scotland. And just as Castile dominated Iberia by its relative size and affluence, so England dominated the
British Isles, and just before James's accession had reduced Ireland to the
status of a dependency by military conquest. But there was one crucial difference from Iberia: each of the British components professed a different religion. England had evolved a unique confessional hybrid in the Church of
England, Calvinist in doctrine, but preserving the institutional structures of
the old Catholic Church. That was why the Church of England had always
contained a vocal minority of committed clergy and laymen who regarded its
reformation as incomplete, and saw it as their religious duty to finish the
work. These were the English Puritans. Scotland had an established
Presbyterian Church. The great majority of the Irish had remained Catholics,
but their religion was outlawed and the reconquest vested effective control in
the minority Protestant settler community. This confessional diversity meant
there was a long agenda of religious issues that needed to be confronted, for
the prevalent European wisdom applied – that in the long term no community could live in peace and security if there was religious diversity.

  Like any normal European kingdom, England had been at war intermittently for decades, and its peaceful interlude developed in 1604 when the
new ruler, James VI and I, negotiated an end to the deadlocked conflict with
Spain, while the Irish rebellion was finally crushed. Like the rest of Europe,
England was a highly devolved structure, a mosaic of counties and corporate
towns, each governed by oligarchies of their wealthiest inhabitants, the
counties by the local peers and gentleman landowners, who held offices
under the crown as lords lieutenant, sheriffs and justices of the peace, and

met together regularly in the shire Quarter Sessions to settle the county's affairs. The town governments were regulated by royal charters which conferred legal authority on their corporations. But this highly devolved system was moderated by factors favouring central control. England was an economic free market: there were no internal tolls or customs barriers and few privileged monopoly companies, while guild controls had largely atrophied. This had enabled something like a modern market economy to develop to a level well beyond what prevailed over most of the continent. England also had a uniform legal system, the common law, administered by a corps of judges who sat in the central courts in London and took the law into the provinces when they went on circuit to hold the local assizes. The lawyers got their legal training in the Inns of Court in London, which were also open to gentlemen, who commonly sent their sons to learn the rudiments of law. The legal and landowning elites, unlike those of most continental societies, shared a common culture. But, most important, the network of local communities was linked by the English parliament. The leading landowners, who held peerages, came together with the bishops of the church in the House of Lords, while the communities elected representatives to the House of Commons. In parliament, king, Lords and Commons jointly held sovereign power to levy taxes and pass statute laws that were binding over the whole kingdom. In addition, it was possible to promote private bills through which individuals and groups could seek to secure their sectional interests. It is clear that one unintentional result of private bill legislation was to strengthen public interest in parliaments as a valued means of resolving community problems. Because the English parliament was not divided between the customary three Estates, each seeking to promote its sectional advantages, it was a viable means of negotiating a national political consensus binding on the royal government and its subjects equally.

The new king faced problems in two main areas: one was religion. A distinctive feature of English religious beliefs was a paranoid fear of popery. The English had come to see themselves as the leading Protestant nation, a compound of the historical memory of the Marian persecution, horror stories of Catholic brutalities on the continent and the experience of the Spanish Armada of 1588. This promoted the belief that England was the special target of popish plotting, masterminded from Rome and led by the Jesuits, to destroy their Protestant faith: the Gunpowder Treason of 1605 gave this paranoia a powerful boost. King James, a solid Protestant himself, was also a seeker after religious reconciliation and hoped that by negotiation with Catholic powers a peaceful settlement of the confessional confrontation could be found. To those subjects who saw popery as the ultimate religious perversion and the pope as Antichrist, any dealings with Catholic powers were suspect; so, for example, the peace with Spain in 1604 was by no means universally approved. This unhappiness was reinforced by the ongoing Puritan agitation for further reform of the church, which produced the Millenary Petition of 1603, in which a group of concerned clergy and laymen asked for removal from church services of what they called 'relics of popery' and for a concentration on the sermon and a preaching ministry as the core religious activities. The king arranged a conference of the parties at Hampton Court in 1604 which failed to establish consensus, and led the king to see the Puritans as dangerous disturbers of the religious peace and a potential challenge to lawful authority. This opened the long confrontation between the Stuart kings and their more zealous Protestant subjects.

But the most immediate problem was public finance. Accepted wisdom was that in peacetime the crown funded the government of the country out of its traditional hereditary revenues from land, feudal dues and customs. Only in time of war, or similar emergency, was it entitled to seek extra tax revenues through parliament. Accepted wisdom had been overtaken by reality, the general sixteenth-century inflation and the rising costs of warfare. The reality was that the English monarchy was underfunded in peacetime. The problem was that the taxpayer, as represented in parliament, did not accept this reality, but blamed any shortfall on extravagant court expenditure and outright corruption. It was unfortunate that James's notorious inability to handle money stimulated the misunderstanding. On the one hand the king's ministers were, like their continental counterparts, driven to dubious fiscal practices to boost revenue, mainly by using the prerogative powers of the monarchy like the authority to levy customs duties, or the selling of titles of nobility, or the exploitation of the king's rights of feudal superiority, like wardship. The parliamentary critics could denounce these, and even suggest that the king was trying to break out of the lawful constraints imposed by the need to get consent to taxation. This drew the common law courts into the dispute. There was nothing special about using the courts to resolve issues arising from the use of royal authority. The French *parlements* did this regularly when registering royal decrees, certifying their compatibility with legal norms. But that was on the initiative of the crown. In England at this period the common lawyers, led by a charismatic Chief Justice, Sir Edward Coke, were developing an idea that the common law, basically a law of property, could also resolve constitutional issues, because the 'liberties' of the subject, such as those specified in Magna Carta, were also his property as much as his house or land, and could not be taken away without his consent. This concept elevated the twelve common law judges to the role of constitutional referees between the crown and the subject.

The one serious attempt to deal with the funding problem, by an agreement between crown and parliament, was the 'Great Contract' of 1610. The king traded fiscal rights which were seen as objectionable in return for a perpetual additional revenue from parliamentary taxation; it foundered through the mutual suspicions of both sides. The king was able to carry on by using a range of fiscal expedients until the crisis of the Thirty Years War opened in 1618. James, as king of England, the leading Protestant power, and as father-in-law of the Elector Palatine, could not stand aside. His overriding aim was to negotiate a settlement, but even diplomacy was expensive. In 1621 parliament was called, principally to provide funding, but this exposed a division running through the ruling elites from the royal court down over the policies to be pursued, basically diplomacy or war. From 1621 parliaments were used by the rival factions to pursue their agendas, by putting pressure on the king. An example arose in 1621, when the House of Commons was persuaded by the war party to present a reasoned memorandum to the king on what he should do. The king rejected the whole idea as an outrageous intrusion on his right to conduct foreign policy. This turned a normal political faction fight into a constitutional issue when the House of Commons sent a remonstrance claiming that parliament was the 'Great Council of the Realm', empowered to discuss any matter of concern to the whole kingdom, and offer its advice, whether the king asked for it or not. In response the king dissolved the parliament. This set the scene for the complex politics of the 1620s. Court politics became focused on the royal favourite of both James and his son Charles I, who succeeded in 1625, the duke of Buckingham. He came to dominate policy and patronage, while the rival faction sought to remove him. This culminated in their attempt to use parliament in 1626 to impeach him as an evil councillor, withholding tax grants until the king submitted. This kind of manoeuvring intensified as the field of controversy widened. When Buckingham did convert to the military option after 1624, the military operations he directed against Spain and France ended in humiliating disasters, at the root of which was lack of adequate funding. Much more dangerous was the development of a religious dimension to the disagreements. A faction developed in the Church of England, usually labelled 'Arminian' – more realistically they were a clericalist faction – led by William Laud, which aimed at reclaiming for the church some of the power, influence and property that had been lost to the laity at the Reformation. They also emerged as hard-line exponents of absolute, divine-right monarchy. In 1625, the new king and the favourite made a fatal decision to support their programme. It was fatal because in the international crisis of that decade, the Arminians could be and were accused by their enemies of being crypto-papists. The king and Buckingham succeeded both in provoking the basic anti-clericalism of the secular elites, and the basic emotional anti-popery hysterias of the broader community.

When the king dismissed the parliament of 1626 in order to save his favourite, he proceeded to demonstrate the basic weakness of parliamentary tactics – that the amount of taxation they were offering was in any case unrealistically low. The king went on to demonstrate that he could use his prerogative power to raise funding: he successfully levied a forced loan in 1627, used his powers to compel local communities to recruit and billet troops at community expense, and when a group of opposition gentlemen challenged the legality of his proceedings, the king had them imprisoned without trial. The signs are that he could have succeeded in going it alone,[1] had the military operations not ended in disaster. In the parliament summoned in 1628 a last effort was made to repair the breach between the crown and the dissatisfied factions among the elite. A legal challenge to the king's use of arbitrary imprisonment in the 'five knights case' had failed and exposed the weakness of relying on the judges as referees. They had to agree that normal liberties were infringed by the king's actions, but ruled that this was covered by the king's ultimate sovereign power to order whatever was necessary for the safety of the kingdom, and of that necessity the king was sole judge.

A negotiated outcome produced the Petition of Right of 1628, a legal definition agreed by the two Houses and the king of the issues raised, most fundamentally that there could be no taxation without consent in parliament, and that the right of *habeus corpus,* which derived from Magna Carta and forbade imprisonment without trial, should not be denied by prerogative action. Formally the petition simply stated what the current legal position was, and was not an encroachment on royal prerogative power. In fact it was a public declaration that the royal government had acted illegally and must desist. In August 1628, the murder of Buckingham could have cleared the way for restoring basic consensus. The king was willing, but required a return to the fundamental problem of the underfunding of the monarchy. The opposition factions, rightly suspicious of the sincerity of the king's acceptance of the petition, were inclined to pursue other grievances first, not least the alleged threat presented by the Arminians to the church. The king lost patience and dissolved parliament, producing the scene in 1629 when the radicals in the Commons defied the royal order to adjourn to pass a final resolution setting out their basic demands, and denouncing those who opposed them as enemies of the king and kingdom.

It is usual to see the personal rule of Charles I from 1629 to 1639 as a conscious experiment in the viability of royal absolutism.[2] This is to give it a coherence it lacked. Certainly the king was trying to reinvigorate the machinery of government. There was no new favourite and the Privy Council became the centre of the executive government. It extended its authority over the local communities through the Book of Orders of 1631; it tried to reinvigorate the county militia system, and through the lords lieutenant and their deputy lieutenants, ensure the militia was properly equipped and trained, all at local expense. The process extended to Ireland, where the king's lord deputy, the earl of Strafford, reasserted control from London and managed to make the Irish administration yield a modest revenue surplus. One of its best-known aspects was the introduction of Arminian programmes into the church, led by Laud as archbishop of Canterbury after 1633. Opposition clergy were purged and recalcitrant laymen disciplined, opposition was intimidated by show trials in the Court of High Commission and the Star Chamber, Laudian ideas on ceremonial were forced on the parishes, and a determined campaign was launched to end lay exploitation of tithe and ecclesiastical properties, and to enforce the moral authority of the ecclesiastical courts over the laity.

On the surface it was remarkable, after the turmoil of the 1620s, how little overt resistance there was. Leaders of the parliamentary opposition in 1629 were imprisoned and held until they submitted or, in the case of the most outspoken, Sir John Eliot, died in prison. The petition offered no protection to them. The fiscal expedients, like distraint of knighthood, effectively a forced levy on the gentry, were grumbled at, but paid. It is significant that the king might have launched a thorough purge of local officeholders, seeking to replace them with committed loyalists. It is interesting that he did not do so. He expected obedience from local leaders, even if they had records of opposition, and generally it was given. These survival tactics among the local elites, however, left large numbers of unreliable personnel in key positions should a new crisis arise.

The test of the system came over ship money, a royal demand for an annual levy on the whole kingdom for money to sustain the royal navy. The king set annually what each community must pay, and ordered his sheriffs, all unpaid local gentlemen, to see it collected. There was resistance but, significantly, at first it was confined to rating disputes about the assessments. The rate of collection was usually above 90 per cent – extraordinarily good for any form of tax. However, the critics of the regime saw an opening for a legal challenge and, in 1637, John Hampden refused to pay his assessment on the grounds that it was illegal, and the case was brought before the 12 common law judges. The basic case was that ship money was unlawful under the Petition of Right; if the king judged there was a need to strengthen the navy, then he should summon parliament to authorize funding. The crown case rested on the assertion of the king's ultimate sovereign prerogative to judge what was necessary for the defence of the realm. The crown won, though three of the judges did declare that the levy amounted to illegal taxation without consent, and two more found legal technicalities in favour of Hampden. The verdict, therefore, was seven to five. This looks like a severe setback for royal authority, but the interesting consequence was that after a pause in payments while the case was being determined, there was almost full compliance with the levy of 1638.

It is difficult to come to any firm assessment of the experience of the 1630s.[3] Against the general public compliance, and undoubted progress being made in some parts of the programme, historians can show that financial underpinning was weak and the king was dangerously dependent on anticipations of revenue. Also, because the government was still basically underfunded, it lacked professional bureaucratic support. The number of paid servants of the crown, most of them in the legal system, amounted to some 600, most holding office for life. The king of England had fewer paid officials nationally than the king of France in the province of Normandy alone. The whole structure rested on the voluntary unpaid service of members of the local elites, and though they refrained from open opposition, they could and did use their positions to obstruct orders they disapproved of. Finally, it is to be noted that Charles I particularly antagonized the powerful merchant oligarchy that controlled the City of London. Political control of the capital, and financial control of commercial credit systems, made them particularly dangerous malcontents, as events would show. But, on the other hand, in the absence of some severe challenge to the system, of which there was no sign internally, those who did defy the system and suffered for it, like the Puritans Prynne, Bastwick and Burton in 1637, attracted demonstrations of public sympathy, but triggered no action. There seemed no reason why the pursuit of the royal policies should not continue indefinitely.

The challenge came from Scotland. James VI and I had hoped that his union of the crowns could be followed by some measure of institutional convergence between the two kingdoms, but quickly found there was no enthusiasm for this in either country. After decades of harsh experience ruling in Scotland, the king was wise enough to proceed cautiously. The big change for the Scots was the transfer of the royal government to London. This involved all the problems of absentee kingship that appeared in the Habsburg government of Portugal or Catalonia. Although the king successfully devolved administration to a group of reliable Scottish nobles, and found, as he boasted, he could rule Scotland from London by his pen, the grip of the royal administration was loosening. Even so, James succeeded in introducing some further royal control of the Kirk, particularly by reintroducing bishops to the ruling structure, trimming back the autonomy of Presbyterian kirk sessions, and largely dispensing with the General Assembly. Charles I had no such experience of Scotland, and showed himself singularly insensitive to Scottish opinion. He aspired to pursue policies of extracting more revenue from Scotland, in particular by threatening to recover ecclesiastical assets taken over by the nobility at the Reformation, and this linked to his other main endeavour to bring about substantial convergence between the Kirk and the Church of England. The continued existence of a strongly Calvinist Church north of the border encouraged the Puritan opponents of the Laudian programme in the Church of England. For example, it was impossible to stop Scotland being used as a channel for importing and distributing polemical religious material into England. Charles had set about reinforcing the authority of the bishops in the Kirk and, in 1637, without any wide consultation with the Scottish elites, ordered the introduction in the Kirk of a new service book, modelled on the English prayer book. To the clergy and many of the laity the new service book was cryto-popish; furthermore, it was a blatant English imposition on Scottish affairs. The introduction of the service book triggered riots in Edinburgh, which the Scottish Privy Council was unable, perhaps unwilling, to control. The unrest developed into rebellion in 1638 with the circulation of a National Covenant to defend the true religion. In 1640 Charles I, determined to suppress the rebellion by force, faced a Scotland in which the covenanters were in control and had raised a substantial army.

The British revolutions, 1640–1660

There is an extensive literature debating the causes of the English Revolution of 1640–60, many predicated on the idea that there must have been major dysfunctions in English society.[4] Yet a glance at England in 1639 shows no signs of such dysfunction. There were various discontented groups who disliked the royal policies. The court opposition faction of the 1620s was led by a group of Puritan-inclined nobles, like the earls of Bedford, Northumberland and Holland. Their gentry clients included John Pym, the established House of Commons spokesman, John Hampden, their friends in the City and sympathetic Puritan clergy. It was they who had organized the ship-money confrontation, and in the crisis of 1640 they were in some kind of collusion with the Scots. But they were in no sense revolutionary. Their aim was to persuade the king to change his advisers and his policies in favour of their recommended line: a more robust, Protestant foreign policy, an end to Laudian 'innovations' in the church, the advancement of the godly reformation in religious life and the vigorous promotion of the commercial and colonial interests of the kingdom. It seems reasonable to assume that, but for the Scottish rebellion, itself the unnecessary result of the king's ignorant political fumbling, there would have been no serious political instability in the England of the 1640s. The Scots were the immediate cause of the 'English Revolution' when their army invaded England.

One great weakness of the opposition to Charles's policies had been the loss of their best political forum in parliament. A parliament was the ideal means of enabling the different strands of opposition to meet and agree on common action. Because of the Scots the king summoned a parliament for April 1640. He expected strong financial support for resistance to the Scots, based on traditional English chauvinism, and was prepared to offer concessions on ship money in return. Pym in the House of Commons managed to block any such deal, and prepared to promote a remonstrance calling for negotiation with the Scots. To evade this, the king dissolved the parliament and pursued the war with his existing resources. These proved woefully inadequate, and the attempted mobilization exposed ominous signs of non-cooperation in the local communities. The result was that when the Scottish and English armies clashed at Newburn in August, the English fled, suggesting low morale and motivation, and the king was forced to sue for an armistice. The result decided the immediate outcome of the crisis. The Scots insisted that, until a settlement was made, their army would occupy Northumberland and Durham and be maintained at the king's expense. This meant that the king had to summon the English parliament again, and that until the settlement was completed in the summer of 1641, the opposition in England could count on pressure from the Scots' army to force concessions.

With this backing, Bedford's group set about persuading the king to admit them to public office and adopt their programme. They secured a Triennial Act, ensuring that in future parliaments would meet once in three years, even without a royal summons, and then launched impeachments of leading royal advisers. The most dangerous of these, the earl of Strafford, was put on trial before the House of Lords, charged with treason. It became the crucial test of strength, as Strafford put up a vigorous defence against a bad legal indictment and it seemed increasingly likely that the House of Lords would not convict. Attempts to negotiate a compromise by putting the opposition leaders into office collapsed when their leading exponent died in the spring, and the opposition resorted to violence. They decided to circumvent the trial by passing an Act of Attainder against Strafford, declaring him guilty. They got their allies in the City to organize menacing mob demonstrations at Westminster to intimidate the House of Lords into passing it, and reinforced their own power base by an Act that this parliament could not be dissolved without its own consent. This stripped Charles of his last constitutional weapon. When he attempted to save Strafford by refusing consent to the Act of Attainder, the same mobs besieged the royal palace until he gave way. This put effective political power in the kingdom into the hands of the two Houses, who now felt safe enough to send their Scottish allies home, and proceeded with legislation dismantling the royal programme of the 1630s.

These measures should have resolved the crisis and enabled normal constitutional government to resume, based on consensus between king, Lords and Commons. Two factors stood in the way. First, Charles I, though reduced to impotence, was determined to reassert royal authority and clearly regarded the concessions forced from him as invalid. This was made clear when he insisted on travelling to Scotland in August 1641, ostensibly to oversee the completion of the settlement with that kingdom, but in reality to buy Scottish support for recovery of his power in England by making whatever further concessions the Covenanting party demanded. The second was the development of divisions over the future of the church. At the start of the parliament, militant Puritans, based mainly on London had presented the Root and Branch Petition, demanding the abolition of episcopacy and the ceremonial based on the prayer book. It was at once clear that this was deeply divisive and split the opposition coalition, many of whom wished to retain the Elizabethan settlement in the church, while eliminating the Laudian 'innovations'. The basis for the development of a constitutionalist royalist position, based on defence of the church, had been established. By the autumn of 1641, Pym and his allies were struggling to keep control and had already lost support in the House of Lords. They decided to reinforce their position by drafting the Grand Remonstrance, a long historical review of events since 1625, suggesting that these represented a popish plot, with the Laudians subverting the church, and evil councillors seeking to seduce the king with the prospect of creating absolutism. This derived greater urgency when another outside intervention radicalized the situation in England and eventually led it towards civil war.

This was the Irish rebellion of October 1641.[5] The political crisis in England, and the well-grounded fear that a victorious Puritan faction was likely to call for new repressive measures against Catholics in Ireland, resulted in planning an uprising to break the Protestant settler control, and then negotiate a settlement respecting the rights of the Catholic majority. Although an attempt to seize Dublin was thwarted, much of the rest of Ireland fell under rebel control, and the process involved violence against the Protestant minority. No one in England seriously contemplated negotiating with Catholic rebels; all agreed that an army would have to be raised to crush the rebellion. But by law any such army would be raised and commanded by the king, putting into his hands an instrument for recovering his power. The parliamentary leadership could not permit this; they drove the Remonstrance through the House of Commons, and the extent of divisions was measured by the final vote. It was approved by nine votes in a very full House and then ordered to be printed, with the clear intention of arousing mass public support for the parliamentarian position. The Remonstrance was accompanied by a petition, partly devoted to tackling the House of Lords by a demand for removing Catholic peers and bishops from membership, but partly an open bid to control the executive government by the demand that in future the king should only appoint such councillors as the two Houses approved. As the crowds were again summoned from the City to intimidate the House of Lords, the City Common Council elections in December 1641 produced a majority supporting Pym's positions, and ensuring his control of the capital. This was the king's opportunity to present himself as the guardian of the traditional constitution, seeking to provoke the opposition into some flagrant illegality and rallying traditionalist sentiment around the monarchy. It was a tactic that could have worked but for the incurable political incompetence of Charles I, who in January 1642 made a bungled attempt to arrest the parliamentary leaders in the House of Commons. When this failed, his credibility was in ruins and he hastily fled from the capital to seek support in the provinces.

It then took more than half a year for actual armed conflict to begin. The negotiations between the king and the two Houses only revealed that the gap between them was irreconcilable. In March 1642 the two Houses took the revolutionary step of passing the Militia Ordinance, a resolution of the Houses, without the king's consent, to begin raising forces for the defence of realm under commanders nominated by themselves. To justify this blatant infringement of royal authority, they had to assert that the two Houses were the Great Council of the realm and the representative of the whole community, whose advice the king was bound to follow. This was made explicit in their terms for a settlement, the Nineteen Propositions of June 1642, which required the king to surrender all his independent authority into the hands of persons nominated in parliament. His position would be reduced to being a political symbol only. The king responded in August by formally raising his standard at Nottingham, declaring his opponents rebels and calling on his subjects to arm in his defence.

It is quite wrong to imagine the first civil war, from 1642 to 1646, as a clear confrontation between two sides in the English community.[6] It was apparent from the first that there was a strong neutralist tendency: in some counties there were attempts by formal neutrality pacts to stand aside from the conflict, and in the later years the Clubmen movement sought to neutralize their districts by forming local defence forces to exclude both belligerents. Initially both sides had to accept a high level of decentralization. Within each local community there were power struggles between committees of activists, and both sides based their administrations on the local committees. Since these committees were the actual source of most revenue and supply, neither side found it easy to develop a coherent national strategy. The sinews of war were dissipated in seizing local power bases and holding them by garrisons. The local communities were unwilling to contribute men and money for operations outside their territories.

The parliamentary side had major advantages. They had unbroken control of the capital, London, the surrounding counties and East Anglia. This did not mean there were no royalists in this area, but they were forced into passive acceptance. Since this was also the most advanced region of the kingdom economically, it gave parliament a solid power base. London in particular was the greatest port, so giving parliament control of the bulk of the customs revenue; it was the only major financial centre able to produce cash loans on a large scale; and it was a major reservoir of manpower. As long as London was under parliamentary control, the king could not win the war, but until 1645 he had enough resources to field armies in each campaigning season, adequate to keep the conflict going on fairly level terms militarily.

The English civil war, like most such conflicts, compelled the participants to adopt methods that would have been unacceptable under normal conditions and thus became a radicalizing force. This can be seen over public revenue, the root problem behind England's original political crisis. Both sides began by appealing for loans from their friends, and seizing the resources of their opponents. Parliament sequestered the properties of the church, and of all who declined to declare their loyalty, or actively supported the king. Then in 1643 it developed two decisive new revenue raisers. One was the Assessment, based on ship money, whereby each community was assessed to pay a stipulated sum, while a local committee, nominated by the two Houses, undertook the collection. This established for the first time in England a standing direct tax, at first levied weekly, then monthly, assessed and collected locally, which became the model for direct taxation for the rest of the early modern era. It proved remarkably efficient, especially since the committees were empowered to use force against recalcitrant taxpayers. Then in 1643 the excise was introduced as a national indirect tax, initially mainly on alcoholic beverages. The collection was farmed out to syndicates of businessmen, but the money came directly to the central treasury, whereas much of the Assessment was drawn on for local expenditure. The excise was bitterly opposed in the country and caused widespread riots, but by using military force where necessary, it became established and was seen as an ideal security for raising cash advances. In this way England, for the first time, acquired a modern tax system capable of raising revenue on a quite unprecedented scale, which was one of the most important long-term results of the civil wars.

It was inevitable that, in the absence of a quick victory, both sides looked for outside support to break the deadlock. The Scots had initially stood aside from the conflict, though the Covenanter leaders knew that if parliament were defeated, their own position in Scotland would be exposed to a victorious king. In 1643 the parliamentarians negotiated an alliance. The Scots engaged to send a substantial army into England in support of parliament's cause. The price was that the English would pay for its upkeep, they would also have to set up a joint command and, most important, they must agree to radical reform of the Church of England, specifically abolishing episcopacy, and seeking the maximum convergence between the Scottish and English churches. The parliamentarians would willingly have evaded this religious requirement, though their own religious radicals, particularly in London, welcomed the support it gave them. The Scots insisted on a Solemn League and Covenant to which both sides were to be sworn. This then became an obstacle to any negotiated settlement of the religious issues in England. The king, disappointed in Scotland, looked instead to Ireland, where he authorized his lord deputy to negotiate a truce with the Catholic rebels, which would enable military assistance to be sent into England, which began early in 1644. The king could not have made a worse choice of ally. Parliament had always alleged that the royalists were a conspiracy of crypto- and open papists; they could now allege that the king intended to bring hordes of murderous Irish papists over to destroy English Protestantism. Some prominent royalists found they could not accept this, and there is evidence that it gave a major boost to parliament's war effort.

The most successful of the parliamentary armies by 1644 was that of the Eastern Association, where the participating counties had agreed on an effective central support system. It had also given an opportunity for a local gentleman, Oliver Cromwell, to demonstrate his military talents as an organizer of cavalry. Cromwell, himself a strongly radical Protestant, had the perception that the effectiveness of an army could be raised if its manpower was ideologically motivated. There is evidence that Cromwell put this into practice in recruiting cavalry for the Association, looking for recruits committed to godly reformation. In the summer of 1644, the Scots army arrived in England and linked up with the Eastern Association army to try and clear the royalists out of northern England by capturing their stronghold in York. A royalist force under their leading commander Prince Rupert, the king's nephew, moved to relieve the city and met the combined Anglo-Scottish force at Marston Moor. This gave the parliamentarians their first major strategic victory, the royal army was shattered, with Cromwell's cavalry playing the leading role, and Yorkshire and most of northern England was brought under parliamentary control.

But the success was not followed up. The Scots and the Association armies went their separate ways and, during the autumn, the king led a successful campaign in the west and restored the military deadlock. In a major political crisis in London, those on the parliamentary side who wanted further negotiation to end the conflict faced those who demanded that parliament reinvigorate its war effort by establishing a properly supported, professional army, free of local constraints, and seek a military decision. This led to the Self-denying Ordinance, which made a clean sweep of the existing command structure, and the New Model Ordinance, which established a new, professional force under the command of Sir Thomas Fairfax, with Cromwell as his Lieutenant General in command of the cavalry, most of which was transferred from the Eastern Association army. This force, fully re-equipped from resources provided by the City, and initially receiving fairly regular pay, took the field in 1645 and destroyed the king's main field army at the battle of Naseby in June. It then launched a vigorous campaign to seize the king's base areas in the West Country, while the king found that at last his own resources had run out. The royalist areas were no longer willing to provide more money and recruits for what they now saw as a lost cause. It took until mid-1646 for the New Model Army to mop up the remaining royalist areas, but then the king acknowledged defeat and surrendered to the Scots army at Newark. His efforts to enlist their support broke down on his firm refusal to subscribe to the Covenant, and in December the Scots sold him to the English in return for a substantial contribution and withdrew to Scotland. The king was now a prisoner of the parliament. This settled nothing. The king was faced with Anglo-Scottish terms for a settlement, the Newcastle Propositions, which would reduce him to a puppet ruler and make him agree to the punishment of his supporters, and above all to take the Covenant as the basis for the church settlement. It seems clear that he was willing to risk any extremities to himself personally rather than yield any of the basic sovereign powers of the monarchy. This obduracy left the victorious parliamentarians at a loss.

They were also under heavy pressures to achieve a quick settlement, for the war, with its breakdown of the normal machinery of social control, had unleashed a flood of unrest and generated some popular radical movements. This was more serious because, since 1644, their own establishment in parliament and among the Puritan clergy had split. There was objection to the strict, intolerant Presbyterian religious settlement being proposed on the basis of the Covenant. A small minority of clergy, with backing within parliament, wanted something allowing for a degree of congregational freedom within a national church, allowing a 'liberty for tender consciences'. This movement, the Independents, was in effect calling for a measure of religious toleration for Protestants. By 1646 it was becoming apparent that the Independent view had strong support in the New Model Army, appealing precisely to the sort of men that Cromwell had been recruiting. Conservatives of all kinds increasingly came to see the army as an obstacle to a settlement. It is apparent that after the fighting ended, when the army was inactive in its encampments, some kind of corporate political consciousness was developing among the soldiers, who conceived that they had won the war and were entitled to a voice in the making of the peace.[7]

The result was that, in 1647, the majority in the two Houses made a clumsy attempt to disband the army, without settling its professional grievances over arrears of pay or the need of the soldiers for legal indemnity for their wartime actions or, most importantly, respecting the army's sense of corporate identity. This provoked a mutiny: the rank and file elected representatives to an Army Council, and publicly demanded redress of their grievances before disbanding, and asserted they were 'no mere mercenary army', but had been enlisted to defend the liberties of the people, and were entitled to be consulted over any settlement. The generals, Fairfax and Cromwell, in order to keep things under control, agreed to join with the men and support their demands. They bid for a settlement by a coup, seized the king from his parliamentary minders, and tried to negotiate a settlement directly with him. The terms offered to Charles, in the Heads of the Proposals, were generous by comparison with what parliament offered, but he simply treated the offer as a chance to divide his opponents and recover his freedom of action. This caused political chaos, with the king seeking whatever advantage he could get, the army leaders using their strength to force the parliamentary leaders to address the grievances of the soldiers, and the parliamentary leaders seeking escape by a new effort to negotiate with the king and produce a settlement based on the traditional government by king, Lords and Commons.

Resolution came through renewed civil war. In 1648 desperate conservatives, former royalists, and the more conservative Scottish Covenanters launched armed risings to restore the king to the throne. In the summer of 1648 the army crushed the two main insurrections in Kent and Essex and in South Wales; then Cromwell went north to meet the invading Scots and utterly defeated them at Preston. In November the army, now in complete command of the country, moved back. Before they left on this campaign, the council of officers had held a prayer meeting at Windsor. It resolved that if they returned victorious, they would bring the author of the new troubles, Charles Stuart, 'that man of blood' to account for the evil he had caused. Cromwell seems to have accepted that the army's victory expressed God's judgement of the king's policies. When a defiant parliament voted to pursue negotiations with the king for a settlement, Cromwell and the officers, and their parliamentary allies, organized a coup, seized London, and through Pride's Purge reduced the House of Commons to a Rump of their own supporters. The king too was seized and brought to London to stand trial, and in January 1649 Charles I was executed.

The Rump of the 1640 parliament, which executed the army's orders, nominally contained about half the original MPs, but the bulk of them rarely attended. Its working core was down to some 70 hard-line collaborators with the army. It claimed to act as the voice of the people of England but, aware of the implausibility of the claim, promised to seek a fresh mandate as soon as security permitted. In the meantime, the Rump abolished both the monarchy and the House of Lords, and assumed full sovereign powers, with an elected Council of State as the executive. The new Commonwealth was tolerated by most, as the only working government on offer: most early modern Europeans would agree that any government was better than none. But the Rump was seen by most for what it was – the political tool of the army leadership, which in 1650 passed to Cromwell as Lord General. Under his leadership, the army broke the Irish rebellion in 1649. When the Scots, who had repudiated the regicide, invited the new claimant Charles II to come to Scotland and take up his throne, Scotland was invaded, and in two years of campaigning, ending with the victory over the invading Scots and royalists at Worcester, this third civil war was brought to an end in September 1651.[8]

Since the regicide, the Rump had provided a vigorous and effective administration. It had sustained the army in its re-establishment of order in the three kingdoms; it had supervised the confiscation and sale of the properties of the crown and the church and stabilized the public finances; it had launched a vigorous policy of promoting trade through the Navigation Act of 1651; and, when this produced armed confrontation with the United Provinces, it launched a successful naval war on the Dutch. It had settled the religious problem by simply repealing all the legislation making church attendance compulsory, thereby creating a broad toleration for Protestants. It was planning an incorporating union with Scotland. It had not taken any steps to secure a fresh mandate by holding elections, although it had proclaimed that all just power derived from the people and was vested in their elected representatives. The reason for this was strictly pragmatic, as any conceivable free election would sweep the Rump from power. It held power only by grace of the army, which in itself ensured its rejection by almost the whole community. But when the army came back from the wars in 1651, its leaders, not least Cromwell, were looking for something more.

They wished to transform England, Scotland and Ireland into a godly Commonwealth, fit to be the leading actor in promoting God's plans for the world. Holding elections for a new representative would be the first step. Under intense army pressure, the reluctant parliamentarians began to consider how that could be done. Then, early in 1653, Cromwell and the officers had a re-think. They too came to see that an election would produce an unacceptable result. The Rump must surrender its powers to a nominated assembly of representatives of the godly community, which would draft a constitution for the new society. This would obviously leave effective power in the hands of the army. It seems[9] that, in the end, the Rump decided to risk an election to break free of army control. It was this design that provoked Cromwell, in April 1653, to take a troop of musketeers into the House of Commons and disperse the Rump.

The remaining history of the English republic is a series of desperate attempts by the army to legitimize its exercise of the sovereign power. This proved impossible, because no representative body of civilians could be assembled that was willing to do this. It was Cromwell who, when reproached for the failure of the government to secure popular consent, stated the basic problem, saying, 'I am as much for government by consent as any man, but where shall we find that consent?' They tried a nominated assembly of representatives of the godly, the Barebones Parliament, then a written constitution in the Instrument of Government, making Cromwell chief executive with the title of Lord Protector, but controlled by a Council of State nominated by the army, whose advice he was bound to follow, and an elected single-chamber parliament. When that met it immediately began demanding changes in the constitution, to eliminate the entrenched power of the officers. The Protector first purged the parliament and then, when even this failed to produce compliance, dissolved it. This was followed by an experiment with military rule. The country was divided into military districts, supervized by a Major General supported by a local militia. This aroused such popular hostility that the Major Generals themselves lost their nerve, and another elected parliament was called in 1656. This time its membership was purged in advance, but even then the members had an overriding aim to shake off army control, and sought to do this by offering Cromwell a constitutional revision, based on the proposal to make Cromwell king and in this way restore the traditional form of government. This plan fell in face of the determined opposition of the officers, who readily grasped how their position would be endangered. Cromwell, who knew his real power lay in the army, felt obliged to refuse. Eventually a new scheme was devised, with Cromwell still as Lord Protector, and a new nominated second chamber created, which effectively protected the interests of the army. This destroyed the whole rationale of the original proposal, and when the new scheme was tried in 1658 it failed in face of new attacks from the Commons on the power of the army. The parliament was dissolved, and no new initiative launched before Cromwell's death in September 1658.

Cromwell had nominated his son Richard to succeed as Lord Protector, but he lacked his father's personal ascendancy over the army, being an essentially civilian figure. A power struggle began among the leading officers which ended in total political chaos by the end of 1659. It was resolved when the commander of the army in Scotland, General Monk, having carefully purged his own troops and entered into negotiation with influential civilian figures, including royalists, entered England with his troops on a simple programme of promising free elections to decide the future government. The army factions could generate no coherent resistance and the survivors of the Rump Parliament were reassembled and compelled to reverse Pride's Purge, producing a majority for formal dissolution and fresh elections. The outcome was what would have happened after any free election since the regicide: an overwhelming majority for the restoration of the traditional government by king, Lords and Commons. Charles II returned to claim his throne in May 1660 to general acclamation.

Historians will probably never arrive at a consensus on what the English Revolution signified, but by most criteria it appears that it was a non-event. Studies of local power structures show an interesting pattern. The original civil conflict tore apart traditional elites in the counties, and the parliamentary side, in setting up its county committees, often drew in gentlemen of low status, who would normally have been excluded from government. This process can be seen accelerating up to the regicide, and then slowly reversing. Particularly after the establishment of the Protectorate, old ruling families began to return to local government. With the Restoration the process speeded up, so that after 1660 the local power structures in the English counties resembled those of pre-1640. There had been no lasting break. Similarly, studies of land ownership reveal a remarkable continuity. Although at the peak of the Revolution large amounts of land came on the market, sold by royalists to pay their composition fines, some confiscated outright from royalist magnates, plus the lands of crown and church sold off after 1649, in the end the old structure of land ownership survived remarkably intact. No significant class of new landlords arose from the sales. Some of the weaker royalist gentry families succumbed; most survived. After 1660, and a negotiated return of crown and church lands, the basic structure of English landholding was very close to what it had been before 1640. There had been no revolution there.

For possible long-term change we must look at religious life. For nearly two decades the control of the established Church of England had been interrupted. During the first civil war, while the elites quarrelled over the future structure of the national church, religious radicalism had found free expression in the form of numerous sects, mostly insignificant in size and influence, but some deeply alarming to orthodox religious opinion. The most important developed after 1650 in the Quakers, who uniquely became a substantial, national movement, and with their open challenge to all traditional hierarchies seemed a dangerous threat to the basic culture of rank and deference. But while Cromwell and the army held power, the manifest eagerness of the established elites to crush the radicals was frustrated. This may have contributed to the mood, after Cromwell's death, for a speedy re-establishment of the traditional order. The concept of a national church sustained by tithes was never seriously challenged. The attempt of the parliamentarians to substitute a strict Presbyterian establishment after 1646 was frustrated by the army and Cromwell. But the result, under the Protectorate, was a national Protestant church of no fixed doctrine, and stripped of any coercive powers, alongside the free existence of radical sects who, as long as they were Protestant, were unmolested by authority.

This was guaranteed because of the religious commitment of Cromwell and the officers, who saw what they considered the 'people of God' as the main agents in the working out of God's plan for mankind. But since no one living could be sure exactly who the people of God were, since God works in mysterious ways, Cromwell held it essential that their freedom to express what God put in their minds must not be obstructed. As he once remarked, he would rather see Mohammedanism tolerated in England than run the risk of obstructing the mission of God's chosen people. This position really was revolutionary, for it struck at the most basic ideas of a society where authority was transmitted down from on high through the established hierarchies. It struck at the whole structure of deference. And it transpired that after 20 years of suspension the old hegemony of the restored Church of England could not be reinstated. Open religious dissent and pluralism had taken root in English society and became a permanent feature. In this respect England, by comparison with most other contemporary societies, was religiously pluralist. But even this was not revolutionary in the end. Established society learned to live with dissent and the elites found their basic right to rule was not really being challenged. Orderly government was compatible with religious dissent.

In the later 1640s there had also been a brief emergence of secular radicalism in the Leveller movement. This had grown out of the struggle for individual choice in religion, and widened into a claim of individual right to participate in government. The English Levellers represent the first appearance in European history of a coherent movement advocating democratic participation as the basis for legitimate political authority. The movement inspired by Lilburne, Walwyn and Winstanley excites the modern observer because it is articulating the basic arguments for a democratic society. But it also demonstrated that in the world of the seventeenth century there was no place for such ideas. The Levellers terrified the established ruling elites, but their ideas evoked no widespread response among the common folk of seventeenth-century England. They were only dangerous during the brief period from 1647 to 1649, when Leveller propaganda won ground among the soldiers of the New Model Army, until Cromwell succeeded in reasserting officer control. Democracy was an idea whose time had not yet come. It is significant how many of the secular radicals of the 1640s turned back to religion in face of failure, many joining the Quakers. Religion was still the dominant mode of thinking in all levels of society. The Levellers are historically interesting, but wholly marginal as a political phenomenon.

If we look to define what had changed by 1660, one obvious answer is that English society had, belatedly, faced up to the requirements of the military imperative. In the 1620s English attempts to deploy military power had been pathetically inadequate. Under the stress of civil war, the English learned how to raise the kind of revenue needed to sustain war and, in the New Model Army and the reconstructed navy of the 1650s, how to build up effective armed forces. The administrative structures of the army and navy were developed and professionalized, particularly the officer corps of the navy and the administration of the admiralty commission. In the 1650s the English navy was effectively projecting English sea power on an oceanic scale. The army demonstrated what it could do within the British Isles by defeating the king, finally establishing the English conquest of Ireland and successfully carrying through the only English military conquest of Scotland, and made its debut in continental campaigning at Dunkirk in 1658 with spectacular success. England had reasserted its position as a major military state. Further, it had used its strength to launch the aggressive commercial and colonial policies foreshadowed by the Navigation Act of 1651, and had entered the competition for commercial and colonial hegemony on which its future development was to be built.

The United Provinces

In seventeenth-century Europe, the United Provinces, seven sovereign provinces allied through the Union of Utrecht to secure their independence from Spain, were in every respect exceptional. They were a small community of about 1.2 million inhabitants in 1600 and perhaps two million by 1700, but by any material standards the wealthiest in Europe. They had enjoyed a modest prosperity in the sixteenth century, based on an advanced agriculture, free of feudal landlordism, in one of the most urbanized regions in Europe, producing a steady surplus for the urban market. They had a technically advanced fishing industry, exploiting the rich North Sea herring shoals, and through their advanced food-processing techniques they supplied much of Europe with their salted fish. To carry this they had good river communications into the centre of Europe and, again partly because of technical advances in ship construction, had a large share of the coastal carrying trade. This basic economy then took off in the last decade of the sixteenth century.

The success of the economy was stimulated by securing the territory from Spanish invasion, and by the flight of Protestant refugees, businessmen and skilled artisans from religious repression in the Spanish Netherlands, and reinforced by the success of the republic in closing the river Scheldt and strangling the trade of Antwerp, then the great commercial entrepot of Europe and a major centre of financial services. By 1600 Antwerp's position was being overtaken by Amsterdam, which remained the financial services capital of Europe until well into the eighteenth century. That was symbolized by the establishment of the Amsterdam Wisselbank in 1612: in the absence of a monarchy, with its inevitable tendency, under financial pressure, to try to requisition assets and to manipulate the coinage, the Amsterdam banking system offered absolute security, backed by a solid currency which held its value almost constant up to the French Revolution.

Amsterdam became the commodity market of Europe, fed by the growth of Dutch commerce, which first penetrated the Baltic and took over from the Hanseatic League the rich Baltic grain trade, then entered the Mediterranean and drove out most of the local and English competition from the Levant trades, and broke into the Spanish and Portuguese colonial trades, at first by covert infiltration. In 1600 a substantial share of the supposedly Spanish exports to America were in fact supplied from Amsterdam and a considerable share of the American silver ended up there. Penetration became official policy when, in 1600, the Estates General chartered the United East India Company to trade openly with the Portuguese East Indies. This company, in which the Estates General were shareholders only, developed into a state within the republic, directing and financing the expulsion of the Portuguese and English from the oriental spice trade and setting up a chain of settlements to service their enterprises: a Dutch empire run by private enterprise with striking success. The Truce allowed the company to pursue its East Indies trade, but held up the formation of a sister venture, the West India Company, designed to break into the Americas, establishing bases in the Caribbean to trade with the Spanish colonies, and above all aiming to take over the hugely profitable Brazilian sugar trade and ultimately annex Portugal's Brazilian settlements.

These developments were the basis of Dutch oceanic trading, added on to the vastly larger, and more productive, European carrying trade. On this basis the United Provinces were the dominant naval power in Europe. Since Amsterdam was the financial capital, and awash with money looking for investments, the Dutch throughout the century were financing European rulers in their warfare and funding industrial and commercial enterprises as far away as Russia – in fact wherever there was a profit to be made. It is this economic miracle, which, though there was a partial recession in some branches after the renewal of the war in 1621, was expanding again in the mid-1640s and did not show serious signs of tapering off until the 1670s: then the Dutch textile trades began to lose to the rising competition from England and France, the general agricultural depression hit farm prices, and the Baltic grain trade had passed its peak. But though from then on the United Provinces experienced continuing relative commercial and manufacturing decline, the position of Amsterdam as leader of the financial services industry survived.

This urban-based market economy was not evenly spread through the seven provinces. It was based on Holland, and to a lesser extent Zeeland and Utrecht. The four inland provinces were nearer the European economic norm, agrarian-based and politically dominated by noble landlords, though even here surviving feudal burdens were marginal, and the agriculture was technically advanced and relatively profitable.

Historians tend to see the history of seventeenth-century Europe as one of advancing development of monarchical absolutist states, driven by the imperatives of the armed power struggle to create ever bigger armed forces. In so far as there was such a trend, the United Provinces, under that same military imperative, survived and flourished by preserving everything that was supposed to stand in the way of building a competitive, military–bureaucratic fiscal state. The original Union of Utrecht had been an alliance to defend provincial autonomy from the attempted encroachments of a centralizing ruler. To ensure this continued, the monarchical executive had been eliminated, and sovereignty vested in the seven provinces collectively, whose delegates came together in the Estates General sitting in the Hague in permanent session. Delegates were mandated by their provincial Estates, each province had one vote, and the convention was to seek consensus. Provincial autonomy could be interpreted to mean that no province was bound by a resolution to which it had not assented.

The Estates General was not a government and there was no head of state; it was not a legislature, as law-making was left entirely to the provinces themselves; and there was no central judiciary. Above all it had no direct power to tax. The Estates General was a conference of ambassadors authorized to organize the collective defence of the Union and to handle its foreign relations. Each year the size of the military establishment and its costs were determined by the Estates General, and the money was raised by quotas on the provinces, according to a virtually unalterable division. It was then up to each province to raise and forward its revenue quota. In 1641, in a typical budget proposal, some 87 per cent of the proposed central expenditure was for defence, 4 per cent for servicing the common debt, and 9 per cent for administration. The Estates General disposed directly only of a small excise revenue on salt that gave less than 1 per cent of its revenue; the proceeds of customs duties, which provided 12 per cent; and the taxes levied on the generality lands, conquered from Spanish control during the war. The remaining 80+ per cent of revenue came from provincial quotas.

This should have been a recipe for military disaster, leaving the central administration chronically starved of cash-flow, even if the quotas were eventually paid in full and on time – an unlikely outcome. In fact the United Provinces consistently maintained the best system of frontier fortresses and garrisons and the most reliably paid field army and navy in Europe, attested by their ability to draw recruits from all over Europe into their service. The explanation was that their war efforts were entirely financed by borrowing on public credit. That was why the public debt of the Union rose from 5 million guilders in 1607 to 80 million in 1715. In any other political context this would have spread ruin. The basic technique for borrowing was one widely used: government bonds carrying fixed rates of interest were issued on the security of specific tax revenues. The Spanish juros and the French rentes were public securities of this type. Being subject to the hazards of periodic bankruptcies, they needed high rates of interest. The Dutch securities were administered by the States of Holland, whose quota provided 60 per cent of the revenue; their currency backing was secure, and there were no bankruptcies, hence the interest rates were low, usually around 4 per cent or less. The Estates General could rely on its loan issues being fully subscribed by voluntary and enthusiastic lenders; they were one of the safest investments in Europe. By 1700 the Dutch had more money invested in public securities than in land and property combined.

This would seem the full explanation why the military imperative did not drive the United Provinces down the road of installing a powerful central executive to cope with the demands of war. One further factor was that the United Provinces did not have a monarchy seeking to pursue dynastic advantage, sometimes at the expense of the common welfare. Their whole existence derived from their having got rid of it. They did have the ghost of monarchical power in the office of stadholder, always vested in a member of the princely house of Orange. The stadholders had been the old royal provincial governors; now they were the salaried agents of the provinces, serving under a contract which defined their powers: principally rights of patronage in appointing members of the magistracy and some other local officers. The office was separate in each province, and at no time in the seventeenth century did one man hold the office in all seven provinces. Friesland, in particular, usually chose its stadholder from a junior line of the Orange family. In addition, the senior stadholder was usually also a servant of the Estates General in the capacity of Captain and Admiral General, hence commander of the republic's armed forces, and in that capacity had more patronage in appointing officers, and also the power to decide whether the army could be used in the maintenance of public order inside the republic. The stadholders of the Orange family were also major landowners and there is good evidence that all the seventeenth-century holders of the office had aspirations to acquire princely sovereignty over the provinces, keeping up a quasi-royal court in their palace at the Hague.

The true powerholders in the republic were the regent oligarchies who ruled its cities. The Netherlands had shared with most of Europe the custom of vesting control of corporate towns in a small executive elite of their more substantial citizens, with a broader-based citizen assembly. There were still a few towns which retained this system in the United Provinces, but by the time of the revolt, most town government was in the hands of a closed corporation of their wealthiest families, who filled any vacancies by co-optation from their own ranks. It was not wholly closed – families would be dropped if they lost their wealth and demography ensured that others became extinct – but it is apparent that turnover of families was slow. These regent oligarchies ran the cities in normal circumstances. There was also a professional magistracy, often appointed by the stadholder, but from lists of candidates presented by the city. They could represent trainee regents waiting for vacancies.

There were two urban sectors the regents did not fully control. One was the Calvinist clergy: here the regents usually appointed and paid the town preachers, although this did not prevent militant clergy denouncing those aspects of regent policy they disapproved of, most commonly their willingness to tolerate Protestant dissent and their reluctance to enforce repressive laws on the Catholic minorities. The regencies tended to be strongly Erastian in their views of the church. The other was the urban militia. This consisted of self-governing companies, recruited from solid, propertied citizens who defended and kept order in the cities. But since they were self-governing, and came from a social stratum below that of the regents, they could be decisive in the event of popular urban protests, demonstrations and riots. The threat from below was one the regents could never ignore, and if they did lose control through the defection of the militia, their sole resort was to appeal to the stadholder to send regular troops, which he might or might not agree to do. Generally the regents ruled unopposed. Though clearly set apart from their fellow citizens, they remained resident in their communities and closely linked to the commercial community, even if their families had become wealthy enough to leave trade and live as *rentiers*. They were rightly perceived as sharing the values and aspirations of the propertied citizenry, and therefore generally trusted.

The regents, however, were not just masters of their communities. The united regents of the Holland cities were also, normally, the ruling elite of the republic. The reason why an apparently incoherent alliance of seven sovereign provinces did not disintegrate politically was that, in the power structure of the Union, the province of Holland was dominant. The fact that it contributed 60 per cent of the Union quotas and administered the public debt of the republic meant that no major political decision could be made if the province of Holland opposed it. The ruling body in the province was the Holland States, a composite assembly of nobles who had one collective vote, which they usually vested in the stadholder, and 18 corporate towns, each with one vote. These included Amsterdam, but excluded the Hague. Thus if the Holland regents were united, they controlled the Holland States, which in turn controlled the Union and gave it its remarkable political cohesion. That made a central executive government superfluous. The Estates General elected a Council of State, of 12 members and the stadholders, to carry out its policy decisions. This was served by embryonic government departments. The Chamber of Accounts, under an Advocate Fiscal, audited expenditure, except that large areas were outside its remit, not least the whole naval administration, which was run by the five provincial admiralties. There never was a consolidated Union budget. Since the Estates General had assumed responsibility for the maintenance of the border fortresses and their garrisons, there was a sub-committee of War under the Council of State, and a Mint Chamber to control the currency.

The coordination of the work of the Council of State fell to the Grand Pensionary, an officer of the States of Holland, who shared with the stadholder the day-to-day direction of affairs. This administration had only an exiguous supporting bureaucracy. It is difficult to determine its precise extent, but it is generally agreed that the Estates General ran its administration with at most some 300 paid servants. There was no danger of this group, which had no corporate existence, growing into a controlling national bureaucracy, which was further assured because the great bulk of the ordinary administration of public affairs was reserved to the individual provinces. While there was broad consensus, particularly among the regent oligarchies, and the business life of the community was prospering, this chaotic system of devolved government worked well enough – probably better, and certainly more economically and with less blatant corruption, than any other contemporary government.

Yet from time to time the consensus came under threat. In 1600, public life was dominated by two powerful individuals, the Grand Pensionary, Johan van Oldenbarneveldt and the senior stadholder, Prince Maurice. Oldenbarneveldt forced the conclusion of the Truce in 1609 against the wishes of Maurice, a clear case of a united Holland exerting its power in the Union, and created a tension which mounted as the end of the Truce approached. Naturally Oldenbarneveldt wished to renew it; the prince was generally for resuming hostilities. But it was typical of this period that a religious controversy precipitated the crisis. The split which shook international Calvinism after 1600 originated in the United Provinces, with a challenge to orthodox belief from the university professor Jacob Arminius.[10] When the confessional controversy began to divide communities, and opened a rift between Amsterdam and the regents of some of the other Holland cities, the prince saw the possibility of undermining Oldenbarneveldt. Maurice promoted the demand for a synod to resolve the issues. This met at Dordrecht and condemned the Arminians. A populist protest movement, supported by the prince and worked up by the Calvinist clergy, demanded their suppression. It challenged the regents in Holland, who were confessionally divided. When Oldenbarneveldt, in desperation, tried to assert that Holland's contingents in the army were ultimately under the control of the province, the prince could claim that the Union was in danger of breaking up. With a certain amount of mob coercion, which Maurice did nothing to discourage, the Orangists carried through a coup which led to Oldenbarneveldt's trial and execution in 1619, followed by a severe Orangist purge of the town regencies.

The legacy of factional division that this created persisted. Families that had split in 1619 into republican or Orangist factions seem to have retained their traditional commitments, creating the basis for new crises in future. But, in the short term, after the death of Maurice, his successor Frederick Henry worked to restore consensus. During the dangerous phase of the new war, the stadholder's authority rose. For a time he had a special Secret Committee of the Council of State set up in which, with the collaboration of the Pensionary, he secured substantial personal control of military and foreign policy. But when it became apparent, by the mid-1640s, that the regent oligarchies wanted to put an end to the war, the prince accepted this.

His son, William II, who became senior stadholder in 1649, had other ideas, and was eager both to pursue an expansionist foreign policy and to extend the political authority of his office. In the post-war wrangling about demobilization and future military establishments, he sought to reopen the controversies of 1618 and challenge the hegemony of the Holland regents, who in turn were threatening to withhold their quota to the Union budget, or reclaim provincial control over the army units which the province funded. William attempted an armed coup, arrested a group of opposing regents, and took troops to Amsterdam, demanding admission into the city. This was refused, and the dangerous stand-off was then resolved by the sudden death of William in 1650, leaving an infant heir, the future William III. Whether things would have been different if William II had lived is a matter for speculation, but all the signs are that neither William nor any other ambitious member of the family could have taken control of the Union while Holland stood opposed. It is to be remembered that the princes of Orange did not have the possibility of setting themselves up as neutral arbiters in the Union; they had been active partisans in domestic politics since the days of Maurice.

In the circumstances, the Orange cause was paralysed by the long childhood of William III, though his ambitious mother did her best to keep the Orange interest alive. The initiative passed to the Holland States, who in 1653 found able leadership in the De Witt brothers, John De Witt becoming Pensionary in that year. He consolidated his position by negotiating an end to the damaging naval war with the English republic, and was glad, as part of the settlement, to give assurances that the Orange faction would be kept out of power. For the time being Holland promoted a resolution in the Estates General to leave the stadholderate vacant, and replace the post of Captain General by an army commander appointed by the States General. During the 1660s De Witt successfully resisted an Orangist revival, but was compelled to provide some official position for William. In 1668, the Holland States passed the Perpetual Edict, abolishing the post of stadholder and vesting its powers in the States. The post of Captain and Admiral General would in time be revived for William, with a seat in the Council of State.

Whether De Witt could have prevented William from claiming his family inheritance indefinitely is uncertain. There was a gathering Orangist protest movement, embracing all the interests that resented the long predominance of the De Witt regime. In the end it was toppled by foreign policy disaster – the French invasion of 1672. Despite the growing signs after 1668 of the French king's aggressive attitude, and the openly hostile commercial and tariff policies being promoted by Colbert, no adequate military preparation to resist invasion had been made, and French troops quickly overran most of the republic's territory, stopping only when the dykes were opened in Holland and the approaches to Amsterdam flooded. The regents would have been willing to buy peace by extensive territorial concessions to Louis, but this triggered a populist Orangist protest movement, demanding effective resistance. At the last moment, William was restored as Captain General and stadholder in the summer of 1672, but he declined to stop the protests headed by the urban militias and the city mobs, which culminated in August in Amsterdam, when mobs murdered the two De Witt brothers. William was then able to use mob pressures to change the delegations to the Holland States and secure authorization for a purge of city governments, which was extended across the other provinces as the French were compelled to withdraw. The purges were far-reaching in the regencies throughout the Union, except in Friesland, which retained its loyalty to the younger branch of the family, yet the Orange triumph did not last long. By 1677 Amsterdam came back under republican control and led a reaction against Orange triumphalism in favour of restored provincial independence. This was encouraged by a growing protest at the often corrupt and unscrupulous methods of William's local agents and new appointees, and by a growing realization that William wanted to use the United Provinces as the core of a European coalition to resist Louis XIV's aspirations to establish a Bourbon hegemony. This was unappealing to the commercial interests in Holland, especially after Louis sought to detach them by offering trade and tariff concessions. Once more the Holland regents demonstrated that, when the province enjoyed internal unity, the Union could not be governed without their cooperation. William soon came to see that he would have to compromise with the Holland regents before, aided by new and alarming signs of Louis's aggressive intentions, he was able to restore cooperation and make the United Provinces the anchor for his coalition war against Louis after 1688.

P A R T

II

THE EMERGENCE OF THE GREAT POWERS

5

Towards 'Absolutism': Variations round a Theme

France

In 1661, on the death of Cardinal Mazarin, Louis XIV announced that he himself would become the active head of the government. This was no empty gesture: Louis was by nature a diligent and hard-working administrator, and he had a model of kingship, based on the intellectual rationalism that was coming into fashion. The image he pursued was of a ruler who systematically informed himself about the condition of his kingdom and listened to professional advisers who would debate the options in his presence, then relying on his own inherent rationality to make decisions. Once he had decided he expected his servants to execute his orders without any further discussion. He told Colbert, who had presumed to question a decision in 1671: 'After I have heard your arguments and those of your colleagues and have given my opinion on all your claims, I do not even wish to hear further talk about it. After a decision I give you, I wish no word of reply.' He worked within a highly centralized system of administration. The core institution was the *Conseil d'en haut*, a select body where the king met with the three chief ministers for war, foreign affairs, and finance according to a fixed weekly routine. The impression is that in this body there was real freedom of discussion, though that cannot be demonstrated because, for the sake of confidentiality, no minutes of the discussions were taken. The execution of policy was supervised by regular sessions of the *Conseil des dépêches*, also attended by the king, which supervised the despatch of the royal commands. There was a third, larger Council of the Realm, consisting of about 30 senior officials, which had a broad remit, including the exercise of the royal judicial functions. All these institutions were run by the king's appointees, drawn from the ranks of the *robe* nobility.

During the reign of Louis XIV, the central administration developed its own permanent staff of executive agents who could be sent out into the provinces to supervise the execution of royal policies. The intendants were recruited almost exclusively from the *maîtres de requêtes*, a corps of legal officers attached to the *parlements* who had purchased their offices, and were drawn from the upper ranks of the *robe* nobility. The use of such men on special missions had revived quickly after the Fronde, but became systematized after 1661. The king was careful to choose his agents personally, and an intendant was appointed to each of the 26 *généralités* into which the kingdom was divided. At first they were given a supervisory role over the existing authorities, and were moved around at frequent intervals to prevent them from getting too intimate with the local elites. In the 1690s it was decided to make the institution permanent, and they became chiefly responsible for supervizing revenue collection, and to fulfil their extended responsibilities began the appointment of local sub-delegates, who purchased their offices and became part of the established local administration. The kingdom had then acquired a new and comprehensive layer of administration, distinguished by its being national in scope, and the intendancy became the backbone of French royal administration until 1789. One function of the intendant, emphasized after 1661, was to collect and feed back information. The central government, with its emphasis on rational decision-making led by the king himself, had an insatiable appetite for facts and figures. Yet to keep the new ruling machinery in perspective, it was extremely small in size. It has been estimated that the king, with three ministers, 30 councillors of state, about 90 masters of requests, and a few hundred clerical assistants, were trying to administer a large and diverse kingdom with some 20 million inhabitants. In fact they were obviously heavily dependent on the cooperation of some 60,000 venal officeholders to make the system work. These were secure in their positions and entrenched in the local power structures, and had to be bargained with to secure their compliance with instructions.

The most important venal officers were the members of the eight *parlements*, which divided the kingdom between them. They not only maintained law and order, but also had wide local administrative responsibilities. Crucially, the *parlements* were the only institutions in the kingdom with a legal right to evaluate the royal actions and criticize them openly. This was because all royal decrees, including fiscal decrees, had to be registered by each of the *parlements* before they could be legally enforced. The *parlements* could decline registration or insist on amendments if they judged the decree was not in accord with the fundamental laws of the kingdom. The king could override their objections by holding a *lit de justice*, in which he personally took back the authority he had delegated to them and then commanded registration. The disadvantage of this was that *parlements* had their own ways of obstructing such enforced decrees, the most obvious one being to decline to prosecute or convict offenders against them. In the long run, the administration of the kingdom could not function without the *parlements'* cooperation. Despite serving an absolute monarchy, the French judiciary had security of tenure guaranteed by purchase. It is true that in 1673 the king forced acceptance of a decree requiring the *parlements* to register legislation and apply it without protest, and then, if they wished, submit remonstrances. This did appear to muzzle them for a time, but events at the end of the reign were to show they had not been effectively intimidated.

The reign of Louis XIV witnessed a sustained drive, led by the king, to assert his absolute authority throughout the kingdom, and to bring it under effective[1] central control. In the first years of the reign the leading ministerial figure was Jean-Baptiste Colbert, who had made a career as Mazarin's business manager, and came from an established dynasty of *robe* nobles. He was a ruthless, professional workaholic character, dedicated alike to the king's business and his own advancement. By his death in 1682, Colbert had become immensely wealthy and his relatives had colonized key parts of the ruling establishment. A son, a brother and a cousin were bishops, four sisters were abbesses, his brother was first an ambassador, then foreign minister, and three of his daughters married dukes. The scale and ambition of Colbert's projects were extraordinary. First he directed an extensive judicial inquest into the financial system, putting the previous controller Fouquet on trial,[2] prosecuting tax-farmers and forcing them to compound for their alleged frauds and embezzlements. Then with the establishment of a new Royal Council of Finance he set about establishing a proper ministry of finance and enforcing adequate accounting systems on the revenue officers. He rationalized the main tax-farms, set about redeeming state debts, began a drive to recover the crown's demesne lands, had some success in rationalizing the collection of the *taille* and did in fact manage to reduce the level of collection. It is possible that, by 1670, the ordinary crown revenues and expenditure were in balance, or even showing a surplus, and the costs of administration were sharply cut back.

Then he embarked on programmes for developing the kingdom's economy by expanding industrial capacity, particularly in textiles, using government regulation, concessions for entrepreneurs and tariff protection with undoubted success. By 1700 France was a major producer in most branches of textile manufacture. He tried to stimulate foreign trade in imitation of Dutch practices, establishing a subsidized East India Company and West India Company, pushing forward French colonial activity in Canada and the Caribbean, and getting a major sugar-refining industry established. Internally he tried to stimulate trade by improving communications: the canal linking the Atlantic coast to the Mediterranean was his work. He tried to diminish the number of internal customs barriers and tolls within the kingdom; and he virtually refounded the French navy as a major fighting force, reforming the admiralty administration, providing professional bureaucratic support to develop the necessary infrastructure of naval bases and shipyards, and tackling the problem of recruitment through his maritime inscription. With the encouragement of the king, Colbert set about trying to rationalize the chaotic mosaic of legal systems in the kingdom. Ultimately they would have wished to establish a uniform law code for the whole kingdom, but realized this was impractical. The several major law codes that he promoted did not attempt to codify the content of the law, but tried to achieve uniform administrative structures and procedures.

It is extremely difficult to assess the real content of Colbert's achievement, to distinguish what resulted from his initiatives and what probably represented natural economic growth. But he did firmly establish the idea that it was the right and duty of central government to maintain active intervention over all branches of economic activity, and established the governmental machinery to do this. He was adding an important new dimension to the activities of government. It was done because Colbert and the king shared the common economic ideology which historians call mercantilism.[3] This was based on the observation that increasing wealth represented increasing power for the state, and the belief that the economic system was, like the political system, an open-ended power struggle, in which one country's economic gain must be another country's loss. Colbert did try to enlist the voluntary support of the trading community by inviting its participation in the Council of Commerce he set up in 1664, but it never really flourished. This would only confirm his repeated complaints that merchants and manufacturers were too engrossed in their private profits and traditional practices, and must be compelled by government action to advance the general interests of the kingdom. Overall, Colbert's labours give a good illustration of the gap between the rationalizing aspirations of the absolutist state, and its capacity to realize them. The vision was not lacking, but the power certainly was.

Running in parallel, but also very much in competition with Colbert's domestic reform programme, was the major military reform being promoted by a rival administrative dynasty to the Colberts, the Le Telliers. They had colonized the war department for decades, but after 1661 produced an outstanding bureaucrat and administrator in François Le Tellier, marquis of Louvois, Colbert's great rival. Tension was inevitable, for over 70 per cent of the revenues that Colbert was so successfully expanding was spent on the army and, of course, this competed with his plans to invest in the economy. The French army was transformed after 1660. One indicator of change is size. In the mid-1660s there was a standing force of about 50,000 men which, when the first serious war began after 1672, was rapidly expanded to 250,000. In the next major war from 1689 to 1697 it reached maximum size at around 400,000. In the last war of the reign it never exceeded 380,000, but by then the normal peacetime standing force stood at 150,000. The army was serviced by a comparable expansion of its administrative machinery. Under Louvois, the secretariat of war expanded and professionalized. By 1680 the secretariat had developed into seven sub-departments specializing in particular branches of administration. It was adopting regular bureaucratic procedures, acquired a central archive, and produced ever more letters. In the 1660s it was issuing about 4500 letters a year, by 1690 about 10,000, and in 1706, 13,000.

The type of army that emerged has been called by historians a state commission army. It had two chains of command, one military between the department and the officer corps, and one civilian, run by *robe* nobles and civilian contractors. It was a commission army because the king appointed the officers, who thereby owed personal loyalty to the crown alone. The crucial appointments were the captains and colonels, who actually recruited the companies and regiments and met the initial costs of raising them; thereafter they received pay from the crown according to the number of soldiers they had. They were almost always chosen from the sword nobility, and the colonels owned their regiments, being responsible for paying and equipping the men. These commissions were venal, and the costs of fitting out the units came in addition, yet there was no shortage of applicants for commissions. Although the colonels and captains, being in financial control, could find ways of making extra profits, and the patronage they exercised could be turned to advantage, they appear to have been willing to sacrifice money for the prestige and status a commission carried in society. At the lower officer level, it appears that a lieutenant could expect to make a modest living from his pay, and the poorer families of the sword nobility grasped the opportunity to exchange dull rural poverty for a socially acceptable career. It was not the least of the factors binding the nobility into the structure of the absolute monarchy.

The state commission army was a hybrid form that ended the system of private contracting, but still left the crown, as employer, with shared control at regimental level. Above that the commissions to the higher command were not venal, and a colonel promoted to this level would be required to sell his regiment. The direction of military operations was now exclusively vested in the king. Over time the war ministry tightened its control over the regiments; they became part of the standing army, except that extra units raised during a war might be demobilized at the end, but here the practice of retaining surplus officers on half-pay was introduced. The king raised his own elite regiment, the *régiment du roi*, under its colonel, Martinet, whose fierce disciplinary drives made him legendary. This regiment was held up as the model the whole army should follow. Slowly standard drills, standard clothing and standard weapons were introduced.

The army was steadily being moulded into a homogeneous, professional fighting force. Louvois, as war minister, waged unending battles of attrition to get the colonels to comply with the norms laid down; they could not be coerced, since they owned their regiments, and success was partial in such matters as requiring the officers to be on duty full-time. A colonel had to be allowed up to eight months annual leave of absence in peacetime. Nor was there any formal military training for officers, except in the specialist arms like the artillery. It was assumed that a nobleman was qualified by right of birth.

But a major element in imposing control was on the supply side, where the war ministry had a second administrative department concerned with feeding and supply. This was staffed by *robe* nobles, working through private contractors, and supervized by intendants of the army. In wartime, the aim remained to sustain the armies at enemy expense by operating in enemy territory, but even this became an organized process. The armies were not left to plunder and requisition indiscriminately: the system of levying contributions in cash and kind was systematized, so that the productive capacity of the occupied areas was not destroyed. In addition a commissariat was established for such essentials as ensuring bread supplies to troops on the move, and providing transport and some basic medical services. One major development was the establishment of magazines, stocked in advance with grain and other necessities, so that the army's movements need not be dictated by the need to find food.

The overall benefit to society at large was to diminish the 'tax of violence', which armies had commonly levied even in friendly territory to billet, feed and clothe the troops through forced requisitioning. In France itself, military routes were established, with magazines, or permanent arrangements with local communities to service troops passing through at standard prices. The order which a strong central administration could establish must have been another strong motive for the absolute state to be seen as conferring benefits as well as costs. For most of the army it was possible to use volunteers, and these were not necessarily the dregs of society. The French army, which had used substantial numbers of foreign mercenaries, was increasingly manned by the king's own subjects, many from the urban sector. In the 1680s, the expansion of warfare led to the development of reserve forces. Using the ancient prerogative right to call on all able-bodied men to serve in defence of the kingdom, in 1686 the *milice royale* was instituted. Throughout the kingdom a quota of the local manpower, selected by ballot, was conscripted into the militia, which was equipped and trained at crown expense, and was initially reserved for home defence. But in the Spanish Succession war, after 1701, militia regiments were required to serve with the field armies outside their home districts. The communities were being forced to make this additional contribution to the military potential of the crown, and it was not popular.

The development of this semi-professional state military establishment was the major achievement of the absolute state: evidence of how that state developed in the first place as an instrument for the waging of war. There is an interesting debate among historians whether the army should be seen as the creator of the modern, fiscal bureaucratic state, or the result of its success in getting control of the resources of the community.[4] In the French case it does seem as though the administrative developments launched under Louis XIV after 1661 created the conditions which made this enlarged and modernized military machine possible. If so, at some point the relationship shifted, for by the 1690s it became apparent that the demands of the military establishment were threatening to destabilize the new administrative structures. They certainly ruined Colbert's attempt to control and rationalize the kingdom's finances. The two great wars that ended the reign, the Nine Years War and the War of Spanish Succession, occurred in the context of a Europe-wide decline of agricultural prices, causing falling rents, and in France in 1693–4 the worst famine of the century, which may have caused nearly 10 per cent mortality, followed by a less extensive subsistence crisis in 1709–10. It became apparent that the swelling military expenditures were outrunning the capacity of the regular fiscal system. One sign was the virtual abandonment of naval war after 1692 in favour of privateering. Even Louis XIV did not have the resources to sustain a world-class army and navy simultaneously.

By 1694, the king had accepted that the war must be wound up by negotiation and peace bought by concession: the war effort was being funded by the revival of all kinds of financial expedients and borrowing, culminating in the *capitation* tax, a direct tax, for the duration of the war, which overrode the normal tax exemptions of the elites. This was revived during the Spanish Succession war in the form of the *dixième*. What is perhaps surprising is how the monarchy was now strong enough to enforce such a basic break with tradition at the lowest point of its fortunes, and that in the event the levels of compliance were good. Louis XIV's government just survived the financial strain of the final war without bankruptcy. However, the process exposed a basic weakness of the supposedly absolute monarchy. The wars in fact put the monarchy at the mercy of what contemporaries referred to as the 'financiers'. This seems to cover a distinct social sub-group of bankers, businessmen and investors, reckoned at some 4000, who between them formed the syndicates that advanced the cash needed to pursue the war. The details of their business methods are obscure: they were not anxious to advertise their proceedings, nor was the crown. So it remains unclear where their liquid funds actually came from. But it is clear that some came from Amsterdam, so that Dutch investors were actually financing Louis's war against the United Provinces; it is also now known that quite large investments were made by the French high nobility. These had to be concealed by the use of middlemen, since it would be publicly unacceptable for a nobleman to be seen participating in commerce. What it seems to amount to is that the upper levels of the French elite, who were fairly successful in protecting their assets from taxation, were instead lending their surplus funds at high rates of interest, secured on present and anticipated revenues of the crown. The monarchy was left hopelessly indebted and unable to escape from the clutches of its creditors, who were its own subjects.

But there is another side to government: its authority depended as much on successful image-building as on actual power. After 1661 Louis XIV, who had a talent for theatricals, put on a continuing show to entertain and dazzle the subjects, in which he was the central figure as the all-powerful Sun King. One aspect was his ostentatious patronage of science and the arts, which produced the brilliant official culture of late seventeenth-century France. Literature, drama, music, ballet, painting and architecture were all harnessed to projecting the image. It all came together in the spectacular show palace of Versailles, built at great expense over nearly two decades. After 1682 it became the official seat of the royal government. In the palace the king lived by elaborate protocols from the moment of his official waking each day to his final retirement, all emphasizing how he personally stood at the centre of affairs.

The palace was a royal residence, the physical seat of the government and a stage set. But it was more; it was a device for neutering the French nobility and binding it to the personal service of the king. At its peak, some 10,000 persons were resident in the palace, some were the working members of the administration, most were sword nobles, with their families, who held honorary posts about the king's person and competed strenuously for his favourable attention. The lubricant of the system was patronage, for the king had an inexhaustible supply of favours, great and small, which only he could bestow. The court was a great market place, and the elite nobles and officials who had direct personal access to the king could not only get their own share of favours, but more importantly could help retail them to aspirants lower down the social scale. On the strength of their access to the king, they could build up clientage chains reaching down into the provinces, boosting their personal status and prestige, and of course they expected payment for their services. That was why it was more important for a great noble landowner to reside at Versailles, and exercise the privilege of handing the king his shirt during the royal toilet, than to stay at home on his provincial estates playing the role of feudal landlord.

In a kingdom that had no formal national representative institutions, Versailles was the single centre to which every part of the kingdom had to resort. There the king had most of the makers and shakers of his kingdom collected together, where he could observe them and exploit their appetite for power and influence by the basic tactic of divide and rule. Nobody who had experienced Versailles could be in any doubt who ruled France. There was plenty of evidence over the years that the image of the power of the monarchy was a public relations triumph. Compared with the turbulent history of the kingdom in the decades before 1660, the king's mastery of his subjects seemed a reality. There was the gradual elimination of popular protest, riot and rebellion. This did not happen suddenly; serious provincial disorders continued to occur for a time – there were two major uprisings in 1675, in Bordeaux and in Brittany – but now they were swiftly put down without the crown having to make concessions. This was not just because the king now had a powerful army, though Brittany was one instance in which the army was sent in to restore order. Generally, if force had to be used, the local militias sufficed. This in turn was because in almost every case of popular unrest, the local elites refused to become involved, and were willing to assist the reassertion of royal authority. In the absence of assistance from the elites, most uprisings collapsed from within. A process of convergence between the monarchy and the corporate elites which largely ran society had developed, and they recognized their mutual interest in keeping the lower orders in obedience.

The king and his council could issue their orders, and the intendants carry them down into the provinces, but there they came up against the mosaic of local corporations, feudal nobles, provincial Estates, *parlements*, municipal corporations, guilds and the venal officeholders, without whose acquiescence things just did not get done. The royal agents had to negotiate, relying more on the trading of favours than threats of royal anger and reprisals for non-performance. The crown always had some leverage: for instance, the heavy indebtedness of most of the smaller towns was used by the royal government to turn their magistracies into royal servants. The independent authority of the provincial governor, a local territorial magnate, as the military arm of royal power in the provinces, was steadily undermined as the new military structures rendered them redundant. The king and his ministers knew their limitations. They knew that most often any proposal for radical change would be opposed by existing vested interests. Colbert and his master would have liked to abolish internal tolls and customs barriers that impeded free trade inside the kingdom, but they knew it could not be done, just as any attempt to codify the laws and establish one uniform system over the whole kingdom could never be imposed on the existing legal oligarchies. Even a comparatively straightforward proposal to introduce uniform weights and measures throughout the kingdom, again to assist the growth of trade, was beyond the regime's power to enforce. Colbert's maritime inscription – his attempt to rationalize and even out the burden of providing sailors for the royal navy, which fell on the coastal parishes, and which on paper looked to be advantageous for all parties – fell in face of stubborn local non-compliance, which after years of exhortations and threats he was unable to overcome.

Overt coercion could generally only be applied to unpopular minorities, as in the case of the Huguenots. Their continued toleration under the Edict of Nantes now contained no political threat to royal authority. But it was a continuous irritant to the Catholic majority, who had a powerful institutional voice in the church, whose cooperation was assiduously cultivated by the royal government. It is also clear that the Huguenots' very existence was felt as unacceptable by the king himself, not because he was outraged by their heretical views, but by the public affront to his absolute command of his subjects through their continuing to profess a faith different from his own. Further, for the first three decades of the reign, Louis pursued a series of confrontations with the papacy. For a time the pope was refusing investiture of new episcopal appointments in France and at one point the king himself was excommunicated. He very much needed both to boost his public reputation as a Catholic monarch, and to secure the support of his own clergy. So from the beginning of the personal rule, Louis connived at policies of attrition aimed at making the position of his Huguenot subjects more difficult, and pursued parallel policies of conversion, offering tax exemptions and cash grants to converts. This seemed to be succeeding, and the Protestant nobility, facing social ostracism and isolation, defected in some numbers. Yet the hard core of urban artisans and rural peasant communities held out. By the 1680s there were many voices around the king, led by the

Louvois family, suggesting the use of force to step up the pressure. There were successful local experiments in using punitive billeting on Huguenot communities which seemed to produce results. Further, the king, a widower by the 1680s, and fallen under the influence of his new partner, Madame de Maintenon, was undergoing some kind of religious conversion, renouncing the notorious loose living that had characterized his younger years. So he came to believe the persuasions put to him that at the current rate of conversion the problem was almost solved, and it would be a great international demonstration of his power and his religious commitment if he revoked the Edict. It would certainly be enthusiastically received by the Catholic majority. In 1685 the Edict was withdrawn, and all subjects were required to conform to the Catholic religion, while open exercise of the Protestant religion became criminal. Protestant clergy must convert or go into exile. To encourage compliance, local government agents were encouraged to use military intimidation, launching the notorious practices of the *dragonnades*.

In one sense, the Revocation was a triumphal demonstration of the ability of a powerful military monarchy to crush a deviant minority. Protestantism in France was reduced to a small, clandestine remnant. When, in the Spanish Succession war, the rural Protestants of the Cévennes rose in the Camisard revolt, and maintained a guerrilla war against the royal troops for some years, in the end they were crushed, mostly by using the local militias. But from a different viewpoint, the monarchy could not stop the emigration of tens of thousands of its Huguenot subjects into Protestant Europe, some of them bearers of technological skills, some wealthy bankers, along with their embittered clergy, which not only gave an economic boost to their host communities, but spread active black propaganda about the French regime among Louis's enemies. It was beyond the administrative capacity of the regime to seal its borders. While it is easy to exaggerate the harm the emigration did to the kingdom, it is likely that Catholic opinion and the royal government thought any damage was a price well worth paying for re-establishing the religious integrity of their community.

There is an interesting contrast in the king's attempt to silence another religious dissident group, the French Jansenists, who did attract considerable public sympathy. The Jansenists were a strict Augustinian tendency within the Catholic Church, who in France had established a base in the twin monastic establishments at Port-Royal, just outside Paris. The Jansenists were religious purists and highly critical of what they saw as the tendency of the church to compromise its principles for worldly ends, in particular in its relations with secular princes. They were peculiarly hostile to the Jesuits, whom they accused, with some justice, of cosying up to the lay authorities in their own pursuit of power. An eminent French historian has argued that 'Jansenism was an exact counterpoint to absolutism. It stalked it like a shadow, contradicting it, dating it, leaving its mark upon it.'

The aristocratic inmates of Port-Royal had a record of public criticism of royal policies going back to the days of Richelieu, and were identified as a dangerous, subversive challenge by Louis XIV. They angered the king in his quarrel with the papacy by open disagreements, and in a society where public opposition was not allowed, they gathered around themselves a loose coalition of malcontents, including all the many enemies of the Jesuits within the church, and many anti-clericals among the laity, who probably had little grasp of their austere Jansenist theological positions. In the 1690s Louis decided to make his peace with the pope, and one piece of common ground was papal hostility to Jansenism, which among other things encouraged the parish clergy to question traditional hierarchical authority in the church. King and pope joined forces to suppress Jansenism in France, but found considerable popular sympathy for the Jansenists, among clergy and most dangerously among the lawyers of the *parlements*, who had always had strong anti-clerical tendencies. The king could not get legal sanctions against the dissident groups enforced. Although at the very end of his reign, in 1713, Louis at last managed to force through the *parlement* legal recognition of the papal bull, *Unigenitus*, which comprehensively denounced the Jansenists as heretical, they survived to become a centre of running criticism and dissent for the eighteenth-century Bourbon regime. Once more the real limitations on the capacity of the absolute monarchy to impose its will had been demonstrated.

This is not to deny that royal absolutism, as it was developed in France under Louis XIV, was able to meet the challenge of the military imperative and its associated power struggle, by securing enough command of the resources of the kingdom to create the most powerful military machine in the contemporary world. For a time, after 1679, it looked as though a position of European hegemony might be within the king's grasp and this was no slight achievement. But in the end the aspiration fell foul of the basic rule of the international power game: that any player who looks likely to achieve total dominance will generate a coalition of other players to block him. Louis XIV died in 1715, leaving his kingdom more powerful in every respect than it had been in 1661. But he looked back in disappointment at the realization that the old dynastic competition had not been superseded; it had merely been raised to a higher level of organized violence.

The Austrian Habsburgs

The Austrian Habsburgs gave a distinctive response to the challenges of war, which diverges from the tendency towards a centralized, bureaucratic fiscal state so apparent in most of Europe. The senior title of the Vienna Habsburgs was that of Holy Roman Emperor, which they held, with a brief interruption after 1740, until the Empire itself came to an end. The reign of Ferdinand II from 1618 to 1637 demonstrated in the Thirty Years War how seriously he took his position, and saw the last sustained effort, by combining confessional politics with political and military coercion, to make the Emperor the effective executive head of the Empire. The failed attempt to enforce the Edict of Restitution after 1629, followed by the Peace of Prague in 1635, which would have recognized the Emperor as the exclusive military leader of the Empire, but fell short of the kind of authority Ferdinand had been seeking, probably mark the limits of what was possible in the contemporary context. The war also showed how the ambivalence of the Vienna Habsburgs over where their priority lay, with the interests of Empire, or the separate interests of Habsburg dynastic expansion, was another reason why there were limits to what they could achieve as Emperors. During the war a strategy developed, which was followed by the three successive rulers, Ferdinand II, Ferdinand III from 1637 to 1657, and Leopold I until 1705. It was a political–confessional strategy based on the assumption that the foundation of their authority mainly rested on the re-establishment of the supremacy of the Catholic religion in their territories and the elimination of religious dissent. Some historians identify this as 'confessional absolutism', a variant that made the church, not the secular state, the basis of the ruler's power.

History regularly shows that, except by military terrorism on the most ruthless scale, it is not in the power of any ruler to eliminate the institutions of an old established society and substitute something entirely different.[5] But circumstances do, on occasion, make possible far-reaching changes, and they did this for the Vienna Habsburgs when the Bohemian revolt was crushed in 1620. The Bohemian ruling elites, noble and burgher, were exposed to the universal penalties of treason, their leaders executed, and their properties made forfeit to the crown. The opportunity existed for Ferdinand to purge and reconstruct the Bohemian kingdom. Because Ferdinand was desperately short of funds he handed over the process of con-fiscation and sale to a local consortium of mainly native noblemen, with some help from Dutch bankers, so that when Ferdinand did make a settle-ment in Bohemia in 1627, this new self-made noble mafia[6] was already entrenched in power by a massive takeover of the landed estate of the kingdom and its associated feudal jurisdictions. The nobles were well on the way to eliminating the surviving power of the burghers. The purged urban communities emerged loaded with debts, deprived of their town lands and their autonomous town governments, and were then exposed to uncon-trolled economic competition from an aggressive and entrepreneurial nobility and their rural enterprises. The peasants stayed where they had been long before 1618, the servile tenants of the landlord elite.

But the conservative restructuring of the Bohemian constitution in 1627, at a meeting of the Estates, showed that Ferdinand II was not seriously inter-ested in radical secular reform, whereas he was resolved to drive all religious dissenters out of the kingdom. This was officially ordered in 1628 and sub-sequently enforced. Otherwise the old constitutional structure, based on cooperation with the Estates, both central and provincial, was reinstated. Ferdinand restored the Ecclesiastical Estate to the Diets, which generally supported the crown; the Burgher Estates were weakened by the economic decline of the urban sector; and the Estate of Nobles dominated the proceedings. The Diets had retained their sole power to grant and administer the direct taxation that was the most important crown revenue.

The administration of the kingdom remained in the hands of officials elected by the local nobility. The effect is seen in the history of one policy Vienna did try to enforce in Bohemia: the full re-establishment of the Catholic Church, and particularly its parish structure. This involved expelling the Protestants, and the landowners often obstructed that if it meant they lost valuable labour power. Bohemia was slowly re-Catholicised, but even at the end of the century underground Protestantism lingered on. The problem was funding: what had been the parish endowments, secularized at the Reformation, had now passed into the hands of the new Catholic landlords, and they persistently and successfully blocked the return of the endowments to the church. The long process of reconversion had to be executed by a clergy inadequate in numbers and poorly funded. All the pressures exerted from Vienna could not break the impasse.

There was a more revealing confrontation in the 1680s. The landlords had used their governmental power to increase their demands for labour services on the peasants, particularly to support activities like food-processing and brewing which they had developed. They legislated to forbid the peasants appealing from feudal jurisdictions to the royal courts. Leopold I is on record as recognizing that his peasant subjects were being intolerably burdened, as he received their petitions, particularly on a visit to Prague in 1680. This stimulated a wave of peasant unrest, and Leopold issued the *robot patent* of 1680, limiting labour services to four days a week. This had the effect of arousing peasant expectations and causing even more widespread disorders. He then had to authorize the local nobility to restore order by force, which was brutally done. The peasants were left to their fate in face of the reality that the king in Vienna was unable to coerce his nobility without creating anarchy. Landlord control was assisted by economic trends which favoured the wealthier landlords over the lesser. Once the chaos of the war years was over, a numerically small oligarchy of magnate families emerged, ruling major accumulations of land and carefully protected by laws of entail, who effectively controlled the kingdom. The Lichtensteins, for example, controlled nearly a fifth of all the lands in the province of Moravia. The revised constitution of Bohemia of 1627 had made the monarchy hereditary and asserted its sovereign rights; the Catholic Church had been reinstated, at least legally, and the religious dissenters expelled. But it remained the case that the kingdom of Bohemia was ruled by a narrow oligarchy of feudal landlords, with whom the ruler had no choice but to collaborate.

The position in the Austrian lands of the Habsburgs was in some ways different. The devolution was, if anything, more marked. The five Austrian provinces were autonomous and there was no central Diet for their common affairs. On the other hand, although there were, in 1600, entrenched

Protestant nobilities in some provinces who controlled the provincial diets, the Catholic Church had never been dispossessed and remained a major landowner in its own right. The powers of the local Estates were the same: they sanctioned and administered all direct taxation, which was hypothecated for the upkeep of the army. The administrators chosen and paid by the Estates controlled the revenue and expenditure and arranged recruiting, billeting and military transits. It was obvious that Ferdinand II, who had made a name even before his election as Emperor for forcibly expelling the Protestants in his duchy of Styria, would face open resistance from the Austrian Protestants, and use this to justify confessional cleansing. Protestant clergy, burghers and peasants were obliged to convert or leave. Nobles were put under pressure and excluded from all public functions and most in the end converted or left. A few established Protestant families hung on in Lower Austria into the 1690s but then they too disappeared. Beyond this no new state-building was called for in the Austrian duchies, although research suggests that their administrations functioned quite efficiently. It helped that in the Habsburg territories both noble and church lands were subject to the land tax which continued to provide the bulk of the crown's regular revenue. It was enough for the Habsburgs to maintain a standing army of some 50,000 after 1648 from the revenues of their hereditary lands, and to double that in the 1690s. The Habsburg army was, like the French one, a state commission army: basically the colonels raised and owned the regiments, but it lacked the inspection and supervision which Louvois imposed on the French forces. Considering the population base in the Habsburg lands was, at 7–8 million inhabitants, around 40 per cent of the French population, it represented a considerable achievement. There was a major increase in the tax burdens, yet once the religious factor was eliminated, there was little sustained protest. This was one instance in which devolution to the provincial Estates worked well.

In the seventeenth century there was no institutional Austrian state and the conglomeration of hereditary lands belonging to the dynasty had no official name, much less a clear common identity. Yet an embryonic state structure was emerging. Originally the imperial Council, the *Hofrat*, was for the whole Empire. In the 1620s a sub-committee for the hereditary lands developed as the *Geheime Rat* which was originally a small executive of leading councillors. Under Ferdinand III it was greatly expanded in the interests of patronage, and from it emerged a more exclusive *Geheime Konferenz*, as the chief policy-making forum. Even then this body was simply consultative; it was not a government department in control of its own bureaucracy. Bureaucracy developed around another growth of the 1620s, when a separate *Hofkanzlei* grew away from the imperial chancellory. This was a central secretariat and its presiding officer, the *Hofkanzler*, became the leading member of the administration. In 1654 it developed into a formal collegiate ministry handling foreign policy, internal policy and justice. In the 1690s it developed further when a separate Bohemian chancellory was established. Yet it was hardly a central government, for it controlled neither finance nor war.

Although the main tax revenues were in the hands of the Estates administrations, the crown did have other revenues: domain income from its own lands, income from mining royalties and customs duties. The crown also raised money by selling favours, titles and appointments, and this was boosted because, as Emperor, the Habsburg rulers could market imperial offices and favours. Indeed there was a system for the sale of titles of nobility and offices in the Empire at a fixed tariff. Offices were effectively sold in the hereditary lands as well. New appointees had to put down a large payment as security for good behaviour, theoretically returned on retirement, but often not. In addition officeholders were expected to contribute forced loans from their salaries in times of need. But there was no central public treasury, only a Chamber office, originally for domain revenues. The *Hofkammer* was a central audit department, but even so its remit did not extend to the direct taxation raised by the provincial Estates. And the actual collection and spending of the Chamber revenues was itself devolved down to its provincial sub-departments. Finally purely military policy, direction of operations, was undertaken in the military council, the *Hofkriegs Rat*, but that had no control over revenue or the other functions devolved to the Estates.

The third component of the Habsburg hereditary lands was the medieval kingdom of Hungary, an elective monarchy. Hungary was not part of the Holy Roman Empire, so here the Habsburgs' authority rested on their election to the Hungarian crown. However, soon after its acquisition in 1526, Hungary was overrun by the Ottoman Turks. The central plains were kept under their direct rule, the north-eastern mountain province of Transylvania was nominally an Ottoman vassal state under a native prince, while the north-western counties remained under Habsburg control as Royal Hungary. During the sixteenth century Hungary was deeply penetrated by the Reformation: the largely German towns became Lutheran, the numerous nobility and gentry tended to Calvinism. In particular, the princes of Transylvania became militant Calvinists, and during the Thirty Years War, with Ottoman connivance, intervened on several occasions against the Habsburgs.

Hungary had an aristocratic constitution which the king was sworn to respect, with a two-chamber Diet, an upper house of titled noblemen and bishops and an elected lower house of delegates from the counties, who were the core of the kingdom's government, together with a handful of urban delegates. In the absence of the king, the Diet elected a viceroy, the Palatine, to exercise the royal powers. Thus Hungary was a self-governing kingdom, attached to the other hereditary lands by the personal dynastic link. When the Habsburgs attempted to introduce their dynastic strategy into Hungary they met real resistance. There had been some fumbled efforts early in the century to reintroduce Catholicism into Royal Hungary, which was one reason why the Transylvanian princes were generally hostile. Then, during the wars, the surviving Hungarian Catholic bishops had been making some headway converting magnate families in Royal Hungary, who were interested in gathering power and influence at the court of Vienna. By the 1660s,

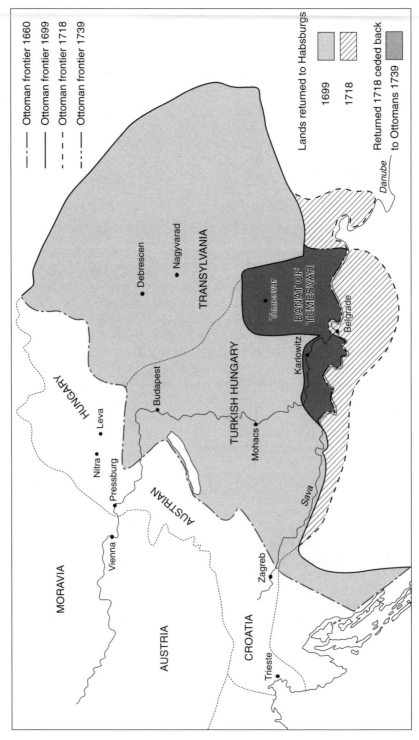

Map 5.1 The European re-conquest of Hungary

Legend:
— · — Ottoman frontier 1660
——— Ottoman frontier 1699
— — — Ottoman frontier 1718
— ·· — Ottoman frontier 1739

Lands returned to Habsburgs
1699
1718

Returned 1718 ceded back to Ottomans 1739

MORAVIA

AUSTRIA

Vienna

Pressburg

Nitra

Leva

HUNGARY

AUSTRIAN

Budapest

Debrescen

Nagyvarad

TRANSYLVANIA

TURKISH HUNGARY

Mohacs

Temesvar

BANAT OF TEMESVAR

Karlowitz

Belgrade

Danube

Sava

Zagreb

CROATIA

Trieste

the upper chamber of the Hungarian Diet had a Catholic majority and the Protestant gentry felt threatened.

Leopold I, like his two predecessors, had no state-building ambitions except in the one area of religion, to which he was utterly committed. In the atmosphere of the 1660s, however, there were factions at the Vienna court who might be described as modernizers, and who would have wished to see a strong central government develop, and like most contemporary politicians were interested in the new mercantilist programmes of economic development, whose implementation depended on the backing of a central state administration. They formed an active lobby group at the court. At the same time a new opening developed towards the east. Hostilities with the Ottomans had been suspended since 1606: they had been preoccupied with internal problems and then by the long struggle with the Venetians over Crete. But now the Ottoman government was again contemplating a forward move on the Habsburg frontier which led to war in 1663. From the Habsburg point of view, war with the Ottomans had one major advantage: as Emperors they could demand military support from the princes of the Empire for a crusade against the infidel, and this succeded in 1663. Even Louis XIV was moved to send a token contingent to the army which, in 1664, inflicted a major defeat on the Ottoman forces at the battle of St Gotthard. It was the first clear demonstration that western military technology was now superior to the outdated methods of the Ottoman armies.

Leopold resisted pressures to exploit the success and lead a counter-attack into Turkish Hungary. He was worried about the intentions of Louis XIV and the situation of the Habsburgs in Spain, so he made a quick peace with the Ottomans at Vasvar. But from then on there was a keen eastern faction at his court, urging that the future of the monarchy lay in the Balkans. In Hungary, in addition to growing gentry fears of the Catholicizing tendency of Leopold's regime, there were those nobles who were disappointed at the failure to pursue the liberation of Turkish Hungary. The malcontents got some encouragement from Louis XIV who was preparing the ground for his Dutch war, and in 1670 rebellion broke out in Royal Hungary and was defeated. This offered Leopold the same kind of opportunity that Bohemia had given Ferdinand back in 1620. It was typical of Leopold's piety that he did not feel he could revoke the Hungarian constitution, to which he had sworn at his accession. But he was willing to listen to advisers who urged the exploitation of the rebel defeat to crush the Hungarian Protestants. It was decided to set up a parallel regime under a military government, the *Gubernium*, based on the establishment of garrisons throughout Hungary to be paid for by the Hungarians. The regime then set in motion the familiar policy of forced conversion or exile, with the confiscation of Protestant properties. In return a savage guerrilla war broke out, with the rebels finding bases in Turkish Hungary. When the regime put Protestant clergy on trial for sedition, and sent some to row in the galleys, it became a scandal throughout Protestant Europe.

From 1673 the Empire was at war with Louis XIV, and Leopold had Protestant allies to consider. In addition there were signs that the Ottomans might move again and in 1679 he entered into negotiation with the Hungarians. At the Diet of Sopron in 1681, a settlement was agreed. In return for making the crown hereditary in Hungary, the constitutional government was restored and the *Gubernium* disbanded. Where Protestantism was established in the kingdom, it would remain tolerated. After 1686 it was clear that the Christian counter-attack after the siege of Vienna would recover the whole of the medieval Hungarian kingdom, including Transylvania. This was another opportunity for a general reconstruction in Hungary but Leopold, characteristically, held to the settlement of 1681 as the basis for the government of the reunited kingdom. This settlement was ratified at the Diet of Pressburg in 1687, though Transylvania, the most intransigently Protestant part, was detached from the rest of the kingdom and set up as an autonomous province with guaranteed religious freedom.

The Habsburgs had always maintained a very cosmopolitan court and drew in advisers from all over Europe. The higher military command under Leopold, for example, was largely staffed with outsiders, including many Italian noblemen, in the same way the rudimentary central institutions in Vienna drew in many foreign recruits, some fired by the absolutist enthusiasms prevalent all over Europe from the 1660s. They found life at Vienna frustrating; economic projects were launched and regularly failed, in part for lack of sustained governmental support. After the fall of the long-standing Chancellor Lobkowitz in 1674, a group led by a German university-trained lawyer, Johan Hocher,[7] and committed to strong government, became influential in the *Geheime Konferenz*, and lobbied powerfully for harsh repression and radical reform in Hungary, yet failed to get Leopold's full consent. In 1680 this group was commissioned to investigate the financial administration, with a view to establishing a unified central treasury. They came up with the proposal in 1681 for a new *Hofkammer Ordnung* to meet this requirement. It would have needed all the support possible from the Emperor to carry such a scheme in face of the stubborn opposition of the provincial magnates, whose Estates administration was threatened by any centralizing project. Leopold was not the man to undertake such a confrontation. The scheme came to nothing and the Habsburgs managed without a central finance administration for some decades more after 1680.

The case of the Habsburg shadow state does demonstrate that the absolutist model was not the only viable way to mobilize resources for war. The apparently loose and incoherent Habsburg regime sustained tolerably successful campaigns on several fronts at once against Louis XIV. Of course they had help. The Dutch and, after 1690, the English supplied cash subsidies. Vienna was rescued from Ottoman attack in 1683, and then the great Christian counter-attack was launched in the Balkans, with substantial contributions from the princes of the Empire and the active help of the papacy, which authorized the use of the wealth of the church to sustain the war. But all the profits of the conquest accrued to the Emperor, very significantly enlarging his dominions at other people's expense. The regime was also quite successful up to 1700 in raising credit, which plugged the gap between revenue and expenditure both internally and abroad. In the right context, it was still possible to cope with the new problems of modern war on essentially traditionalist lines.

The end of Habsburg Spain

The other branch of the dynasty also sought to survive by traditional means with less success. One indisputable fact is that after Philip IV made his peace with France in 1659, with the intention of forcing Portugal back into its allegiance, it became obvious that Spanish military capacity had collapsed. This can be measured in various ways. The army of Flanders, that had once dominated western Europe, was demobilized down to a shadow of its former strength, and when tested in war in 1667, 1673–9 and 1689–97 was quite incapable of defending the Netherlands from French invasions. It later became apparent that the capacity to defend the Pyrenean frontier was also lost. In the war after 1689, the province of Catalonia was repeatedly invaded by the French army, supported by naval forces with uncontested command of the coastal waters, and in 1697 the city of Barcelona fell to a French siege. Spain was involved in every European conflict between 1667 and 1697, but her military contribution to the coalitions against Louis XIV was marginal. Even more strikingly, Spain proved incapable of defeating the Portuguese secession. Since the 1640s a very damaging war of frontier raiding had devastated the resources of a swathe of frontier districts on both sides, without producing any military decision. In 1662 Spain mounted a full invasion and, despite some initial successes, only stimulated the Portuguese to raise their own field army, which by 1667 had fought the invaders to a stalemate. In that year Spain gave up the attempt. It is true there were external factors involved. The Portuguese had received loans, military advisers and mercenaries paid for by Louis XIV, Charles II of England and the United Provinces, all interested in promoting Portuguese independence. Even so, the inability of what had been the most formidable military state in Europe to defeat the Portuguese was dramatic evidence of its decline.

There was no obvious change in the overall conditions in Spain to account for the collapse.[8] The American trade held up quite well through this period, with steady returns of bullion. Only it seems clear that of goods shipped out through Cadiz to the colonies, perhaps 5 per cent were of Spanish origin; the bulk were French or Dutch. Consequently much of the incoming bullion was not actually landed on arrival; around 60 per cent was sent on directly to the real suppliers of the goods. Spanish industry was uncompetitive, even though there was a pool of cheap labour to be drawn on. Some research suggests that, overall, more than 60 per cent of the population were permanently unemployed or otherwise unproductive. Basically it seems that high levels of government taxation, diversion of capital into unproductive public loans, the power of guild controls to stifle innovation or competition, and currency instability combined to discourage manufacture, while constant bouts of inflation favoured imports of manufactures. Spanish agriculture, like that in most of Europe, entered a long phase of falling prices after the 1660s. After 1660 some economic revival took place in selected regions. The Basque provinces and Navarre, autonomous under the Castilian crown, with their own laws and currencies, and the lands of the crown of Aragon, particularly Catalonia and Valencia, avoided the currency instability of Castile, while the tax levels were lower. Here there was evidence of a definite, though still fairly modest, economic recovery in the second half of the century. Barcelona was beginning to get a foothold in the colonial trade, Valencia developed a successful production of raw silk. But this was offset by the continuing stagnation in the main provinces of Castile, which had to provide the bulk of the public revenues.

Despite this discouraging record of stagnation and decay, Spain remained remarkably stable internally through the last decades of the century. The two biggest armed protest movements of the 1690s both occurred in the crown of Aragon. The basic reason has been suggested by the historian H. Kamen when he wrote:

> By the late seventeenth century, Spain was probably the only west European country to be completely and unquestionably under the control of its titled aristocracy ... it is unlikely that there was any significant change in the status or function of the aristocracy during the seventeenth century.

He is not the only historian to see the society as essentially an aristocratic republic. The reason is the extreme level of devolution of authority throughout the Spanish kingdoms. One factor is the consistent grants of jurisdiction, made in return for cash advances, to the titled nobility and the urban corporations, which in turn were being increasingly penetrated by the nobility. These grants meant that law enforcement and revenue-raising were vested in the local community, the *pueblo*, usually a town and its dependent rural hinterland, or in the feudal landlords. In the crown of Aragon, where by law the judicial system was retained under direct royal control, the outcome was the same, since in Aragon the royal judges were elected by the *cortes*, which the nobility controlled. The main taxes were farmed out as *assientos*, or fell under the jurisdiction of the *cortes* of Castile, which maintained its own assessment and collection machinery. The same groups also administered most of the *juros*, the annuities on which so much of crown revenue was raised, using the taxes raised locally as security for the interest payments. It made no difference when, after the reign of Philip IV, the *cortes* of Castile no longer met. The administrative structure was maintained, and the crown, instead of negotiating with the towns through the *cortes*, dealt separately with its constituent corporations.

The broad result, which shocked the advisers of the new Bourbon regime after 1700, is that Spain combined high levels of taxation with low government revenue, since most of what was raised was spent locally. One estimate is that about 112 million ducats were being levied as taxes in Castile, of which 20 million were actually coming into the royal treasury in Madrid. This problem was compounded by the restricted tax base. At the bottom of society was the large unemployed population, incapable of yielding much by way of taxes, and the quite substantial elite of nobles, those claiming *hidalgo* status, and almost anyone who held any kind of public function, who enjoyed substantial tax exemption. It is possible to cite a small community with 60 households, of whom 46 were tax-exempt. But the 46 owned two-thirds of the community's property. The crown was not entirely without some independent resource: in partnership with the pope it could draw a substantial subsidy from the church, and could effectively tax the exempt by cutting the interest payments on *juros*, which, in the reign of Charles II, consumed 50–75 per cent of the revenue. It could sell offices and titles, which was the universal practice. And since it appears most purchasers invested for the status conferred, rather than from an expectation of financial advantage from office, it was possible to create supernumerary offices with no salary and sell them. When noble titles and entry into the military orders were marketed under Charles II, the number of titled noble families in Castile doubled. The reality was that the crown's revenue came largely as a result of endless complex negotiations between the central administration and the localities, which meant that in the end the levels of taxation were kept down, but that the government's ability to wage war was crippled. A monarchy that had once been able to fund an army of 70,000 professional soldiers in the Netherlands alone, found that in the 1660s it could field only some 20,000 men for the re-conquest of Portugal, since the total military establishment for the whole peninsula was just over 30,000 men.

The grip of the nobility extended to the central government machinery itself: the bureaucratic councils to which all policy proposals were referred. These were recruited from the titled nobility, while their expertise came through the university-educated *letrados*, themselves children of the nobility educated at the elite universities like Salamanca. The overall effect of this pervasive aristocratic hegemony, combined with the entrenched vested interests of local communities, was an impenetrable barrier against reform, since all proposals for change had to entail the reduction of the entrenched privileges of the existing powerholders. A further factor inhibiting change was the mental isolation of the Iberian community. On the whole the intellectual changes that were exciting the elites all over western Europe by the 1650s, had very little impact in Spain. This was in part because the Inquisition was vigilant against anything that could be condemned as heretical, which certainly included some of the new scientific and philosophical ideas. The low levels of education – general illiteracy in Spain was far higher than the European norms – also contributed, as did chauvinistic Iberian pride, which held that Spain's own distinctive culture was superior to and independent of the rest of Europe. The immediate reaction to any new concepts imported from over the Pyrenees tended to be negative. The monarchy of Charles II did not join in the rush to imitate the model offered by Louis XIV.

The main political reason for the stagnation in late Habsburg Spain, however, was the common historical joker, dynastic failure. Much effort has been expended trying to specify the mental and physical capacities of the last Habsburg king, Charles II, who succeeded as a child in 1667, but he was the sad product of generations of intensive inbreeding. In some degree he was mentally retarded and physically deficient. The practical effect has been summarized as: 'he was unable to rule personally: he failed to arouse respect from those in closest contact with him, mainly Castilians: and his inability to produce an heir created wide-ranging international disputes over the succession'. The regency was assumed by the queen, a political incompetent who depended on her Jesuit confessor, Father Nithard. His influence was bitterly resented by the court nobility and the grandees which created paralysis of the central administration through faction struggles. The system had no solution for this except Philip IV's illegitimate son, Don John, who became the focus for the opposition. He led an open public campaign for the dismissal of Nithard, culminating in a march on Madrid, which forced Nithard to retire. This may be Spain's first military *pronunciamiento*. Don John then retired to his power base in Aragon, as the queen promoted another obscure favourite, Valenzuela, whose main interest was in exploiting the patronage at his disposal. In 1675 the king was declared of age, and Valenzuela became formal first minister. Discontented aristocratic factions turned to Don John and this led to his instalment as head of government in 1676. This change, which seems to have had wide support among the nobility, revealed that Don John did not really have a coherent political programme, though there was naturally a purge of the administration. He died in 1679 in the middle of a financial crisis, after the humiliating Peace at Nymegen in 1678.

Proposals for modernization of the government revived in 1679 under a new first minister, the duke of Medinacoeli, a serious reformer. There was a *junta de comercio* set up in 1679 to promote trade and industry, though it is unclear whether it ever functioned; a definitive currency stabilization was carried out in 1680 and a technical expert put in charge of the Council of Finance. The office of the *Despacho*, the personal secretariat of the king, whose secretary also doubled as secretary to the Council of State, was given wider authority in an attempt to get a more focused administration. The government planned to end tax-farming, reduce the overall level of taxes, and spread the burden more widely. It is significant that, after two years of trials, the taxation changes were dropped. Consultations in the provinces showed that the proposals aroused deep suspicion, and any further action was stifled within the Council bureaucracy.

In 1684 a new leading figure entered the government, the count of Oropesa. Oropesa was an admirer of French administration. His programme involved further reforms of the Council of Finance and of the bureaucracy generally, and reforms to the church to reduce the numbers of clergy and superfluous monastic institutions and to limit the powers of the Inquisition. Oropesa met the same obstruction from vested interests and court rivals as other would-be reformers. The king remarried in 1691, and the new consort, chosen in Vienna to strengthen Habsburg influence at court, allied with Oropesa's domestic rivals to dismiss him. Thereafter, as events focused increasingly on the succession problem, the queen's German advisers took control, while the war ended in military defeat and a new state bankruptcy. Government was paralysed by the intense faction struggles between the grandees and the German advisers, yet one clear consensus did arise: that whoever succeeded Charles II, there should be no partition of any part of Spain's dominions. In this last act of chauvinistic defiance, the near moribund Spanish monarchy brought down on itself and Europe the disastrous War of the Spanish Succession.

6

The Evolution of the British State: A Different Model

Circumstances had forced the English Commonwealth to develop a modern military capacity. An effective army and navy had been maintained, backed up by a radically transformed taxation system and an improved central administration. But the Commonwealth had failed to win consent from the ruling elites for the changes, primarily because the army had refused to reinstate the religious uniformity and discipline that was held to be necessary to maintain an ordered hierarchy in society.[1] Yet there was an underlying wish to restore consensus. A consistent feature of the history of the interregnum was the failure of the defeated royalists to organize any effective armed challenge to an unpopular regime. There was no stomach for renewed civil war. The republic was not overthrown; it disintegrated once Oliver Cromwell's charismatic leadership was removed, revealing how it did not have, and never had had, widespread public acceptance. General Monk, the officer who contrived the Restoration, had sensed that stability must be built on the return of traditional modes of government, basically by the consensus of king, Lords and Commons. He persuaded the king to secure an invitation to return on the basis of the Declaration of Breda, which promised a full amnesty, the disbanding of the army with payment of its arrears, and a religious settlement to be negotiated, with provision for 'a liberty for tender consciences'. This and the other outstanding issues were to be settled in a free parliament. This proved instantly acceptable and Charles II returned unarmed, to general acclamation.

The result was a remarkable tribute to the capacity of the English governmental system to generate negotiated compromise. Both crown and parliament were reinstated with their former powers. If anything the crown was strengthened by explicit confirmation of the king's position as head of the executive power and sole commander of all armed forces, with rights of appointment to all public offices in church and state. It was affirmed that it could never be lawful for a subject to resist the royal authority. Then, in the

Corporation Act of 1661, the crown was empowered to intervene in municipal corporations, to ensure the loyalty and religious conformity of their membership. But the position of parliaments was also confirmed; they had sole power to approve taxation and the kinds of expedients Charles I had employed in the 1630s to sustain his government were outlawed. Indeed nothing similar was even attempted after 1660. It was also clear that the Arminian bid to assert an autonomous authority for the Church of England was rejected. The royal supremacy over the church was in future exercised jointly by king, Lords and Commons. Further, the Triennial Act of 1641 remained in force and parliaments had to be summoned at least once in three years, recognizing that royal government without parliament was no longer feasible. There was also a remarkably successful land settlement: the lands confiscated during the interregnum from king, church and defeated royalists, and sold off, were returned to their former owners on terms giving reasonable compensation to the purchasers. It seems that this Restoration was a fair reflection of the reality that there had not been any fundamental revolution in the power structure. The outsiders who had held local authority during the interregnum in many places mostly disappeared into the social obscurity from which they had emerged. The peerage, ignominiously dismissed in 1649 as useless, resumed their places in the House of Lords, and the restored upper chamber tended to increase its power and influence, relative to the Commons, after the Restoration.

But the settlement left major isssues unresolved. One was public finance. There had been an attempt to grapple with this problem; it was calculated that the crown needed a revenue of £1,200,000 a year for the normal expenses of government, and most authorities accept this was a reasonable sum.[2] But in the first decades after 1660 the revenues which were supposed to produce this sum consistently fell short, and the king was burdened with heavy and rising debt and was compelled to go back to parliament to ask for augmentation. The problem was eventually solved in the 1680s by a combination of improved administration, the establishment of the Treasury as a central ministry of finance, the gradual move from revenue-farming to direct collection by professionalized bureaucracies under the Treasury, and above all a major expansion of the economy from the mid-1670s which swelled the customs and excise receipts. By the end of Charles II's reign his income was comfortably in excess of £1,200,000, and during his final years from 1681 to 1685, he felt no need to summon parliament. The more intractable issue was religion. Initially there were serious negotiations to make a restored national church more inclusive, so as to reincorporate most of the Protestant dissenters. But the bishops and clergy and former royalist gentry were determined to prevent this. They played for time in the Convention Parliament, and in its successor, elected in 1661, the initial mood was an uncompromising demand for full restoration. A new Act of Uniformity restored a fully episcopal church, with the prayer book services and the thirty-nine articles. All the clergy had to swear acceptance or face expulsion; all the laity were required to attend their parish churches. This obligatory membership was an affirmation of both religious and political conformity, since holders of public offices were required to be church members. The result was a schism and in 1662 several hundred dissenting ministers left their benefices, followed by a substantial number of the laity. This was the birth of English Protestant dissent as an organized movement. The dissenting ministers and their congregations were liable for the statutory penalties for non-attendance at church and the Conventicles Act and the Five Mile Act severely restricted the public practice of their faith. Legally they could only worship in private households. It was the intention of the framers of the settlement that, over time, the dissenting movement would be eliminated, but although there were periods of intensive harassment by fines and imprisonment, particularly severe against radicals like the Quakers, the dissenting congregations survived. The restoration of a comprehensive national church was unattainable, and the dissenters were a reality that government would have to come to terms with.

There was a further significant change in respect of the armed forces. Here the reformed admiralty administration for the upkeep of a standing navy was maintained after 1660. The funding sometimes fell short, though parliament tended to be receptive to requests for extra money for the navy. This reflected consensus expressed in the Navigation Act of 1660, committing the government to sustain and develop foreign trade and colonies. In full contrast, parliament had been eager to provide the funds to disband the Cromwellian army. In their view, in peacetime, no army was needed in the kingdom and security could be achieved by an invigorated militia. This was organized on a county basis under the lord lieutenant and his deputy lieutenants at local expense. Although the crown appointed the lord lieutenant, it had little option but to vest the office in a leading local landowner, usually a peer, and the militia was firmly under local control. It proved adequate for the maintenance of domestic order. The king's wish for the maintenance of a standing professional force was denied. But using his position as sole commander of the armed force, Charles II did manage to retain a small royal army, initially about 5,000 men, funded out of his existing revenues. It was not a serious field force, but as a royal bodyguard it secured Charles II from becoming a prisoner in his own capital, as his father had been in 1641.

The settlements after 1660, despite the deficiencies, could have provided the basis for a working system of government. They preserved the highly devolved political structure, with most day-to-day administration vested in the county communities and borough authorities, but welded together by acceptance of the common law, and by the institution of parliament for working out consensus through statutory action. It was now reinforced by a new factor, the experience of the interregnum. Among the ruling elites of the gentry landowners and the restored clergy there persisted a dread that it might recur. Nobody of significance wanted a new civil war and the authorities were at first paranoid about the dangers of a fresh breakdown of social controls, which was why, initially, religious dissent, rightly seen as a major factor in the revolution, was subjected to harsh repression. There was a genuine desire to see the monarchy powerful and effective, and hence some disposition in parliament to support this. It was apparent in the Dutch war of 1665–7, which had strong popular support as a bid to cripple Dutch commercial competition. Parliament readily voted substantial subsidies, using the parliamentarian assessment system, and in fact their grants did cover the full costs of the war, in complete contrast with the attitudes towards finance in the 1620s.

It would appear that if Charles II was careful, he was well placed to develop and expand the authority of the monarchy by using powers of patronage and working with the elites through cooperation with parliament. Unfortunately he had characteristics that stood in the way. Charles II was the ablest and most politically intelligent of the Stuart kings, but he did not have any clear political agenda, was disinclined to work steadily at the business of government, and was unwilling to submit to the financial disciplines necessary in view of his restricted revenue. Further, he clearly resented his dependence on parliamentary grants and was seeking ways of breaking free. But in one area he did have an agenda, and that was religion. Charles was not a religious man, but during his continental exile he had been impressed by the Catholic monarchies, and probably in 1660 was a crypto-Catholic himself. He was also aware that, during the civil wars, the English Catholic community had been the most consistent supporters of the royalist cause, and felt some obligation to alleviate their oppressed position in his own kingdoms.

This tendency, though perhaps praiseworthy in itself, was politically suicidal in face of the ingrained anti-popery paranoia of English Protestant society. There was an alarming expression of this in 1666, when the great fire of London was firmly believed to have been the work of the papists, as the monument set up to commemorate it clearly stated. As early as 1662 the king attempted to use his prerogative power to issue a Declaration of Indulgence, remitting the penalties on religious dissenters. The tactic was to use the cover of relieving Protestant dissenters to facilitate comparable reliefs for the Catholics. There was an instant reaction from the two Houses, denying the king had any such prerogative power and forcing him to withdraw his Declaration. It says little for his political sense that in 1672 he tried again, and this time in alliance with Louis XIV, for a carve-up of the United Provinces. The new Declaration of 1672 proposed that Protestant dissenters be allowed freedom to worship publicly, while Catholics would be permitted the private exercise of their religion. When parliament met in 1673, with the war in full flow and the king desperate for funding, the Commons would not consider that until they had issued a formal denunciation of the Declaration as illegal, and followed this up with the Test Act, which required anyone holding a public office to prove his religious credentials by taking communion in the Church of England. This flushed out Catholics in high places, and the king's brother, James duke of York, heir presumptive, who had converted to Catholicism, had to resign his office as Lord Admiral. This exposure did irreparable damage to the credibility of the monarchy. When the king sought to intervene in the European war in 1677, this time against Louis XIV, and got funding from parliament to raise an army of 12,000 men, there was widespread suspicion that he might try to use it for a military coup. When the war ended before the army had taken the field, parliament immediately called for the army to be disbanded and voted money for this.

Suspicion of the dynasty's religious integrity had wrecked an experiment led by the earl of Danby between 1674 and 1678, based on a combination of the king declaring his commitment to the Church of England and working on the members of parliament and the gentry in local communities, with the aid of crown patronage, to get additional financial support for the crown. A growing opposition faction at court, led by the earl of Shaftesbury, mounted a counter-campaign among the public, reviving the scenario of an international popish plot to establish an absolute, Catholic monarchy in Britain. It was the first attempt by an aristocratic court faction to mobilize public opinion in order to secure control of the House of Commons and force a change of government on the king. It represented a novel experiment in party politics. In order to mobilize support in the local communities, Shaftesbury and his colleagues went on speaking tours, financed polemical literature and established a party headquarters in the Green Ribbon Club in London. Their aim was to overthrow Danby's ministry and force a dissolution of the parliament elected in 1661. Their breakthrough came with the discovery of Titus Oates and his story about a Jesuit conspiracy to assassinate Charles and in the confusion seize control of the kingdom. This tissue of lies was readily accepted in a society already conditioned to believe in popish plots and, for a time in 1678–81, it created near panic in society. Before it settled, a number of priests and innocent Catholics had been judicially murdered to wide public applause.

The crisis tested the authority of the monarchy almost to destruction. When Charles II accepted new elections in 1679, the Shaftesbury faction, now called Whigs, controlled the Commons. They determined to force the issue by excluding James from the succession on the grounds of his catholicism and then forcing the king to appoint them to office. The attempt extended over the three Exclusion Parliaments of 1679, 1680 and 1681. Shaftesbury's ability to stir up public emotions over popery maintained his control of the Commons, but the king discovered how to use the royal control of the executive to counter this. He was strengthened throughout by the support of William of Orange, married to James's elder daughter Mary, who declined to countenance any tampering with the succession. This left the Whigs without a plausible alternative successor. Then the king and his advisers found that they too could exploit growing alarm among the elites that the crisis could lead to a new civil war. This appeal to popular fears grew more effective as the sheer implausibility of the popish plot scenario became apparent. In the 1680 parliament the king was able mobilize the House of Lords to reject the exclusion bill and royalist supporters began to form their own party organization, accusing the Whigs of being republicans and religious fanatics. When the last Exclusion Parliament was summoned to Oxford in 1681, where the university was a powerful royalist and Anglican influence, the king took his lifeguards to Oxford to prevent any attempted interference by the London mobs. When his offer of safeguards on a Catholic successor was rejected, as he expected it to be, the king dissolved the parliament, and put out a public declaration of his loyalty to the Church of England and his determination to defend the ancient constitution from subversion. In effect he was daring the Whigs to resort to rebellion, which they were not then prepared to do.

The government initiated a counter-attack.[3] First it found how to use the courts to destroy the Whig movement, dismissing unreliable judges and using its power to appoint the sheriffs, who selected the juries, to set up show trials of its opponents. In 1683 Shaftesbury had to flee to Holland to escape treason charges. A purge of Whig sympathizers began. Since many were entrenched in borough corporations, the crown could attack them through its power to recall and modify borough charters. An attack on London in 1682–3, which ended in the forfeiture of its charter, and a loyalist takeover of City government, was decisive. By 1685 50 boroughs had had their charters renewed, and a bonus was that a loyal corporation was a powerful influence in any parliamentary election. In the counties, the administrations were purged in a similar partisan spirit. The regime's commitment to the church was advertised by a fresh round of persecution of dissenters urged on the local authorities. The crown's finances were now satisfactory with the increase in revenue, and the danger of war was diminished by a secret agreement with Louis XIV that Charles would stand aside in current European conflicts in return for a modest annual subsidy. There were also moves to strengthen crown control in the peripheral kingdoms of Scotland and Ireland, and to build up small military establishments from their revenues. Yet what happened in Britain in the 1680s was not the result of a determined policy of building royal absolutism. Charles had no such policy and nor did James, though he was a notoriously authoritarian personality. The reaction from Exclusion was based on the fears in a deeply conservative establishment of renewed internal disorder, and resentment of Anglicans at the stubborn survival of dissent. In the Anglican church there was an orchestrated output of argument in favour of divine right and absolute non-resistance to a lawful sovereign, which seems to have been widely acceptable. The system was put to the test when Charles died in February 1685.

James II succeeded his brother peacefully, and when radical Whigs raised a popular rebellion in the West Country in favour of Charles's bastard son the duke of Monmouth, it was brutally crushed by the royal army and judiciary. The parliament elected in 1685 had a strong royalist majority and readily voted James a larger revenue than had been given to Charles. James had no financial problems in his brief reign. His subsequent conduct must be seen in context. His heirs were two Protestant daughters, Mary and Anne, both with Protestant husbands. His second Catholic marriage was childless after 12 years. Since he never considered tampering with the succession, his strategy was to secure legal reliefs for the Catholic community, strong enough to protect them during the probable continuation of Protestant rule. He proposed to parliament in 1685 to allow Catholic worship and repeal the Test Acts that prohibited Catholics from holding public office. The Tory majority refused to consider any breach of the Anglican monopoly on office-holding. James spent a year using his prerogative to install Catholics in office, while lobbying individual members of parliament in favour of his programme, but met with so little success that the parliament was dissolved. From early 1687 a new strategy was launched. The king issued a Declaration of Indulgence, which suspended all repressive legislation on religious dissenters. This would hold until a new parliament could meet to legalize toleration. The policy was a gamble on religious toleration proving acceptable, combined with a determined use of royal power to influence a parliamentary election. There was intensive lobbying of local elites, a new round of modification of borough charters, this time to open them up to Protestant dissenters, and a purge of central and local administration, down to the JPs and the lieutenancy that controlled the militia. In England, Scotland and Ireland the size of the standing army was increased, and where possible Catholics given commissions, though they never amounted to more than a quarter of James's officer corps.

The success of the strategy is arguable[4] since the proposed elections were never held. The international crisis in Europe intervened. After 1678 William of Orange made it his life's mission to build a coalition to restrain the ambitions of Louis XIV. Britain would have been a valuable addition to the Alliance; hence William's concern for his wife's claim to the succession to the throne. In 1687, William sent missions to England to establish the position of James and leading subjects. James demanded William should support the dynasty; some opposition leaders suggested William should intervene to restrain the king's Catholicizing policies. In December 1687 William and Mary announced publicly that they were opposed to any repeal of the Test Acts. Shortly after, it was revealed that James's queen was pregnant and in June 1688 she gave birth to a prince, who now became heir to the throne, cutting William and Mary out of the succession. At that point William began to prepare to lead an armed intervention in England. There the open opposition to James's programme was growing. The leaders of the Church of England became so alarmed that they opened discussions with Protestant dissenters, offering some toleration in return for a united front of Protestants. Then in 1688 James issued a new Declaration of Indulgence and ordered it be read out in all churches. Seven leading bishops petitioned to be excused on the grounds that the Declaration was illegal. They were charged with seditious libel, but such was the force of Protestant opinion that the

trial judges split and a London jury acquitted them. There was a wave of
demonstrative Protestant rejoicing extending to the soldiers of the king's
army. In June a group of peers and the bishop of London wrote to William
inviting him to come over to protect the Protestant constitution. At the same
time there was a campaign, encouraged by William and Mary, suggesting the
birth of the prince was suspicious. In November, William successfully landed
an army at Torbay, declared he came only to secure the liberties of the
English people and began to advance on London. James then threw his
throne away, perhaps as the result of a nervous breakdown. First he planned
to take his army to challenge the invaders, then retreated from confrontation, at which point his supporters began to melt away. Negotiations
between the king and William were opened, with no mention of deposition,
only that there should be a free parliament elected, which would undoubtedly demand strong legal safeguards for the Protestant ascendancy. While
these were progressing, James panicked and fled to take refuge with Louis
XIV. William occupied London and was invited by a committee of former
members of parliament to assume control of the government until the new
parliament could decide on a settlement.

The Revolution of 1689

It is obvious that the English Revolution of 1689, with its spin-off in
Scotland and Ireland, was in the strictest sense a historical accident. It would
not have happened if James II and VII had not been a Catholic, and England
a society deeply hostile to what it called popery. Nor could it have happened
if William of Orange had not intervened. Neither of these had anything to
do with deficiencies in the political structure, except that by the 1680s the
English had come to link the idea of popery with the idea of repressive, arbitrary absolutist monarchy. This was encapsulated in the popular Whig
slogan, 'no popery and wooden shoes'. The old Whig historicism that saw
1688 as the final realization of England's manifest destiny as a law-bound,
constitutional monarchy is clearly untenable, but the fact that it arose from
unexpected contingency goes far to explain its ambivalent outcomes.[5]

When the Convention Parliament assembled in 1689, there was only a
fringe group of radicals who perceived an opportunity for remodelling the
constitution. The great majority in both Houses wanted to patch over the
crisis with as little change as possible. There was, however, no support for
restoring James directly, while the existence of the prince was simply
ignored. Direct succession was impossible because James's elder daughter
Mary would not accept the crown unless William was recognized as co-sov-
ereign. The House of Lords nearly voted for a regency to gloss over the
breach in the hereditary succession of the monarchy, but the Commons preferred their own fudge – that by deserting his office, James had abdicated
and the throne was vacant and should be offered to William and Mary as

joint sovereigns. If Mary predeceased her husband, the succession passed to William alone. There was a minority who realized the implications for the nature of royal authority if the line of hereditary succession was broken. A substantial group of Anglican clergy and a few lay officeholders could not accept this and left public office. The great majority affected to believe it had made no difference, helped by the fact that no new constitutional conditions were imposed on Willliam and Mary. They subsequently accepted the statutory Bill of Rights passed several months after their accession. This struck one further blow at hereditary succession by stipulating that Catholics were barred from succession to the crown. This was driven by religious prejudice not politics: the statute did rehearse all the alleged violations of law committed under James II, but few remedies were enacted. The dispensing power was no longer to be abused, the coronation oath now specified that the king must govern according to laws laid down in parliament, and it was forbidden to maintain a standing army in peacetime without consent in parliament. It was stated there ought to be frequent parliaments, but no provision was made to ensure this, nor was anything done to protect the electoral system or proceedings in parliament from attempted manipulation by the crown. Even the religious settlement was fudged. The dissenters had been promised relief as a reward for rejecting James's offer of toleration. There was another attempt to reach agreement that would re-admit them into the established church that quickly proved impossible, and the resulting Toleration Act of 1689 merely lifted the legal penalties on most forms of non-conformist Protestant worship, while leaving dissenters excluded from holding public office or entering the universities. Perhaps this was a significant shift: it meant formal legal recognition that England was a multi-confessional society, except that the legal restrictions on Catholics were actually made harsher. The established Anglican Church never recovered from the ending of its monopoly and it remained internally divided thereafter between a high-church faction, which still aspired to recover its exclusive status, and a broad church faction, willing to accept the new dispensation.

The changes in British constitutional systems that were put in place after 1689 arose, as had the original break in 1688, from the force of events. The most important of these was that William took the kingdom into two successive wars against the France of Louis XIV, which necessitated the development of new methods of government. The wars compelled close cooperation of royal government and parliaments if the necessary funding was to be provided; they forced new methods of raising the public revenues; the necessity for the crown to find ways of working with parliaments meant that future government in Britain required formal power-sharing between the crown and the political elites. This was compounded by William being a foreigner, and by the war requiring long absences on the continent. He had to find native political managers who could put together the necessary parliamentary support for the the government. The dependence of the crown on parliamentary revenue was recognized in 1694, when William traded in the crown's independent revenues for a civil list: in effect a parliamentary salary for managing the civil government. Any remaining possibility of re-creating an independent royal executive was ended.

The structures of parliamentary politics were complex. The crown always had a solid core of support, particularly in the Lords, from those who made their career in court service. These men provided an essential element in any working administration. At the other extreme there were truly independent back-bench members of the Commons, genuinely representing a strong current of public opinion, which was instinctively opposed to strong central government and the taxation and interference with local autonomies it entailed. This 'Country' position was deeply conservative, often militantly anti-dissenter and sympathetic to high-Anglican policies. It was also xeno-phobic and instinctively opposed to the land war on the continent, though sympathetic to supposedly profitable naval and colonial alternatives. It implied contrast with the 'Court' groupings and was especially powerful under William. The basic, anti-government aspirations of the 'Country' appeared in the Act of Settlement of 1701, which regulated further the Protestant succession by including the Hanoverian line, and enacted such safeguards as requiring royal decisions to be formally confirmed by the Privy Council, and barring those holding public office from sitting in the House of Commons. The Court–Country antagonism co-existed with the revival of political parties, which were the normal result of any political regime that needed support from an elected assembly. Key factors in the revival of Whig and Tory parties, which now became a permanent feature of British politics, were the Triennial Act of 1694, requiring an election every three years, and the end of formal press censorship after 1695, allowing the proliferation of polemical pamphlets and a newspaper press so necessary for the politiciza-tion of public opinion. Another factor was religion; broadly, the Tories were inclined to support the high-Anglican positions, while the Whigs favoured a comprehensive church and were in favour of extending the rights of the Protestant dissenters. The parties, while remaining attached to their basic positions, were also bound into the Court–Country divide, in that the party enjoying royal favour would usually adopt Court positions on the need for strong government, while the party out of power would tend to take up basic Country positions as well. After an initial period of confusion while the king and the Court factions adjusted themselves to the changed face of politics, William III found he could best work with the Whigs, and their aris-tocratic 'Junto' that had mastered the techniques of parliamentary manipu-lation and were firm in their support for the king's foreign policies.

There was a further force changing the face of politics, which could be called the rise of the money power in Britain. It is true that in 1688, and perhaps for nearly two centuries afterwards, British society was ruled by a landowning oligarchy, as was nearly all of Europe. But the substantial eco-nomic expansion of the economy since the 1670s, on the back of oceanic trades, and import and re-export of oriental and Caribbean products, together with the rising profits of the Atlantic slave trade, in which the British were becoming major participants, was creating unprecedented accumulations of commercial wealth. From the beginning of the wars in 1689, governments and parliaments were faced with the need to produce funds on a hitherto unimagined scale. It was obvious from the start that even raising the comparatively efficient land tax, which hit the landlords hardest, could not produce the necessary cash-flow, and so revenue was used as security for public borrowing. The technique of government by deficit financing was established. In 1694 the decisive step was taken of a parliamentary chartered bank, the Bank of England, to act as manager of the mounting public debt, which was now recognized as a funded national debt. One unplanned function it served was as security against any reversal of 1688, which would throw the legitimacy of the national debt into question. In effect, though, it meant no government could afford to ignore the monied interests from the commercial and banking sector, who alone could keep any government afloat while they were willing to lend. From the viewpoint of the landed interest, which was paying the land tax, it seemed all the profits were being drained off to the money power. Since many of these financiers were also dissenters, and some were Jewish or foreign, like French Huguenot refugees and a substantial group of Dutch investors, the whole development was a provocation, particularly to the less affluent landlords, and did much to reinvigorate a combined Country–Tory opposition, which found its own able political manager in Robert Harley. When the war ended in 1697, the king and his Whig managers found the House of Commons increasingly unmanageable, as the alliance demanded drastic tax reduction and the disbanding of the army, and eventually sought to force a change of royal policy by impeaching the Junto leaders. William steadily retreated, eventually asking Robert Harley, the Country–Tory leader, to take on parliamentary management.

From 1700 partisan politics developed as both sides found populist causes to reinforce their appeal. The Junto, always identified with the war, was able to exploit the provocative behaviour of Louis XIV after he accepted the Spanish succession for his grandson. When James II died in exile, and Louis recognized his son as James III of England, a patriotic, francophobe reaction set in, which the Whig leaders eagerly exploited. At the same time the Tories now publicly took up the high-Anglican cause. From 1697, led by an able publicist, Dean Atterbury, they had been calling for a revival of Convocation, the general assembly of the Church of England to sit alongside parliament, and they launched a 'church in danger' campaign, alleging that a combination of dissenters, materialists and atheists was threatening the very survival of Christian belief in the kingdom, helped by the tolerance of the broad-church bishops installed after 1689. In 1701 Tory leaders insisted on reviving Convocation and it became a standing public forum for anti-Whig and anti-dissenter propaganda.

The behaviour of Louis XIV did, nevertheless, mean broad acceptance in Britain that there would be a new round of war. The Tories conceded this, though they argued it should be primarily a naval and colonial war. Then, early in 1702, William died and Anne became queen. She has often been misrepresented as a Tory partisan and a high-church fanatic but this is clearly wrong.[6] She did pride herself on her English descent and her devotion to the church, in implied rejection of the legacy of William. But, in fact, like any politically aware monarch, she detested party politics, realizing how the predominance of either party would be a constraint on the freedom of the crown to determine policy, and she retained this attitude until her death in 1714. Thus, although on her accession there was a purge of surviving Whig officeholders, the administration she installed was built around the duke of Marlborough, whom William had installed as coalition Captain General in the Netherlands, and whose wife Sarah was the queen's personal intimate. Marlborough was also, in effect, foreign minister too. Sidney Godolphin, an experienced financial expert and friend of Marlborough, headed the domestic administration as lord treasurer. This combination ensured a vigorous prosecution of the new war, with the full support of the queen, and those Tories who criticized the war, and were stirring up confessional strife by promoting the Occasional Conformity Bill to stop dissenters qualifying themselves for office by a token attendance at Anglican communion, angered her, for she saw the whole high-church agitation as implying that religion was under threat, even though she was in charge as Supreme Governor. In return the Whig Junto was giving tacit support to the ministry, particularly as the war proceeded favourably after Marlborough's triumph at Blenheim in 1704. There was a further success with the negotiated union with Scotland in 1707. This arose from the discontent of the Scots at the way they had been taken for granted after 1688, and they had used the opportunity to carry through their own much more radical revolution and gone on to emphasize their separate identity, culminating in the Scottish Act of 1703, specifying that on the death of Queen Anne, Scotland would choose its own Protestant successor, different from that in England. The English response was to call their bluff by threatening reprisals if the Act were not repealed, but then offering negotiations for a full parliamentary union of the kingdoms. The terms offered, and a generous use of incentives on the Scottish leaders, secured the Union Treaty that came into force in 1707. This removed the danger that separation would have represented for England's international position.

It was at this point that the political system operative since 1689 began to disintegrate. Public opinion was moving against the continuation of the war from 1708, and the queen moved with it. The Whigs and Marlborough, who were determined to fight on, could no longer depend on the queen's support, and their position was further undermined when the public impeachment of a high-Anglican preacher, Sacheverell, roused violent mob action in London calling for an early peace. In consequence, the queen began to work with Harley and the Tories, first dismissing Marlborough as Captain General, then authorizing secret negotiations with Louis XIV for a separate peace, the terms for which were agreed in 1711.

This meant Britain deserting her continental allies and in the end forcing them to seek peace too. At home a general election was held in 1710 which produced a strong Tory majority. This should have brought political stability, and might have done so but for the intervention of the succession question. The heir under the Act of Settlement was the aging Sophia, Electress of Hanover, who died in 1714, so that her son succeeded as George I. He was an active military leader who admired Marlborough, wanted to continue the war on Louis XIV, and bitterly hated the new Tory ministry led by Harley and Viscount Bolingbroke. By making peace after 1711 they had simultaneously consolidated their power in parliament and with the queen, and painted themselves into a corner. Queen Anne was visibly declining in health, the succession was approaching, and the new Hanoverian sovereign would certainly dismiss the Tory ministry. Yet the only way of preventing it would be to scrap the Act of Settlement and arrange a succession for the Stuart pretender. Since he, in turn, refused to consider conversion to the Church of England as the price of restoration, that option too was closed. In the end, although the Tories secured an even larger majority in the election of 1713, the ministry was being eroded from above. A substantial number of Tories broke with the party and declared their support for the Hanoverians. They joined with Whig magnates to put pressure on the dying queen to dismiss Harley, now earl of Oxford and lord treasurer, from his key post, which would have made him president of the Regency Council on the queen's death, and to appoint the veteran Whig duke of Shrewsbury. Under his guidance a smooth Hanoverian succession was achieved.

In retrospect it is perhaps misleading to talk of a 'revolution settlement' after 1689. Rather it repeated the Restoration experience of leaving difficult issues unresolved. In time it settled the fate of the associated kingdoms of Scotland and Ireland by putting them firmly under English hegemony. The year 1689 certainly struck a damaging blow at the sanctity of hereditary succession to the crown, although, except on the plane of ideological politics, that made little practical difference. The monarch, as both William III and Anne proved in their different ways, was in charge of the government. It was also true that 1689, or more strictly the burdens of the wars that it caused, meant that royal government also needed the participation of parliaments. Yet there are very few instances where the monarch had to abandon personal positions in face of parliamentary pressures, William did so to some extent after 1697, and so did Queen Anne under Whig pressure after 1708, though she soon regained control. What was obvious was that, in normal circumstances, neither Lords nor Commons aspired to take over for themselves the executive power vested in the monarchy. It remained true that the royal ministers needed ways of influencing parliaments. Normally this was done through power brokers whose leaders sat in the Lords, and it is significant that no government was overthrown by adverse votes in parliament. On the other hand, a parliament with a strong party identity could not be disregarded, while an electorate that was becoming increasingly politicized was also becoming increasingly volatile, as the swings from Tory to Whig and back again in Anne's later years showed. The quest for a system that would create a stable balance between king, Lords and Commons, with occasional populist inputs from the electorate and the mob, remained for the Hanoverians to pursue.

7

Developments on the North-Eastern Periphery

Brandenburg Prussia

The Hohenzollern dynasty was one of the Empire's oldest, and its princes had been involved in the medieval colonizing drives to carry German settlement and culture east of the Elbe river. It held lands scattered over the Empire, with their core in Brandenburg, which had long been an Electorate. In 1599 a family compact ruled that the core territories should pass intact by primogeniture. In 1600 these comprised Brandenburg, together with the duchy of Prussia which was outside the Empire and held as a vassal of the Polish crown. After 1610 the family acquired the Rhine duchies of Cleves and Berg, though the legal processes were not completed until 1666, and in the 1630s they made a claim to the succession in Pomerania. These lands had nothing in common except their dynastic allegiance, and were widely scattered geographically. Apart from the Rhine duchies, which resembled the United Provinces, with a powerful urban sector, the territories were ruled by a German landowning nobility, structured in two tiers: a small exclusive group of titled nobles, and a larger class of knights who tended to be grouped under the patronage of their local magnates. Their once significant urban sector had declined severely in the six-teenth century, but in the east the nobility had engaged profitably in the Baltic grain trade, using serf labour for extensive domain production. They had used their dominance of the local Estates to control public revenue and set up their own fiscal administrations independent of the ruler, in return for assisting with his debts. All the territories subscribed to the Lutheran confession and when, in 1606, the Elector and his successors converted to Calvinism, they found that the integrity of the Lutheran church settlement could not be infringed.[1]

Depite an attempt to stand neutral in the early phase of the Thirty Years War, Brandenburg found itself caught in the fighting, particularly after the Swedish intervention in 1630, when they were intermittently allied to the invaders, or subjected to Swedish military contributions. The consequent population loss by 1650 was not made good for nearly a century. In 1640 the inheritance fell to an Elector who was both ambitious and well educated at a Dutch university, Frederick William. His ambition has been described by the German historian H. W. Koch:

> Prussia as a state is a work of art, a Renaissance State in the true sense of Jacob Burckhardt's term … During the reign of the Great Elector, a major constituent principle of this new state became visible, namely a kind of étatisme, an ideology of the state community, which subjected dynasty, aristocracy and subjects alike, and which represented a revolutionary break away from the the still prevalent feudal, dynastic conceptions.

The Prussian state that eventually developed was an artefact; there was no 'natural' basis for its existence.

Frederick William, the 'Great Elector', achieved his creation through an opportunistic foreign policy. He declared once: 'clever and intelligent rulers adapt themselves to circumstances on each occasion, and not to that which represents the greater right, but what possibility and contingency offer and permit'. He began by tacit collaboration with the Swedes, gaining a breathing space to lay the foundations of a small army of his own. At Westphalia he agreed to facilitate the peace by dividing Pomerania with Sweden. In return he received as compensation four large secularized bish-oprics in north Germany, which left him the biggest territorial prince in the Empire. He then sought to enlarge his army, but found the Estates of his various territories resisted any idea of contributing jointly to a common army, just as Olivares had discovered in Spain. So he had to bargain, and began with the Brandenburg Estates, where a deal was struck with the nobility, the *Abschied* of 1653. In return for an annual grant of land tax on their tenants, limited to six years, the Elector confirmed their privileges, their exemption from taxation and their feudal powers over their peasants. It was a typical arrangement for a partnership in exploitation between rulers and nobilities that was often the basis of the military–fiscal state. There was no confrontation in 1653, though in 1659, when the grant expired, the Elector simply continued collecting it, and met with no serious protest.

The Elector joined Sweden's aggression on Poland in 1655, in return for a promise of sovereignty over Prussia. With an army to offer he was a useful ally and showed skill in transferring his support to the eventual winners. His reward, in 1660, was the sovereignty over Prussia, recognized by treaty. It has been said that Prussia was not a state that acquired an army, but an army that developed into a state. This began during the war with the establish-ment of the war commissariat, the *General Kriegskommissariat*, which itself collected the taxes and organized the upkeep of the army. This, however, was also a cooperative development: in each taxation district, a nobleman, often already working for the local Estates administration, became the agent of the war commissariat, so that some convergence of the two administra-tions developed. After 1660 the Elector wanted to develop his tax base by levying a general excise in Brandenburg. Here he did meet immoveable opposition from the nobility, and in the end did a separate deal with the towns, which agreed to make a perpetual grant. This had the advantage of splitting the towns from the nobility, and indeed made their attendance at the provincial Estates unnecessary. It also enabled the war commissariat to appoint an excise officer in each town, so that it now had a network of fiscal agents throughout Brandenburg. By the death of the Elector in 1688, the war commissariat was a central fiscal agency for all the Elector's lands. Their control was less secure in the Rhine Duchies, where the towns were powerful in the Estates, able to look to the United Provinces for support, and appeal to the Emperor for the maintenance of privileges. A compromise had to be struck leaving their Estates with the right to consent to tax changes.

The most testing situation arose in Prussia after 1660. There, local administration was firmly in the hands of the Prussian Estates, controlled by the nobility and familiar with the gentry liberties that prevailed in Poland. Further, the city of Königsberg was a powerful, self-governing trading city. In Prussia, Frederick William needed time to wear down resistance to central control. In a visit in 1661–3 he managed to get the Prussian Estates to recognize his sovereignty, while asserting their continuing constitutional rights. Resistance in Königsberg had to be discouraged by military occupation. In 1669, the Prussian Estates met again to consider taxation and it needed a mixture of negotiation and coercion over several years to secure what he wanted – a perpetual revenue in land tax from the nobility and an excise in the towns.[2] The Elector had his own extensive domain lands in all his different provinces, and for these a remarkable technician administrator, von Knyphausen, laboured over many years after 1683 to create an efficient central administration based on the Elector's Chamber. He reformed the accounting procedures, changed the leasing policies and commuted rents in kind into cash payments. A total domain revenue of near 300,000 thalers in 1660 had risen to 1,500,000 thalers by 1689. The Elector was a keen mercantilist: one of his reasons for wanting Pomerania was the possibility of developing a maritime trade and founding a colonial trading company. He subsidized attempts to start manufactures, but the basic lack of capital and skills and guild resistance ensured most of these failed. Where he did have success was immigration, a process put under the war commissariat. The Elector was a genuine believer in religious toleration, which he extended as far as Catholics and Jews, but his major enterprise was the open invitation after 1685 to settle Huguenot refugees on favourable terms. They brought in various skills as well as capital: they introduced advanced farming methods, set up successful textile manufactures and provided officers for the army. They settled extensively round Berlin, making it into a substantial city, which by 1700 was strongly French in culture.

It is a mistake, however, to see Frederick William as creating the classic Prussian state system. The army was not run by local noblemen; most native nobles showed little enthusiasm for army service. It was a state contract army, run by its colonels, and only towards the end of the reign did the Elector establish his right to approve appointments of junior officers. It had a permanent command structure and a general staff but these, and much of the central administration, were staffed by Calvinist immigrants. In some branches they held 80 per cent of the leading positions. Also the different branches of the administration remained separate; the Prussian bureaucracy had still to be developed. In fact, Frederick William disliked bureaucrats. He wrote once: 'the more servants, the more thieves'. Yet the position of international importance to which he had always aspired still eluded him when he died in 1688. He continued his pragmatic foreign policy, but after 1660 it brought no major gains. In 1673 he came out against Louis XIV and promoted a patriotic revival in the Empire against the outsiders. It was then that he circulated his pamphlet, *Remember that you are a German*. In the war he raised some 45,000 troops, though this was heavily dependent on foreign subsidies, and he succeeded in overruning Swedish Pomerania, whose possession was his primary war aim. Yet in 1679 he was forced to return it by Louis XIV, who wanted to maintain Sweden as a force in Germany. For all his exertions he emerged from the war with only some minor territorial adjustments in Pomerania, and found that many of the promised subsidies were never paid. His immediate reaction was to offer himself as a client to Louis XIV, seeking to replace Sweden as the French ally in the Empire, in return for a French subsidy. The relationship became badly strained, particularly by the Revocation in 1685 and evidence of Louis's expansionist designs in the Empire. Frederick William switched his support to the alliance being created by William of Orange. The brutal truth behind these manoeuvrings was that, with all his efforts, Frederick William was still regarded as a mercenary to be hired by the real powers of Europe, not a participant in his own right.

Brandenburg–Prussia is often seen as the extreme example of a military state, whose sole purpose was to sustain its army. That was not how Frederick William, a rather conservative ruler, perceived it. He warned his heirs that they must always respect the laws and constitution of the Empire, and despite the centralizing drive behind his policies, in his testament of 1680 he contemplated establishing separate principalities for his younger children after his death. His testament of 1667, for the guidance of his heirs, is traditionalist. One dominant theme is personal piety: 'It is and remains pre-eminently the moral obligation of a legitimate ruler that he shall fear, love and keep before his eyes the God that made him and established him as ruling lord over so many lands and peoples.' Yet his language does suggest the concept, which was to develop in the next century, that rulers were the divinely appointed guardians, rather than the owners of their lands. He wrote: 'You must love all the subjects God has given you, without distinction of religion, as a true father of the country, willingly seek to further their profit and their advantage in all reasonable things, develop trade and strive to increase the population, especially in Brandenburg.'

Frederick William got his contemporary title, the 'Great Elector', because of his rather minor success against a Swedish invasion force at Fehrbellin in 1675, commonly rated as the first real defeat of a Swedish army since the days of Gustav Adolf. This was a gross exaggeration, but somehow the episode caught the imagination of Europe at the time. His real claim to be a significant historical figure is as the ruler who launched developments that in time enabled Prussia to become a major European power. The development faltered under his son and successor Frederick III. For the first decade of the new reign he kept his father's advisers and allowed their policies to continue. Frederick showed more of the conventional aspiration of the rulers of his day for public assertion of his status through display, through showpiece palaces and patronage of the arts. His father had specifically warned him 'not to maintain too extravagant a Court', but this ideal was progressively abandoned. He did have serious policy aims in view, in particular he wanted to raise his dynastic rank by acquiring the title of king. He could not do this within the Empire, as neither the Emperor, nor his fellow Electors would have permitted such a development. But he proposed to become king in Prussia, which was not in the Empire. He had followed his father's choice of the imperial cause in the new round of warfare that opened in 1688, and hired out his army to the alliance. When he realized that he would get nothing of substance out of the peace settlement of Ryswick in 1697, while his neighbour, the Elector of Saxony, was elected king of Poland, he blamed his father's ministers and dismissed them. Brandenburg was still being treated as a hired mercenary. The Elector now concentrated on making sure that in the next round of the war, sure to be triggered by the Spanish succession, and for which the Emperor needed all the allies he could find, Brandenburg would be rewarded.

The policy worked: he got a special privilege from the Emperor exempting his lands from imperial jurisdiction. This meant his subjects there could no longer appeal to the imperial courts against their ruler, and in 1703 he set up his own court of appeal. The same year the formalities of recognizing Frederick as 'King in Prussia' were completed. The distinction meant that within the Empire he still ranked as an Elector. Frederick combined the new war with lavish expenditure on advertising his new royal status. The result was that by 1710 the regime was heading for bankruptcy, and an opposition began to form at court around the crown prince, Frederick William. The crown prince had very firm ideas of how he would take up and develop his grandfather's policies, but he had to wait until Frederick died in 1713 to get the necessary freedom of action. In the eyes of the historians, Frederick III cuts a poor figure compared with his father and his son, yet in contemporary terms the achievement of a royal title was a substantial advance. It gave the Hohenzollern Electors a special recognition and was a step on the way to the higher status that the Great Elector had aspired to.

The Scandinavian kingdoms

In the seventeenth century the lands around the Baltic, the Scandinavian peninsula, and Poland and Russia, stretching across the great European plains, had a history divergent from, but at times interacting with, the core territories of western Europe and the Iberian–Mediterranean zone. The century witnessed a marked process of convergence that would in time integrate these peripheral territories and their political systems into the mainstream of European civilization. The Baltic grain trade had been one economic force when, under Dutch management, it became a vital food supply, and in its wake Dutch entrepreneurs took their capital and technical skills into Sweden, Poland and Russia. The grain trade lost its central importance after mid-century, but was partially replaced by the growing trade in naval stores, mast timbers, tar, hemp for ropes and sail cloth, following the growing demand from the new military states for navies. The United Provinces defended its commercial interests by several naval interventions in the Baltic to determine the outcome of local power struggles. Even so the political history of the region remained only intermittently linked to the power politics and wars of the core lands.

Denmark–Norway

Denmark–Norway, the kingdom most nearly linked to the core of Europe, since its rulers, as dukes of Holstein, were princes of the Holy Roman Empire, was the remnant of what had been a union of the three kingdoms, Norway, Denmark and Sweden. Sweden had finally broken the union in the 1520s and established its independence, leaving behind a destructive legacy of mutual hostilities. Norway was a peripheral part of the joint kingdom. It had its own provincial administration, directed by a Governor General appointed from Copenhagen. It was usually a passive participant in the political struggles both international and domestic. The detachment of Norway showed itself during the repeated Swedish–Danish wars of the period through the custom in the frontier parishes of agreeing local neutrality pacts, to which central governments were always bitterly opposed. In 1600 Denmark ranked as the leading Baltic power because it held the lands on both sides of the Sound which controlled the entry and exit from the Baltic. The Danish crown levied tolls on all shipping and, especially while the grain trade flourished, enjoyed a very substantial income. In the 1620s Christian IV had a revenue surplus of 1.5 million thalers annually, and was a significant international money-lender.

This gave the king an independence within the kingdom he would not otherwise have enjoyed, for the Danish monarchy was elective, and though hereditary succession was the custom, at each accession the new king had to grant a charter, which defined his powers. Denmark was in fact an aristocratic monarchy. The Danish nobility in the sixteenth century had become a closed oligarchy of some 200 families, whose lands, nearly half the cultivated land in the kingdom, were legally protected and could not be sold to outsiders. The nobles were technically of equal status and there were no titles, but in time an internal elite emerged of about 12 families, who sat in the Council, and usually held the chief offices. Council members were appointed by the king for life, and the charter for Christian IV established that sovereign power was held jointly by king and Council. Further, although the crown had extensive lands, these were leased out to nobles as administrators, giving them control over tax collection and jurisdiction over the peasants.

Christian IV's independent income had enabled him to assert himself in the war with Sweden of 1611–13, which should have enabled Denmark to close Sweden off from direct access to the North Sea through Älvsborg, but the Swedes unexpectedly managed to pay off the huge ransom demanded. Even so, Denmark's leading position was asserted. The same independence, and his status as prince of the Empire, enabled Christian to enter the German conflict in 1625, very much against the will of the Council, but there he came to grief and in the process the first hostile occupation and devastation of Jutland started Denmark's seventeenth-century economic decline.

The crown had to be bailed out by the Council agreeing to a substantial war taxation, while the king's accumulated financial surplus was lost. The Council oligarchs then determined to keep the king's propensity for foreign ventures under control. But Denmark had been dragged into the process of creating a military state. Between 1628 and 1645 the levels of taxation increased five times under Council control. In 1637 it was decided to maintain a standing army but the Council controlled the war commissariat set up to administer it. In 1645 the Council reinforced its position by a law fixing its membership. The king still had leverage, since the day-to-day conduct of government was in his hands, the Council only met periodically, and he could exploit factional rivalries within the oligarchy. But the total military disaster of the 1643–5 war, which brought a second devastation of Jutland and ended in territorial losses at the peace of Brömsebro, signalled clearly that Sweden was now the leading Baltic power. In the Westphalia negotiations, Denmark could play no significant part and gained nothing, compared to the spectacular confirmation of the international role of Sweden.

Christian IV died in 1648, and his heir Frederick IV, young and inexperienced, had to accept a charter drafted by the Council, and ratified by the Estates, which left him under strict Council supervision. It looked as though Denmark, in adapting to the demands of the new power politics, might defy the general European trend towards royal absolutism and centralization. Yet the position of the monarchy as the divinely appointed source of local authority was not being challenged by the Council nobility, and the king had some resources, one important one being the unstinting support of the Lutheran Church, whose clergy had many grievances against the abuse of power, as they saw it, by an anti-clerical nobility. And in times of crisis, like the Swedish invasion of the home islands which threatened Copenhagen itself in 1658, it was the king who led a patriotic movement to defend the capital and earned the confidence of the Copenhagen burghers, the only significant urban power in the kingdom. The Council administration inevitably took the blame for the military disasters of 1658–60. The Treaty of Roskilde of 1658 marked the lowest point of Denmark's fortunes, involving major territorial concessions to Sweden, including Bornholm and the Trondheim province of Norway. Most important was the cession of the province of Skåne, which meant the loss of Danish control of the Sound. Intervention by the United Provinces and the Emperor helped Denmark, after the sudden death of Charles X, to recover Trondheim and Bornholm in the Treaty of Oliva in 1660, but in the outcome the prestige of the Council was damaged, and that of the king improved. The Council had proved unable to direct the war effectively.

When the Estates were summoned in 1660, the nobility was divided and demoralized. This produced a political outcome, very rare in early modern history, where the king was able to work with the two commoner Estates to break the power of the nobility. The king granted new privileges to the Copenhagen burghers and could rely on the clergy. When a programme of fiscal and administrative reform was advanced by the commoners, and blocked by the nobility, it was the clergy who suggested that the king be invited to resolve the problem and be empowered to rewrite his accession charter. Under a veiled threat of violent coercion, the nobility gave way. The new charter was the first formally absolutist constitution in Europe. As summarized in the Royal Law of 1664, it ascribed all sovereign power to the king alone, who made all public appointments, was supreme judge, could legislate at will and raise revenue at his discretion. Any resistance to the royal will would be treason. The crown ceased to be elective and would descend by hereditary divine right. The only formal restriction on the royal power was the obligation to uphold the Lutheran religion. At one stroke Denmark had become a model absolute monarchy, though whether the commoners who had contrived the coup of 1660 had anticipated this outcome cannot be known. The Estates were not to meet again until 1849. It can only be said that, in the end, it was the common people, not the nobility, who carried the burden of the new dispensation.

The old nobility certainly lost their hegemony. The new regime removed their tax exemption, the legal protection of their property, and their monopoly of high office, but also their personal liability to military service. They were not subject to any reprisals, but were gradually pushed into marginality in the new government. Where, before 1660, the old families had held almost all the higher posts in government, by 1720 this shrank to a quarter. They were slowly absorbed in the new service nobility created by the crown. This was funded by a massive shift in land ownership: the crown now put most of its own land on sale to finance the creation of the new salaried service class. This was open to commoners and foreign nobles, and the Table of Ranks of 1671 established that status in society went according to official rank, not birth. But in reality a new nobility was created. The higher offices in royal service conferred noble status on the officeholder, and after 1693 this became hereditary. The titles of count and baron were introduced, and their landed estates were recognized under the titles and protected by entails. There is no doubt that, in the early stages of the process, before the new oligarchy consolidated, the system did offer openings for upward social mobility and advancement on merit for able commoners.

As the new nobility consolidated its power, it became clearer that the peasant would ultimately pay the bill. The regime established a reformed land tax, based on a scientific valuation of all the lands in the kingdom. The collection of the tax was to be the responsibility of the landlord, who was given increased jurisdiction over his tenants. This was further enhanced when the military system was remodelled on the basis of peasant conscription, instead of reliance on mercenaries. The landlords were to administer the conscription too, and to make it effective the peasant families were bound to the estates. The new nobility were to be sustained by a new serfdom. The landowners could use their administrative powers to impose harder leases on the tenants and step up their liability to labour services. And although the Danish peasants remained legally free men, with access to the royal courts, these courts themselves, with their traditional jury system, could be manipulated by the noble administrators.[3]

The Danish experience could suggest that, for the evolution of a modernized, military state, absolute monarchy offered the best model. This was not just because of the theoretical advantage of having a powerful, autonomous, centralized executive, with control over legislation and taxation. For as long as the prevailing mentalities survived, which traced all lawful authority back to a ruler with a divine mandate, in a society structured from top to bottom on a hierarchy of command, absolute monarchy seemed natural and fitting. There have to be good reasons why, in Denmark, a well-entrenched aristocratic oligarchy surrendered without a struggle, while the commoners who sought to unseat them turned automatically to the rather uncharismatic sovereign, who symbolized legitimacy and stability. It could be said that authoritarian, absolute monarchy was the flavour of the century, and perhaps what needs explaining more is why a few exceptional societies did not adopt it.

The Swedish empire

The course of development in the kingdom of Sweden–Finland in 1600 was uncertain. The founder of the Vasa dynasty of kings, Gustav Vasa, after leading a successful struggle for independence from Denmark, had gone on to build a strong executive monarchy, and reinforced it in 1543 by securing the consent of the Diet to declaring the monarchy hereditary. He also re-endowed the monarchy by introducing the Protestant Reformation, transferring to the crown the substantial landed endowments of the church. In 1593 at the Diet of Uppsala it was finally resolved that the kingdom adhere to the Lutheran confession. Sweden was unusual for its time in possessing a written constitution in the land law first codified around 1350. It had provided for an elected

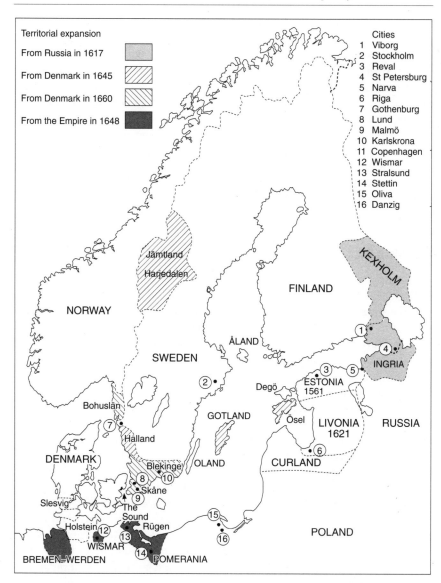

Map 7.1 The Swedish empire

monarchy, but with strong executive powers, which were to be exercised with the advice of a Council of native noblemen and leading clergy: after the Reformation the clergy were removed. The crown had been endowed with a large landed property, which was declared inalienable, and was intended to cover the normal costs of government. If there were need for additional taxation, or major questions of policy, such as making war and peace, or legislating changes to the land law, then the king was to consult with the community of the realm. By the sixteenth century this consultation had been institutionalized as meetings with a Diet of four Estates, clergy, nobles, burghers and peasants, consulting with the king and the Council and seeking consensus.

The Swedish nobility derived from the elite of landlords who rendered cavalry service with the royal army, and in return were exempt from personal taxation themselves, and could claim reduced rates of taxes and conscription for their tenants. In the 1570s the titled ranks of count and baron were introduced, endowed with lands to support their titles over which they had some powers of jurisdiction. They became the leading group within a relatively small and compact nobility. The nobility attended the Diet in person and asserted a degree of pre-eminence for their Estate. The Estate of the Clergy consisted of the bishops and elected representatives from each diocese, and claimed to act as a general consistory for the church. The Estate of Burghers consisted of elected representatives from each of the chartered towns. Most of these settlements were in reality large villages endowed with exclusive trading rights over the produce of their hinterlands. Stockholm was the only town with any substantial commercial activity, and all the towns were aware of their dependence on the royal power that had created them. Finally there was the unusual survival in Sweden of an Estate of Peasants. All Swedish peasant farmers were legally free men, with access to the royal justice, but fell into three groups. The tenants of the nobility with their tax exemptions comprised about one-third, and they were not represented in the Estate; their lords were held to speak for them. The remainder were tenants of the crown, owing taxes and services, and containing an elite group, the tax peasants, who enjoyed security of tenure and hereditary leases provided they paid the taxes assigned to their farms. They were in effect freeholders; the other crown tenants were tenants at will. Peasant society was organized in groups of parishes constituting the legal district of the hundred. The hundred was governed by the regular sessions of the hundred court, where a royal presiding officer sat with a local jury and disposed of criminal and civil cases, and also acted as a local administration. The ecclesiastical parishes were governed in the same way; the priest, usually elected by the parishioners, worked with a parish council and dealt with all aspects of religious life in its community. It was the hundred court which elected the peasant representatives to the Diet. This meant that in Swedish society there was a high level of local popular self-government, and direct access to decision-making centrally through the Diet meetings. These worked to a written agenda, determined beforehand by the king and the Council, but also provided for each Estate to present grievances to the crown for adjudication and redress.

In 1600 the system had been destabilized by the dynastic dispute caused by the election of the direct Vasa heir Sigismund as king of Poland, where he converted to Catholicism. On his accession to the Swedish crown, his uncle Charles had led a resistance on confessional grounds, which split the nobility. Charles reinforced his position by populist appeals to the commoner Estates in the Diet and in 1600, after a show trial before the Diet, had the leading opposition nobles executed. He moved from regent to king as Charles IX, but was left facing a resentful noble opposition at home, and a war with Poland across the Baltic, which was not going well. When he died in 1611 there was a new war with Denmark, which had started badly.

The new king, Charles's son, was Gustav II Adolf, and was an able, ambitious and unusually well-educated man, who possessed a powerful personal charisma. He entered into a lifelong partnership with the leading opposition magnate, Axel Oxenstierna, who was equally gifted. They began with a charter of privileges to the nobility in 1611, confirming to them exemption from personal taxation, trial by their peers, legal safeguards on noble lands, which could not be sold to commoners, and preferred access to higher public offices with assured salaries. The Council was reinstated as the central decision-making body under the crown. In 1617 the nobility were formally incorporated as an Estate in the Diet. They were organized in three distinct classes, the titled counts and barons, other noble families whose members had served on the Council, and the untitled nobility. They were to constitute a House of Nobility, and though the crown retained freedom to create new nobles, such grants now had to be accepted and registered in the House of Nobility before they took legal effect. In Diet proceedings, the nobility would vote by class, and since two classes constituted a majority, the predominance of the higher nobility over the untitled was assured.

The working partnership of crown and nobility set about a range of reforms. As a measure of centralization two new appeal courts were established, with a mixture of nobles and commoners, to supervise and standardize the work of the hundred courts. The senior high court in Stockholm became a collegiate ministry of justice. Oxenstierna himself, as Chancellor, headed the royal secretariat and also acted as foreign minister. The chancery was also developed into a collegiate ministry at the centre of government. The development of a strong central administration was completed by the development of the Chamber as the central ministry of finance, and two colleges for war and the admiralty. These ministries were directed by magnate officials and coordinated by the royal secretaries in the chancery, who issued the documents implementing policy decisions, and by the Council, which had its representative in each ministerial college. The lower levels were staffed by full-time, salaried professional administrators. It remained to link the central government to the localities, and this was done at the hundred level by making the presidents of the hundred courts trained lawyers appointed by the government, and then by a network of provincial governors. These were senior and experienced administrators, not natives of their provinces, with broad authority to supervise all governmental activity there. They were strictly answerable to the crown and were salaried public servants.

The reinvigorated government raised new taxes through the Diet, reorganized the armed forces and equipped and trained them in the new military arts. This army was not a crown contract army, but a professional force led by native noblemen and recruited from the native population by a regular system of conscriptions authorized by the Diets. It was the professionalism and morale of the new forces that lay behind the remarkable successes of Sweden in the Thirty Years War. A further factor was the development of a native armaments industry. Sweden was a major producer of iron and had the largest copper deposits in Europe. A combination of Dutch entrepreneurial skills and capital and German mining technicians upgraded Sweden's extractive industries, and developed processing plants and manufacturing facilities which supplied the army with standardized equipment.

The war effort, continuous from 1611 to 1648, was grounded on a basic national consensus. Policies were debated in Council and the major decisions, like that to go into Germany, were put before the Diet for approval. Naturally the tax demands were never popular, but they were based on formal consent and legal process, and mitigated by the consistent policy of making foreigners contribute much of the costs of war. The levels of war taxation actually fell in Sweden after 1632. The drain of repeated conscriptions was certainly resisted by evasion and desertion, and the heavy drain on young manpower in the countryside has been shown to have caused measurable depopulation. But again, the conscription was based on law and custom, and the consensus meant there was no serious resistance from the general population. The real triumph of the system was how it survived the king's death in 1632 and the 12-year regency for the child Christina until 1644. Oxenstierna formalized the reformed government system in the Form of Government, presented to the Diet in 1634 and alleged to have been approved by Gustav Adolf before his death. This emphasized the role of the high nobility in the regency government, vested in the great officers and the Council, and in effect placed the government in the hands of a tight inner group of some 30 magnate families, linked by increasing inter-marriage. It did maintain coherence, though naturally there were internal differences over specific lines of policy and the share-out of patronage. Yet the regency period showed the restraint of the oligarchy, which had an open opportunity while the direct power of the monarchy was suspended. There was little evidence of blatant corruption, while the regency emphasized the respect due to the concept of royal authority. There was no attempt to make constitutional changes to reduce royal authority, unless the Form of Government itself be seen as such. It was almost always justified as a temporary arrangement for the period until the new sovereign was able to take up her functions.[4] In 1644, Christina was recognized as exercising the full traditional powers of the crown, and had no problems asserting her will, for example over securing a negotiated peace quickly, against the views of Oxenstierna and the Council.

The Peace of Westphalia brutally demonstrated how Sweden's international pretentions had depended on subsidization by war contributions and foreign subsidy from her allies, both of which ceased. It had been a policy of Oxenstierna, with the king's approval, to use the crown lands to reward public servants. Much of their revenue consisted of peasant produce, not cash, and although they could not be legally alienated in perpetuity, they could be leased for the lifetime of a reigning sovereign. This had been done and Oxenstierna had intended to find new, modern cash revenues, hopefully from customs and excises, to replace the lost income. In Christina's last years, with financial crisis pressing, the rate of dispersal increased until by the 1650s the point was being reached where most of the desirable properties had been leased out, exclusively to members of the nobility. The commoner Estates in the Diet had always protested at the policy, since it was their taxes that rose to fill the revenue gap created. Furthermore, the peasants on royal properties granted out to the nobility feared their new landlords would seek to undermine their tenurial conditions and even, in the longer term, reduce them to serfdom. At least their delegates in the Diet repeatedly said as much.

When the Diet met in 1650 to consider the financial crisis, there was a remarkable joint initiative by the three commoner Estates (a *reduktion*) suggesting that the grants of crown land be resumed and their own burdens relieved. The initiative was a petition to the queen to act, and any suggestion that the Estates were presuming to dictate policy was specifically denied. In fact this reveals the underlying strength of the absolutist concept, since the Swedish commoners, who were showing a quite unprecedent level of political consciousness, could only envisage a remedy coming from the absolute ruler exercising her sovereign powers. They certainly had no concept of taking up those powers themselves.The nobility were naturally outraged at what they saw as a blatant attack on their rights. The queen, who was already considering the possibility of abdication, simply used the initiative to improve her own freedom of manoeuvre. The succession crisis was resolved in 1654 by the queen's abdicating in favour of her cousin, who became king as Charles X Gustav. But part of the settlement was a gesture of appeasement to the commoners, by agreeing to implement a partial resumption of grants up to one quarter. The immediate fiscal problem was little affected, the oligarchy did not press the resumption policy with any urgency, and a solution was sought in renewed imperialist expansion leading to the wars of 1655–60. Although these brought significant territorial gains from Denmark, they failed completely in Poland and demonstrated a second time that without foreign support Sweden did not have the resources to sustain a prolonged war on several fronts. When the death of Charles X brought a new, prolonged regency for the five-year-old Charles XI, it was vested in the queen-mother and the great officers of the realm, all of them members of the oligarchy.

The debates in the Diet of 1660 revealed the growing unwillingness of the commoner Estates to leave power in the hands of the oligarchs. The Form of Government was re-introduced and modified. The regents must seek the approval of the Council for policy decisions, and then in turn be answerable to the Estates. The Diet should meet at least every three years, and had to approve appointments to the higher offices. It was perhaps more significant that, in response to commoner demands, it was specified that the Form of

Government applied only during the regency, and that when the king came of age he would exercise the full royal sovereignty. The fear that the oligarchs might abuse the regency to extend their own power and influence was openly expressed. It was further shown in the demand for a strict state budget to be established and supervised by the Diet. It was strongly asserted that no alienation of crown properties could legally take place under a regency.

At the head of the regency government was the richest magnate in Sweden, Count Magnus de la Gardie, who was Chancellor. The declared policy, set out in 1661 by the magnate treasurer, G. Bonde, was to avoid further military involvements and achieve a steady state balanced budget, so that the kingdom could become truly independent. This aim was never achieved, and the failure was bitterly criticized in the two Diets of 1664 and 1668. The reality was that the budget could not be balanced unless the oligarchs and their clients had been willing to sacrifice some of their own financial privileges. The situation came to a head in the Diet of 1672, which was to declare the king of age and authorize his coronation oath. The commoner Estates were neurotically suspicious of oligarch designs to limit the royal authority for the future, and it was now apparent that the nobility itself was divided. There was a rising generation who had attached themselves to the young king and hoped to displace the influence of de la Gardie, but equally there was a growing anti-oligarch faction among the untitled nobility, who complained that they were excluded from public offices, and demanded that in future appointments should be made on merit, disregarding social status. There was a faction among the oligarchs that had hoped to modify the coronation oath and subject the new king to the obligatory supervision of the Council, but the opposition in the Diet made this impossible. There was an impressive consensus, stretching into the nobility, to restore unfettered royal authority, and this was done. The Estates in the Diet showed no interest in the possibility of extending their own participation in government, only in ensuring the oligarchy's power should end.

After 1672, de la Gardie continued to direct policy under the young king, who was still too inexperienced and immature to impose his own policy. The intractable financial problem remained, and an escape was sought through a subsidy agreement with Louis XIV as part of his preparations for the Dutch war. Sweden would mobilize a force in Pomerania to intimidate the north German princes into non-intervention. De la Gardie had gambled on being able to avoid actual military intervention and lost. In 1675 Sweden was at war against a coalition extending from the Emperor to the United Provinces. All Sweden's German territories were overrun, while Denmark launched an invasion to recover Skåne. For Sweden the war was a disaster. Dutch naval power swept the Swedish navy from the seas, and though, after the battle of Lund in December 1676, the Swedish army led by Charles XI in person steadily drove out the Danish invaders, the peace in 1679, with only marginal losses of territory in Germany, was imposed by Louis XIV, who demanded a restoration of the status quo in north Germany.

The war was a decisive experience for Charles XI. He had established his personal prestige as a successful warrior king, but was deeply humiliated by the outcome and determined it would not be repeated. He would make Sweden powerful enough to stand on its own in international affairs. Johan Gyllenstierna, who became Charles XI's chief minister during the war, had almost certainly converted the king to a plan of post-war reconstruction.[5] In the two wartime Diets, the commoner Estates and nobles like Gyllenstierna had openly blamed the oligarchy for Sweden's weakness, accused them of misusing public funds and demanded restitution. They also demanded that the resumption of crown lands be extended. The king and his advisers proposed to summon a Diet and use it to enact a programme of financial reforms based on these demands. When the Diet met in October 1680, the king simply indicated to the Estates the urgent need to rebuild the kingdom's defensive capacity and ensure it was adequately and reliably funded in future. It needed no pressure from the king to establish an enquiry into the alleged misconduct of the regency government. The Estates readily agreed to establish a tribunal to assess its guilt and impose financial restitution, since this would involve only the oligarchs themselves, or their heirs, and would relieve the fiscal demands on everyone else. It also threw the oligarchs on the mercy of the king, who alone could, if he chose, mitigate their penalties.

This probably inhibited them from any vigorous resistance, either in the Council or the House of the Nobility, to the tribunal, or the following proposal for a comprehensive resumption of alienated crown lands. This demand might have produced a united resistance among the nobility, since the sacrifice would fall entirely on them. But attempts to rally resistance in defence of the rights of their Estate failed when the king's spokesman Admiral Wachtmeister moved an amendment that small beneficiaries should be allowed to retain their grants. This broke the nobles' united resistance and the resumption was approved by all four Estates. Then, as the session ended, it became apparent that the retribution on the regency magnates was to be extended to the Council as well. The threatened Council members alleged that the Council, as an established constitutional body, could not be called to account for its actions. The king then demanded that the Diet clarify the status of the Council and this produced the Declaration of the Estates which was registered as a binding resolution. It started by asserting: 'Your Royal Majesty, as an adult king who rules the kingdom according to law and lawful custom, as your own hereditary kingdom granted by God, is solely responsible to God for your actions.'

It went on to deny that there were any constitutional restraints on the discretion of the king, and that the Council had no autonomous authority and its advice was not binding on the king, who consulted it as he saw fit. As far as the evidence goes it seems likely that this public definition of royal absolutism represents an overwhelming contemporary consensus. The implications were spelled out in subsequent Diets. In 1682 it was established that the absolute royal power included the right to declare law without needing to seek confirmation in the Diet, and the absolute right to dispose of the crown lands, either by granting or recalling grants, which made limitation of the resumption agreed in 1680 invalid. In 1686 the Diet agreed to allow a partial repudiation of the crown's debts, using such dubious techniques as a retrospective reduction of interest. All this was argued to follow logically from the basic recognition of the king's sovereign rights, sanctioned by God.

The new powers were put to use for a major reconstruction of almost all the institutions of the kingdom. The basis for all the rest was the recovery of financial self-sufficiency. Already in 1680 the king had set up a budget office, where every year the state budget was drafted, approved personally by the king, and then enforced. The system used was to identify all the standing charges of the government, and then assign to each one a specific revenue source. The resources came from the recovered crown lands, and the whole of the rest of the reign saw a relentless campaign, led by the royal officials, to track down and reclaim more properties. On the king's death, when the process was still going on, the nobility had surrendered nearly half their lands. It was a formidable administrative challenge to complete this process, but at the Diet of 1693 the king claimed the budget was now balanced and fixed, and it is probable the claim was true. In addition funds had been found for substantial reductions of the public debt.

Then there was radical reform of the armed forces. This was funded out of the recovered revenues, guaranteeing housing and a reliable salary payment for the officers and the cavalry troops. For the infantry a territorial system was adopted. The peasants in each province contracted with the king to recruit and, in peacetime, to house and clothe a specified number of infantry soldiers, who were to be ready for instant service. In return, the old burden of conscription was abolished. The system was made to work by careful planning and constant royal supervision. The men could be regularly trained, and yet live as civilians in their villages and contribute productive labour. The king had solved the problem of how to sustain a standing army of some 60,000 professional soldiers at an expense the community could afford. The navy was reorganized on similar principles, and established in a new, purpose-built naval base at Karlskrona.

The government machinery was distinguished by its professionalism. The crown officials were trained and qualified men who, once the budget was got under control, were regularly paid. They worked under the close personal direction of the king. Charles XI was a pious and dedicated ruler, unimaginative, contemptuous of display and ceremonial and a workaholic, who inspired little affection but a good deal of respect. He had a strong sense of equity: he expected all subjects to perform their respective duties but also upheld their rights. While quite unsentimental about the common people, he defended their right to be heard and informed. At Diet meetings, the royal officials would present reports on their work and justifications of royal policy. Despite Charles's strong assertions that kings were not answerable to anyone but God, he behaved as though subjects should be informed. The bureaucracy managed to process the flow of petitions which came up from the subjects and which were always given an official response. The king defended the rights of parishioners to have a voice in choosing their priest, and could be harsh on royal officials, or officers in the army who were caught abusing or oppressing their inferiors.

Swedish absolutism functioned with a very low level of coercion. There were only a handful of political prisoners, no political executions, and an almost complete absence of popular protest. Various factors helped to produce acceptance. Sweden enjoyed confessional uniformity: except along its eastern border, the Lutheran Church was unchallenged. Its institutions were overhauled in the church law of 1686, which lasted unchanged into the nineteenth century. The law represented the king's most typical administrative form, the issue of a rule-book for the clergy and laity throughout the kingdom. The church both provided religious services and acted as a government agency. It controlled all education and was supposed to ensure that all its parishioners were basically literate; it operated the censorship; and the parish clergy were the chief communicators between crown and subject. They disseminated government information and collected vital statistical information on population and the economic state of their parishes. The parish priest would also be the voice of the common man, helping to draft petitions and see that they were transmitted through the official channels. The Lutheran clergy had always preached a doctrine of submission to lawful authority; they had captive audiences and a monopoly of communication. They were also deeply aware how much their status in society depended on the willingness of the crown to uphold it, for there were plenty of laymen who questioned whether they were getting value for money, while the nobility would have liked to extend their influence over church patronage.

Perhaps the most remarkable feature of the absolutism was how it held the loyalty of the nobility in face of policies that, in effect, confiscated much of what they had come to regard as their landed property. After 1680 most of the old oligarchy adapted to the system and returned to some form of public service. A man like Bengt Oxenstierna, a major sufferer from the resumption served Charles XI as Chancellor and foreign minister. For the nobility in general, the system offered compensations by providing steady paid employment in military and civil service. The wealth that was taken from them through resumption came back in part in salary and was more equitably distributed. The nobility had always been primarily a service nobility and this did not change. But the nobility itself did, in a more egalitarian direction, since it was the king's policy to be generous in creating new titles. When a Table of Ranks was introduced it established a regular career pattern for public servants. Once the qualifiying level was reached, a commoner bureaucrat would be ennobled, and those already noble who worked up the system could expect promotion to titled rank. This process diluted the exclusiveness of the nobility, swelled their numbers, and also promoted social mobility. All this contributed to the stability of the system. However harshly Charles XI treated his nobility, he never failed to sustain their status as the senior Estate in society. By keeping entry open and providing reasonable career prospects, he secured the acceptance of the new regime. It is noteworthy that when, after 1718, the nobility got the opportunity to dismantle the new structure, they made no effort to do so.

Charles XI and his advisers had found a viable answer to the problems that had destabilized Sweden since her precipitous rise to international power in 1648. It depended on becoming a satisfied power, content to defend the status quo. The king had set up a military structure capable of providing adequate defence at a cost the economy could sustain, and he resisted the powerful temptation to use his new strength to pursue more foreign adventures. He had also defused the dangerous social tensions that had become apparent from 1650, and produced a social balance which most of his subjects could live with, confident that the royal government was committed to maintaining equity between the Estates, and was imposing something like equality of contribution from them all. That was why it proved so widely acceptable.

The Polish–Lithuanian Commonwealth

In the sixteenth century the once powerful Polish monarchy had been steadily transformed into a gentry Commonwealth, with an elected king as its presiding officer. This made it clearly a different kind of society from those of the European core. Polish society had a nobility which recognized no titles except that of prince in Lithuania, and claimed the legal equality of all noblemen. There was no formal register of noble families but entry into the nobility required the formal acceptance of the Diet. Between 1601 and 1764, only 549 such promotions were recognized. In reality there were ways round the restriction for anyone with a plausible claim to the status. One of the easiest was to arrange for a collusive action against the claim of title in the courts and procure a verdict of recognition. Along with formal equality of status, Polish noblemen retained the Slavic custom of partible inheritance which worked against the development of consolidated landed estates. By law the *szlachta* were a legal Estate, each member of which was exempt from personal taxation and could only be prosecuted before a tribunal of fellow nobles. They had the exclusive right to own noble land; were exempt from urban jurisdiction if they lived or traded in towns; and they had full manorial jurisdiction over their peasants, including the right to exact unlimited labour services, all formally established in law.

The Commonwealth had been restructured in 1569, when its two component societies, Poland and Lithuania, converted a purely dynastic union into a formal political union by accepting a joint Diet. Officially it remained a federal union, for each part retained its own laws and separate political identity. But the liberties of the Polish *szlachta* proved attractive to the Lithuanian nobility, and a process of polonization set in, by which Lithuanian culture was steadily assimilated to Polish. The union was ruled through the Diet, consisting of the king, the senate of magnates, the great officers of state and the bishops, and a chamber of deputies consisting of gentry elected by their fellows in local provincial diets, and delegated by their electors. The Diet met every two years for a statutory session lasting six weeks. It was already well established by 1600 that resolutions of a Diet should be voted by unanimity. The king was elected at a special coronation Diet, where every nobleman was entitled to attend and vote and again the final choice required unanimity. On election each new king had to agree to a *pacta conventa*, setting out the conditions on which he would rule. The king was the head of state, and was always accorded the formal respect due to his office. His most important power was that of nomination to the 2500 public offices, many of them sinecures, coveted for the status they conferred. He also had an endowment of crown lands, perhaps one fifth of the kingdom. These rights were constricted by the rule that crown officers, and tenants of the crown estates, which had to be leased out, were appointed for life. The king also commanded the standing forces of the Commonwealth, which he was also expected to maintain out of his revenues. There was the Frontier Guard in the Ukraine, some 4000 strong, to shelter the Commonwealth from Tartar incursions – this was the 'Quarter Army' funded by the hypothecation of a quarter of the crown land revenues – and a 'Crown Army' which in the early seventeenth century had a peacetime establishment of some 12,000 men. These forces were levied on the crown commission model and recruited from mercenary volunteers. Technically, the Polish armed forces had a good reputation, and they regularly defeated the Russians and inflicted some notable defeats on the Swedes. Their heavy cavalry, the Polish Hussar regiments, were especially effective in a theatre of operations that often involved fighting over long distances in thinly settled lands with poor communications.

From the 1560s, Poland had established religious toleration, since the Reformation had left it a confessional confusion. The majority faith remained Roman Catholicism, but most urban communities were Lutheran, many of the nobles were Calvinist, and Poland had communities of a heretical sect, the Arians, while to the east there were Orthodox congregations, and in the Ukraine the distinctive Uniate Church – Orthodox in ritual, but recognizing the supremacy of the pope. The Catholic Church was established, a major landowner with some 14 per cent of the total, and its bishops sat in the senate. It had taken up the Counter-Reformation doctrines of the Council of Trent and was steadily regaining lost ground by 1600. Poland was one of the most successful regions of Jesuit missionary work and their network of colleges provided most of the education available. After the 1650s the revived Catholic Church was strong enough to begin undermining the toleration, and particularly after the aggressive Swedish invasion of 1655, an assertive Catholicism became part of the culture of Sarmatianism, claiming that Poles and Lithuanians were the descendants of a once-imperial

Sarmation nation. This emphasized their exclusiveness and rejection of western values.

The urban sector of Polish society was small and in steep decline by 1600. The nobility had undermined their powers of self-government and their trading privileges. A handful of cities was entitled to send delegates to the Diet, but they were treated with open contempt by the nobility. The only major, almost autonomous, city was the port of Danzig, centre of the Baltic grain trade. Most Polish towns were large agrarian villages, with recognized local markets. The vast majority of the population were peasant farmers or labourers, living in village communes, which exercised the local self-govern-ment found all over Europe, but although there were groups of free peas-ants, and in the Ukraine free settler communities of peasants and Cossacks, nearly all the rural population were the serfs of noble landlords, bound to the land by law and wholly under seigneurial jurisdiction. The nobility were rather numerous by contemporary standards – it is reckoned at least 7 per cent of the population enjoyed noble status – but their legal equality was not reflected by their social structure. At the lower end were a landless, noble proletariat, driven to find a subsistence as clients of the magnate elite; above them were noble families that farmed their small properties themselves. There were whole villages where all the farmers claimed noble status. The real landed nobility began with those who owned at least one village commune and could exploit the labour of its peasants. Even these seigneurial lords often scraped a bare subsistence and were attracted by the advantages of clientage under the magnates. These latter were the true ruling elite, the 2 per cent of the nobility who owned 75 per cent of all land by 1700. The Zamoisky family, one of the few to maintain an entail for its possessions, had 10 towns, 220 villages, 100 manors and about 100,000 tenants in the eighteenth century. These vast accumulations, mostly launched on the back of the sixteenth-century agrarian upswing, and big enough to survive eco-nomic recession and war devastation, were almost independent republics of their own. The Polish magnates by the eighteenth century were probably among the richest in Europe and controlled the destiny of the Commonwealth through their wealth, their clientage networks, their grip on public offices, and private armies that could rise to 5000 armed retainers.

The history of early modern Poland is usually taken as illustrating the fate of those communities that stubbornly refused to respond to the imperatives of the growing militarization of Europe. This was not how the *szlachta* saw things. They gloried in the 'golden liberties' of the Polish nobility, often openly envied by nobles elsewhere. The centrality in the affairs of the Commonwealth of the Diet proceedings required an exceptional freedom of speech and discussion of public affairs. The Poles recognized the European drive towards the absolutist state as a possible solution of their problems and consciously rejected it. They well understood that a strong monarchy with a standing army spelt the end of the kind of liberty they treasured. So the whole nobility set their face against the development of a strong state.

That was the whole point of the device of the *liberum veto*, the best-known and most criticized feature of early modern Polish history. There is much misconception of its significance and effect.[6] It is true that in the Diet of 1652 a single nobleman successfully claimed that his one dissentient vote nullified the whole legislative work of the session. From that time on the majority of Polish Diets ended without completing any business. Outside observers saw it as suicidal self-indulgence, deliberate promotion of anarchy and political insanity. The Poles themselves saw it as proof of the sanctity of their liberties. The veto made almost any reform programme impossible, but that was precisely what it was meant to do. A Diet member remarked in 1669: 'there can be no novel measures introduced in the Commonwealth without danger and great disturbance'. The nobility valued their ability to block any attempt to bring them under some external authority. They were contemptuous of the other European nobilities that submitted to absolutism; they flaunted their Sarmatian culture, refusing to adopt western costume and clinging to their distinctive oriental style of dress. But the Polish nobility were neither blind nor insane. They were aware of the negative consequences of the veto and devised means to get round them. When a Diet failed it was constitutional for any group of nobles to form a confederation, in which they could unite in support of some specific programme. Confederations operated majority voting. If they got enough support they could prevail and overrule a Diet decision or, more often, a Diet refusal to decide. The critics were of course right in the long run: the Commonwealth eventually came to grief in the partitions. But they saw that danger too, and decided it was a risk they could live with in order to preserve their liberties.

Basically, the history of early modern Poland is the record of repeated attempts by the kings to push Poland along the road to authoritarian government, of the success of the magnates and their clients in preventing this, and of the price the Commonwealth paid at the hands of external predators. The first Vasa king, Sigismund III, started the cycle. He was both a modernizing absolutist and a zealous, counter-reform Catholic, who was resisted by the gentry for involving Poland in his dynastic ambitions in Sweden, and by the Protestants for his confessional aggression. On the strength of his striking victory over Sweden at Kirkholm in 1606, Sigismund proposed that majority voting be adopted for the Diet and an enlarged standing army be secured by perpetual taxation. There was an armed confederation formed in protest, which the king managed to defeat. But when in 1611 he put his programme to the Diet, it was rejected. Even so, the reign saw a general eastward drive by Polish magnate landlords into the largely unsettled territories of the Ukraine. They were helped by Poland's clear military superiority over the Russians, which enabled them, by 1618, to seize much of White Russia, including the city of Smolensk. Gradually the frontier zone, thinly settled by free colonists and Cossack mercenaries, was brought under landlord control, against the resistance of the largely Orthodox population, which Sigismund tried to force into the Uniate Church.

His son secured election in 1632 as Ladislas IV. He was a pragmatic conciliator and he was ready to revert to religious toleration. Frustrated in his desire to enlist Poland in his claims on the Swedish crown, he turned to the Ukraine, where he promoted schemes to compromise with the Cossack settlers by agreeing to enlist some of them into the frontier defence force. But his many attempts to embark on military enterprises, either against Sweden or Russia, were blocked by the refusals of Diets to fund them. His last venture, before his death in 1647, was based on enlisting Cossack support for an attack on the Ottomans. During the interregnum after his death, the Ukrainian Cossacks and serfs found a leader in a Ukrainian nobleman, Bogdan Chmielnitsky, who saw the opportunity and persuaded the Tartars to join in a massive, anti-landlord rampage into Poland. The Polish forces were swept aside and the new king, John Casimir, was plunged into prolonged border warfare. In 1654 Chmielnitsky turned to the tsar and offered him the allegiance of the Ukraine, which was accepted. There was a renewed Polish–Russian war in which Smolensk was soon lost, followed in 1655 by the Swedish invasion. After the Swedes left in 1660, John Casimir attempted a counter-attack on Russia, but was forced into a new treaty with Russia in 1667, in which Smolensk returned to the Russians and the Ukraine was divided along the Dnieper, with the tsar taking the east. The following year, John Casimir, finding the Diet obdurate in its refusal to consider constitutional reform, abdicated.

The period between 1648 and 1667, which some contemporaries called 'the deluge', was a major factor in Poland's decline as an independent participant in the international power struggle, and its transformation into a victim of the armed predators who surrounded her territories. The economy had suffered serious structural damage after 20 years of continuous warfare, mostly fought over Polish territory. It has been estimated that the population fell by a quarter. The Baltic grain trade was shrinking and the Polish economy went into prolonged recession. Since it experienced a further round of devastating war from 1700 to 1721, economic recovery was long delayed. The ruling elites were clear that any positive structural change in Poland could only occur at the expense of their own status, and that was a price they knowingly refused to pay. In the context of a weak monarchy, a handful of magnate families competed for power and showed no compunction about inviting foreign powers to intervene and assist them.

National resentment of their country's humiliations at the hands of foreigners had led the lesser nobility, at the election of 1668, to choose a native magnate, Michael Wisniowiecki, for king. He was continually harassed by magnate factions subsidized by Louis XIV, and his brief reign climaxed in a disastrous war against the Cossacks and the Ottomans. In 1673, the magnate Jan Sobieski won a major military success at Xotin over the invaders. In the election Diet of 1674, Sobieski was the native candidate and won. Sobieski's priority was to make the crown hereditary in his own family. In search of new military triumphs he persuaded the Diet to authorize a crusade against the Ottomans, which led him into an alliance with the Habsburgs, and Poland's last appearance as an independent force in Europe. Sobieski led the international army that relieved Vienna in 1683. But his domestic position was consistently undermined by magnate intrigue, encouraged by Louis XIV, which meant that, after 1685 until the end of the reign in 1697, five of the seven Diets were blocked by factions in alliance with the French. Sobieski's lack of domestic support forced him to conclude a definitive peace with Russia in 1686, confirming the loss of Smolensk and eastern Ukraine, as an inducement to the tsar to enter the Turkish war.

At the election Diet of 1697 there was a straight power struggle between a French candidate and a Habsburg client, Augustus II of Saxony, who, in consequence of quick military intervention after a dubious election process, secured the crown. He had a clear design to make the crown hereditary, intending to use professional Saxon troops to intimidate opposition. He was quite prepared if necessary to trade parts of the territory of the Commonwealth to purchase foreign acceptance. To win domestic support he planned, in collusion with Denmark and Russia, to attack and annex Sweden's provinces of Livonia and Estonia. This aggression precipitated the Great Northern War of 1700–21, in which Poland became a helpless victim in a foreign power struggle.

The failure of the attack on Charles XII and his devastating counter-attack into Poland with the aim of deposing Augustus succeeded in 1703. A new coronation Diet under Swedish protection declared Augustus deposed. But when Charles XII insisted on the election of his puppet king Stanislas Lesczynski, the magnates split, and in 1704 there was a confederation to reinstate Augustus under strict conditions, which he had no choice but to accept. But the confederation also secured the military and political support of Peter the Great, precipitating a bitter civil war between the confederates and the adherents of Charles XII. This was resolved by the Swedish disaster at Poltava in 1709, after which Augustus was invited back under Russian protection. But all attempts to institute reforms and give the Commonwealth a stronger military capability fell before internal resistance. In 1713 Augustus again brought in Saxon troops to reinforce his authority, but a powerful resistance, supported by Peter, ensured his failure. At a Diet in 1717, under heavy Russian pressure, the Saxon intervention was ended. Reform was still debated among some of the noble factions, but nothing enacted. The prevailing mood among the *szlachta* was expressed in 1699 when the magnate Stanislas Lubomirski published *De Vanitate Conciliorum*. This accepted that major structural reform was impossible and advocated a strong defence of the existing system, leaving the longer-term outcome to divine providence. Some Poles found compensation in the promotion of the Sarmatian ideals, stressing Poland's distinctive native culture, and taking out their frustrations by new measures of persecution against the surviving confessional minorities. In 1718–20 there was a last effort, inspired by an anti-Russian coalition, to strengthen the position of Augustus and establish a barrier against further

Russian interference in the west. This was firmly and finally defeated after Peter and Frederick William of Prussia agreed in 1720 that their best interests would be served, not by exploiting Poland's weakness for territorial gain, but by maintaining that weakness indefinitely, by joint action to preserve the Polish constitution unchanged. Partition was postponed for a further 50 years, while Poland survived, in effect, as a Russian protectorate. The era of relative peace and stability that followed, in combination with the general change of political mood in eighteenth-century Europe and a return of economic expansion after 1750, generated a new drive to modernize the Commonwealth. When that seemed to be likely to produce real change, it was crushed by the partitions.

Russia

It is a fact of European history, painfully being re-learned since 1989, that Russia is different. Since the fifteenth century, when the grand princes of Moscow at last secured independence from the Tartars, there had been trade and other relations between Moscow and western Europe, but Russia was cut off by the religious barrier of its adherence to the Orthodox faith. Both sides of the divide regarded the other as dangerous and heretical schismatics. This strengthened after the fall of Constantinople and the subsequent conquests of the Ottoman sultans, leaving Russia as the only surviving independent Orthodox community in the world. Church and people combined in accepting the concept of 'the Third Rome'. Holy Russia was the providential guardian of the true faith, with the duty of keeping it untarnished until the Second Coming. Hence all external influences were regarded as potentially subversive and were rigidly excluded.

The grand prince or tsar of Moscow and all the Russias maintained his authority by practices derived from the Mongol conquest. He was a truly absolute ruler, vested with unlimited authority to rule his lands and their inhabitants, whatever their rank, as he saw fit. All the tsar's subjects, even the very highest, accepted being called his 'slaves'. Clearly the system was very different from the feudal monarchy, with its devolution of authority, that had developed in the west. In reality there had to be power-sharing, first with an exclusive, hereditary caste of nobles, the *boyars*, whose chiefs carried the title of 'prince' and were mostly related to the ruling family. They were recognized as the customary advisers of the tsar and sat in the council of *boyars* (the *duma*) which was the principal agency of the executive government. They formed a very exclusive group, ranked according to a complex set of precedence rules, the *miestnichestvo*, regulating entitlements to offices. The *boyars* also possessed hereditary family esates, making them considerable landowners. Below them the tsars created a rank of servitors, principally for military service on horseback, who were rewarded with grants of land, *pomestie*, which were strictly tied to the performance of public service. Within this class of servitors a division had opened between

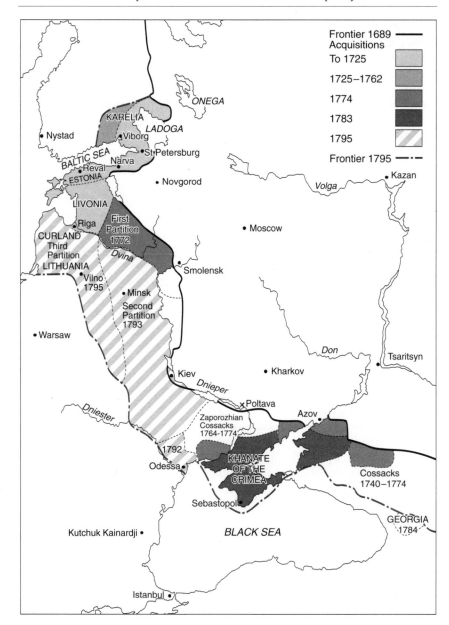

Map 7.2 The Russian empire 1689–1795

the Moscow servitors, who because of their proximity to the ruler had the best choice of appointments, and the provincial servitors, who constituted the cavalry which was the backbone of Russian armies, and survived on smaller grants of land. The provincials were bitterly resentful of the preferences enjoyed by the Moscow elite. There was also a system of bureaucratic departments in Moscow, the *prikazi*, which had grown on an ad hoc basis to meet particular administrative needs. They handled the paper work and record-keeping for the government and were staffed by officials, mainly recruited from the Moscow service gentry, who were full time salaried administrators. The other governing institution was the church, ruled by its patriarch, who although he acknowledged his subordination to the autocrat, following the Byzantine tradition, had some of the characteristics of a co-ruler with the tsar, since the Orthodox Church was the visible symbol of the identity of Russian society.

The total dependence of society on the authority of the tsar was painfully demonstrated by the crisis known as the 'time of troubles', caused by a combination of dynastic failure and a dire economic crisis caused by bad harvests and epidemics. By 1600 different factions among the leading *boyar* families were promoting a variety of dubious claimants, supposed to be lawful heirs, and two major foreign candidates, both Vasas, one Polish, one Swedish. It was the urge to block the foreigners that enabled the patriarch, with a broad popular following, to build a force strong enough to expel the Poles from Moscow, and in 1613 call an Assembly of the Land, *zemsky sobor*, which in theory represented all levels of society, and which recognized Michael Romanov as tsar. It is to be noted that they did not elect him;[7] the whole concept of subjects usurping the right of God to determine who should rule was alien to Russian tradition. The Russian historian Klyuchevsky commented: 'to elect a tsar was to their minds as incongruous as to elect one's father or mother'. Michael was recognized as being by descent the divinely chosen ruler, with the same unrestricted power as his predecessors.

Michael Romanov is generally written off as a weak ruler, and it took time to stabilize his authority. The disappointed Swedish and Polish claimants had to be bought off, the Swedes at Stolbova in 1617, the Poles in 1619 by the surrender of Smolensk. This last secured the release from captivity of the tsar's father, the Patriarch Filaret, who until his death was the actual head of government.

The restored monarchy faced two major problems: the peasant problem and the military inferiority of Russia to its western neighbours. As late as the fifteenth century the Russian peasantry had been free tenant farmers either of the lay landowners, the church or the crown. By 1600 most of them had become serfs, tied to the land and subject to the seigneurial control of the landlords. Economic insecurities, leading to peasant indebtedness, and also putting pressure on landlords to maximize their returns, had inexorably eroded their liberties, and the tsar had no choice but to support the landowners, for they could only render their service to his regime if they had the labour necessary to maintain their estates. A further important factor was Russian territorial expansion. In the sixteenth century the southern border, exposed to Tartar raiding, had been secured by establishing a military frontier of soldier-settlers, an attractive alternative to hard-pressed peasants in the interior. Beyond that were the open lands of the Ukraine, with the possibility of peasant escape to join the free Cossack communities. On top of this, the Russian eastward drive into Siberia was under way; indeed the first pioneers reached the Pacific shore in the 1650s and came up to the Chinese border along the Amur river in the 1660s. The government in Moscow encouraged the pioneering movement, and serfs who escaped into Siberia to join it were usually left undisturbed by the authorities. When the population losses of the 'time of troubles' are added, there was a severe labour shortage, such that the landlord class practised kidnapping serf labour from one another, and naturally the poor provincial servitors were vulnerable to the aggression of Moscow-based *boyars* and service gentry. Something had to be done to stabilize the rural labour force.

The military problem was one of technical obsolescence. Russian forces consisted of the *streltsi*, a militia of musketeers some 60,000 strong, normally distributed as garrisons in the principal towns, where they were permitted to pursue secondary livings as artisans, much like the contemporary Turkish Janissaries. Over time they had developed into a conservative, hereditary caste, whose military skills fell behind the new standards of western warfare. The other component was the cavalry force made up of state servitors, and called out as needed for campaigns. They were both struggling economically, finding it difficult to meet their obligations, essentially amateur, and again falling behind western standards. These forces had suffered repeated defeats at the hands of the Poles and the Swedes. The tsar and the *boyars* came to see that something must be done, and once Michael was established, with some reluctance, the government began to hire foreign mercenary officers to raise western-style regiments. It was done reluctantly because these heretical aliens threatened the purity of Orthodox culture, and they were joined by others, mainly Dutch entrepreneurs, called in to develop a modernized armaments industry. The main Russian military–industrial complex at Tula, near the Urals iron-ore fields, was started up in this way. This demonstrates a very characteristic process, whereby the military imperative forces backward societies to modernize or perish, however distasteful this may be to their native culture. The first experiment was a disappointment; the new regiments constituted most of the army that tried to recover Smolensk from the Poles in 1633–4 and were defeated. For a time the process was halted, but then soon resumed. By the 1680s, nearly 80 per cent of the Russian military establishment consisted of western-type regiments, and the foreign officers were being replaced by natives. The provincial servitors were increasingly ordered to do their service in the new regiments, and the making of new *pomestie* land grants virtually ceased. This in turn brought with it the need for central government to raise new tax revenues to fund its expensive military habits.

The consequences soon showed. Michael died in 1645 and was succeeded by his son, Alexis. Alexis proved a more politically active ruler, was reasonably well educated and had some familiarity with western culture. Though sharing the native conservatism, he was not neurotically opposed to adopting western technologies. In his early years he was guided by his tutor, Morozov, and court faction flourished, while dubious projectors offered revenue-raising schemes. It was one of these, for a salt tax, that inspired a serious revolt in Moscow in 1648, where the urban taxpayers, the *streltsi*, who were becoming conscious that their services were less in demand, and servitors struggling with the labour shortage, ran amok in the capital. It was noticeable that they followed the contemporary practice of blaming their grievances on evil councillors, not on the tsar himself, but his efforts to pacify the rioters failed until he permitted them to lynch some of the alleged villains. In order to rally the servitors, he agreed to the calling of a *zemsky sobor* and authorized it to revise the laws. Little is known about how this was done, except it was a rushed process, and in 1649 the *zemsky sobor* adopted the revised code, the *Ulozhenie*. The main provisions of the code were aimed to tie the peasants to the land. All peasants were now subject to taxation and placed under the jurisdiction of their landlords, who became responsible for tax collection. The seigneurial jurisdiction of the landlords was confirmed, with no limits set on the demands they could make. Above all, flight was criminalized, and fugitive serfs could be pursued and recovered by their masters without limit of time. It was a clear instance of the sovereign and his ruling elites combining to maximize their exploitation of the unprivileged majority. Similar measures were included to tie down the urban taxpayer. The code also stressed the unlimited authority of the tsar, threatening severe penalties for any kind of disobedience, and made a significant incursion into the autonomy of the church by establishing a new government department to supervise and intervene in its affairs.

The events of 1648–9 seem to have determined Alexis to assert himself. He responded to the Cossack appeals to take up the protection of the Ukrainian Cossacks against the Poles, and in 1653 another *zemsky sobor* was called to ratify this. The measure was consistent with the growing interest of Alexis in asserting that Moscow was the natural protector of all Orthodox communities, the seed of future pan-Slavism. He also set about reinvigorating the church in partnership with the Patriarch Nikon. This proved to be a disastrous error. Both Alexis and Nikon, while strong traditionalists, were open to useful ideas from outside. One source in religious matters came through Kiev, a centre of Orthodoxy, but with active connections to Poland and the west. This was not Nikon's main inspiration, though both he and the tsar were impressed with aspects of Catholic counter-reform. They recognized a need for a better-educated clergy, and attached more weight to preaching as one of the main duties of the clergy. Nikon wanted to strengthen the claims to universal primacy of the Russian church by bringing it into line with ideas taken from the Greek patriarchate at Constantinople. The importance of printing was appreciated, and Nikon introduced a new printed service book, which incorporated some innovations in church rituals as used in Constantinople.

This was the beginning of the Old Believer schism in the Russian church. The actual alterations were marginal but, as soon as the new rituals appeared, a substantial minority of clergy and laity denounced them as not only heretical but the work of Antichrist, a prelude to the coming of the Apocalypse. Their leader, the archpriest Avvakum, took literally the mission of the Russian church to keep the faith pure and unchanged to the world's end. He wrote:

> Alas poor Russia. What possessed you to seek Latin customs and German practices? … Although I am a foolish and untutored man, I do know that everything handed down to the church by the holy Fathers is pure and holy. I hold it unto death as it was given to me. I change nothing in the eternal truth. It was laid down before our time – let it be so for ever and ever.

The Old Believers denounced Nikon's church as diabolical and formed their own separatist congregations, defying the most brutal repression from church and tsar. Some groups chose mass suicide rather than submit. Nikon and the tsar had offended one of the most cherished beliefs of Russian society – its divine destiny as the bearer of pure Orthodoxy. The schism proved impossible to eradicate and damaged the authority of church and state by its mere survival. It provided a moral justification for defying authority to almost any kind of dissident movement. It was notable how the *streltsi*, an increasingly alienated group, hostile to change, adopted the Old Believer position. It can be argued with some plausibility that once the church lost its ability to represent the whole Orthodox community, it came to be regarded as a tool of an oppressive regime. This was reinforced when Nikon was disgraced by Alexis for defending the autonomy of the church as spiritual leader against the lay power. A deep fracture had opened up in the heart of Russian society.

This manifested itself in another revolt in Moscow in 1662, in protest at a government devaluation of the currency. The *streltsi* of the garrison openly supported the rebels, but this time, unlike 1648, the new army troops were brought in and the rebels crushed. The regime was asserting its grip over its subjects. It did so again in 1667, after the greatest Cossack-peasant rising of the century under a Cossack leader, Stenka Razin, who denounced the new burdens the military state had loaded on the peasantry. It took a major campaign by the new army to save Moscow itself from being threatened, and then to destroy and punish the rebel host.

In the last years of Alexis there were signs that westernizing tendencies were developing in court circles. For a time the *boyar* Ordin-Nastchokin was the leading figure, a promoter of western, mercantilist measures. He made peace with Poland in 1667 as a first step towards a more western-directed foreign policy. He pressed too hard for Alexis and fell from power in 1671. He was succeeded as a westernizer by Prince Golitsyn, who in 1686 took Russia into its first alliance with the west, joining the Habsburg crusade against the Ottomans. He talked about other westernizing measures, but no major domestic reforms resulted. The death of Alexis was followed by a short reign of his eldest son Theodore, and then a new dynastic crisis. Alexis had fathered children from different marriages and in 1682 none was of age, so a regency was established under the Princess Sophia until the most viable of the offspring, Peter, came of age. It may be that Sophia planned to seize the throne herself; if so she was stopped by a court conspiracy in 1689 – an anti-westernizer faction with the help of the Moscow *streltsi* and the patriarch. This was done in the name of young Peter, though it was unlikely he was involved.

The reforms of Peter the Great

Peter did not take on active direction of the government until 1694, and his true assumption of personal control began after his tour of western Europe in 1697. Peter was a freak by any standards. He was the only physically and mentally robust male born to the Romanov dynasty from the death of Alexis until Alexander I. He was entirely Russian in background and remained so throughout his life. His basic attachment to the Orthodox religion never wavered, nor did his drive to end dependency on foreign advisers and technicians. Although famous for his restructuring of the Russian nobility as a service nobility, to be promoted on merit not birth, he retained a belief that the highest posts should, where possible, be preserved for 'distinguished families', the old *boyar* elite. It is difficult to determine whether he had any consistent plans, but it appeared that his basic strategy, whether consciously formed or not, was to adopt western methods, so that Russia could compete on level terms in the European power struggle, while retaining the basic distinguishing values that constituted the Russian identity.[8]

Peter offers one of the most consistent proofs of how European civilization was driven by the military imperative: it drove Peter for his whole life. At the same time he was a consistent pragmatist, willing to try almost anything that promised to produce results. The process began in childhood, when he was left free to consort with the foreign community in Moscow. This was the period when he began personally training his own western-style regiments which later became the guards regiments. He also acquired the very non-Russian passion for naval development. One of his main concerns on his European tour, and during his first active campaign, was to build warships for a drive to reach the Black Sea and take the Ottoman fortress of Azov. The tsar's methods combined a passion for education in the broadest sense with the crudest kind of violence. He sponsored a whole range of educational institutions, in the first instance to teach military skills, but he certainly aspired to spread education among the clergy and even into the general population. It must be said that there was no internal enthusiasm for his schools and most came to nothing. He also pioneered state-sponsored journalism to explain and justify his policies, and one distinctive and characteristic initiative was his orders to the nobility to attend social evenings in 1718: 'a free meeting in a house which encompasses both pleasure and business, where people can meet and converse about all manner of things and learn what is passing around them'. On the other hand was the violence. The most dramatic episode was his suppression of the revolt of the Moscow *streltsi*, almost certainly instigated by conservative forces encouraged by Sophia to block his westernizing policies. Some 700 *streltsi* were publicly executed, with Peter himself wielding the axe on some, after which the surviving *streltsi* were disbanded. Peter assumed that nothing could be achieved without violence in a Russian context. He remarked in 1723, 'was not everything done by force and are not people grateful for what has resulted?', to which the brief answer is no.

All his life he faced the inertial resistance of traditionalists. The Patriarch Adrian, resisting orders to state officials to cut their traditional beards, declared: 'God did not create men beardless, only cats and dogs ... the shaving of beards is not only a foolishness and a dishonour, it is a mortal sin.' The *boyar* Prince Golitsyn, who as governor of Astrakhan was ordered to construct a canal linking the Volga and the Don, said: 'God had made the rivers to go one way, and it was presumption in man to think to turn them in another.' Construction lapsed. Perhaps Peter's most striking use of force came in 1717, when he killed his son and heir Alexis. Peter realized that if Alexis came to the throne he would endeavour to reverse his father's reforms. Peter's lifelong struggle to change basic mentalities failed, except among the elite, who with their shaven faces, western dress and adoption of western social norms showed no strong desire to return to tradition after Peter's death. But among the common people, who saw their tax burdens double between 1700 and 1724, and who were subjected to repeated levies of manpower, not just for the armed forces, but for Peter's economic enterprises and the construction of his new capital at St Petersburg, Peter was the Antichrist. The split that resulted between the world of the elites and the culture of the masses was one of Peter's most lasting achievements, and the resulting alienation between rulers and ruled became a fundamental structural fault built into Russian society, which seems to survive into modern times.

This was not what Peter had envisaged. His proclamation to his army on the eve of the battle of Poltava declared:

> Either Russia will perish, or she will be reborn in nobler shape. And they must not think of themselves as armed and drawn up to fight for Peter, but for the tsardom entrusted to Peter by his birth and by the all-Russian people ... of Peter it should be known that he does not value his own life, but only that Russia should live, and Russian piety, glory and prosperity.

It was Peter who introduced the double oath of allegiance, to the state first, then to the tsar, and insisted the interest of the state was superior to that of the autocrat who was its servant. It was a vision few shared. Pososhkov, an enthusiast for Peter's policies wrote despairingly: 'The great monarch works hard and accomplishes nothing: there are few who help him. The Tsar pulls uphill alone, with the strength of ten, but millions pull downhill. How then shall the work prevail?'

Peter's reign down to the death of Charles XII in 1718 was a period of unremitting warfare. Initially he had envisaged expanding against the Ottomans, but the decision of the Habsburgs to make peace with them in 1699 made the policy unviable. Instead, without much thought as to the consequences, he joined the attack on Sweden planned by Augustus II. To do this the new style army was rapidly enlarged under foreign colonels and engaged in the siege of Narva. In December 1700, Charles and his army of 12,000 attacked the 40,000 besiegers and routed them. Fortunately for Peter, Charles then plunged into his Polish campaigns, giving Peter the chance to reconstruct his army. He devised a new conscription system, launched a series of fiscal experiments involving some 30 new taxes, set about expanding his armaments production, and ordered the service nobles to join the army's ranks. The new forces made steady progress against the local Swedish defenders, and when the invasion came in 1708 Peter had about 100,000 men in his new army uniformed and equipped with modern weapons and largely officered by natives. They could meet the Swedes on level terms, and at the battle of Poltava destroyed the Swedish field army. From then on, Russian armies were technically the equals of – and some think tended to be superior to – those of the other European powers right through the eighteenth century. From 1704 Peter was committed to expansion in the Baltic. He first established a naval base at Kronstadt, then resolved to build an entirely new capital at St Petersburg and developed a Baltic fleet that also proved able to meet the Swedish navy on equal terms.

Over the years, Peter conscripted the whole of society into the support of his military machine. The reconstruction of peasant society was settled with the census of 1724 and the institution of the 'soul tax', set at 70 kopeks a year for every taxpayer, which became the basic Russian revenue until the abolition of serfdom in the nineteenth century. This finally institutionalized serfdom. All taxpayers, rural and urban, were tied to their communities and subjected to the jurisdiction of their social superiors, who were responsible for the payment of taxes, conscriptions and the levies of forced labour.

The counterpart of this was the forced service of the nobility. The key reform here was the Table of Ranks of 1722. There were 14 ranks in all, in the military and civil service. Entry and promotion were based on merit, and officials had equal status: 'whatever their birth, they become the equals of the best and most ancient noble families, and enjoy the same dignity and advantages.' Anyone reaching rank 8, if a commoner, was automatically registered as a hereditary noble. All the nobility were required to serve, and to see that their children were given appropriate education. Service was now salaried, but the former servitors with *pomestie* lands were allowed to retain them. There was an attempt in 1714 to enforce a rule of primogeniture, the aim being to force younger sons into service, but even Peter could not enforce a break with the tradition of partible inheritance. He was constrained to try and enforce the rule of universal service. In 1722 a special college, under the direction of the *Heraldmeister*, took on the task of identifying and registering the noble families and ensuring that all their members entered service. Together with ranks, western titles of nobility were introduced, though the pre-eminence of the old *boyar* families was retained. The Russian nobility were converging with western nobilities except that, under Peter, compulsory service prevented the development of the parasitic nobles, who were a feature of most western societies. In theory those who refused to serve could have been downgraded and lost their lands. It seems probable that under Peter the nobility were heavily burdened. Basically there were not enough of them to service a fully developed system of central administration and officer the armed forces, even though the records suggest that there was a very considerable expansion in the number of noble families between the 1680s and 1730. The result was that much of the actual work of government was devolved on to the elected officials of the village communes and the municipalities, which perhaps facilitated some mitigation of the legal burdens on the taxpaying commoners.

Peter also carried out restructuring of the government machinery. In his early years Peter's restless activism tended to inhibit the development of regular institutional administration. He was an admirer of the Swedish absolutist model, and favoured a system of collegiate governing institutions. The traditional council of state, the *duma* continued to function at least down to 1707, though membership was increasingly confined to working administrators. In 1711 Peter established the Senate, modelled on the Swedish Council, as the central government college. At first it showed that Russians were not culturally adapted to the collegiate way of conducting business – indeed at least one of the early senators was illiterate – and members tended to intrigue against colleagues to gain Peter's favour. But over the years the Senate did settle down as the core administrative body. A policy of rationalizing the governing *prikazi* into modern bureaucratic institutions followed. By 1717 they had been arranged into nine collegiate ministries. But since they were staffed from the old *prikazi*, it appears that in reality much of the old system survived within the framework of the new. As Klyuchevsky remarked, 'the reforms did not prevent Russians doing things in their own way'. To counter this, Peter retained the old Russian system of installing an inspectorate of crown officers, the *fiskals*, inside the governing structures to observe and denounce misconduct. In 1722 he installed a chief inspector in the Senate, the Procurator General, to act as the tsar's personal superviser. This obviously tended to inhibit the development of responsible collective work in the institutions.

Peter was least successful in his attempts to establish a modern system of local administration. The old government system in Moscow had never had much close control outside the environs of the capital. The practice had developed of sending a governor, or *voivode*, out into the provinces as the central government's agent. His remit was vague and no salary attached to the post. He was explicitly permitted to accept gratuities from the people he governed. This was still the basic position in 1700. In 1708 the country was formally divided up into provinces, the *gubernia*, with an officially appointed governor, a prosecutor, and a team of assistants to deal with conscription and tax and grain collection. At first there were 11 provinces; then, in 1718, the system was further elaborated, with the number of *gubernia* raised to 12 and the institution of 50 counties, with one appointed *voivode* per county, and these were sub-divided into districts with an appointed commissar. The officials were all salaried and answerable to the new government colleges and the Senate. To strengthen the local authorities there was provision for the local nobility to elect assessors to work with the appointed officials. It is interesting that this proposal failed everywhere: the local elites had no wish to participate and central government had to appoint the assessors. There was a similar experiment to establish urban self-governing bodies, exempting their towns from the jurisdiction of the provincial governors. These too all failed for lack of local participation and the towns were taken back under provincial control. It was typical of Peter's unsystematic thinking that after 1724, when the soul tax system was finalized, a network of military districts was superimposed, each district supporting one regiment, and the army took over the work of local revenue collection. Their boundaries cut right across those of the new local government system, and the military and civil authorities were plunged into endless jurisdictional disputes. Yet, however chaotic the system may appear to have been, it was for the most part retained after Peter's death and worked well enough to sustain the position of Russia as a first-rank military and naval power.

One area where Peter produced permanent administrative change was the church. When the patriarch died in 1700, the office was deliberately left vacant and the tsar assumed overall direction, with two clerical collaborators, Stefan Yavorsky, made exarch in 1700, and the archbishop of Novgorod, Feofan Prokopovich. There was consistent pressure from Peter for more clerical education, and for recognized professional qualifications for ordinands. There was also pressure to rationalize the monastic sector, reducing its numbers and enforcing stricter observance of the rules of the monastic life. This enabled Peter to sequester what he regarded as superfluous endowments for the secular budget. In 1721 the government of the church was entrusted to a collegiate government, the Holy Synod. Its statutes declared that:

> From the collegiate system the state has no need to fear the rebellion and disturbance, that can arise from the spiritual rule of a single individual, for the common people cannot distinguish spiritual power from the power of an autocrat ... but think he is a second sovereign with similar or greater powers.

The Synod was presided over by a chief procurator, who was always a layman, and the College was pledged to 'accept the monarch of all Russia, our gracious sovereign lord, to be final judge of the College'. Opinion is divided over the longer-term effects of the Petrine reform of the church. Some see it as a necessary modernization and invigoration of church life, others argue that by making it clear that the church was now a department of state the reform further alienated the official church from the ordinary believers. It is certainly clear that the power which the patriarch had held in 1613 was gone for ever.

Peter had brought about irrevocable changes in Russian society. After his death in 1725, despite the deep and bitter hostility to many of his measures, it was never possible to reverse them. The westernized elites did in fact come to appreciate the value of the changes for themselves. But the resulting system was only superficially comparable with the emergent royal absolutisms of the west. The westernized Russian elite might look like their western equivalents, and the new institutions were openly copied from western models, but the values and mentalities of the Russians remained alien from those prevailing in the western European world.

8

The Second European War, 1660–1721

The treaty between Louis XIV and Philip IV in 1659 should have ushered in a period of prolonged international peace. Only the local conflicts between Spain and Portugal and Russia and Poland remained. A third theatre of war, the Ottoman frontier, flared up briefly. The Ottomans had been having a difficult century, with a succession of decadent sultans, a military establishment that was conservative, and becoming technologically obsolescent, and the end of the imperial expansion, whose spoils had sustained the Ottoman empire in its glory days.[1] Yet a line of tough-minded Albanian adventurers of the Köprüli clan had secured an almost hereditary grip on the key office of grand vizier, and with the help of some well-directed terrorism, engineered a revival of Ottoman military power. The Venetian republic discovered this in its losing battle to defend its outposts in Crete. The Köprüli revival also displayed its strength on the Habsburg military frontier and in 1663 open war began between the Emperor and the Ottomans. Leopold had not wanted the war, which compelled him to call the imperial Diet to ask for military aid. The call for a crusading war against the infidel had popular appeal all over Europe and the imperial troops inflicted a crushing defeat on the Ottomans, demonstrating the superiority of European military techniques. But in 1664 Leopold threw away his advantage and concluded a quick peace with the Turks at Vasvar, restoring the status quo, an early signal of his preoccupation with developments in the west. The Ottoman frontier reverted to an uneasy peace.

There are many reasons why the pacification of 1660 was so brief, but all relate to the basic reality that Europe, which had always been a warrior culture, was now much better organized for war than it had been in 1600. The emergent military–fiscal states were essentially war machines. The business of their rulers was to make war. As a modern commentator remarked, wars were not events, but a continuous process, as much part of the European culture as the weather.[2] The fact that most powers were dynastic states, regarded as the proprietory possessions of their rulers, added to the instability. The dynastic rulers shared the common ambitions of any contemporary property-owner, from nobles down to peasants. These were to preserve, and if possible to enlarge, the family inheritance. Over most of Europe, rulers were able to insist that subjects pursue their ambitions by peaceful means – purchase, marriage and litigation. But there was no comparable restraint on the princes, who habitually resorted to force to settle their claims. There was a further incentive to use force – what would now be called the creation of a public image. This is what Louis XIV and his contemporaries signified by the word *gloire*: perhaps the best English translation is 'reputation' or 'prestige'. Thomas Hobbes had stated clearly a basic truth about human nature: that men are naturally driven to seek power over others as the only way to guarantee their own welfare and security. War is the highest expression of this impulse.

But while power is ultimately based on physical force, in normal circumstances it rests on reputation. People will not often resist those that they *believe* to be powerful; rather they will seek to ingratiate themselves with the powerholders. Monarchs knew that if they wished to be able to rule their subjects securely, they must preserve a public image as men, or occasionally women, who possessed power. This explains why the rulers of early modern Europe – and their modern successors are really no different – were locked into an open-ended power struggle, as Hobbes pointed out they must be. Their survival depended on demonstrating their power, and this they did through war, or the threat of war. The most vicious aspect of this competitive power game was that there was no escaping it. Those who refused to play would fall victim to the crowned mafia bosses of the European world.

Louis XIV, who wrote his *Mémoires* as a handbook for his successors on how to be a king, always claimed that the absolute monarch operated by the rules of reason. The monarch saw to it that he received the best possible information and advice, and then made his decisions on the basis of rational calculation. In 1660 rational calculation suggested that the power of Louis's kingdom was such that he had no further need to reinforce it. The main dynastic rivals, the Spanish Habsburgs, had lost their former superiority. After 1660 the kings of Spain proved unable, without the help of allies, even to defend their core territories, much less exert any international power. Their cousins in Vienna were beginning to build a power base in their hereditary lands, assisted by their unshaken hold on the imperial crown, but were in no position to launch a serious challenge to the power of Louis XIV. The money power of the United Provinces was a more serious competitor, and their apparently effortless superiority in trade and commerce was irksome, but not threatening. The republican regents who directed foreign policy, led by the De Witt brothers, were allies of Louis XIV. The one obvious threat to the relationship was Louis's unconcealed dynastic ambition to acquire the Spanish Netherlands. Although he was willing to share the booty with the United Provinces, the De Witts and most of their compatriots, preferred the southern Netherlands to remain intact as a buffer zone between themselves and France. The Empire was no threat because of Mazarin's skilful diplomacy which had exploited the French position as a legal guarantor of the Westphalia settlement. He had made treaties with the princes guaranteeing their internal autonomy, and blocking any attempt by the Habsburgs to reinvigorate the imperial authority. Mazarin's *Reinbund* locked the western principalities into a pro-French alliance. In the British Isles the newly restored Stuarts had to secure their restoration internally, and Charles II personally was an admirer of Louis XIV, and most of the time a willing client. But the most important component of French predominance was military power. Finally, Louis's security rested on the supremacy of the French armies. This was repeatedly demonstrated between 1660 and 1700, perhaps most convincingly during the war of 1688–97, when Louis fought almost the whole of Europe, without a single ally, and held it at bay.

In 1660 Louis XIV was the premier monarch in Europe and recognized as such. Reason should have told him that for the foreseeable future it would be possible, using the diplomatic skills that Mazarin had developed, to concentrate on preserving the status quo, but there was no chance of this happening. Louis was young, ambitious and imbued with the militarist ethos of European civilization. It was unthinkable that he should possess such power and not seek to use it to emphasize and enhance his supremacy. It is true that Louis showed awareness of the risks, as he remarked, 'the more one loves *la gloire*, the more one ought to be sure to achieve it safely'. Generally he tended to follow this rule and be content with limited, basically defensive objectives. But all power corrupts, and Louis was given to lapses. There were periods when his sense of his own power carried him away. The Dutch war of 1672, or the period after 1679 when, as the Great Elector wrote, 'France has already become the arbiter of Europe ... henceforth no prince will find security except with the friendship and alliance of the king of France', were examples of this. In the period 1679–84, he had a prolonged fit of aggressive bullying, expressed in the policy of 'reunions' or the revocation of the Edict of Nantes. He even had hopes of taking the imperial crown from the Habsburgs. These rampages were usually short-lived and his normally calculating and cautious nature prevailed. He got a reputation throughout Europe of being an aggressive expansionist, with the inevitable result that the other rulers formed coalitions to restrain him.

Some of Louis's lapses from rational calculation arose from a stubborn adherence to principle at the expense of expediency. This seems true of his revocation of the Edict of Nantes, his recognition of the exiled Stuarts as kings of Britain after 1689, or his refusal to tamper with the laws of divine hereditary succession by insisting that his grandson, who became Philip V of Spain in 1700, retained his hereditary right to the succession in France. It needs very little rational analysis to work out how counter-productive these principled actions were. It was unfortunate for Louis that the one legitimate use he could have made of his military predominance would have been to head a crusade to drive the Ottomans out of Europe. This was ruled out, partly because France had thriving trade with the Orient, based on agreements with the Ottoman empire, but more seriously because the territorial gains of such a crusade would go to strengthen the Vienna Habsburgs. So apart from making token gestures by assisting the Venetians in the 1660s, or the Empire in 1663, Louis usuallly saw the Ottomans as a force whose survival weakened his main rival. Finally, the most rational and calculating ruler cannot avoid the interventions of contingency, or divine providence as contemporaries saw it. The international relations of western Europe from 1660 to 1715 were dominated by the problem of the Spanish succession.

Even before the death of Philip IV in 1667, no one expected his one surviving son, Charles II, to live very long, or to produce offspring. The evidence suggests that Mazarin, in arranging the marriage of Louis XIV to Philip's elder daughter in 1659, despite her formal renunciation of her claims on the succession, knew as everyone else did that such renunciations were valueless. The succession to divine-right monarchies was disposed by God, not men. Mazarin intended that Louis XIV should acquire a claim on the inheritance. After the death of Philip IV in 1667, Louis advanced a very dubious claim that the laws of inheritance in the Spanish Netherlands gave prior claims to an elder daughter over a son and therefore, by right of his wife, Louis should inherit. There had been meticulous military planning for seizure, and Louis in person marched into the Netherlands with his army, but the Spanish commanders sensibly contented themselves with token resistance, and the campaign was an almost bloodless triumphal progress for the king. It was spoiled when De Witt got together with Britain and Sweden in an alliance that threatened war if Louis annexed the province. Being unprepared for a general conflict, Louis drew back and contented himself with a few border towns.

The opening of the Dutch war of 1672 was a model of the capacity of an early modern state to plan and conduct a successful war. Louis XIV was determined to punish the ruling oligarchs of the United Provinces for presuming to interfere in 1668. He secured the non-intervention of potential allies of the Dutch and enlisted Charles II of England in a plan to destroy and parcel out the United Provinces, leaving a rump state for the prince of Orange. Louis would dazzle Europe by his lightning war and gratify his own subjects who would profit by the economic assets taken from the Dutch. The Spanish Netherlands would become untenable, squeezed from two sides by Louis's power. In the summer of 1672, the French armies conquered some four-fifths of the republic and were poised to take the rest. The Dutch regents were taken by surprise and offered to surrender, but the triumphant Louis posed such humiliating terms that the prince of Orange, William III, who had just assumed military command, was able to engineer a populist revolt against the Holland regents, purge the town governments and install his own partisans. At the height of the coup the two De Witt brothers were murdered by mobs in Amsterdam. The dykes were opened, flooding the approaches to Holland, and the French halted, while William organized the defences and the Dutch admirals fended off the English navy. Louis became nervous about the exposed position of his army, as Spain declared war, and feeling in the Empire encouraged the Emperor to appeal to patriotic senti- ment and join in. Louis was facing his first coalition war, and withdrew his armies from most of the United Provinces, but then demonstrated his superi- ority by defending his frontier against the Empire, while steadily advancing into the Spanish Netherlands. At the same time the regent class in Holland lost enthusiasm for the war once Louis made advantageous offers of a settle- ment, while William III suffered repeated setbacks campaigning in the south. In 1678 a general settlement was made at Nymegen; the United Provinces regained all their territory and were given a favourable commercial treaty with France. The Emperor and Spain were in no condition to pursue the war without Dutch support, and had to buy off the French by letting them keep their conquests: strategic fortress towns on the Netherlands frontier, the province of Franche-Comté, a Spanish enclave contained within French ter- ritory, and lands along the frontier with the Empire in Lorraine and Alsace. The completeness of the French success was demonstrated in 1679, when Louis, merely by threatening to send in his troops, forced Sweden's enemies to give up their conquests from Louis's only continental ally.[3]

The period from 1678 to 1684 saw the most sustained outbreak of oppor- tunist expansionism in Louis's reign, crowned in 1685 with the expulsion of the Huguenots. The Emperor was paralysed by revolt in Hungary and clear signs of a coming offensive drive by the Ottomans. William III was locked into a domestic struggle with the reviving power of the regents in the republic, who were satisfied with the outcome of the war and concentrating on their commercial interests. Louis embarked on a round of legal chicanery, the policy of 'reunions': seizing any territories which could be claimed as feudal dependencies of the new acquisitions of 1678. It was not pure oppor- tunism; there was an underlying strategy to round out the frontiers of the kingdom and then render it impregnable by building a fortress line directed by a military engineer of genius, Vauban. Force was used as necessary, most notably in seizing the Protestant free city of Strasbourg in 1681, and re-intro- ducing the Catholic confession. As the Ottoman invasion developed into the siege of Vienna in 1683, and the forces of the Empire turned east, there were further pickings. In 1683 a desperate Spanish government actually declared war on Louis in the hopes of attracting help. William would have responded, but the Holland regents refused to permit it. Louis moved in and secured more gains, culminating in 1684 with the capture of the great fortress of Luxembourg. Louis then decided to secure his winnings, and offered a settle- ment if his existing gains were legally recognized. The Emperor was not ready to go that far, but lacking support in the west, reluctantly accepted a 20-year Truce at Ratisbon, leaving Louis in possession of his gains.

The territorial advance stopped there, but apart from turning on the Huguenots, and reviving bitter confessional passions all over Protestant Europe, Louis entered on a dispute with the papacy, and humiliated the republic of Genoa by a devastating naval bombardment of the city. All this fed a bitter propaganda war, greatly helped by the Huguenot refugees, that began to lose him support. Charles XI of Sweden ended his French alliance after 1682, Brandenburg defected in 1686, while in the United Provinces the regents were alarmed by aggressive new French tariffs and became ready to collaborate with William III, who now engineered a new coalition, the League of Augsburg, committed to upholding the settlements of 1678.

This became possible because the eastern campaign, after the relief of Vienna in 1683, turned decisively in favour of the international Christian armies who were doing much of Leopold's fighting for him. By 1686 the whole of Hungary was recovered, reconstituting the traditional hereditary territories of the Habsburgs, and the armies were moving south into the Balkans. Leopold was personally never committed to a drive to the east beyond this. His attention was firmly fixed on the Empire and the Spanish succession. To his mind the eastern conquests were valued as opening the way for a new advance of Catholicism into conquered lands. They were, in any case, of little material value to the Habsburg state in their current devastated condition, and Leopold improved his military potential mainly by eliminating any future danger of an Ottoman attack on his rear.

Louis and his advisers became increasingly concerned at the consequences, sensing the military balance was beginning to move against them. In 1688 a crisis arose over the question of the succession to the ecclesiastical Electorate of Cologne, long held by a client of Louis XIV. This was now threatened and led Louis into what he conceived as a swift, pre-emptive strike, to convert the Truce of Ratisbon into a definitive peace, and French troops moved towards the Rhine. The plan began to unravel at once. Louis was aware that William III was planning an intervention in England in 1688, but accepted assurances from James II of England that he could deal with it. In the autumn of 1688, William was able to take his expedition to England while Louis was preoccupied in Germany. Louis had not anticipated that James would flee and that William would take control of the British Isles and add them to his coalition; nor had he expected the military power that England could exert through its navy, and an army in the Netherlands that built up to 70,000 men. Even so, Louis was able to fight, single-handed, a coalition of almost every other power in western Europe, and on the tally of battles and sieges lost and won, emerged an easy military winner. The defensive strategy was begun brutally by the deliberate devastation of the Rhine Palatinate in 1689. This was a policy positively encouraged by Louis himself, and involved the deliberate destruction of all property, crops and livestock, though the inhabitants were given the opportunity to leave, and even to resettle in French Alsace.[4] It was an unprecedented act of military terrorism, intended to make operations along the German borders impossible. It failed in that and handed his enemies excellent propaganda material.

This Nine Years War of 1688–97 developed into a war of attrition. There were few successful military actions, with the exception of William's securing of Britain and Ireland and the continuing victories of the Holy

League armies against the Ottomans. By 1693, Louis was ready to end it. He wrote in October: 'The success of my arms, upon which the benediction of God continues to rain, has not erased from my heart the desire I have to make a good peace.' At that point, on balance, he was on top, and the hostile alliance was beginning to crack under the strain.[5] Then the French war effort was struck a heavy blow by the harvest failures of 1693–4, which brought famine and falling revenues in France. In 1695 the French battle fleet had to be laid up and resources put into privateering warfare. Louis was now not only looking for peace, but willing to make concessions to secure it. That year William III won his first major success in the Netherlands war by the capture of Namur. But he too now accepted that the original aim of the alliance, to restore the status quo of 1659, was unattainable. Active negotiations began for a settlement between William and Louis, who got a major boost at the last moment by capturing Barcelona and effectively occupying Catalonia. But he only planned to keep it until the conference at Ryswick worked out the necessary exchanges.

The peace of 1697 was no humiliation for Louis XIV, but it did mark a recession from his original primacy. In the Empire he gave up virtually all his winnings since 1678 except the city of Strasbourg. It is an interesting reminder of contemporary priorities that he fought successfully for a provision that, where the territories he was restoring had been converted to Catholicism under French occupation, there would be no attempt to reverse this.[6] Spain recovered all losses in the Netherlands since 1678 and the return of Catalonia. The United Provinces were once more given access to trade with France on the conditions conceded in 1678. William of Orange was formally recognized as king of England.

The new-style military–fiscal states had produced meagre results. Armies and navies were bigger, more professional, more successfully controlled from the centre, and better supplied and equipped, but in the west at least they were incapable of achieving decisive results, since they cancelled one another out. Only against the Ottomans, where the Christian forces had a clear technical superiority, were major, irreversible power shifts achieved. Further, it was clear that none of the participating powers were able to fund their war effort from their revenues. All the participants fought the war by supplementing regular revenues with the proceeds of war contributions from occupied territories. This did restrain the physical and human destruction in the war zones, and even produced conventions governing the legitimate demands an occupying force might make, but, in addition, all the combatants had to resort to government borrowing, and ended the war with much expanded public indebtedness. The most successful participants were England and the United Provinces, where loans were guaranteed on the public faith of the parliament and the Estates General. The United Provinces had been creating long-term funded government debt for most of the century, but it was a new development in England. However, after some early experimentation it was stabilized in 1694 with the parliamentary chartering of the Bank of England, which assumed responsibility for servicing the long-term debt. The French were driven more to short-term borrowing, from the venal officeholders and through the issue of *rentes*, and in the last critical years of the war by an experiment in taxing the exempt elites through a universal property tax. It is unclear how the Habsburg war effort, which was on a more modest scale than that of the other major combatants, was funded. The Habsburgs were quite successful in getting outsiders to pay for their war, particularly the Turkish campaigns where the imperial contributions, and those of the Holy League powers led by the papacy, were a substantial help. It is also apparent that the Habsburgs had some success raising foreign loans, mostly in the United Provinces, on such securities as the crown mineral royalties. It is a fact that, although by 1697 all the belligerents were hard-pressed to finance a continuing war, none were actually forced out by financial failure. For rulers, especially those with a reliable funded debt, there seemed to be an endless supply of credit at quite reasonable rates of interest. Those less well secured often had to pay much more. The Habsburgs were borrowing from their court Jew at Vienna, Samuel Oppenheimer, at rates up to 30 per cent. His death in 1703, and the subsequent failure of his firm, nearly bankrupted the Habsburg war effort, exposing its precarious funding base. What remains largely unexplored so far is where all the capital that was lent to fund the wars came from. Estimates of the total costs of war in western Europe and the Balkans between 1688 and 1715 work out at £5–600,000,000. The European economy was clearly producing large surpluses, which were then squandered on the unremitting round of warfare.

However, some recognition of the destructive cost and futility of the contemporary wars seems to have penetrated to some of the participants, most noticeably Louis himself and William of Orange. The impulse came from the growing awareness that the problem of the Spanish succession was becoming critical, as Charles II of Spain sank towards his end. European rulers had been thinking about the problem for decades. Neither the Bourbons nor the Habsburgs would accept that the other should secure the undivided inheritance, since this would destabilize the dynastic power structure. The obvious solution was to pass the central inheritance of Spain and its empire to a third party, accompanied by some compensatory cessions of parts of the inheritance to the senior claimants. Fortunately, in 1697 there was such a claimant, the electoral prince of Bavaria, and the first partition agreement between Louis and William gave him the Spanish crown, which was agreed to by Charles II himself. The treaty then awarded securities and compensations to the other claimants, mainly by a carve-up of the Spanish dependencies in Italy and the Netherlands. The British and the Dutch would have their commercial interests in Spain and the colonies secured, and the United Provinces would get a line of barrier fortresses in the southern Netherlands as protection against French attack. This partition had two weaknesses: the Emperor never gave his agreement to any partition arrangement, insisting on his dynastic right to the whole succession, and since he had wound up the war with the Ottomans by the Treaty of Carlowitz in 1697, he was prepared to fight. Then the electoral prince died, reopening the whole issue. A further partition treaty was cobbled up between Louis and William, allowing a Habsburg succession in Spain, with Louis being compensated in Italy, but it was never even communicated to Leopold, and was rejected by Charles II who, as his parting gift to mankind, made a will offering the undivided inheritance to a grandson of Louis XIV, and if he declined, to the second son of Leopold, the Archduke Charles.

For Louis XIV this was an offer he could not refuse[7] and his grandson was swiftly installed in Madrid as Philip V, while French troops secured the Netherlands. War could still have been avoided, if William were satisfied with commercial concessions in Spain for England and the United Provinces, with perhaps a naval base for England in the Mediterranean and the fortress barrier for the United Provinces. The Emperor and Louis could then be left to fight out the division of Italy, which was Leopold's first target. But such an outcome demanded tact and restraint on the part of Louis XIV, and instead he suffered his last bout of reckless arrogance, a not uncommon phenomenon in lottery winners who get the first prize. The existing Dutch garrisons were expelled from the Netherlands, commercial concessions in Spain were secured for French merchants, Louis declined to give concrete assurances that the crowns of France and Spain would always be separated and – his crowning folly – on the death of James Stuart, Louis provocatively recognized his son as James III of England. This was probably crucial in swinging opinion in the English parliament to accept the necessity of a new war. In 1701 William was able to resurrect his Grand Alliance, and negotiation with Louis was broken off. The Alliance did not specify what would happen to the Spanish succession. The indications are that William would have accepted Philip's succession if the other conditions were fulfilled, but the Alliance guaranteed the Anglo-Dutch interests and awarded Italy to the Emperor.

When William III died unexpectedly in 1702, the momentum for war was unstoppable. Indeed, Prince Eugene the Emperor's senior general had already opened the Italian campaign, and in May 1702 the Alliance declared war. Initially the war went in favour of Louis. This time, apart from Spain, which was a military liability that had to be propped up with French troops, he had an ally in Bavaria, nervous about the revival of Habsburg power in the Empire, and in Italy the duke of Savoy was an ally, though early Austrian successes in Italy had already persuaded him to consider changing sides. The one sign of French weakness was the inability to send out a battle fleet to challenge Anglo-Dutch control of the seas. On land Louis was able, until disaster struck, to maintain a rough parity of numbers with the Allies, but the land war developed a new feature. Both the duke of Marlborough, Allied commander in the Netherlands, and Eugene, the Austrian commander, revived the role of the set battle. Their joint expedition into Germany in 1704 resulted in the battle of Blenheim, where Louis's main army and that of his Bavarian ally were destroyed. It was probably the first battle to change the course of a war in western Europe since Nördlingen in 1634. It drove French troops out of the Empire and gave possession of Bavaria to the Emperor, who squeezed it ruinously for war contributions. The following year the duke of Savoy finally defected, and Eugene cleared northern Italy, while other Habsburg forces conquered Naples. Marlborough moved back into the Netherlands and in two further set battles, Ramillies and Oudenarde, drove the Franco-Spanish forces out and prepared for an invasion of northern France. The revival of the decisive role of battle in warfare probably owes much to the personalities of Marlborough and Eugene, who realized this was a war that could not be decided by sieges with a view to subsequent exchanges of winnings at the peace. But it can also be linked to the general adoption of the ring bayonet, making pikemen redundant, and the replacement of the matchlock musket with the flintlock, greatly improving reliability and rate of fire, which together made it possible to increase infantry fire power on the battlefield to the point where it could break opposing formations by significantly increasing killing rates.

In 1703, in order to win over Portugal as an ally, the Alliance publicly declared their aim of installing the Archduke Charles and deposing Philip V. The Anglo-Dutch fleets entered the Mediterranean, secured Sardinia and Sicily for the Habsburgs, captured Gibraltar in 1706, and mounted an expedition to install Charles on his throne. This backfired, for while he was well received by the lands of the crown of Aragon, and established in Catalonia, Castile rallied to Philip V against this alien intrusion. Although Madrid was briefly captured twice during subsequent operations by the Allies, they were unable to subdue Castile. But the Allies continued to believe that military victory was possible, a belief not seriously shaken until the disastrous battle of Malplaquet in 1709, an allied victory which inflicted as much damage on the victors as the defeated French army, and prevented Marlborough invading France at a crucial moment. The war then repeated the experience of its predecessor, in that Louis's war effort was struck with economic and financial disaster.

The war had again been financed on both sides by borrowing, and the Allies, sustained by the financial markets of London and Amsterdam, and based on funded borrowings at reasonable interest rates, had a marked advantage over Louis. While the war was going well, he managed to raise a series of short-term loans through the banking community of Geneva, several of whom were Huguenots, who did not let that consideration stand in the way of business. But in 1709 harvests failed all over Europe in face of adverse weather conditions,[8] revenue was so hard hit that Louis's tax-farmers, who handled the indirect taxes, declined to renew their farm, and bankruptcy seemed imminent. For a period Louis lost his nerve and cast about to end the war on almost any terms, including the abandonment of Philip V. The peace negotiation of 1709–10 failed due to two miscalculations: that France was now so weak that if necessary the Allies could continue the war to final victory, and that, if necessary, Philip V would give up his throne if offered some modest personal compensation. Both were wrong. To the surprise of Louis himself, Philip refused to go voluntarily. When the Allies then insisted that Louis himself should remove Philip by force he refused. That was a dynastic humiliation too far. Encouraged by Malplaquet, and some evidence of a patriotic rally among the subjects to whom he publicly appealed, Louis determined to fight on. The most concrete evidence that there was a public response was the successful levying of the revived property tax, the *dixième*, payable by the tax-exempt elites. It was retained for the duration of the war.

At that point it was the Alliance that began to unravel. This was because it became increasingly clear that Louis and Philip V were prepared to concede to the maritime powers their essential requirements: guarantees that the two crowns would not be united, the Dutch barrier in the Netherlands, favourable commercial concessions from Spain, and the cession of Gibraltar as an English naval base for the Mediterranean. The process was speeded by the fall of Marlborough and the installation of the Tory ministry in England in 1710. By 1711 the English and French governments had agreed terms for a general settlement and the English withdrew from the continental war, though they continued to pursue colonial gains against the French in Canada. It took a further four years after 1711 before first the United Provinces, and then the Habsburgs, realized that without the support of Great Britain, as it became by the Anglo-Scottish union in 1707, they could not win against Louis XIV. At the end the princes of the Empire realized that the only remaining issues were the Emperor's dynastic ambitions in Spain and Italy which were not their concern, and this added to pressures for a settlement. In 1714 the French won a major victory over Eugene's army at the battle of Denain, finally re-establishing the military reputation of the French armies, and ended the war.

The treaties of Utrecht, which the Emperor did not sign, though he acknowledged them, and Rastatt which was his separate settlement with the Bourbons, were explicitly based on a wish to establish a balance of power as the basis for a secure peace. The British emerged with almost everything they had wanted in 1702, with the addition of some colonial concessions at the expense of French Canada. So did the United Provinces. The southern Netherlands now passed to the Habsburgs, but the Dutch got their guaranteed barrier, with the Emperor agreeing to carry part of the cost of its maintenance. The main Habsburg gain was control of Italy, though Sicily had to be ceded to the duke of Savoy, together with a royal title, as reward for his services in the war. The settlements of 1715 left unsolved problems, mainly concerning Italy, since Philip V and Charles, who had become Emperor in 1711 on the death of his brother Joseph, had not exchanged formal recognitions, and were still technically at war. Further, any balance of power was continually challenged by the dynastic principle and its erratic workings. It is significant that nearly all the major European conflicts after 1715 were labelled wars of succession. The war of 1702 was only the first of a series. In

1715 itself the succession in Britain was briefly challenged by the exiled Stuarts, with a full-scale rebellion in Scotland and some sympathetic support in England, but that was efficiently crushed by the new Hanoverian regime. When Louis XIV died in 1715, after his family had been decimated by a series of deaths in 1711, France faced a long regency for a five-year-old child. By the 1720s it was obvious that an Austrian succession crisis was developing, as it became clear that Charles VI would be the last male Habsburg. This triggered the next major round of general warfare in 1740.

In 1715 there was still a war in northern Europe which had begun in 1699 when the rulers of Denmark, Saxony–Poland and Russia planned an aggression against the young Charles XII of Sweden. This Great Northern War was fought out parallel with the Spanish succession war, but the two conflicts only impacted on one another sporadically. The north-eastern European periphery was still loosely bound in with the European core, it was not wholly detached. Even in 1700 the two maritime powers, who had a strong concern in the Baltic as a source of naval stores, assisted Charles XII to deliver a knock-out blow to Denmark by a direct seaborne attack on Copenhagen. Thereafter their influence was used to restrain any thoughts in Denmark of re-entering the war. Even in the turmoil of the general war after 1702, the western powers could not fail to mark the striking and almost unbroken successes of the Swedish army against Peter and Augustus II. Then, after five years of campaigning in Poland to install his own puppet king, Charles decided to settle the conflict by marching into the Empire and occupying Augustus's Saxon Electorate. He quartered his army there, rebuilding its strength through 1706–7, and both sides in the western conflict approached him to either enlist his support or urge him to turn east again to settle accounts with Peter. Since that had always been his intention, the danger of a Swedish intervention in the west was illusory, but in the general power game, a player with Charles XII's reputation as a warrior could not be ignored.

Charles did turn east, and met his fate at Poltava in 1709. While he languished in Ottoman territory from 1709 to 1713, trying to persuade his hosts to attack Russia, the predators fell on his territories in the north. Peter had secured his hold on Sweden's Baltic provinces, Livonia and Estonia, by 1710, and then moved on to the occupation of Finland in 1714. In Germany the Prussians took over Swedish Pomerania in alliance with Denmark, and the Elector of Hanover secured Bremen-Verden. In 1713 Charles made a dramatic reappearance in the west to organize the defence of Stralsund, the last surviving Swedish possession in Germany, but had to surrender it, escaping back to Sweden with every intention of continuing the struggle. This led Peter into a bold penetration into the west. In 1715 he brought his army into Germany and established a base in Mecklenburg, hoping to coordinate his allies in an invasion of Sweden from the south. His appearance in their own backyard thoroughly alarmed the western rulers, who looked with distaste on Peter as an alien barbarian, but one in possession of a formidable armed force.

In particular, the north German princes and the Emperor had no desire to see Peter established in Mecklenburg. Peter spent 1717 visiting some of the western courts and his reception persuaded him that they would not accept him as an equal partner, nor did they want Sweden wholly eliminated and Russian ascendancy established in the Baltic. The German princes, including the Elector of Hanover, who was now George I of Great Britain, would have been willing to work with Charles, at the price of his German lands, to recover his losses to Peter in the east. This was impossible while Charles lived, since he had no intention of making any concessions as long as he could scrape some military forces together. Only with his timely death in 1718, and the end of the absolute monarchy in Sweden, could the necessary peace treaties be made, in which Sweden gave up all her lands in the Empire except a small portion of western Pomerania. It was then planned that, with assistance from George I and the British navy, Sweden should be enabled to recover her lost territory from the Russians. However, the financial crisis of the South Sea Bubble in Britain in 1720 put an end to the intervention plan. The Swedish government had to make the best terms it could with Peter in the Treaty of Nystad of 1721. The most obvious result of the northern war was displacement of Sweden as the leading Baltic power. The fact that her place would be taken by Russia, as a major new participant in European power politics, was not immediately obvious, but in retrospect the final integration of the eastern frontier zone into the European power system began after 1721.

PART

III

THE END OF THE OLD REGIME

III

9

Changing Mentalities

Science

There are historians who will argue that the most important single development in the history of Europe from 1600 to 1789 was the birth of modern science. It can equally be argued, from the point of view of the Europeans who lived through those years, that science had almost nothing to contribute to their lives. Modern scientific investigation began with the Greeks, and the take-off point that was to change the world can be dated at will.[1]

A reasonable beginning is the publication by Copernicus of his small Latin text *De Revolutionibus ...*, in 1543, which claimed to demonstrate mathematically that, contrary to Aristotle and centuries of belief, the Earth was not stationary at the centre of the universe, but spun on its own axis every 24 hours at unimaginable speed, and simultaneously moved in a circular annual orbit, together with the other known planets, round the Sun. Almost nobody took any notice, partly because only a trained mathematician could understand it, partly because even the most ignorant peasant could have seen it was nonsense. His senses told him the Earth was solid, and not in motion, and his eyes confirmed every day how the Sun and the planets moved round the Earth in their orbits. If it had been true it would have had disturbing implications. First, it contradicted explicit biblical texts, accepted as the Word of God, and this was unthinkable. Second, it blew apart the whole description of the universe by Aristotle and his christian commentators, which said the universe consisted of two distinct components. The inner circle was formed by the Earth and the Moon, where there was endless mutability and change; this was the theatre of God's providential design for the human race and stood at the centre. Beyond this was the immutable world of the chrystalline spheres, set in perpetual circular motion round the Earth, carrying the Sun, the planets and the fixed stars. In that sphere of perfection, nothing ever changed. The laws of earthly physics did not apply.

A small elite of mathematicians, who did understand Copernicus, were excited by his arguments and worked away to develop them. The Danish nobleman Tycho Brahe, with his gifted assistant Johannes Kepler, spent years observing the heavens, calculating the orbits of heavenly bodies, and discovering further impossible things. The Nova, a new star visible to the human eye, suddenly appeared in the chrystalline realm where nothing ever changed, and the comet of 1577 made its appearance and was tracked passing through the chrystalline spheres, which was also impossible. Kepler, the dedicated imperial astrologer to the Emperor Rudolf, finally worked out the mathematics of the planetary motions, showing that they did not move in circular orbits at constant speeds, but in eliptical orbits with the Sun at one focus. They accelerated as they approached the Sun and slowed down as they moved away, and these motions were governed by mathematical laws. But Kepler, like Copernicus, was incomprehensible even to educated laymen. The breakthrough was the work of the Italian mathematician Galileo, a convinced Copernican, an experimental scientist and a gifted writer, who began to publish his discoveries in the vernacular in terms comprehensible to the educated reader. His work on the laws of motion, elucidating such phenomena as impetus, inertia and acceleration with the aid of experiments, showed how it would be possible for planetary bodies to maintain perpetual motion in space, and how the Earth could rotate without those on its surface being thrown off by centrifugal forces.[2] Then he used the observational powers of the newly invented telescope to show that the surface of the Moon was not smooth, that the number of the stars was vastly greater than had ever been imagined, that the universe was incredibly large, and, most dramatically, that Jupiter too had moons, which under Aristotelian orthodoxy was impossible. Any layman with a telescope could see these things for himself.

Galileo's place in history derives from his gifts as a publicist, and he used them in a campaign to discredit the whole Aristotelian scientific system as utterly mistaken. He was in effect telling the European intellectual establishment it needed re-educating. He went on to grasp the nettle of religion. In his *Letter to the Grand Duchess* of 1616, he argued that the physical sciences must be detached from theology. On religious questions, the theologians were entitled to pronounce as experts; in the world of natural sciences they were laymen, and the qualified scientists pronounced, and if what the scientists said seemed to contradict Scripture, or religious tradition, then Scripture must be re-interpreted to conform with scientific truths. This was to challenge the ultimate status of the church as the final judge of truth about the world. Belatedly, at Galileo's trial before the Inquisition, the church mobilized to stamp out the challenge. In an earlier age they would have succeeded; in the seventeenth century it was too late. Galileo was silenced, but nothing the Roman Church could do would stop admirers publishing his ideas in the Protestant sector. Not that the Protestant confessions were not also alarmed by the challenge, but in countries like the United Provinces or England the churches no longer controlled the machinery of repression, while printing supplied the technology for the rapid spread of novel ideas.

The genie was out of the bottle and could not be put back. It is arguable that much of the success of the scientific project was due to the English statesman, Francis Bacon, who articulated the whole idea of science as the key to the betterment of the human condition. In works like *The Advancement of Learning*, he pointed out how unsystematic experiment had given the world such tools as gunpowder, the magnetic compass and printing. If society were willing to fund systematic, collaborative scientific research, surely many more useful inventions would result; man could learn how his environment worked, and thus how to exploit it for his own purposes. Bacon, like Galileo, appreciated that for this to happen science and religion must be separated into autonomous spheres of knowledge. But if his project were pursued, he affirmed that all mankind could look towards a future of incremental material betterment. It was this prospect, that applied science could give man control of his environment that sold the scientific project and encouraged the flood of new discovery and theories that from the 1650s was continent-wide and unstoppable, except in places like Italy and Spain, where the Inquisition still had the power to suppress it, and even then not totally. A European scientific community developed, institutionalized by the creation of academies: informal, like Gresham College in the City of London, or official, like the English Royal Academy of 1662 or the French Academy of Sciences set up under Louis XIV in 1666. Science was now an acceptable part of official culture. Neither churches nor academic establishments in the universities could stop it, though they tried.

In 1637, René Descartes published his mould-breaking *Discourse on Method* which proposed the radical step of literally scrapping all existing knowledge of the workings of the material world and starting again by logical, mathematical deduction from axiomatic first principles. He developed a purely mechanical picture of a world where there is no material phenomenon that does not have a direct physical cause governed by mathematical laws. The exception is the free-thinking human mind, which can investigate the material world while not being part of it. Descartes' method was, of course, scientifically useless: the system he and his disciples derived from it was nonsense. But its basic message was not lost – that in the material world nothing was to be taken for granted until demonstrated beyond doubt. Authority based on written texts only, and sanctioned by immemorial custom, was rejected, and with it the very foundations of European culture. It remained for Isaac Newton, in his *Principia Mathematica*, to produce a final synthesis of the laws which control the physical world that held good until the challenge of Einstein in the twentieth century.

In evaluating the impact of the scientific movement there is one outstanding fact to be faced. In the period down to 1789, the benefits promised by the Baconian propaganda and by Descartes, and very specifically by the charter of the English Royal Academy did not materialize. There was very little technological advance that derived from the work of the scientists. They had long set themselves the task of discovering how to find longitude at sea and failed completely; it was a working clockmaker who produced the first reliable chronometer. In the fields of medicine and public health, it is notorious that nothing was achieved. The microscope was invented, revealed the world of bacteria and helped to expose the detailed structures of body parts, but nobody discovered how to put this knowledge to practical use.[3] There were of course developments related to the spreading acceptance among the elites of the scientific world-view. The drive to collect and classify precise information did enhance the efficacy of government, enabling systematic bureaucratic administration to develop, and such activity was one of the most important remits of French intendants. It was possible to improve techniques for accounting, mapping and surveying. Yet it is notorious that when it was proposed to apply such techniques to standardize and rationalize traditional methods of revenue-raising, they met such determined resistance from vested interests that few such schemes got beyond the paper planning stage.

Besides the general acceptance of the new scientific ideas among the elites, which did take place – Aristotelian science was utterly discredited by the 1660s – the actual results were marginal. It is notorious that although some kinds of superstition, like witchcraft beliefs, were increasingly rejected by the elites, other forms of irrationalism, such as astrology, transmutation of base metals to gold, belief in prodigies, monstrosities, ghosts and all kinds of charlatan trickeries flourished undiminished. Louis XIV may have founded his Academy in 1666, but it did not prevent the great court scandal involving alleged magic and sorcery that engulfed the royal mistress, Madame de Montespan in the 1670s. A British ambassador in Sicily in 1772 reported:

> There is not a Sicilian in the polite circle but can ask how you do in three languages, talk of Newton and Descartes ... but this their knowledge is to such a wonderful degree superficial ... the men seem universally to affect a tone of society foreign to their real characters.

As for the lower orders of society, it is reasonable to deduce from the record that they remained largely untouched by the scientific movement. More typical of their reaction was the outcry in England in the 1750s, when parliament at last adopted the Gregorian calendar and there were popular disturbances protesting at the alleged 'nine lost days'. The authorities all over Europe eventually called a halt to witch persecutions, but that evidently did not result from popular demand. Folk beliefs in magic, curses and the 'evil eye' flourished quite undisturbed, and attempts to introduce vaccination against smallpox met the most determined resistance.

The most evident result of the scientific breakthrough seems to lie in its largely unintended erosion of the certainties of the traditional culture. This was not because the scientists were unbelievers; almost none of them were. Even Newton spent much of his later life seeking a scientific interpretation of the prophetic books of the Bible. It was the fact that the religious beliefs that were the foundation of European culture were so vulnerable to materialist scepticism. Religious values were losing their status as uncontested, axiomatic truths, and the churches had to defend their claims from persistent questioning. For example, one of the key works of the period was Pierre Bayle's *Dictionnaire historique et critique*, which asserted:

> Any particular dogma, whatever it may be, whether it is advanced on the authority of the Scriptures, or whatever else may be its origin, is to be regarded as false if it clashes with the clear and definite conclusions of the natural understanding.

He wrote in connection with the comet of 1681, that 'it is purest delusion to suppose that because an idea has been handed down from time immemorial to succeeding generations, it may not be entirely false'. It would have been difficult to make a more damaging attack on the roots of a culture imbued from top to bottom with the sanctity of precedent and the wisdom of ancestors. The impeccably orthodox Catholic priest, Pierre Simon, published his *Histoire critique du Vieux Testament*, writing purely as a philologist. He did not deny that the men who had compiled it might have been divinely guided, but asserted that, even so, the text was as prone to human error as any other. Bishop Bossuet, one of Louis XIV's most active supporters, was himself a Cartesian, though he admitted: 'I see preparation for a great onslaught on the Church in the name of Cartesian philosophy.' He had Simon's book suppressed, and Simon responded in 1702 with his own new text of the New Testament. When the Council of State considered whether this too should be suppressed, there was general reluctance. Fleury remarked, 'Crusades! We are past all that kind of thing.' That remark perhaps encompasses precisely the shift in mentality that took place after the 1660s among the elites. The Christian religion continued to be the principal way in which most people interpreted their experiences and expectations. But growing pressure within the elites for rationalist values to be accepted as the criteria for human action was throwing religion on the defensive and preparing for the emergence of such ideas as Deism, as the intellectuals despaired of being able to reduce the pretentions of orthodox confessional religion within rationalist bounds.

The arts and culture

Potentially the arts were an important element in maintaining the power structures of early modern Europe. In a population that was still predominantly illiterate, public display through ritual, ceremonies, pictures and buildings was a direct means of conveying ideas to the common people, and demonstrating the relative power and wealth of the rulers. Parallel with official elite culture, there was the traditional culture of the ordinary folk. It has been keenly debated among historians how these two cultures were related.[4] It is suggested that this was the period in European development when the elite and popular cultures diverged, as the traditional communities of the medieval world broke up and the elites withdrew from participation in community rituals and customs. This certainly did happen in some places at some times. It was seen in seventeenth-century England when Puritan clergy and their lay supporters, using their control of local magistracies, tried to suppress those aspects of folk culture they classified as godless. The persistent campaigns to end the profanation of the sabbath, forbid dancing and feasting and close down the alehouses, all of which played a vital role in sustaining popular culture, display an aggressive hostility. The efforts of urban magistracies all over Europe to discipline the poor and the vagrant display a similar antagonism. But this sort of evidence is difficult to interpret; activist Puritanism was always a minority taste. There is contrary evidence of the anti-Puritan elites exploiting populist support in a common front against Puritan assertiveness. In England, the general celebration of the Restoration after 1660 was a genuine popular manifestation. It was never difficult, at times of political tension, to raise 'church and king' demonstrations in defence of what were conceived as common traditional values which all levels of society shared.

Reliable information about popular mentalities in this period is limited, but we know that, irrespective of time or place, this culture was steeped in tradition. It was permeated by magic beliefs and rituals, and enforced community rules against deviants by popular sanctions. Popular culture created a market for appropriate types of literature, circulated round the rural communities by the packmen, pedlars and printers who found a profit in selling ballads and pamphlets, especially those relating horrendous crimes and disasters, along with religious tracts and accounts of miraculous happenings. These provided the staple content. But probably the commonest printed material in lower-class households was the almanac, issued annually, and combining astrological predictions and guidance with summaries of recent happenings and miscellaneous practical advice on household problems. This was a popular culture that co-existed peacefully alongside the culture of the elites and they had some common elements. Interest in almanacs, prophecy and astrological lore was something both cultures shared.

Public art is a reflection of the values of the society from which it comes. The high culture of the seventeenth century reflected the twin insecurities that haunted its elites about the future of their religious establishment and the whole structure of authority in the context of confessional disunity. It showed in literature where, for example, the works of Shakespeare contain little reference to religious doubts or uncertainties, while mid-seventeenth-century writers like Pascal or Milton are haunted by them. The response is everywhere to turn inwards, to cultivate soul-searching. This is common to Jansenism in the Catholic Church, to Puritanism among the Calvinists, and to the Lutheran mysticism in Germany. A similar turning inwards developed from the struggle of the Catholic Church, first to halt the advance of Protestantism, then to roll it back. The Catholics had an advantage over the Protestants. Protestantism was a religion of the word, based on combining preaching with reading of Scripture, and adherents had specifically rejected images and ceremonial and drama as educational tools. The Council of

Trent itself had accepted that the abuse of images needed to be controlled, but they recognized that appropriate art forms had a central role to play.

The spearhead of the Counter-Reformation had been the Jesuits, and they placed a high value on the use of public display to symbolize the power and mystery of the faith, which produced the art described as baroque. Nobody has succeeded in defining precisely what baroque art is,[5] except that it is characterized by extravagant, even strident decoration, and riotous forms and shapes, intended to generate emotion, and is a repudiation of the rationalism and intellectualism of the Renaissance humanists like Erasmus. Baroque art is meant to arouse a sense of awe, wonder, reverence and excitement, intended to awaken the spiritual longings of the individual. The aim is not to make him think, but to make him feel. In the 1590s the Jesuits built their model church in Rome, Il Gesu, which became the model for other churches they built or recovered in the Netherlands, in southern Germany and in Poland, which were their most successful missionary areas. But while the Jesuits were out in the field, the popes in Rome engaged in massive building projects meant to assert the power and the glory of the post-Tridentine church. The prevailing style of government of the Roman Church was nepotism. Each successive pope, after election, made a sweep of the papal appointments and installed members of his own family, the papal nephews, who then made the most of their chances while their patron survived in office. Pope Paul V brought in his Borghese family, and their great palace, with its massive art collections, became a public gallery. Then Urban VIII brought in the Barbarini. Both popes concentrated on the task of rebuilding St Peter's in the most extravagant baroque style, and the Barbarini employed the most reputable of the baroque artists, Gianlorenzo Bernini, to complete the job, which he worked on for nearly 20 years. Until the 1660s Rome was the artistic capital of Europe.

The promotion of baroque art by the Catholic Church emphasized one aspect of the art world in the early modern period: that the artists had to seek their patronage from churches, rulers and aristocratic magnates, and consequently their work had to advertise and promote the aims and values of their patrons. Most high art of the period was government propaganda. This can be seen just as well in Lutheran Germany. The Lutheran Church did not patronize pictorial art, but it was keen to promote religious music. And since the Lutheran Churches were subordinate to the secular powers, this again was government promotion. The Lutheran equivalent of Rome as an artistic centre was probably electoral Saxony and its court at Dresden, but Lutheran free cities like Augsburg and Hamburg used public funds to keep composers like Heinrich Schütz and Buxtehude in fairly steady employment, and supported the players and singers to perform their works. They, like Bernini in Rome, were advertising the prestige and status of their patrons.

The outstanding illustration of art as publicity was found at the court of Louis XIV, where it was enshrined in the great palace of Versailles, which among other functions was an art gallery, concert hall and theatre. This was openly organized by government; Colbert, among his many functions, was superintendant of buildings. He spelled it out to Louis in a letter of 1663:

> Your Majesty knows that in lieu of magnificent acts of warfare, nothing betokens more the grandeur and spirit of princes than buildings; and all of posterity measures them by the standard of these superb buildings that they have erected during their lives.

In 1672 the king established a royal academy of painting to lay down the rules of acceptable art work. Here too, Colbert established an intendant-like official, C. Lebrun, as controller of arts to supervise the work of the artists who were officially commissioned. The manufacture of the official images was comprehensive under Louis XIV. Music was led by Lully; the tragedies of Racine and Corneille, and the satirical comic dramas of Molière, were staged in the royal theatre with official approval; and the Gobelins tapestry workshop was a state manufacture. The court itself was a non-stop dramatic performance with its rigid protocols and daily ceremonial, and in his younger years Louis himself would perform in ballets and masques, all consciously glorifying the Sun King, Louis's chosen symbol. There was nothing unique in what was being done at Versailles; it had been tried elsewere, though on a much more modest scale. Charles I of England practised the promotion of royal authority through protocol at Whitehall in the 1630s, using his court artists Inigo Jones and Ben Jonson as impresarios for the masques that were then the fashionable form of dramatic performance, and he even found an improbable contributor in the great Puritan poet John Milton, though a critic might wonder, in view of Charles's eventual fate, just how cost-effective these methods of boosting royal authority were. The model on which both Charles and Louis drew was the ritual of the Habsburg courts at Madrid and Vienna, which carried the baroque idea to its limits. However, Versailles culture was baroque with a difference, in art as in politics. Louis XIV sought rationality, although Versailles was baroque in the sheer scale of the operation, and took much inspiration from Bernini, who worked for Louis in the 1660s on the upgrading of the Louvre, the principal royal palace in the capital. Also, Jesuit influences were strong at the court, but French baroque was combined with a degree of classical formality and restraint compared with its Italian models.

It is apparent that somewhere between the high official culture of the courts and the low culture of the people another level of private cultural activity also existed. This is most obvious in the realm of literature, with the expansion of every kind of print culture. Censorship was a restraint everywhere, but a wide market for serious books existed. There was also a market for prints of well-known buildings and paintings for those who would never see the originals, or afford paintings of their own. At all times and places, the majority of published work was religious and the demand for collected sermons and guides to pious living was steady. But poetry and the various early experiments with fiction writing also sold; otherwise a book like

Grimmelhausen's *Simplicissimus* would not have been around to form the European image of the horrors of the Thirty Years War. There was also commercial theatre: the English Restoration dramatists, despite the opposition of the churches and Puritan authorities of London and other provincial centres, managed to make a living from their work.

The most striking illustration of the emergence of a commercial art culture was naturally found in the urbanized, commercial society of the United Provinces. Not only was Amsterdam the international capital of the publishing world, and the freest from censorship until England abandoned its licensing laws in 1695, but it produced its own art, completely distinct and alien from baroque high art, for a private commercial market. Foreign visitors marvelled at the existence of original paintings in ordinary affluent Dutch homes. Of course much Dutch art was officially sponsored – Rembrandt's *Night Watch* had been commissioned by the city militia company and the magnificent Amsterdam town hall was a burgher mini-Versailles – but Dutch art was a commercial enterprise, one aspect of a developing consumerism among the affluent, who felt able to spend part of their earnings on purely decorative art works for their private residences. The art itself naturally illustrates the values of Dutch urban culture, just as baroque art reflects the values and aspirations of its royal, aristocratic and ecclesiastical patrons. In doing so, however, it announces the emergence of a new layer of elite society, definitely far above the labouring majority, and well below the noble elites, which would one day become a bourgeoisie with cultural values of its own.

The baroque culture, as modified through Versailles, continued to dominate Europe after 1700, when the hegemony of French art and cultural fashion was established. Louis XIV himself was changing his tastes in his later decades, particularly after he became religious under the influence of Madame de Maintenon in the 1680s, with piety and rationality gaining ground. The importance of art as propaganda remained undiminished. It was Louis himself who ordered the first salon exhibitions of paintings for the public at Versailles, and in the eighteenth century this became an established routine for showing the latest art trends to the public. But his last major palace building, at Marly, reflects a more domestic style of living, away from the public theatre of Versailles. The underlying cultural tensions were exposed during a prolonged debate within the French Academy between the 'ancients' and the 'moderns'. It produced no clear result, but in effect the 'moderns', with their rationalist inclinations, came out on top. Elsewhere, princes all over Europe were imitating Louis, so far as their resources allowed.

The original Italian baroque ecclesiastical style still flourished, and indeed was carried over the Alps into central Europe, expressed in churches and monasteries throughout Bavaria and the Habsburg lands. It produced the small church of St Johannes Nepomuk in Munich, the great pilgrim church at Vierzehnheiligen on the Main, and the showpiece monastery of

Melk in Austria. It was a pointer to changing values, however, that ecclesiastical building was outstripped by the palace building which provided the absolute monarchies all over Europe with suitable public temples where their power could be seen and worshipped. In Vienna, Leopold commissioned Fischer von Erlach to outbuild Versailles with his new palace of Schönbrünn, though in the end finance required it to be scaled down. The palace in Stockholm was rebuilt after the disastrous fire of 1697 in French baroque style. In Russia the Italian, I. Rastrelli, improved the huge Winter Palace in St Petersburg, followed later by the Peterhof and Tsarskoe Selo as summer residences in the countryside. In Dresden, Augustus II built the Zwinger, less a residence than a stage set, while in Portugal the great monastery–palace of Mafra was built on the wealth produced by Brazilian gold. Only the British monarchy failed to produce its Versailles. William III remodelled Hampton Court, but his priorities lay elsewhere, and the first Hanoverians were not builders, at least not in Britain, where they could not have afforded it. Instead, Britain, under the guidance of Vanbrugh and Hawkesmore, built Blenheim for the duke of Marlborough and Castle Howard, as monuments of the power and wealth of the aristocracy. Later in the century Robert Adam, with the landscape gardener Capability Brown, got to work rebuilding the country seats of the British ruling elite on a more modest scale. These increasingly expressed a shift in taste from the extravagantly monumental to the domestic in this kind of power building.

The trend towards a more restrained baroque had become apparent quite early on the continent, with the modification of baroque magnificence into the rococo style. This was a restrained and more rational version of baroque art. It seems as though the need to advertise wealth and power by massive display was no longer so urgent, and the amenities of comfortable living were receiving more consideration. Rococo style was taken up enthusiastically in central Europe, especially Bavaria, and became dominant for a time in France. There a major change had occurred on the death of Louis XIV. The regent, Philip of Orléans transferred the seat of government from Versailles to Paris. This gave a great boost to artistic activity and social life in the capital, as court nobles built or refurbished their Parisian town houses, and a vigorous *salon* life developed: not only formal exhibitions of art works, but as informal social gatherings for the discussion of public affairs and the arts. They were often presided over by aristocratic ladies, or even the wives of the great financier and banking families, who had never moved to Versailles. The court moved back to Versailles after some years, but Paris had become the home of a parallel, or even competitive, cultural world. The rococo style, exemplified in paintings by Watteau and Poussin the supreme court painters of the mid-century period, was directed at Versailles by Madame de Pompadour, a woman of good taste and discrimination. Her patronage extended over all branches of the Arts. The development of the royal porcelain works at Sèvres was under her supervision and she represented a changing attitude to art. The rococo period seems to be the first to value art as an end in itself, aimed at the creation of aesthetic pleasures. This assurance, that there was no longer the need to impress through display, was expressed by the marquise du Châtelet in the 1740s, who remarked: 'We have nothing else to do in this world but seek pleasant sensations and feelings.' Apart from Poussin and his unashamed hedonistic art, this also produced the eighteenth-century fashion for the Venetian art of Canaletto and Tiepolo that swept Europe. Focused on Venetian townscapes, it preached no moral message, but reflected how Venice, once a great commercial power, now lived off the aristocratic tourist trade and was a leading centre of the emerging leisure industry. The paintings exude the quiet confidence and self-satisfaction of the ruling elites.

This relaxed mood could not and did not last. A new wave of moral earnestness swept through society in the mid-eighteenth century. For Catholics it was expressed by the spread of Jansenism, in the Protestant world by north German Pietism, and in Britain by Charles Wesley and the Methodists, whose missionary journeys began in the 1730s. In the secular world it was a common theme of Enlightenment publicists whose project was educational: art, like other human activities should serve useful and moral ends. In England, during the reign of Queen Anne, the earl of Shaftesbury, a noted critic of the arts, had laid down that they must be both moral and useful. He wrote: 'the knowledge and practice of the social virtues, the familiarity and fervour of the moral graces are essential to the character of a deserving artist and just favourite of the Muses'. This was taken up by Diderot, the leading *Encyclopédiste* and correspondent of crowned heads round Europe: 'To show virtue as pleasing, vice as odious, to expose what is ridiculous, that is the aim of every honest man who takes up the pen, the brush or the chisel.'

The struggle against hedonism and frivolity had been launched. The art historian usually labels the new mood as neo-classicist, and apart from Diderot sees as its leading exponents the English painter Sir Joshua Reynolds, the first president of the new Royal Academy in 1768 and portrait painter to all the best families, and the German academic Johan Winckelmann, whose *Geschichte der Kunst des Altertums* first appeared in 1764. Reynolds set out his ideas on the educational mission of the artist in a series of 'Discourses' to the Academy.

> The Moderns are no less convinced than the Ancients of this superior power existing in the art [of painting]: nor less sensible to its effects. Every language has adopted terms expressive of this excellence ... It is this intellectual dignity, they say, that ennobles the painter's art, that lays the line between him and the mere mechanic; and produces those great effects in an instant, which eloquence and poetry, by slow and repeated efforts, are scarcely able to attain.

Winckelmann had the conviction that classical Greek art represented the peak of human achievement and was the model from which all subsequent true art must derive. To do him justice, he did not advocate copying Greek art, but adopting its aspirations. He had a profound influence on the emergent German *Aufklärung*.[6]

The changes that came over European artistic life in mid-century can be seen as having various sources, most of which point to future change. The rococo period had developed during the quarter century of relative stability that followed 1715, which had encouraged the feeling of security in elite society. This was shattered by the return of war between 1740 and 1763, until Europe's rulers once more had fought themselves and their societies into exhaustion. It was this experience that undermined complacency and, fed by the Enlightenment, produced a general sense that there must be reform, most concretely expressed in the endeavours of the 'enlightened despots'.[7] There was convergence between public, aristocratic culture, and the spread of a private commercial culture.

This latter had moved its centre from the United Provinces into Great Britain, and gave to British culture, for the first time, a leading role on the wider European scene. This was most marked in print culture, since censorship was virtually ended in 1695, and not only did all kinds of book publishing expand, but in particular a flourishing newspaper and periodical press emerged. This had a conscious educational programme directed at the emergent educated and affluent middle sector. The *Spectator* of Addison and Steele systematically encouraged the adoption of 'polite' values, and soon became seen as a classic source, widely quoted all over Europe. Anglophilia spread fast and was an inspiration for one of the most important books of the century, Montesquieu's *L'esprit des lois*.[8] The exclusive exoticism of aristocratic culture was criticized, as in John Gay's *Beggar's Opera*, which satirized the Italian opera being marketed in Britain by G.F. Handel. The reaction produced the alternative *opera buffo* in Italy, and the popular *Singspiel* in Germany, forcing Handel to change over to oratorios, with great success. In Great Britain, where there was no dominant court culture to hold them back, institutions like the theatre, the commercial public concert and the subscription library developed, as did a distinctive art form, the novels of Fielding and Richardson, which described and justified the new social values. At the time, few foresaw what an explosive mix might be generated when the polite and aristocratic cultures converged.

10

Change in the Economy and Society

The economy

The economic development of Europe after 1700 combines features that can seem contradictory, including obvious signs of growth and development together with the widespread survival of traditional practices. This leaves room for historians to differ about the precise contours of the processes of expansion, and about how far the European economy really was being tranformed prior to the events of 1789.[1] But no one challenges that the overall picture is one of a lasting change of economic direction for Europe as a whole. Broadly speaking, the seventeenth-century recession came to its end around 1710 and signs of growth appeared, which then accelerated after 1740. The key indicator is population. Most of Europe had experienced stagnant or declining population after 1620. But it is reasonable to assume that the population increased from 118 million to 187 million during the eighteenth century, and that this was the start of a population expansion that would continue unbroken into modern times. Figures for individual countries support the general trend. France, about 20 million in 1700, was at 22 million by 1750 and 27 million by 1800. England at 5.5 million in 1700, was at 6.1 million by 1750 and 9.2 million in 1801. Italy in 1750 stood at 15.5 million and reached 18.1 million in 1800. Spain, which had been one of the hardest hit countries in the preceding century stood at 8.2 million in 1717, 9.3 million in 1749 and 11.5 million in 1797. The causes are obviously complex; areas with apparently similar contexts can show quite different levels of development. For example, in the eastern Baltic the epidemics of the 1690s, followed by continuous and destructive campaigning in the Northern War, left Finland on the north shore, and Livonia and Estonia on the south, depopulated and devastated. On the southern shore, a full recovery of population had still not been achieved by 1800, while on the Finnish side the surviving population of 300,000 had risen to 832,000 by 1800. As is usually the case with population movements it is difficult to pin down the causes. One feature was the disappearance of continent-wide killer epidemics, which had ravaged Europe since the Black Death. Plague appeared on a limited scale in Marseille in 1736, and in Italy in 1743, and then retreated to the frontier zone with the Ottomans. There was no medical advance to account for this, but there was the more systematic enforcement of quarantine regulations, which could not cure the disease but could prevent its spread. There were still plenty of other killer diseases, like smallpox, which were uncontrolled, but it does seem that over the century death rates probably fell somewhat, and that, mainly through earlier marriage, birth rates increased.

This suggests that the rising population is connected to economic expansion, since otherwise the rising numbers would have triggered a Malthusian crisis. While subsistence crises following harvest failures did still occur – indeed one of them, in 1788, is often confidently advanced as a significant trigger for the French Revolution of 1789 – they were less frequent. The adverse climatic conditions of the previous century, which some historians have described as a mini ice age, had a last fling in 1709, after which climate improved.[2] There were still other natural disasters to be coped with, like the great Lisbon earthquake, or the persistent outbreaks of cattle disease which ravaged northern Europe in the middle decades of the century and hit Dutch agriculture particularly hard. On the other hand, the improved governmental systems developed after 1660 were capable of more effective relief measures when subsistence crises did occur. It is also apparent that food production increased; some experts say it broadly kept pace with rising numbers. It would have been expected that with more labour being available new land would be brought into cultivation, and this was done. There were two almost empty, and reasonably fertile, areas available for settlement recovered from the Ottoman frontier: in Hungary and then in the Ukraine, as the Russian empire established its grip on the region. The best-known area for emigration and settlement was the North American colonies, but it has been calculated that the migration into the eastern border lands was considerably greater.

It could also have been expected that rising demand, which underlay the reversal of food prices after 1740, when they began a steady upward trend, would have facilitated investment in new farming methods. It was once believed that the eighteenth century witnessed a dramatic agrarian revolution, led by Britain, where a combination of new machinery, new crop rotations in place of leaving land fallow every two or three years, better stock-breeding, connected with names like Jethro Tull, Thomas Coke of Holkham, and Viscount Townshend, the enthusiast for turnips as a fodder crop, swept the traditional farming regime aside and revolutionized productivity. It is now realized that the reality was more complicated.[3]

These techniques had been known and written about in Europe for more than a century before and had indeed been practised in parts of the United Provinces, England and a few other favoured regions during the sixteenth and seventeenth centuries. They were not the only examples of agricultural innovation in selected regions; in Mediterranean Europe, maize had proved an advantageous crop, as had the cultivation of rice in the Po valley. Europeans knew about these methods and their potential, but for the most part chose not to adopt them, so that in Germany, in 1800, 60 per cent of cultivated land was given over to growing grain in the traditional way, while each year 25 per cent of the land was left fallow. Even the steady rise in rental income, resulting from rising prices and abundant labour, did not induce either landlords or their tenants to try out or invest in new techniques. In so far as landlords were enjoying rising incomes, they chose to invest the profits elsewhere. This is an example of how the rooted conservatism of early modern societies blocked change. The nearly universal practice of communal cultivation of village lands was a standing obstacle to new methods.

Rulers and their servants had mixed attitudes. In Germany, for example, rulers tended to practise the protection of the peasant commune, which they valued as a reliable source of steady tax revenue. Those who were persuaded of the potential of change to raise production, and hence taxable capacity, often found traditionalist opposition too powerful. A good case was King Frederick William I of Prussia, who spent years of effort trying to repopulate the eastern borders of East Prussia after the plagues and war damage that began in 1709. He found that even the use of mounted police to patrol the new settlements could not force the peasants to abandon their traditional farming methods or stop them running away if pressed too hard. The most immediate and inexpensive way to raise food production quickly was also widely known – the cultivation of potatoes. Eventually this did catch on, most notably in Ireland, and was spreading fast by 1800, but it too was stubbornly resisted at first. However, it is not safe to blame the forces of tradition alone. Market forces had a part to play. If farmers were to be persuaded to abandon the patterns of local subsistence farming and raise marketable surpluses, they needed a market to supply. The traditional peasant agriculture had always had to produce a saleable surplus to get the money needed to pay taxes, rents and tithes. They could sell these surplus products in their local market towns. To go beyond that, they would need a steady demand, which existed only in scattered areas. The most important were those where the level of urbanization led to a strong demand for agricultural produce. The big capital cities like London, Paris or St Petersburg provided this, so in the Ile de France commercial farming flourished, as it had long done in Holland, which had had a unique intensity of urban development. The problem was intensified by the difficulty of overland transport of bulk produce, which was uneconomical to carry over long distances, over bad roads, or up rivers clogged by toll barriers. A consignment of produce sent up the Rhine from Basel to Rotterdam would pay tolls 38 times en route. It seems, therefore, that although agricultural production in Europe did increase substantially after 1740, just about enough to avert a subsistence crisis in face of rising numbers, the potential increases that could have been produced by adopting new methods were not realized.

Manufacturing followed a similar pattern to agriculture. There were two well-established types of manufacturing: the more traditional was urban production under strict municipal and guild control. This was the equivalent of subsistence farming; it developed to supply restricted local markets and the regulatory systems sought to share out the available market so that all the recognized producers, who were organized as family businesses or were skilled artisans who worked at home, could expect to make a living. Competitive marketing was not part of the tradition; indeed there was still powerful moral condemnation of excess profit-making or aggressive sales techniques. The basic urban trades were developed to service farming. Textiles and leather work, tool-making, food-processing, milling and brewing and specialized services, such as lawyers, doctors and tax-collectors, were found there. The ordinary small town lived by providing these services for its rural hinterland in addition to its most basic original purpose, the provision of regular markets for the farmers' produce. Larger towns could develop more specialized trades, like printing and book-selling, potteries and glass-making. These too would usually be small, family businesses. Even the really big manufacturing enterprises such as mining and quarrying, ship-building and some forms of military contracting, were commonly devolved to teams of sub-contractors.

There was another manufacturing sector: the rural trades operated on some variant of the putting-out system, where a capitalist entrepreneur provided the raw materials for home working in the countryside, free from urban and guild regulation. Most of this was textile manufacture, though basic metalwork, like pin, chain and nail-making, could also be produced on this system. The towns and the guilds tried their best to suppress such uncontrolled competition, where the wages were lower and quality and price controls not enforced. But even though governments sometimes disapproved of rural industry, on the same grounds that it was difficult to police and could upset local arrangements, it was so advantageous to the entrepreneurs and to the home workers, to whom it gave employment in the dead seasons of the farming year for the whole family, and above all was a source of cash for paying taxes and other burdens, that it was unstoppable.

The evidence suggests that industrial production in all its forms was expanding after 1740. There are signs of growing specialization in some areas, and production did move around as local circumstances changed; for example, much of the manufacturing industry in the United Provinces failed in the face of competition from areas where wages were lower or conditions more favourable. In the course of the eighteenth century they lost much of their textile trade. Leiden, once a leading centre, had 36,000 cloth workers in 1680, 17,000 in 1752. The herring fishery shrank when the fish shoals moved closer to the Scandinavian coasts and Swedish and Danish fisheries benefited. Ship-building contracted as it lost its technical superiority and its cost advantages to countries like France and Britain and as the mercantilist policies in competitor states cut into the European carrying trade which the

Dutch had dominated so successfully in the seventeenth century. That leaves the question of why the still dominant Amsterdam money markets did not invest their abundant capital into reviving manufactures and shipping, but manifestly they preferred to invest in state securities or foreign investment, not least in the English national debt. At least part of the answer is the lack of a strong central government and legislative machinery to direct investment or protect local manufactures.[4]

The area where there was major growth and change in the eighteenth century was in commerce, both locally within Europe, and more spectacularly in the long-distance colonial and oceanic trades. Here too there were factors holding back development, though over the whole continent, governments, in principle, sought to encourage and expand commercial activities. The most obvious bottleneck was transport, which prevented the economical transport of bulk goods, so that in times of local subsistence crises the food surpluses that did exist, or could have been created by investing in productivity, could not be moved to where they were needed. Governments tried to improve the road networks – the improvement of Peter's original St Petersburg-to-Moscow highway cut journey times by three-fifths by the 1780s. The first Bourbon king of Spain planned to build a national road network like that in France, which had some of the best roads in Europe, dating from Colbert's original development programmes, though in Spain little was achieved on the ground. In France in 1747 a new *Ecole des ponts et chaussées* was established whose introduction of improved techniques put the French system even further ahead. Typically in Britain improvement was left to private enterprise, in the form of turnpike trusts, to build lengths of toll road, though this could be helped by using parliamentary legislation. The trouble was that even if the roads were improved, long-distance bulk transport overland remained uneconomic and was little improved over the century. A much more productive area of investment was in canal-building, because bulk transport by water was a paying proposition. Governments all over Europe built canals, though in Germany, for example, even when the canals were built, the main river systems were riddled with toll barriers. In Spain topography was a block on canal-building: the lie of the land was simply unfavourable. The prime development areas were Russia, where government could commandeer abundant forced labour, and where the canal linking the Volga river system to St Petersburg made a crucial addition to the prospects for internal trade, and Britain, where again private enterprise, reinforced by parliamentary legislation, facilitated the development that really began when the duke of Bridgewater's canal linking his coal pits to the Mersey was followed by a true canal-building boom that covered the whole country in an extensive network, and had a key role to play in the coming industrial revolution. Over the century, the improvements in water transport, supported by some technical improvements in ship construction, chart-making and navigation systems, did something to relieve the transport bottleneck.

The general increase in commerce can be observed in most parts of the European world and its overseas peripheries. Traffic on the Rhone increased by 70 per cent between 1740 and 1790; the Sound tolls confirm that the number of ships passing in and out of the Baltic rose from around 4000 a year in the 1730s to 12,000 in the 1790s. It is difficult to ascertain the full volume of this increase in local trading because reliable statistics are unevenly available. It is much easier to document the progress in the oceanic trades, which took European exports out to the colonial and oriental markets; the centrally important African slave trade to the plantation colonies in America; and the rising imports into Europe of colonial produce. One estimate suggests that the expanding East Indies trades consisted of 25 per cent spices, 10 per cent pepper, 33 per cent textiles, especially Indian calicoes, and 20 per cent, tea and coffee, the two new drinks, which were exotic luxuries in 1660 and articles of common consumption by the 1760s. The trade was seen as so advantageous that after 1715 governments in Sweden, Denmark, Prussia and the Austrian Netherlands were prepared to support the founding of their own East India companies to compete with the established Dutch, English and French companies.

In the American trades the breakthrough went back to the establishment of the Brazilian sugar trade after 1650, followed by the expansion of the Caribbean plantations, which made Caribbean sugar islands a central focus of the colonial warfare of the period. In 1763 the French government readily traded its colony in Canada for the return of its captured sugar islands. Sugar, the master product, was supported by tobacco, rice, dyewoods, furs and hides and bullion. Spanish colonial silver production entered a new phase of development after 1740, and was supported by the discovery of gold in Brazil. Then there was the Newfoundland fishery, shared uneasily by Britain and France, and a major source of foodstuff for all Europe. These trades all interconnected: the gold and silver brought back from America funded the Orient trades, since demand for European manufactures among the oriental empires was limited. Triangular trades developed, including the notorious slave trade, in which Britain took the major share, whereby goods could be taken to Africa, traded for slaves, the cargoes disposed of in the plantation colonies, and their produce returned to Europe, and then often re-exported to those countries that could not participate directly. This was enormously profitable, and is now recognized as a main source of the capital that went to finance the British economic take-off at the end of the period.[5] As the British colonies of settlement began to expand after 1700, they provided growing markets for manufactured goods.

The net effect was of course that Europe was getting steadily wealthier out of the proceeds of colonial exploitation. This could be seen in the growth of the Atlantic port system. Cadiz retained its monopoly of the Spanish colonial trade and was a growth point in its economy; Lisbon flourished; the British Atlantic ports, Bristol, Liverpool, Glasgow, now shared with London the British export and import trades; and even the more marginal continental enterprises in Scandinavia and Hamburg contributed to their more modest development. Perhaps the most spectacular expansion took place in France. Coffee imports through Marseille grew seven times between 1660 and 1675; Bordeaux, once the trade routes reopened after 1715, managed to treble its colonial imports in three years from 1717 to 1720; and it is now accepted that, after 1760, the rate of French participation in the oceanic trades, and the resulting re-export and processing industries like sugar refining, was outstripping that of Britain. The France of the late eighteenth century was not economically underdeveloped, but internally divided, with highly prosperous seaports – Marseille, Bordeaux, Nantes, La Rochelle and their hinterlands – and inland centres like the Paris basin, and Lyon, capital of the European silk trade and a major banking centre, co-existing with the wide provincial areas where the agrarian economies remained stuck in their traditional methods of production.

It is significant that the new products were not necessities. Europe had survived for centuries without these products and could no doubt have continued to do so. This implies that there was now surplus wealth, so that some of it could be spent on luxuries and leisure goods. All but the very poorest participated; labourers smoked tobacco, and tea and coffee, once exotic luxuries, were being consumed by farmers and artisans; all classes consumed sugar. Yet the constraints on economic development – the transport problem, popular conservatism and traditionalism, guild controls on manufacture, the small-scale artisan style of production – remained. Most recent accounts agree that in 1800 Europe was still in a proto-industrial phase of development, and not likely to break out quickly. The whole system was locked up with the mercantilist controls imposed by government, aimed not at spreading prosperity for its own sake, but at taxing the proceeds of any expansion to sustain the real purpose of the state, the effective waging of war. Much of the increased product was diverted to that end, which could in itself be economically stimulating. The naval dockyard complexes at Deptford and Portsmouth were the biggest economic units in Britain and sustained flourishing local communities. But to illustrate how resources were allocated, it is worth noting that, in the 1780s, Great Britain had £2.25 million invested in its navy, when the total capital value of the West Riding woollen manufacture was £400,000.

Capitalist take-off in Britain

Anyone in a position to survey the European economy as a whole in the 1790s would be likely to conclude that while there had been major expansion of activity and wealth production, it had largely taken place through traditional methods. The changes had been quantitative rather than qualitative. But British expansion had been in a class of its own. Its export trades had doubled between 1700 and 1750, and expanded fourfold betwen 1750 and 1800. Although the oceanic trades made a major contribution, still more than half of Britain's trade was with continental Europe. It is calculated that British gross domestic product was growing at an average 0.7 per cent a year from 1700 to 1760 and slightly faster than that into the 1780s, from £50 million to £92 million a year. There has been some tendency to overplay the supposed agricultural revolution as the basis of this prosperity.[6] Certainly from about 1740 prices were rising and taking farming income up with them; landlords and those living off landed income, like the established clergy, experienced new levels of affluence, and some of this was being invested in the economy. One sign of that was the first surge of Enclosure Acts going through parliament after 1760. Yet it appears that the transformation of British farming to capitalist production for the market, involving the elimination of the small freeholder, had some way to go even at the end of this period. In the countryside a quarter of the land was still worked by small freeholders, and the reduction of smallholders and cottagers to the level of landless labourer still had some way to go. In 1700 there had been 3.5 landless villagers for every two property owners; in the 1780s it was five to two. The immediate effect was less to drive the poor off the land, as to impoverish them, relative to the propertied. The traditional rural economy was disturbed, but not yet transformed. Agriculture was losing ground to commerce and manufacture in the overall economy: it is estimated that by 1780 it had declined from 34 per cent of total output to 25 per cent, while manufacture rose from 20 per cent to 25 per cent. Even so, Britain was a long way from becoming an industrial economy, and its government was firmly in the hands of its aristocratic and gentry landowners, even if over half the workforce was now engaged outside agriculture.

What can be observed in Britain, even in 1700, was a society interested in industrial and commercial growth, and a ruling elite willing to invest private capital in it. So the parliament of landowners backed development with appropriate legislative underpinning, while private resources funded road- and canal-building, and invested in mining, manufacture and maritime commerce. Further, government was prepared to put the military power of the state behind the expansion: the investment in a large navy was used to seize colonies and trading rights from rivals like France and Spain, and the Navigation Acts both stimulated the growth of shipping and ensured that the profits of the expanding overseas empire remained in British hands.

The industrial revolution, when it did come, involved the achievement of mass production by power-driven machinery. By 1712 the first primitive steam engines had been installed to pump out Cornish tin mines, and their use was later extended to coal pits. Their technical limitations prevented them being put to wider use until the development of the improved steam engine by Boulton and Watt in the 1760s. This could be adapted to driving powered machinery, which was beginning to develop from Arkwright's weaving frames and Crompton's spinning mule in the 1760s, which in turn led to the first true factory production in the cotton industry. At first water was the principal power source and remained so for some decades, but by 1800 steam power was spreading fast. At first a more important development was the substitution of coal for wood or charcoal in industrial processes. This broke the stranglehold of limited charcoal production that held back the expansion of metallurgy. Abraham Darby first used coke for producing pig iron in the 1740s and the first big iron works based on the technique was the Carron works at Paisley in 1760. The use of coal was extended to making wrought iron in the 1780s. The result was that British pig iron production grew from 20,000 tons a year in 1720 to 250,000 tons in 1806, while the output of coal rose from 2.5 million tons in 1700 to 10 million tons in 1800. The industrial revolution was starting up in Britain by 1800, when it had made little impact on the continent. The Swedish and Russian iron manufacturers were still using charcoal then, and becoming increasingly uncompetitive. The new British technologies were known on the continent but little used. One rare exception was the development of machine-powered cotton manufacture in Catalonia in the 1780s. Still, it is necessary to note that even in Britain the impact of the new methods was limited in 1800. Most British manufacturing was still at the level of small, artisan production carried out by established proto-industrial methods.

The historians continue to debate why this crucial development occurred in Britain.[7] It has been mentioned that the ruling elites were positively inclined to economic enterprise, and willing to invest in it and encourage it by law. This contrasted with most of the continent, excepting the United Provinces, where governments often had to force economic innovation on societies that were at best sceptical or indifferent. European elites readily accepted the intellectual case for development, but were much less likely to be willing to get engaged in it themselves. There were favourable economic factors. Britain had a reliable banking and credit system from the 1690s, its labour force was legally free and not tied to the land, and the levels of taxation on the poor in Britain were usually well below continental levels, so the idea of using mass production for mass consumption was feasible. Also Britain had a significant entrepreneurial class, an urban-based monied elite, which was often barred by non-conformity from aspiring to enter the nobility or gentry, which was the ultimate aim of most successful entrepreneurs in continental countries. Non-conformists were prominent among the early entrepreneurs. Making money in business was their only road to social advancement and status. Finally, Britain was free from damaging economic interference by a powerful royal court presided over by an absolute monarch and driven by the fiscal demands imposed by the dynastic power game. No doubt the Hanoverian kings would have behaved like their royal colleagues had circumstances allowed, but because of the dynastic shift after 1714 in Britain it was beyond their powers.

11

Social Change

When historians saw the events of 1789 in France as a 'bourgeois revolution', this implied that there had been social changes enabling a rising middle class to challenge the hegemony of the existing ruling elites, who were classified as 'feudal'. Recent research into social structures during the eighteenth century has raised doubts whether such changes had in fact occurred.[1] A recent historian, Jeremy Black, has remarked:

> The weight of the past was never more apparent in eighteenth-century Europe than in the distribution of wealth, status and power within society. The influences that affected this distribution were similar to those of the previous century and there was little change in the methods by which the social position of individuals was determined or could be altered.

Despite the changes in the European economy that were led by the opening up of the oceanic trades and the new wealth that they brought in, most of Europe was still a subsistence-based, agrarian society with a low and inelastic system of production. Even after the modest growth in the economy after 1740, the surpluses available to support the lifestyles of the elites were still restricted, so that the methods of extraction by which they secured these surpluses remained firmly in place.

It is very difficult to generalize about the conditions of the European peasants. They were the prime producers everywhere, and remained so until the end of the century. In Russia some 90 per cent of the population can be classified as peasants in 1700, and the figure in 1800 had not changed significantly. The same can be said of France; despite the growth of prosperous commercial communities in the coastal cities, most Frenchmen in 1789 were peasant farmers, as they had been in 1700, and their legal status and economic condition had changed only marginally. The most significant division of the peasantries is that between eastern Europe and the west. It is broadly true that the majority of peasants in eastern Europe were serfs, legally bound to their landlords, who would normally be noblemen, for only noblemen could acquire serf estates. Serfdom prevailed because eastern Europe was thinly settled, land was plentiful, but labour was scarce, and the best-known feature of eastern peasant life was that the serf was subject to various kinds of forced labour. The amount could vary widely from Poland, where it was legally unlimited at the landlord's will, to the Habsburg lands, where there were at least notionally legal norms decreed by the ruler and it was the policy of the government to make a serious effort to enforce them.

Generally levels of labour service were negotiated with village communes, which took collective responsibility for the delivery of labour services, as they did for other obligations. Given the shortage of labour, even the individual serf tenant farmer had some scope for negotiating his terms of service. These could vary with the levels of peasant affluence. A peasant with draught animals and carts got a lower rate of demand than a landless cottager, and might be able to afford to hire substitute workers. This was certainly common in Brandenburg–Prussia and other parts of the Empire where labour service was prevalent. Peasants could also mitigate the rigours of forced labour by their style of working; forced labour has always tended to be relatively inefficient, and the peasants had, over many generations, devised tactics for easing their burdens. That was why some landlords preferred to commute labour service for cash, and use that to hire wage labourers. All over the region there were also communities of peasants who were legally freemen, either small freeholders, who are found as a substantial 10 per cent minority in East Prussia, or holders of hereditary tenant farms. Even in Poland and Russia minorities of free peasants survived. If, as seems to be the case, one force of change in the period was the population increase after 1740, which led in time to falling real wages and rising rents, the serf in eastern Europe, where labour remained in short supply, was to some extent protected from further exploitation. This suggests it is unsafe to assume that the unfree peasants of the east were necessarily worse off than the free peasants in the west. It is not at all certain that the landless labourers in southern Spain, who got an uncertain living on the vast estates of the grandee landowners, were better off than a serf in Russia or Poland, who in some respects enjoyed greater security. In any case, even legally free peasants were never really free, except for the small elite groups of freeholders. French peasants generally had legal tenure of their holdings, and serfdom had largely disappeared from France, but they still had labour services to perform for the crown, and sometimes for their landlords, in the form of the compulsory *corvées* to which they were liable. Even the peasant freeholders of Sweden had such services to perform on fortification works and, most onerous, the obligation that existed in many areas for the peasants to provide unpaid transport or cartage services for royal troops or officials. Other well-known burdens are seigneurial hunting rights over peasant fields, while the peasants themselves were forbidden to take game. Of course the peasants had defences against this too. They could poach and, if occasion offered, get together and collectively remove the game themselves, just as they could find ways of absenting themselves from *corvées*.

Historians are increasingly coming to the view that the distinction between serf tenure and free tenure, subject to seigneurial and crown demands, might not be all that great.[2] In the end the peasants had to manoeuvre as best they could in face of landlord pressures in order to moderate the rate of exploitation. Legal protection did exist in some societies where peasants were allowed resort to the royal courts, but it was uncertain. The legal system was firmly in the hands of the local nobility, so that resort to law against a landlord meant appealing to tribunals which, even if notionally royal courts, were in fact readily influenced by the local landlords and their agents. Such figures as can be collected suggest that levels of exploitation varied quite widely. Usually, after providing for his subsistence, the peasant paid rent and service to the landlord, taxes to the state and tithes to the church. If the lands of the Habsburg monarchy are taken as an illustration, a peasant in Moravia was paying 35 per cent of what he produced, in Bohemia 41 per cent, in the Austrian provinces between 41 and 50 per cent. Labour services, which crown policy sought to limit, ranged from three days a week in Bohemia to only 40 days a year in neighbouring Moravia. In both cases, and judging by the way these legal limits were periodically reaffirmed, it is likely the full local control exercised by the nobilities of both provinces meant that these legal restrictions were often disregarded with impunity.

One of the most irksome conditions of the peasant life, for those who sought to better their personal situations, was the narrowness of the escape routes. For the young unmarried man soldiering was a possibility, since conditions for rankers were somewhat improved in the new state armies, but it was a long shot. In Russia a serf who volunteered for military service could receive personal emancipation for himself and his family on discharge, though the odds on any individual surviving long enough to claim his reward were not good. Migration to a town was possible in some areas, but for an unskilled, migrant labourer the employment prospects were poor; it would have been of little avail in Russia, where escaped serfs could be legally recovered. There was the possibility of moving to Siberia, where landlordism did not develop and the local authorities were keen to have more settlers. Migration was generally discouraged, as in Prussian Silesia, where peasants were attracted to work in mining until the local landlords complained to the king, who decreed they could only leave with their lord's permission. There were, as everywhere in eighteenth-century society, hierarchical distinctions within peasant society, based mainly on wealth or family status within the community. There was always an elite of families that occupied communal offices, collected taxes, chose army recruits and allocated services, acting as agents of the authorities. Sometimes they loaned money or tools and animals to less affluent neighbours. But no peasant could forget for long that, in the overall social structure, his kind were second-class subjects, if indeed they were regarded as full members of society at all.

The elites were ambivalent about the peasantry. Any thinking person knew that their labours supplied most of society's basic needs. After mid-century the economic doctrines of the physiocrats, like Quesnay, who saw agriculture as the main producer of real wealth, argued that the land would yield more if the peasant were a free, independent producer with material incentives to improve output. Among the enlightened chattering classes, emancipation of the serfs was being urged by leading publicists, like the finance minister Necker in France, Antonio Genovesi in Naples and Joseph von Sonnenfels, adviser to Joseph II, in Austria. Further there had always been some moral unease among the religious over peasant oppression. There was also the fashionable sentimental myth of the happy rural idyll that led Marie Antoinette and her courtiers to play at being shepherdesses at Versailles. Many governments were conscious of the need to protect the peasant, as the principal source of tax revenue and army recruiting. The Habsburgs were leaders in this, and in principle both Frederick II in Prussia and Catherine II in Russia wanted serfdom alleviated or abolished. Yet almost nothing effective was done. Joseph II did grant personal freedom to the peasantry and sought to regulate labour services, but Catherine, while contemplating recognizing the free peasants as a legal Estate, which would have done nothing for the majority of serfs, drew back, while Frederick in Prussia, while extending his reform notions to the tenants of crown estates, recognized openly he could not force the noble landlords, the backbone of his army and government, to give up their powers over their peasants. Serfdom remained legally confirmed in the major Prussian law code of 1796. Most contemporary government systems were basically partnerships between princes and aristocratic landlords. Without the voluntary goodwill of the latter, the former could not function. And while the surviving records are full of the liberal intentions of landlords and government officials, the unofficial records are full of remarks betraying that to many landlords, peasants were an inferior life form and a threat to orderly society if not kept under strict discipline. Even to liberals, the peasants seemed ignorant, superstitious and ineducable. A progressive landlord who tried to introduce agricultural improvement was as likely as not to meet suspicion and resistance from his tenants. There was a basic wisdom that told the peasants that not only was all departure from custom dangerous in itself, but that any improving measures that would enrich their landlords would in the end impoverish them. The English cottagers and labourers certainly learned this lesson the hard way. So there was a vicious circle, a mutual incomprehension between classes, that stood in the way of agreed reforms.

With rare exceptions, like Sweden, where the peasants were a legal Estate, the peasantry was excluded from political participation above the village level. At that level they could negotiate with authority, and if dissatisfied might try litigation or petition to higher authority. Occasionally, when authority was obdurate, peasants would riot and enclosures or oppressive bailiffs and officials would be attacked. Government was accustomed to this, and could deal with it by force if necessary, though most preferred negotiation. In most of Europe the old, large-scale peasant insurrection, the *jacquerie*, had died out, until it flared up spectacularly in France in 1789, a warning of how dangerous reform might be. Once the peasants had heard tell of the intentions of the National Assembly to abolish feudalism, they made a preventive strike to forestall possible landlord resistance. There were others, like the serious peasant uprisings in Bohemia in the 1780s, where awareness of the reforming plans of Joseph II and a particularly severe subsistence crisis coincided.

Peasant rebellion was generally confined to the eastern borderlands. They contained an explosive mix of weak central control and the Cossack model of a free frontier society without landlords or religious animosities between Orthodox peasants and Polish Catholic landlords in the Ukraine, or Uniate peasants and Calvinist landlords in Transylvania, and everywhere between impoverished peasants and Jewish shopkeepers and bailiffs. It was on the eastern borders that peasant rebellion could flare up into a mass protest, often including murderous pogroms against every vestige of official culture, and naturally against the Jews. The last of these was the Pugachev uprising in 1773. It began among frontier cossacks, the Yaik cossacks, and recruited both agricultural and industrial serfs, Old Believer sectaries and the support of Bashkir frontier tribesmen. Pugachev claimed to be the murdered tsar Peter III, unfortunate husband of Catherine. His programme was simply to destroy landlordism and establish a free peasant society. Although it shook Catherine's government, coming at a point when she was trying to wind up the current war with the Ottomans, the time was gone when this kind of anarchic turmoil could defy the organized forces at the disposal of the contemporary military state. It was crushed in 1774, and proved to be the last of its kind in Russia before 1906.

The history of the peasantries in the eighteenth century suggests that their conditions were often harsh and oppressive, that there was some awareness among the elites that this ought to be alleviated by government action and adoption of new farming methods, but that the vested interests and fears of the landlords, who controlled government and politics, stood in the way of radical action. Joseph II came near to breaking up his empire by persisting in his attempts to liberate the peasantry in the 1780s. Among the peasants themselves, their sheer insecurity in face of natural disasters, which no one could control, and man-made disasters like destructive warfare had bred a deep fatalism, a culture of acceptance of things as they were as dispensations of divine Providence. Peasants lived from harvest to harvest, struggling for bare survival, and wasted little energy on speculating how things could be different. When the French revolutionary armies marched out with their call to the peoples to liberate themselves from the feudal oppressors, they met with determined peasant hostility wherever they went. European society, which treated its peasants so harshly, had been in no danger of being overthrown by spontaneous agrarian insurrection.

A survey of Europe in 1789 would show that in almost every existing society, with some marginal exceptions like Norway, the United Provinces and the surviving city states, plus some small exotic examples like Friesland and some of the Swiss cantons, their ruling elites were landed nobilities. Even nobilities that had originated as urban, trading elites, like the Venetian or Florentine nobilities, had acquired landed status by 1700. Superficially there was a wide variety in the size, wealth and privileges that each nobility enjoyed in its own society; but this makes no difference to the basic reality about who ruled eighteenth-century Europe. The basis of the nobles' power was their control over local administration. This could be grounded in seigneurial right – the jurisdiction they enjoyed over their tenants. With the exception of Britain and Sweden, seigneurial courts and jurisdiction existed all over Europe. Sometimes it was comprehensive, virtually excluding central authority, as over most of serf Europe, Russia, the Habsburg dominions, the Baltic provinces, and much of Iberia, Sicily and Naples. Sometimes it was more a matter of status conferred by seigneurial title, like hunting privileges and the profits from collecting seigneurial dues, as in most of France and western Germany. But seigneurial status was eagerly sought, irrespective of how much power it actually conferred. Dutch regents purchased manors which yielded little but an honorary title, and manorial titles, frequently sold by Italian princes to those looking for enhanced status, were eagerly purchased.

Wherever labour services were a crucial part of the noble economy, seigneurial jurisdiction was vital, and noblemen expected government to help enforce their rights, whether positively, as in Russia with its fugitive serf laws, or Denmark, where after 1660 the crown had endowed a new service nobility, with land grants that carried seigneurial powers, in return for noble administration of tax collection and conscription. This was reinforced twice after 1700 by royal decrees defining the extents of landlord authority. In Britain, where seigneurial rights had virtually been abandoned, gentry control of local government was secured through the county bench, where they sat as justices of the peace, supported by the lord lieutenant, nearly always a local peer, and the gentry deputy lieutenants who controlled the county militia. A similar power system operated in Hungary and Poland, where the lower nobility had virtually autonomous control of the counties.

The nobilities were also entrenched in the machineries of central government. Where there were active representative institutions, as in Britain, the *pays d'états* in France, the Austrian Netherlands – indeed almost all the Habsburg dominions – in Sweden, where the Estate of the nobility dominated the Diet, and Poland where they entirely controlled the Diets, power lay with the nobilities. In executive government almost all the higher posts were held by nobles, or if the holders were commoners on appointment, they became ennobled in the course of their careers. In Britain during this period four-fifths of senior ministerial appointments went to peers. The peerage controlled the House of Lords and by 1786 peers could influence the elections to 210 seats in the House of Commons, where the sons of peers also sat in significant numbers. The remaining seats in the Commons were mostly held by lawyers or landed gentlemen. In France, from the reign of Louis XIV onwards, no commoners held high government office with the exception of Necker, who was both a foreigner and a Protestant and therefore barred from entering the nobility. Further, between 1718 and 1789, three-quarters of French noblemen holding ministerial office came from families with at least three generations of noble descent.

In the countries where there were formal Tables of Rank, ennoblement came automatically on reaching the prescribed level of seniority. Noblemen could also be found in high places in the churches. The Empire had a rule requiring nobility by birth for entry to some cathedral and monastic chapters. That apart, throughout Catholic Europe, it was common for the higher positions in the church to be held by noblemen. In France there was a steady increase in noble penetration of the episcopate and by 1789 nobles held 97 per cent of the bishoprics. In Hungary the more prestigious clerical appointments usually went to magnate families. In Lutheran countries it was uncommon for members of noble families to enter the church, but in the Church of England, as the century progressed, the episcopate was increasingly colonized by the nobility, and in all of Europe noble landowners held rights of patronage over church livings. The English peerage controlled 14 per cent in 1800, and gentry families many more. In addition, noblemen and women dominated the royal courts and enjoyed rights of access to the presence of the sovereign. This was a valuable source of power and influence, through which noblemen could construct patronage networks reaching down into society. They also had a virtual monopoly of senior diplomatic appointments.

A major source of recruiting of nobles was the creation of service nobilities in the emergent military–bureaucratic states. In Denmark, for example, a small and exclusive pre-1660 nobility was supplemented by a new titled service nobility arranged according to the official Table of Ranks and endowed with grants of crown lands. This same process of dilution through enlargement is found in Sweden. There was a novel principle of egalitarianism built into the Tables of Ranks, since precedence was supposed to depend on service rank and not on hereditary status. In theory, a commoner who held an office would outrank a nobleman by birth holding a lower office. It did not happen much in the real world. Even an enthusiast for promotion on merit, like Peter in Russia, recognized the existence of the old *boyar* noble families and accorded them a special legal status in his system. The biggest professional field for the expanding service nobility was always the army. In general the officer corps were made up of noblemen, and the expanding military establishments greatly enlarged career prospects. They also boosted noble power and influence; for example, where armies were organized on the state commission system, as they were in France, Prussia and the Habsburg lands, captains and colonels were the proprietors of their companies and regiments and acquired a valuable asset, through the funds they administered and the patronage over commissions they controlled. Indeed, state service must have been a lifeline for many of the less affluent noble families, offering paid employment that was compatible with their noble status.

There is little sense in the eighteenth century that the position of noblemen as the natural ruling elite in society was threatened. On the contrary, the nobility was a growth industry, with the commoners outside their ranks clamouring to get in. Generally a nobleman had a legal right to his superior status in society. This was marked by a range of public legal distinctions attaching to noble status, expressed in forms of address, entitlement to special legal procedures, often safeguarded by trial by his peers, and exemption from humiliating punishments. In social intercourse the nobleman enjoyed precedence, as he usually did in seating in church, or placement in public ceremonials. These were such important public tokens of status that disputes over precedence were many and bitter. Usually noblemen could expect tax privileges, though a blanket exemption from all public taxation was being steadily eroded, and in some countries had never existed. The English peerage and gentry had always paid public taxation, so had the Polish nobility, though where they did pay, the nobility was often well placed to control the assessments. The Swedish nobility had always claimed tax exemption as one of their most cherished privileges, but in practice had acquiesced in its repeated infringement. So in the end did the French nobility: from the 1690s they paid the new property taxes levied to meet the costs of war, and continued to do so through until 1789.

It is as difficult to generalize about nobilities as it is to generalize about peasantries. There was the obvious distinction between the relatively expanded nobilities in countries like Poland, Hungary, Spain and even Britain, if the English untitled gentry is regarded as the equivalent of the lesser nobility of the continent, which they certainly thought they were. In such systems there were very wide distinctions between the magnates at the top of society and the impoverished family that clung to its status by birth but had little else. Spain was perhaps peculiar in having a class of *hidalgos* that included working artisans. This disturbed Spanish governments who would have wished to eliminate them. The poorest Polish nobles were similar, as were some of the landless Hungarian nobles. They were protected by law, but like their English counterparts, having no formal legal privileges, simply lost public recognition and sank back into the ranks of the commoners. It was certainly not the case that all noblemen were affluent, though it was the case that most affluent people were nobles. The main exceptions to the rule were the commercial and monied elites of Britain and the United Provinces. Within the ranks of nobilities there were enormous disparities of income. If some Polish noblemen were landless and penniless, there were magnate families owning complexes of estates the equivalent of a small principality. The same was true of the Habsburg nobilities or the Spanish grandees.

On the whole, European nobilities were expanding in the eighteenth century, a sign of the vigour and importance of their order. It was a demographic fact that if there had not been recruitment of commoners, hereditary nobilities would have been doomed to eventual extinction. In the United Provinces, where there was no sovereign authority empowered to grant new titles of nobility, their numbers were slowly and inexorably shrinking with the passage of time. Those already in the exclusive club did not always welcome expansion. Where the nobles themselves had some control, as they did in Poland and Sweden, the tendency was to resist enlargement. In Sweden there was a persistent attempt to shrink the number of noble families. In most of Europe, where sovereigns had the power to ennoble, it was so convenient and lucrative that they used it freely. One of the attractions for the Habsburgs of holding the imperial crown was its exclusive right to grant titles in the Empire. By the eighteenth century there was a regular procedure and a fixed tariff operative for the acquiring of imperial titles.

The Spanish monarchy had long sold ennoblements: the relatively new stratum of titled nobles, less than grandees but above the ordinary *hidalgo*, expanded from 533 to 1323 families during the century. By contrast, the British crown kept the peerage exclusive. There were 167 peers in 1710, and still only 220 in 1790; and of the new titles nearly 90 per cent were given to members of families connected to the existing peerage. In France entry was open to all who could pay because of the unusual extent of the system of venal officeholding. There were categories of office, like *sécretaire du roi*, which could be treated as sinecures and conferred instant nobility, and after some years of tenure, hereditary status. The existing nobles naturally responded by forming sub-categories which competed for status within the system. The best known to historians is the distinction between *noblesse de robe* and *noblesse d'épée*, the latter claiming to be a superior nobility of blood. They in turn drew distinctions between the truly distinguished families, noble since 1465, and the majority of later creation. But there were further distinctions between princes who were sovereigns in their own right, the princes of the blood, the *ducs et paires* and the ordinary marquises and barons. The French crown did not have to create many nobles by patent; the nobility was inexorably expanding, and the crown reaped a useful income from the process. The lively demand from commoners to win entry into the ranks of the nobility showed that it was a vigorous and expanding part of European society right up to 1789. Even the reformers and thinkers who turned a critical eye on the system of noble privilege during the century rarely advocated abolition. The assumption that all societies were hierarchical in structure, and could not function otherwise, was rarely questioned. Radicals like Rousseau might express a preference for a true aristocracy of merit over the existing system, but he accepted that there had to be social ranking. It is true that the Americans, when they came to draft their constitution, did deliberately forbid the introduction of titles of nobility into the new republic, and the French Revolution developed an intense hostility to the noble class on ideological grounds, but more recent work on the French Revolution has shown how successfully the French nobility survived this onslaught to re-emerge as the social elite after 1815.[3]

If there was to be a successful challenge to the hegemony of the nobilities over eighteenth-century society, since they dominated the landed sector, it would have to develop from the urban sector. Urban Europe, like its peasantries and nobilities, experienced diverse fortunes in the eighteenth century. It may be true that overall the urban sector was expanding over the period, but certainly not in a uniform manner. Some towns were in decline. This was true of some of the imperial free cities, though not all – Hamburg was a major exception. In the United Provinces, Amsterdam continued to be a major entrepot and financial centre, but many of the Dutch towns were stagnant or declining. In Sweden, Stockholm had been steadily growing in size and affluence up to around 1750, then went into decline. On the other hand, the naval town of Karlskrona, founded on a greenfield site in the 1680s, was by 1700 the third-largest town in Sweden, one of many reminders of how the activity of the emerging military states could have significant economic consequences. In Russia, St Petersburg had grown from nothing into one of the major cities of Europe after 1700. When Catherine II reorganized local government in Russia in 1775, a whole series of new towns had to be developed as the new provincial capitals, and 216 had been founded by 1786. At the end of the process, some 10 per cent of the Russian population could be classified as urban. Another example of state-building leading to major urban growth is Turin, the planned capital of the emergent Italian principality of Savoy-Piedmont. It became a flourishing centre of administration, trade and manufacture and helped the development of enlarged satellite towns in the principality to service its growing economy. But commercial factors could also drive urban expansion, as the oceanic trades fed the rising ports of the Atlantic seaboard, from Gothenberg in Sweden down to Bordeaux, whose population grew from 45,000 to 81,000 between 1700 and 1790. The other French Atlantic ports saw comparable expansion, as did Bristol, Liverpool and Glasgow.

If it is possible to show that there were centres of commercially led urban expansion like those mentioned, it is not possible to show that their successful citizens were seeking to challenge the landed nobilities for control of their societies.[4] Urban society reflected the structures and values of the culture as a whole; in particular, it was highly decentralized and internally structured along hierarchical lines. By 1700 there were still many parts of Europe where the urban sector had a voice in representative bodies, and where Estates still met it was usual to have a burgher Estate included. Where this had atrophied, as in the case of the *cortes* of Castile, or Brandenburg, it seems the town elites were willing to give up formal representation in face of the rising authority of the central government. They could do better for themselves in separate negotiation with the ruler and his officials, who could offer them real protection against, for example, the encroachments of the landed nobility. Where they did remain represented there is a marked lack of evidence of any significant political initiatives associated with their Estates. In Sweden after 1718, when the Diet successfully exercised effective supervision over the monarchy, the burghers were usually willing to yield leadership to the nobility, contenting themselves with lobbying for their sectional interests. In Britain where, in theory, borough seats in the House of Commons constituted four-fifths of the total, there was no thought that the urban sector might use this to challenge the control of the landlords, who in fact occupied most of the borough seats with the willing consent of the local community. The larger cities, led by the corporation of London, did elect their own citizens to represent them, but they proceeded by lobbying and trading favours, there was never the remotest sign that the urban members would pursue their own political agenda. It is significant that, in the most economically advanced society of its day, the commercial interest felt no need to bid for control. The reality was that by seeking consensus, rather than confrontation they secured in Britain the most commercially friendly governments in Europe.

In any case, commerce and industry were not necessarily the basis of urban societies. In Britain, the spa town of Bath flourished in the century as a centre of leisure services and tourism, an example followed by other lesser towns where mineral springs of good repute were marketed successfully. Then there were the garrison towns that existed all over Europe. Berlin was one such, where the military and their auxiliary services were the main basis of its urban development in 1700. In places like Toulouse, a city of 60,000 inhabitants in the 1760s, it was the existence of the *parlement* and a university which sustained a community described by Arthur Young as 'almost without manufactures or commerce'. Besançon contained little except a *parlement*, but that supported a flourishing community of lawyers, whose families made up its ruling elite. Such communities, which lived by servicing the prevailing political order, were unlikely to develop as centres of political agitation to change it. The emergent military–fiscal states were in any case watchful over any risk of the urban sector mounting a political challenge to their authority, even if they had been so inclined. Louis XIV in the 1690s had established a royal official, the lieutenant of police, to supervise local government in the main urban centres, though he, like all other officials, found it expedient to engage in dialogue rather than confrontation with the local elites. When it was felt necessary to round up vagrants and beggars in Paris in 1749, it was the lieutenant who organized it, but the municipal authorities were offered bonuses for cooperating in the exercise. The towns of Brandenburg–Prussia were brought under firm central control by the intrusion of the royal official, the *Steurrat*, to organize not only taxation, his original remit, but the policing of the towns as well. In Russia, where Peter had positively tried to establish urban self-government, he found the local communities unwilling to take any responsibility, and gave up the attempt. Administration was supervised by provincial governors and local garrison commanders.

There is in fact almost no record of urban resistance or challenge to central government in the eighteenth century. Urban riots and demonstrations did occur, but they resembled the parallel peasant protests, being provoked by local problems, most often subsistence problems, where town government failed to take adequate remedial action. If central authority did get involved, it would be when the town elite feared they were losing control and asked for help. This was the case in the worst urban disturbance of the century in London. During the Gordon riots of 1780, the mob, fired up by anti-Catholic hysteria, roamed unchecked through the city, doing a signifi-cant amount of looting and burning. Control was not regained until a very reluctant lord mayor authorized the army to intervene. Among the other infrequent incidents of major urban revolt was the rioting in Madrid in 1766, apparently a combination of food riots with an admixture of popular xenophobia. Here the mob controlled the city for four days and the king had to make an undignified flight from the capital. Yet Madrid was easily settled by negotiation, and there is strong reason to believe that the the troubles were being exploited by a court faction seeking the overthrow of an unpop-ular administration. There is no evidence that the citizens were disloyal to the monarchy.

In reality the whole structure of urban society was inimical to the devel-opment of any such action. Early modern towns were basically defined by being corporate holders of liberties, granted by charters from higher authority. That authority could be a sovereign prince, the church or a feudal magnate. But a liberty always means in that context a privileged exemption from the rules governing the rest of society. Urban liberties were often seen as abusive grievances by those who did not enjoy them; hence they were under intermittent critical attack. So the first requirement of urban society was to engage the protection of higher authority by collaborating with it. Some examples of urban independence and assertiveness can be found in the United Provinces, where the towns had secured their autonomy after the rebellion against Spain, although even there occasions arose, as in the crisis of 1618, or again in 1672, when the town oligarchies lost control and had to appeal to the stadholder and the army to intervene. The reality was that the great days of city states and urban autonomy had long gone by 1700. The Italian city republics had mostly become absolute monarchies, except Genoa, now a shadow of its former self as banker to the Spanish monarchy, and Venice. After a brief imperial revival at the turn of the century, which proved very short-lived, Venice lingered on as a theme park for the enter-tainment of Europe's nobility.

Towns throughout Europe were ruled by the oligarchies that made up their elites. In times past these had been subject to election by fellow citizens; by 1700 either election had been dispensed with, and the governing body was a closed corporation, recruiting by cooption, as with the Dutch regents, or there was an identifiable group of families from whose members the town corporations were selected. These were more likely to be *rentier* families that could 'live nobly', that is without actually working, or the wealthiest mer-chants or bankers. In the smaller provincial towns, where there might not be such people, the officers of the leading trade guilds might constitute the ruling elite of the community. The main criterion for being in the elite group was always adequate personal wealth, giving the ability to sustain the burdens of public office. The officeholders had to have time free to conduct community business, to be affluent enough to meet the costs of public display that went with officeholding and to be of sufficient social status to be able to negotiate effectively with the higher authorities. Even Dutch regent families would be downgraded if they lost their wealth. Generally, holding high office in town government was not economically rewarding, as evidenced by the many town statutes that made officeholding a compulsory obligation, and levied fines on those who refused to serve when their turn came.

The rewards of office were clearly firstly the demonstration of recognized public status already achieved; secondly reinforcing that status through the patronage that went with office; and finally by being in a position to be of service to the higher authorities, and perhaps win promotion into the nobility. A recent historian has suggested: 'for many a merchant or rentier in an early-modern city, the pursuit of wealth was only an instrument by which to gain some form of social recognition'. Noble status was the ultimate prize.

The overall impression is that urban elites were not generally led by the entrepreneurs in their communities but by the established families whose aspirations were socially conservative. They did not want to change the existing social order, only to advance their position within it. Beneath the established ruling group of families was the larger category of citizens or burghers. These were mostly economically active merchants, manufacturers and artisans with businesses to run, even if often on a very modest scale. The definition of who was a citizen or burgher varied from place to place, but usually it involved being the head of a household and economically self-supporting; that is, able to pay his share of the municipal taxes and perform the humbler civic offices. Yet these people too were an elite – usually, except in Britain, members of a guild. The recognized burghers were often as little as a fifth of the population of their communities. The evidence about the aspirations of the various merchant and trade guilds suggests they remained faithful to their medieval traditions. They existed not to maximize production and earnings, or to win new markets by aggressive competition. Quite the contrary, they existed to guard the privileges of their craft or trade against outsiders or competition. The tendency was to restrict the number of new businesses, make the processes of gaining recognition as a master more lengthy and expensive, bar the entry of outsiders into their trade and have rural competition outlawed.

The guilds too were socially and economically traditionalist. This meant that they could be seen as an obstacle to development by reforming governments which wanted to expand production and commerce, or were influenced by the truly entrepreneurial investors and projectors who did appreciate the potential of freeing up production and marketing from legal restriction. On balance, however, though monarchs like Joseph II in Austria, and at times Louis XVI in France, and some of their advisers, were persuaded of the potential of freer trade, and tried to advance it in face of stubborn guild resistance, most appreciated that the system of controls was an important part of the machinery for maintaining orderly government in the urban sector. The need for this was reinforced by the fact that the majority of the urban population were outside the ranks of the elites, the guildsmen or the burghers. They were the labouring poor, usually casually employed, crowded into tenements, owning no property and paying no taxes. Since these people were not economically self-sustaining, they had to be relieved at the expense of the municipality in hard times when employment was unavailable, or when a subsistence crisis arose and food prices meant hunger even for those who had work. Beneath this social layer there was an underworld of migrants, not recognized as being lawful inhabitants at all, who lived by their wits, often by crime and begging.

There was a variety of institutions and practices for coping with the danger these people presented. It was one of the main arguments for the public control of markets that the price of the basic essentials for the poor must be stabilized, and most urban governments acknowledged some obligation to fund relief measures. The expense of traditional relief methods and the declining public acceptance of begging and indiscriminate relief of paupers encouraged a growing movement to set the poor to work in public institutions or workhouses. The trouble was that no early modern state had the administrative or fiscal resources to run such systems on the scale that would have been needed. The sense of the precariousness of the social order in the urban sector encouraged the authorities to combine repression and control with the provision of some minimal public welfare to keep the urban poor from rioting. In the last resort they would need the power of the central government if the worst happened and things got out of control. The awareness of danger by the urban elites did not encourage thoughts of challenging the established structure of authority.

The eighteenth-century urban economy, and the social attitudes of the elites who ruled in the towns were overwhelmingly conservative. Nearly all the proposals for social renewal which were floated after the 1760s on the basis of Enlightenment thinking, and sometimes urged on communities by the authority of the enlightened despots, could count on meeting obstinate resistance from the vested interests at all levels of urban society. It is difficult to see, in the situation that actually existed, much evidence of a developing revolutionary challenge to the established order. That said, it is plausible to argue that the expanding urban sector, and overall it was expanding, was an agency for promoting change and undermining traditional thinking. For if the towns and their rulers were not themselves leading demands for reform, they were developing an environment in which reform movements could develop and flourish.

There was a growth of both a consumer society and a leisure society in eighteenth-century Europe, and the evidence comes from the urban sector. It was there that the services for such developments were located. Shops were an urban phenomenon, as were professional medical services, and towns were where the educational facilities were situated to meet the rising demands for a better level of education and professional training. They were also the places where the government agencies and law courts were situated, together with the professional lawyers, whose services were in constant demand among the propertied classes. The towns had the theatres, the libraries, the bookshops, as well as the newpapers and the periodicals that met the growing demands of those with the money to buy them and the leisure to read them. The elites were drawn in to balls and dances and other occasions for social gathering – the new societies and discussion groups which helped spread the ideas of the Enlightenment necessarily established themselves in towns. Further, the urban environment, for all its conservatism, was one in which concerted action for social betterment was actually possible. Urban governments were pioneering measures to improve public health, promoting rebuilding, installing drainage and organizing the removal of refuse, paving the streets and lighting them, building theatres and assembly rooms, developing more effective policing, providing public parks and promenades. In their way towns were both stimulating informed debate about traditional values and the possibility of ameliorating reforms, and providing working models of the sort of change for the better that was actually possible through concerted public action. Further, some of the ideas being discussed among the educated elites, such as that society could be changed for the better, filtered down to the lower orders in urban society. The elites were making the mistake of talking too freely in front of the servants, not realizing that in urban society levels of education and literacy were much higher among the working population than they were in the villages. When the revolution did come, it was not to be led by a revolutionary urban elite, for no such group existed, but the towns did provide the only environment from which the reformers and revolutionaries could launch their challenge.

12

A New Search for Political Stability

The treaties of Utrecht, Rastadt and Baden were a major attempt by the leading European states to create a stable balance of power in Mediterranean and Atlantic Europe and with it a lasting peace. When the Treaty of Nystadt, in 1721, brought the Northern War to an end, rulers and their ministers had an opportunity to reinforce the new order and postpone the coming of the next general war. Their efforts brought nearly a quarter-century pause, during which the wars that were fought were limited and local. The European power game had not changed, but all the players needed time to build up their strength before embarking on the next round of general conflict.

Great Britain

After 1689, although Britain had managed to build a powerful military state that had proved itself in two successful wars against Louis XIV, domestic political stability had not been achieved, and in 1714 the society faced a change of dynasty and a disputed succession. By the Act of Settlement, on the death of Queen Anne, the crown was to pass to the Protestant claimant, now George, Elector of Hanover. He had no claim on the affections of his new subjects, except his Protestantism. This was a substantial asset; the evidence is strong that the English and the lowland Scots had come to build their national identity round their Protestantism.[1] The English saw themselves as God's chosen Protestant nation, and at the same time identified 'popery' with absolutism and tyranny. The revolution of 1689 had proved divisive, for although the united elites welcomed the establishment of a Protestant succession, they were not agreed about the political outcome. This had created a constitutional monarchy which had very significant powers, but could not govern without the cooperation of parliament, which represented the whole body of Protestant property-owners. The divisions of the elites were expressed through two political parties, the Whigs and the Tories, competing for popular support. The Tories represented those conservative forces that basically rejected two of the results of 1689: the loss of the legitimacy which was conferred on monarchy by divinely sanctioned hereditary succession, and the weakening of the exclusive authority of the established Church of England by the grant, in the Toleration Act of 1689, of limited legal recognition of the rights of Protestant dissenters. These had been the foundations of traditional kingship. Their Whig opponents, while equally committed to the monarchy and the national church, were reconciled to the changes, which they saw as the necessary price of preserving a Protestant succession.

The reign of Queen Anne had intensified party strife, and as attitudes to the war became party issues, the succession too became a party issue. The Elector had been a committed opponent of Louis XIV and regarded the change in British policy under the Tory administration that took power after 1710 as a betrayal of the cause. Everyone knew that if the Elector succeeded to the throne, the Tory administration could not survive the new king's hostility. That was why, in the last years of the queen, the Tory administration of Robert Harley and Bolingbroke had canvassed the possibility of restoring the Stuart succession, by inducing the Old Pretender to convert to the Church of England. When James III, as he claimed to be, refused to consider the idea, the Tories split, some openly expressing support for the Hanoverian succession, others prepared to gamble on a Stuart restoration, or at least build such a grip on government that they would be able to bargain with the Hanoverians. Thus the succession of George I in 1714 could have caused civil war. In Scotland it did, with the formidable rising of 1715, showing how there the Stuart cause provided a rallying point for the many Scots who had remained unreconciled to the Act of Union of 1707, and aspired to restore Scotland's independence. The Scottish rebellion failed because the parallel Stuart insurrection in England was anticipated and stifled by swift government action.

The new king had immediately dismissed the Tory ministry and installed a Whig administration, whose very political survival depended on the success of the new dynasty. After suppressing the 1715 rebellions, the ministry set about consolidating its hold on power. It ingratiated itself with the king by providing British money and naval support for his plans to halt Russian infiltration into the Baltic and north Germany, and then set about re-establishing political stability at home. After 1715 there was a far-reaching partisan purge of Tory officeholders from central and local government, accompanied by measures to control parliament itself: the statutory triennial elections for the House of Commons were seen as a weakness, and in 1716 the system was changed by the Septennial Act. Less frequent elections were much easier to manage, and it proved that, by systematic use of the political patronage available to government, both the elections and the subsequent political conduct of the MPs once elected could be effectively influenced. The aristocratic leadership of the Whigs attempted to make the

House of Lords equally secure by the proposed Peerage Bill of 1719, putting statutory limitations on the future creation of peers, but the career ambitions of their own parliamentarians and their wealthy commoner supporters forced the dropping of that measure. Even so, over time, as Whig hegemony over the government consolidated, control of the House of Lords was increasingly secured by such measures as the appointment of Whig bishops, while natural and political erosion reduced the Tory peerage from 40 to 20.

While the Whig aristocrats manoeuvred for government and court places, and involved themselves in what really mattered – foreign affairs and diplomacy, which were the king's main concerns – the actual business of organizing the political controls fell to the commoner, Sir Robert Walpole, a Norfolk country gentleman who combined a genius for political fixing and dealing with proven competence in handling public finances, one of the great post-war issues facing the country. The war had left the country with a much increased national debt, and ways had to be found of managing this economically. Walpole grasped how the key to domestic political power lay in the Treasury. Public opinion could be won over by good management resulting in lower taxes, combined with security for the public creditors by measures acceptable to the financial and trading interests. Above all, by the patronage attaching to the Treasury through the jobs and favours which it could dispense, members of the elites could be influenced, if not entirely controlled. Walpole's patronage was systematic, ruthless and all-embracing; no mercy was shown to the disloyal. Historians are still arguing about how strong Jacobitism was in the Tory party,[2] whose organization survived and usually assured them of about a quarter of the seats in the Commons. In the 1730s, under the leadership of the former Jacobite, Bolingbroke, the party called for a restored consensus in politics, implying their acceptance of the Hanoverians and a readiness to enter a coalition which could end Walpole's monopoly of power. Walpole himself successfully used the Jacobite danger to rally opinion and brand the Tories as disloyal. Within the period of his effective hegemony, from about 1725 until 1741, he had consolidated a one-party state in England and turned Scotland's parliamentary representation into a Treasury pocket borough.

The system was openly corrupt but not unprincipled. Walpole adhered to the basic principles of Whiggism: support of the Hanoverian succession, public adherence to the revolution of 1689, political control of the Church of England and political reliefs for Protestant dissenters, public support for the promotion of trade and commerce, prudent management of the public revenues and low taxation. This led to a foreign policy aimed at avoiding continental wars, in so far as the dynasty's commitment to its Hanoverian territories allowed, by promoting the balance of power in Europe, while pursuing British growth overseas. It was a conservative regime and reform proposals, like attempts to repeal the Test and Corporation Acts to give full political rights to dissenters, were not pressed in the face of determined parliamentary resistance.

Walpole also suffered defeat on his one major innovative project, the attempted reform of the excise in 1733. The excise was becoming the most important source of public revenue, easier to levy than direct taxes, and the one revenue entirely managed and collected by professional, salaried government agents. Because they were established over the whole kingdom, and were a powerful element of government patronage, but above all because they were efficient, the excisemen were deeply unpopular. The other big indirect revenue, the customs, was less threatening because it was regularly mitigated by smuggling, which was a major industry in parts of Britain.[3] Walpole proposed to exchange customs duties for excises, freeing up imports and exports, cutting out the smugglers, and providing extra revenue that could be used to reduce the land tax. It was a sound, modernizing reform, but easily attacked by a vociferous opposition of combined vested interests, fed by insinuations that it would reinforce the scope of Treasury patronage. Walpole had to abandon his plan. It was a warning that public opinion could not be manipulated beyond certain limits. On the other hand, Walpole was not threatened, since throughout he had the firm support of the crown.

This had not been easily gained. George I was not initially well disposed to Walpole, until he demonstrated his usefulness during the South Sea Bubble crisis in 1721. The South Sea Company had developed during the war to exploit the opening up of the Spanish empire to British merchants. This was partly realized when Spain reluctantly awarded the *asiento* for the slave trade to Britain and permitted an annual trading voyage to Spanish America. The expected trade bonanza had not materialized and the company was looking for new opportunities, culminating in a scheme to privatize part of the national debt, some £30 million of which was taken over by the company. The hopes of profits, exploited by corrupt financial interests including government ministers, led to a wild boom in South Sea shares, followed by a spectacular crash, which shook the whole political and trading community. It was Walpole who used all his manipulative and parliamentary skills in a campaign of damage limitation, which restored financial confidence while protecting leading ministers from possible criminal proceedings and preventing the downfall of the administration. Walpole was recognized as the necessary political manager and accepted as such by George I. He then managed the very difficult feat of surviving the change of monarch in 1727, for the new king, George II, had established the family tradition of venomous hatred of his father and all who were associated with him. Walpole had managed the transition through his business relations with the queen, Caroline, whose influence was a main support of his ministry until her death in 1737.

When Walpole fell from power at last in 1741, he had stabilized the British political system along lines that held good for the rest of the century. The key to successful government was a ministry secure in the support of the crown, the necessary basis for any government, and able to handle policy and patronage to secure majority support in the two Houses of Parliament, which represented the views of the property-owners. It was also wise to respect the prejudices and emotions of the wider populace, which was usually content with the role of passive onlooker at the political game, but which could become dangerous if roused, in a society with freedom of debate and publication.

France

The French monarchy also faced a succession problem on the death of Louis XIV and it threatened the governmental system he had developed. This combined giving the sword nobility a share in power through the court at Versailles, while the business of administration and policy-making was reserved to the *robe* nobles who ran the ministries and sat on the ruling councils. Its relative success had depended on the untiring supervision over both sides of the system exercised by the king. A series of deaths in the royal family during 1710–11 had removed nearly all of Louis XIV's direct male heirs, leaving one surviving great-grandson, who became Louis XV at five years old. Until he was able to marry and produce an heir, the succession remained uncertain. The strongest claimant was Philip V of Spain, but he was debarred by the peace settlements; that left the collateral Bourbon lines of Orléans and Condé.

Louis appointed his nephew Philip, duke of Orléans, as regent, but also nominated a council that was to share his powers. By a swift coup, Philip, with the cooperation of the *parlement* of Paris, had the full powers vested in himself. The regent had two obvious aims: first to safeguard his own claim on the succession if Louis XV should die, and then to open up the central government to his fellow magnates and regain aristocratic control. The ministries were replaced by seven governmental councils, each presided over by a member of the high nobility. The seat of government was moved from Versailles back to Paris, and to win the vital support of the *parlement* necessary to validate the changes, its traditional rights of remonstrance against royal policies, restricted by Louis XIV in 1673, were restored. The new system of government quickly foundered; it was abandoned in 1718 and the old ministries reinstated. The magnates had neither the professionalism nor the inclination to give their lives to routine administrative duty. But in the absence of a strong-willed monarch who would impose his authority on the aristocratic factions at his court, the return of the high nobility to active politics survived. From 1715 to 1789, French government was determined by the struggles of aristocratic factions at court for office, favour and influence over the king.

The main preoccupation of government, apart from dynastic and foreign affairs, was public finance. France, like the other belligerents in the recent wars, was left with a huge public debt, which had to be serviced. The regency, like its counterpart across the Channel, fell for the schemes of a financial entrepreneur, the Scotsman John Law. He offered a financial packet in 1717, like the South Sea scheme in Britain, built around a colonial trading company with a government monopoly, the Mississippi Company, which would also take over management of the public debt, and in Law's scheme was authorized to issue a paper currency, a sure recipe for disaster once the expected profits of the company were slow to materialize. This duly came in 1720 when the scheme collapsed, carrying large numbers of speculators down with it. The actual long-term damage from the failure was limited, but the memory of it inhibited most future attempts in France at radical financial restructuring. French governments continued to operate the fiscal system established under Louis XIV until the final crisis of 1789.

This system was more viable than used to be imagined. The older view was that because a whole network of privileges prevented government taxing the wealthy, governments depended on borrowing from the financial sectors both at home and abroad, while tax was collected by venal office-holders and tax-farmers, who took inordinate commissions on what they collected. The French public certainly came to believe this image, and the *financiers* were standard hate figures, blamed for all the ills of government. Research is now revealing a more complex and sophisticated system which, despite its weaknesses, worked well enough most of the time.[4] The financiers were not an autonomous class of alien money-lenders who were bleeding France white. They were interrelated with the French nobility, being either members of noble families, like the Colberts, or agents of the higher nobility, who with the provincial elites put up the cash for government borrowing. A recent historian, P. R. Campbell states: 'The financial system relied on the Court nobility and the provincial elites for funds ... these were made available through the nobles' own agents, who were the financiers.' The crown could not tax its wealthy subjects, but provided it kept their goodwill it could usually borrow what was needed.

In 1722 Louis XV was declared of age and moved back to Versailles. Orléans continued to head the administration until his death the following year, and was followed as first minister by the equally aristocratic duke of Bourbon. One of his agents was the aristocratic cleric, André-Hercule de Fleury, who had impressed Louis XIV as a hard-line opponent of the Jansenists, and was rewarded with the guardianship of the future Louis XV. He had won the unwavering respect of the young prince and retained his full confidence until his death in 1743. For Bourbon, Fleury was the essential link to the king. Bourbon had plans to clear up the aftermath of the Law disaster, and imposed a deflationary policy which in 1725 finally stabilized the French currency. His downfall was the project for replacing dependence on borrowing by introducing a general property tax. This was unacceptable to all the components of the elite, clerical and noble, and Bourbon rapidly lost control of court politics. Fleury worked on persuading the king to dismiss Bourbon and he then became effective first minister, though he avoided holding ministerial office. Promotion to cardinal gave him status, and he secured his position with the king by his close control over access to the monarch, and was present at all audiences.

The ministry of Fleury from 1726 to 1743 gave French government a period of unusual stability; indeed he can be seen as the last effective head of government before 1789. He had affinities with Walpole, with whom he maintained a long working relationship, based on a policy of avoidance of war. The succession problem was resolved through the marriage of the king to a daughter of the ex-king of Poland, Stanislas Lesczynski, which served its purpose when a son and heir was born in 1728. Bourbon's property tax was dropped, but under the Controller General of finance, Orry, financial affairs were left to the controller and the intendants. Orry renegotiated the *cinq grosses fermes*, the customs farm that collected the bulk of the indirect taxation. The resulting professionalization of the service produced a model of regular administration, such that when Frederick II wanted to restructure the Prussian excise system in the 1760s he hired French experts to supervise it. Although there was no powerful central ministry of finance comparable to the Treasury in Britain, the many bureaux of finance that operated in Paris, and not in Versailles, provided a competent administration in normal times. It was quite capable of producing annual budgets, and it is probable that by the later 1730s ordinary revenues and expenditures were balanced.

The Fleury regime rested on his control of the king, and consequently of the ultimate source of patronage and favour. A competent manager like Fleury could master the ongoing struggle of court factions and reduce politics to endless vain intrigues to unseat him. The one force that gave Fleury real political difficulty was religion. The Jansenist movement in the French church represented a typical activist minority. The Jansenists wanted a religious awakening, and saw the established hierarchy of pope and bishops as standing in the way. Louis XIV, at the end of his life, launched a vigorous repression of the movement, in alliance with the pope, and secured from him the bull *Unigenitus* of 1713, which comprehensively condemned Jansenist doctrines as heretical. But his attempts to enforce the bull in France ran up against the old Gallican tradition of the *parlements* that papal authority in France could only be exercised with their authorization. Fleury himself had become identified with firm repression, since he could see the dangers if the Jansenists were allowed to challenge established authority, and he was concerned at any possible threat to religious unity in the kingdom. The Jansenists, who by the 1720s were supported by some 20 bishops including Noailles, the archbishop of Paris, and perhaps some 7000 of the parish clergy, were at most 5 per cent of the whole clerical order, but were especially strong and vocal in the Paris region. They had many lay sympathizers and, more important, a dedicated group of lawyers in the *parlement*, who were willing to assert the supremacy of the law over the church. The Jansenists also appealed to a wider public through their preaching and publishing, and ran a uniquely successful underground weekly paper, the *Nouvelles ecclésiastiques*, which was strongly critical of public policy in general, and which the authorities never succeeded in silencing for long.

Whether or not the Jansenists realized the significance of their activities, they were politicizing public debate and creating a public opposition which was to have wide political consequences. Fleury had been wary of precipitating a confrontation because of the trouble it might cause with the *parlements*, but in 1730 he formally declared that *Unigenitus* was legally enforceable in the kingdom. The Jansenists' supporters in the *parlement* organized formal protests, which they had a legal right to publish, and they insisted that the enforcement of the bull would be unlawful and an infringement of the legislative authority vested since time immemorial solely in the *parlement*. In a pamphlet published in 1732 the danger of political escalation became apparent. The writer asserted that the issue was one of the fundamental laws of the kingdom. He claimed:

> When it is a question of something in which the people has an interest, it cannot be decided in the Council of State. The king can only contract with his people in the Parlement, which being as old as the crown, and born with the state, is the representation of the whole monarchy.

It is unlikely, in 1732, that the lawyers who subscribed to such rhetorical assertions were seriously challenging the sole sovereignty of the king. Their claim was part of a well-recognized bargaining process through which the parties could find a consensus without losing face. Such assertions of right were advanced with a view to trading them in. Apart from the convinced Jansenists, who saw themselves as God's elect with a mission to witness to religious truth, the *parlementaires* in 1732 were focused on the defence of their claim to have full jurisdiction over clergy and laity.

But whatever the players in this power game intended, it triggered a series of increasingly aggressive confrontations, arising out of the king's determination to suppress the Jansenists, and the *parlement*'s determination to defend its rights of jurisdiction. This escalated when the bishops tried to hit back by refusing the sacraments to unrepentant Jansenists, who appealed to the *parlement* for protection which the lawyers were happy to provide. The climax came in 1753, when the *parlement* drafted a general remonstrance to the king defining their view of the rule of law:

> The fundamental law of the State constitutes a reciprocal and eternal relationship between the prince and his descendants on the one side, and the subjects and their descendants on the other, by a sort of contract which orders the sovereign to reign and the people to obey ... the Laws are the sacred knot that makes this commitment indissoluble, the King, the State and the Law constitute one inseparable unity.

The remonstrance, which was printed, implies that the *parlement* has an ultimate power of veto over any royal act it deems contrary to fundamental law. The king refused to accept this remonstrance; the *parlement* declared that if it could not remonstrate as necessary it could not function at all, and went on strike. As the work of the courts ground to a halt, and this included not only settling litigation and prosecuting criminals, but also many important administrative functions, the king sought in vain for a way to break the strike. After trying to send the judges into provincial exile, he finally purported to set aside their jurisdiction and replace it by a new tribunal, the *Chambre royale*, but the legal corporations over the kingdom made difficulties about recognizing it. In 1754, after nearly a year of confrontation, the king backed down, negotiating secretly for a compromise on the *parlement*'s disputes with the clergy, and the *parlement* then resumed its full functions.

The king's attempt at coercion had failed and it was entirely his own fault. The outcome of this first round of the struggle between the church establishment, backed by the king, and its Jansenist critics, supported by the *parlement*, was nothing abnormal by the prevailing rules of the political game. Early modern societies were agglomerations of privileged interest groups, engaged in unceasing competition with one another for relative status and advantage. It was the business of sovereign rulers to moderate the process, to preserve traditional relativities, and to mediate to forestall confrontation. Louis XV, by taking sides on behalf of the church hierarchy, had failed in his duty and produced a potentially damaging challenge to his personal authority.

This did not mean that the French system of government was breaking down. For most of the time it functioned as satisfactorily as that of any other contemporary kingdom. While Fleury lived and guided the king, affairs remained under control. On Fleury's death in 1743, the king announced that in future he would assume personal direction of affairs, which indeed he endeavoured to do, but never mastered the vital management skills necessary for the effective performance of his functions. The subsequent, increasingly obvious failings of French government reflected, not the unworkability of the system, but the incompetence of its manager.

Bourbon Spain

The entry into Spain of the new Bourbon king, Philip V, and the subsequent war in the peninsula enabled some lasting modernizations to be introduced. The Spaniards were unlucky in their rulers and victims of the dynastic lottery. The new Bourbon dynasty proved little better than the Habsburgs they replaced. Philip V showed repeated signs of mental instability, including a nervous breakdown in 1724, when he abdicated. He was sustained initially by the French advisers seconded to assist him, Jean Amelot and Jean Orry, but they were removed under the influence of his second queen, the Italian Elizabeth Farnese, who was both unintelligent and ambitious. The French ambassador wrote in 1717: 'The king is visibly wasting away, through excessive use he makes of the queen. He is utterly worn out.' The reign lasted until 1746 under a king who really had nothing to contribute to government. His successor Ferdinand VI also proved mentally unstable, finally descending into insanity in his last years. He too was emotionally fixated on his Portuguese queen. The Spaniards had to wait until the accession of Charles III in 1759 before they at last got a sane and competent personality on the throne.

Reform and modernization in Bourbon Spain owed nothing to its own king. The initial phases were carefully orchestrated by Louis XIV himself through the advice he gave to his grandson. At first the whole future turned on the fortunes of war, with the Allied invasion of the kingdom of Aragon on behalf of the Habsburg claimant. This revealed that the new dynasty was firmly rooted in the loyalty of Castile: the Allies twice managed to capture Madrid and twice withdrew in face of local hostility. In Aragon support for the Habsburgs was solid only in Catalonia, which maintained its position until 1714, when it was abandoned in the peace settlement. In Aragon and Valencia the coming of the Habsburg aroused some populist support against the local feudal elites, which the Allies encouraged. The elites in response looked to the Bourbons for protection. After the decisive battle of Alamanza in 1707 drove the Allied forces back to the coast, the opportunity was seized to bring about the constitutional unification of the kingdom, by the abolition of the *fueros*, the local privileges of the kingdom of Aragon. In the decree, the aim of the new regime was set out as 'to reduce all the kingdoms of Spain to obedience to the same laws, customs, practices and tribunals, each equally subject to the laws of Castile'. In the subsequent reorganization of government in Aragon two basic Castilian principles were enforced: that the king, as sovereign, stood above the law and that he had full powers to levy taxation. In return the subjects of Aragon had equal access to office and patronage with those of Castile.

The reality fell somewhat short of the aim. In order to eliminate aristocratic power which dominated the Council bureaucracy in Madrid, Amelot set about replacing it with a new system, supervised by a council of state, the *despacho*, with five ministries for the various departments of state under it. The staff of the new institutions was drawn from outside the traditional elite of aristocratic graduates of Salamanca, and involved a major expansion of the nobility – some 200 new titles were granted under Philip V. Now the core of the government should have been the secretary of the *despacho* working directly under the king. In fact the old bureaucracy fought back successfully, securing the retention of the former Council of Castile, whose remit was extended to the whole kingdom. Their reactionary influence caused the long struggle to set up an intendancy on the French model, first mooted in 1703; it was finally established on a nationwide basis in 1733. The standing army was reformed after 1704, with a regular command system, but plans to introduce conscription were consistently blocked by conservative provincialism, so that the peacetime establishment of 70,000 was quite modest by contemporary standards. The navy reforms starting from 1714 established a permanent infrastructure round the new naval base and dockyard facilities at El Ferrol, and a navy ministry was established from 1726 but, as with the army, growth was constrained by lack of experienced seamen and the absence of any adequate system for conscription. The church was subjected to more intense lay control in the new concordat worked out with the papacy in 1734.

One major area where modernization was slow was in the public finances. Orry managed to achieve a respectable 20 per cent increase in the yield of existing revenues through improved administration by 1716, and this was increased by a further 50 per cent by the 1750s. But repeated attempts to reform the tax system failed. Only in Catalonia, after the re-conquest of 1714, was it possible to enforce a major tax reform. All subsequent plans to extend it to the rest of Spain failed. The vested interest of the elites in keeping their extensive exemptions from taxation stood in the way of change. Despite the revenue increases that were secured, and a fairly steady growth in American trade on which the crown continued to levy substantial impositions, there was probably a continuing deficit in government income. If the dynasty had produced more capable leadership, the modernization of Spanish society might have been carried further.[5] What is certain is that the personal inadequacies of the first Bourbon kings permitted conservative interests, working through court faction and intrigue, to frustrate most of the reformist initiatives of the professional administrators in the *despacho*.

Two successful reforming monarchs: Piedmont and Prussia

The feeble performance of the first Spanish Bourbons contrasts starkly with the state-building achievements of two dedicated, strong-minded rulers, each of whom consolidated a new kingdom in this same period. The first was Victor Amadeus II, who in 1675 became duke of Savoy-Piedmont, a buffer principality that had stood between the rival French and Spanish contenders for control of Italy. The main asset of her rulers was that the principality controlled most of the main Alpine passes between France and Italy. The dynasty had originated on the French side of the mountains in Savoy, but during the seventeenth century deliberately chose to establish its capital on the Italian side at Turin, which was systematically developed as an administrative and industrial centre, prosperous enough for its municipality to act as banker for the public debts. Its society was seigneurial: the dukes had been steadily selling rights of manorial jurisdiction to the noble landowners and most local administration was firmly in their hands. In Savoy and Piedmont there was a governing Senate, with powers based on those of a French *parlement*, staffed by a local *robe* nobility which, as in France, was increasingly merging with feudal nobility. For most of the seventeenth century the principality was dominated by France which had established garrisons in the two key fortresses of Pinerolo and Casale, and the young Victor Amadeus, during the ascendancy of Louis XIV, had no choice but to accept French protection.

In 1690 Victor Amadeus made a bid for freedom by joining William III's coalition against Louis, and got back Pinerola as the price of reverting to neutrality in 1696. When the next war began in 1702, Piedmont was allied to Louis XIV, but successfully changed sides and collaborated in alliance attempts to invade France from the south. In the process Victor Amadeus picked up enough Allied subsidies to bring his army up to 24,000. At the peace settlements he got his reward: Casale was recovered and some extra territory on his border with Milan was added. Most importantly he was granted the island of Sicily, with a royal title, which he subsequently had to exchange for Sardinia, but still with the title. He was now in business in the international power game. In order to become an independent player, he needed to consolidate his domestic position by applying the techniques now familiar in western Europe for constructing an absolute monarchy.

From 1697 the development of a controlling ministry of finance, the *Generale della finanze* was begun, and at the same time an intendancy was instituted, whose duties were mainly concerned with revenue-raising. These institutions began a sustained attack on the tax exemptions of the elites: they began examining land titles, with a view to expanding the crown estates, and from 1690 to 1711 launched a general land survey to act as the basis for a reformed tax system. After the war there was further development of the central administration. A Council of State was set up, supervising eight ministries. The central treasury became the Council of Finance with a permanent accounting and audit department attached. In this institution the annual budgets were framed. The nobility was offered the possibility of military service in the standing army and could purchase venal offices in the administration. From 1717 the sale of seigneurial jurisdictions was resumed, open to all who could pay, and purchase conferred automatic nobility. Victor Amadeus entered into a long and bitter dispute with the papacy over church patronage and reducing clerical exemptions from taxation, which he won in 1724. In order to develop a service nobility and professionalized clergy, the university of Turin was reformed and entry into the clergy and the civil service was reserved for Turin graduates. The land survey had been completed in 1711, but even a strong ruler like Victor Amadeus hesitated to use it as the basis for a new general land tax. However, in 1731 he felt secure enough to go ahead. The Piedmontese land tax became a model for other reforming rulers. In 1729 his administration had completed a codification of the law and was promoting vigorous mercantilist policies for trade and manufacture, which increased 250 per cent between 1700 and 1750. Successful entrepreneurs were freely rewarded with titles of nobility.

The achievement of Victor Amadeus was one of the major success stories of the early eighteenth century. He created the most powerful, independent Italian principality, and yet his motivation remains obscure. He was a secretive personality, and left little record of his thoughts.[6] He had the characteristics of a successful absolute king and had a good grasp of political realities, making the development of an effective army his priority, and a workaholic dedication to the business of government. His basic motive seems to have been advancing the glory and status of his dynasty. The ease with which he traded Sicily for Sardinia suggests he had a detached attitude to the subjects over whom he ruled, and he made no effort to integrate his new possessions into the main body of the state. The price of rise in international status was infliction of a decade of destructive and costly warfare on his subjects. Nobody thought of asking them if they felt it was worth it.

King Frederick William I of Prussia, who succeeded his father Frederick I in 1713, was a similarly dedicated personal ruler. Most historians now agree that he was the real creator of the classical Prussian state.[7] There was a cultural factor involved in this development which is often overlooked and is difficult to describe concisely: the spread of Pietism among the Brandenburg–Prussian elites. A major weakness of the Great Elector Frederick William's state-building exercise had been the confessional conflict between the Calvinist rulers and their Lutheran subjects. While the Hohenzollerns had not tried to force their belief on their subjects, they had relied heavily on foreign Calvinists to run their military and civil services and invited Calvinist refugees like the Huguenots to settle in their lands, which antagonized their Lutheran subjects. Pietism was developed by Philip Spiner, whose major book, the *Pia desideria* had been published in 1675. His principal follower, August Francke, worked firstly from Leipzig in Lutheran Saxony, but in face of the hostility of the local clergy transferred to Berlin in 1690.

Pietism was a doctrine of religious activism, central to which was a conversion experience leading to a life of service to God's cause. King Frederick William was a convert, who described himself as an 'administrator for God', and dedicated himself to creating in his own dominions a state similarly committed. Frederick William and Francke established a partnership and the Pietists were encouraged to colonize the principal university of the kingdom at Halle. Chairs were endowed in cameralist political studies and Pietist academies encouraged, which provided an attractive modern training for and an entry qualification into both military and civil service. In 1718 a Pietist was installed as chief army chaplain and the army was used to indoctrinate both the officer corps and the common soldiers and their families. For the nobility, Frederick William established a Military Cadet Corps Academy in Berlin to which nobles were encouraged – in some cases, it was alleged, forced – to send their children and where they got a firm Pietist training. From 1717 to 1740, this Academy had 90 per cent of its graduates commissioned into the army, and by 1740 they provided half the officer corps and a quarter of the civil service. This was the basis of the common culture of the Prussian state built around the concept of the Christian duty of its subjects to serve God through service to the state. Pietism had the further advantage of being acceptable to both Lutherans and Calvinists and thus resolving the confessional divide and dissolving provincial loyalties among the elites.

The core of Frederick William's project was to build up the standing army into uniform regiments and to nationalize it. Although the key officers, the captains and the colonels, remained in part proprietors, since the funding of their units was in their own hands, the army was strictly controlled, and increasingly the personnel was drawn from the king's own subjects, though the Prussian army always had a substantial minority of foreigners in its ranks. The final major reorganization came in 1733, when the cantonal system of recruitment, similar to the Swedish *indelningsverk,* was adopted. General conscription was abolished and instead each canton had to provide a specified number of recruits for regular army service, usually about one man from 40 peasant households. Once he was trained, the soldier would spend much of the year on leave at home, liable to recall at any time. His officers would usually be from local landowning families. On this basis, Prussia maintained one of the largest and best-trained standing armies in Europe.

The king's aim in central administration was to establish a uniform system which would cover all the provinces of the kingdom. He began on his accession by a drastic reduction of the royal court, which he regarded as a frivolous extravagance. The budget for the royal household was cut by three-quarters, with corresponding reductions in personnel, the money saved going to finance the army and the civil service. He also unified the finance departments into a *Generalfinanzkasse,* constituting a ministry of finance whose competence covered the whole kingdom. In 1723, he drew all the central administration, civil and military, into his General Directory, divided into four executive departments, which prepared policy recommendations and implemented them. They worked to a fixed timetable each week, with the king allotting one day to working with each. But the main policy decisions were collective, made at a general meeting of the whole Directory. The central departments maintained their own collegiate agencies at the local level. Although the civil and military treasuries were kept separate, they were subjected to a single audit department and budgetary disciplines were strictly enforced. Self-sufficiency was the standing aim of the Prussian system. Frederick William intended to expand the crown domain and carry through a systematic land survey, both to recover properties usurped by local elites and to provide the basis for a proper land tax. It was typical of these early modern regimes that this could not be done. The land tax could only be introduced into East Prussia, where nobles were not tax-exempt; elsewhere noble privilege stood in the way. But, at the end of the process, the crown estates had been expanded to about one-third of the total cultivated land.

The Prussian administration was drawn from diverse sources. The upper levels were increasingly recruited from native Junker families, though only if they were professionally qualified. Educated burghers were encouraged, as were other university-trained professional administrators, and at the lowest levels increasing use was made of retired NCOs, with the advantage that this saved the king from having to pension them off. Local administration had to be devolved, but in the urban sector the power of the excise commissioners was virtually emasculating local self-government, and in the countryside the appointment of the key official, the *Landrat*, was made centrally – Frederick William made it a rule that the appointment go to an outsider. This did not essentially weaken the control of the local Junkers over their home districts.[8] Pietism favoured a controlled economy geared to promotion of the common good and was against unchecked private enterprise. Frederick William invested much labour and many resources into promoting useful economic development. The most ambitious were his land settlement schemes, based on religious toleration for Protestant immigrants, with favourable rental and tax privileges. These were established in Pomerania and in eastern Prussia, which was devastated by the wars and epidemics after 1709.

Manufacture was also given government protection, especially textiles. For example, the contracts for army uniforms were reserved for native artisans. Garrison towns could also become centres of economic growth; the soldiers paid for their subsistence out of wages, which could be a considerable boost to urban economies. Frederick William was a fanatical militarist, and his personal indulgence was the special regiment of grenadiers, recruited from men over six feet tall, who were lured by pay, or kidnapped by the king's agents from all over the Empire. They were financed by his personal *Soldatenkasse*, which was topped up by the substantial contributions expected of all state servants on appointment. But Frederick William had a basic political integrity; he took his own Pietism seriously and pursued his ideals unwaveringly. The building of the Prussian state was his duty to God, as he affirmed in an outburst over the obstructions of provincial particularism: 'I shall destroy the authority of the Junkers: I shall achieve my purpose and stabilize the sovereignty like a rock of bronze.' More striking in a committed militarist was his belief that war could only be justified if it served God's purposes. He warned his heir in 1722:

> I beg you not to begin an unjust war, because God has forbidden unjust wars. You must give an account of every man killed in an unjust war ... That is a hard fact. Therefore I beg you, keep your conscience clear before God and you will enjoy a happy reign.

He followed his own prescription, even if his son conspicuously did not. He felt that the seizure of Swedish Pomerania in the Northern War, his only major territorial conquest, was just, since the Hohenzollerns had always had a plausible dynastic claim on the territory. Otherwise he offered a rare example of an early modern military ruler, with a large and effective army and sound public finances to sustain it, who resolutely refrained from using it for opportunistic expansion and genuinely aspired to keep the peace.

13

The Stabilization of the North-Eastern Borderlands

The ending of the Northern War in 1721 was based on the collapse of two once significant powers, Poland and Sweden, and the emergence of one major power, Russia. Poland had been fought over and ravaged by epidemics, and all attempts to preserve some kind of independent monarchy had failed. The weakness of the central government can be seen by comparing its annual crown revenue, about 8 million zloty after 1700, with the incomes of the magnate families who dominated society: M. Radziwill had a revenue of 5 million, S. F. Potocki had 3 million. These were the super-magnates; the average income of the leading magnate families was around 300,000 zloty. But this, in turn, compares with a landed gentleman owning one or two villages with an income around 2000 zloty a year. As always, prolonged warfare and devastation had hit the small property-owners hardest; the wealth and influence of the magnates had enabled them to survive the wars, even to profit by them, while lesser men were forced to seek shelter by begging their patronage and protection. The fate of Polish society was firmly in the hands of the magnate families and their clienteles, and they in turn survived by dealings with the external powers. The last attempts of the Saxon king, Augustus II, to legislate on military reform were blocked in successive Diet sessions in 1719–22, and in each case the wrecking veto cast was due to the influence of foreign powers. But they also reflected the mentality of the *szlachta*. The Diet of 1719 resolved: 'the free voice, founded on the right of veto … is the finest jewel of the free nation of this Commonwealth'. Augustus continued his scheming to contrive some real authority for the crown down to his death in 1732, but the combination of internal opposition and foreign support for the status quo foiled all his endeavours.

After 1718 Sweden experienced an episode unique in the history of the period – the deliberate dismantling of an absolute monarchy. In his last two years, Charles XII and his minister, the Holsteiner baron Görtz, had run a radical wartime regime that largely bypassed the established governmental procedures of the Swedish kingdom. Although there was no public protest against this royal dictatorship, there was high-level conspiracy to end it, and the king's death in action in 1718 could have been an assassination – the only remedy left to the subject under absolutism. Whether accidental or not, his elimination was eagerly exploited by the Swedish ruling elites to ensure that his kind of uncontrolled royal absolutism would not recur. A revised constitution stripped the crown of almost all independent authority and all its actions had to be sanctioned by the Council of State, whose members had to be approved by the Diet, and which was collectively answerable to the Diet for its conduct of the government. The sovereign power was vested in the four Estates, but effectively exercised by the Secret Committee, elected at the beginning of each Diet, on which the Peasant Estate was not normally represented.

The period from 1719 to 1772, in which the Swedish Diet exercised the sovereign power, is commonly and misleadingly referred to as the 'Age of Liberty'.[1] This exaggerates what the changes involved. The people who ruled Swedish society after 1719 were essentially the same people who had run it under the absolutism, and had been content to do so until the actions of Charles XII highlighted the dangers of the system in the wrong hands. What happened after 1718 was not a change from absolutism to representative government in Sweden. It was a transfer of absolute power from one agency to another. The Diet ruled just as absolutely as kings had done and claimed that no subject could challenge its actions. Those who ventured to do so were severely repressed. The Diet represented the collective memberships of the four Estates, which excluded labourers and servants, and also substantial numbers of men of property and education, who were not members of one of the Estates.

This would not have mattered if the system had delivered effective government, but conspicuously it did not. This was partly because the fear of a strong executive power created a system of checks and balances which made decisions difficult to arrive at and encouraged the formation of factions. Further, as a result of the war, Sweden had a standing deficit which had to be filled either from taxation, which no system of that kind could easily agree on, or from elsewhere, which in this case meant getting subsidies from interested foreign powers. The Diet was in effect ready to put the country's foreign policy up for auction and the interested powers, mainly Russia, Great Britain and France, were willing to bid. Foreign money was channelled through the embassies to Swedish faction leaders who promised collaboration, and used by them in turn to build up internal client networks, loosely grouped in two main factions of 'Hats' and 'Caps', who contested with each other control of Diet proceedings. For those who find it difficult to understand why early modern people were so acceptive of absolute monarchy as a political system, it is instructive to look at the Swedish 'Age of Liberty', which represented the most available alternative power structure – absolute oligarchy. The old peasant wisdom – better one master than a hundred – was not perhaps far wrong: the Peasant Estate continued to advocate a stronger kingship.

The place of Sweden and Poland as eastern powers was filled by the Russian empire, the name Peter the Great gave to his reformed polity in 1721. Yet although Peter pressed on with his reforming agenda up to the moment of his death in 1725, the structure of his empire appeared vulnerable at the weakest point of monarchical systems – the question of the succession. Perhaps because of Peter's misfortune with his son and heir Alexis, done to death for alleged conspiracy in 1717, there was no clear law of succession laid down for the empire. The absolute powers of the autocrat extended to the right to name a suitable successor. The result was that, from 1725 until 1763, the empire functioned without an effective adult ruler. This is not to deny that the two empresses, Anna and Elizabeth, were strong, even formidable personalities, but beyond installing themselves in power and keeping it neither had any clear political agenda; their personal interests lay outside politics. The period therefore was a significant test of the viability of Peter's construction.

The immediate succession passed to Peter's widow, Catherine, who survived until 1727, to be followed by his grandson, Peter II. There was a power struggle at court between the supporters of Petrine reform, led by his favourite Menshikov, and the families most closely associated with Peter II, the Dolgorukys and the Golitsyns. In the process some pieces of the Petrine system were abandoned. A Privy Council was established in 1725, taking over control from the Senate, and the proposed Petrine rationalization of provincial governments was dropped. Under Peter II, the Dolgorukys and Golitsyns got control of the Privy Council and moved the seat of government back to Moscow. If they had any clear plan to go further towards restoring the pre-Petrine system, it was cut short by the death of Peter II in 1730. In a desperate bid to maintain their hegemony, they called up the Princess Anna, as the most senior adult Romanov, and induced her to sign a constitutional compact, giving the Council a power-sharing role with the empress. The reaction was interesting: this did not give a starting signal for the introduction of limited monarchy into the empire – on the contrary, the service nobility, who saw the attempted coup for what it was, encouraged Anna to repudiate her concessions and reclaim the full autocratic powers. One memorandum of protest, circulated during Peter's funeral, declared:

> God forbid that it turn out that instead of one autocratic sovereign, we have tens of absolute and powerful families, and thus the nobility will decline completely and we will be forced, more painfully than before, to make obeisance and seek favours from everybody.

The short answer to the question of how the autocracy survived this long period of dynastic instability with its authority intact is that autocracy is what Russia's ruling elites preferred. They were not ignorant of what was happening just over the borders in Sweden and Poland, but had no desire to follow their examples. The rejection of the attempted reaction in 1730 was effected by the guards regiments, who emerged as one of the principal supports of the Petrine reforms. The government moved back to St Petersburg, the Privy Council was abolished and the Senate reinstated as a collegiate administration. In the immediate aftermath of 1725, the army had been partially demobilized, but the basic military establishments for the army and navy were maintained, making Russia one of the leading military powers in Europe throughout the eighteenth century. The Russian armed forces proved technically the equals of the best military establishments in the west, perhaps even better. They were the only opponents to inflict shattering military defeats on the otherwise invincible Prussian army of Frederick the Great.

Recent studies have thrown more light on the underlying stability of the Russian imperial regime. The changes imposed by Peter had in fact proved less radical than they appear on the surface. An examination of the ruling elites around 1730 has shown that in spite of the Table of Ranks, and the principle of advancement on merit and open entry into the service hierarchy, only some 50 significant new service families had entered the system. Most were Baltic–German nobles from the provinces annexed from Sweden, who remained as a conspicuous elite group in Russian government. Otherwise, in 1730, the top posts were held by members of the pre-1689 Moscow elite, the old *boyar* families, and the privileged Moscow service gentry. It can also be shown that the new ministries were heavily recruited from the traditional Moscow families that had run the pre-Petrine *prikazi*. These top families had their power base in the guards regiments, where they provided four-fifths of the officers. In effect, what Peter seems to have achieved was, as a recent historian, B. Meehan-Waters, put it, 'to ensure that the privileged elite became a qualified elite, so that they might more effectively spend their lives in the service of the State'. In Russia, as in the western absolutisms, the basic social realities dictated that even the most autocratic rulers had to have the collaboration of their noble landlords to maintain a working administration and provide the officer corps for their armies. Absolute monarchy was always a power-sharing arrangement between the haves at the expense of the have-nots. On the death of Anna in 1740, the infant heir Ivan VI was pushed aside, again by intervention of the guards, in favour of the empress Elizabeth. In 1761 she was succeeded by her nephew as Peter III. He made a promising start by issuing the first general decree releasing the nobility from the obligation to lifetime public service, but also made a fatal mistake. Driven by his unbalanced admiration for all things Prussian, Peter tried to impose reforms on the guards regiments. In 1762 they conspired with Peter's estranged wife to depose him and install her in his place as the Empress Catherine II. She then provided Russia with nearly 35 years of strong imperial government, ending for a time the dynastic deficit.

Through this period of politically incompetent autocrats,[2] the governing elites kept the empire going as a working concern, consolidating their own power within it. The foreign policy of the empire was directed largely by two individuals, the Baltic–German noble Ostermann from 1725 to 1741, and after him the native Russian noble, Bestuzhev-Rjumin until 1758. The regime successfully asserted Russia's place as a participant in the dynastic power game, defending Russia's Baltic hegemony at the expense of the weakened Sweden, and generally maintaining a protectorate over Poland. In the east, the Russians crossed the Bering Strait and began to penetrate Alaska, while to the south, the Kazakhs accepted Russian protection. Beyond them the Bashkirs were conquered and a new southern Orenberg province was established. The economy was slowly expanding, noble estates benefited from the recovery of world prices after 1750, there seems to have been a favourable balance of foreign trade, and the public finances were stable. Against this background there was evidence of a slow cultural change within the noble landlord class.

The Petrine reforms, although anchored in the service principle, had in effect conferred allodial status on noble estates, which was reinforced when the landlords assumed the collection of the poll tax. Educational standards among the nobility were rising, basic literacy was general, and at the top a more cosmopolitan, elite culture was developing. There was significant legislation in 1736 which weakened the service principle by recognizing that one member of any family could remain at home to manage the affairs of the family estate. But a general survey of noble engagement in active public service by 1760 seems to indicate that as many as 70 per cent of the adult male nobles were not actively engaged in state service. This would make Peter III's official abrogation of the universal service principle more a recognition of reality than a radical reform. But, even so, in these interim years from 1725 to 1762, the professional administration grew steadily. In 1725 there were about 6000 state servants to administer the empire. By 1762 this had grown to 16,500. About two-thirds of these posts were essentially clerical and held by commoners, but the real positions of power were held by nobles. There was no sale of office in Russia, and most of these people were career officers, though it was possible to switch back and forth between military and civil office and even hold both simultaneously.

It was this remarkably small group of full-time state servants that kept the momentum of the Petrine reforms alive, although the dynastic instability of these years did undoubtedly undermine the Petrine vision of a well-ordered police state administered by trained professional bureaucrats. Although government by an executive Senate supervising collegiate ministries remained, it was undermined by the prevalence of power struggles at court to influence the sovereign. Evidence suggests that the concept of collective decision-making could not really function when the possibility of pursuing personal advantage at court was open to the Senate members. As Nikita Panin remarked of the reign of Elizabeth, 'the power of persons' was weakening the 'authority of State institutions'. The dynastic instability also made high politics a risky game. There was no western concept of a rule of law in Russia. Those who fell from favour would not only lose office but faced loss of estates and exile, if not worse. Perhaps a reminder that Russian high politics were different was the emergence, after the return of the government to St Petersburg in 1730, of a revived Chancellory for Secret Investigative Affairs, which was consolidated under Major General A. Uchakov, who directed it until 1744. This department was running a political police system which maintained a permanent element of terrorism through its spying activity and known ruthlessness in suppressing opposition conspiracy.[3] Even the guards regiments were not immune from its attentions. This gives some plausibility to the assessment of V. Bashkurov, about the structure of the Petrine empire:

> The tsar was the autocrat above, the landlords were the autocrats below and under them, without right or voice, were the common people, their subjects ... In such a State only the autocrats were free, only they were real people: the all-Russian Autocrat was free beyond measure, the freedom of the small autocrats was limited by the boundaries of their estates, and by the supreme autocrat, sitting on high.

But without the services of the small autocrats, the whole system would have become unviable, and the unlimited freedom of the tsar at the top was illusory.

14

The European Power Game,
1715–1740

Europe, being basically a predatory, military culture, has never experienced peace in the full sense of total absence of armed conflict between its constituent societies. But what passes for peace – the absence of active general hostilities involving all the major players at once – has at times prevailed. The years from 1715 to 1740 represent such a pause. It resulted not from any absence of conflicts between the powers, but from a temporary unwillingness to resolve them by war. Most of these conflicts were dynastic, about which crowned head was to get which bit of European real estate: this was the basis of the confrontation after 1715 between the Spanish Bourbons and Charles VI over the post-war carve-up of Italy.

These were compounded by the several uncertainties over dynastic succession in Britain as long as a realistic Jacobite challenge existed; in France until Louis XV was safely married and produced a male heir; and above all in Austria and the Empire, which made the Austrian succession the main issue in the diplomacy of the period. It arose because the Emperor, Charles VI, was the last male Habsburg, which raised two problems: first who would inherit the hereditary lands, second what to do about the imperial succession, which could only go to a male candidate. The senior female Habsburgs were the two daughters of Charles's elder brother, the late Emperor Joseph I. But they were already married to two of the Electors, Bavaria and Saxony. If either sister got the inheritance, it would in effect fall to their husbands, who would in addition almost certainly be elected Emperor. The Habsburg dynasty would be reduced to a historical memory.

The solution to this dynastic problem, devised by Charles VI, was the Pragmatic Sanction, drafted in the 1720s when the Emperor accepted that he would not beget a male heir. The Pragmatic Sanction was a Habsburg family compact, whereby the daughters of Joseph I renounced their hereditary claims in favour of the daughters of Charles VI, the eldest of whom was the Archduchess Maria Theresa.[1] That done, there were two further steps needed: first, to find a credible princely consort for her from some modest family that could not pretend to outrank the Habsburgs, and trust that the union would renew the male Habsburg line; second, was to consolidate this arrangement by securing the election of the spouse as Emperor after Charles VI, thus keeping the imperial throne warm for the renewed male Habsburg succession. There was little difficulty in persuading the Estates of the Habsburg lands to accept Maria Theresa as heiress. But to secure the succession, Charles VI needed to get international recognition as well. This issue destabilized European politics for two decades and then caused the next round of general warfare that began in 1740. It confirms the priority of dynastic politics over all other considerations in the power games of early modern Europe.

However, before Europe's rulers and their ministers focused on the big issue, there were other outstanding matters arising out of the peace settlements. One concerned the Baltic where Peter the Great's final victory over Sweden was viewed with alarm by the Elector of Hanover who was, after 1714, the king of Great Britain, George I. As Elector, he feared renewed Russian armed interventions in north Germany, and as king he feared for Britain's essential supplies of naval stores, which mostly came from the eastern Baltic lands ceded to Russia in the Treaty of Nystad. Through the 1720s there was intermittent Anglo-Russian tension, which brought British fleets into the Baltic to inhibit any aggressive activity there from the Russian side. George I was neurotic about the 'Russian peril'. It was only after his death in 1727 that the two powers recognized there was really nothing to fight about: a flourishing trade in naval stores was to their mutual advantage, as was recognized by the establishment of full diplomatic relations between the two powers in 1731, followed by some decades of fairly harmonious cooperation to uphold the status quo in the Baltic region.[2]

The Baltic problem was unlikely to cause a major war, since the issues were marginal to most of the other powers. The same could not be said of the problem of Italy. The peace settlements of 1715 did not cover the antagonisms of the Emperor and the Spanish Bourbons. Philip V did not recognize the Habsburg gains in Italy, while Charles VI still formally claimed to be rightful king of Spain. This smouldering conflict was intensified after 1716 when Philip V married the Italian princess, Elizabeth Farnese, and submitted to her domineering personality. Farnese brought with her an ambitious Italian cleric, Alberoni, who was promoted to cardinal and became chief minister. Her preoccupations were purely dynastic. Since Philip had already produced an heir for Spain, she was concerned to find suitable princely inheritances for the children she might have by him, and eventually there were two, the princes Don Carlos and Don Philip. Since Philip V had a standing resentment at the loss of Spain's Italian possessions, he readily fell in with the schemes of Alberoni for recovering them by force, after which they would provide suitable appanages for any princes. The window of opportunity was the Emperor's preoccupation with a new war against the Ottomans, which came to a successful conclusion with the Treaty of

Passarowitz in 1718, giving Charles VI control of most of Serbia, including the great fortress of Belgrade. But Austria had no naval power, while Spain did, and while the Emperor was occupied in the Balkans in 1717 a Spanish naval expedition successfully seized Sardinia from its Habsburg garrison. In normal circumstances this was the point where France should have reactivated the Bourbon family compact and supported the Spanish enterprise, but in 1716 the regent and his foreign minister Dubois had already concluded an agreement with Great Britain to work together for a peaceful resolution of outstanding problems.

The French had signalled their sincerity by expelling the Old Pretender and his family from French territory, and then a formal treaty between the two powers pledged to sustain the post-war settlement. Faced with the Spanish challenge in Italy in the following year, Britain and France offered to mediate a settlement between the Emperor and Philip V, based on mutual recognitions of each other's possessions. Charles VI would get Sicily from Victor Amadeus in exchange for Sardinia, thus saving his face over the Spanish seizure. Philip and Alberoni, who were mobilizing a new naval expedition for 1718 for further conquests in Italy, refused the offer. Charles VI, realizing that without a navy of his own he needed Anglo-French support, reluctantly accepted and formed, with the United Provinces, the Quadruple Alliance of 1718. The British fleet then destroyed the Spanish naval expedition off Cape Passaro.[3] It took two more years of Anglo-French threats and persuasions to bring the Spaniards to agree to negotiate on the basis of the terms offered.

At this point the Pragmatic Sanction became part of the problem and the quest for its international recognition the predominant concern of Charles VI. The sheer anarchy of the power game was never better illustrated than during the 1720s as the rulers tried to find advantage in a swirl of overlapping disputes. At one point in 1725, Charles VI and Philip V, tired of being pushed around by the Anglo-French alliance, suddenly came to terms, exchanging mutual recognition and a Spanish recognition of the Pragmatic Sanction in return for rather vague assurances of Austrian support for Spanish claims against Britain over American trade, Gibraltar and Minorca.[4] This then linked up with an ambitious commercial project of Charles VI to establish his own East India Company based on the Netherlands' port of Ostend, which aroused the commercial fears of Britain and the United Provinces, who came together to get it suppressed. As tensions rose over the Baltic between Britain and Russia, Austria entered an alliance with Russia, while in 1726–7, Britain and Spain began a low-intensity undeclared war over Gibraltar and the *asiento* agreement.

There could easily have been a general war in the later 1720s but for two factors: after 1726 Fleury had established firm control over French foreign policy and he was prepared to continue cooperation with Great Britain to find negotiated solutions; and with the passage of time Charles VI gave heightened priority to securing the Pragmatic Sanction. The final twist came when Walpole, in 1730, took personal control of British foreign policy.[5] By a direct approach to Charles VI, without consulting Fleury, Walpole secured a general settlement. The basis was the recognition of the Pragmatic Sanction by Great Britain and Spain. In return the Emperor suppressed the Ostend Company and accepted the transfer of the duchy of Parma as an inheritance for Farnese's elder son, Don Carlos. George II also got imperial confirmation of his title to Bremen-Werden, which his father had seized from Sweden during the Northern War. Other powers now fell into line and recognized the Sanction, culminating in its ratification by the Diet of the Empire in 1732.

Cardinal Fleury had remained passive during this process, but a change of French policy was decided, since Charles VI was now much strengthened and the Emperor had chosen Francis Stephen, duke of Lorraine, as the appropriate husband for Maria Theresa. This would add Lorraine, the strategic territory on France's northern border, to the Habsburg dominions, an outcome Fleury could not accept. He resolved on preventive action to cut back on Austrian expansion, and encouraged the foreign secretary, Chauvelin, who led an expansionist faction at Versailles, to engineer an anti-Habsburg coalition of German princes, wary of any increase in Habsburg authority in the Empire. The conflict that followed was a limited European war, limited because the maritime powers Great Britain and the United Provinces stood aside, being reassured by Fleury that in any event there would be no attack on the Austrian Netherlands – a promise that was honoured. The trigger was the death of Augustus II of Poland, which led a faction in Poland to seek to break the Russian protectorate by electing a native king, Stanislas Lesczynski, the deposed candidate of Charles XII, who was now also the father-in-law of Louis XV. It was clear that dynastic honour alone required French support for his candidature and he was easily elected at the Diet of 1733. It was equally obvious that the choice was unacceptable to Russia or to Austria, as it would facilitate Bourbon influence in their sphere of influence, so they intervened militarily to drive Lesczynski out and impose their favoured candidate, Augustus, Elector of Saxony. His election was secured by force, and Lesczynski was driven into exile. The Saxon Elector was installed as Augustus III, and in return ceded the Polish duchy of Courland to Russia and gave formal recognition to the Pragmatic Sanction.

Fleury was realistic enough to see that France could not challenge the Russian control of Poland.[6] Instead, in the autumn of 1733, he launched a swift, surprise counter-attack in the west against the Emperor. A French army crossed into the Empire and seized Lorraine, a Piedmontese–French force overran the duchy of Milan[7] and, in November 1733, Louis XV and Philip V signed a new Bourbon family compact. They would cooperate to secure Naples and Sicily as a further inheritance for Farnese's sons, and also work together to combat British imperial expansion in the Americas and seek the recovery of Gibraltar. Early in 1734 Spanish troops came into Italy and easily overran Naples and Sicily, where the new Austrian regime had become widely unpopular. The merits of Fleury as statesman were revealed when, after these striking successes, that had involved little serious fighting, he stopped and offered to negotiate. When Chauvelin and the activists at the French court pressed for further conquests, Fleury had them dismissed. Fleury could afford to wait, since he held solid bargaining counters and Charles VI had no prospect of mounting a military riposte. He needed allies and subsidies, but Britain and the United Provinces refused to intervene, while in order to keep his only active ally, Russia, he agreed to support a Russian attack on the Ottomans which was launched in 1736. Unhappily, the Austrian campaign in the Balkans proved a disaster. The Emperor had to settle on Fleury's terms: it took until 1739 to complete all the diplomacy, but military operations in western Europe virtually ceased in 1735.

The settlements were a triumph for Fleury, who demonstrated that if Great Britain stood aside, France was the dominant power on the continent up to the borders of the Russian Empire and its dependencies. The Polish complication was ingeniously resolved: the exiled Lesczynski became duke of Lorraine, a title Francis Stephen renounced on marrying Maria Theresa. On Lesczynski's death, Lorraine would pass by inheritance to the crown of France, and this happened in 1766. In return, the status quo in the Empire was maintained and Louis XV now guaranteed the Pragmatic Sanction. In Italy there was a redistribution of territories: Piedmont gained another strip of land in the Po valley; the duchies of Parma and Tuscany were assigned to the Habsburgs, consolidating their control of northern Italy; while Naples and Sicily were assigned to the Spanish Bourbons, but on condition that they remain independent, and not reincorporated in the Spanish empire. Finally, Fleury mediated in the war with the Ottomans, where the Emperor had to purchase peace by giving up Austrian conquests in Serbia.

When the French negotiators were tying up the last details of a comprehensive peace settlement in Europe, the next war was just beginning. Although Great Britain under Walpole had resolutely refused to get involved in the conflicts on the continent, she had been embroiled in embittered disputes with Spain over colonial trade. During the 1730s the Spanish government had been trying to control the steady spread of illicit trading between her American settlements and British, Dutch and other interlopers. Spain established a privatized force of *guarda costas* who made their profits from prize money from the cargoes and ships they seized. This angered the British trading interests, and Britain being an open society they lobbied vigorously in parliament and outside against the alleged Spanish outrages, culminating in 1738 with the appearance of a Captain Jenkins before the House of Commons, displaying a severed ear, allegedly cut off by over-zealous *guarda costas*. Neither Walpole nor Philip V's ministers wanted a war, but the Spaniards would not compromise the principle of maintaining a trade monopoly in their empire, and Walpole could not hold out against a surge of imperialist and jingoist public opinion. In October 1739, Britain declared war on Spain. Both the Bourbon powers had been building up their navies, Britain had no allies, and Fleury agreed to work with Spain to check British commercial aggression. In 1740 French ships sailed to the Caribbean to assist the Spanish war effort.

The post-1715 peace, or rather phase of limited wars, was ending. Its history clearly points to the viciously destructive nature of the contemporary power system. As long as dynastic rulers pursued advancement of their status by the acquisition of additional territory, with accompanying subjects and revenues, there would be no peace. The treaties of Utrecht had formally subscribed to the idea of a balance of power. But that provided not stability but endless readjustment, if only because dynastic instability was constantly disturbing it. The previous general war had been fought over the Spanish succession, the next one would be over the Austrian succession. The balance concept assumed continuing adjustments: one player's gains must be balanced by compensatory rewards to the other players. The years after 1715 demonstrated that, given the participants were all militarized societies, the disputes over compensation would in the end be resolved by war.

15

The Last European War of the Ancien Régime, 1740–1763

Phase 1: 1740–1748

This was a war that should not have happened. By 1739 the Austrian succession question was settled by the general acceptance of the Pragmatic Sanction. It was launched, unintentionally, by the new king in Prussia, Frederick II, known to history as Frederick the Great. He had inherited the military machine developed by his father, which enabled Brandenburg–Prussia, a relatively poor society of some 2.25 million people, to sustain a standing army of 80,000 men. The subsequent history of the Prussian army has led to the assumption that in 1740 it had acquired technical qualities that made it superior to all its opponents.[1] This was not the case, though probably its standards of training were unusually high. The key to its superiority lay in logistics: the Prussian army was throughout better fed, better clothed, and above all more reliably paid than any of its rivals. And it possessed decisive leadership from a monarch who was not so much an original military genius, but a competent commander with clear and realistic ideas of what could be accomplished, and the status and prestige to ensure that they were put into practice.

Frederick himself recorded that in part he acted out of youthful thirst for reputation. 'My youth, hot headedness and thirst for glory ... the satisfaction of seeing my name in the gazettes and then in history carried me away.' That may have been true, but his opening campaign, to seize the Austrian province of Silesia in one surgical strike, was a hard-headed calculation. Silesia would be an invaluable strengthening of his kingdom; it was a populous and economically advanced region, adjacent to his core territory of Brandenburg, with an industrial potential that Prussia had so far lacked. The time was right: Charles VI had just died, Maria Theresa had had no time to consolidate her grip on the inheritance, and her most dangerous ally, Russia, was undergoing a succession crisis on the death of Anna. In October the Prussian army moved into Silesia, without warning or justification, met only token resistance, and secured control. Frederick then offered to purchase it from Maria

Theresa. When she refused, and in early 1741 sent troops to recover it, they were defeated at the battle of Mollwitz in April, and all subsequent Austrian attempts to drive the Prussians out failed.

Nobody had anticipated this development. The initial response of Louis XV to the crisis was to affirm non-intervention: 'In these circumstances I do not want to be involved at all, I shall wait, hands in pockets, unless they try to elect a Protestant as Emperor.' But the temptation to profit from the situation, possibly to extinguish the Habsburgs as a major dynasty, and establish French hegemony was too strong. Fleury tried to control events, but the militants at the French court, led by Marshal Belle-Isle won the king over to intervention. Belle-Isle was sent on a mission to the imperial Diet to secure the election of the Elector of Bavaria as the new Emperor, Charles VII. At the same time he formed a coalition of predators to take the Habsburg dominions apart. French aid was promised to Frederick to keep Silesia; Belle-Isle himself led a Franco-Bavarian army which moved into Bohemia and western Austria and secured the allegiance of the local Estates to the new Emperor; Philip V and Farnese were encouraged to send troops into Italy to carve up Habsburg lands there; while in Sweden, where the French-subsidized Hat party had bought control of the Diet, the Hat administration were encouraged to launch a war of revenge on Russia while its government was paralysed by the succession crisis, thus pre-empting a Russian intervention in the west. Maria Theresa's cause looked lost, except for a swing of opinion in Great Britain in favour of intervention. This was led by the king, George II, fearful for the future of Hanover under a French puppet Emperor, and made possible by the fall of Walpole, and his replacement by Carteret, an old-fashioned Whig seeking to re-create the Grand Alliance against the Bourbons. Britain formed an alliance with Maria Theresa, providing subsidies and hiring an army of German mercenaries to operate from Hanover.[2] Maria Theresa herself took a dramatic initiative in 1741 when she appealed to the Hungarian Diet for support. In return for constitutional concessions, the Hungarians formally elected her queen of Hungary and provided military assistance. She was still desperately dependent on British subsidies, and during 1742 was persuaded by Carteret to make peace with Frederick by ceding Silesia, and to buy the support of Charles Emmanuel to fight the Bourbons in Italy with an offer of more territory. In 1743 the tide of war turned. Frederick used his disengagement to make urgent improvements to his army. The fighting had revealed that although the Prussian infantry was excellent, the cavalry and artillery were weak, and the king set about correcting this. Maria Theresa now turned on Bavaria and occupied it, making Charles VII a refugee under French protection, while George II led his mercenaries to a victory over French forces at Dettingen, and the French retired from German territory. During 1742–3, the attempted Swedish attack on Russia was easily repulsed under the new empress, Elizabeth, and Sweden was forced to buy peace by ceding further territory in Finland. There was now the possibility that Russia could enter the conflict, and if so it would be on the Austrian side.

In 1743 the war was nearly deadlocked and might well have been wound up. One problem was the weakness of French leadership. Louis XV had declared after the death of Fleury that he would take charge but he had little idea what to do. Amelot wrote to Belle-Isle in January 1743: 'this war has been prolonged without our being able to see any way out of it: the king is bearing all alone, all the weight of it, we are today much less further on than at the beginning'. The problem for the French leadership was the lack of some clear strategic aim, as Amelot obviously perceived. In the end Louis XV decided to revert to the policies of his predecessor and made a new family compact with Philip V. France would join the Spanish invasion of Italy, though she had no claims of her own to pursue, they would jointly revive the naval war against Britain, and France would open up a new front by invading the Austrian Netherlands. In 1744 this was put into effect: Louis XV at last declared war on Britain and Austria. A proposed invasion of Britain in 1744 was foiled by bad weather, but good progress was made in the Netherlands, and Frederick decided to forestall any Austrian recovery by another lightning strike. He re-entered the war and for a time overran Bohemia. In Britain public feeling was turning against what seemed a futile conflict in Germany and Carteret had to resign. William Pitt began to make a name for himself as a critic of continental involvements by Britain. A new government headed by Henry Pelham and the duke of Newcastle was installed at the end of the year, but it had no clearer idea than the French how to bring hostilities to a successful conclusion.

In January 1745 a new turn brought the German conflict to an end when Charles VII died. His succcessor in Bavaria sought peace and was willing to see the imperial crown revert to the Habsburgs. Frederick, who had success-fully beaten off all Austrian attempts to recover Silesia, was anxious to settle, and after Francis Stephen was elected Emperor in September, the British forced Maria Theresa to accept the loss of Silesia as the price of peace. The British government had been surprised in 1745 by the expedition of the son of the Stuart pretender to Scotland, which caught them off guard as he raised the highland clans in a bid to re-assert Scotland's independence. But the prince's spectacular invasion of England was a doomed enterprise: the population remained passive towards the invaders, but there was very little popular support.[3] It appeared that although the Jacobite cause had served as a sentimental protest position, the reality was quite different. It was appreciated that a restored Jacobite regime could only survive under French protection, and this was quite unacceptable to Protestant public opinion. It only remained for the elimination of the Scottish basis of Jacobitism, after the victory at Culloden in 1746. Following the initial, brutal military reprisals on the Gaelic community, the abolition of heredi-tary jurisdictions and use of the Forfeited Estates Act were intended to intro-duce English-style landlordism into the highlands. At the same time the Pelham ministry had a deliberate policy of opening up careers in the army and the colonies, in particular to Scottish applicants. A major sign of change in highland Scotland came in the next war, with the raising of Highland regiments in the British army. The full integration of Scotland into the British empire had begun.

Although peace negotiations between France and Britain opened in 1746, showing both major protagonists wanted to get out of the conflict, it continued to be deadlocked. In Italy the Austrian and Piedmontese forces had a good year in 1746 against the Bourbon invaders, but there too military stalemate set in. In the Netherlands the French commander, Marshal Saxe, won a striking victory over Allied forces at Fontenoy in 1745, went steadily forward to overrun the whole territory, and in 1747 threatened the United Provinces with invasion. Although this triggered an Orange revival and restoration of the stadholderate for the first time under one ruler, William IV, it did not result in any revival of the Dutch will to fight. It was made clear that any pretensions of the United Provinces to be a major power were gone. In the end, it is arguable that British naval power decided the issue. In 1745 the navy took a firm grip on the English Channel, and there was little prospect that the Bourbons could do anything to assist the Jacobite uprising. At the same time the North American colonists, with naval support, captured the French fortress of Louisbourg, commanding sea access to Canada in 1745, while a systematic blockade of French and Spanish trade with the Americas began to take effect. The French were hit by harvest failures in 1747, but more serious were the warnings from the controller of finance, Machault d'Arnonville, that bankruptcy was threatened, mainly because the blockade had seriously reduced the customs revenues, and the raising of further credits was becoming difficult. The British parliament was hearing rising complaints about the high levels of wartime taxation, but in fact the English financial system held up well. The war in the end cost Britain £43 million, of which some £30 million were raised by borrowing. Even so the servicing of this debt was still manageable, and although the British public might see the burdens as intolerable, the French certainly had the impression that Britain could keep the naval war going and afford the hire of mercenaries on the continent. In 1748 the British had paid £500,000 to hire a Russian force to come into Germany, but the war ended before it got further than Poland.

The war was finally concluded by the general peace of Aix-la-Chapelle in 1748. Austria was the main loser, since although the dynasty had survived, and recovered the imperial crown, the loss of Silesia was a major defeat and carried with it the fact that Prussia must now be considered an equal power in Germany. After making peace in 1745, Frederick had retained an army of 140,000 men and, unlike Austria, could maintain it out of his domestic revenues. Austria also sacrificed lands in northern Italy: Parma and Piacenza went to the Spanish Bourbons and another piece of Milan went to Piedmont. Yet this did settle Italy until 1789: Philip V died in 1746 but his successor, Ferdinand VI, was no friend of the Farnese branch of the Bourbons and had no further claims of his own in Italy. In 1752 Ferdinand concluded a treaty with Austria, in which all outstanding issues between them were settled. Maria Theresa was further humiliated because throughout the war she had depended on British subsidies that had provided 20 per cent of her wartime revenues, and her armies had proved so inferior to that of Frederick II. Austria had, in effect, ceased to be an independent great power. Maria Theresa tolerated the peace because of her determination to re-establish her independent military capacity. Britain and France ended by trading in their respective gains and the conflict was drawn. In spite of the wholly successful conquest of the Netherlands, it was restored in its entirety to the Habsburgs. Yet on balance Britain was the clear winner. She had forced France to near bankruptcy, she had demonstrated that Jacobitism was dead as a serious political force, and Louis XV once more had to expel the Stuarts from his territory. And Britain had demonstrated, after an uncertain start, that her naval power was more than able to face down the combined efforts of the two Bourbon monarchies. Further, it soon became apparent that the personal authority and prestige of Louis XV had suffered serious damage before a public opinion that could not accept a settlement which, in effect, gave nothing to France after years of costly warfare.[4] The surrender of the Netherlands, after the brilliant campaigns of the French armies there seemed inexplicable. The Treaty of Aix-la-Chapelle gave rise to a popular saying in France: *bête comme la paix*, 'as stupid as the peace'.

Phase 2: A creative pause, 1748–1756

Frederick II remarked of the peace: 'This general pacification resembles rather a truce in which all parties profit from a short period of repose and look for alliances, to be better placed to take up arms again.' But few had Frederick's clear and cynical powers of analysis, and when hostilities recommenced the political scenario had changed. The new king of Spain and his minister, Carvajal, were serious about wishing for a period of peace. Besides the settlement with Austria in 1752, they sought a settlement of the almost forgotten Anglo–Spanish disputes that had originally begun the war. The Spaniards dropped the issue of the return of Gibraltar, disbanded the *guarda costas* in the Caribbean, and bought out the trading rights of the South Sea Company. They wanted to strengthen the Spanish economy and establish self-reliance and independence. The Russian government of the Empress Elizabeth, which had been poised to intervene in the campaign of 1748 on the Austrian side, took a continuing interest in any further developments in central or northern Europe and had shown it had the capacity to make its intervention effective. This was particularly a concern for Frederick, since the one respect in which his analysis was absolutely correct was that Maria Theresa meant to recover Silesia by war as soon as the internal reconstruction she was planning had produced results and suitable alliances were put in place. An alliance with Russia would be a more direct threat to Frederick than any other.

Frederick used the pause to pursue the first round of his reform programme. Although his father had left a centralized administration in the Directory, Frederick disliked its collegiate working practice. He declined to involve himself in the regular collective policy sessions, seeking to bypass the Directory by dealing directly with department heads. He was unhappy with its recruitment; his father had used a large proportion of commoners and aliens in the civil service, while one of Frederick's most consistent aims was to build the Prussian state on the loyalty of the Junker landlords. He deliberately recruited Junkers into the higher levels of the civil service at the same time as he was giving them a near monopoly of military commands. His *Political Testament* of 1752 was explicit about this: 'a sovereign should regard it as his duty to protect the nobility, who form the finest jewel in his crown and the lustre of his army'. At local level the appointment of the key rural official, the *Landrat*, was made in consultation with the local assemblies of noble landlords. Frederick suspected that the collegiate system was creating a corporate bureaucracy that would be an obstacle to change. In this he was, of course, correct. One of his early measures was to add a Fifth Department for economic development to the Directory. It tended to be systematically obstructed by the established departments, and in the end was retained largely as a statistical section, while the actual work of promoting economic growth was done by contracting with the Berlin commercial community. Indeed the launching of initiatives through special commissions, rather than the machinery of the Directory, was a feature of his government.

When he faced the question of how to assimilate Silesia into his kingdom, he did not place it under the Directory. To the end of his life, Silesia was controlled by a separate administration under a president answerable only to the king. The province was a mosaic of ecclesiastical and feudal jurisdictions, with a self-governing urban sector, and largely administered through its Estates. It had the further problem of containing a large Catholic community, which the Habsburgs had always promoted, although as a consequence many of the Protestant community welcomed Frederick as a protector. Because Silesia was a conquest, Frederick enjoyed a freedom of action he could not look for in his own kingdom, with its long-established legal rights. The Silesian Estates were simply abolished and so was urban self-government. Instead the Prussian dualism was established: an urban sector closely supervised by an appointed royal official, in this case the burgomaster, and paying tax through the urban excise, and a rural sector governed through its noble landlords by the *Landrat* system. This was achieved by negotiation with the native nobility, but advantage was taken to sweep away the old Estates-based tax system and introduce a model Prussian land tax. This rapidly increased the Silesian revenues fourfold.[5] After 1745, the Silesian population as a whole stayed loyal to Frederick. He was able to negotiate working arrangements with the local Catholic hierarchy; being an unbeliever himself, Frederick had no problems with full religious toleration. He left church property alone, restricted

ecclesiastical courts to strictly religious issues, and established a joint tribunal to settle demarcation disputes. Once the Catholic community was
convinced the toleration was genuine, they settled down quite contentedly.

But for Frederick the most urgent task of the truce period was to consolidate and improve his army. By 1745 his reserve fighting fund of 10 million
thaler had been reduced to 6 million and urgent measures were taken to
build it up again; it had reached 13 million by 1756. The enlarged army
establishment of 140,000 was enormous in relation to the population
resources and this was one reason why a large proportion of the rankers
were aliens – half or more. Experience taught Frederick that such a large
force could not be maintained over a long war out of his own resources, so
he was preparing the army for swift and decisive action. This was the doctrine set out in his *General Principles of War* which described the strategy to
be employed: this required careful advance preparation, systematic opera-
tional planning, and the capacity for swift execution. Before the next war
began, Frederick had tackled problems of weapons and equipment, largely
through his own commercial contractors, brought his cavalry and artillery
up to standard, and above all intensified the training and drill, allowing tactical flexibility in action, through which he claimed a small well-trained
army could expect to meet and defeat superior forces.

The Austrian territories had lacked central decision-making bodies in
1740 beyond the Secret Council (*Geheime Konferenz*), a rather large advisory body. The territories were administered through their local Estates,
with a separate chancellory for Austria, Bohemia, Hungary and
Transylvania, and Councils for Italy and the Netherlands. During the war
some adjustments occurred: in 1742 a central *Hof und Staatskanzlei* was
established, whose president, the *Hofkanzler* became in effect foreign minister. But the basic weaknesses remained. The army was still a state-contract
force – a collection of autonomous units controlled by their colonels.
Recruiting and billeting were controlled by local Estates officials, and its
main financial support, the Contribution, had to be voted and administered
through the Estates. There could be no central finance ministry, and even the
chamber revenues, including most of the indirect taxes, were committed as
security for the state debt and administered by the Vienna Bank.

During the war Maria Theresa became impressed by the reform plans of
a Silesian administrator, Friedrich Haugwitz, who in turn admired the
success of the Prussian system. In 1748 a major reform plan was launched.
The basis was to find funding, 14 million florins, for an army of 108,000.
This would be achieved largely by raising the Contribution, which was
doubled to 10 million florins. It proved possible to persuade the various
Estates to agree to this and the missing 4 million were to come from
Hungary. This did provide a large boost to the revenues. The controversy
broke out over the administrative reforms: Haugwitz proposed to amalga-
mate the Austrian and Bohemian chancellories. A new advisory council for
internal affairs, the *Konferenz in Internis* was set up, and to execute policy a

Directorium was created on the Prussian model, combining control of administration and finance, with the establishment of local offices, the *Deputationen und Kammern*, all to be staffed by salaried public officials. It was the clear intention that these bodies would in time replace the local Estates' control of affairs. This part of the plan met the most determined local resistance and, in May 1749, it was simply imposed by royal proclamation. Even if this reform had worked as intended, it still did not apply to Hungary, Italy or the Netherlands; nor did it establish a central treasury. It was not practicable to force the Estates to yield control of the Contribution, or to free the chamber revenues from their commitment to the debt. Nor did they reduce the formidable autonomous financial and administrative power of the church.

The Haugwitz reforms, with all their imperfections, did increase central control and it was possible to begin systematic military reform which started to provide the Habsburg state with a modern army. On the other hand they showed the limitations of early modern absolute monarchy. Maria Theresa could order change and override local protest on paper, but when it came down to actually getting in the money and raising the recruits, the cooperation of the local elites had to be negotiated and this weakened the new structures.

It can be argued that the decline and fall of the Bourbon monarchy in France started seriously after 1748 with Louis XV's growing loss of public credibility. There were grounds for this. The king never had a serious political strategy beyond his basic belief that it was his duty to safeguard the power of the monarchy and transmit it undiminished to his successors. It did not help that he was a shy and retiring personality and his only regular public appearances outside the court rituals at Versailles were for his passionate pursuit of the hunt. It was unfair because he was in fact a hardworking, conscientious administrator. The king and his two favourite ministers of the 1750s, the controller of finance, Machault, and the secretary for war, d'Argensen, saw the lessons of the war to be that France had little to gain from an active policy on the continent. They favoured building up naval and colonial power with a view to an eventual confrontation with Great Britain. French overseas trade swiftly recovered from the wartime blockade and was developing vigorously, and the French Caribbean colonies were coming into their full potential production.

But it was also the period when the ideas of the French Enlightenment were spreading in society. A new generation of lawyers entered the *parlements*,[6] enthused by the constitutional ideas of Montesquieu in particular, and his distinction between absolute monarchy, which was legitimate because it operated within a framework of law, and despotism which was a corruption to which monarchy was always liable. There was a very influential publication in 1753 by a *parlementaire* lawyer, Le Paige, called *Lettres historiques*, which discussed the threat of despotism and assigned to the *parlements* a special responsibility for resisting it in France. Le Paige claimed that the *parlements* were ancient institutions, coeval with the monarchy itself, and had always shared with it the exercise of sovereignty. They had a representative role, certifying to the subject that the royal policies were in accordance with law, and transmitting to the king the legitimate grievances of the subjects. Their rights to participate in the process of legitimating royal actions could not be overridden by resort to the royal Council, which represented a lower order of authority. This provided an ideological basis for a mounting confrontation between royal power and the *parlements*.

It arose from a fusion of two sources of conflict: in 1748 Machault produced a fiscal reform programme to bring the public debt under control. He planned to establish a proper sinking fund for the long term debt. This would come from a new general tax, a *vingtième*, which would be a 5 per cent property tax, and was justified on the grounds that it would be socially equitable. There was a massive public protest from the privileged elites and it had to be forced through the Paris *parlement*, which voted 106–49 for a remonstrance against it. Then it ran into the determined resistance of the clergy and the provincial Estates, particularly in Brittany and Languedoc. In 1750 an Assembly of the Clergy made a vigorous defence of its ancient fiscal exemptions against the tax. It was here that the second source of conflict became involved – a bitter revival of the Jansenist controversy. From 1746 there was a new, confrontational archbishop, de Beaumont, a militant opponent of Jansenism. In his drive to enforce *Unigenitus* he adopted the tactic of refusing the sacraments to those who would not certify their acceptance of the bull. There were publicized cases of Jansenists dying without the last rites rather than give in, and the victims appealed to the *parlement* for protection, which was readily given and this asserted its superior jurisdiction over ecclesiastical law. Since the king made the anti-Jansenist cause one of his most consistent lines of policy, he too became involved in a series of bitter public controversies with the *parlements*, where the new arguments about the threat of despotism were freely employed. In order to support the clergy, in 1751 the king and Machault had to give in over the *vingtième* on the clergy, which greatly stimulated the protest movement among the other privileged groups.

In 1753 the *parlementaires* complained of the threat of despotism, which of course they blamed on the self-interest of evil councillors, and went on strike. After more than a year of public debate and controversy, the royal government had to give way and the *parlements* resumed their usual functions. The attack on the Jansenists was tacitly abandoned and so was Machault's fiscal reform programme. It was against this background of domestic failure that Louis XV's government reluctantly entered the new war. To rally opinion behind it, in 1757 both d'Argensen and Machault were dismissed.

In Great Britain at the end of the war there was a strong Whig administration in office, led by the duke of Newcastle, who directed foreign affairs, and his brother Henry Pelham, who managed the Treasury. Their aim after 1748 was to keep the peace and embark upon a financial reconstruction: with major savings on military expenditure, the land tax could again be cut back to 2 shillings in the pound, and the interest on most of the national debt reduced from 4 per cent to 3.5 per cent. This was a success and demonstrated the resilience of the British financial structure. Even Dutch investors often preferred to put their money into British funds. The maintenance of the peace was threatened by two developments. In 1754 Henry Pelham died, necessitating a reconstruction of the ministry and, in spite of the peaceful intentions of both the British and French governments, they found themselves drifting into confrontation in the American colonies. The problem was beyond the control of either government. By the 1750s the white settlers in Britain's North American colonies had increased to near 2 million and the area of settlement was pushing inexorably westwards. The French in Canada had about 6000 settlers and even fewer in the vast tract of Louisiana. To give some security in face of such disproportion, the French government maintained a substantial garrison of regular soldiers in Canada, acutely aware that in a war it might be difficult to reinforce them. They adopted the obvious survival strategy of trying to restrict British expansion along the line of the Alleghenny Mountains, setting up a line of military posts reinforced by alliances with the native American tribes, for whom the British settlers presented a threat to their existence. In 1753 the French established a military base at Fort Duquesne in the Ohio valley and expeditions by the colonial militias to drive them off failed. After Pelham's death, the weakened ministry was assailed by factions around the king, assisted by ambitious opposition politicians like Henry Fox and William Pitt working up a genuine public opinion that favoured an aggressive imperial policy. In 1755 the government yielded and agreed to send regular troops to America, backing them up with a naval blockade to prevent any further French reinforcements reaching Canada. When the British expeditionary force under General Braddock was massacred in 1755, the government stepped up seizures of French shipping. The French government refused to be provoked and in the end it was the British government, pushed by public opinion, that declared war on France in 1756.

Newcastle had been hampered by Britain's continental problem as it became clear in the 1750s that the old alliance with Austria and the Netherlands to restrain France was no longer an option: the United Provinces were set on staying neutral and Maria Theresa was fixated on Silesia. In 1755 the problem was Hanover, which the king insisted on defending, and which was obviously vulnerable to French attack in case of war. In 1755 Newcastle first sought assistance from Russia to intervene in Germany, but also approached Frederick. He was aware that Austria and Russia were intending to attack him, and by the Convention of Westminster in January 1756 agreed to cooperate in preventing foreign troops intervening in Germany. This move deeply offended Louis XV. The king and the French Council in February 1756 decided to accept the offers coming from Vienna for cooperation between the Habsburg and Bourbon families. In May 1756 the first Treaty of Vienna bound France and Austria to a defensive alliance: Austria would be neutral in any Anglo-French war and, if

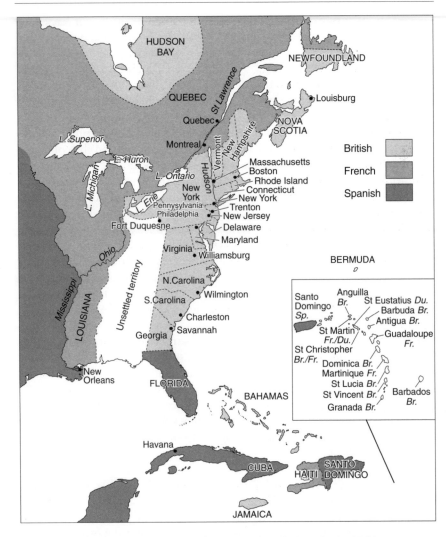

Map 15.1 European settlements in North America in 1756

any other power attacked France, would give military assistance. France gave an equivalent promise and broke her alliance with Frederick. This was meant to give France freedom to prosecute her naval war with Britain and Austria time to get together with Russia to crush Frederick.

The Seven Years War, 1756–1763

This reversal of centuries of dynastic rivalry was the 'Diplomatic Revolution' of 1756. It was intended, like so many of these plans, to postpone or even prevent the outbreak of a new general war, and its effect was to precipitate one. Frederick, now without any ally on the continent, and seeing the open preparations of Austria and Russia to attack him, repeated his coup of 1740 and attacked first. In August 1756 the Prussian troops suddenly invaded Saxony and effectively occupied it, allowing the Elector to take refuge in his Polish kingdom. The move had been carefully planned. A Prussian military administration took over Saxony and seized its resources for the Prussian war effort. In the end Saxony provided a third of the financial costs and considerable numbers of recruits. The Prussian military machine had also been strengthened. In 1754 Frederick had set up a Sixth Department in the General Directory to control the supply and logistics of the army; its plans for supplying the armies on campaign, through its Magazine Administration, gave the Prussian army the inestimable advantage over its opponents that its men were always tolerably paid, armed and fed. As the king left to take command, the Directory was charged with assuming domestic government, giving priority to the demands of war.

The Prussian administrations, despite enemy occupations of East Prussia and the Rhine duchies, and Pomerania being continuously subject to military operations, managed to keep up the flow of tax revenue and recruits without resorting to ruinous levels of exaction. From 1757 to 1761, Frederick was receiving British cash subsidies, but towards the end he was driven to debasing the currency to survive. The size of the army was maintained at around 140,000 men, but the quality inevitably declined over time: by 1759 half the original officer corps had become casualties and the infantry was diluted with unreliable Saxon conscripts and mercenary contingents under foreign officers. Fortunately for Frederick, the problems of his principal opponents were even more severe.

Strategically the sudden move into Saxony, meant to frighten the potential enemies into pulling back, failed. The original defensive arrangement between Louis XV and Maria Theresa developed into a coalition; Russia formally allied with Austria for a joint attack; the Holy Roman Empire voted assistance to the Emperor; French influence in Stockholm brought Sweden in to attack Frederick in Pomerania. On paper such a combination should have crushed him, and in 1757 things went badly. His attack on Bohemia ended in failure and demonstrated the improved fighting power of the Austrian armies. Russian troops moved into East Prussia and the French invaded Germany. Frederick concentrated his forces in his central territories and used the advantage of united command, interior lines and superior logistics to beat back the uncoordinated Allied offensives. The year ended with a brilliant strike: on 5 November he shattered a French-led force at Rossbach and exactly one month later destroyed an Austrian army at Leuthen.

This severely discouraged the Austrians. They found that in spite of the improved fighting capacity of their troops, the high command proved sluggish against an opponent like Frederick, and above all the logistics failed. The Haugwitz reforms simply did not deliver the improved administrative efficiency they had promised, in part because they had never been effectively enforced. The central Directory, a tight body of seven members as set up, had swollen to 21 members by 1754, and the Chancellor, Kaunitz, admittedly always critical of the Haugwitz system, claimed in 1761 that instead of centralizing and concentrating power, it had turned an original four central agencies into 18.[7] Certainly its financial resources did not stand the strain of war at all well. During the conflict Austrian tax revenues totalled about 240 million florins, and the government managed to borrow a total of 243 million florins from domestic loans, some of them forced loans. But all this did not suffice and by 1761 the government was using a form of paper money guaranteed by the Estates. Although, during this war, the Austrians were fielding armies of 180,000 men or more, the administrative and financial system proved incapable of sustaining such an effort. By 1761 Kaunitz was advising Maria Theresa that they would have to make peace without regaining Silesia.

Austria changed to a defensive strategy after 1757, hoping that attrition and Russian pressure would bring victory. It was indeed the Russians who bore the brunt of the fighting in 1758 and 1759, and their armies not only stood up to the Prussians but inflicted on Frederick some of his worst defeats, while in summer 1760 Russian forces occupied Berlin, though they evacuated it after extorting a large war contribution. Yet the Russians could not force a result, in part because their commanders were acutely aware that Elizabeth's health was declining, and that her successor, the tsarevich Peter, was a fanatical admirer of all things Prussian, and would certainly stop the war if he succeeded to the throne. More crucially their liaison with the Austrian commanders was poor, so that Frederick never faced an effectively coordinated offensive, and that in turn reflected the reality that Maria Theresa and her advisers were nervous about Russia becoming the dominant partner in central Europe. Yet Frederick nearly despaired at times. After the disastrous defeat at Kunersdorf at the hands of the Russians, he wrote: 'Our losses are very considerable, of an army of 48,000 I have less than 3000 men left. All flee and I am no longer master of my men ... This is a terrible mishap and I shall not survive it ... to tell truth I believe all is lost.'

But his will to persevere proved strong enough, and his enemies' blunders repeatedly saved him from final disaster. After a bad first half of 1760, he gathered enough troops and energy to defeat the Austrians twice, at Liegnitz in August and Torgau in November. It was after that that the Austrians became ready to settle, but Elizabeth insisted on another round in 1761, which was as indecisive as all the others except that Prussian resources were now critically low. In that year Britain had a change of government, which was looking for peace, and Frederick's subsidies were withdrawn. Then, in January 1762, Elizabeth died, and as expected Peter at once made peace with Prussia. Although he was deposed by his wife Catherine after six months' reign, she decided to remain neutral. The Austrians, left alone against Frederick, made peace by the Treaty of Hubertusberg in February 1763, restoring the territorial status quo of 1756.[8]

The Seven Years War had always been two distinct struggles loosely linked together. The fight for hegemony in central Europe went on parallel with the naval and colonial war between Great Britain and the Bourbons. One factor here is the development of British opinion in mid-century, carried forward by a sustained expansion of British trade and manufacture, in which overseas trade with the Americas and India was the leading sector. The fast-growing colonial economies in North America had a major input as expanding markets for basic manufactures, like textiles and metal goods. The plantation colonies, besides supplying produce for re-export to Europe, were also an insatiable consumer of African slaves, a trade now dominated by Great Britain. That must be one reason why the British public took imperial policy seriously and in the 1750s, through the press and parliament, they compelled the reluctant Pelham–Newcastle ministry to do the same in face of the French challenge. A broad political grouping developed in support of imperialism, which after the death of Pelham forced its way into the ruling coalition, with William Pitt as its populist mouthpiece and support from the court faction that had built first around Frederick Prince of Wales until his death in 1751, and then revived under his ambitious widow and her young son, the future George III, who was deemed of age in 1756.

He and his mother rejected what they saw as the narrow dependence of the first Hanoverians on the Whig oligarchs, and were enthused about the idea of a patriot king, who would lead a new political consensus, rising above partisan strife. Their leading political adviser was the Scottish nobleman Lord Bute. When the new war, in 1756, opened badly for Britain with a successful French seizure of Minorca, public opinion forced the Newcastle Whigs to broaden their power base by taking Pitt into a reconstructed government as Paymaster General, but in fact minister in charge of the war. Pitt shared with Frederick the advantage of having a well-conceived, war-winning strategy. One part of it was, on the strength of his populist standing, to give British subsidies to Frederick, in order to keep French forces tied down in Germany and save Hanover from attack. But his basic strategy was naval, and he was ably seconded by the naval commander, Lord Anson, who ran an extremely effective regime at the admiralty during the 1750s. This made the most of British superiority in finance, shipbuilding capacity and reserves of experienced seamen to maintain a British navy equal in strength to France and Spain combined. Indeed the French fleet was dominated throughout, not venturing to offer battle, and allowing the British to strangle their oceanic trade and then pick off their colonies in combined operations. This demanded major financial resources. British war expenditure averaged £13.7 million a year, and at its peak in 1760 topped £90 million. This was sustainable because the British government could borrow huge sums at 3.5–4 per cent. For instance, in 1758, 22 private consortia in the City readily underwrote a loan of £8 million. The investments not only came from the City. By this time country banks were developing to channel investment, and considerable purchases of British securities were funded in Amsterdam.

The results were dazzling. Apart from blockading the French coasts and mounting amphibious raids on French ports to tie down military strength, the British had conquered French Canada by 1760, and then proceeded to mop up the French sugar islands in the Caribbean and take French slaving stations in West Africa. In India the troops of the East India Company, led by Clive, established the predominance of the British over the trade of the sub-continent.

Until 1759, Spain, crippled by yet another royal insanity, which struck Ferdinand VI in his last years, kept outside the struggle. His successor Charles III was an exception among Spanish monarchs – entirely sane and healthy, industrious and interested in rational reform. Unfortunately he had an obsessive hatred of the British, and fearful at the extent of British success, rashly entered a new Bourbon family compact in 1761 and declared war on Britain in 1762. Pitt had seen it coming and resigned in 1761 when his colleagues refused to sanction a preventive strike at Spain. George III had come to the throne in 1760, and he and Bute correctly perceived that for the patriotic taxpayers the war had gone on long enough. The king was now seeking a negotiated peace to make way for domestic political reconstruction. But the sheer impetus of the Pitt naval strategy meant that the British, in 1762, easily seized Havana and Manila from the Spaniards. In February 1763, coincidentally with the Peace at Hubertusberg, the Treaty of Paris was concluded with the Bourbon powers. This ended French colonization in North America with the cession of Canada. The British also rounded out their colonies by taking Florida from Spain in exchange for Manila and Havana. The French recovered their principal sugar islands in the Caribbean, but felt bound, out of dynastic loyalty, to transfer their remaining North American possession, Louisiana, to Spain. These were moderate terms compared with what Pitt had wanted, but apart from a few disgruntled imperialists and francophobes, British opinion was content with the settlement.[9]

The poor performance of France in the Seven Years War merits comment. In terms of resources, France was certainly the equal of Great Britain, though it can be recognized that in terms of a naval and colonial conflict the British did have major advantages. There is no reason to suppose, however, that given leadership of the quality provided by Frederick or William Pitt, French resources could not have been mobilized to much better effect. There was a basic strategic problem. France was engaged simultaneously in two wars, when her opponents, Prussia and Britain, could focus on one of them. French resources did not extend to supporting two major conflicts at once, one continental and one maritime. Navies in fact tended to cost more than armies in terms of investment in facilities and upkeep, and to keep up a world-class navy and a world-class army together was probably beyond the capacity of any early modern European state. The French leadership should have made a clear strategic choice and followed it, which to some extent they did in 1759, when they revised their alliance with Austria and French military intervention in the continental war was downgraded to hiring auxiliary contingents for Austrian service. But by that time France had lost the maritime war beyond possibility of recovery – the change of strategy came too late.

But this fact illustrates the further problem that the French government had weak and indecisive leadership from the king. Where Britain entered the conflict on a wave of popular patriotism, France was locked in embittered domestic disputes between the royal government and the *parlements*. The confrontation of 1753–4 had only shifted the balance of power further against the royal authority. As the international crisis intensified, aristocratic factions at court, grouped round the duke of Orléans and a clique of senior sword nobles, now sensed opportunities for extending their power from the court to the administration. There, since Louis XIV's day, they had been excluded and the great *robe* families had become entrenched. There was unusual scope for court faction because Louis XV himself had been hesitant both over getting involved in war and, once he had concluded the Austrian alliance, where to direct his main effort. The alliance with the Habsburgs was such a breach with generations of tradition in French policy that it had a divisive effect: public opinion was at best lukewarm towards it. Its most obvious consequence, the humiliating defeat of the French army by Frederick at Rossbach, did nothing to increase support. Also war brought out the problem of imposing wartime taxation, an issue certain to generate argument with the *parlements*. In 1757 there was talk of another judicial strike. Instability was reflected in a rapid turnover of ministers, particularly the office of controller, which was held by five different appointees between 1754 and 1758 when Louis XV had to sacrifice his favourite minister, Machault, the advocate of unpopular taxation projects, to appease the critics in the *parlement*. In a letter to the infanta in Madrid he revealed his own weakness. Factional pressures, he wrote, 'have done everything to force me to dismiss Machault, a man after my own heart: I shall never be able to console myself'.

A weak government was not equal to directing a successful war against such formidable opponents as Pitt and Frederick. It was not until late 1758 that ministers with a clear programme and real political ability emerged to lead the administration: the duke of Choiseul and his brother, who managed to stay in charge of French government until 1770. They were clear that the priority for France must be the maritime struggle with Britain and continental involvements must be avoided. The Choiseuls accepted that the current war was lost, and were already looking for peace, though they were unable to resist a final gamble on the Spanish entry into the war strengthening their bargaining position, particularly once Pitt had resigned, and the new king and his chief minister were known to be eager to settle.

Some commentators enthuse over the Seven Years War on the strength of the extraordinary triumph of the will represented by the performances of

Frederick and the Pitt administration. Unquestionably, after a shaky start, the British had a good war, and were demonstrating how their political and social system was laying the foundations for a period of British hegemony in international affairs. But a more detached assessment suggests that this had been a peculiarly pointless conflict, particularly in view of its unusual destructiveness. Yet that may have been one of its only merits. The conflict had indeed tested the system of international relations almost to destruction. All the participants, once they began counting the costs, seem to have emerged with the resolution that at least there should be another creative pause, and even that a future general conflict on this scale should be avoided, as indeed it was until the French Revolution changed everything. After 1763 the European governments entered a phase of constructive rebuilding, with the conscious intention of establishing a better international order. Behind this tendency was the shift in European mentalities that historians like to call the Enlightenment.

16

The Enlightenment

Historians have problems deciding what the Enlightenment was,[1] but they cannot fail to see how in the course of the eighteenth century there was a shift in the mentality of the European elites, and that this influenced rulers and their advisers and encouraged the emergence of a whole new branch of government – domestic policy. Rulers now recognized a duty, in addition to promoting their dynastic interests, maintaining the established religion, defending their realms from attack and upholding the royal authority within the kingdom, to use their sovereign power to promote the material welfare of their subjects. This in turn reflects the growing belief that society could be improved by human intervention, and the well-being and happiness of their subjects increased. The Enlightenment was a process through which much of elite society came to change their assumptions about the world they lived in and the way it functioned.

Its intellectual pedigree could be traced back to the Renaissance and the Reformation, but its immediate causes are to be found in the scientific movement of the seventeenth century. Then belief had been based on one authority, which could not be challenged – Christianity – and which assumed that the destiny of mankind was pre-determined by God's Providence, which operated in ways inaccessible to merely human reasoning. Bossuet had reminded men that:

> The long sequence of particular causes which make and break empires, depends on the secret commands of divine Providence ... what our uncertain counsels mistake for chance is a design elaborated in a higher council, in that eternal council which comprises all causes and effects within a simple unity.

The work of Bacon, Galileo, Descartes and Newton had offered a cautious challenge to this iron law of Providence by defining a part of God's creation, the material world, as open to human investigation, since it was regulated by God-given laws of natural science, which any normal human intellect could understand. In this way men would be able to understand and manipulate the material world for their own betterment. It was pointed out earlier that this claim was potentially subversive of the dominance of religious dogma over the European mind. This was not intended, as Descartes had been careful to say: 'above all we will observe as an infallible rule that what God has revealed is incomparably more certain than all the rest'. Yet only 50 years later Pierre Bayle was claiming, 'every individual dogma ... is false when refuted by the clear and distinct perceptions of natural reason': Bayle had cast aside the caution of the early scientists. By 1700, the churches were on the defensive against the challenge of science and readier to accept Newton's model of a law-bound universe in which God had indeed decreed the laws of nature, but was also bound by them and became the divine clockmaker, with a largely passive role of supervising his creation, and at most making occasional adjustments to keep the machinery running smoothly.

It is Newton whose thought stands at the heart of the Enlightenment. Its greatest pioneer, Voltaire, made his public reputation promoting Newtonian science in France. The core idea of the Enlightenment was based on the confidence created by the Newtonian synthesis that the material world should be subjected to constant critical investigation by human reason. Rationality was the key to understanding, and was indeed the defining characteristic of being human. The possession of reason was what distinguished humans from all the rest of creation. An important contribution to the development had been John Locke's *Essay on Human Understanding*, whose explanation of the laws controlling human intelligence, which was claimed to be present in everyone, suggested men could indeed become the masters of their world. A recent historian, N. Hampson, asserts: 'Locke appeared to have disclosed the scientific laws of the human mind, which would allow men to reconstruct society on happier and more rational lines.' The relative peace of the period 1715–40 favoured the spread of Enlightenment ideas through educated European society. Among the favourable circumstances were the beginnings of the economic upturn and the end of the long recession, the surge in the oceanic trades, and the growing interest of governments in material improvement.

A generally optimistic belief in an essentially benevolent creation awaiting development is displayed in the English poet Pope's *Essay on Man*, published in 1733. If there appeared to be defects in nature, this was because man did not yet fully appreciate its workings. The message was supremely complacent:

> And spite of Pride, in erring Reason's spite,
> One truth is clear, whatever is, is right.

Natural law would ensure a favourable outcome for mankind, since:

> Two principles in human nature reign:
> Self-love, to urge, and Reason to restrain.

As 1750 approached it was clear that the centre of Enlightenment had moved to France; the *philosophes* had arrived. The single most influential

Enlightenment text, Montesquieu's *L'Esprit des lois*, was published in 1749. It made a new classification of governments into the despotic, where the power of the ruler was unrestrained, and the balanced polity, which could be a monarchy or a republic, which operated under a rule of law. To achieve this balance was needed. The power of the ruler should be mediated through corporate bodies, who would ensure a just balance between the power of the government and the rights and welfare of the subjects. The book was immensely influential: reprinted 22 times in its first two years, it spread in translations all over Europe. It was a model Enlightenment analysis of the workings of government, based on the study of existing regimes and subjecting them to rational analysis in order to discover the laws controlling them.

Then in 1750 came the first volume of the compendium of Enlightenment thinking, the *Encyclopédie*, a subscription project intended to provide a compehensive record of current knowledge, but also including interpretive essays on key general principles. Its publication was facilitated by the appointment of Malesherbes as official censor in France from 1750 to 1763, the period during which the work was being published. He was broadly supportive of the project, which conservative circles in France, both in the church and the *parlements*, would gladly have seen suppressed. The *Encyclopédie* is in many ways the core of the Enlightenment project, a reminder that the *philosophes* were not a political party, much less a revolutionary conspiracy. They were educators, and their publication was designed to spread information, on the assumption that all that stood in the way of the general improvement of the human condition was ignorance and superstition. There is no doubt of the rapid spread of Enlightenment values among the European elites. There were 3931 original subscribers to the *Encyclopédie*, drawn by necessity from the upper levels of society, since it was expensive. In time cheap editions appeared, and a quantity of tabloid-style summaries aimed at the lower levels of society, though these of necessity could only reach the literate. The impression is that a version of Enlightenment thinking did trickle down to the urban artisan level, but probably penetrated very little into rural society. In fact, action based on enlightened principles was more likely to be opposed than approved by the masses.

A basic principle of the Enlightenment was general religious toleration. This was rarely popular anywhere. When Voltaire involved himself in the Calas case, the last example of the execution of a Protestant in France, he was applauded by the elites, but not by the wider public. Generally toleration was unpopular. The worst protest disorders in Britain in this period were the Gordon riots in 1780, inspired by demagogic exploitation of popular anti-popery. There were earlier riots in Britain against the emancipation of Jews, and even against the adoption of the Gregorian calendar in 1752, which was also of course popish. The *philosophes* quickly had to face the fact that the lower orders were hostile to their projects. While enlightened ideas swept through educated society, the great popular mass movement in Britain was the evangelical revivalism of the Wesley brothers. Their highly emotional populist preaching, outdoor services, and stress on original sin and the need to repent and be reborn led to the Methodist movement, the very antithesis of Enlightenment values. The strength of the popular response underlines that the poor inhabited a different mental world from their social superiors.[2]

That was one powerful reason why the Enlightenment was never a democratic movement. Its leaders soon realized that the lower orders were uneducable, and hence were driven to a paternalist approach. The reformed society would have to be imposed from above. Voltaire wrote: 'It is expedient the people should be directed, not that it should be educated; it is not worthy of teaching', while D'Holbach concluded: 'atheism, like philosophy and every profound and abstract science, is ... by no means suited to the common people'. So the *philosophes*, far from desiring the overthrow of existing governments, looked to them to use their authority to implement the reforming programmes. Even so the Enlightenment agenda was inevitably one of liberalization for all ranks of society. All men, by virtue of being rational beings, were born with basic personal rights derived from natural law. Since all men had some ability to make personal choices, religious coercion was unacceptable and forms of faith were a matter of choice: hence the need for religious toleration. Beyond that, in a society governed by a universal natural law, all men should be treated equally under the laws which controlled their society. So the movement was opposed to irrational, that is unearned, privilege, and favoured taking away the privileges of established churches, of nobilities, particularly their feudal rights and jurisdictions, of urban corporations and guilds and of professional incorporations. In this way privileges would go, but basic rights to legitimate property under the law would be assured. Further, since the *philosophes* rejected the idea of authority based on revelation, they had to consider the basis of authority in society, and were driven, like Montesquieu, to supposing it must be based on some kind of contract between the rulers and the ruled. This not only underpinned their demand for a rule of law, which was held to embody the original contract, but suggested that in the process of legislation and government there should be some element of consultation between the rulers and at least their propertied and educated subjects, who were qualified to participate in rational discussion of public affairs. They also suggested that rationality required a review of existing laws, not only to make them non-discriminatory, but also to humanize them by eliminating cruel and unnecessary punishments and the use of torture, which was widespread in contemporary judicial systems. In the same spirit, fiscal systems should be rationalized and unjustified discrimination and exemptions eliminated.

It is necessary to stress that this was not an organized or a political movement. It was a tendency that took wide hold on the thinking of Europe's 'polite society'. What it did was to start a widening public debate. The most obvious concrete evidence of this was the increasing number and circulation of printed matter – books, pamphlets, journals and newpapers.

This was then multiplied in effect by the growth of education at all levels. N. Hampson suggests:

> Despite the enormous variations within European society, the gentlemen of Europe formed more of a social club in the eighteenth century than at any time before or since. Court society almost everywhere and the gentry in the more civilized areas, shared a common language and a common culture.

Rousseau certainly oversimplified when he claimed: 'there is no longer a France, a Germany, a Spain, not even England, there are only Europeans. All have the same tastes, same passions, same way of life.' But for a time it seemed to be true.

However, even as the *philosophes* were spreading their ideas, problems over their application began to be apparent. One shock that caught the imagination of all Europe was the Lisbon earthquake of 1755, which devastated the city and killed tens of thousands. How was this to be reconciled with the idea of a benevolent natural order? Opponents of the Enlightenment argued forcefully that it was a warning from God against the rising tide of scepticism and irreligion. Maupertuis pointed out how much in nature seemed positively hostile, and increasingly the original optimism, expressed in Pope, was diluted. Those who still rejected divine Providence were either driven, like the Scottish thinker David Hume, to accept that first causes were unknowable, or like D'Holbach in *Système de la Nature*, in 1770, to argue that there is no purpose in Nature:

> The whole cannot have an object, for there is nothing outside itself towards which it can tend ... Men have completely failed to see that Nature, lacking both good and evil intentions, merely acts in accordance with necessary and immutable laws.

The original project of man creating a brave new world had to be modified.[3] It was now reluctantly conceded that universal happiness was probably not attainable. Voltaire announced his conversion from his earlier optimism about progress through rationality in 1759, when he published *Candide*. This enormously popular, picaresque novel, which went through eight editions in its first year, was a sustained satire on the naive optimism of the first wave of Enlightenment thinking. Just a year before, Helvétius had published *De l'esprit*, in which, while accepting that utilitarianism was now the only basis on which rational judgements could be formed, he also perceived that, in the end, an ethics based on this kind of purely material calculation was not likely to promote individual freedom: it would tend to constrain the individual to conform to society and the result would be that the individual would be 'forced to be virtuous'.

It was these problems that concerned the last of the major Enlightenment thinkers, Jean-Jacques Rousseau. He did not deny the role of rationality, but asserted that to give it the exclusive right to determine behaviour was to ignore an equally vital part of being human – the role of feelings, manifested as the promptings of the heart, as sentiment. As early as 1749 he had insisted that human beings were not just animated calculators; each was a unique individual. 'I feel my own heart and I know men. I am differently made from any of those that I have seen.' He developed his ideas in the best-selling *La Nouvelle Héloïse* and *Emile*, published in 1761 and 1762, in which he argued for the cultivation of sensibility and spiritual awareness of the individual through education, since it must be sensibility, not calculation, that determined behaviour. He wrote: 'Oh man! Look not further for the author of evil. That author is yourself. There is no evil apart from that which you inflict or endure, and both come from yourself.'

The only legitimate basis for a just society was the mutual consent of its members and that could not be transferred or delegated. But when faced with the necessity of explaining how a working society could operate on the basis of the free consent of each individual, he was driven to the concept of a 'general will' that would emerge from all the citizens merging their individual wills in a common sovereignty. For this to be possible education would be needed to develop 'sentiments of sociability, without which it is impossible to be either a good citizen or a loyal subject'. And if this educational process did not condition the individual, 'in order that the social pact shall not be an empty formula … whoever refuses to obey the general will shall be constrained to do so by the whole body'. It is in consequence possible to see Rousseau as arguing for unrestricted, direct popular sovereignty based on individual freedom of choice, or to see his ideas as a blueprint for a totalitarian society.[4]

One result of the general debate that Enlightenment thought stimulated was the science of economics. The physiocrats – writers like Quesnay, Dupont de Nemours and Mercier de la Rivière – argued that the laws of nature had provided the way to material welfare through enhanced production. Based on the observation that nature has provided that growing crops can produce surpluses, if men were free to follow nature's laws, wealth would inevitably accumulate. This required the recognition that ultimately agriculture was the source of wealth, and the physiocrats argued for allowing market forces free play. They advocated abolishing controls and creating a free trade in food grains, which ran counter to centuries of European tradition. Adam Smith, in his *Wealth of Nations* had a more sophisticated analysis, but it was based on the same fundamental concept, that there was a law of nature which ensured that if economic enterprise were free of counter-productive controls and restrictions, then the whole society would benefit from the increase in wealth it would produce. Smith asserted there was a providential law that: 'Every individual asserts himself to find out the most advantageous employment for whatever his capital can command. The study of his own advantage necessarily leads him to prefer what is most advantageous to the society.'

Whatever the merits of the ideas advanced in this field, its importance is the way it reflected a turn round in the general mentality of the European elites. N. Hampson has remarked that: 'the Enlightenment was an attitude of mind rather than a course in science and philosophy' and that its consequence was that 'most people – for the first time perhaps in modern history, preferred their own age to any that was gone before'. The underlying belief in the possibility of progress that has driven European civilization since this period had taken root. But it was an evolutionary mentality; there was an absence, except on the radical fringes, of any expectation of transcending the existing social systems. The assumption was that 'the future would be a rectified version of the present'. And while there was difference of opinion about specific programmes of action, which had to be adapted to local contexts, there was a broad consensus that because all men had been created as rational beings, they had natural rights which should not be denied by arbitrary authority or outdated privilege and tradition. Very few contemporaries appreciated how measures based on such principles must, in the end, subvert the very foundations of a culture built for centuries on hierarchies of power and privilege.

17

Enlightened Despotism: The Enlightenment in Action

By 1763 almost all the European rulers were engaged in programmes of domestic reform or took up such programmes as part of their post-war reconstruction. Many of these were openly defended in terms of Enlightenment thinking. Since most of these powers had some kind of absolute monarchy, the concept of enlightened despotism was invented by historians, though it was present in contemporary thought. In 1767 Le Mercier de la Rivière, in *L'ordre naturel et essential des sociétés politiques*, argued that the most effective form of government was a 'patrimonial and legal despotism', and that was a view generally acceptable to the *philosophes* themselves, notably Voltaire and Diderot, who readily corresponded with rulers like Frederick II and Catherine II in the clear expectation that they could be effective instruments for implementing Enlightenment ideas. It is also a tacit recognition that there was no popular support for most of their ideas from the lower levels of society. If there was to be reform it would have to be imposed by authority on a resistant society through its ruling elites. However, if the Enlightenment had been only a body of moral precepts, it could be expected to have had minimal impact on actual political action. Rulers and ministers did express their acceptance of Enlightenment ideas but applied them in part for purely pragmatic reasons, at the root of which was the eternal imperative to maximize the war-making potential of their subjects. Above all they sought new sources of revenue and more efficient systems of administration, and all knew how existing personal, corporate and ecclesiastical structures stood in the way of modernizing their societies. If the proposals put forward by the *philosophes* had not promised to promote these practical ends, then the interest in them of rulers and statesmen would have remained academic.

It is because of this that some historians have sought to deny that enlightened despotism was ever more than, at best, a cynical public relations exercise for the rulers.[1] They note the limitations of the results achieved and the frequent retreats in face of opposition. This was most obvious in the eventual failure to abolish serfdom, or the very cautious approach to the basic concept of religious toleration. Above all they have noted how, when rulers approached the issue of power-sharing with an institution or assembly representing the elites, they tended to back away. The best-known example is that of the Archduke Leopold in Tuscany, who got as far as drafting a constitution for the duchy, which it was then decided not to implement. The idea of enlightened despotism is now used in a more realistic approach, which recognizes that policies should be appraised in terms of the specific contexts within which they operated. These set limits which rulers could not safely ignore, as Joseph II demonstrated during his personal reign in Austria after 1780. It is also being pointed out that the will might be present, but the means were lacking. At the heart of the whole Enlightenment project was the need for education: here a principal obstacle to change were the established churches and their clergy. Yet there was no conceivable source of teachers for any kind of extended educational facilities outside the ranks of the clergy. It was a major bottleneck for any enlightened reformer.

Enlightenment projects did not have to start from scratch in Europe. Rulers had always acknowledged a Christian duty to promote the welfare of their subjects from their basic function of dispensing justice. The German natural law theorists of the late seventeenth century, Pufendorf, Thomasius and Wolff, had developed the concept of a natural contract between rulers and subjects, based on their duty to advance the subjects' material as well as spiritual welfare. This line of thought had been taken up in Protestant universities and had produced the cameralist civil servants who were active in royal courts over much of the Empire, creating the *Polizeistaat*,[2] which was a working institution long before the *philosophes* began to attract widespread attention. The cameralists would have found nothing novel in the view expressed by Archduke Leopold in his *Testament* that 'a ruler, even a hereditary ruler is only a delegate, a servant of the people, whose cares and troubles he must make his own'. While the historian needs to be careful in evaluating the work of the enlightened despots, it is undeniable that there was a wave of reforming projects, linked to the Enlightenment concept of increasing human welfare by the application of rational policies, from the 1750s until the outbreak of the French Revolution.

Reform in the Iberian kingdoms

It can be argued that the Iberian kingdoms were a special case, since the influence of Enlightenment culture stopped at the Pyrenees. There were individuals, some in power as ministers or consultants to government, who expressed commitment to Enlightenment ideas, and in Spain Economic Societies promoted the study of foreign thought and were often active in promoting new developments in education and economic activity. But there was also the most rooted opposition to new ideas, based on religion. The Erastianism and anti-clericalism that became so widespread elsewhere had a lesser impact in Iberia. The emancipation of the New Christians, descendants of Jewish converts, was unacceptable in societies that made a cult of 'purity of blood' – the need to prove that there had never been any taint of Jewish blood in a family over the generations, which could legally disqualify people from holding public positions. The Portuguese reformer, Antonio Sanchez, noted after the passing of laws abolishing discrimination: 'can this law extinguish from the minds of people ideas and thoughts they have acquired from their earliest years?' The short answer, of course, is no. Further, in both Spain and Portugal, the Inquisition still controlled thought and prohibited the publications of the Enlightenment; when they were admitted to Portugal, it was in censored versions which excised all matter considered offensive to the Catholic faith. The truly popular movement in Spain, which united the king and the common people, was the campaign to get papal recognition of the cult of the Immaculate Conception of the Virgin, who was regarded as the special protector of the kingdom.

The artificiality of introducing alien concepts of progress into mentally closed societies like these was first exemplified in the career of Sebastian de Carvalho e Melo, son of a modest service gentry family, known to historians by his later title, marquis of Pombal. After a diplomatic career, he was recalled in 1750 to become a minister to the new king, Joseph I, and came to win the entire confidence of a monarch whose main interests were hunting and opera. He rose to full power in the aftermath of the Lisbon earthquake of 1755, when he personally directed the relief measures and then rebuilt the city. The new Lisbon was a model of eighteenth-century town planning, entirely controlled by the state. Portugal had been comfortable in the first half of the century, the era of the Brazilian gold boom, which made the monarchy financially independent, though most of the proceeds had been invested in prestige building projects like the huge monastery–palace of Mafra. The real economy, the wine export trade and the colonial trades, was controlled by foreign investors, with the native businessmen employed as their commission agents.

In the 1750s Pombal concentrated on trying to claw back economic control from the foreigners. His main instrument was the use of state-supported monopoly companies, which should be powerful enough to defeat the alien competition. These were established for the Douro port wine trade and for the main colonial trades. Native investment was encouraged and ennoblements were freely dispensed to successful entrepreneurs, to the disdain of the established nobility. It so happened that at the end of the process these companies were dominated by Pombal's extended family and clientele.

Pombal's status as an enlightened ruler is tainted by his spectacular brutality against opponents. When a conspiracy of conservative aristocrats attempted to stop him by assassinating the king in 1758, a show trial was held after which conspirators of the highest social rank were publicly broken on the wheel and burned alive, an affront to social rules that shocked polite European society. Pombal went on to implicate the Jesuits in the conspiracy. Their missionary settlements in Brazil, and generally conservative influence, were identified by Pombal as an obstacle to his plans, and on the basis of their alleged plotting, the Order was suppressed in Portugal, its members brutally persecuted, and its properties seized. Following that, Pombal confronted Rome over clerical appointments and successfully asserted the state's control of the church. Pombal's economic policies were mostly traditional mercantilist measures, but an entrepreneurial business community, with the Pombal clique at its heart, did develop, and by the 1770s a significant revival of domestic manufacture by state monopoly companies with heavy protectionist cover had developed, driven by the quest for economic self-sufficiency. Programmes were instituted to extend educational facilities and remodel the conservative, clericalist university of Coimbra to make it suited for the production of enlightened administrators and clergy.

It is difficult to evaluate Pombal's achievement, in part because it was so intensely personal and depended on the support of a king who had little claim to be enlightened, but whose unwavering support kept Pombal in power. The real difficulty is seeing through the public facade of reforming legislation, which eventually covered most aspects of Portuguese life. Pombal's career confirmed that reform would have to be enforced from above on a resistant and conservative society, and thereby exposed this fundamental weakness of the Enlightenment project. When Joseph I died in 1777, Pombal was immediately disgraced and was lucky to escape a show trial and execution. Although he had achieved a permanent strengthening of the Portuguese economy, the eagerness with which much of his work was reversed by successor regimes after his fall from power indicates the superficiality of his modernizing project. Certainly his ultimate aim – to revive Portugal as a significant and independent imperial power in the European system, which was not wholly fantasy, given the great potential wealth of Brazil – was nowhere near being realized.

The history of enlightened reform in the Spanish kingdom shows many interesting parallels with Pombal's endeavours, but also significant differences. First, Charles III, who succeeded in 1759, was a capable and concerned ruler. It is arguable whether Charles qualifies as 'enlightened', for he was not intellectual and did not read or write theoretical works. He was conventionally pious and, like most sovereigns of the time, addicted to field sports, which occupied half of most working days. But he was sane, healthy, a good family man, sociable and communicative. He was experienced in administration, for he had had a spell as king of Naples–Sicily before transferring to Spain. There he had worked with reforming ministers, some of whom he brought with him as advisers. And he had an agenda to pursue – the revival of Spain's former status as a leading imperial power, which was the basis of his ingrained anglophobia, for he saw British imperial ambitions as the most important threat to be overcome.

Spain was not entirely closed to Enlightenment influences. The Inquisition certainly hindered circulation of foreign writings although Montesquieu's ideas were known, but the *Encyclopédie* was forbidden and in general it was some members of the urban elites and reformist bureaucrats who were acquainted with foreign thinking. On the other hand, Spain did have a tradition of fairly open discussion of public policies going back to the *arbitristas* and the development of the local Economic Societies after 1765. The spread of a critical public press after 1761 meant that informed discussion was developing in elite circles, which the government did not attempt to prevent. The obstacle to reform was the conservative grip of corporate interest groups. The church was a major power in the land: apart from still having, in the Inquisition, the means to suppress deviant religious thinking, it was a major landowner. In Castile it held, in mortmain, 15 per cent of the cultivated land; over the whole kingdom it can be calculated that the church enjoyed 20 per cent of the national product. Although the crown now had full control of episcopal appointments, the clergy asserted their traditional exemption from ordinary taxation, though in reality they had always had to submit to making 'donations' out of their revenues. Then the nobility were entrenched in their ownership of seigneurial rights over some 68 per cent of the cultivated lands, and were the controlling elite in many urban corporations, where the policy of sale of offices had opened the way for this development. Since, in early modern societies, for ordinary people most government was local government, it is easy to see how, although in law the Spanish monarchy had highly centralized authority over the kingdom, in practice government had to be negotiated with the real powerholders. This can be illustrated from one of the reform attempts by Campomanes in 1766. He introduced a new level of urban government by adding elected officers, the *alcaldes*, with a broad remit, hoping this would enlist the lesser townsfolk in breaking down the grip of the venal oligarchs. It failed: the established elites had little difficulty integrating the new elected officers into the oligarchy so as to retain control. It had been unrealistic in the early modern social world to expect anything different.

Charles III had a rough experience shortly after his accession, when he entered the new Bourbon family compact of 1761 and found that his armies performed indifferently in the resulting frontier warfare with Portugal, and that the British swiftly seized Havana and Manila. Years of intermittent investment in the navy had produced disappointing results. This naturally only hardened his determination, after 1763, to rebuild his power by reforms at home and in the empire, in order to prepare for a replay in more favourable circumstances. He had brought with him a group of Italian advisers, with the marquis of Squilace as finance minister, and the marquis of Grimaldi as secretary of state. They were reinforced over time by native appointments, usually university-trained lawyers from modest noble families, like Campomanes – taken on to the Council of Castile in 1762 and later the most important of them – Jose Moñino, count of Floridablanca, who replaced Grimaldi as secretary in 1776 and then held the office until 1792. Since Charles III increasingly withdrew from active leadership after 1777, Floridablanca became effective first minister for the rest of the reign, working through a highly professional council of leading ministers, the *Junta de Estados*. These men shared a broad reformist programme with many Enlightenment features.[3] They formed a professional, salaried bureaucracy drawn from the middling ranks of the nobility. The real top-level aristocracy, the grandees, were systematically excluded, though being entrenched in their entailed estates and extensive feudal jurisdictions they remained a power to be reckoned with.

There was an interesting reminder of this in 1766, when the reformers introduced one of their key reforms, a free market in grain. This broke with centuries of tradition, led to a rise in food prices, and then to urban riots, the most serious of which, in Madrid, forced the king to flee from the capital, which was controlled by the protestors for nearly a week. Royal authority was quickly reasserted and not openly challenged again, but the king and his ministers, in an echo of events in Portugal in 1758, chose to accuse some of the grandees and the Jesuits of involvement, and in 1767 the Order was expelled from the monarchy and its properties seized. This opened the way to major reforms of the universities, breaking up the privileged *colegias majores*, former Jesuit strongholds, whose graduates had established a grip over appointments to the higher levels of the administration. The whole educational curriculum was to be modernized and geared to the training of servants of the state.

Indeed, after the disturbances of 1766–7, the way was open for the bureaucrats to press their reforming plans in many areas of government. Yet the record of solid achievement remained modest and some major projects failed altogether in face of resistance. The regime tried to promote a rationalized single tax, payable by all. It was Floridablanca himself who described how this project failed:

> I have done all I can to implement the plan for a single tax, prepared in the previous reign and continued in this, and after immense expenditure, juntas of experts, scrutiny of the tax rules, all printed and circulated, there have been so many thousands of appeals and objections that they have frightened off and intimidated the office of the single tax, and it has been impossible to proceed further.

That was an extreme example where years of effort by the reformers ended in total failure. But most of their projects faltered in the face of the vested interests opposed to them. For example, the feudal jurisdictions were seen as a barrier to progress. The crown did stop further sales of jurisdictions and attempted to claw back those that were open to legal challenge. This effort to roll back feudalism failed, as it lacked radical will. Floridablanca's instructions made this clear:

> It is not my intention to harm the lords of vassals or destroy their privileges, it is the duty of courts and fiscals to examine carefully

what they hold, and to seek to incorporate in the crown all alienated jurisdictions, in accordance with existing privilege and laws.

This was a realistic approach – the government needed the acceptance of the feudalists in order to operate – but it was also an approach that ensured failure. Campomanes was, in principle, of the opinion that 'all privilege is odious'. But he could not act on it. He also wrote: 'politics are not derived from general principles ... it is the consideration of actual circumstances which forms political judgement'.

The reformers wanted to do something to curb the Inquisition, an institution somewhat decayed but still dangerous to attack. In 1768 they cut back its control of censorship, it fought back and in 1776 a reform-minded intendant of Seville was arrested and successfully prosecuted for heresy, while in 1778 it launched an investigation into Campomanes himself and the king had to intervene to rescue him. Once more pragmatism prevailed; Enlightenment thought left no place for an institution like the Inquisition, but Floridablanca wrote: 'It is important to favour and protect this Tribunal, but care must be taken that it does not usurp the regalian rights of the crown, and that on pretext of religion, it does not disturb public order.' The Inquisition, like feudal jurisdiction, was too powerful to confront head on, even by this absolutist regime.[4]

The reconstruction of Spain's imperial power was one of the main concerns of government policy, but it too could not be carried through. The poor performance of the army in 1762 led Charles III to hire a foreign mercenary general to reorganize it on the Prussian model. Changes did occur: a modern regimental structure was put in place; the domestic armaments manufacture was developed. The officers, recruited from the lower nobility, were offered a career structure, though the salary levels were low. Their *esprit de corps* was boosted by the introduction of the *fuero militar*, a distinctive feature of Hispanic military establishments ever since. All soldiers were exempt from civil jurisdiction and from some categories of taxation, and were exclusively under military jurisdiction. But the modernization stopped at the supply arrangements. These were left to the civilian intendancy and the soldiers were still expected to buy their own food in the open market and hire their transport services from the local communities. Further, all attempts to introduce conscription had to be modified in face of local resistance, based on widespread claims of exemptions, leaving only the poorest peasants at risk. The army had to recruit whole regiments of foreigners, and even then the fairly modest target strength of 80,000 men in the regular establishment was rarely achieved. Some authorities suggest that the actual effective peacetime strength was nearer 30,000, a feeble figure for a state of Spain's size. Expenditure on the navy was kept quite high but, although a respectable battle fleet was constructed, it was chronically short of experienced seamen and professionally trained officers.

The sustained attempt to strengthen imperial control over the colonies and win back a higher share of colonial trade for the domestic economy had more success. In fact the American colonies had enjoyed a long period of substantial self-government since the seventeenth century. Quite apart from the basic reality that colonial government, like domestic government, had to be negotiated between the crown and the local elites or, as a recent historian, J. Lynch, put it, 'the metropolis looked for collaborating elites, the colonies for conniving officials'. Venality of office was normal, so that by 1750 most of the key administrative posts, and the judiciary, were in local hands. The new imperial policies were launched in the 1750s when the sale of offices was stopped. From then on metropolitan Spaniards were increasingly appointed to posts in the administration and the church; only 23 per cent of such appointments after 1750 went to locals. Then, after 1763, a colonial intendancy was established and officials sent out from Spain with broad visitatorial powers. Colonial exploitation of the Indian populations was controlled and the local defence forces reorganized and financed out of local revenues, though this did mean an expansion of colonials in the officer corps. An enthusiastic reformer, José de Galvez, was appointed to head the Council of the Indies in 1776 and the pace of reform stepped up. The biggest change was the gradual winding down of the monopoly trade through Cadiz between 1765 and 1789, after which all Spanish ports could trade freely to the Americas. Barcelona made the most use of this, and its trade was in Catalan produce, so that gradually the share of Spanish manufactures and produce in the American trade began to increase. After the 1780s, Spanish America was booming and emigration from Spain increased, as did government revenues and the volume of trade. New provinces were established in Buenos Aires, Chile and Venezuela. For the time being, the underlying reality that the Spanish government was imposing its direct control more effectively, and drawing off substantially increased revenues from trade, mining and local taxation, was accepted by the colonists, against the background of rising prosperity.

The absolutist regime in the Spain of Charles III had some substantial improvements to its credit. Yet most historical commentary tends to stress the limitations of the achievement. One recent summary by C.C. Noel concluded: 'in 1788 the flourishing condition in which the Monarchy seemed to be was partly illusory'. The basic reason is that any superficial comparison between developments in Spain and the contemporary developments in France and Great Britain leaves Spain looking backward. Charles III's project of restoring Spain to its former status as a major imperial power had clearly failed. The whole Enlightenment project in Spain was being forced from above on a society rooted in traditional conservative values. Feudalism, 'superstitious' religion, provincialism and suspicion of all outside influences were still entrenched in 1788. The intended beneficiaries were alienated from the programmes of the government. They tolerated the regime because in practice it was careful not to infringe the basic rights of the traditional elites, and because in the early modern world royal authority was not lightly challenged anywhere. But the subsequent course of Spanish history has repeatedly demonstrated how powerful the traditional values and institutions have been. Even the French Revolution came to grief when it tried to carry its ideas across the Pyrenees.

Enlightenment reforms in Italy

The Italian principalities offer significant evidence of the practical application of Enlightenment ideas and their potential for promoting lasting changes in society. On the one hand, eighteenth-century Italy did produce its own school of Enlightenment thinkers, who were admired well beyond the borders of Italy. They were preceded by the writings of the pre-Enlightenment historian and theorist, Giambattisto Vico of Naples, who made a deep impression with his emphasis on the continuities of historical development and their importance in understanding social structures.[5] Ironically, it was because the Enlightenment reformers in Italy tended to disregard Vico's ideas that they nearly all failed to produce lasting change. But Italy was not, like Iberia, outside mainstream thinking, and at least two of the Italian thinkers had a major input into the wider European movement. Ludovico Muratori, a pioneer advocate of rational reform in the Catholic Church, published a seminal work in 1747, *On the manner of a well-ordered Devotion*. He advocated the removing of baroque excesses from ritual, raising the standards of the parish clergy and redistributing wealth away from the monastic sector in the church, which fitted well with the Jansenism and anti-clericalism of Enlightenment thought, though Muratori himself was unswervingly committed to the Catholic faith. Cesare Beccaria wrote one of the most influential Enlightenment texts: his *Crime and Punishment* of 1764, which became the legal reformers' handbook for rationalizing and humanizing criminal justice.[6]

On the other hand, much of the most successful reform projects in Italy had nothing to do with the Enlightenment at all. The reforms of Victor Amadeus in Savoy-Piedmont have been outlined earlier, but they included centralization of government, rationalization of taxation based on accurate land surveys and valuation, a consistent attack on feudal jurisdictions in his law code and a successful application of a modern university curriculum for the training of public servants in his educational reform. Victor Amadeus must rank as the most effective modernizing ruler in eighteenth-century Italy, but both chronologically and by temperament he was in no sense part of the Enlightenment. In the duchy of Milan, the early Habsburg administration had also implemented a similar survey-based tax reform and abolished the sale of offices before 1750. By contrast, in the kingdom of Naples–Sicily, from the installation of the Bourbon rulers in 1734 into the late 1790s, there was a succession of enlightened, intellectually aware ministers. Bernardo Tanucci is the best known of the Neapolitan administrators who strove intermittently for nearly 20 years to promote reform against the determined resistance of the dominant feudal landlords, the church and the urban corporations. His efforts to use the confiscated properties of the Jesuits after 1767 to establish settlements of small peasant proprietors and his persistent efforts to rationalize the judicial structures of the kingdom came to nothing. In the 1780s another group of even more convinced reformers, led by Filangieri and Palmieri, tried to centralize and rationalize the tax system. It has been noted by a recent study that: 'Naples, in the second half of the century had a more stimulating intellectual life than any other Italian state and produced a greater volume of challenging political speculation.' Yet it remained by any measure the most backward region of the peninsula. The fact that, from 1767, King Ferdinand IV was, like most Bourbons, politically inept and gave no consistent support to the reformers did not help, but probably was of little consequence. No amount of well-meaning reform projects or enlightened publication could make headway against the entrenched power of the landlords, clergy and lawyers determined to block it.

The potential of enlightened absolutism to produce lasting modernizations was tested almost to destruction by the two Habsburg brothers, sincerely devoted to Enlightenment ideals, Joseph II in Milan and Leopold I in Tuscany. The reforms begun in Milan before 1750 were carried forward. A Supreme Economic Council, under Gianrinaldo Carli, pressed on with tax reform and the opening up of trade and manufacture from guild restrictions. These changes were pressed with due caution, as were measures for restricting the accumulation of ecclesiastical property through mortmain, or loosening the clerical grip on censorship. When Joseph II came to power after 1780 he found such pragmatic gains unsatisfactory. In 1781 he set up an Ecclesiastical Commission and set about abolishing the tax exemptions of the church, closing monasteries and establishing a Jansenist seminary in the university of Pavia to train the parish clergy for the whole duchy. In 1786 Joseph abolished most of the existing governmental structure, establishing a new central government divided into ministries, a full system of intendants to control local administration, and a central judiciary, that swept away the whole pre-existing system. The result was local outrage, and by his death in 1790 the whole duchy was on the verge of open, conservative revolt.

His brother Leopold, on the other hand – perhaps the most truly dedicated of all the enlightened despots – sought to avoid this kind of confrontation and carry his subjects along with his changes. From 1767 Leopold liberated the trade in grain, began reducing the power of guilds, ended tax-farming and began the reform of administrative structures and the judiciary. In 1786 his new criminal code abolished capital punishment and torture. A Jansenist programme of church reform confined church courts to purely religious issues, suppressed some monasteries and abolished the Inquisition. But when a general church synod revealed the strength of both clerical and popular resistance to further reforms, he drew back. Leopold's most significant, almost unique, move was to draft a constitution for Tuscany in 1782, which would have made it a power-sharing monarchy with an elected assembly to safeguard the rights of the subject. The sequel is instructive: almost all Leopold's advisers opposed the constitution, while Joseph in effect vetoed the project since it would get in the way of his plans for the closer integration of the Habsburg lands. So it remained a paper project. But even more significant was the effect when Leopold became Emperor in 1790 and handed over the government of Tuscany to regents. A wave of popular protest and rioting swept the duchy, demanding a reversal of many of the church reforms, an end to the free market in grain and the return of price controls. The force of traditionalist feeling was such that the new regime felt obliged to give in. Leopold had explained his constitution as intended to return to the subjects their 'full natural liberty'. The subjects showed in unmistakable terms that they did not want it.[7] The society the reformers were trying to improve showed no appreciation of this at all.

Cameralism, *Aufklärung* and Enlightenment in the Empire

It can be argued that Germany produced its own version of Enlightenment, which shared with the French one the desire to improve the human condition by rational reform, but differed in its basic acceptance of traditional social structures, such as feudal landlordism and established churches, lacking in particular the distinctive secularist, anti-clerical critique of the *philosophes*. It can be seen as much more of an evolutionary development than a call for new beginnings. Cameralism was a late seventeenth-century development, derived from the ideas of Pufendorf, Leibniz and Christian Wolff, and reinforced by the input from Lutheran Pietism. Its strength lay in the Protestant German universities whose graduates were trained in a curriculum dominated by law and designed for the education of public servants.

The Empire was mostly a mosaic of small principalities, all of them feudal and hierarchic in structure. Cameralism had offered their rulers in the first place a blueprint for rationalizing their governments and increasing their revenues and had early recognized the relation between prosperous subjects and taxable capacity. So as rulers increasingly recruited and relied on the cameralist civil servants, the classic *Polizeistaat* had developed, in which the absolute ruler accepted ever wider responsibilities for promoting the welfare of the subject. The rulers were by training warrior aristocrats, and often strove to maintain top-heavy military establishments: some, like the Hessian princes, could make a living by hiring out their armies to the great powers. Princes also took commands in the armies of the major powers; but this left them even more reliant on the skills of their cameralist administrators to ensure their patrimonial territories were competently governed. It is noteworthy that although many of these principalities were ecclesiastical, ruled by prince–bishops or abbots, this made little difference.

The ecclesiastical rulers were drawn mainly from princely families and were not career clergymen. Further, being technically celibate, they had no personal dynastic ambitions to pursue. Nor did they have any reason to maintain large military establishments and the taxes to support them, so that the same cameralist policies were pursued as in the secular principalities, even extending to practising religious toleration, like the archbishop of Trier in 1783, for the cameralists had long understood how the offer of toleration to minority confessions could pull in good-quality immigrants who would promote economic growth.

Hereditary succession could throw up occasional irresponsible rulers, like Charles Theodore of Bavaria, who reversed earlier reform programmes to maintain a luxurious court of 2000 retainers which consumed a fifth of the public revenues, or Charles Eugene of Württemberg, with delusions of grandeur, who really did say on one occasion 'I am the state.' Even with poor-quality rulers, the cameralist administrations could usually protect the basic stability of their principalities. A classic case of this was Hanover after its Electors became kings of Britain. The administration there had a deserved reputation for efficient and progressive government.

The German principalities offer a variety of working examples of pure enlightened despotism in action. The principle of absolute monarchy was never questioned, even in those principalities which still had functioning meetings of the Estates. These would stubbornly seek to defend their sectional privileges and immunities, but showed no inclination to claim any kind of power-sharing with the princely executives. These were being enlightened well before the Enlightenment had been launched. The German *Polizeistaat* developed professionalism in administration: public servants were trained, paid by regular salary not fees and gratuities, and sought to pursue policies based on information and analysis. There was a spreading enthusiasm for collecting statistics, making land surveys and mapping their territories as the basis for investing public effort and funding into improved economies and services. Immigration was subsidized, new trades promoted: almost every principality at some time aspired to start a silk manufacture, beginning with the cultivation of mulberry trees for the silk worms. On the whole they stayed with established mercantilist practice. There were moves to open up some trades, weaken guild restrictions, break up monopolies. The governments approved private enterprise in principle, while recognizing that the small scale of private capital accumulation necessitated public investment. Almost everywhere they preserved the traditional control of markets in basic foodstuffs and regulation of wage rates and accepted responsibility for providing relief in periods of subsistence crisis. Paternalism extended to promoting basic health and hygiene regulations, even to compulsory fire insurance schemes.

When the Enlightenment did get under way, it certainly influenced the German rulers and their officials, but they could build upon a whole range of practices that had anticipated many of the Enlightenment programmes.

The most obvious extensions of state policy were found in law reform and education. The German principalities readily adopted the policy of clarification and codification of the laws, and measures to simplify and speed up legal process. In the second half of the century they were also adopting at least parts of Beccaria's programme for humanizing the law by eliminating torture and reducing capital punishments. The other area where major initiatives were implemented was in the whole field of education. The modernization of university curricula was extended, and serious attention given to organizing mass education. In Hohenlohe-Öhringen the prince declared: 'The foundation of a state comes not from masses of crude, uncivilized and ignorant men. Only a civilized, well-led and well-disposed people can give strength, wealth, power and happiness to a country.'

These principalities were small and compact enough to experiment with schemes for general primary education. They moved towards secularizing the schools by paying adequate salaries to teachers, while requiring proper professional qualifications; they standardized curricula, introduced examination and testing, and sought to enforce compulsory attendance. In the informal sector governments subsidized educational journals, encouraged the foundation of academies, learned societies and reading rooms, and funded prize essay competitions on social improvement.

The German *Aufklärung* ran parallel with the wider Enlightenment after 1750, but retained its own local characteristics. Because it developed naturally out of the established practices of the German principalities, it had a distinctively more conservative character. The German reformers also met the kind of traditionalist protest that occurred elsewhere. Popular prejudice objected to religious toleration, the ending of witch-hunting, changing farming practices, cultivating potatoes, setting up lightning conductors. But the German authorities were careful to avoid confrontations on major issues by leaving price and market regulation in place, and perhaps above all by avoiding anti-clericalist confrontation with the established churches and their clergy. These principalities were probably also structurally suited to reform experiments. They were compact enough to be controlled by contemporary administrative techniques and their rulers were on occasion carried away by obsessive pride and status-seeking to misuse the proceeds of public revenue, but as they were too small to be principal actors in the power game, the rulers and their ministers could reasonably focus their attention on domestic problems. In these conditions, rationalization could produce modest improvements at an acceptable cost. After 1794, the French were disconcerted to discover that the Germans mostly had no wish to be liberated from regimes with which they were comfortable.

18

The Big Three and Scandinavia

Frederick the Great and Prussia

If enlightened despotism existed then Frederick II was its most significant and successful practitioner. Contemporaries certainly thought so. Goethe wrote from Strasbourg: 'we looked towards the North, and from there shone Frederick, the Pole Star around whom Germany, Europe, even the world seemed to turn'. Frederick's credentials look impeccable. He wrote to Christian Wolff, just before his accession: 'Philosophers should be the teachers of the world and the teachers of princes. They must think logically and we must act logically.' He could not have summarized the Enlightenment project more concisely. His friendship with Voltaire is famous, his correspondents included most of the leading *philosophes*, and he himself wrote intellectual treatises, like the *Anti-Machiavel* in 1739 or the *Essai sur les formes de gouvernement et sur les devoirs des souverains* in 1777. And he was completely consistent in support of the Enlightenment tenet that the obstacle to progress was superstition and ignorance. He laid down at the beginning of the reign that there was to be complete religious toleration: 'All religions must be tolerated, and the sole concern of officials is to ensure that one denomination does not interfere with another.' From his private correspondence it is clear he thought all confessional religious dogma was superstitious nonsense, though some kind of religious belief was probably necessary for keeping the lower orders in obedience. He was consistent in promoting law reform, first putting all his weight behind the reformer Samuel Cocceji, who by his death in 1755 had created a new central judiciary for the kingdom, centralized in a ministry of justice in Berlin, and staffed by salaried judges, who had to pass professional examinations to qualify for appointment. The king insisted the law must treat all equally. He declared: 'whether it is a prince accusing a peasant, or the other way round, the prince is equal to the peasant before the law'. One of his first official acts was to abolish judicial torture, the use of capital punishment was reduced to a low level, and among his last major projects was the initiation of the full codification of Prussian law.[1]

Once he settled down to peaceful development after 1763, he followed a working routine, by which he began around 5 a.m. and worked through to

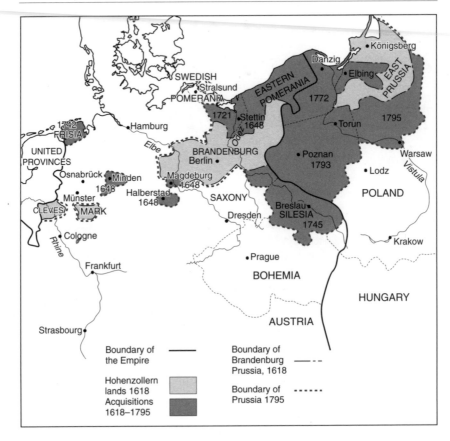

Map 18.1 Brandenburg–Prussia 1618–1795

5 p.m. He was of course not making all the policy, which would have been impossible, but the policy which was prepared by his officials, and brought to his working cabinet in Potsdam, was decided by the brief memoranda in the king's hand. This he did out of duty. In his *Political Testament* of 1752, Frederick defined his conception of the role of the ruler:

> Here we have, in general, the duties which a prince should carry out ... he should often recall to mind that he is a man, just like the least of his subjects; if he is the first judge, the first general, the first minister of society, it is not so that he can indulge himself, but so that he can fulfil the duties involved. He is only the first servant of the state.

He believed government rested on contract, irrevocable certainly, which bound the ruler to protect the interests of his subjects, and always to pursue the general welfare of his society above any interests of his own. There has been no lack of critics to assert that his actions fell far short of the ideals he professed.[2] It can appear that he was basically profoundly conservative, and his aim was less to reform society than to preserve its hierarchical structure. It was Frederick, not his father, who made it public policy to build his state around the feudal landowners, the Junkers. His *Testament* says: 'An object of policy of this state is to preserve its noble class.' At the opening of the reign he reversed his father's campaign to claw back crown lands that had passed into Junker possession: 'the officials shall be forbidden, on pain of death, to harass the nobility and to resurrect old claims against them'. He repeatedly asserted that the nobles were 'the finest jewel in his crown and the lustre of the army'. He tried to stop impoverished nobles selling their lands to commoners and encouraged them to protect their properties with entails. After 1763, when war damage threatened many noble families, he established special credit facilities for rebuilding the estates. The Junkers had prior claim on all army commissions and the higher civil service appointments. Frederick was willing to suspend policies of appointment on merit to public service to safeguard such positions. In the army 90 per cent of the officer corps was noble, and commoners commissioned during the war were quickly squeezed out in the demobilization after 1763.

These were most distinctly anti-Enlightenment policies. He is also criticized for his policy on serfdom, which in principle, like all Enlightenment thinkers, he condemned in the strongest terms as a stain on human society. It is fair to say that Frederick did uphold the rights of peasants to resort to the royal courts for protection, and that he did pursue policies of emancipation of crown tenants, but he drew back from attempting to force the same policy on his nobility. In Pomerania, where the peasant conditions were particularly harsh, he withdrew a project for alleviating them in face of the corporate resistance of the landlords. His defence was realism: he accepted that to abolish serfdom would overturn the whole rural economy, and it could not be done. Frederick had told Cocceji in 1754: 'The slavery of serfdom still continuing in Pomerania seems to me so cruel and to have such a bad effect on the whole country, that I really would like to have it completely abolished.' In 1777 he referred again to the problem: 'One rightly despises the abuse and thinks that only will-power is necessary to abolish the barbaric custom ... If one tried to abolish this loathsome custom at a stroke, one would cause upheavals throughout all agriculture.'

An equally serious criticism is that Frederick was an unapologetic militarist. The army was his first concern in all circumstances. After 1763 Frederick maintained a standing army of some 180,000 men that consumed 70 per cent of the public revenues, while about 16 per cent of the population was engaged in military service. One of the better-known historical aphorisms, usually attributed to the French comte de Mirabeau, was that 'the Prussian monarchy is not a country which has an army, but an army that has a country, in which, as it were, it is just billeted'. It is true that the Prussian administration maintained a very close linkage between the civil and military establishments. Not only did Junkers, usually from army service, get preference for the higher administrative jobs, but many of the lower clerical posts in the public services were filled by retired NCOs. In fact Frederick laid it down that 'any man of good breeding who is not a soldier is a miserable wretch'. Again Frederick's justification was pragmatic and realist. In a world of military predators, Prussia was vulnerable and his vast military establishment justifiable. After 1763, when it could be argued that the army had been used to secure a valuable new territory for the kingdom, the king waged no more wars of conquest; the brief confrontation with Austria in 1778 was a defensive gesture. The purpose of the army was deterrence, but for this to be effective its size, constant public display, spectacular drill and discipline were essential constituents of the process. The other, unspoken, purpose of the army was as the bonding agent that held together a society composed of several different component parts. The evidence is that the military ethos became internalized by the king's subjects. A French traveller noted: 'The ordinary people in Prussia, even among the lowest classes, are imbued with the military spirit, speak with respect of their army, know the names of their generals, refer to their feats of arms.'

For the nobility it became a necessary way of life. The Prussian Junkers were not, as a class, a very affluent nobility. Even the top families were modestly endowed by comparison with the magnates of Bohemia or Poland. Although their economic prospects improved, along with the rest of Europe's landlords, in the economic recovery after 1750, they needed the earnings from state service, plus the subsidies which Frederick provided after 1763, to remain economically viable.

Frederick did launch a sustained reconstruction programme for his devastated kingdom after the war. From the very beginning the surplus stocks of the army and the labour of the soldiers were diverted into emergency programmes, the debasement of the currency was stopped, and the budget surplus quickly restored.[3] On top of the military expenditures and the financial aid to the Junkers, he drove through extensive resettlement schemes to attract immigration and boost his population. Over the reign he seems to have settled some 250,000 colonists in almost 1500 new villages. In the end this was expected to pay off as it added to the number of taxpayers in the kingdom, but in the short term the policy absorbed very substantial public funds. Critics observe that Frederick's economic development projects were backward looking, deriving from seventeenth-century mercantilist programmes rather than the Enlightenment. But since the central Enlightenment policies of moving towards private enterprise and free trade regulated by the market usually came to a bad end wherever they were practised at that stage of European development, Frederick's economic conservatism may have served his kingdom well.

In the development of the second pillar of the mature Prussian state, the central bureaucracy, Frederick was similarly conservative and pragmatic. The Directory and its provincial chambers was left largely as Frederick found them in 1740. He was never satisfied with it because he suspected, with good reason, that it was developing its own corporate agenda and, like most such institutions, tended to be an obstacle to change.[4] Frederick added the two new departments, the Fifth for the economy, and the Sixth for army supply and maintenance, but his general inclination was to circumvent possible bureaucratic obstruction by setting up alternative agencies. He did this for Silesia from the beginning: it retained its own provincial government, separate from the Directory, until the end of the reign. The other new acquisition, West Prussia, taken from Poland in the partition of 1772, was, however, integrated under the Directory. It was a problem with any established institution like the Directory that although it was meant to execute the will of the ruler and implement his policies, in fact its officials found that to achieve reasonable results and a comfortable life, it was best to seek agreements with the local elites and to adapt the royal policies to local circumstances. In the end a cosy working relationship generally developed between the central administration and the local communities. The Prussian administration went down the same development curve as the French intendancy and lost its radical potential as an agency for change.

After the war Frederick decided to remodel the collection of the excise, his principal indirect tax revenue. This had been a Directory function, with the *Steuerrat* supervising the levy of the tax in each town. Frederick hired 200 French consultants to set up the *Régie*, which eventually employed 2000 officials. The Directory was bitterly opposed to its loss of control, but the king persisted and evidence indicates the reform was a success. Those historians who have contrasted the efficiency of Prussian administration with the chaos in France find Frederick's decision puzzling. One historian considers that the new institution, the *Régie*, 'was not a great financial innovation, but a strike against the Prussian bureaucracy'. This is consistent with Frederick's appointment of Ludwig von Hagen to reform the Directory. He became its head in 1766 and sought to end the practice of collegiate decision-making that had been built into the Directory from its first establishment. He multiplied specialist sub-departments, organized a State Bank under the Directory; and reinvigorated the *Oberrechnungkammer* and its provincial offices to establish centralized financial control. In his new departments, career bureaucrats and technical experts worked together, and it was under Hagen that the central bureaucracy adopted the systems of professional training and qualifying examinations for entry, which had been tried out in the judiciary reforms.

Most recent historians of Frederick's Prussia have tended to emphasize both his personal conservatism and the conservatism of the elites through whom society was governed. The king's father had distrusted the Junkers, and sought to reduce their influence, while Frederick was deliberately putting them at the heart of his system and accepting the limitations which this imposed. Frederick decided that the *Landrat*, the key local official, who was generally recruited from the wealthier Junker families, and whom Frederick William had insisted on appointing himself, was now, in effect, elected by his fellow landlords: the king chose from candidates they nominated. The

Landrat was the key to continuing Junker hegemony over rural society. He ensured that the formally absolute Prussian state was in practice a system of power-sharing. As C. T. W. Blanning commented, the power of the king stopped at the boundary of the Junker's estate.

There will always be debate whether Frederick's Prussia was a model of enlightened absolutism or only an unusually efficient *Polizeistaat* on the cameralist model. There is a good case to be made for Frederick. His lifelong advocacy of the basic Enlightenment programme of bringing the light of reason to bear on the problems of society was not empty posturing. When Frederick decided that serfdom could not be abolished, he was being rational – in that context it could not. Kant, who was a leading Enlightenment philosopher and a subject of Frederick, accepted his credentials:

> If it is now asked whether we at present live in an enlightened age, the answer is: No, but we do live in an age of enlightenment ... The obstacles to universal enlightenment, to man's emergence from his self-imposed immaturity, are gradually becoming fewer. In this respect our age is the age of enlightenment, the century of Frederick.

An English visitor in Berlin, John Moore, was surprised at the freedom of public discussion and the availability of books and pamphlets, often critical of royal policies. But he added: 'a government, supported by an army of 180,000 men, may safely disregard the criticisms of a few speculative politicians and the pen of the satirist'.[5] Frederick's Prussia was no earthly paradise; life for common folk was hard, as it was everywhere. But the regime did offer a basic security; the kingdom was at peace and internally stable. The tax burdens were heavy but they were also stable. The state was solvent and the money collected was not squandered on conspicuous consumption by the ruling elites. Conscription was a burden, but the native Prussian conscript could live as a civilian for much of the time. In times of subsistence crisis effective state-organized relief could be depended upon. The educational facilities available to the ordinary subject were some of the best in Europe. The common subject would not congratulate himself on the enlightened principles of his ruler – they were a concept above his understanding – but he would know that if he accepted his place in the social hierarchy, and followed the rules, a tolerable existence was possible.

Maria Theresa, Joseph II and the Habsburg lands

The hereditary lands of the Habsburg dynasty had had no formal existence as a political society before the Pragmatic Sanction. And even then they could only be defined by the allegiance they owed to the dynasty. Austria and Bohemia were part of the Holy Roman Empire; the entirely independent kingdom of Hungary was not.[6] Legally, only the common dynastic allegiance connected Hungary to the other lands. The outlying provinces in northern

Italy, cut off by the Alps, and the entirely detached Netherlands existed as separate territories and there had been no move to assimilate or incorporate them into the central block. This structure was a major obstacle to implementing any reform policies, enlightened or not, in the Habsburg lands. Most government was local and, since they were all more or less feudal societies, was devolved to the local Estates. These usually represented clergy, titled nobility, untitled nobility and some vestigial urban participation. In practice they met in full session once a year to hear proposals from the ruler, which now they rarely even debated, since the absolute nature of royal authority was unquestioned. In the Austrian Estates in 1765 the abbot of Melk declared: 'we must absolutely obey, when her Majesty absolutely commands'. Thus the main business, the annual renewal of the Contribution for the army, went through unopposed, even though over the period it was steadily increased. Even the 1748 doubling of the Contribution by Haugwitz caused no trouble. Compensating factors were the right of the Estates themselves to present grievances, to which the ruler was expected to respond, and the fact that the administration of the levy, and the officials who handled it, were the agents of the Estates Committee, set up after each session to handle current business. They could mould the central policies to suit local requirements. Hungary as always had its own system. It actually had a constitution that reserved all offices to natives, and though the Diet rarely met, it had full legislative power. More importantly, local government was run under the county system. The Hungarian *komitat* was an autonomous institution, controlling justice and administration, presided over by a royal sheriff, working with a county assembly of the nobility, who ran the administration.

The Haugwitz reforms of 1748, modelled on the Prussian system, and bitterly resisted by the Estates and conservatives in Vienna, had not performed well during the war. They were under attack from prince W. A von Kaunitz, who was Chancellor from 1753 to 1794 and dominated both the foreign and domestic policy of the dynasty under Maria Theresa. In 1761, the Haugwitz structure was remodelled. There was a small Council of State to consider policy options and report. Most important policy initiatives came up through this body which stood in for the absence of a legislature. Routine domestic administration remained under the Austrian and Bohemian court chancellery. Hungary, Italy and the Netherlands retained their separate administrations. In each province there was a *Gubernien*. This was a body of salaried central officials, who executed central policies, necessarily in collaboration with the local Estates administrations. The government of Austria and Bohemia employed some 20,500 officials: 7500 crown servants, 1500 Estates' officers and 11,500 officers in urban government. The feudal administrators, bailiffs and stewards of the landlords provided a further level of control. The kingdom of Hungary had a similar mix totalling some 15,000 officials.

It remains unclear what the overall effect of the undoubted increase in numbers of professional, salaried officials was. The direct influence of magnates at the top of the system may have diminished and there was probably some assimilation between the royal officials and the Estates' officials – both in the end were mainly recruited from the middle ranks of the nobility. But administrative coherence was weak. There was endless inter-departmental rivalry and evasion of responsibility. Yet when Galicia, a territory that had no local Estates, was annexed from Poland in 1772, the Austrian system of joint administration was installed there, so that a new local Estates administration had to be constructed.

The Kaunitz reforms, like almost everything done under the Habsburg government, were never completed. The development of one central treasury was blocked, as were the attempts to modernize accounting procedures. Introduction of double-entry book-keeping was abandoned in face of the institutional conservatism of its officials. However, after 1763, fairly comprehensive and systematic financial records were kept, and analysis of these suggests that substantial progress was made towards achieving financial self-sufficiency. The first step was a windfall. Maria Theresa's husband, the Emperor Francis, died unexpectedly in 1765, and turned out to have been a capable businessman, for he left a huge cash legacy of 18 million florins. This was mainly used to launch a sinking fund for the accumulated crown debt. After an abortive experiment with a new credit bank guaranteed by the Estates in 1767, a scheme for the Vienna City Bank to make controlled issues of paper notes in 1771 was successful. The government debt was then under control. There were few new revenue sources after 1763, but the government was pushing up the Contribution, not by raising the rates – they were stabilized after 1763 – but by eliminating exemptions. The Contribution was essentially a tax assessed on real property, and the principle was established that it was payable regardless of the status of the owner. In effect, the Habsburg government succeeded where both Frederick and the French monarchy failed and eliminated the principal tax exemptions of the clergy and the nobility. The net revenues had reached 55 million by the mid-1780s. The standing army steadily increased to 200,000, overtaking the Prussian army and went up to over 300,000 in times of war. This certainly strained the system, but did not break it, and the monarchy survived financially to 1789 without recourse to deficit finance.

The monarchy was ruled after 1765 by a triumvirate. At the head was Maria Theresa, who held on grimly to final authority until her death in 1780. She was a paradoxical figure and impervious, indeed hostile, to the French Enlightenment, being devoutly religious and utterly opposed to toleration of disbelief or heresy. She accepted Protestantism in Transylvania and Hungary, where it was established by law, but in 1771, scandalized at discovering congregations of Protestants in Moravia, she pressed hard to have them expelled. It needed the combined pressures of Kaunitz and Joseph to persuade her that this was no longer acceptable in civilized society. She was not intellectually inclined, and emphatically did not correspond with Voltaire and his like. Yet though brought up in the tradition of Austrian baroque piety, with the Jesuits as its main support, she began to convert in the 1760s, influenced by her Dutch physician van Swieten and the spreading movement in the Empire for Catholic reform as advocated by the Italian Muratori, and in end she took a Jansenist confessor. As a result, in cooperation with Kaunitz and Joseph, the Jesuits' grip on university education was broken, and when the papacy finally disbanded the Jesuit Order, she made no attempt to defend them, welcoming the use of their properties to finance educational reforms. There was also a sustained attack on the privileges of the church through a vigorous assertion of lay supremacy. But Maria Theresa was always at heart a traditionalist, though willing to make radical changes on pragmatic grounds. It was her influence that ensured the slow uneven progress of reform, for while willing to lend her authority to reform in principle, she was liable to empathize with conservative protest and unwilling to exert pressure to overcome it. She had genuine respect for tradition and privilege: it was her consciousness of having sworn to uphold the Hungarian constitution that prevented any radical action in Hungary while she lived. She had an instinctive realization that even absolute rulers have to seek consent if policies are to succeed.

This put her on a collision course with her son Joseph, who recognized no such restraints. He was not formally educated in Enlightenment ideas, though over time he became familiar with them, nor was he an intellectual of Frederick's calibre. But in fact he accepted all the main attitudes of the *philosophes* and the basic strategy of using rational analysis to sweep away ignorance and devise measures to improve human happiness. Joseph wrote to his brother in 1768: 'love of country, the welfare of the monarchy, that is genuinely the only passion I feel, and I would undertake anything for its sake'. In a circular to officials in 1783 he declared: 'each man should have no other aim in all his actions but utility and the welfare of the greatest number'. He lived up to his principles and his support for religious toleration was unconditional; though he remained a Catholic believer all his life, he thought hierarchy absurd. He wrote: 'our parents can give us nothing more than physical existence, and for that reason there is not the slightest difference between a king, a count, a burgher or a peasant'. When he got sole power at last he abandoned court life, turned the Hofburg palace into offices and the royal hunting reserve into a public park, and took up residence in a modest villa. With the death of Francis in 1765 he became Emperor, and was recognized by his mother as co-regent. That year he produced a 40,000-word memorandum setting out his aspirations to reform and improve almost every aspect of public life. This also reveals his limitations: he never saw the contradiction between his advocacy of freedom of expression and of the individual, and his unrestrained appetite for legislative regulation of all aspects of life.

He offered a more mature version in a *General Picture* he wrote for his brother Leopold in 1768. In this he seems to accept the more pragmatic and realistic policies of his mother and Kaunitz. A recent biographer, D. Beales comparing it with the radical aspirations expressed in 1765, notes that he writes as 'a reforming statesman, working conscientiously, knowledgably and rationally within the existing system, to strengthen the state and benefit the people'. But in both documents he exudes the sense of his personal responsibility to take control and act decisively. His position after 1765 was intolerably difficult, since his mother affected to take him into partnership but insisted on controlling everything. And she was devious, trying to use Kaunitz as cover for her own resolve to keep him under restraint. Joseph shared with Frederick a passion for militarism. He said on his death bed: 'To be a soldier has always been my profession and my favourite occupation.' He scarcely let a day pass without attending some military exercise, and in 1766 an ambassador noted: 'He enjoys talking, not only with the officers, but even with the common soldiers ... He is happy discussing anything to do with the conduct of war.' It was thus reasonable that Maria Theresa should allocate direction of army policy to Joseph, and this she agreed to do. Yet when a new commander-in-chief was to be appointed in 1768, she deliberately selected General Lacy, knowing that he was opposed to some of Joseph's policies.

So for 15 years, Joseph, bursting with the desire for radical action, was frustrated at every turn by his mother's conservatism. It was remarkable they managed to maintain a stormy but workable relationship. This owed much to the third member of the ruling triumvirate, Kaunitz. In his long career, first as foreign minister, which was always at the centre of his power base, and after 1761 as the guiding influence in the Council of State, Kaunitz was accepted by both mother and son as an indispensable support, and she certainly used him unscrupulously to control her son. The three of them played a game in which one or the other would threaten to resign if they did not get their way, then the other two would rally round to rescue the partnership. In 1773 there was a showdown, when all three declared they would retire simultaneously. It was Joseph who blinked first; he seems to have felt he was too isolated to accept sole responsibility. In effect, it has been pointed out, Maria Theresa and Kaunitz made the decisions; Joseph was the loyal opposition, particularly after 1773 when he seems to have accepted that he must wait patiently for the succession.

He spent the next seven years endlessly travelling and inspecting and making policy recommendations that the other two usually blocked or watered down. Joseph acquired an unusual personal familiarity with all his territories and their problems. He even met fellow rulers, like Catherine II, Frederick, and his brother-in-law Louis XVI. He seems to have concluded that there remained much to be done in pursuit of the increase of the general welfare of the subject, and hardened in his belief that real change must come from above. In a memorandum to his mother in 1771, Joseph asserted:

Y[our] M[ajesty]'s departments and ultimately the Council of State ascribe all mistakes to the provinces, which blame the Departments, ministers and ultimately the Council of State, which shuffles the responsibility on to the Departments. In this vortex of folly the only sufferer is the peasant and the worthy citizen.

The overall result was that, until 1780, policy-making at the centre was erratic and major issues were fudged. One such was Hungary and its autonomy. In 1764 the Hungarian Diet was convened with the aim of effecting reforms. At the centre of these was the desire of Maria Theresa and Kaunitz to alleviate the conditions of the peasantry, and thus undermine the power of the feudal landlords in Hungary. The Diet proved uncooperative, opposed the reforms and pressed its own long lists of grievances for redress. Maria Theresa decided to dispense with the Diet, which did not meet again until 1790. New legislation on peasant rights was introduced on royal authority in 1767, and some effort made to use government patronage to recruit collaborators in the Hungarian administration. But Maria Theresa resisted to the end the pressures from Kaunitz and Joseph for authoritarian policies that disregarded the Hungarian constitution. She preferred negotiation with local interests, with the result that little had been done for the peasantry by 1780, though in other fields, like education and military reform, some changes were pushed through. In effect Maria Teresa had decided to leave Hungary alone, and at least ensured that the magnates, the church nobility and the local bureaucracy remained loyal to the Habsburg regime.

There was a peasant problem in Bohemia, precipitated by the major subsistence crisis of 1771–2. Here both Joseph and his mother agreed that agrarian reform was urgently needed, and that the local administration, firmly controlled by the landlords, was obstructing this. The open knowledge of this conflict finally set off a peasant revolt in Bohemia in 1775, which needed a major military campaign to restore order. In this case it was Maria Theresa who, after 1774, was arguing for abolition of serfdom in Bohemia, Kaunitz and Joseph who held back. A new law regulating labour services was promulgated, but it was Joseph who insisted on working locally, with the crown promoting negotiation on individual estates between landlords and peasants to agree on new conditions of tenancy. Most histories agree that over time there was a significant alleviation of peasant conditions. In these episodes the practical parameters within which enlightened reform could be pursued are revealed. The crown had the legal power to decree reforms, but the local elites had the ability to delay and frustrate them, simply because the day-to-day running of government was in their hands, and short of using force to impose a radical change of government structures there was no way round. Progress would depend on the government's use of patronage to negotiate some cooperation from the local powerholders. Both Frederick in Prussia and Joseph in Bohemia came to the same conclusion: serfdom was uncivilized and abhorrent, but abolition was impractical.

Joseph could claim some achievements for his programmes as he waited for power. One was the abolition of judicial torture; another was the moderation of the censorship: Joseph got permission for a popular, German-language theatre in Vienna. This might seem trivial, but in fact a popular theatre was a potent medium for introducing reformist ideas among the lower classes. It was responsible for the first productions of Mozart's *Magic Flute*, using the vernacular in place of Italian, and imbued with Enlightenment idealism. Joseph also got his way over tariff policy for the monarchy. Joseph's tariff policies, which were implemented in 1775, favoured a free-trade area internally and encouraged international trade by moderate tariffs. But these marginal achievements were a poor return for years of effort. As one of the Habsburg princesses, his sister Eleanora, remarked: 'This poor prince ... he will never be happy, I think he aims at the good, he takes more trouble than many others to find it, it is pointed out to him, but he has never yet done it.'

Joseph's opportunity came in 1780 when Maria Theresa died after 40 years of ruling the hereditary lands. In the ten years of his personal government, Joseph II was the model enlightened despot. Except in the field of foreign policy, where he accepted the need to share policy-making with Kaunitz, he took all major decisions himself after consulting with expert advisers. These were strictly confined to their specialities, so Joseph talked to Kolowrat and Zinzendorf on financial policy, Kessel on religion, Sonnenfels on education. The Council of State, very much controlled by Kaunitz, remained a forum for policy discussion, but the Emperor was not bound by its opinions. Joseph attempted to implement the Enlightenment project and promote the public welfare. He declared that, since 'Providence and Nature have made all men equal ... forms of government ... must be in accordance with the general good of the greatest number.' He also saw no obligation to make concessions to conservative, or ignorant, unenlightened protests. He wrote: 'one has to begin with first principles derived from the nature of the object and one must not take into account customs, which are just prejudices, even if they have endured for a century or more'. The trend was illustrated by the fact that while the number of effective advisers at the centre was nearly halved after 1780, compared with the previous decade, the number of royal decrees, which had run at around 100 a year, shot up to 690 a year under his personal rule, when 6206 reforming edicts were published in nine years.

His most effective project was in the field of religious reform. Joseph, who remained a committed Catholic believer, first asserted complete secular control over the church. He insisted that the relations of the local churches with the papacy must be mediated through the government in Vienna, imposed a new oath of allegiance on the bishops, and then enforced his ideas on improvements. Central to these was the internal redistribution of resources, from the monastic sector to the parish clergy. After 1780 the number of regular clergy fell from 25,000 to 11,000, which meant that monasticism was retained, even though 530 monasteries were dissolved. The numbers of the parish clergy rose from 22,000 to 27,000, and their mission was redefined, with the emphasis on pastoral care of the ordinary parishioner along Jansenist lines, and the elimination of superstitious ceremony and excess ritual. Clerical education was taken under state control; all clergy were to be educated in 12 official seminaries, with strict secular control over their curriculum. The general conclusion of historians is that the quality of religious life in the community was substantially enhanced by the reforms. They were combined with the effective establishment of full religious toleration. With the objection of his mother removed, Joseph issued the patent of 1781 which granted complete freedom of worship to all Christian denominations and full rights of citizenship regardless of religious confession.

A series of provincial regulations removed most of the legal disabilities on the Jewish community. Here he was restrained by pressures from Kaunitz and the Council who, with good reason, feared populist reaction to any such measures. As a result of the reforms, religious liberty in the Habsburg lands was far in advance of that in contemporary Britain and measured up well to Enlightenment standards. Joseph's educational reforms were biased by his insistence that education should be vocational: but his Educational Commission, led by Gottfried van Swieten and boosted by re-allocated funds from church reform, gave priority to extending primary education, with general literacy its first objective, while keeping the curriculum for the common folk focused on useful knowledge. Both religious conservatives, who saw the new schools as spreading heresies, and the peasants, who objected to the expense, opposed the reforms. The evidence suggests that there was significant improvement in literacy rates in some parts, and access to social improvement by educational qualification was increasingly possible.

Joseph had long accepted that serfdom was an unacceptable survival from the unenlightened past. He had to recognize that the attempted alleviations introduced in the 1770s and the attempts to legislate reduction of labour services and irksome feudal restrictions on individual freedom were being successfully obstructed by the landlords at local level. On a visit to Transylvania in 1783, ten years after the introduction of reforms, he noted: 'everything is just as before ... magistrates, lords and landowners exploiting subjects'. There was a series of reforming decrees from 1781 for the different provinces, ordering reductions of labour services, granting personal legal rights to the peasantry, and opening up the protection that royal courts could offer. In 1785 Joseph tried to extend these to Hungary, where the power of the landlords had proved an insuperable obstacle to change. In 1783 he embarked on his most radical project to combine reform of taxation with peasant emancipation. This had to wait on implementation of a single universal land tax, which decreed that taxation on the peasantry must leave 70 per cent of peasant income for the upkeep of his family and payment of local taxation and tithe. The 30 per cent would be divided between the public revenue and the landlords, who would thus be compensated for surrendering their feudal rights. The scheme was ready for implementation in 1789, but by then the general collapse of Joseph's authority and the intensity of landlord resistance, especially in Hungary, then on the edge of revolt, caused it to be postponed indefinitely.

One solid success was to drive through the codification of the criminal law, enacted in 1787. This incorporated the principle of equality before the law, abolished the death penalty for most offences, and abolished such crimes as witchcraft and heresy. Equally striking was his virtual abolition of censorship after 1781. This was done on basic Enlightenment principles, though he drew the line at irreligion, pornography and social subversion. He wrote:

> Criticisms, if they are not slanderous are not to be prohibited, no matter who their targets may be ... for every lover of the truth must rejoice to be told the truth, even if it is conveyed to him by the uncomfortable route of criticism.

On balance the new publications were positive towards the reforms and indicated that there was an enlightened public opinion, though it represented an essentially aristocratic intelligentsia and the common people remained sceptical or hostile.

It was the drive for a centralized uniform administration over all his territories that wrecked the reform programme. Joseph, impatient at the obstruction he found among the provincial elites, was determined to confront it. In the last years of Maria Theresa, despite the disputes with the Hungarian Diet of 1764, her unwillingness to challenge Hungarian privilege had enabled a reasonable working relationship to be achieved with the Hungarian nobility and clergy. Joseph was provocatively bent on changing this. He refused to be crowned king in Hungary, which would have involved swearing to uphold the constitution, and made clear his intention to assimilate Hungarian administration into that of the rest of the monarchy. So even policies that did have some support in Hungary, like the decision to incorporate Transylvania into Hungary, or the toleration now assured to Hungarian Protestants, failed to win support for his other proposals. When they were combined with his planned tax and agrarian reform of 1789, it brought the Hungarian nobility to the verge of armed rebellion by the time that Joseph died in 1790. Even this fell short of the anarchy he caused in the Austrian Netherlands. There the province had enjoyed virtual autonomy under the Habsburg governor, Charles of Lorraine, from 1741 until his death in 1780. He had been a progressive absolutist and the province had flourished in the absence of war after 1748, assisted by government protectionist policies and public investment in communications. But to an enlightened eye, the administration and laws of the province were deeply feudal. Even before 1780, this situation had drawn Joseph's attention, but his mother had warned him to let well alone. She wrote: 'I do not believe anything needs changing in the essentials of the constitution and forms of government. It is the only happy province and it has provided us with so many resources.'

Joseph had a bad experience there: his plans to get possession of Bavaria by exchanging it for the Netherlands collapsed in face of general international opposition, as did an attempt to secure the re-opening of the Scheldt and hence of the port of Antwerp to international commerce. Joseph was forced into a humiliating climbdown.[7] This seems to have convinced him that at least he would enforce the modernization of the government and laws of the province, ignoring the fierce local protests. When his own governor in the Netherlands responded to local protests by offering major concessions, Joseph recalled him and decided to use force to get his way. The result was an open armed uprising, a popular anti-Enlightenment revolt, uniting the elites and the common people. When Joseph died he had completely lost control there.

Joseph came to grief by taking the Enlightenment too seriously; he assumed that the eminent rationality of his project must win the hearts and minds of all but a handful of obstinate reactionaries. He misunderstood the society in which he lived. He had stated in one of his early memoranda of 1761 that 'everything exists for the state: this work contains everything, so all who live in it should come together to promote its interests'. The problem was that the Habsburg dominions were not a state and never had been. They were a heterogeneous collection of provinces, bound together only by the loyalty of their inhabitants – elites and common people too – to the Habsburg dynasty. The power of the ruler had always been patrimonial and specific to the individual territory. At the end of his life Joseph seemed to appreciate his error and began the process of reversing some of his policies in order to save his inheritance from disintegration. The interesting point to note is how easy this proved to be. When Leopold succeeded as Emperor, and continued the retreat from the reforms, there was little difficulty in regaining the allegiance of Hungary and the Netherlands. The truth was that the whole Enlightenment concept was elitist: its ideals had never won the hearts and minds of most contemporaries. On the contrary, in so far as there was populist awareness of what was proposed, reactions tended to be negative. Ordinary believers did not want their religious practices modernized, villagers did not want to be forced to send their children to schools, which caused expense, loss of their labour and exposure to teaching they suspected to be godless. The ruling elites might find much Enlightenment thinking attractive, but if implementation meant they had to give up their hold on local administration, if ending serfdom reduced their income, if equality before the law meant giving up centuries-old privileges, they wanted at least compensation and safeguards that their whole social hegemony was not being threatened. Enlightenment reforms required great caution if they were to work and become accepted. Joseph had operated as though no such constraints applied. On his death bed, he proposed the terms of his own epitaph: 'Here lies a prince whose intentions were pure, but who had the misfortune to see all his plans collapse.' Kaunitz was more brutal when he wrote in January 1790: 'Everything is as bad as it could possibly be and there is little hope for the future, despite all my best efforts. It is frightful that despotic obstinacy has brought this great monarchy to its present state.'

Russia and Catherine II

Catherine II came to the throne of the Russian empire without any hereditary entitlement. Her husband, Peter III, from whom she had long been estranged, was deposed after only some six months on the throne by a conspiracy of guards officers who represented the aristocratic elite. Peter the Great's Table of Ranks had officially recognized two levels of noble family: 136 'distinguished' families, basically the old Moscow *boyar* elite; and the 2849 'undistinguished' families. They had been running the empire since his death. Within the distinguished group, a further group of families had established a hereditary dominance in the top four ranks of the Table of Ranks, which included control of the guards regiments. It is unclear how deeply Catherine was involved in planning the deposition and subsequent inevitable murder of her husband, but she had no dynastic claim, for Peter had left a son, the future Tsar Paul, and at most Catherine could have claimed a regency for him. In these circumstances Catherine was very much the agent of the guards officers, and clearly they could have dictated terms of succession, but they followed the Russian tradition of autocracy and passed over the chance to limit her authority. Her choice for first minister in 1762, Count Nikita Panin, did suggest setting up an appointed Council of State, whose members would hold office for life, which would share decision-making with the empress, but Catherine rejected the idea of any limitation. Her absolutism caused her some embarrassment, since she always made a point of displaying her enlightened credentials, and she was aware that Montesquieu, whose ideas she constantly cited as shared by herself, had classified Russia as a tyranny. She claimed Russia was a special case on account of its vast geographical extent and that 'the sovereign is absolute: for there is no other authority than that which centres on his single person, that can act with a vigour proportionate to the extent of such a vast dominion'.

Her formal qualifications as an enlightened despot were impeccable. She was a genuine intellectual, who had read steadily through the works of the *philosophes*, and for years she maintained a lively correspondence with many of them. She went so far as to invite Diderot to visit Russia and advise her on reform, though it is difficult to show that this had much real effect on her policies. She declared: 'one should be good, and avoid doing evil, as much as one reasonably can, out of love of humanity'. She subscribed to the importance of the rule of law: 'It is in the interests of the state, the laws of which must ever remain sacred to monarchs, because they last for ever while subjects and rulers disappear, that men should be judged according to law.' She praised liberty: 'The soul of everything, without you all is dead. I want the law to be obeyed, but I want no slaves. I want the general aim of making people happy, but no caprice, no fantasies, no tyranny that might undermine it.'

It is a matter of record that some of her actions embodied Enlightenment aspirations. She dismissed censorship as 'productive of nothing but ignorance, and must cramp and depress the rising efforts of genius'. She effectively abolished it for many years in Russia. In 1783 the establishment of private printing presses was authorized, while Catherine had sponsored a society for the translation of foreign books, and in that same year charged the Russian Academy with the duty of supporting its work. In fact nearly all the main works of the Enlightenment, including the *Encyclopédie*, were freely available in Russia. She further encouraged educational and critical periodicals, and actually contributed articles of her own to some of them. She duly embarked on codification of laws, and was clear that torture was not acceptable, 'contrary to all the dictates of nature and reason'. It was not totally abolished, but the whole revision was based on the Enlightenment programme of humanizing the system, reducing capital punishment and establishing equality before the law. In the 1780s she was encouraged by her meetings with Joseph II to copy the Austrian plans for educational reform. As with all such schemes, problems over funding and staffing, and resistance from the unenlightened, meant that success was limited. Estimates of the numbers of pupils by the 1790s can vary from 20,000 to 60,000, but there was some real achievement.

Catherine also pursued her ideals in the field of religion. She began by vigorous assertion of the right of the secular ruler to supervise all forms of religious activity. One early measure which was based on this was the secularization of church property and the using of the proceeds to fund her programmes. This had the incidental effect of changing the status of the serfs on these properties to that of state peasants, who enjoyed the best-established legal position in the hierarchy of peasant society. But having asserted the right to supervise, Catherine proceeded to establish a general religious toleration, which went beyond that established by Joseph. The legal disabilities of the Old Believers were largely removed, the position of the Catholic Church was legally recognized, and the process was extended to recognizing the rights of the Muslim community, for whom a Muslim Spiritual Assembly was set up in 1786. Finally the Jews were given extensive civil rights, and an area was designated along the western borders, the Pale of Settlement, where they were free to form their own communities.

Catherine also followed the usual Enlightenment prescriptions for developing economic activity. The most striking achievement was the dynamic agrarian expansion into the southern lands won from the Ottomans, with a substantial influx of new settlers. It has been claimed that 'this Russian expansion remained unparalleled in the scale, scope and rapidity with which it was carried through'. Peter's College of Manufactures, with its tight control over industry, was abolished in 1779; before that, in 1775, a manifesto gave freedom to all kinds of industrial entrepreneurs, regardless of social rank and most of the commercial monopolies were wound up. Over the reign as a whole there was a major expansion of the economy: both agriculture and manufacturing showed significant increases in production; foreign trade may have increased as much as five times; and there was a strong surplus on Russia's balance of trade.

Catherine's credentials as an enlightened despot are most often challenged over the reforms in government and administration, and the issue of serfdom. The empire was divided out into very extensive governments and districts under a head appointed from the centre. But the payment of local government officials had been discontinued and it is apparent that both judicial and administrative officers were left to make a living by selling their services to clients. The effect was that the grip of the centre on government in the provinces was minimal. Much contemporary evidence suggests a high level of internal insecurity and armed feuding among noble factions and simple banditry were common. In the end it was the army that held things together. Peter's aspirations to bind the nobility into lifelong state service were also eroding. Even before Peter III's abolition of compulsory service in 1762, the nobility were showing more interest in developing their landed properties, which were now legally regarded as hereditary. After Catherine had consolidated her hold on power she set about a reform of the administrative structures.

In 1764, salaries for all public officials were introduced. This was seen as requiring more intense central supervision, and the system of procurators and government inspectors – enforcers in modern terminology – was enhanced. One of Catherine's most important collaborators was the Procurator General, A. A. Vyazemsky, who held the office from 1764 to 1792. The procurators were to enforce new regulations against corrupt practice and abuse. An Enlightenment touch was the general instruction to the provincial governors and their subordinates that they were to make the furtherance of the public welfare their priority. Further, the collection of the poll tax was finally taken back from the military and transferred to the civil administration. This all points towards a desire to establish an effective, professional administrative system throughout the empire. In 1765 there followed the most interesting and ambivalent of Catherine's initiatives, the Legislative Commission. This was the first representative assembly for the whole empire since the *zemsky sobor* ceased to function in the seventeenth century, and was to be the last before the state *duma* of 1906. It was composed of delegates elected and mandated by the different classes of society. It contained 29 deputies representing the central administration, 142 nobles, 209 urban taxpayers and 200 delegates from the state peasants' communities and the tribal societies of the borderlands.

Catherine issued a formal *Instruction*, a programme which contained suggestions for ways in which the betterment of society might be advanced. The idea was that the Commission would put recommendations to the sovereign, on the basis of which she would issue decrees. The *Instruction* laid down that the autocracy was inviolable, but it contained a range of suggestions, more than half of which were copied from the works of Montesquieu and included the separation of functions between the judiciary and the civil administration, general law reform based on the principle of equality before the law and the establishment of legal rights for the different classes of society. A draft section on serfdom was not included in the final version.

Otherwise the specific proposals tended to reflect Enlightenment thinking on humanitarianism and utilitarianism as principles of government, the *Instruction* was also printed and made available to the reading public. The experiment with the Legislative Commission was Catherine's Enlightenment show-case. Her critics can point out that it had limited practical outcomes. It has to be said that this was partly its own fault, since while it was in session, from 1765 to 1768, the records of the debates show little inclination among the delegates to do more than defend their sectional interests. No leadership emerged to direct its debates towards positive conclusions. The major issues like serfdom were debated, but while it was criticized, no consensus emerged on what should or could be done, except the tacit recognition that the whole social structure was bound up with retaining it. The Commission's work illustrates a feature of Russian society that many still identify in our own time – the absence of civic consciousness or a willingness in the subject or citizen to accept collective responsibility for the direction of public affairs. It cannot be known whether the Commission could have produced any significant agreed recommendations, for the outbreak of the first Turkish war in 1768, followed by the first partition of Poland in 1772, absorbed the government's energies and the Commission was prorogued. There followed the greatest social crisis of the reign, the Pugachev rebellion; when order had been restored in 1775, there was a general amnesty and a new round of reforming activity began. But the Commission was never recalled, and there is little sign that it was regretted. It can be seen as a typical, ideologically driven mistake. It does reflect one of Diderot's main ideas, but the context was wrong. It has been noted that 10 per cent of the elected delegates of the nobility were illiterate. Many Commission members would have been quite ignorant of Enlightenment thought or would have found the proposals largely alien to their mental world.

The Pugachev revolt was not initially a rising of serfs: it had started as a Cossack protest against government policies which sought to restrict the privileges of the Cossack communities. Pugachev himself showed some political awareness and as the revolt spread northwards into regions of serf agriculture, held out the Cossack model of free peasant communities as a general model. Although serfs provided only some 30 per cent of Pugachev's supporters, his programme demanded abolition of serfdom and he denounced landlords as:

> Disturbers of the Empire and destroyers of the peasants: catch, execute and hang and treat them in the same way they, not being Christian, have dealt with you, the peasants. With the eradication of these opponents and villainous nobles, each may find peace and a quiet life that will continue for ever.

His call seems to have been answered. Some estimates suggest as many as 5 per cent of the nobility may have perished during the course of the revolt, and the material damage was extensive. There was never any danger of the regime being overthrown by the revolt. The rebels had always been internally divided and once the necessary military force was brought to bear they were easily defeated. But it may have alarmed Catherine into dropping reform of serfdom from her agenda. She had remarked to Vyazhemsky that 'if we do not agree to reduce this cruelty and moderate a situation intolerable for human beings, then sooner or later they will do it themselves'. Yet, after 1775, among all her other reforming projects, nothing was done to alleviate serfdom. In the light of Pugachev it is not difficult to see why she, like Frederick II, concluded that, in the circumstances, emancipation was impractical. The difference was that he still thought that some official protection against exploitation should be implemented. She, faced with levels of exploitation that sometimes exceeded those to be found in the west, put her distaste on record but then did nothing.

The amnesty of 1775 marked the beginning of a new round of reforms focused on the modernization of provincial administration. It was a long-term process, still incomplete in 1796. By then the original 25 provinces had increased to 50, and they were sub-divided into nearly 500 districts. The costs of the system, in which the officials were salaried, rose from 1.7 million rubles to 11 million, which reflected the rise in the number of officials from 12,000 to 27,000. The system was based on specialization of function: justice, administration and finance were separated out. The other persistent feature was the provision that the centrally appointed officials work with elected assessors from the localities, so that of the final 27,000 officials, some 10,000 were elected. Further levels were added later: local policing was vested in urban provosts and rural land captains, in each case with elected assessors. Police in the cameralist sense of public welfare and economic development also involved the participation of locally elected boards.

At present the state of research means that it is unclear how the new machinery actually worked.[8] There was a bottleneck in the supply of trained personnel, courses in public law in the university of Moscow were only started up in the 1760s, in the early stages 17 per cent of noble applicants for public service posts were found to be illiterate, and many of the early official staff were supplied by retired army officers. These problems eased with time and the spread of education and there is no doubt that the reforms, for the first time, gave the empire a comprehensive local administrative structure, though it remained true, right through to 1917, that relative to the size of the country and its population, Russia was the most thinly governed of the major powers. The other obvious feature of the system is that the elected elements showed no inclination to contest the ultimate authority of the appointed officials. There seems to have been no interest in power-sharing from below. Participation by elected representatives was just another duty imposed by the autocrat.

The next series of structural reforms came in 1785 with the establishment of formal Estates, with individual legal rights, which of course excluded the peasants. This is probably linked to the concept from

Montesquieu of the erection of 'intermediary authorities' between the ruler and the subjects. The Charter of the Nobility established nobles as a legal corporation. In every district the nobles who owned estates there formed an Assembly and elected a marshal as their presiding officer. They were granted personal rights: to trial by their peers, security for their poperties, exclusive access to certain categories of public appointment, and the exclusive right to own serfs. The legal criteria for being recognized as noble and a clear hierarchy based on heredity and service seniority were prescribed. But it was one of the functions of the marshal and the Assembly to monitor the local registers of recognized nobles. A comparable charter was issued for the urban dwellers. They were ranked purely by the criterion of their capital value, and had an analogous system with an elected provost and a general assembly. They were also given specified individual rights like the right to trial by their peers. A third charter was drafted for the 'free' peasantry, the tenants on the crown estates, with similar provisions for self-administration as an Estate, but this was never implemented. There exist other plans, in draft, for restructuring the central government and even for introducing some participation by elected assessors there, but they too were shelved. If it was the intention that this policy of establishing self-governing Estates should provide the kind of 'intermediary authority' advocated by Montesquieu, it failed. The Estates were vigorous enough in asserting their sectional privileges against other subjects, but against the autocracy they showed no inclination to assert themselves.

The opening of the second Turkish war in 1787 brought domestic reform activity to a halt, and the outbreak of the French Revolution seems to have alarmed the aging ruler, who by 1790 entered a final reactionary phase of the reign. Catherine once told Diderot, in justifying the modest progress being made in implementing his ideals in Russia, that 'what I despair of overthrowing, I undermine'. She may have persuaded herself this was the case, though there is very little hard evidence to substantiate the claim. The idea that the Enlightenment programmes could be implemented in any radical sense in the kind of society existing in late eighteenth-century Russia was simply unreal, and Catherine knew it. She lacked the resource, which her contemporaries in the German lands enjoyed, of a substantial body of professional administrators, commoners and nobles, with a cameralist training in law and administration at university, reinforced by the influence of Pietism, with its ideal of disinterested public service as a way of life. That no doubt has much to do with the quite disproportionate role of the Baltic German nobility in public service in Russia. They were the one section of the tsars' subjects who had been exposed to the German cameralist culture. On the other hand, it is fair to accept that Catherine's reforms, whatever their limitations, undoubtedly did improve the working of government, and certainly sought to improve material conditions in the empire. Catherine's Russia was not obviously seriously backward by comparison with other major European powers. What is clear is that, in the

European power game into which Russia was now fully integrated, her ruler was one of the major players.

The eastward shift in the European power struggle

The general pacification of 1763 inaugurated another quarter-century pause during which there was no general war between the European powers. This had enabled rulers and their ministers to invest time, energy and sometimes considerable funding into domestic reform, which was broadly based on the Enlightenment agenda of material improvements in the lives of the subjects that it was the duty of rulers to promote. It is easy, in the warm glow of approval which the changes tend to elicit in historians, to overlook what the main purpose of the modernizations was to enhance the power of the state relative to other states. The aim was to create a more affluent, better-educated body of subjects, who could pay more taxes and provide more efficient public servants for the civil and military establishments. For the dynastic competition still exerted its murderous imperative over rulers. International relations remained in a Hobbesian state of nature – an endless struggle for power that was ultimately resolved by resort to war. Apart from a few utopian idealists no one, from top to bottom of society, could conceive of an escape from this vicious circle.

The most the working statesmen could conceive of was some measure for moderating the damage that unrestrained warfare inflicted on all the participants. This aspiration had been written into the Treaty of Utrecht. Its proclaimed purpose was 'to confirm the peace and tranquillity of the Christian world through a just equilibrium of power (which is the best and most secure foundation of mutual friendship and lasting agreement in every quarter)'. But against this was the reality, expressed by Montesquieu, that 'the spirit of monarchy is war and aggrandizement'. A commentator in the 1760s concluded: 'in the end everything depends on power'; and another noted: 'The struggle for the balance of power is, in effect, the struggle for power.' It is best summed up by the marquis d'Argensen, a French minister who had seriously sought for a better basis for international relations:

> A state should always be at the ready, like a gentleman living among swashbucklers and quarrellers. Such are the nations of Europe, today more than ever; negotiations are only a continual struggle between men without principles, impudently aggressive and greedy.

The idea expressed at Utrecht was obsolete before it was written, since it derived from an era of two competing super dynasties, Habsburg and Bourbon, around whom the lesser participants could group themselves. The survival of the latter depended on ensuring that neither of the superpowers achieved hegemony. But after 1715 there were not two, but five 'great powers': France, Austria, Britain, Spain and the United Provinces. By 1763 this had been modified: the United Provinces had given up, Spain retained delusions of grandeur but had lost its reality, and in their places had emerged Prussia and Russia. This in itself meant the balance had shifted towards the east. This was then reinforced by the deliberate decision by the French ministry of Choiseul to postpone any continental activity in favour of preparing for the next round of colonial and commercial confrontation with Britain. This meant that apart from some feeble attempts to intervene in Poland, France became a passive onlooker. Further, it knocked all real content out of the Austrian–French alliance, which was still maintained on paper, but in reality ceased to function. Since Great Britain was almost wholly preoccupied with colonial and commercial problems, and was further going through a phase of political instability after 1763, it too became a spectator of European developments. That left three powers, Prussia, Austria and Russia, all seeking a period of domestic reconstruction and avoidance of general war, but each on the watch for any opportunity of territorial gain, and in the name of maintaining the balance of power insisting that any increase of territory by one must be accompanied by equivalent compensation for the others. This guaranteed that no stable balance could be achieved, for since the three main participants were of roughly equal potency, and wanted to avoid war, they could not hope to gain territory from one another. Any accretions would have to be at the expense of their weaker neighbours, and there were two potential victim states that offered rich pickings – Poland and the Ottoman empire, both ex-powers entering into terminal decline. Finally there was the chance card – dynastic accident – that at any moment could create new openings.

The second of Poland's Saxon kings, Augustus III, had proved ideal. Without any urges of his own to change things, he was content to leave his subjects to enjoy their golden liberties while putting himself under Russian protection. He found collaborators in a grouping of noble clans, the Poniatowskis and the Czartoryckis, often referred to as 'the Family'. They had a modernizing agenda, but accepted that neither the internal opposition nor the foreign powers would permit its implementation, and settled for exploiting the patronage that collaboration with Augustus and his Russian patrons could offer. Augustus III died inconveniently in 1763 and offered an opening for Catherine and her minister Panin, who wanted to stabilize the position in northern Europe by developing a group of client states in Poland, Denmark and Sweden. As they saw it, a third Saxon king in Poland would risk making the Polish crown hereditary. Further, they knew Louis XV was interested in reviving the French interest in Poland and supported a Saxon succession. Catherine judged that Russian control could be strengthened by pushing a native candidate, and had just the man in Stanislaus Poniatowski, whom she had known intimately in the past. At this point Frederick saw an opening. The war had taught him that the opponent to fear was Russia, and now, in return for a defensive alliance with Catherine, he joined her in securing the election of Poniatowski. Russian troops were sent in to ensure the election Diet did what was required.

When the new king Stanislaus showed signs of trying to implement a modernization programme, by limiting the use of the veto and strengthening the powers of Poland's central government, Catherine had to remind him and his followers who really ruled there. From 1766, Catherine flashed her enlightened credentials by demanding that Poland establish religious toleration for its Protestant and Orthodox minorities. This touched an essential pillar of Polish identity and there was powerful internal resistance to conceding toleration. The Family organized a Confederation, Russian troops moved in to help, a Diet was called in 1767, and several opposition members were arrested and taken to Russia. The Diet then voted the programme Catherine wanted, established toleration, and made some cosmetic reforms of serfdom, like removing the lord's powers of life and death over recalcitrant serfs, and making it a crime for a nobleman to kill a serf, while reasserting the right of veto over political decisions in the Diet. In return Russia would guarantee the territorial integrity of Poland. This stimulated all the opponents of the Family to form the Confederation of Bar, whose basic programme was to reassert the traditional constitution and end Russian domination. The evidence suggests this was a genuine popular resistance movement, and a guerrilla war was maintained against the Russian occupiers and the collaborators.

The Austrian leaders saw these developments as excluding them from Poland, and extended some military assistance to the Bar Confederacy, while using the insecurity created in the frontier zone as an excuse, in 1769, to seize a slice of Polish territory which they claimed belonged to the kingdom of Hungary. Normally the Russian troops would have crushed the Confederation of Bar, but in 1768 Russia was involved in war with the Ottomans and wanted Poland settled quickly. At this point Frederick suggested a partition, to which, in 1771, Catherine agreed. Maria Theresa and Kaunitz were initially opposed to the idea of partition, since it was clear the other two had most to gain from it, but Kaunitz decided that since he could not stop it without a general war for which he was not ready, Austria should join in and a share-out of the booty was agreed between the three powers. They took about a third of Poland's territory and population: Prussia got West Prussia, creating a land link between East Prussia and Brandenburg; Russia took large areas in Livonia and White Russia, strengthening her western border; Austria took Galicia, her first big territorial gain since the loss of Silesia. In 1773 Russian troops ensured ratification of the partition by a Polish Diet. The three powers then solemnly guaranteed the reduced Polish state and the Bar Confederacy was crushed. Stanislaus accepted his position as a Russian client, working under the supervision of the Russian ambassador Stackelberg as a kind of colonial governor. The squeamish, at the time and later, condemned the partition as a moral outrage, blatant armed robbery. The realists saw it as a major success for realism in international relations. A potential European war, which nobody wanted, was averted. The French government, which retained a sentimental attachment to

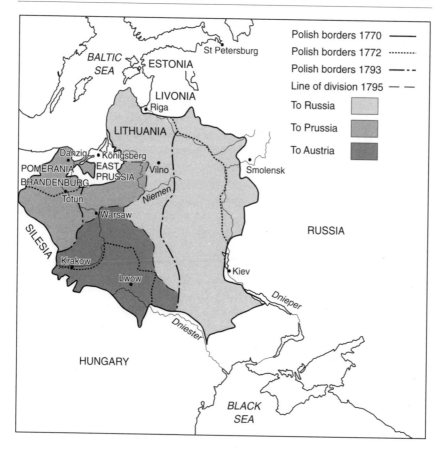

Map 18.2 The partitions of Poland

Poland, recognized that it could not intervene to any good effect, and sensibly decided not to. The partitioners got their loot while maintaining the balance of power and, it could be argued, even Poland gained.

Stackelberg proved a benevolent supervisor and Stanislaus was allowed to develop a modest programme of modernization. At the Diet of 1773 a new executive Council was elected by the two chambers of the Diet, and all the royal acts required its confirmation. This new central executive was granted enhanced tax revenues and powers to limit the influence of the magnate class, who were further restrained, since most had properties in the lost territory, which served as pledges for good behaviour. Naturally the rivals of Poniatowski were looking for openings to weaken his regime, and this needed to be boosted in a Diet and Confederation in 1776, again held under Russian military pressure, which further strengthened the powers of the new executive, particularly over the Polish military establishment. The opposition, who organized themselves as the Patriots, were sufficiently subdued for Stackelberg to agree in 1780 to withdraw most of the Russian occupation force. Under this relatively benign regime, Poland was opened up to the Enlightenment. Stanislaus had made a start in 1765, by allowing the establishment of private printing presses, while also establishing a new Cadet School for the nobility, with a curriculum heavily influenced by the German cameralist ideas. In 1773 the Diet, anticipating the coming suppression of the Jesuits, who remained popular in Poland, established an Educational Commission to take over their assets and apply them to developing a school system based on Enlightenment ideas and using Polish as the language of instruction. This was followed up by the Educational Ordinance of 1783, which envisaged a comprehensive system of national education. A proposed new legal code that would have put restrictions on serfdom was blocked by the conservatives, but torture was abolished, urban self-government reformed and invigorated, free trade established, and a modest economic growth developed.

One reason for Frederick's proposals to partition Poland had been his concern, shared by Kaunitz and Maria Theresa, at Russia's military successes against the Ottomans after 1768. It was the Ottomans who provoked the conflict, but by 1772 Russian forces were established along the Black Sea littoral and the Crimea had been occupied, while in the Balkans the provinces of Moldavia and Wallachia were seized. Catherine declared her intention of keeping her gains, and reinforced this by further military successes in 1773–4. In the Treaty of Kutchuk-Kainardji in 1774, Catherine, still embroiled in the Pugachev rising and pressed by Kaunitz, gave up the Danubian provinces, but retained her new footholds on the Black Sea, while turning the Crimea into an independent Muslim state, which would clearly be a Russian protectorate. Perhaps more important for the future, Russian shipping secured free access to the Black Sea and the right to pass through the Straits into the Mediterranean, and the Ottomans recognized a Russian right of intervention in the Ottoman empire as protector of its Orthodox Christian communities. The gains from the Ottomans, added to the lands gained in the partition, were a substantial boost to Catherine's power and prestige. It was natural for the Habsburgs to look for a balancing compensation, and in the 1770s the Electorate of Bavaria offered a target. The Wittelsbach Elector was aging and childless and died in 1777, leaving as his heir another Wittelsbach Elector, Charles Theodore of the Palatinate. He too had no legitimate children, but did have a considerable illegitimate family whose futures he wished to secure. Here Joseph could help, as Emperor, to place them in suitable sinecure positions in the Empire. In return Charles Theodore signed over nearly a third of Bavaria to the Habsburgs. This was a coup that would represent a significant enhancement of Habsburg power in Germany, and none of the other powers would tolerate it. The French government made it clear that Joseph would get no help from his supposed ally if a war should break out. Frederick was most strongly opposed, and since Russia was an ally, felt free to risk using force.

As the Austrians occupied their acquisitions in Bavaria, the Prussian army attacked Bohemia and the War of the Bavarian Succession was begun. But it failed to develop: Frederick secured no early military success and neither side wanted to try and force the issue. Negotiations for settlement began immediately, since Maria Theresa was determined not to engage in a new war with Frederick and, supported by Kaunitz, who also thought it risky, she opened negotiations for a settlement without informing Joseph, who rather fancied his role as commander-in-chief. It was now a question of finding a face-saving compromise, and France and Russia offered mediation. A peace treaty was concluded at Teschen in May 1779, which gave the Habsburgs a much reduced slice of Bavarian lands, while paying off Frederick with two minor claims he held on territories in the Empire. The episode was an interesting balance between the restless search by rulers to find new pieces of real estate they could claim, and the reluctance of all involved to precipitate a major European war. This was demonstrated by both combatants mobilizing formidable armies and then being careful to avoid a battle.

The next round was influenced by two factors: first, a shift in Catherine's strategic outlook, following the success of the Turkish war. This combined with the declining personal influence of Panin as her adviser and the rise of that of Prince Grigori Potemkin, one of her lovers. Potemkin was an enthusiast for expansion to the south-east, and was made governor of the new lands acquired in 1774, where he instituted a vigorous policy of settlement and development. He sold his enthusiasm to Catherine, who at least entertained prospects that eventually Russian power could be installed in Constantinople itself, and a great Christian empire re-established. The other factor was the death of Maria Theresa in 1780, putting Joseph in full control of policy, except to the extent that the aging Kaunitz remained influential and was usually a restraining factor. Joseph read the disappointing outcome of the Bavarian affair as showing the need for an arrangement with Catherine. In 1781, after a personal meeting between the two, a secret agreement was concluded to support each other's expansionist plans. Catherine got in first by annexing the Crimea in 1783. Now it was Joseph's turn to have a new go at Bavaria. There, Charles Theodore was now installed as Elector, but could be offered an exchange – the Austrian Netherlands. He was willing, but his heir the duke of Zweibrücken objected and was backed in his objections first by the French, and then by Frederick's intervention, his last significant initiative, in organizing a 'League of the Princes' in the Holy Roman Empire, with the aim of blocking any extension of Habsburg power in the Empire. Since Catherine declined to do more than express sympathy, Joseph had to give up on Bavaria in 1785. It was now Catherine's turn again, though her new move against the Ottoman possessions was provoked by them declaring war in 1787, after Catherine, having taken the Crimea, made it very clear she had further plans for expansion at their expense. Joseph hesitated over joining in, as his alliance with her required, but in the end got involved, and after a shaky start the two allies made major gains against the Ottoman forces. On Joseph's death in 1790, his successor Leopold pulled out, leaving Catherine to mop up and secure more Ottoman territory at the peace treaty of Jassy in 1792.

The last act of the old power game, before the French Revolution restructured it, was the final partition of Poland. The settlement of 1772 had satisfied Russia and Austria, and Frederick II, who had designs on Polish lands, but was prepared to wait. When he died in 1786, his successor Frederick William II took up a plan for Prussia to help Poland shake off Russian control by offering to guarantee her continuing independence, in return for which Poland would cede to Prussia the territories that interested her. In 1788 the opportunity appeared to have come. Catherine was now heavily involved in the new war with the Ottomans, and in addition threatened with attack by Gustav III of Sweden, who was looking to win back territories lost to Russia since 1721. Then in 1788 a new Polish Diet met, and also saw an opportunity. Evidence suggests the Diet was driven by an underlying russophobia, which rejected the modest reforms permitted by the Russian protectorate. Some of their leaders had been excited by the successful struggle of the American colonies against Britain, but Prussian encouragement was probably decisive in spurring the Diet to challenge Russian control. In 1789 the Diet voted to abolish the Council of State and proceeded to draft legislation for a modern, hereditary constitutional monarchy, sweeping away the veto and proclaiming basic civil rights for all except the serfs. This emerged as the proposed constitution of May 1791, which generated an outburst of patriotic enthusiasm. The Diet also planned to raise a modern army of 100,000 men.

It seems likely that Catherine would have preferred to keep the arrangements of 1772 in place, but the actions of the Diet had clearly made this impossible. In May 1792, Catherine organised a Confederation of collaborationist magnates against the new constitution. This Confederation of Targowica appealed for help, and Russian troops invaded and quickly defeated the Polish forces. Stanislaus, who had been active in promoting the new constitution, offered his capitulation in July 1792. Catherine hesitated some months before deciding to accept a proposal from Prussia for a second partition. This was implemented during 1793, when a new Polish Diet was compelled to accept the reduction of Poland to a rump state of 4 million inhabitants, with Prussia and Russia dividing up the remainder. Further, the Diet voted to restore the old political order and accepted a treaty re-establishing the Russian protectorate. This settlement might have endured longer, but for the reaction of the Polish Patriots, led by Kosciuzko, who organized a national rebellion in the spring of 1794. It took until the end of the year for the Russian and Prussian forces to defeat the rebels, but it sealed the fate of Poland. In 1795 the three powers, for Austria now came back in to claim a share, agreed to put an end to the independent Polish state. It was a logical final solution. It is also the ultimate monument to the realities of the European power game. It was self-sustaining and endless. Once Poland was gone, the surviving players would seek new victims to devour.[9]

Enlightened absolutism in Scandinavia

The Danish absolute monarchy was a victim of dynastic accident. King Christian VI, who reigned from 1766 to 1808, was mentally ill and incapable of ruling, though the situation was partially alleviated after 1784 when the crown prince Frederick was made co-regent. The central issue of reform in Denmark was necessarily agrarian. The prevailing quasi-feudal regime developed after 1680 tied the tenant farmers closely to their landlords, in respect of military service obligations, taxation and labour services. By the 1750s there were signs that enlightenment ideas were causing some members of the ruling landlord class and the state bureaucracy to regard this system as increasingly obsolete, and from 1757 a government Land Commission began consideration of reform. This was the background to the brief burst of absolutist reform activity by the royal favourite J. F. Struensee. For two years from 1770 to 1772 he anticipated all the mistakes of Joseph II in driving through reform programmes without consultation or consent. The royal government ordered radical reductions in labour services and embarked on a series of Enlightenment policies. It is usually claimed that the relaxation of censorship was Struensee's undoing, for he was personally unpopular, aggressively Germanic and contemptuous of Danish tradition, and notoriously owed his position to being the lover of the queen. In 1772 a coup at court secured his dismissal, and much of his proposed reform programme was halted or reversed.

If Struensee exemplified the wrong way of implementing enlightened reform within the parameters of an absolute monarchy, the second period of reform, after the court coup which established the regency in 1784, was a model of how caution and moderation could produce lasting results. A team of noble reform ministers led by A. P. Bernstorff, effectively first minister until 1797, and Christian Reventlow, presided over an era of piecemeal reform, often based on local experiments. The basic emancipation of tenants was first tried out on crown estates, and showed that secure, hereditary tenure was more practicable than creating peasant freeholds. Reventlow's aim was:

> To make these peasants an example ... for their brethren to follow and to make the formerly unappreciated Estate of the peasants into a hard-working, happy and upright people, from whose prosperity all other Estates will blossom, and on whose loyalty and courage the king can rely as fully as on the most secure defence.

The government waited until 1786 when a new Agrarian Commission set to work, and in 1788 a decree abolished the old conscription system that had tied the peasant to his estate. After this breakthrough the regime gradually pressed further emancipatory measures over time, avoiding the build-up of collective protest from landlords. Landlords and tenants were encouraged to negotiate new forms of tenure and credit banks were established to enable tenants to buy out onerous services and dues. The process was also eased because in effect it emancipated a peasant elite; the rural poor – the cottagers and labourers – may well have found their meagre securities undermined by it. At the same time, other enlightened reforms were promoted, religious toleration widened, free trading established and guilds restricted, and a primary schooling system and a new poor relief regime introduced. The Danish reforms were an example of how a resolutely absolutist regime, proceeding circumspectly and supported by the slow spread of Enlightenment thought among the elites, could achieve lasting improvements without threatening the basic stability of the society.[10]

Developments in neighbouring Sweden started from a different base: the system of Estates' sovereignty, combined with a purely symbolic royal power still prevailed down to 1772. The four Estates represented privileged minorities in society, which excluded the majority of the population. All the Estates had a restrictive attitude to membership and fiercely defended their exclusivity. On the other hand, Swedish society was becoming more integrated into the common European culture and Enlightenment ideas were spreading. The long Hat dominance of the Estates was brought down by the failed intervention of Sweden against Prussia in the European war. It left a legacy of mounting public debt and raging inflation of the unsecured paper currency used to finance the war. In 1765, the Caps, who had identified themselves as a reform party heavily subsidized by Anglo-Russian funding, swept to control of the Diet. After purging the Council and the administration, they did enact reforms, the most important of them being the abolition of censorship, and opening up a wide-ranging public debate. At its heart were the demands of the commoner Estates for the limitation of noble privileges, above all their reserved right to occupy most of the higher and more prestigious public appointments. The nobility put up an impassioned defence and, as the Diet was increasingly deadlocked by the controversies, the commoner Estates insisted that if necessary a majority of the Estates could overrule the objections of one dissenting Estate.

In 1769 the Hat leaders among the nobility approached the king for support in forcing new elections, for the Cap regime had forfeited much of its popular support by its deflationary policies, which were causing widespread discontent in the community. The bargain was that, if successful, a Hat government would agree to an extension of the crown's authority. The tactic was for the king to go on strike and refuse to sign any documents. When the Cap Council tried to bypass this by using a name stamp, the senior civil servants in turn declined to accept unsigned documents as valid. This succeeded in producing a new Hat regime, but its leaders, once in power, went back on their assurances to the king. Instead the former social strife was renewed. Then in 1771 the king died, to be succeeded by his son Gustav III.

Gustav had all the qualifications for Enlightenment monarchy. He had been brought up on enlightened principles, was particularly influenced by de la Rivière's *L'ordre naturel et essentiel des sociétés politiques* and was familiar with the writings of Bolingbroke's *Patriot King*, both of which recommend a strong king ruling in the common interest. Gustav had been in France at the time of his accession, looking for French subsidies to sustain a royalist coup that he already had in mind. He declared in his first speech to the Diet:

> Born and educated among you I have from my earliest youth learned to love my country ... My utmost wish is to rule over a happy people; the height of my ambition to guide the steps of a free nation ... You have it in your power to be the most fortunate people in the world.

The king's subsequent efforts to mediate between the commoners and the nobility to secure an agreed accession charter failed and in the summer of 1772 the king organized a coup in Stockholm, supported by the guards' officers, and imposed a new constitution on the Diet. This provided for a stronger, but constitutional kingship; the Diet kept its rights over taxation and legislation, but would now meet when summoned by the king, who would also appoint the Speakers of the Estates. The Council was no longer elected by the Diet but appointed by the king. The most striking feature of this monarchist coup was the total absence of resistance to it. The events took place against the background of the worst subsistence crisis in Sweden for decades, while the Diet stood paralysed by factional disputes over Estates' privileges. It is clear that to a wide public they appeared irresponsible and self-seeking, while the king was creating a plausible image as dedicated to reform policies that would rise above faction. He was allowed to make an attempt to demonstrate what enlightened absolutism could do for the whole community.

The new regime did launch a programme of enlightenment reforms. There were measures to help the peasantry to acquire the freehold of their farms, currency reform to produce a stable silver currency, the freeing of internal trade and reduction of guild restrictions, law reform, the abolition of torture, religious toleration for Protestants, admission of the Jews, reform of the administration to eliminate sinecures and corrupt practices, and the strengthening of the armed forces. This seemed to be in the spirit of what the king proclaimed in 1772, yet at the same time there were negative manifestations. The most serious was in 1774, when Gustav re-introduced strict censorship of the press. At his first Diet in 1786 he was surprised and angered by the opposition expressed there. He had been looking for approval of his achievements and proposed measures to increase the royal powers and the revenue but found both commoners and nobility united in opposing them.

Gustav was losing his Enlightenment enthusiasm and looked to foreign policy for the kind of success that would enhance his position. He was frustrated by the growing power of Russia in the Baltic, and discovered that his French patrons could do little to help him. When Russia became embroiled in the second Turkish war in 1787, Gustav resolved to try on his own, with a military strike against St Petersburg while Russian forces were engaged against the Ottomans. This proved dangerously unpopular among some of the nobility, particularly in Finland, where dissident nobles conspired to seize control and offered to put the province under Russian protection. At a meeting at Anjala, they issued a manifesto denouncing Gustav's regime as tyrannical.[11] The proposed land and sea attack on St Petersburg was blocked by the strength of the Russian defence and the war became deadlocked. In order to stabilize his authority, Gustav summoned the Diet in 1789 with a new set of radical programmes. The king had been soliciting the support of the commoner Estates by proposals for enlarging their rights at the expense of the nobility and won their support for the Act of Union and Safety, which greatly extended the royal powers. Although acceptable to the commoners, it was bitterly resisted by the nobles, even after the arrest of some of their spokesmen. Finally the king declared that the consent of three Estates sufficed to approve the legislation, and the new constitution was carried. A new royal absolutism had been established. After this the commoners got their rewards. The public service was now made open to commoners on equal terms with nobles, and advancement was to be based on merit, while commoners were entitled to purchase types of property previously reserved to the nobility. This internal success was, however, offset by the failure of the Russian war, which was concluded in 1790 on the basis of the status quo. Domestically that left Gustav with a legacy of debt and financial disorder, but how he would have developed his policies is unknown, for in 1792 a group of dissident nobles successfully plotted his assassination.

In some respects Gustav III did act out the role of the enlightened despot in the way that some Enlightenment thinkers had recommended. But he also dramatized the dangers underlying the concept. The king's indulgence of his personal longings for military glory and international reputation diverted him from the consistent pursuit and consolidation of his domestic projects. At the end he seemed to have found a winning formula in his brand of royalist populism, but then learned the hard way that government under the *ancien régime* needed at all times, if not the enthusiastic support, at least the general acquiescence of the noble landlords and military elites. Their grip on the fundamentals of social power and control could be weakened, but not in the end disregarded, except at a heavy price.

19

Alternative Models

The deviant line of development in the eighteenth-century United Provinces is linked to their experience of economic decline. There is some difference of opinion over the extent of the decline, and general agreement that it was not universal.[1] But agriculture picked up again after 1750 and rents and land values held up. It is probable that the decline in shipping was relative to the growth elsewhere rather than absolute. A diminished Baltic trade survived and a growing colonial trade flourished. Finally the United Provinces remained the second-largest banking and financial services provider in Europe. In general the regent class, largely *rentier* in this period, remained affluent.

But it may be that the precise extent of the economic decline was not the important point. The radical Patriot movement which emerged was based on a perception that their society overall was degenerating. A recent commentator, S. Schama, has suggested: 'Their express sense of decline, especially in those departments of the economy that the Dutch had long assumed to be their forte, surely contributed to the sharpening of disquiet which in due course grew into rebellion.'

The history of the Enlightenment in the United Provinces is distinctively different from other parts of Europe. The United Provinces should have provided a favourable environment, for the Dutch were not only the most literate society in Europe, but were still the centre of the European publishing industry. Yet although the works of the *philosophes* were printed there, they do not seem to have had the expected impact on Dutch thinking. The Dutch made a major contribution to European intellectual life, but concentrated on research into the natural sciences, where they led in the movement away from Cartesian science to Newtonian science. What was lacking was the sceptical attitude to religion and tradition that characterized the thinking of the *philosophes*. In matters like Deism and natural religion, the Dutch tended to be conservative. Broadly speaking, Dutch thinking retained its religious dimension after the mainstream Enlightenment had moved away from the concept of a world ruled by God's providence. It gave a special aspect to the Dutch approach to reform. Where the Enlightenment sought to improve society by rational analysis and the rejection of superstition and tradition, the Dutch tended to see reform as the recovery of a lost past. They wanted to recreate the conditions that had made the republic great, which they felt had been lost through moral decline. Dutch society did not want to modernize.

The possibility of renewal became real during the later stages of the War of the Austrian Succession, when the United Provinces were invaded by French troops and their relative military impotence was exposed. The invasion, which was never a serious threat, created political panic, and tradition was followed in turning to the prince of Orange, as stadholder, to save the republic. Spontaneous Orangeist populist movements, encouraged by the British, threatened the regents. In the outcome the prince of Orange, William IV, was invested with the office of stadholder in all seven provinces, something none of his predecessors had achieved. The Orangeist mobs had a programme of establishing popular militias, which would hold the administration of the regent oligarchs to account. Yet William declined to promote the movement in order to reinforce his own authority on a partisan basis. On the contrary, he exercised a moderating influence, preferring to negotiate with the regent oligarchs, to establish compromises and avoid any radical purging of urban administrations. This was particularly evident in Amsterdam, Haarlem and Leiden, where the stadholder sent in federal troops to restrain Orangeist excess, and ensure that the reform of their governments stopped short of a radical purge. He concentrated on installing his own local political agents in the localities and using his powers of patronage to build up his local control. William had been offered the opportunity to act as a reformer on Enlightenment lines and had deliberately declined to do so. When he died in 1751, his heir was a child and did not come of age until 1766. During this period the regents were able to recover some of the power they had lost in the crisis. By 1753 they had full control in Amsterdam and were powerful enough to keep the United Provinces neutral in 1756, when the regent for the young William V, a Hanoverian princess, would have wished to intervene in support of Britain.

It was perhaps more important that in the 1750s a wide-ranging public debate began in the republic about how to recover its lost power and prosperity. This was aided by the growth of political clubs and societies and a major increase in the number and variety of political books and journals being circulated. Both Orangeists and Republicans sought ideological arguments to justify their positions. The outcome was the political education of the literate and the educated. William V proved to be an ineffective political leader, though his Prussian wife tried to encourage him to assert his authority. He tended to maintain a conciliatory line, and sought to work with the regents, but it proved impossible to agree on a programme to reinvigorate the army and navy. The province of Holland was unwilling to sanction spending on the army, the inland provinces took the same attitude to naval expenditure. This was a dangerous policy of drift against a background of spreading politicization in the community. It was largely an urban phenomenon, and involved the political awakening of the small urban property-owners, tradesmen and professional people, led by reform-minded members of the urban elites. They called for a return to society's moral roots in religion and the broadening of citizen participation in government, making the regent oligarchs answerable for their administration, but this went along with a basic conservatism and localism. There was little inclination to modernize the institutional structure of the union, or to restrain its devolved federalism by strengthening the central authority.

The crisis broke because of the American war. Public opinion was strongly in favour of the rebel colonists, and indeed the Dutch economy did well as a neutral power with the capacity, through its Caribbean colonies and extensive shipping, to run a contraband trade in arms and other supplies to the colonists. The popular movement was also stimulated by the political debate launched by the American Revolution, and the American example of popular resistance headed by self-governing people's militias was especially relevant to Dutch experience. In the end, in 1680, the British government decided to end the blockade-running by declaring war on the United Provinces. This exposed their failure to maintain the armed forces and the war brought a British blockade of commerce, with heavy losses of trade and shipping and a string of military disasters. An increasingly vocal public opinion, now calling itself the Patriot movement, blamed the stadholder and the Orangeists for the disaster. The rich and extensive polemical literature of the period maintained the themes of the earlier debates. All sides based their arguments historically on Dutch experience and their remedies were restoration-oriented.

The most influential exposition of the Patriot cause was published during the war by Baron van de Capellen, entitled *Aan het volk van Nederland*. The main argument was historical: the true liberty of the people had been usurped in 1581 at the original establishment of the union, and power had been vested in the regents supported by the stadholders. The popular institutions of local authority, the town militias and the guilds, had lost their rights to be consulted. Citing the American example, the baron called for the formation of popular militias to take back the lost liberties. These were to be controlled by citizens' councils, independent of the town regents, and would elect their own officers.

In 1784, new-style urban militias, calling themselves 'Free Corps', began to form spontaneously. The centre of the movement was Utrecht, where a national Convention of Free Corps was assembled. Their political programme was based on the aspirations of lesser urban property-owners: there was to be an end to all religious discriminations and sectional privilege. The urban corporations would be reformed, and entry to the corporations was to be open to all citizens, with advancement on merit alone. In 1785 a further convention adopted an 'Act of Association' which bound the movement to restore a true republican constitution for the United Provinces. In face of mass street demonstrations and petitions, the regents of Utrecht agreed to cooperate. As the movement spread, supporters of the stadholder tried to organize resistance. William V was stirred to action by the obvious political challenge to his authority, and by the encouragement and funding offered by the ambassadors of Britain and Prussia. In the key province of Holland, the Patriots seized control during 1785–6 against strong Orangeist resistance. They controlled the Holland States and forcibly suppressed Orangeist activity. After disorders in the capital, the Hague, the Holland States took control of the city and the stadholder left. In the same period the Patriots took control of the province of Overijssel. At this stage the regent oligarchs in Holland and Utrecht began to see the Patriots as a threat and turned to the stadholder for support. During 1787 the Patriots drove them out of Amsterdam and Rotterdam, and their leaders considered summoning a National Assembly, seeking French support for their cause.

The stadholder made his first counter-attack by sending troops to secure the province of Gelderland. By this point, the States General could no longer function and the country faced civil war. It was probably the action of the Patriots in arresting the wife of the stadholder in 1787 that outraged the sense of the royal dignity of the new Prussian king, Frederick William II. Prussian troops invaded the United Provinces and the Patriot movement collapsed. Their militias were not inclined to risk fighting Prussian regular soldiers and the Patriot leaders fled, to re-emerge later as clients of the French Revolution. William V was obviously presented with another opportunity for the strengthening of the central government. He did not take it, preferring to reinstate the traditional system of working with the regent oligarchs.

It is tempting to see the events in the United Provinces as some kind of overture to the French Revolution.[2] Yet the evidence suggests that the Patriots were not, and had never been, revolutionary. They did not want to destroy the system of elite control that governed their society, as it did all other contemporary societies. They wanted to be admitted to a share in it. The Patriot movement does show that economic and social developments in later eighteenth-century Europe, particularly the relaxation of censorship, the spread of education and literacy, and the activity of all kinds of voluntary societies geared to the aim of social betterment, were politicizing a wider section of the property-owning classes. They now wanted to be included in the ruling circle, but that meant admission to the existing power structures, not their replacement. The Patriots had more in common with the contemporary British radical critics of the political system than they did with the future French revolutionaries. The Patriot collapse before the Prussian intervention, after years of demonstrating their supposed political muscle in street brawls and mass demonstrations, showed they lacked the capacity or the will to fight for what they wanted. This all suggests that the revolutionary threat to the established order of society, despite what happened in France, was really lacking in substance. The nobles, urban oligarchs and legal corporations were still in firm control of their world. A contemporary commentator on the Dutch disturbances, the marquis de Reyneval, remarked:

> In order to emerge from their state of nullity, the bourgeois are asking to take part in government ... the result of this new order of things is as simple as it is certain. The bourgeois, once having become something in the political order will emerge from their apathy and at the same time force the populace to return to the most absolute insignificance.

The Prussian dispersal of the Dutch radicals in 1787 demonstrated, with comparatively little bloodshed, what Napoleon Bonaparte realized in revolutionary Paris a few years later – that any amount of radical rhetoric, sloganising and popular demonstrating can be swiftly dispersed by a timely 'whiff of grapeshot'.[3]

Britain and her empire after 1763

After 1763 it is likely that Great Britain, with Ireland and the colonies, was the most powerful state in Europe, or indeed in the world. This was because it was structured differently from the great continental monarchies. Like all early modern societies it was highly devolved and most government was local government. The authorities that affected the daily lives of the people, that enforced the laws and settled their disputes, were the lords lieutenant and the justices of the peace in the counties, and the urban corporations. They were largely self-appointed and above all wholly self-financed. The difference from the continental monarchies showed at the level of central government. The British governments were appointed by and answerable to the king, but could only function with the consent of the two Houses of Parliament which controlled taxation and to a degree expenditure, and had, through statute, the exclusive power to legislate. Thus participatory government – power-sharing – was the basis of the British system. Behind this were two further levels of difference. First Britain was a money power, and the money was primarily generated through trade and commerce. Governments were run by great aristocratic landlords since ministries were almost wholly recruited from the peerage, but this political hegemony of the landlords, replicated at lower levels by the control of the localities by gentleman JPs, disguised the existence of the money power. Wars were financed by borrowing to a much greater extent than taxation. In 1758 a consortium of 22 City financiers could readily contract to raise £8 million for the year's war expenditure. This was possible because Britain had a viable system of public finance centralized in the Treasury, a reasonably professional and uncorrupt fiscal bureaucracy particularly in the excise service, and taxes secured on parliamentary consent. The revenue from the taxes could not pay for more than about a third of the costs of war, but its reliability could assure subscribers to government loans that the interest would be promptly paid in full. Uniquely in Europe, the British governments did not have to worry about a possible state bankruptcy, and they could maintain the world's biggest navy and hire soldiers with a freedom denied to their rivals. But perhaps the best evidence of the power of money was the consistency with which the Whig landlord oligarchs made the protection and furtherance of commerce the basis of their public policies.

The second factor was an unusually high degree of participation by a politicized public opinion. There had been no effective press censorship since 1700. Governments could still try to restrain hostile authors and publishers by using the laws on seditious libel, but these had little effect. The result was the massive expansion of newspapers, daily and weekly, central and local, periodicals, books and pamphlets. These were available on subscription and through the growing availability of bookshops, reading rooms and libraries, and increasing numbers of clubs and societies were devoted to spreading knowledge and discussing public issues. These appeared on the continent too, though Britain with its higher literacy rates probably led, mostly because in Britain there were openings for the legal participation of the common people in public affairs. Here parliamentary elections and by-elections were important. Although most people had no vote, that mattered less because most elections were uncontested. A local election was a community affair, fuelled by the hospitality provided by candidates, where local views could be freely expressed: public opinion mattered. Despite the bizarre electoral system, there were enough open constituencies where voters had to be wooed to make a difference to the outcome of a general election.[4] In addition to this there was in Britain relative freedom to petition parliament and to engage in street demonstrations, some connected to established celebrations, like 5 November, others organized when some urgent public issue aroused mass reaction. Public opinion was not only manifested in opposition to government; there was activity in support of policies that represented a national consensus.

Historians have identified the growth and consolidation of a national identity as politicization seeped down beyond the ruling elites, resting on the two basic emotions, anti-popery and patriotic imperialism, with the Bourbon powers identified as the enemies of Britain's commercial and colonial primacy. This public opinion could be an embarrassment for governments, for it could be exploited by charismatic politicians like the elder William Pitt, in the war of 1756, as the popular spokesman for an aggressive imperial policy. Britain's emerging primacy grew out of the advanced condition of her economy, which produced the wealth that underwrote it. From mid-century, when population began to rise, followed by rising agricultural prices, Britain was in a phase of rapid economic growth. There was a slow-down after 1763, but the growth resumed and after the mid-1780s soared ahead. Distinctive features of this were the level of urbanization, rising to 20 per cent towards the end of the period, and the rise in agricultural productivity following the enclosure movement, which was based on parliamentary

Enclosure Acts. This affected about a fifth of the cultivated land and reflected a major capital investment in an increasingly commercialized agriculture. By 1789, nearly half the working population was employed outside agriculture. This did not mean that the industrial revolution had arrived, for factory production and machine power were only really developing after 1790, but it did signify the growth of 'proto-industrial' developments[5] that arose from rising domestic consumer demand and the flourishing export trades both to Europe and the colonies. There is also the significant evidence of investment in infrastructure: the growth of turnpike trusts to build a better road network – these too based on parliamentary bill procedures – and from the 1770s the rapid development of the canal system. There was public investment in urban improvements, drainage, paving and lighting of streets and the provision of civic amenities like parks and assembly rooms. All this reflected an economy whose consumers had money to spend.

There was for a long time a tradition that the young George III came to the throne in 1760 with a political project to change the constitutional balance in favour of a stronger monarchy. The ideas are said to have come through his tutor, and then closest political adviser, the Scottish earl of Bute. The reality seems to be that the king and Bute did believe that, since 1714, the traditional leadership of the monarch in government had been usurped by the Whig government and parliament. Bute may have wished to regain the right of a king to choose his ministers and to be properly consulted by them over the direction of policy. There is no evidence that they planned to subvert the independence of the House of Commons by the improper use of royal patronage. In 1760 a very strong ministry was in office, with Pitt coordinating the running of the war with great success, and the duke of Newcastle competently managing war finance and parliament. The king certainly had the impression that he was being disregarded by both men.

George III was the first sovereign since Queen Anne who was born and educated in Britain, and he was quite uninterested in his Hanoverian Electorate. He aspired to end party domination of government by rebuilding a patriotic consensus around his own person. At the new court a few Tories were admitted to office, and gradually the exclusion of known Tories from official positions was ended. This came at a time when the old party system was collapsing. With the death of Jacobitism and the advent of a native monarch, followed by the admission of Tories into government, the Tory party withered away. The Tory traditions did not, but those who still took them seriously tended to merge into the Country opposition with dissident Whig groups. This process then impacted on the Whig party, which, in the absence of an opponent, began to break up into competing factions, grouped round the leading magnates. There has been controversy over the basis of this political system since Namier's radical revisionism. That suggested a period in which politics was an ongoing struggle over patronage and place, and that party and ideological politics went into abeyance; in recent years, party politics has made a comeback as an interpretation.

The reality was that a working administration had to be appointed by the king, but could only function if assured of enough support in the House of Commons to carry its budget and its legislative projects. At the core of any voting majority had been a block of MPs and peers who would support any government approved by the king – the Court party or king's men, about 150 in the Commons. They were held together by patronage and had no partisan commitment. At the other extreme were a block of independent members of parliament, the Country opposition, perhaps around 100 MPs, whose support could be solicited on particular issues but not relied on. In a House of over 500 members, a majority had to be constructed by adding to the Court party enough of the factions into which the old Whig oligarchy had split. The resignation of Pitt in 1761 gave the king the chance to introduce Bute into the government and in 1762, when the main Whig faction led by Newcastle voted against the proposed peace terms, they were dismissed. The king and Bute took the opportunity offered for a major purge of Whigs and their clients from their public positions. It may have been the intention that Bute, with the full support of the king, would construct a non-party administration, strengthened by a redistribution of patronage. If so, Bute proved unequal to the task: as a royal favourite and a Scot he was an outsider and in less than a year retired from government to a post in the royal entourage. This enabled the opposition to assert that Bute was secretly controlling government from the court, and that there was an intention of subverting the independence of parliament by improper use of patronage.

The king found a new leader in George Grenville, an able administrator and good House of Commons manager. But Grenville complained of the continued influence of Bute over the king, and demanded that the king should take advice only from his ministers. In 1765 the king tried to escape Grenville's bullying over this and asked Newcastle to form a government. Newcastle died the same year and leadership of his Whigs passed to the marquis of Rockingham. Rockingham renewed Granville's complaints that the king was taking advice from Bute and, with more justification, that the court was not using its influence to ensure that the Court party in parliament voted with the ministry. In mid-1766 Rockingham resigned and the king turned to Pitt, who offered to form a non-party administration and restore political consensus. The attempt failed disastrously. Pitt refused to become First Lord of the Treasury, which went to the duke of Grafton; Pitt himself became Lord Privy Seal and made the further mistake of taking a peerage as earl of Chatham and going to the Lords. On top of that his health broke down and the grand design of constructing a broad-based non-party government collapsed. The administration staggered along, partly because the opposition remained divided. Rockingham went into opposition but could not hold his faction together and by the next election in 1768 his group had shrunk to 57 MPs. In that year Chatham resigned and went into opposition with his small personal following.

The governmental instability of the 1760s was the result of the break-up of party politics combined with the ambitions of a king who lacked the charisma or political skills to be his own political manager, and by the personal collapse of Chatham. The damage to governmental authority and credibility was illustrated by a novel outbreak of populist radicalism that rocked the weak administrations of the period. There was an established Tory populist tradition of seeking to break the Whig monopoly of power by demanding greater responsibility of the House of Commons to the electorate.[6] In 1763 an obscure MP, John Wilkes, had set out to boost his fortunes by political journalism. He realized the unpopularity of Lord Bute and in his paper, the *North Briton*, launched a demagogic campaign against Scots in general and their alleged sinister influence at court in particular. In 1763, in issue no. 45, his paper suggested that the king himself was conspiring against his ministers. This went too far, and the Grenville ministry issued a general warrant for the apprehension of the perpetrators, which led to Wilkes' arrest by ministerial order. Wilkes fought back in the courts and won, obtaining a legal ruling that general warrants were 'unconstitutional, illegal and absolutely void'. Wilkes became a popular hero, a symbolic protest against the prevailing oligarchy. However the ministry launched further charges in the House of Commons and Wilkes fled to the continent.

There was a pause until the election of 1768 when Wilkes returned and successfully fought Middlesex, a London constituency with a large popular electorate. He won but was expelled by the Commons and re-arrested, causing some popular rioting in London, then stood again at the by-election, won again and was again expelled. The process was repeated and this time the Commons declared his defeated opponent elected for the seat. His cause became a popular movement, political societies were formed in his support, and he went on to publicize a string of radical causes, including the freedom of the American colonies, full religious toleration and parliamentary reform. A new wave of populist politics developed, with badges and cockades displayed at public meetings and processions in support of his various causes. The practical outcome was limited. The authority of the oligarchy had been publicly defied, Wilkes went on to become lord mayor of London, and in 1774 he got back into parliament. He was left unchallenged and both general warrants and the Middlesex election proceedings were formally annulled, while in the 1774 election a handful of radical MPs were returned. The Wilkite agitations drew support from the small tradesmen and artisans. They never solidified into a coherent political movement that threatened the establishment, once political stability returned after 1770. There was a growing political awareness and even some demand to be included in the process of consultation among the petty property-holders, but as yet they were content with demonstrating within the existing system.

A more serious development of the 1760s was the conscious adoption by the Rockingham Whigs of an ideology of party and their assertion of the legitimacy of loyal opposition. Their reduction to a rump of 57 MPs must have stimulated the desire to go beyond waging guerrilla war in the House of Commons over issues like Wilkes and the Middlesex elections. In 1767, Rockingham hired Edmund Burke as his political secretary, and Burke entered parliament next year. Burke was a gifted politician, orator and polemicist and he gave the Rockinghams an ideology, notably in his pamphlet *Thoughts on the Present Discontents* of 1770. This alleged that constitutional liberties, and especially the integrity of parliament, were under threat from 'secret influence', generated by the court's abuse of patronage. It outlined a reform programme, 'economical reform', to cut back the network of sinecures, pensions and favours that were undermining the independence of MPs. Burke argued that it was the duty of publicly minded subjects to organize as a party to educate and lead public opinion in support of their agreed programme. After 1766, the Rockinghams developed a party organization, with a London headquarters, the appointment of provincial agents and their own newspapers – the best known the *Annual Register* – and a continuous critique of government policy was maintained. The Rockinghams were a party, and not a faction, because they were pledged to act together on their declared principles, and agreed only to enter government as a party, with their leader as First Lord of the Treasury, and with full control of public appointments, though they did not rule out the possibility of coalitions.

The Rockinghams had some years to wait before reaching their goal of forming a government and implementing their programmes. For after 1768 George III at last found a political manager who was sympathetic with his views and prepared to work with him, yet was also a skilled House of Commons politician and political tactician. Lord North had entered the government as Chancellor of the Exchequer in 1767. In 1770, when the duke of Grafton retired, North became First Lord and led his ministry for the next 12 years. His relation with the king was one of trust, so that the king was willing to leave North and his colleagues to carry on the business of government without interference. From the beginning he was helped by the dissidence among the opposition. The Rockinghams and Chatham failed to work together, and as the government stabilized there was an erosion of the opposition as career politicians joined the government ranks. North was flexible enough to ride occasional parliamentary defeats, and after a successful general election in 1774 looked impregnable. In addition he ran a competent administration, which managed to maintain modest budget surpluses and in 1773 made a start on reducing the debt. He seemed to have inaugurated an era of political stability until he stumbled over the problems of the American colonies.

This became an issue in domestic politics after 1763. Prior to that British colonial policy had been confined to promoting and regulating trade between the colonies and the mother country, and defending them against threats from the Bourbon powers. The Caribbean plantation colonies and the 13 mainland colonies had been left to develop their own institutions, but the basic pattern was a royal governor appointed from London working with an elected colonial assembly, which claimed rights comparable with those of parliament over taxation and legislation. Since the legislatures determined and paid the salaries of the local officials and maintained their own militias for local defence, they were in effective in control of the local administration. Imperial legislation, like the Molasses Act of 1733, intended to stop the colonies trading with the French sugar islands, was simply unenforceable. It was the Seven Years War that had first brought to the notice of the British government what they regarded as the insolence and non-cooperation of the colonial governments. Further they were acutely aware that the national debt had doubled because of the war, and intended that in future the colonies should contribute to the costs of imperial defence. They took it as axiomatic that the British parliament had full powers to legislate and tax in the colonies, as it did in all parts of the king's dominions.

The new activist imperial policy was first revealed in the arrangements for Canada, with its 80,000 French Catholic settlers. It was given a provisional regime retaining its French institutions and separating it from the other colonies. Further, its boundaries were enlarged southwards to the Ohio river, and lands between the Great Lakes and the Ohio were kept for the native Indians and closed to settlement. This policy was extended by the establishment of the Allegheny mountains as the western boundary of settlement, again to appease the Indians who had mounted a dangerous general uprising against settlements in 1763. These arbitrary restrictions were resented and disregarded by the colonists. Then Grenville introduced a series of Acts to tighten imperial control and make the colonists contribute to the expenses of administration. The Sugar Act of 1764 was designed to set up a local customs administration capable of enforcing the rules of the Navigation Acts. The Quartering Act obliged the colonies to meet the costs of billeting the British garrison troops. Finally the Stamp Act of 1765 imposed an imperial tax on the colonists, intended to provide an independent revenue. The force of the colonial reaction took the British government by surprise. Nine colonies sent representatives to a congress to coordinate resistance. The basic principle urged by the colonies was their claimed basic right as English subjects to 'no taxation without representation'. Their protests were reinforced by a call to boycott British imports, which was enforced by local direct action and intimidation of officials.

In Britain there were those, led by the king and Grenville, prepared to resort to force, but public opinion and the Rockingham ministry, shaken by the success of the boycotts, decided on conciliation. The Stamp Act and the Sugar Act were repealed, though to save face the ministry passed a Declaratory Act, asserting that the British parliament did have the right to tax and legislate for the colonies. Chatham's Chancellor of the Exchequer, Townshend, made a new approach in 1777, by levying customs duties on imports into the colonies and specifying that the revenue would go to funding the salaries of the imperial administration. It was also intended to provide strengthened enforcement measures against unlawful colonial trading. This renewed the colonial protests, there was direct action by the colonists, and British troops were sent to maintain order, since the colonial authorities declined to do so. This in turn led to a new trade boycott and once more the British backed away from confrontation. By 1770 the offensive measures were repealed, except for the duty on tea, retained as an assertion of parliament's sovereign power in the colonies. This was enough to keep the colonial protest movement alive, with the colony of Massachusetts and its capital Boston the organizing centre of activism. It was there that in 1773 the local patriots seized a cargo of tea in the harbour and dumped it in the water.

The North ministry decided on firm action to restore imperial authority. Up to then there had been vigorous public debate on the issues on both sides of the Atlantic, and the Rockingham Whigs had come out for conciliation, but the Boston Tea Party swung opinion in Britain behind North's measures. In 1774 a series of Acts closed the port of Boston, proposed to alter the terms of the Massachusetts Charter, allowed some offences in Massachusetts to be tried outside the colony to avoid recalcitrant local juries, and enforced local payment of the costs of a British garrison. At the same time the offensive settlement of the Canadian government was finalized in a statute. The attempt to isolate Massachusetts and crush the resistance at source proved a mistake. It stimulated a broad protest and resistance movement through all the colonies, whose representatives met in a Continental Congress in 1774. The Congress authorized a general boycott of British trade, established committees in each colony to enforce it, demanded the repeal of the measures against Massachusetts and laid down conditions for a definitive settlement that amounted to autonomy for the colonies under the nominal sovereignty of the British crown. The British government now sought a compromise, while stepping up its repressive measures, but after armed clashes between British troops and the colonial militia at Lexington and Concorde in 1775, the activists among the colonists moved steadily towards the proclamation of independence in July 1776.[7]

With hindsight it becomes apparent that the British cause was hopeless. The heart of the matter was the impossibility, in an age of sailing ships, of conducting a war across 3000 miles of ocean that was too dangerous to cross in winter. Forces mobilized in Britain were not ready for action in America until mid-summer. A delay of up to three months in exchange of communications meant plans made in Britain were constantly overtaken by events, and any coordinated campaigning was extremely difficult. When the troops did arrive they faced the classical colonial war problem: they were operating among a hostile population and they were at a disadvantage when they moved out of their coastal bases from guerrilla warfare against their supply lines. Unpreparedness in 1776 had left the colonists almost a whole year to organize a provisional government and establish an army under General Washington that succeeded throughout the war in avoiding a decisive confrontation but simply by keeping the field tied down considerable British force. More probably could have been done to organize the estimated quarter of the colonists who stayed loyal to Britain, but they were generally despised by the British command, which had not appreciated that the conflict was in part a civil war, in which the American side had no scruples in exercising intimidation against suspected British collaborators, to whom the British were unable to offer effective protection. Finally there was the crucial factor of morale. The colonists had a clear war aim to which they could relate, based on long-established British traditions going back to the Glorious Revolution of 1688. They could plausibly represent George III and his evil advisers as comparable with James II. The British were never so clear what the basis of their war was. Although public opinion supported firm action in 1775, the idea of making war against fellow Protestant Englishmen was repugnant to many, and there was always an outspoken minority, which tended to grow as the military operations repeatedly failed, who advocated conceding independence, and a radical fringe beyond that, represented by publicists like Tom Paine, who suggested that the Americans were setting an example in asserting their basic political rights that the English might well follow for themselves.

As always, the best chance of success would have been a swift military response to the rebellion at the start, but this was impossible. The main British force in 1775 was trapped in Massachusetts and had to be evacuated to the British base in New York, where they stood on the defensive. It was not until 1777 that Lord Howe, in command in New York, was reinforced and moved out to capture Philadelphia, before turning to the decisive campaign, a joint advance in the Hudson valley by Howe, and an invasion force under General Burgoyne coming south from Canada. If successful this would have isolated the New England colonies from the rest. In the event coordination over such distances through hostile territory caused the operation to fail. Burgoyne was trapped by the colonists at Saratoga in late autumn and forced to surrender. The impact of Saratoga was dramatic in giving credibility to the American cause.

From the first, European powers, mainly France, had seized the opportunity to embarrass Britain and to make a profit by supplying arms and volunteers for the colonial cause. The Americans had agents at the European courts soliciting help, and the French, who were in any case inclining to intervene, were persuaded by Saratoga to enter the war. A formal treaty bound the French to an alliance with the colonists to secure their independence. Saratoga had an equal and opposite impact in Britain. It seems to have broken the morale of Lord North, who responded with a peace offer approved in parliament offering far-reaching concessions short of independence. But although a conciliation commission went to America in 1778, the Americans, secure in their French alliance, declined to compromise on independence. Militarily the British in America were thrown on the defensive, Philadelphia was evacuated, and troops and ships were withdrawn to defend the Caribbean settlements from Bourbon attack. In 1779 things got worse: Spain entered the war, reluctantly at first, being aware that it too had extensive colonies of settlement for which the American rebellion was a bad precedent. For a time this tipped the naval balance in favour of the Bourbons, the control of the Channel was in doubt, and the French fleet cut loose in the Caribbean, capturing Granada and St Vincent. In 1780 the British launched their last major bid for victory in America, although by now the tide of domestic opposition to the war was rising, and calling openly for accepting independence. Motions in the House of Commons for an early peace showed Lord North's majority steadily eroding. A new army was sent under Lord Cornwallis to roll up the colonies from the south; Georgia and South Carolina were secured and Cornwallis prepared to invade Virginia.

In 1781 the French and Spaniards launched their peak effort in the Americas and kept naval supremacy, capturing Tobago and west Florida, but above all French ships and troops helped the Americans to corner Cornwallis and his army in Yorktown. With no possibility of relief from the sea, Cornwallis was compelled to capitulate in October. It was the effective end of the American war and Lord North, on receiving the news, remarked 'It is all over'. Although, in the course of 1782, the British at last managed to reassert their naval superiority with a crushing defeat of the Bourbon navies in the Caribbean, at the battle of the Saints, there was no serious thought of continuing the war.

One new factor was a threat of parallel trouble in Ireland. Since the settlement of 1690 Ireland had been under a Protestant landlord ascendancy. The original Catholic proprietors were almost eliminated, the leadership of the Catholic peasantry fell to the priests, and their resentments flared up only in occasional outbreaks of rural banditry against the landlords and their agents. As in America, the British government had been content to leave control in the hands of the landlords who controlled the government and parliament in Dublin. As part of Townshend's drive to strengthen imperial control, from 1767 the London government began to enhance its direct grip on the Irish executive, which attracted the protests of the settler ascendancy. A Patriot movement developed, led by Gratton, for the repeal of Poyning's Law, and the Act of 1722 asserting the supremacy of the British parliament over Ireland, and was encouraged by the developments in the American colonies. Under cover of the invasion threat after 1778 an Irish volunteer movement was launched to set up a local militia, together with a threatening agitation for the recognition of Irish self-government. By 1782 this was added to the British government's problems.

The anti-war opposition after 1778 was divided into two groups: the Rockingham party, in which a new spokesman had emerged, the charismatic Charles James Fox; and the following of the earl of Chatham, who had died in 1778, now led by Shelburne. They managed to cooperate in harassing North's failing ministry, until in February 1772 a motion to end the war failed by a single vote. North resigned. This launched a bitter struggle between the king, determined not to hand over government to a party, but to preserve his own prerogative to appoint ministers, and the Rockinghams, determined to assert their claim for full ministerial control of appointments. The king was able to force the Rockinghams to enter government in partnership with Shelburne in order to negotiate a peace. That proved the easy part. By 1782 both France and Spain were feeling the financial strain of the war and were interested in ending it, encouraged by the evidence of reviving British naval power. Once the British accepted the full independence of the former colonies, the Bourbons were glad to close down the war with some modest gains. The French kept Tobago in the Caribbean, had their Newfoundland fishing rights extended, and got back their slaving station in Senegal and some small concessions in India; Spain got Florida and Minorca. Shelburne in particular had counted on Britain recovering her trade with the former colonies in a short time, which she did, and overall the war, far from weakening Britain, was a prelude to the very marked economic advance after 1785.

The new ministry was now able to take up reform projects blocked under the North regime, particularly the Rockingham policy of 'economical reform'. As the North ministry declined, the opposition campaign was reinforced by the argument that the unfortunate outcome of the war further illustrated the need to reinvigorate the parliamentary system and remove improper interference with its independence. Already in 1780 the opposition had succeeded in passing the Dunning resolution that 'the power of the crown has increased, is increasing and ought to be diminished'. Now it was possible to proceed with Burke's bill to abolish a number of sinecures and pensions, and reduce the king's civil list income. It was not in fact very radical, but it set a trend towards financial reforms which was further developed under Pitt the younger after 1784. The new ministry also settled the Irish crisis by conceding full independent powers to the Irish parliament. In July 1782 Rockingham died and was succeeded as leader by the earl of Portland, which in reality put the leadership of the Whig opposition into the hands of Fox. The party demanded that the king now appoint Portland First Lord and allow him to distribute the offices, but the king was resolved not to allow this, and promoted Shelburne to First Lord, sending the Portland party into opposition. As part of the new ministry the king appointed the young William Pitt, a member of Chatham's old following, as Chancellor of the Exchequer, his first entry into government.

The Shelburne ministry fell in February 1783, when motions critical of the peace terms were carried and a new crisis developed. The Whigs demanded once more that Portland be made First Lord with full control of patronage. The king refused, being particularly incensed by the growing relationship between Fox and the Prince of Wales, who was now adopting the familiar role, as heir to the throne, of patron of the opposition.[8] It was Fox who forced the issue by negotiating a coalition with Lord North. This proved a feasible way of constructing a majority administration, but in view of the past hostility of the Whigs to North looked like sheer political opportunism, and went down badly with large sections of public opinion. It is also now apparent that it was not just the opportunism that offended, but the open intention to force the king's hand and deprive him of his rights to appoint the ministry.

In the end, in April 1773 the king agreed to accept the coalition, but in terms making it clear he did so under protest. It is also now known that the king was being advised by William Pitt on how to bring the coalition down. The opportunity came over a new India bill: the coalition proposed that a parliamentary board of commissioners be given supervisory power over the East India Company, including the power to approve appointments. Since the company disposed of some very lucrative posts, the bill could be seen as a bid by the coalition to get control of this patronage and perhaps perpetuate itself in office. When the bill got to the Lords, the king let it be known he would regard any who supported the bill as enemies of the monarchy. It was defeated, and the king dismissed the government, appointing Pitt as First Lord in a new administration. It was a minority government and for some three months was repeatedly defeated in the Commons, but each time, as the king indicated his resolve to uphold it, the opposition vote diminished. By March 1784 the margin was down to one vote, and the king dissolved parliament. In the ensuing election Pitt's management skills and disposal of full royal patronage secured a majority of 100 for him in the new parliament. It proved to be a constitutional turning point and inaugurated a new period of stable government. The revival of party which the Rockinghams, Burke and Fox had brought about had not convinced public opinion that it was proper to allow a political party to usurp the basic right of the crown to influence the composition of the government. It is a clear indication that society on the whole was still content with traditional political practice and suspicious of proposals for change.

This is consistent with the history of the demands for reform outside parliament in these years. The radical movement of John Wilkes had pursued various campaigns, with a central theme: hostility to oligarchic, irresponsible power. This used ideas from Locke and the Glorious Revolution to assert that oligarchy was inconsistent with the rights of Englishmen. The general effect was to spread political consciousness among social strata that had previously been uninvolved. In 1771 a group of radicals in London took up the cause of parliamentary reform, through the London Constitutional Society. Wilkes resisted this development. In general his propaganda had been strongly chauvinist in tone, denouncing Scots and foreigners and defending English tradition, which included the system of parliamentary representation. So when in the 1770s the radicals took up the cause of the American colonists, as fellow Englishmen demanding their political rights, the movement was temporarily halted. During the patriotic surge against the independence of the colonies, the radicals found themselves under attack as unpatriotic.

The mood changed after 1778 to one of blaming the North ministry for mishandling the American crisis. The radicals took up the Whig theme that it had been improper influences on policy which had caused the disasters. The formal reappearance of radical protest came from Yorkshire, where Christopher Wyvill organized a campaign among the gentry, through county meetings, criticizing government failings and demanding economical reform on the lines set out by Burke, and in addition parliamentary reform, to protect parliament from improper manipulation by the court. The proposed remedy was triennial elections and redistribution of parliamentary seats from decayed boroughs to the counties. On this basis a nationwide petitioning movement was generated in 1780. Since the Wyvill movement was based on restoring the independence of the House of Commons, and not the extension of the franchise, it was taken up by the Whig opposition. It was a London radical association, founded by John Cartwright in 1780, that promoted the cause of electoral reform based on annual parliaments, universal male suffrage by secret ballot and equal constituencies, which would make parliaments truly representative. This was quite unacceptable to the Rockingham Whigs, but some leaders, including Fox, Shelburne and the young William Pitt took up Wyvill's programme. Pitt moved motions for the redistribution of seats in 1782, 1783 and finally in 1785. Fox had had to drop reform as part of his coalition deal with Lord North. Wyvill tried to support the proposals by a renewed petitioning campaign, but it became apparent that once the war was ended, and the government crisis resolved, there was no strong popular demand in the country for parliamentary reform, even of a limited kind.

There had been a brutal reminder of the sort of issues that were capable of setting off a mass popular intervention in politics in the Gordon riots of 1780. There a populist agitation, based on the rooted anti-popery hysteria of the British, triggered by some very modest proposals to relieve the legal disabilities on Catholics, brought mobs on to the streets of London, controlling the city for several days and causing serious damage to property. They were a sharp reminder of the precariousness of authority in eighteenth-century Britain. No such militancy could ever have been mobilized in favour of parliamentary reform. Wyvill had tapped in to the discontents of the propertied classes, aroused by the war and the perceived incompetence of the government, and the short-term economic disturbance they had caused. The resulting surge of activity had soon subsided when the stimuli were removed. What Wyvill had achieved, following on the experience of the Wilkites before him, was to increase political awareness, and to do so in a more ordered and focused way than Wilkes had attempted. The petitioning movement of the 1780s provided the model for later single-issue campaigns for change within the traditional political system.[9]

The basic stability and conservatism of British society, which is confirmed by the radicals' failure to change it, was confirmed by the course followed by Pitt's ministry once it was established in power after 1784, until everything changed in consequence of the revolutionary war. Pitt came into office with an established record as a reformer. Not only had he been the leading Commons' spokesman for parliamentary reform, he was also known to favour action on the slave trade and the granting of full civic rights to Protestant dissenters by repealing the Corporation and Test Acts. But quickly came to accept that these reforms could not be carried without breaking up his majority. Instead he concentrated on establishing better government at home and in the empire. He was able to exploit the expanding economy to reform the tax structure and to increase the professionalization of the revenue departments. In the last budget before the wars, in 1792, he could claim a 47 per cent increase in government revenue since he came to office, and a promising start to reducing the national debt. He continued the economical reform programme of eliminating sinecures and improper patronage and settled the problem of the East India Company in his India Act of 1784. Pitt steered a careful course on the economy, negotiated the trade agreement with France in 1786 and balanced the claims of those commercial interests who wanted government protection against the others, who had been persuaded by the doctrines of Adam Smith to favour free trade. He was helped by the decline of the Whig opposition which although it upheld its party organization and cohesion, was losing public support. The Fox–North coalition of 1783 had undermined Fox's credentials as a reforming leader, since it seemed to exemplify the worst features of unprincipled faction politics. The impression of irresponsible opportunism was reinforced by the association of the opposition with the Prince of Wales, an unpopular, even scandalous, public figure. Fox's attempt to exploit the relationship through the regency crisis of 1788, when the king was incapacitated by porphyria, was bungled by excessive demands for the full transfer of all the royal prerogatives to the prince as regent. The king's recovery in 1789 was a cause of genuine public rejoicing, while Pitt's position was stronger than ever. In foreign policy Pitt was cautious but effective in pursuing the national interest, with one uncharacteristic lapse in 1791, when he almost got into a war with Russia over her expansion into the Black Sea at the expense of the Ottomans. He handled the Patriot crisis in the United Provinces through Prussian intervention without war, and settled by negotiation the Nootka Sound dispute of 1790, a dangerous colonial confrontation with Spain over rival claims on the Pacific coast of North America.

Great Britain in the 1790s was moving steadily towards that position of world hegemony that was established in the first half of the nineteenth century. The British developments had owed little to the Enlightenment or to the *German Aufklärung*. The British approved of Montesquieu, because he had, somewhat mistakenly, taken the British constitution to be a model of a polity based upon checks and balances that he was advocating. The *philosophes* were French, and so inherently untrustworthy, and even worse were religious sceptics and materialists, at a time when the British labouring classes were being religiously aroused by Methodism and evangelicalism, and the expanding middle classes, increasingly critical of worldly, aristo-cratic lifestyles, were being enthused by Puritan-based moral revivalism. By the standards of the Enlightenment, the English legal system was a disgrace, with its utter lack of codification and its literally hundreds of capital offences, but the English gloried in its gothic complexities and could boast of how John Wilkes could take on the whole might of the English state and win by asserting his legal rights as a free-born Englishman. The successful American Revolution did not inspire the British to make their own declaration of independence – though it did the Irish – because the British assumed the colonists were only asserting those same rights which all Englishmen possessed. This was the period when the figure of John Bull became the standard icon of Britishness, in the press, popular ballads and cartoons. He was legally a free man, enjoyed low levels of tax, was free to say what he liked about his rulers, was materially prosperous, well fed on roast beef, solidly but not extravagantly dressed, and an upright, God-fearing Protestant. He was compared with his French neighbour, crushed by the burdens imposed by a feudal-absolutist monarchy, intellectually and morally crippled by popery, driven to try and supplement his meagre vegetarian diet by eating frogs, and still clumping around in wooden shoes because leather was a luxury beyond his means. That this image was an utter travesty of reality could be observed by anyone who crossed the Channel with their eyes open, but most Britishers never did. Nor was it widely noticed that, since mid-century, with the effects of a rapidly rising population, a steady increase in food prices, and slowly declining real wages, the labouring classes were becoming relatively impoverished; labourers' and cottagers' families did not often have roast beef on their tables. But the propertied classes were flourishing as the economy grew, and the general self-satisfaction, with the consciousness that in spite of America Britain was easily holding her place in the world, made revolution in Britain a very remote prospect.

20

The French Time Bomb

During the 1750s the personal prestige of the French monarchy, in the person of Louis XV, was being seriously weakened. The Austrian ambassador reported: 'A radical change in the spirit of the nation ... the previous real authority and respect for the king are being transformed into a malevolence that is almost seditious and in any case very dangerous.'

In modern terms he was developing an image problem, partly derived from a scurrilous gutter press. This purveyed lurid accounts of his alleged private life, portrayed him as the puppet of Madame de Pompadour and her circle, and accused him of neglecting his royal duty to govern. This was grossly unfair; Pompadour did not interfere in the business of state, except to try to push her candidates for office on occasion, and the king maintained a work routine of attendance at meetings, audiences with ministers, and steady attention to paper work, conscientiously reading the piles of documents requiring his signature. Yet the ambassador was right; the hostile public perceptions were dangerous to an absolute monarchy. One sign of the damage was the increasingly demanding public attitudes of the *parlements*, pushing their claim for a share in the exercise of the royal sovereignty. The *parlement* of Bordeaux told the king in 1756:

> Your Parlement respects, Sire, the authority your Majesty exercises in your Council ... But after having drafted necessary laws there ... your authority is transferred into your Parlement ... It is in that legal Council of the sovereign that, by process of verification and registration, you validate the projected laws.

Two years later the same *parlement* told him that, 'its decrees are the very commands of your Majesty'. The king seemed to lack the will to assert his supremacy in face of these arguments. Even after the Seven Years War started the *parlements* did not hesitate to threaten strike action against proposed wartime taxation increases. When the intendant of Montauban got into dispute with the local *cour des aides*, the king chose to transfer him elsewhere rather than uphold his authority. In 1757 the king had reluctantly sacrificed his Controller, Machault, as a concession to the critics, and he accepted the policy line of the Choiseuls, seeking to cooperate with the sovereign courts. After 1760, again following Choiseul, a keen anti-clerical, Louis went along with an attack by the *parlements* and the Jansenists on the Jesuit Order in France.[1] In 1763 he abandoned another tax reform scheme in face of *parlementaire* criticism, declaring he would rule henceforth:

> not by the sole weight of that authority he holds from God, and will never allow to be weakened in his hands, but by the love, justice and by the observation of the rules and forms, so wisely established in his kingdom.

The Choiseul ministry was engaged in a range of reforming activity after 1763, following its strategy of rebuilding the strength of the kingdom for a war of revenge on Britain. Choiseul accepted that France should, as far as possible, avoid new commitments on the continent; reforms of the army were begun, together with an ambitious naval building programme. At home, the suppression of the Jesuits, finalized in 1764, was followed by a major reform of the monastic establishment, leaving it heavily reduced. These were all measures agreeable to the *parlementaires*, but did nothing to halt their continual critical appraisal of government measures. The *parlementaire* publicity represented their actions as the defence of the rights of the subject against ministerial despotism. A prolonged confrontation began in 1763 with the *parlement* of Brittany at Rennes on this subject, after a bitter dispute with the royal military governor, the duke d'Aiguillon. After an exchange of remonstrances the *parlement* went on strike and was supported by the Estates of Brittany. The government decided to assert its authority, and early in 1766 the king called the *parlement* of Paris into session to register a new royal resolution. After rejecting the claims of the *parlements* to be intermediary corporations, empowered to defend the liberties of the subject, the king declared:

> It is in my person alone that the sovereign power resides ... it is from myself alone that my Courts derive their existence and their authority ... it is to myself alone that the legislative power belongs, independent and undivided ... the whole public order and the rights and interests of the nation, which they claim as a body distinct from the monarch, are necessarily united with my own, and rest only in my hands ... I shall not permit that there shall be any departure from the principles set out in this declaration.

This clear declaration of the royal will was not openly opposed; it was simply ignored by the Estates of Brittany, working to support the *parlement* of Rennes, by the *parlement* of Paris which supported resistance to the government's proposed fiscal reforms, and by the *cour des aides*, all claiming to defend the subjects' rights. In reality the campaign was a defence of privilege by the *parlementaire* elites, who saw both their tax privileges and their administrative powers being challenged by a reforming administration. They represented the problems of government as deriving from the excess profits and corruption of the financiers and tax-farmers, who were an easy target for arousing popular passions. The government represented the enlightened party, seeking to control the debt and make taxation more equitable, as in 1768 when it was agreed to freeze the level of the *taille* permanently. Other privileged groups – opposition factions at court and the sword nobility – realized it was in their interest to support the *parlementaires* in their resistance. The privileged elites were closing ranks, not to demand reform but to obstruct it.

Choiseul and his faction had dominated government through the 1760s and had shown a preference for conciliating the *parlementaire* critics, while the king, for once, remained resolute to reassert his sovereign power. In 1769 in a ministerial reshuffle a new Chancellor, René Maupeou, was appointed, who had a plan to restructure the processes for confirming royal decrees. Those concerning administration and taxation would be sent to a Council, made up of intendants. Early in 1770 Maupeou was reinforced by the appointment of a new Controller, the abbé Terray. Confrontation between Louis XV and the *parlementaire* opposition intensified, and the king became convinced that Choiseul was unreliable on the issue. When in addition Choiseul wanted to threaten war over the Falkland Islands dispute between Britain and Spain,[2] a political coup was planned. In November the king declared he would tolerate no more criticism of his sovereign powers by the *parlements* and they went on strike in protest. At the same time Louis wrote to Charles III to tell him that he was giving priority to restoring authority to the crown: 'I am resolved to get myself obeyed by every possible means. In this situation, a war would be a disastrous event for me and my people.'

The Choiseul brothers were dismissed. The existing magistrates of the sovereign courts were required to give their written acceptance of the new arrangements, and on their refusal they were dismissed. A new *parlement* was installed in April 1771. Six new high courts would exercise the former appeals function of the *parlement* of Paris; venality of offices was abolished in the new courts which had salaried magistrates; the provincial *parlements* were preserved, but purged, and their staff put on salaries. There was a furious protest, led by the peers and princes of the blood, who declined to recognize the new courts. The *cour des aides* protested and was dissolved. Terray now resumed financial reform: the *vingtième* was confirmed as a permanent, universal 5 per cent property tax, and would be levied at double rate until 1781. More important, a new attempt was launched to base it on a permanent, independent assessment. This new authoritarian course was held firm until the death of Louis XV in 1774, and the evidence suggests that the opposition was being worn down, the boycotts of the new courts were weakening, and former protesters were submitting and joining the new system.[3]

The government coup of 1770 gave a major stimulus to the formation of a coherent opposition faction. It was entrenched in the court, where Choiseul and his clients constituted a continuous focus for political conspiracy. The opposition was patronized ostentatiously by some of the princes of the blood, led by the duke of Orléans, and his heir, the duke of Chartres, from the Palais Royale. This developed into a public pleasure garden with free entry, and entertainments, including political oratory, were provided. It was also a centre for organizing and circulating a steady flow of printed material: over 200 pamphlets attacking Maupeou appeared in 1771 alone. These denounced the government and the tax-farmers, and asserted that the ancient liberties of the subject were being systematically attacked by a despotic regime. The resistance movement was a broad coalition of the dismissed magistrates, the provincial *parlements*, the disaffected peers and court nobility, even the Jansenists. These had lost their main enemy when the Jesuits disbanded in 1774, and now the Jansenist parish clergy and their allies turned on the tyranny of the episcopal hierarchy. The opposition began to see itself as a 'patriot' movement, and denounced those who collaborated with the government as betraying society. For the moment they had no clear political programme of their own, beyond seeking Maupeou's dismissal. When they were joined by Malesherbes, from the *cour des aides*, he stressed the basic need for administration to become transparent and responsible, and suggested that the Estates General should be convened to express the people's grievances and work out solutions. The overall effect cannot easily be measured, but the tendency to challenge the legitimacy of royal authority, and to suggest that the government's agents were in effect public enemies, part of a standing conspiracy to despoil and oppress the subject, could not fail to direct attention to the role of the king in allowing these things to happen.

The ministers put up their own justifications, which were based on enlightened absolutism: the royal authority was promoting modernization, equity in taxation and a fairer and more efficient judicial system, and was dealing with anomalies like venality of offices. As proof of their credentials, they could claim the endorsement of Voltaire himself for their programmes. They did not venture to follow the policy suggested by the marquis of Argensen, and published in 1764 as *Considerations on the Government of France*. Argensen had recognized hereditary privilege as the barrier standing in the way of good government. The king should neutralize it by going directly to the people through elected assemblies, making them citizens rather than subjects, and creating 'a republic protected by a king'. This was superficially plausible, but the idea was unrealistic; the institution of monarchy itself was the supreme example of a structure built around legally secured hereditary privilege and holding the structure of corporate rights in equilibrium by the exercise of its role as final arbiter.

The new king, Louis XVI, was a victim of the dynastic system, thrust by accident of birth into a role for which he was poorly equipped. His tragedy is made worse by his genuine good intentions, strong sense of his responsibilities and generally progressive outlook. What he lacked were political skills and charisma; like his grandfather he was a poor communicator and shared with him the habit, when pressed by difficult decisions, of resorting to taciturnity. He had been married since 1770 to the Habsburg grand duchess, Marie Antoinette. She had been intended to be the Habsburg voice at Versailles, but had little taste for politics before the later 1780s. Further, the Austrian alliance had never won public support in France and there was a cloud of prejudice standing in the way of her winning public acceptance. In these circumstances there was little hope that the monarch himself would provide effective leadership, and much turned on whether he would give consistent support to his ministers to overcome the obstacles to change and modernization. His record after 1774 showed that he would not. He was persuaded to abandon the Maupeou programme and to seek conciliation with the *parlementaires*. Under the guidance of Maurepas the new system was disbanded and the old structures and their dismissed members were restored.

But the king wished to push forward reform policies and he appointed Anne-Robert Turgot as his Controller. Turgot was an experienced and progressive intendant, whose work in Limousin had been the model of an improving administration in a backward part of the kingdom. Turgot was a committed enthusiast for the Enlightenment, and particularly for physiocratic ideas. He sent a memorandum to the king in 1775 on the reform of the kingdom, by introducing free trade and sweeping aside outdated institutions. He assured the king, 'In ten years the nation would be unrecognizable.' He began with abolishing controls on the grain trade in which he was unlucky, in that a bad harvest in 1774 had caused a temporary subsistence crisis, bread prices soared and rioting began in 1775. It required a heavy use of troops and legal repression to keep things under control until the next harvest brought relief. This got the minister off to a bad start with the public, but he persisted. With a set of six edicts he proposed the remodelling of finances. The whole guild structure for controlling trade and manufacture was to be abolished and replaced by unregulated trade; the public forced labour for the upkeep of roads, the *corvée*, bitterly resented by the peasants, would be discontinued and the state would take responsibility for communications. A property tax would be levied on the whole community to meet the costs. The outcry from the vested interests adversely affected by the programme was formidable. They rallied round the restored *parlements* in opposition, and Turgot was thrust back on coercing them by use of the *lit de justice*. His enemies got the ear of the king, and since Turgot had tended to patronize the young monarch, indeed told him that: 'you are too young to judge men, and you have yourself said, Sire, that you lack experience and need a guide'. Louis took offence and Turgot was dismissed. His reforms were mostly discontinued.

Turgot is a good illustration of the basic problem. His aims were impeccably progressive, and as an intendant he had taken the lead with experimenting in setting up elected regional councils for consulting public opinion. But, when faced with obstruction from the vested interests, he automatically resorted to coercion and was accused of the same kind of ministerial despotism as Maupeou before him. Had Louis XVI been prepared, as Louis XV had been, to put his full authority behind Turgot, and had Turgot himself listened to the advice of Maurepas to proceed gradually, one reform at a time, something might have been achieved. The Turgot experience revealed how reform from above, imposed on a sceptical public, would be resisted by the community it was intended to benefit. The problem in France, and it appeared elsewhere too, was not that popular demand for reform was being blocked by a reactionary authoritarian government, but that an admittedly authoritarian government, with clear reforming intentions, was being systematically obstructed by a conservative society.

There followed the fateful diversion of French interest to the American Revolution. Turgot had warned Louis XVI that in any new war 'the first gunshot would drive the state to bankruptcy'. Turgot was quite wrong about that, and in any case there was no hesitation by Louis about taking advantage of Britain's difficulties. He was urged on by his foreign minister, Vergennes, a hard-line absolutist who had little enthusiasm for domestic reform.[4] From the beginning it was decided to supply the colonists with arms, and as soon as it seemed likely the rebellion would succeed, the government resolved to enter the war. The time gained had been put to good use preparing the French navy for action. It took more time to convince Charles III to join in, but in 1779 a firm agreement was secured that the Bourbon powers would unite in promoting American independence. Vergennes supposed that the loss of the colonies would restore the colonial balance between Britain and the Bourbons and reverse the disasters of 1763. On the surface he was proved right. In this Anglo-French conflict, uniquely, with no continental complications, France put all her resources into the naval war, and for two vital years, 1780–1, the Bourbons achieved control of the seas long enough to secure the final victory of the colonists. It was also very obvious that the American war did much to restore the credibility of Louis XVI's government with his subjects and there was genuine public enthusiasm for the humiliation of the British. There was a further effect, which worried no one at the time, that the success of the colonists, in asserting what they claimed to be the natural rights of all men to be governed by consent, proved a great stimulus to the reform movement in France, partly through the feedback from French officers and volunteers who had served with the colonists.

The bankruptcy anticipated by Turgot did not materialize, and much of the credit for that was due to the Swiss Protestant banker Jacques Necker, who was recruited as Director of Finance, since, as a Protestant, he could not be appointed Controller. Necker was very much a man of the Enlightenment and an advocate of economic reform aiming at free trade, but was also a pragmatist. He had a much more realistic grasp of public finance, given his background in banking, than professional administrators like Turgot. Necker understood that if government revenue was reliable, governments could always borrow to meet the expenses of war. This was the programme he sold to Vergennes and Louis XVI and to French public opinion, for he also understood how well-aimed publicity could reinforce confidence and facilitate borrowing. Consequently Necker embarked on a programme of fiscal and administrative reforms with the declared intention of financing the war by loans. He launched a retrenchment programme to eliminate superfluous venal offices, realizing that in a very short time money invested in buying out the officeholders would be regained. He succeeded in liquidating several hundred superfluous fiscal offices and another 500 sinecures in the court at Versailles. When the Great Farm for the indirect taxes came up for renewal in 1780, he would have preferred to resume state administration, but he compromised by revising the contracts to ensure that the crown got a substantial share of any profits made above the basic returns guaranteed to the farmers. Naturally Necker's reforms brought him many enemies, though for a time the king stood by him.

In 1781 he broke all precedent when he published his *Compte rendu*, an explanation of the current budgetary situation. This was controversial at the time, and has been since with the historians.[5] It asserted that after his reforms the ordinary budget, that is the peacetime revenue and expenditure, was now in surplus. The national budget had never been exposed to the public before and it was an extraordinary publishing success, selling 20,000 copies and read all over France and in much of Europe. It broke a most fundamental rule of government under the *ancien régime*: that the processes of government – 'mysteries of state' as the English called them – should remain entirely secret. They were held to be beyond the comprehension of ordinary subjects, and even institutions like the British parliament and the Swedish Diet tried to forbid the publication of their proceedings.[6] Necker also proposed the logical follow-up to publication, that subjects should be consulted on policy, and he favoured a gradual extension of provincial assemblies through the kingdom. Necker was well aware of the official hostility his policies were facing, and in 1781 he turned to the king with a request that his status be elevated to that of Controller, with full powers over government expenditure. He threatened to resign if refused, whereat Vergennes and Maurepas told the king they would resign if he conceded to Necker's demands. Louis let him go.

The king clearly had not understood what Necker was trying to do, which was to establish the creditworthiness of the state through openness in government, and thus enable it to raise loans at reasonable rates to cover the costs of war. In doing this Necker gave a hostage to fortune, for after 1781 opposition to the government could cite the *Compte rendu* as evidence that no new taxation was required, and that if the government was in financial difficulty it must be due to mismanagement and corruption. Necker had borrowed some 530 million livres to finance the American war. This was predicated on the assumption that after the war expenditure would return to peacetime levels and the borrowing would stop. This did not happen. The next Controllers, Joly de Fleury and Calonne, sanctioned continuing high military expenditures, reversed most of Necker's economy measures, and continued to borrow money to cover the deficit. When in 1786 the additional *vingtième* approved to meet the costs of war expired, Calonne had to tell the king that the state was effectively bankrupt; there was a deficit for the year 1786 of 112 million livres and credit had dried up.

During the 1770s and 1780s a shift in public opinion was observable, with significant changes of values that could be argued to have constituted a cultural revolution in France.[7] In the nature of things it tended to be led from Paris, but swiftly spread out into the provinces. The spread of print culture in France has already been noted. The government tried to exercise some control, and authors and publishers who pushed too hard could find themselves in prison under the executive order of a *lettre de cachet*. This had little restraining effect and journalism became a major industry. The most famous publisher C.-J. Panckoucke had started by importing his *Journal de Genève*, and *Journal de Brussels* into France, then moved to domestic publication; the *Journal de Paris* was the first national daily newspaper and was followed by the influential *Mercure de France* in 1778. This was the respectable tip of the publishing iceberg; beneath it was what today would be called the tabloid press, specializing in scandals, sensation and soft pornography, in pamphlets, popular ballads and fly-sheets for posting up on walls.[8] Parallel with this was the spread of facilities for public education and debate. This ranged from the Palais Royale, the Orleanist centre of opposition publicity, supplemented in Paris and provincial centres by the *parlements*, usually housed in a Palais de Justice, as in Paris, where booksellers and pedlars could distribute the latest works to the public who necessarily thronged such places on business or out of curiosity. These public meeting places also provided opportunities for oratory, which could reach down even to the illiterate levels of society, who no doubt mostly came to be entertained, but could then be influenced.

There were other cultural channels available. The Paris *Salon* for the public showing of painting and sculpture was an established institution with its annual exhibition, which evidence shows was visited not just by the elite but by the lower orders as well. Here popular painters of the new cult of sensibility, like Greuze and later the great painter of the classical revival David, could find a mass audience. Then there was the popular theatre, alongside the Comédie Française and the Opéra, which were officially sponsored. A network of small popular theatres and cabarets developed, where drama with a critical social or political message was put on before popular audiences. The best-known example is the production of Beaumarchais' drama, *Le Mariage de Figaro* in 1774. The text of the play is distinctly more radical than the libretto of Mozart's opera, and its critique of aristocratic and feudal values was sensational. An aristocratic lady who watched the first performance was swept away by it: 'The Marriage of Figaro is the cleverest thing that has ever been written, excepting perhaps the works of M. Voltaire. It is dazzling, a true piece of fireworks.' There was rapturous applause for Figaro's attack on the hereditary nobility, when he asks Almaviva, 'what have you done to have so much? You have hardly given yourself the trouble to be born, and that's about it.' Louis had wanted to ban the play, but was persuaded to allow the performance after a few cosmetic changes, and was infuriated by its massive public success. Beaumarchais duly got his *lettre de cachet*, but his play continued to be performed.

In the background to these Parisian excitements was the quiet educational work of provincial societies, libraries, prize essay competitions on themes about how society might be improved, masonic lodges, private salons. There was also the oldest publicity agency of all, the preaching of the church, which was where the Jansenist clergy could promote its critique. But before any rush to conclude that this sealed the fate of the *ancien régime*, it must be noted that the exchange of ideas was not one-sided; there was a vigorous defence being put up of traditions and established order, and much of the critical material was apolitical, meant only to entertain and sell. But it tended to dwell on the scandalous and to undermine respect for hierarchy and authority. It was not peddling a coherent vision of a different society, but industriously muck-raking among the failings of the present.

The crucial change in values took place at a higher level. The elites were moving on from the doctrines of the Enlightenment. By now even governments usually subscribed to Enlightenment ideas, as reforming ministers and intendants sought to implement rational improvements in the economy, education, public health and poor relief. But the aim was to improve society as it was, with its hierarchical structure, not to create a new one. These ideas were being outflanked by new trends with more radical implications. Perhaps the most surprising was the popularity of Rousseau's ideas – not so much the political tracts, the *Contrat Social*, but the educational works, *La Nouvelle Héloïse* and *Emile*. These promoted a dream of a moral rebirth of society, a return to basic human virtues, a natural life unpolluted by urban materialism, usually imagined in an idyllic rural setting. Rousseau died in 1778 and became a cult figure, while his burial place, on a peaceful island in a lake, became a place of pilgrimage. It was even visited by Marie Antoinette in 1782. The cult elevated sentiment and the promptings of the heart over reason. The effect was summed up by a modern commentator, S. Schama:

> He created, in fact, a community of young believers. Their faith was in the possibility of a collective moral and political rebirth in which the innocence of childhood might be preserved into adulthood and through which virtue and freedom would be mutually sustained. Just how this was to be accomplished was, in all of Rousseau's writings, notoriously obscure.

The Rousseau effect found support in the French experience of America. With a little stretching of the imagination, the American Revolution, in a society seen as being still primitively rural, could be taken as an example of

Rousseauesque renewal. Leading figures like Benjamin Franklin and Thomas Jefferson were enthusiastically cultivated in polite society when they came to France as ambassadors. The more distant George Washington could be seen as a paragon, a liberator, the true, uncorrupted father of the nation. The success of the Americans was held to prove that moral renewal was possible in the real world. Such dreaming could have dangerous implications. The abbé Robin, an ardent propagandist for the American way of life, described the social relaxations of the American patriots: 'Then officers, soldiers, American men and women, all dance together. It is the festival of equality ... These people are still in the happy time when distinctions of birth and rank are ignored.'

For a hierarchical society, the spread of this kind of egalitarian utopianism was potentially subversive. There was a similar effect arising from the cult of the Roman republic. This was especially taken up by the orators of the kind who performed at the Palais Royale, and who found a role model in Cicero. The history of classical Rome could also be interpreted as an example of Rousseauesque virtues. Readers were assured that:

> there, good morals were cultivated at home and in the field ... justice and probity prevailed among them thanks not so much to laws as to nature. Quarrels, discord and strife were reserved for their enemies; citizens contended with each other only in merit.

The cult of classical virtue as role model probably peaked in the astonishing popularity of David's painting in the Salon of 1785, *The Oath of the Horatii*. The *Journal de Paris* wrote of it: 'one feels in seeing this painting a sentiment that exalts the soul and which, to use an expression of J. J. Rousseau, has something poignant about it that attracts one'. The new sensibility was expressed in action by Marie Antoinette and her ladies playing at being shepherdesses in the grounds of Versailles, or in the campaign for society ladies to breast-feed their infants, so as to return to their roots in nature. It was not the stuff of which revolutions are made. But the aspiration for a moral rebirth of society which it encouraged built up dissatisfaction with the actual world and cultivated a vision of virtuous citizens coming together to build a better one.

One factor in the slow attrition of respect for the old order in France was the growing unpopularity of the queen. It is hard to see Marie Antoinette as more than a victim of circumstances: she was stranded in an often uncomfortable marriage and unwilling to adopt the passive role allotted to Bourbon consorts. She was impatient of etiquette and determined to carve out some sort of private life for herself. Her unconventionality and the clique of companions, male and female, that she drew into her circle provided abundant material for malicious gossip, which the gutter press eagerly circulated. If she had tried to play a political role, she would have been severely criticized, but since she did not, it made her expensive pursuit of social amusement appear that much more frivolous and, in a context of growing financial constraint, irresponsible. Then in 1785 she became involved in the affair of the Diamond Necklace. This was in fact a criminal confidence trick, of which the queen was an unwitting victim, but given the public image that had been building up, various aspects of the affair could be used to portray the queen as avaricious and sexually dissolute. As the national crisis moved towards its climax in the late 1780s, the queen had become a public hate figure.

With the resignation of Necker, Charles Alexandre de Calonne, the leading minister after Vergennes, who had charge of foreign policy, became the new Controller. He was one more enlightened ex-intendant who, on the model of Turgot, was pursuing a scheme of modernization. He is best known through the charge brought by Necker of causing a fiscal disaster after 1783, by continuing high levels of public borrowing – a total of 5 million livres in 1783–6. This was partly facilitated by wider use of foreign loans from Amsterdam and Geneva. They were meant to buy time to launch a scheme of internal reforms, which would, like Turgot's earlier ones, boost the economy. The creation of a free trade area in France by abolishing internal customs barriers was proposed, as was a new attempt to open up the grain trade. The state put up capital to start new industrial projects, often based on British models, and the government made a trade agreement with Britain, which was supposed to stimulate French industry by introducing healthy competition. And, to complete the reform, Calonne revived the attempt to introduce a single direct tax, properly related to the wealth of the taxpayer and allowing no exemptions. Calonne held to the absolutist concept of change directed from above. He made little effort to win over public opinion; rather he shared the view of his colleague Vergenne that an invigorated censorship was called for to silence the flood of critical publications.

Then in 1785 circumstances began to turn against him. The Patriot movement in the United Provinces upset the financial markets there, cutting off a major source of credit. That year brought the first of a series of poor harvests, and the Diamond Necklace scandal broke. In 1786, the last of the extra wartime taxes expired and Calonne discovered that public credit was drying up. In August 1786 he revealed the extent of the crisis to the king, admitting to a large deficit on the current year's budget. The only way out, by getting new credit, would be to raise additional taxation to use as the basis for fresh borrowing. Reversing his earlier neglect of public opinion he proposed to call an Assembly of Notables to ratify a new financial package.

Louis was nervous, but in December 1786 the summons for an Assembly was issued and it met in February 1787. The device was chosen to bypass the *parlement*. The Assembly was chosen from the highest levels of society and government: princes of the blood, nobles of the higher ranks, the leading bishops, leading *parlementaires* and royal officials. The whole experiment was not free of critics. Some of the princes of the blood, like Orléans, were hostile to Calonne's policy, and the marquis de Lafayette was included, though he had a reputation as an outspoken radical. Even so, it could have been expected that a gathering like this, chosen from the top elite groups, would rally round to extricate the monarchy from its current crisis. Calonne presented his package to the opening session, freely admitting the seriousness of the credit crisis and proposing the new single land tax. Elected representative councils, starting at parish level and culminating at the provincial, would be established, and these would be regularly consulted on policy. The *corvée* would be commuted for a money payment, and the free internal market established. Finally he assured the Assembly that henceforth the welfare of the people should be the first priority of royal policies.

The Assembly discussions indicated that its members were prepared to implement much of the programme; the basic strategy of combining tax reform with a representative system was readily accepted, though a strong body of opinion preferred using the Estates General to validate the tax reforms. Instead of attacking the programme, Calonne's many enemies focused on his personal record, including his private financial dealings, which were open to criticism. In desperation Calonne struck back with an appeal to public opinion, the *avertissement*. He claimed that his critics really represented the defence of privilege; he wrote: 'The privileged will be sacrificed, yes – when justice requires it and need demands it. Would it be better to tax the unprivileged once more, the People?'

This desperate populist appeal failed and his enemies at court closed in, representing to the king that it was Calonne himself who was the main obstacle to a settlement. Louis, as was his habit, wavered. He authorized the publication of responses to the *avertissement* and when Calonne demanded his critics be silenced the king abandoned him. In April 1787 Calonne was not only dismissed, but publicly disgraced and exiled to a chorus of public rejoicings.

The last government of the *ancien régime* was headed by the archbishop of Toulouse, Loménie de Brienne. He had good Enlightenment credentials and recruited some notable reformers into his administration, especially Lamoignon who became Keeper of the Seals and Malesherbes who had a reputation with the public for integrity. Brienne was broadly in support of the Calonne reform package, and the king addressed the Notables, inviting them to work with the new ministry in finalizing it. Most of it was agreed to and expanded to include legal emancipation of the Protestant community, the final abolition of torture in judicial process, and the reform of the prison system. But the Assembly proved unyielding on the central issue of the tax reform. This, they insisted, could only be sanctioned by calling the Estates General. Brienne was weakened by Louis XVI, who seemed unwilling to decide and may have been suffering a nervous breakdown. Rather than see power transferred to an Estates General, Brienne decided to dissolve the Assembly and seek to secure the necessary validation of his financial programme through the *parlement*. Brienne seems to have received some assurances from the president of the *parlement* of Paris, d'Aligre, that it would be prepared to work with the ministry; if so d'Aligre had misjudged the mood of the *parlementaires*. The *parlement* met as a *grand chambre*, with the peers in attendance, including opposition figures like Orléans, and the lead was taken by a faction led by a conservative, d'Eprémesnil, a veteran of the resistance to Maupeou, now determined to force resort to the Estates General. The *parlement* promptly rejected both a proposed stamp tax and the new land tax, though they were prepared to accept other parts of the reforms. D'Eprémesnil insisted that 'the constitutional principle of the French monarchy was that taxes should be consented to by those who had to bear them'. So in August Brienne resorted to the *lit de justice* to force registration. The *parlementaires* put up a noisy public campaign of protest and were exiled to Troyes. But it was the government that lost its nerve and in September a settlement was negotiated: the tax proposals would be postponed, the *parlement* would return to Paris and would approve a *vingtième* to be payed until an Estates General convened, not later than 1792.

At the session called to ratify this bargain, the more radical critics maintained their opposition to the deal, and the king, who was in attendance, lost patience and ordered immediate registration. Orléans then openly declared to the king: 'Sire, I beg your Majesty to allow me to place at your feet and in the heart of this Court, that I consider this registration illegal.' He was arrested, but the *parlements* and the new provincial assemblies joined to campaign against the alleged despotism of the ministers. Brienne ploughed on in face of the outcry, and the Chancellor, Lamoignon, launched a radical law reform that was close to Maupeou's scheme and would effectively have ended the obstructive powers of the *parlements*. He made it more attractive by added law reforms, including the abolition of seigneurial jurisdiction. The reaction was that the protest campaign took a violent turn and crowds turned out to defend the threatened *parlements*. The climax came in June 1788 in Grenoble, when Brienne ordered the local governor to enforce the closing of the *parlement* and use troops if necessary. There were confrontations between soldiers and the crowds, and casualties; but the authorities gave way and the governor and the intendant agreed to withdraw the troops from the city. The *parlement* was triumphantly re-installed. This emboldened protests elsewhere, unauthorized provincial meetings of Estates were held and, on 8 August 1788, the French monarchy virtually abdicated its absolute power. Louis XVI had gone through his usual routine, first taking a hard line against the protests, then giving in. He announced that the Lamoignon reforms would be suspended until an Estates General met on 1 May 1789. Brienne had already been told by his financial officials that the government was running out of money. Desperate attempts to raise further credit failed against a background of rising public unrest. On 25 August, Brienne resigned and Necker returned as Controller. He was able, on his personal credit, to raise enough loan monies to keep the administration going until the Estates General met.

The situation in France was now serious, especially as further harvest failures caused an acute subsistence crisis in the winter of 1788–9, with the familiar accompaniment of food rioting. More serious than that was the reality that the kingdom no longer had a government. Although the king and his ministers were still in place, they could no longer be certain that their orders would be obeyed or that the security forces were reliable. The kingdom was in a mild state of anarchy, pending the coming of the Estates General. This did not mean, however, that the Revolution had now begun. The process of calling the Estates General has left a unique and authentic picture of public opinion in early 1789 in the *cahiers de doléance* drafted for the Estates General by every constituency. Broadly the *cahiers* of the privileged Estates of Clergy and Nobility suggest that the propertied and educated classes were near agreement that there should be a constitutional monarchy, based on the principles of Montesquieu. Government would be answerable to a representative assembly, taxation and legislation would require consent, and regular annual budgets would be published. There would be civil liberties, freedom of speech, religious confession and the press, and an end to arbitrary arrest and imprisonment. Most of the *cahiers*, including those of the nobility, were willing to accept an end of seigneurial rights and a basic equality of citizens before the law. In addition they usually recommended a programme of Enlightenment reforms to promote the public welfare.

The *cahiers* of the Third Estate reveal a different order of priorities. These were drafted by lawyers or other members of the propertied classes seeking election to the Third Estate, and politically they usually incorporate most of the constitutional proposals found among the Clergy and the Nobility. But when they articulated the grievances of the peasants and the artisans these tended to be anti-modernization. They wanted to keep controls of the food trades and prices, preserve the communal tradition of village agriculture and maintain guild protection of artisan production. They attacked mechanization and factory production, enclosures and agrarian innovations. While denouncing the insolence and illegalities of the old revenue collectors, especially the oppression of the salt tax regime, they still wanted a strong government that could repress banditry and vagrancy, and hold the social balance between the rich and propertied and the labouring poor. It was a programme distinctly different from the Rousseauesque, Enlightenment plans of the elite.

In the light of the evidence contained in the *cahiers* of 1789, it is still possible to maintain that, while France had been in a state of anarchy since late 1788, and effective government authority had been weakened, this did not mean the situation was beyond control, or that adequate political leadership could not have avoided revolutionary solutions. For one thing, much of the uncontrolled local violence of the period was due to the subsistence crisis and would be alleviated in time, as it had been on innumerable earlier occasions. The disorders were not a call for political revolution. If the *cahiers* are a true reflection of opinion, there was a broad consensus among the propertied elites in favour of a constitutional monarchy under a rule of

law, while the lower orders were basically traditionalist. Evidence of a frustrated capitalist bourgeoisie eager to take control for itself is lacking. This
was because the governments were usually friendly towards the entrepreneurs in their quest for a wealthier society, while there were no serious
obstacles to social advancement: noble status could easily be purchased if
the money was there. The later Bourbon monarchy in France had certainly
been authoritarian, but it had not, on the whole, been reactionary. What it
had lacked was skilled and imaginative political leadership from the top,
and the accident of dynastic succession had meant that under Louis XVI
this would not be forthcoming.

Conclusion: Europe in 1789

There are historians prepared to argue that European civilization was on the brink of revolutionary transition in the last decades of the eighteenth century. Since that is what actually happened in the end, the view has a great deal of plausibility. The European elites had accepted the idea of social betterment through government-led action, whether in its Enlightenment version or in its Germanic version, cameralism, and were acting on it over much of Europe. There was violent political unrest in parts of Europe and its dependencies. Besides the two major upheavals of the American and French revolutions, there were revolts in both parts of the Netherlands, Geneva, Liège, Bohemia, Hungary and Poland, not forgetting troubles in Ireland. The problem lies in showing convincingly that these different events can be explained by some common causal pattern. It has to be demonstrated that there were powerful forces seeking radical change which was being obstructed by the existing social and political structures. The assumption that progress and modernization had converted hearts and minds, and that their realization had run up against a system rooted in tradition and the outdated values of a dying society, has to be proved.

Progress was uneven in different societies, but religious persecution was weakening: the Jesuits were dissolved, monasteries were being scaled down and their resources redirected to social welfare. Legal systems were being reformed and the use of judicial torture and cruel punishments was being discontinued. Money was being invested in improving the social infrastructure, serious efforts were being made to improve educational facilities, and censorship was relaxing its grip. It is difficult to show persuasively that Europe was paralysed by reaction or was unwilling to contemplate change. Further, the actual rebellions or armed protests were often directed against modernizing reform, not the prevailing system – this was certainly the case in the Habsburg dominions under Joseph II – and when the reform programme was abandoned it was remarkable how quickly the Netherlands and Hungary and Italy returned to their allegiance. The most significant evidence is contained in the French *cahiers* of 1789: the labouring classes complained of the oppressions they endured at the hands of their ruling elites but had no political programme for displacing them; while the Patriot revolt in the United Provinces was fixated on the past glories of the Dutch republic not on a vision of a new society.

European civilization was still in reasonably good working order at the end of the eighteenth century. It had managed to come to terms with the truly subversive and destabilizing effects of the Renaissance and the Reformation and had achieved stability combined with a modest level of social improvement. The economy had entered on a long upward curve and substantial new wealth was being generated, though its unequal distribution was as marked as it had always been. In the middle of the social range there was an expanding bourgeoisie, an increasingly affluent consumer society, which would sooner or later have to be accommodated into the political power structure. For the present, however critical the bourgeois subjects might be of aristocratic arrogance, extravagance and immorality, they were not disposed to challenge their social and political hegemony. When the French revolutionary armies offered liberation to the oppressed peoples of Europe, they found they were not satisfying a pent-up demand; on the contrary, neither their presence nor their ideology were wanted. So they settled instead for playing the old European power game in a spectacularly new and successful way. It was their success in that game which compelled the other players to contemplate a radical overhaul of their own traditional methods and beliefs.

Endnotes

1. The European World of the Seventeenth Century

1 The subject of demography in early modern Europe has produced an extensive debate and considerable disagreement. For an introduction to the discussion see *The Fontana Economic History of Europe*, vol. 2 (1974); B. H. Schlicher van Bath, *The Agrarian History of Western Europe* (1963); C. Cipolla, *The Economic History of World Population* (1962); M. W. Flinn, *The European Demographic System 1500–1800* (1962).

2 The subject of epidemic disease and subsistence crises is also controversial. For an introduction to the discussion see: M. W. Flinn, 'Plague in Europe and the Mediterranean countries', *Economic History Review*, 8 (1937): A. Appleby, 'The disappearance of plague: a continuing puzzle', *Economic History Review*, 8 (1937): E. Le Roy Ladurie, *Times of Feast, Times of Famine* (1971). There is a collection of articles from the *Annales* school of French historians in L. P. Burke, ed., *Economy and Society in Early-Modern Europe* (1972).

3 Discussion is especially lively about the impact of the Thirty Years War on Germany. Some contributions to this are: T. K. Rabb, 'The effects of the Thirty Years War on the German economy', in T. K. Rabb, ed., *The Thirty Years War* (1964); S. H. Steinberg, 'The Thirty Years War: a new interpretation', *History*, 32 (1947); H. Kamen, 'The economic and social consequences of the Thirty Years War', *Past and Present*, 39 (1968).

4 The long discussion over the impact of American silver on Europe began with E. J. Hamilton, *American Treasure and the Price Revolution in Spain, 1501–1650* (1934), and 'The decline of Spain', *Economic History Review*, 8 (1937). Among other contributions are: J. H. Elliott, 'The decline of Spain', *Past and Present*, 20 (1961); H. Kamen, 'The decline of Spain, a historical myth', *Past and Present*, 81 (1978).

5 The witch beliefs and persecutions in early modern Europe have spawned a very large literature of varying quality. Major contributions are: K. Thomas, *Religion and the Rise of Magic* (1971); C. Larner, *Enemies of God: The Witch Hunt in Scotland* (1981); N. Cohen, *Europe's Inner Demons* (1975); B. P. Levack, *The Witch Hunt in Early-Modern Europe* (1987).

6 Filmer is often dismissed on the assumption that his ideas were fundamentally refuted in the writings of John Locke. But Filmer's critique of all theories of government that rest on the supposed consent of the governed is not easily dismissed, and was perhaps closer to popular thinking in the seventeenth century than the intellectual concepts of Locke.

7 A pioneering study of a proto-bureaucracy of the period is found in the two volumes by G. E. Aylmer, *The King's Servants* (1961), and *The State's Servants* (1973). The French bureaucracy is treated in R. Mousnier, *The Institutions of*

France under the Absolute Monarchy (1979); and A. F. Upton, *Charles XI and Swedish Absolutism* (1998), claims that something much closer to the modern idea of a bureaucracy can be found in Sweden.

8   There are useful accounts of the devolved system of government in England in D. Hirst, *Authority and Conflict, England 1603–1658* (1986); R. Ashton, *The English Civil War – Conservatism and Revolution, 1603–1649* (1978); and detailed studies in J. S. Morrill, *Cheshire, 1630–1660* (1974), and D. Underdown, *Somerset in the Civil War and Interregnum* (1973).

9   The article by S. T. Perron, 'The Castilian Assembly of the Clergy', *Parliaments, Estates and Representation*, 18 (1998), illustrates several basic realities about the working of early modern representative institutions.

10 The basic survey of the impact of printing on European society is E. L. Eisenstein, *The Printing Press as an Agent of Change. The Printing Revolution in Early-Modern Europe* (1983).

2. The First European War

1   The acceptance of war as a natural feature of European civilization was reflected in the paucity of serious pacifist critiques. Apart from small Christian–pacifist sects whose members refused to bear arms, when the elites discussed a general pacification, as Sully did after 1598, they conceived of it as a cessation of hostilities among Christians, who would then unite to wage crusading warfare against the infidels. Generally, war was treated as both natural and beneficial to society. A parallel was drawn with the medical cure-all of the time, blood-letting: war improved the health of the body politic.

2   The Antichrist was a living reality all over Christian Europe: he figures largely in the Puritan polemics of the English Revolution and was very much alive in seventeenth-century Russia. See, for example, C. Hill, *Religion and Politics in Seventeenth-Century England* (1986); R. O. Crumney, *The Old Believers and the World of Antichrist* (1970).

3   This aspect of the international crisis is easily overlooked, but is analysed in: C. H. Carter, *The Secret Diplomacy of the Habsburgs* (1964); B. Chudoba, *Spain and the Empire* (1952).

4   There is an account of the debate in Sweden over the intervention in the Empire in M. Roberts, *Gustavus Adolphus* (1958) and *Essays in Swedish History* (1967).

5   There is an extensive literature about Wallenstein which leaves much in his career obscure. G. Mann, *Wallenstein* (1976), is authoritative but forbidding; G. Parker, ed, *The Thirty Years War* (1984), and G. Pagès, *The Thirty Years War* (1970), are more user-friendly.

6   See Chapter 1, note 3, and R. Ergang, *The Myth of the All-Destructive Fury of the Thirty Years War* (1956).

3. The Origins of the Modern State: The Absolutist Route

1   There are wide differences among the historians about the military revolution. For an overview, see G. Parker, *The Military Revolution: Military Innovation and the Rise of the West, 1500–1800* (1988); M. Duffy, *The Military Revolution and the State, 1500–1800* (1980).

2   There is a lack of research publication in English on the reign of Henry IV, but see M. Greengrass, *France in the Age of Henri IV* (1984).

3   Historians have been slow to expose Richelieu's successful spin-doctoring techniques. Significant revisionist studies are: J. Bergin, *Cardinal Richelieu and the Pursuit of Wealth* (1985); J. Bergin and L. Brockliss, eds., *Richelieu and his Age* (1995).

4 Historians find difficulty in determining the origins of an institution like the French intendancy. Richelieu made a major contribution, but much earlier use by the crown of travelling commissioners is on record, while Colbert had to rebuild the institution after 1660.

5 The French peasant revolts of the 1630s and 1640s have produced a range of interpretations. It is easy to get the impression that the crown's authority was being tested almost to destruction. But the reality is that Richelieu was able to pursue his policies regardless, and not one of the rebellions succeeded. It is arguable that in early modern European societies successful peasant rebellion was not feasible.

6 The *moriscos* had been nominally Christian for more than a century by 1600, but there is convincing evidence that they had retained their ancestral beliefs. The Christian authorities had done little to invest in evangelization among the *morisco* community. The economic consequences of the expulsion must be speculative but there is reason to doubt the concept of the *moriscos* as a dynamic community of artisans and peasants in a society that seemed to despise productive labour.

7 See Chapter 1, note 4; J. Lynch, *Spain under the Habsburgs*, vol. 2 (1981), gives a good general account.

4. The Origins of the Modern State: Alternative Routes

1 Despite the flood of vocal protest against the king's proceedings, what forced him to call a new parliament in 1628 was the military defeat on the Ile de Ré and the consequent need to raise a new seaborne expedition to help the Huguenots in La Rochelle.

2 The correspondence of two leading members of the royal government, Archbishop Laud and his friend Thomas Wentworth, uses the word 'Thorough' to refer to comprehensive reforms in government, which they felt were necessary. Some commentators have taken 'Thorough' to represent the settled policy of the royal government. In fact, Laud and Wentworth were using the term to indicate what the government ought to have been doing, and in their view was failing to implement.

3 For a spread of interpretations on the Scottish crisis, see C. V. Wedgwood, *The King's Peace* (1955); R. Ashton, *The English Civil War* (1978); K. Sharpe, *The Personal Rule of Charles I* (1992).

4 See I. Roots, *The Great Rebellion* (1966); G. E. Aylmer, *Rebellion or Revolution?* (1986); A. Fletcher, *The Outbreak of the English Civil War* (1981).

5 The Irish rebellion made armed confrontation in England almost inevitable; the one open question was whether Charles I could raise enough support to make an armed challenge to the parliamentary leaders possible. See C. Russell, 'The British Problem and the English Civil War', *History*, 72 (1987).

6 It is now accepted that all the local communities were internally divided by the war and that substantial elements in society sought a 'third way' of non-involvement, from the attempted local neutrality pacts of 1642 to the populist 'Clubman' risings of 1644-5.

7 On the New Model Army, see M. Kishlansky, *The rise of the New Model Army* (1980); A. Woolrych, *Soldiers and Statesmen* (1987).

8 On the Commonwealth phase, see B. Worden, *The Rump Parliament* (1974).

9 Worden has persuasive evidence that Cromwell and the officers had a brief surge of providentialist excitement in 1653, expecting some spectacular divine intervention.

10 'Arminian' was a label used in polemic to discredit any opponent, regardless of his actual beliefs, just as 'communist' was after 1917. But Arminius' views on predestination did in fact subvert the very basis of Calvinist belief, whatever his intention, which made him 'objectively' crypto-papist and an agent of Antichrist.

5. Towards 'Absolutism': Variations round a Theme

1 In all government there is a gap between aspiration and performance. Louis XIV clearly was not in full control of his kingdom, even by 1715. The ongoing saga of his efforts to suppress the Jansenists testifies how far short he was. This is not to deny that over the reign the royal power in the kingdom had been powerfully reinforced.

2 The Fouquet trial for treason was a mockery of justice. He was seen as an over-mighty subject because of his accumulated wealth and patronage, and he stood in Colbert's way. The treason charge made it possible to confiscate his wealth and to demonstrate that the king could strike down even the most powerful of subjects. On the background to this episode, see R. Bonney, 'The secret expenses of Richelieu and Mazarin', *English Historical Review*, 91 (1976).

3 Mercantilism is a term invented by historians to describe the economic thinking and practices of early modern societies. The core concept was derived from the medieval period, that government could and should direct economic activities in the interests of the community as a whole. It acquired a further dimension as part of the international power game, aimed to increase the relative wealth and economic power of the community at the expense of rivals. The basic texts on the subject are: C. Wilson, *Mercantilism* (1958); E. Hekscher, *Mercantilism* (1935); D. C. Coleman, ed., *Revisions in Mercantilism* (1968).

4 Brandenburg–Prussia is the most quoted example of a state that developed out of an army. Sweden is often called a 'military state', but was already a mature civil society before Gustav Adolf made it a major military power. But no state could afford to ignore the military imperative to modernize its forces; those that did, like Poland, paid a heavy price.

5 Perhaps the best example is Russia, where neither the coercive regime of Peter the Great, nor the comparable rule of the Communist party after 1917, succeeded in eradicating the values and mentalities of the old society.

6 The best accounts of the reconstruction of Bohemia after 1620 are: J. V. Polisensky, *The Thirty Years War* (1971); R. J. W. Evans, *The Making of the Habsburg Monarchy* (1979).

7 Hocher represents one strand in Habsburg state-building, provided by cameralist administrators, usually trained in German Protestant universities. They had to struggle with the entrenched clericalist conservatism of the Habsburg court. Hocher was a potential Colbert, who never enjoyed the full support or understanding of his master, Leopold I. See J. P. Spielman, *Leopold I of Austria* (1977).

8 The concept of the decline of Habsburg Spain is still debated by historians. See: J. H. Elliott, 'The decline of Spain', *Past and Present*, 20 (1961); H. Kamen, 'The decline of Spain: a historical myth?', *Past and Present*, 81 (1978).

6. The Evolution of the British State: A Different Model

1 In 1659 'Quaker panic' was developing over the open challenge to the rules of hierarchy by the early Quakers, who were then singled out for harsh repression under the Restoration. But even in the parliaments of 1654 and 1656, there was confrontation between Cromwell and the officers, insisting on liberty for 'the people of God', and the community representatives seeking the reinstatement of traditional religious controls. See R. Hutton, *The Restoration* (1985).

2 There is a comprehensive analysis of the finances of the Restoration monarchy in C. D. Chandamon, *The English Public Revenue, 1660–1688* (1975).

3 The royalist reaction after 1681 is a fact; it was then that Filmer's *Patriarcha* became a bestselling text on politics. But the commitment of either Charles II or James II to a

partisan, Tory programme is subject to debate; there were signs by 1684 of renewed attempts to bring relief to Catholics, and expand the standing army, both policies unacceptable to most Tories. See J. Western, *Monarchy and Revolution* (1972).

4 This question will always be controversial: see J. P. Kenyon, *Sunderland* (1958); J. Childe, *The Army, James II and the Glorious Revolution* (1980); J. R. Jones, *The Revolution of 1688* (1972).

5 The structure and language of the Bill of Rights, or the Toleration Act of 1689, reflect a wish to pretend that nothing much had changed. Real radical change after 1689 was in Scotland and Ireland and developed in England from William III's involvement of the country in the European war: this could only be financed by parliaments. The Whig cult of the 'Glorious Revolution' arose later in response to militant Tory–Anglican revisionism about the 1689 settlement.

6 Queen Anne seems as much influenced by her early infatuation for Sarah Churchill, duchess of Marlborough, and the deep dislike she came to feel for her Hanoverian heirs, as by any personal commitment to Tory principles. See E. Gregg, *Queen Anne* (1980); G. Holmes, *British Politics in the Age of Anne* (1987).

7. Developments on the North-Eastern Periphery

1 This was a rare example of a sovereign of one religious confession ruling subjects of a different confession. When tried by James II in Britain it was a disaster, but the Hohenzollern rulers were intelligent enough not to challenge the position of the Lutheran establishment. They were content to appoint Calvinists to public positions, encourage Calvinist immigrants and appoint Calvinists to university teaching positions. The result was relatively peaceful confessional co-existence.

2 The Prussian nobility long grudged their forcible transfer from Polish sovereignty for they appreciated the liberties of the Polish gentry. To them, the Hohenzollerns and their agents were alien intruders. The real assimilation of Prussia was the work of King Frederick William after 1713. In some ways the characterization of the Hohenzollern state as 'Prussian' is misleading.

3 On the effects on the Danish peasantry, see T. Munck, *The Peasantry and Early Absolute Monarchy in Denmark, 1660–1708* (1979).

4 The legal status of the 1634 'Form of Government' was an issue within the Swedish Estates until resolved by Charles XI and the Diet in 1680. It seems likely that its sponsors in 1634 meant it to be a constitutional law, but it was never confirmed as such by a reigning monarch. The most acceptable interpretation, as expressed formally in 1660, was that it applied specifically in a regency. Magnate proposals then and in 1672 to reduce the powers of an adult sovereign were firmly rebuffed in the Diet.

5 Contemporary speculation and rumour alleged that Gyllenstierna had left a written programme of action for reinforcing absolute monarchy in Sweden. Charles XI secured Gyllenstierna's archive when he died, and it has since disappeared. There is now no firm evidence that any such plan existed, though the basic objection to the idea of such a project is that it would have been redundant. In the eyes of most Swedes, their kings were already absolute, Christian sovereigns. See A. F. Upton, *Charles XI and Swedish Absolutism* (1998).

6 The myths of the malign consequences of the *liberum veto* in Poland are so entrenched that they are difficult to shift. It is a historical absurdity to propose that the Polish *szlachta* were not aware of the problems it caused, or could not have overridden it if they wished. To ascribe the later destruction of the Polish Commonwealth to this one factor represents a profound misunderstanding.

7 There is evidence that some *boyars*, presumably aware of the laws in Poland or Sweden, suggested imposing an accession charter, which would limit the autocratic power. They clearly got a negative response from the *zemsky sobor* of

1613. The proposal would have changed the *recognition* of Michael Romanov as tsar into an election. There was another proposal at the accession of the Empress Anna in 1730, and it too was rejected.

8 In this respect Peter appears, not as a revolutionary mould-breaker, but following the practice developed since 1613 of using western technology while deliberately seeking to preserve Russian traditions and values.

8. The Second European War, 1660–1721

1 The Ottoman empire was a predatory imperialism, whose functioning depended on a rolling process of expansion by conquest. The booty from the wars and revenues from the subject peoples sustained its military machine; but when expansion stopped it became difficult to satisfy the military clans, like the Janissaries. The seventeenth century had experienced such a period of internal instability until the Köprülü Viziers restored the expansion.

2 The historian G. N. Clark was one of the first to recognize that the state of intra-European warfare was accepted as normal. In principle, Christian rulers should have lived at peace with one another, and treaties always spoke of the desire for a 'firm and lasting' peace. But all contemporary testimony, whether it comes from an academic like Hobbes or practitioners like Olivares or Louis XIV, indicates the acceptance of the permanence of recurrent armed conflicts. The structure of the emergent European states reflected this.

3 It was ironic that, by intervening as he did to rescue Sweden in 1679, Louis deeply offended Charles XI, who saw himself as patronized and humiliated, and nursed his resentment to the end of his days.

4 The devastation of the Palatinate was denounced at the time as an unacceptable act of military terrorism, and even some of Louis's commanders and advisers protested at what they saw as an atrocity. Of course the devastation completely failed to achieve its stated purpose of securing French borders from subsequent attack.

5 Louis had not envisaged such a protracted conflict when he acted in 1688, and even before the crop failure he had realized that in spite of a string of military successes there was no more to be gained by prolonging the war.

6 During the peace negotiations, this 'Rijswick clause' caused as many problems as any other single issue. It was a question of image, affirming Louis's claim to be the temporal champion of the Roman Church, but in the Empire it breached the confessional stability enshrined in the Westphalia settlements, and threatened to re-open issues that had been supposedly settled for all time.

7 Historians continue to debate Louis's decision to accept the Spanish succession for his grandson. It was a breach of his commitment to partition, but a realistic appraisal of his options suggests any other choice would have a worse outcome. A war with Leopold was unavoidable in any case. It is Louis's subsequent conduct towards William III and brutal disregard of legitimate Anglo-Dutch concerns that look indefensible. See R. Hatton, ed., *Louis XIV and Europe* (1976); R. Hatton and J. S. Bromley, eds., *William III and Louis XIV* (1967).

8 The subsistence crisis of 1709–10 was evidence of the vulnerability of European society to natural disaster. It was seen as a warning from God, but the disaster did not stop the wars: by 1711 everything was back to normal. Louis XIV's public acknowledgements in 1709 that the wars were imposing intolerable sufferings on his subjects were later revealed for what they were – empty rhetoric.

9. Changing Mentalities

1 In the end Copernicus probably deserves to be recognized as the pioneer of the scientific movement, not so much for the originality of his thought, for he remained

a firm Aristotelian all his life, but because he was not playing mathematical games, like Orême, but believed in the physical reality of his ideas. He was lucky in his timing; it needed the technology of printing and the confessional pluralism emerging from the Reformation to provide a favourable context.

2 The contemporary strength of the common-sense, observational case against, for example, the motion of the Earth, to say nothing of its scriptural support, should not be underestimated. Many of Galileo's experiments were 'thought experiments'; it is doubtful he ever dropped anything from the Leaning Tower of Pisa, and if he had it would not have produced the result he predicted, while his central argument proving the motion of the Earth on the basis of the tidal motions of the seas is completely erroneous. The critics of the new science were not blindly ignoring the irrefutable force of experiment.

3 The invention of the microscope had enormous potential to advance human understanding; yet for a long time it remained an interesting scientific toy. Those who used it had no explanatory framework for making sense of what they observed, or how it might affect the human condition.

4 See P. Burke, *Popular Culture in Early-Modern Europe* (1976): R. Munchemblad, *Popular and Elite Culture in France, 1400–1800* (1985); B. Capp, *Astrology and the Popular Press: English Almanacs 1550–1800* (1979); M. Spufford, *Small Books and Pleasant Histories* (1981); D. Darnton, 'The high Enlightenment and the low life of literature in pre-revolutionary France', *Past and Present*, 71 (1976).

5 See T. Munck, *Seventeenth-Century Europe* (1990), p. 306, for a concise definition of baroque, or the more extended one in D. H. Pennington, *Europe in the Seventeenth Century* (1985), Chapter 7. The main differences are over whether baroque applies to most manifestations of contemporary civilization, or should be confined to the visual arts, architecture and music. In H. Trevor-Roper, ed., *The Age of Expansion* (1969), the section headed 'The Baroque century', has an extensive, lavishly illustrated discussion.

6 The contribution of Winckelmann to the German Enlightenment is discussed in 'The role of the artist in society' in A. Cobban, ed., *The Age of the Enlightenment* (1970).

7 The term 'enlightened despotism' tends to be used interchangeably with 'enlightened absolutism' by historians. See the discussion in the Introduction in H. M. Scott, ed., *Enlightened Absolutism: Reform and Reformers in Later Eighteenth-Century Europe* (1990).

8 On Montesquieu, see L. M. Cranston, *Philosophers and Pamphleteers: Political Theorists of the Enlightenment* (1976); R. Shackleton, *Montesquieu, A Critical Biography* (1961).

10. Change in the Economy and Society

1 An introduction to the debate can be found in I. Wallerstein, *The Modern World System*, vol. 2 (1980); C. Cipolla, ed., *The Fontana Economic History of Europe*, vol. 3 (1973); R. Davies, *The Rise of the Atlantic Economies* (1973); P. Burke, ed., *Economy and Society in Early-Modern Europe: Essays from the 'Annales'* (1972); F. Braudel, *Capitalism and Material life, 1400–1800* (1981).

2 See L. Benfield et al., eds., *The World We Have Gained* (1986); M. W. Flinn, *The European Demographic System* (1998); J. D. Post, *Food Shortage, Climatic Variability and Epidemic Disease in Pre-industrial Europe* (1985).

3 See G. E. Mingay, *English Landed Society in the Eighteenth Century* (1963); J. D. Chambers and G. E. Mingay, *The Agricultural Revolution 1750–1815* (1966); J. Cooper, 'In search of agrarian capitalism', *Past and Present*, 80 (1978).

4 The most accessible account in English for the history of the United Provinces is J. Israel, *The Dutch Republic* (1995).

5 The slave trade is a highly controversial and emotive subject: for an introduction, see O. Rainsford, *The Slave Trade* (1971); D. B. Davies, *The Problem of Slavery in Western Culture* (1966); H. A. Wyndham, *The Atlantic and Slavery* (1935).

6 For a recent discussion, see M. Dainton, *Progress and Poverty, An Economic and Social History of Britain, 1700–1850* (1995).

7 A general overview can be found in E. J. Hobsbawm, *Industry and empire* (1963); T. S. Ashton, *The Industrial Revolution* (1965); E. Dawson, *The Early Industrial Revolution* (1966); P. Deane, *The First Industrial Revolution* (1965).

11. Social Change

1 The problem is to locate the revolutionary bourgeoisie. It is not in dispute that all over Europe a distinct middle class was emerging, differentiated from the nobility above and the artisans and craftsmen below, and this was a new level of 'polite society'. The problem is finding evidence of radical social and political discontent among such people. Their common aspirations seem rather to seek to enhance their status within the existing structures of society and, if successful enough, enter the ranks of the nobilities. See R. and E. Forster, eds., *European Society in the Eighteenth Century* (1969); F. L. Ford, *Strasbourg in Transition* (1958); E. Barber, *The Bourgeoisie in Eighteenth-Century France* (1955); 'Making the English middle class, c. 1700–1850 ', *Journal of British Studies*, 32 (1993); D. Johnson, ed., *French Society and the Revolution* (1976); C. Morazé, *The Triumph of the Middle Classes* (1968).

2 For recent work on the European peasantries, see T. Scott, ed., *The Peasantries of Europe* (1995); J. Blum, *The End of the Old Order in Rural Europe* (1978).

3 For work on the social basis of the French Revolution, see A. Cobban, *The Social Interpretation of the French Revolution* (1964); F. Furet, *Interpreting the French Revolution* (1992); S. Schama, *Citizens* (1989).

4 There is a general account of urban life in Europe in C. R. Friedrichs, *The Early-Modern City, 1450–1750* (1995); see also P. Corfield, *The Impact of English Towns, 1700–1800* (1982).

12. A New Search for Political Stability

1 There has been considerable debate about the development of British society in the eighteenth century: see J. C. D. Clark, *English Society* (1985); L. Colley, *Britons, Forging the Nation: 1707–1837* (1992); R. Porter, *English Society in the Eighteenth Century* (1982).

2 On the involvement of the Tory party with Jacobitism, see B. Lenman, *The Jacobite Risings in Britain, 1688–1746* (1984); L. Colley, *In Defence of Oligarchy, the Tory Party 1714–1760* (1982); J. C. D. Clark, 'The politics of the excluded: Tories, Jacobites and Whig patriots', *Parliamentary History*, 2 (1983); I. R. Christie, 'The Tory party, Jacobitism and the '45', *Historical Journal*, 30 (1982).

3 In the nature of things reliable evidence on smuggling is sparse, but there is good reason to believe that it constituted a significant 'black economy' in the eighteenth century. See P. Langford, *The Excise Crisis and Politics in the Age of Walpole* (1975).

4 See P. Goubert, *The Ancien Regime* (1973); R. Mousnier, *The Institutions of France under the Absolute Monarchy* (1979); J. F. Bosher, 'Current writing on administration and finance in eighteenth-century France', *Journal of Modern History*, 53 (1981).

5 The basic general study of eighteenth-century Spain is, J. Lynch, *Bourbon Spain, 1700–1808* (1989); see also R. Herr, *Rural Change and Royal Finances in Spain*

at the End of the Old Regime (1985), and *The Eighteenth-Century Revolution in Spain* (1958).

6 The inner thinking of Victor Amadeus, beyond the obvious urge to maximize the wealth and power of his dynasty, remains impenetrable. But to most contemporaries his quest for *gloire* would be seen as a natural justification – it was what rulers did. See G. Symcox, *Victor Amadeus II: Absolutism in the Savoyard State, 1675–1730* (1983).

7 This is a revision of earlier accounts that credited his grandfather, the Great Elector, with this achievement. It is difficult to empathize with Frederick William I as a person. His routine brutality of speech and behaviour verged on the insane at times, yet his life's work displays a consistent integrity that is so often lacking in his fellow rulers. It was characteristic that he declined a coronation as a frivolous waste of money.

8 Recent work on Frederick William's administration of East Prussia shows clearly how effective the defence of local custom against centralizing pressures could be, even in face of his relentless bullying.

13. The Stabilization of the North-Eastern Borderlands

1 Swedish historians have debated the merits and failings of the Estates' government in the eighteenth century, and rival schools of history have developed. However it is interpreted, it is clear that the Estates' regime fell far short of any modern concept of a liberal political system. There is a very perceptive analysis of the period in M. Roberts, *The Age of Liberty: Sweden 1719–1772* (1986).

2 Of the autocratic sovereigns of Russia between Peter and Catherine II, Catherine I was an uneducated servant woman by origin; Peter II was an immature adolescent; Anna was a woman of strong personality, with little inclination towards serious politics; Ivan VI was an infant; Elizabeth was another strong personality with limited political interests; and Peter III was mentally unbalanced. The survival of the institution of autocracy in face of this woeful experience is evidence of how deeply it was rooted in the Russian mentality.

3 All known regimes in history have made some use of organized spying on their subjects, and have also received a flow of voluntary information and denunciation from those anxious to pursue grudges or ingratiate themselves with authority. But whereas in Christian Europe even feared institutions like the Inquisition operated under a rule of law, the Russian secret police, in their various manifestations, have never been constrained by law. The creation of an intimidatory political climate, in effect organized political terrorism, seems to have been the reason for their existence.

14. The European Power Game, 1715–1740

1 The selection of Maria Theresa as heiress of the hereditary lands, to the exclusion of her two senior cousins, was an inbuilt weakness of the Pragmatic Sanction. When the moment of truth came in 1740, neither of the two Electoral spouses, or their husbands, who had solemnly affirmed their acceptance of the Sanction, had much hesitation about joining the scramble for the inheritance. For this they had a moral basis of sorts: the working of hereditary succession was a branch of divine Providence and no merely human agency was entitled to interfere with its mysterious working.

2 The acceptance of the Russian autocrats as equal members of the club of Europe's royal families always caused problems. After Peter adopted the formal title of 'Emperor' there was a further protocol problem: the European

community recognized the Holy Roman Emperor as the only potentate of that rank. There was a persistent tendency to relegate the Russian monarchs to the outsider status accorded to the Ottomans or the Moguls.

3 Since no formal state of war existed between Britain and Spain, this action might be seen as international piracy. It was an early example of the persistent British proclivity to assume their naval superiority was a kind of divine right, which empowered them to set the rules of naval warfare. The habit of pre-emptive strikes against potentially competitive navies continued through the two eliminations of the Danish navy in the Napoleonic period to the destruction of the French fleet at Oran in 1940.

4 This episode illustrated the bitter resentment of Spaniards over the concessions the British had extorted from them at Utrecht. These embittered Anglo-Spanish relations for the rest of the century, and repeated Spanish defeats at the hands of the British did nothing to discourage Spain's rulers from seeking redress of their grievances.

5 Foreign policy was the one area where Walpole had to share power with Charles Townshend, who enjoyed the confidence of George II. In 1730, Walpole manoeuvred Townshend into resigning, and got rid of his only serious competitor in the government. See J. Black, *Foreign Policy in the Age of Walpole* (1985).

6 The French government made a token gesture by sending a small force to hold Danzig on behalf of Lesczynski, but after a siege by forces loyal to Augustus, supported by the Russians, surrendered the city and withdrew.

7 The French counter-strikes in Germany and Italy were model operations; the element of surprise secured for Fleury the bargaining counters he needed and he held them until Charles VI recognized he could not retake them and agreed to negotiate. The operation was so economical that French government finances carried the costs without serious disturbance.

15. The Last European War of the *Ancien Régime*, 1740–1763

1 The Prussian army had experienced no serious military operations for years by 1740, and under Frederick William I was something of a 'display army', drilled to technical perfection on the parade ground. When Frederick took it to war, the infantry did out-perform their opponents, but the cavalry and artillery proved deficient. The subsequent ability of the Prussian army to defeat all its opponents, except the Russians, developed after its battle experience under Frederick.

2 The 'Pragmatic army', commanded for a time by George II in person, won a notable victory over the French at Dettingen in 1743, though Britain and France were not then at war. The failure to exploit this success created a rising public opinion in Britain that taxpayers' money was being used in defence of Hanoverian, rather than British, interests. This enabled critics in parliament to create a governmental crisis in 1744, after which George II found himself compelled to accept the resignation of his favourite minister, Lord Carteret.

3 For the last Jacobite rebellion in the British Isles, see B. Lenman, *The Jacobite Risings in Britain* (1984); D. Szecki, *The Jacobites: Britain and Europe, 1688–1788* (1994).

4 In one sense, by 1748 Louis XV had asserted his status as the most powerful ruler in Europe: in both the Netherlands and Italy he had defeated the hostile coalition, with only Savoy as an ally, once Frederick retired with his gains in 1745. But Louis's military power was nullified by the lack of a clear strategic objective once the bid to take the imperial title from the Habsburgs failed on the death of Charles VII. The achievement of Frederick, who single-mindedly pursued a consistent war aim throughout, compares with Louis XV, who entered the war reluctantly in the first place, and then floundered aimlessly in a quest to

get out of it. He had brought his kingdom close to financial collapse for no obvious advantage and this proved seriously damaging to his image both at home and abroad.

5 See P. Baumgart, 'The annexation and integration of Silesia', in M. Greengrass, ed., *Conquest and Coalescence* (1991).

6 A change in attitude was reflected in the more populist tone of *parlementaire* rhetoric; 'depotism' became the central charge against ministerial actions. This meant that when royal ministers were genuinely trying to reform the system by, for example, shifting the tax burden from the poor on to the wealthy, their proposals were systematically attacked as despotism and obstructed. See J. Rogister, *The Parlement of Paris, 1737–1755* (1995).

7 For discussion of the failings of the Haugwitz reforms, see H. M. Scott, ed., *Enlightened Absolutism* (1990); K. L. F. Szabo, *Kaunitz and Enlightened Absolutism, 1753–1780* (1994).

8 The sheer futility of this war, and how what seemed to be a good idea, the 'reversal of the alliances' in 1756, became a disaster for both Louis XV and Maria Theresa is clear enough in hindsight. See the relevant chapters in D. E. Showalter, *The Wars of Frederick the Great* (1981); and Szabo, *Kaunitz* (1994).

9 The change of mood in British public opinion is often linked to the bestselling pamphlet by I. Maudit, *Considerations on the Present German War*, which appeared in November 1760. See R. Middleton, *The Bells of Victory: The Pitt–Newcastle Ministry and the Conduct of the Seven Years War* (1985).

16. The Enlightenment

1 The literature is voluminous and there is unlimited scope for debating whether there was a single movement, the Enlightenment, whether its programme changed over time, or whether the phenomenon was a series of parallel movements, the *Encyclopédistes*, the *Aufklärung* and the Scottish, Dutch and Italian enlightenments. There are good overviews in R. Porter, *The Enlightenment* (1990); N. Hampson, *The Enlightenment* (1981). There was also an opposition to Enlightenment ideas; see R. J. White, *The Anti-philosophers* (1970).

2 This important feature of the history of the Enlightenment, that it was elitist and failed to capture the minds of the common folk, is often overlooked. The more realistic thinkers like Voltaire acknowledged this at the time. See R. Darnton, 'The high Enlightenment and the low life of literature in pre-revolutionary France' in *Past and Present*, 51 (1971): H. Payne, *The Philosophes and the People* (1976).

3 A structural fault in Enlightenment thinking seems to be an assumption that once human beings are released from the constraints of ignorance and superstition they will behave rationally. Rousseau was obviously correct in insisting that there was more to human nature than rationality. There is a comparable structural fault in Marxism, which assumed that once men were liberated from exploitation and 'false consciousness', a new, harmonious socialist society would painlessly emerge. They both use a one-dimensional view of human nature which is at odds with the realities that history has consistently illustrated.

4 The ambiguities in Rousseau's writings about how the general will actually operates has provided abundant ammunition for those political thinkers who seek to criticize the very concept, or possibility, of a democratic, egalitarian society.

17. Enlightened Despotism: The Enlightenment in Action

1 There is a general review of the concept of enlightened absolutism in the 'Introduction' to H. M. Scott, ed., *Enlightened Absolutism: Reform and Reformers in Eighteenth-Century Europe* (1990).

2 The contemporary usage of the German description *Polizeistaat* can be misunderstood by the modern reader to whom 'police state' has a special significance. The early modern *Polizeistaat* was a society where all aspects of the subjects' lives were supervised by its sovereign ruler; this extended beyond law and order to the regulation of the whole life of the community in the common interest of all its members.

3 J. Lynch, *Bourbon Spain* (1989), offers the best survey of the reformist ministers of Charles III. More detailed accounts can be found in L. Rodriguez, 'The Spanish riots of 1766', *Past and Present*, 59 (1973); C. C. Noel, 'Opposition to enlightened reform in Spain, Campomanes and the clergy, 1765–1775', *Societas*, 3, 1973.

4 A general study of the Spanish Inquisition is H. Kamen, *The Spanish Inquisition* (1965). The Inquisition had lost some of its power to intimidate during the eighteenth century, and heresy hunting had declined, but it was still formidable, not least because of the popular support it enjoyed.

5 Vico is now accepted as an important and original thinker: his *Scienza nuova* of 1725 made him a precursor of the Enlightenment. It was an irony that Vico, like several other leading Italian reformers, came from Naples, regarded with some reason as the most socially backward of the Italian principalities.

6 The influence of the writings of Beccaria on penal reform over much of Europe is evident and makes him a major international thinker of the Enlightenment. Muratori's influence was necessarily mainly effective in Catholic Europe, but he too ranks as a leading reform influence; these two names alone are evidence that eighteenth-century Italy was not a stagnant cultural backwater in European civilization.

7 Leopold, in contrast with his brother Joseph, is often put forward as the model reformer, whose realistic appreciation of the need to respect the rooted conservatism of his subjects was the basis of his relative success. But in the end he seems to have had little more success than Joseph in persuading his Tuscan subjects of the merits of adopting enlightened reforms.

18. The Big Three and Scandinavia

1 There is a discussion of Frederick's collaboration with the law reformer S. Cocceji in H. C. Johnson, *Frederick the Great and his Officials* (1975); H. Weill, *Frederick the Great and Samuel Cocceji* (1961).

2 Interpretations of Frederick as a reformer are in G. Ritter, *Frederick the Great* (1968); C. Duffy, *Frederick the Great* (1985); P. Paret, ed., *Frederick the Great, A Profile* (1972); and T. C. W. Blanning, 'Frederick the Great and Enlightened Absolutism', in H. M. Scott, ed., *Enlightened Absolutism* (1990).

3 The war damage was serious – a population loss of 10 per cent and some provinces repeatedly fought over, notably Pomerania and East Prussia – yet the comparatively rapid recovery suggests that the basic social and governmental structures had survived. It may be that the organized levying of war contributions on hostile territory was less destructive than uncontrolled plundering. See D. Showalter, *The Wars of Frederick the Great* (1985).

4 The innate tendency for career bureaucracies with established working routines to develop a corporate identity and become an autonomous power within the state was always a problem for royal absolutisms. Those who confronted an obstructive bureaucracy head on, like Joseph II, tended to come to grief; the skilled operators accepted reality and created alternative lines of command around the obstacle.

5 Over-sensitivity to public criticism is a mark of a weak government; Frederick understood that the chattering classes were harmless when government is

functioning effectively. But the English visitor certainly exaggerated the freedom allowed in Frederick's Prussia; the regime was very tolerant of religious debate, but there were certainly limits on public discussion of politics.

6 The legal status of the Italian provinces, some of which had historically been imperial fiefs, was open to debate. They might be considered parts of the Empire; the Netherlands was not.

7 The debacle in the Netherlands was a good instance of how a political design that looks reasonable on paper can misfire in the real world of politics. It also showed the danger when dogmatic rulers, with a passion for order, cannot resist trying to eliminate anomalies and will not leave well alone. Joseph's intervention in the Netherlands was particularly inept in a contented province, which produced a regular revenue surplus for the dynasty.

8 Because Russia was not a country, but a multi-cultural sub-continent, effective central supervision was peculiarly difficult. The local bureaucratic administrations tended to report back what they knew the central government wanted to hear and concealed unpleasant realities in the well-grounded confidence that they would not be found out. This then becomes a problem for historians in their search for what was really happening.

9 They did not have far to look: the Ottoman empire was evidently destined to repeat the experience of Poland. The process has destabilized international relations ever since, either in the guise of the 'Eastern Question' which so preoccupied statesmen of the nineteenth century, or the problems of the Balkans and the Middle East that plagued the twentieth.

10 Denmark, whose elites had largely shed their imperialist delusions of grandeur, can be compared with a middling, German *Polizeistaat*, where a strong central administration, under enlightened administrators, could produce positive outcomes.

11 The Anjala conspiracy was basically a traditional bid by a clique of disaffected nobles to improve their position by switching allegiance from one sovereign to another. It envisaged Finland following the pattern of the Baltic provinces in 1721 and becoming an autonomous province within Russia. Attempts to claim it as a pioneering assertion of an emergent Finnish nationlism are anachronistic; romantic nationalism was an idea whose time had not then arrived.

19. Alternative Models

1 See E. H. Kossman, 'The Dutch republic in the eighteenth century', in M. C. Jacob and W. W. Mijnhardt, eds., *The Dutch Republic in the Eighteenth Century* (1992); S. Schama, *Patriots and Liberators: Revolution in the Netherlands, 1780–1813* (1977).

2 See S. C. F. van Sas, 'Patriot Revolution', and M. C. Jacob, 'Radicalism in the Dutch Enlightenment', in Jacob and Mijnhardt.

3 Military repression works if the circumstances are right, the commanders resolute and the soldiers willing to shoot. This worked for London in the Gordon riots in 1780, but failed at Lexington and Concorde in the American Revolution in 1775, and in the Grenoble riots in France in 1788.

4 The list of open constituencies, where voting counted, is not confined to the handful with wide popular franchises, but includes most of the county constituencies. Although these did not usually hold a poll, there were intense local power struggles over selecting candidates and shifting political orientation, reflecting swings in the public mood.

5 On the economic development of eighteenth-century Britain, see M. Berg, *The Age of Manufactures: Industry, Innovation and Work in Britain, 1700–1820* (1985); P. Matthias, *The First Industrial Revolution* (1983); J. Rule, *The Vital*

Century: England's Developing Economy, 1714–1815 (1992); G. Holmes and D. Szechi, *The Age of Oligarchy: Pre-industrial Britain, 1722–1787* (1993).

6 Generally a ruling party preferred long intervals between elections, an opposition short ones. The call for more frequent general elections had been a Whig policy when they were struggling for power, and became a Tory policy when they lost it. In other terms, frequent elections was a 'Country' rather than a party issue.

7 The Continental Congress of 1774 was of course internally divided, as was colonial society. It is possible that loyalists may have been a quarter of the population, and were seen as enough of a threat to evoke widespread violent intimidation by the majority. The majority in the Congress would have preferred to retain a form of British sovereignty, but were not prepared to make any significant concessions on their claim to internal self-government in order to preserve it.

8 The phenomenon of a strained relationship between the ruling monarch and the heir is inherent in any system of hereditary succession, though it was unusually strong in the Hanoverian dynasty. Oppositions naturally tried to exploit it by cultivating the support of the heir. Fox could not know, in the 1780s, that it would be 25 years before the prince attained power as regent and he would enter government.

9 The best-known, best-organized and ultimately most successful example of a single-issue campaign was the struggle first to abolish the British slave trade, and then to abolish slavery itself.

20. The French Time Bomb

1 The personality of Louis XV, an intensely private man, not communicative by disposition and an instinctive dissimulator, is a problem for the historians. It is easy to dismantle the image of a rather stupid, irresponsible hedonist, cursed with 'the terrible sexual appetite of the Bourbons'. The legend of the Parc aux Cerfs, his private brothel just outside the palace gates, which he visited nightly, was fantasy. Louis was intelligent, well-read and industrious. But his record as a political manager looks mediocre compared with that of Louis XIV, and he appears weak and vacillating in political crises until his final assertion of authority over the *parlements* after 1766.

2 The Falklands Islands dispute was another typical British abuse of their naval superiority to assert a legally dubious claim to sovereignty. Louis was almost certainly right in his decision that the time was not yet come for the Bourbon powers to attempt to challenge British sea power.

3 There are two close studies by W. Doyle, 'The parlements of France and the breakdown of the old regime', *French Historical Studies*, 6 (1969–70); and *The Parlement of Bordeaux and the End of the Old Regime, 1771–1790* (1974). Two studies based on the *parlement* of Paris are J. H. Shennan, *The Parlement of Paris* (1968); B. Stone, *The Parlement of Paris, 1774–1789* (1981). See also D. Echeverria, *The Maupeou Revolution* (1985).

4 Vergennes usually appears as a secondary, background figure in the history of pre-revolutionary France, yet there is a case to argue that from 1781 he was, effectively, the first minister until his death in 1787. In M. Price, *Preserving the Monarchy: The Comte de Vergennes, 1774–1787* (1993), there is a clear picture of how the vicious faction struggles at Versailles, combined with Louis XVI's chronic indecision, undermined the regime.

5 See P. M. Jones, *Reform and Revolution in France* (1995). On the politics: J. Bocher, *French Finances, 1770–1795* (1970); on the budgetary problem: J. Bocher and R. D. Harris, *Necker, Reform Statesman of the Ancien Regime* (1979).

6 See the account, 'Parliamentary sovereignty and royal reaction, 1719–1809', in M. F. Metcalf, ed., *The Riksdag: A History of Sweden's Parliament* (1987). In Britain there was a more protracted struggle to win the right to publish parliamentary debates.

7 A 'cultural revolution' is a nebulous concept, but in Part 1 of S. Schama, *Citizens* (1989), he makes a strong case for a critical shift in values and mentalities coming to a decisive turning point in the reign of Louis XVI. For other views, see V. R. Gruder, 'A mutation in elite political culture: the French notables and the defence of property and participation, 1787', *Journal of Modern History*, 50 (1984): J. Mackrell, *The Attack on 'Feudalism' in Eighteenth-Century France* (1973); N. Hampson, *Will and Circumstance: Montesquieu, Rousseau and the French Revolution* (1983); K. M. Baker, 'French political thought at the accession of Louis XVI', *Journal of Modern History*, 50 (1978); C. Lucas, 'Nobles, bourgeois and the origins of the French Revolution', *Past and Present*, 60 (1973).

8 These are issues that await more systematic analysis than is available at present in English. Contemporary accounts strongly suggest that the circulation of sensational material for the titillation of a mass audience was an extensive business, and though much of this matter is not overtly political, it represented a steady erosion of the credibility of established authority. See R. Darnton, 'The literary underground of the Old Regime', in J. Comer and J. Popham, eds., *The Press and Politics in pre-Revolutionary France* (1987); R. Darnton, *Mesmerism and the End of the Enlightenment in France* (1968).

Chronology

1598 Treaty of Vervins ends war between France and Spain; issue of the Edict of Nantes; death of Philip II of Spain, accession of Philip III.
1603 Death of Elizabeth I of England, accession of James VI of Scotland.
1605 Death of Boris Gudunov, 'time of troubles' in Russia over disputed succession.
1609 Truce between Spain and United Provinces.
1610 Henry IV of France assassinated, regency for Louis XIII.
1612 Death of Emperor Rudolf II, election of Archduke Matthias.
1613 Michael Romanov recognized as tsar by Russian *zemsky sobor*, ends succession crisis.
1614 Meeting of last Estates General in France until 1789.
1617 Treaty of Stolbova ends war between Sweden and Russia.
1618 Revolt in Bohemia triggers Thirty Years War; Synod of Dordrecht in United Provinces, followed by Orangeist coup directed by the stadholder, Prince Maurice.
1619 Death of Emperor Matthias, election of Ferdinand II; Bohemians elect Frederick of the Palatinate king.
1620 Bohemian revolt crushed after battle of the White Mountain.
1621 Death of Philip III of Spain, accession of Philip IV; end of the Truce; Gustav Adolf captures Riga.
1622 Olivares first minister to Philip IV in Spain.
1624 Richelieu first minister to Louis XIII in France.
1625 Emperor hires Wallenstein as commander; Christian IV of Denmark enters the war; Death of James VI/I in Britain, accession of Charles I.
1626 Tilly and Wallenstein defeat Christian IV at battle of Lutter.
1627 Ferdinand II revises Bohemian constitution.
1628 Dutch capture the American silver fleet, financial crisis in Spain.
1629 Emperor issues the Edict of Restitution; Denmark leaves the war; Gustav Adolf makes a truce with Poland; Charles I begins the 'personal rule' in Britain; following siege of La Rochelle by Richelieu, Huguenots submit to Louis XIII in France.
1630 Dismissal of Wallenstein; Gustav Adolf enters Germany; Richelieu survives in office after 'day of dupes', persuades Louis XIII to intervene against Spain in Italy.
1631 Gustav Adolf concludes Treaty of Bärwalde with Richelieu, wins battle of Breitenfeld.
1632 Emperor recalls Wallenstein; Gustav Adolf killed at the battle of Lützen; regency for Queen Christina under Axel Oxenstierna.
1634 Murder of Wallenstein; Swedish army defeated by imperialists at Nördlingen.
1635 Treaty of Prague between the Emperor and Protestant princes in the Empire; France declares war on Spain.

1637 Death of Emperor Ferdinand II, election of Ferdinand III; Dutch recapture Breda.

1638 Beginning of British crisis, National Covenant in Scotland.

1640 Charles I defeated by the Scots, calls parliament; revolts in Catalonia and Portugal against policies of Olivares; accession of Frederick William as Elector of Brandenburg.

1642 Civil wars in Britain begin; death of Richelieu.

1643 Death of Louis XIII, regency for Louis XIV under Anne of Austria; Cardinal Mazarin first minister; Spanish army defeated by the French at Rocroi; Sweden launches preventive war on Denmark.

1645 Treaty of Brömsebro ends war between Denmark and Sweden, with territorial gains to Sweden; New Model Army formed in Britain, wins decisive battle of Naseby; opening of peace negotiations for the Empire at Münster-Osnabrück; death of Tsar Michael, accession of Alexis.

1648 Conclusion of Peace of Westphalia, ends Thirty Years War; second civil war in Britain, Pride's Purge of parliament; death of Christian IV of Denmark, accession of Frederick III; Khelmnitsky rebellion in the Ukraine; revolts in Naples–Sicily; beginning of the Fronde in France, causing civil war.

1649 Regicide of Charles I and foundation of English republic; Cromwellian conquest of Ireland; *zemsky sobor* accepts the legal code establishing serfdom in Russia.

1650 Financial crisis in Sweden, commoner Estates call for *reduktion*; political crisis in United Provinces, death of stadholder William II, De Witt establishes republican control.

1652 First trade war between England and United Provinces.

1653 Cromwell becomes Lord Protector in Britain; De Witt becomes Grand Pensionary in Holland; end of the Fronde in France; Nikon begins church reform in Russia.

1654 Abdication of Queen Christina, accession of Charles X in Sweden; Ukrainian rebels accept sovereignty of Tsar Alexis, triggers war between Russia and Poland, Russians recapture Smolensk; Treaty of Westminster ends war between Britain and the United Provinces.

1655 Charles X invades Poland.

1656 Britain joins France in war on Spain, captures Jamaica.

1657 Charles X begins pre-emptive war with Denmark.

1658 Death of Oliver Cromwell; death of Emperor Ferdinand III, election of Leopold I; battle of the Dunes and capture of Dunkirk by Anglo-French force.

1659 Disintegration of republican government in Britain; Treaty of the Pyrenees ends war between France and Spain, Louis XIV married to the Spanish infanta.

1660 Restoration of Charles II in Britain; death of Charles X of Sweden, regency for Charles XI, Treaty of Copenhagen ends war between Sweden and Denmark, Treaty of Oliva ends war between Sweden and Poland; Frederick III establishes absolute monarchy in Denmark.

1661 Death of Mazarin, Louis XIV starts his personal rule.

1662 Colbert appointed French minister of finance.

1663 Ottoman attack on Austria.

1664 Ottomans defeated by Christian army at battle of St Gotthard.

1665 Death of Philip IV of Spain, accession of Charles II; second trade war between Britain and the United Provinces; Danish Royal Law institutionalizing the absolute monarchy; plague epidemic in London.

1666 Louvois appointed French minister of war; great fire of London; Old Believer schism develops in Russia.

1667 Treaty of Andrusovo establishes truce between Poland and Russia; Treaty of Breda ends war between Britain and United Provinces; Louis XIV begins war of devolution against Spanish Netherlands.

1668 Treaty of Aix-la-Chapelle ends devolution war; Spain recognizes independence of Portugal; first Spanish partition treaty between Louis XIV and Leopold I.

1670 Treaty of Dover between Louis XIV and Charles II for attack on United Provinces; revolt in Hungary against Leopold I; death of Frederick III of Denmark, accession of Christian V.

1671 Leopold I defeats Hungarian rebels, imposes military control in Hungary.

1672 Louis XIV begins the Dutch war, assisted by Charles II; Orangeist coup in United Provinces, De Witt brothers murdered, William III appointed stadholder; Charles XI assumes the government in Sweden.

1674 Britain makes peace with United Provinces; Empire and Spain enter war against Louis XIV.

1675 Sweden invades Brandenburg, defeated at Fehrbellin; Denmark invades Sweden.

1676 Peace negotiations open at Nymegen; death of Tsar Alexis, accession of Theodore III; Innocent XI elected pope.

1678 Treaties of Nymegen end war between France, United Provinces and Spain; popish plot crisis in England.

1679 Peace treaties end war between Sweden, Denmark, the Emperor and United Provinces.

1680 Louis XIV begins policy of reunions; Swedish Estates condemn regency, approve *reduktion*, recognize Charles XI as an absolute king.

1681 Louis XIV annexes Strasbourg; end of popish plot crisis in England, Charles II dispenses with parliaments.

1682 Louis XIV in dispute with papacy over Gallican articles; Tököli rebellion in Hungary, Ottoman attack towards Vienna; death of Tsar Theodore III, Ivan V and Peter I joint tsars; French court established at Versailles; Swedish Estates approve unlimited *reduktion*.

1683 Ottoman siege of Vienna, Jan Sobieski heads Christian army which defeats the Ottomans; death of Colbert, ascendancy of Louvois faction in France.

1684 Truce of Ratisbon between Louis XIV and the Empire; Innocent XI creates Holy League against the Ottomans.

1685 Death of Charles II in England, accession of James II/VII, Monmouth rebellion; Revocation of Edict of Nantes triggers Huguenot emigration.

1686 William III forms League of Augsburg against Louis XIV.

1687 Battle of Mohacs, Ottomans defeated, rapid Christian advance towards Balkans; Diet of Pressburg, Leopold I conciliates Hungarian rebellion.

1688 Louis XIV launches war of the League of Augsburg, devastates the Palatinate; death of Elector Frederick William of Brandenburg, accession of Frederick III; 'Glorious Revolution' in Britain, William III invades, James II/VII flees to France.

1689 Convention Parliament recognizes William III and Mary as joint sovereigns, Bill of Rights; Britain declares war on Louis XIV; Peter I assumes sole power in Russia.

1690 James II/VII invades Ireland, defeated at battle of the Boyne.

1691 Death of Louvois in France.

1692 Anglo-Dutch naval victory at La Hogue, French concentrate on privateering at sea; start of prolonged general subsistence crisis in Europe.

1693 English parliament establishes the national debt; Estates approve final structures of absolute monarchy in Sweden.

1694 Peak of European subsistence crisis; Bank of England established.

1695 William III exchanges financial autonomy of the crown for a parliamentary civil list; virtual end of censorship in England.

1696 Peace negotiations begin at Ryswick; Tsar Peter I captures Azov from the Ottomans.

1697 General peace in western Europe concluded at Ryswick; Prince Eugene defeats the Ottomans at Zenta; death of Charles XI of Sweden, accession of Charles XII; Tsar Peter visits western Europe.

1698 Second partition treaty for Spain between Louis XIV, William III and Leopold I; revolt of the *streltsi* in Moscow, suppressed by Peter I.

1699 Treaty of Karlowitz ends war against the Ottomans; Peter I launches his reform programme in Russia; death of Christian V of Denmark, accession of Frederick IV; Peter I, Frederick IV and Augustus II of Saxony/Poland plan dismemberment of Swedish empire.

1700 Third partition treaty between Louis XIV and William III aborted on death of Charles II of Spain, whose will leaves whole Spanish inheritance to grandson of Louis XIV; Louis XIV accepts inheritance, installs Philip V in Madrid; Northern War begins, Charles XII repels the attackers, defeats Peter I at battle of Narva.

1701 Hostilities between Louis XIV and Leopold I in Italy; breakdown of negotiations between William III and Louis XIV; William III constructs a Grand Alliance against Louis XIV; duke of Marlborough Allied commander in the west; Act of Settlement in England provides for eventual Hanoverian succession; Charles XII invades Poland to dethrone Augustus II; Elector Frederick III of Brandenburg recognized as king in Prussia.

1702 Death of William III, accession of Queen Anne in Britain; Heinsius and States General assume power in United Provinces.

1703 Savoy and Portugal join the Alliance, extend conflict into Iberia; Peter I begins construction of St Petersburg; Rakoczi rebellion against Habsburgs in Hungary.

1704 Marlborough and Eugene win battle of Blenheim, drive French out of Germany.

1705 Death of Emperor Leopold I, election of Joseph I.

1706 Marlborough wins battle of Ramillies, occupies the southern Netherlands; French driven out of Italy; Allied expedition to Spain to install Archduke Charles as king, defection of Aragon and Catalonia from Philip V; Charles XII invades Saxony, forces Augustus II to abdicate Polish crown.

1707 Act of Union unites England and Scotland into kingdom of Great Britain; Charles XII begins invasion of Russia; Allied forces in Spain defeated at battle of Alamanza.

1708 Very severe winter marks new European subsistence crisis; Marlborough defeats French army at battle of Oudenarde, Allies invade France.

1709 Severe financial and subsistence crisis in France, Louis XIV seeks peace; Peter I defeats Charles XII at battle of Poltava.

1710 New Tory government in Britain opens negotiation with Louis XIV for peace; Russia occupies Livonia and Estonia, Denmark re-enters the war, invades Skåne.

1711 Death of Emperor Joseph I, election of Charles VI; Tory government dismisses Marlborough; Treaty of Szatmar ends Hungarian revolt.

1712 Successive deaths of Louis XIV's son and grandson, Philip V renounces his rights to French crown.

1713 Treaties at Utrecht end war between Louis XIV and Britain, United Provinces, Prussia, Savoy and Portugal, and between Britain and Philip V; Charles VI publishes the Pragmatic Sanction; death of Frederick I of Prussia, accession of Frederick William I.

1714 Treaty of Rastadt ends war between Louis XIV and the Emperor; death of Queen Anne, succession of George I of Hanover in Britain; Philip V recaptures Barcelona, ends Habsburg presence in Spain; Charles XII returns from Turkey to defend Stralsund, Russia occupies Finland.

1715 Death of Louis XIV, regency for Louis XV under duke of Orléans; Jacobite risings in Britain defeated, Tories ousted from government.

1716 War renewed between the Ottomans and Austria; marriage of Elizabeth Farnese and Philip V of Spain; Septennial Act in England.

1717 Spain seizes Sardinia.

1718 Charles XII invades Norway, killed at Frederikshall, accession of Ulrika Eleonora and Frederick of Hesse; Spanish fleet destroyed by British at Cape Passaro, ends Italian intervention; Treaty of Passarowitz ends war between Ottomans and Austria.

1719 New form of government in Sweden ends absolutism, gives power to the Estates; Peter I sets up governing Colleges in Russia.

1720 Financial crisis in Britain, South Sea Bubble; financial crisis in France, collapse of John Law's schemes; Savoy exchanges Sicily for Sardinia, becomes kingdom of Sardinia.

1721 Walpole appointed prime minister in Britain; Treaty of Nystad ends Northern War.

1722 Peter I introduces Table of Ranks in Russia; Frederick William sets up General Directory in Prussia.

1723 End of regency in France.

1725 Death of Peter I in Russia, accession of Catherine I.

1726 Cardinal Fleury chief minister in France.

1727 Death of Catherine I in Russia, accession of Peter II, government moves back to Moscow.

1730 Death of Peter II in Russia, accession of Anna, attempt to impose restrictions on the autocracy fail, government returns to St Petersburg.

1731 Treaty of Vienna sets up alliance of Austria, United Provinces, Spain and Britain.

1733 Defeat of Walpole's excise scheme in Britain; first family compact between France and Spain; War of the Polish Succession, Bourbon powers recover Naples–Sicily for Spanish Bourbons.

1735 War between Russia and the Ottomans.

1737 Austria joins war against the Ottomans.

1738 Treaty of Vienna ends War of the Polish Succession, France to get reversion of Lorraine, general international recognition of Pragmatic Sanction.

1739 Treaty of Belgrade ends war between Ottomans, Russia and Austria.

1740 Death of Emperor Charles VI, Maria Theresa inherits Habsburg lands and Hungary; death of Frederick William in Prussia, accession of Frederick II, who invades Silesia; Britain starts colonial war on Spain; death of Tsaritsa Anna, court intrigues over the succession.

1741 Britain pays subsidies to Maria Theresa; Fleury overruled in France, Marshal Belle-Isle organizes anti-Habsburg coalition in the Empire; Elizabeth installed as tsaritsa in Russia; Sweden launches attack on Russia to recover lost lands.

1742 Fall of Walpole in Britain, Carteret pursues active intervention in Germany; Charles Albert of Bavaria elected Emperor as Charles VII, seizes Bohemia; Maria Theresa invades Bavaria.

1743 Treaty of Åbo ends war between Russia and Sweden; second family compact between France and Spain, aimed at colonial resistance to Britain and expansion of Bourbon lands in Italy; death of Cardinal Fleury, Louis XV assumes direction of policy in France.

1744 France declares war on Britain, plans joint Franco-Spanish invasion of Britain.

1745 Death of Charles VII, Bavaria makes peace with Maria Theresa, her husband elected Emperor as Francis I; France invades the Austrian Netherlands, activates the war in Italy; Charles Edward leads a Jacobite uprising in Scotland; British capture Louisbourg in Canada; Maria Theresa makes peace with Frederick II, cedes Silesia to Prussia.

1746 French capture Madras; Charles Edward leads failed invasion of England, pursued into Scotland, defeated at battle of Culloden; George II forced to accept new Whig ministry led by Henry Pelham and Newcastle, seeks to end continental war; death of Philip V in Spain, accession of Ferdinand VI; new king seeks end to Spanish involvement in war.

1747 France overruns Austrian Netherlands; Orangeist coup in United Provinces, William IV of Orange becomes stadholder of whole United Provinces.

1748 Treaty of Aix-la-Chapelle, ends hostilities between Britain, France, Austria and Spain.

1749 Tax reform in France, strong protests from the Assembly of the Clergy; Haugwitz reforms of Habsburg administration begun; publication of Montesquieu's *L'Esprit des lois*; reform programme in Spain under Ensenada, introduction of intendants.

1750 Pombal appointed chief minister in Portugal.

1751 Publication of first volume of the *Encyclopédie*.

1753 French *parlements* issue remonstrance on rule of law, judicial strike follows; Kaunitz appointed Chancellor by Maria Theresa.

1754 Death of Pelham in Britain causes government crisis; William Pitt leads call for strong imperial policies; armed confrontation between French and British colonists in America.

1755 British troops sent to America, naval blockade of Canada; Lisbon earthquake.

1756 Frederick II concludes Convention of Westminster with Britain; launches preventive strike by occupying Saxony, triggering Seven Years War; reversal of the alliances, Treaty of Versailles for cooperation of France and Austria against Prussia; alliance of Russia and Austria against Prussia; Britain declares war on France.

1757 Pitt–Newcastle ministry formed; Frederick defeats French army at battle of Rossbach and Austrian army at battle of Leuthen; Pitt concludes subsidy agreement with Frederick; second Treaty of Versailles, full alliance between France and Maria Theresa; Clive defeats French in India at battle of Plassey.

1758 British capture Louisbourg and French West African trading posts; duke of Choiseul appointed first minister in France.

1759 Russians defeat Frederick at battle of Kunersdorf; British navy eliminates French navy at battle of Quiberon; British capture Quebec; Pombal expels Jesuits; death of Ferdinand VI in Spain, accession of Charles III; Voltaire publishes *Candide*.

1760 Death of George II in Britain, accession of George III; British capture Montreal, Russians occupy Berlin briefly; Frederick defeats the Austrians at battles of Torgau and Liegnitz; Kaunitz establishes Council of State in Austria.

1761 Third family compact between France and Spain, Charles III enters war with Britain; Pitt resigns; Rousseau publishes *Emile*.

1762 British capture Havana and Manila; George III appoints Lord Bute as prime minister; death of Tsaritsa Elizabeth, accession of Peter III; Peter III makes peace with Prussia, emancipates Russian nobility from compulsory state service; Peter III deposed in favour of his wife Catherine in palace coup, then murdered.

1763 Treaty of Paris between Britain, France and Spain; Treaty of Hubertusburg between Austria and Prussia; confrontation between Louis XV and Estates of Brittany; Wilkes challenges power of general warrants and wins.

1764 Expulsion of the Jesuits from France; Hungarian Diet rejects reform proposals from Maria Theresa to alleviate the position of the peasantry; Catherine II secures election of Stanislas Poniatowski as client king of Poland, permits some modernizing reforms.

1765 Stamp Act seeks to tax American colonies; organized resistance among colonists, meeting of Stamp Act congress, trade boycott by colonies threatened; death of Emperor Francis I, Joseph II elected, becomes co-ruler with Maria Theresa; Archduke Leopold assumes government of Tuscany, embarks on extensive reform programme.

1766 Chatham ministry in Britain; Stamp Act repealed, Declaratory Act asserts sovereign power of British parliament; Townshend duties imposed on tea and other items, evokes continuing colonial protest; Louis XV confronts the *parlements* with formal assertion of the absolute sovereignty of the crown, protest and resistance continue; Campomanes enters government in Spain to promote reforms; major protest riots in Madrid, Charles III flees the city; Frederick II introduces new excise tax; Lorraine incorporated into France; Rockingham becomes leader of Whig party, advised by Edmund Burke, committed to reform, goes into opposition.

1767 Catherine II summons the Legislative Commission to review whole of Russian law.

1768 Ottomans declare war on Russia, meetings of Legislative Commission suspended; Wilkes contests Middlesex election and wins; expelled by Commons for blasphemy and imprisoned; twice re-elected in defiance of Commons; Confederation of Bar in Poland to resist Russian intervention.

1769 Colonial resistance to Townshend duties leads to rioting and trade boycotts, British government decides to repeal the duties, except that on tea.

1770 Wilkes released, leads popular movement for radical reform; Burke publishes *Thoughts on the Present Discontents*; George III secures appointment of Lord North as prime minister; Falkland Islands crisis threatens war between Britain and the Bourbon powers, Louis XV draws back, dismisses Choiseul; appoints Maupeou Chancellor and resolves to confront opposition from *parlements*.

1771 Major subsistence crisis in Bohemia and peasant unrest; Maria Theresa and Joseph II resolve on reforms; Gustav III elected king of Sweden, resolved to strengthen the monarchy; Louis XV and Maupeou abolish the *parlements* and set up a new judicial structure in France, defy protests.

1772 First partition of Poland, by Russia, Prussia and Austria; Gustav III carries out absolutist coup in Sweden.

1773 The Boston Tea Party; North government decides on punitive response, initially supported by public opinion; outbreak of Pugachev revolt in Russia, mass rising against landlords; Order of Jesuits dissolved.

1774 Fierce colonial resistance, Continental Congress meets in Philadelphia, organizes boycotts, demands full autonomy; British government sends troops to America; Treaty of Kutchuk-Kainardji ends war between Russia and the Ottomans, recognizes tsar as protector of Christians in Ottoman empire; death of Louis XV in France, accession of Louis XVI; Maupeou reforms reversed, Turgot becomes Controller.

1775 Suppression of Pugachev revolt, Catherine II implements reconstruction of local government in Russia; peasant uprisings in Bohemia, Joseph II initiates gradual emancipation of the peasantry; war between Britain and the colonists begins at Lexington and Concorde, Congress rejects British conciliation offer, insists on full self-government.

1776 American Declaration of Independence, Congress assumes government, begins negotiations with foreign powers; British evacuate Massachusetts; Louis XVI and Vergennes decide to assist the Americans, Turgot replaced by Necker as Director of Finance; Charles III appoints Floridablanca as chief minister in Spain, to pursue reforms.

1777 British lose control of New England with capitulation at Saratoga; death of Elector Max Joseph of Bavaria without direct heirs, Joseph II attempts to secure Bavaria.

1778 France declares war on Britain, recognizes American independence; Americans reject British attempt at conciliation, British evacuate Philadelphia; War of the Bavarian Succession, Frederick II invades Bohemia, negotiations begin at once.

1779 New family compact, Spain enters the war; French naval successes in Caribbean, attempted Franco-Spanish invasion of Britain abortive; split in British public opinion on the war, Rockingham Whigs accept American independence; campaign by Wyvil for radical parliamentary reform; Treaty of Teschen ends Bavarian war.

1780 Russia leads campaign against British blockades, forms the Armed Neutrality; Britain declares war on the United Provinces; new British expedition wins control of the Carolinas; death of Maria Theresa, Joseph II takes control, embarks on reform programme.

1781 Necker publishes full financial statement in his *Compte rendu*; advocates elected assemblies; Vergennes forces his resignation; Joseph II makes alliance with Catherine II for cooperation against the Ottomans; internally decrees full religious toleration for Habsburg lands, embarks on reconstruction of Catholic Church; British surrender at Yorktown, government accepts American war is lost.

1782 Resignation of Lord North; Shelburne government opens peace negotiations; Burke carries economical reform bill, first motion in Commons for parliamentary reform.

1783 Treaty of Versailles ends American war; political crisis in Britain, George III forced to accept the Fox–North coalition, king works with William Pitt the younger to overthrow the government; uses Lords to defeat government's India Bill; king dismisses government and appoints Pitt prime minister; Catherine II annexes the Crimea; Calonne, new Controller in France facing state bankruptcies; attempts new modernization policies, which are widely opposed; Joseph II plans comprehensive tax reforms and full emancipation of the peasants.

1784 Pitt wins general election in Britain, political stability returns; Pitt embarks on extensive financial and governmental reforms; Joseph II proposes to exchange the Netherlands for Bavaria, meets general international opposition.

1785 Frederick II organizes League of Princes in the Empire to stop Habsburg expansion; Anti-Orangeist opposition in United Provinces; Patriot party forms armed militias, begins takeover of provincial governments; Catherine II consolidates Estates system for Russia, issues charters of privilege to nobility and townsmen.

1786 Calonne tells Louis XVI the state is bankrupt, proposes to call an Assembly of Notables; death of Frederick II in Prussia, accession of Frederick William II; disorders in United Provinces threaten overthrow of stadholder William V.

1787 Assembly of Notables in France approves part of Calonne reforms, insists tax reform be referred to an Estates General; Calonne dismissed, Brienne appointed Controller, dismisses the Assembly, tries to secure acceptance of reforms through the *parlements*, with promise to call Estates General by 1792, *parlement* refuses; Brienne attempts to replace *parlements* with new court system and elected provincial assemblies; Prussia sends troops into the United Provinces, restores authority of the stadholder; Ottomans declare war on Russia.

1788 Popular movement and riots in France in support of the *parlements*; Louis XVI promises an Estates General in 1789, Brienne replaced by Necker; reform Diet in Poland, embarks on modernization; Joseph II's proposed reforms for the Netherlands and Hungary provoke rebellion; Austria enters war against the Ottomans; Gustav III of Sweden launches attack on Russia.

1789 Meeting of the Estates General in France triggers revolution; Netherlands and Hungary in full revolt against Joseph II; Gustav III extends royal powers in Sweden.

1790 Death of Emperor Joseph II, Leopold II elected Emperor; pacifies Netherlands and Hungary; Treaty of Varala ends war between Sweden and Russia.

1791 Polish Diet approves new constitution, Catherine II organizes to overthrow it.
1792 Treaty of Jassy ends war between Ottomans and Russia.
1793 Second partition of Poland; patriotic resistance suppressed by Russian troops.
1795 Third and final partition of Poland.

Genealogies

402

Habsburgs

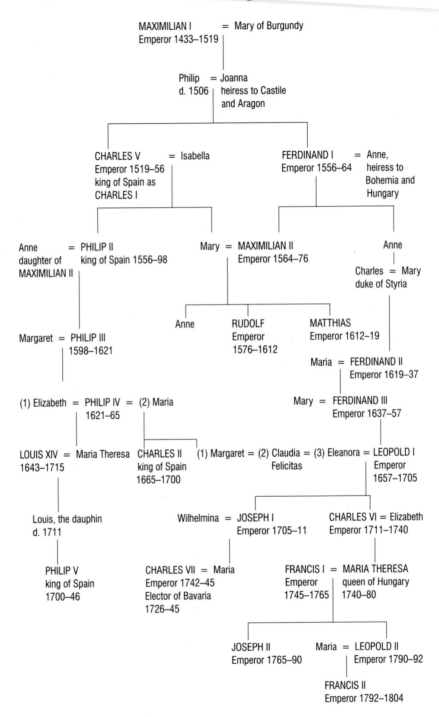

Bourbons

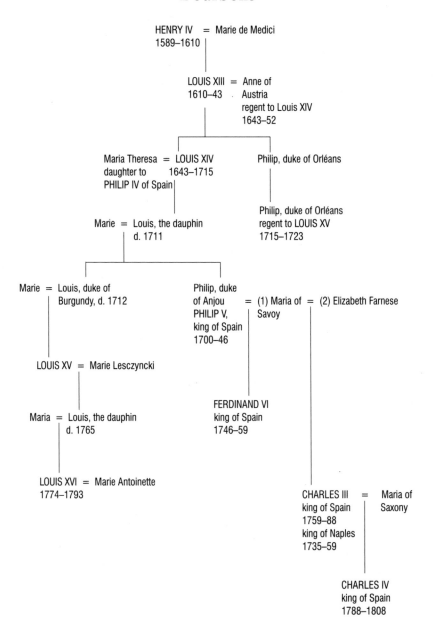

HENRY IV = Marie de Medici
1589–1610

LOUIS XIII = Anne of
1610–43   Austria
regent to Louis XIV
1643–52

Maria Theresa = LOUIS XIV   Philip, duke of Orléans
daughter to   1643–1715
PHILIP IV of Spain

Philip, duke of Orléans
regent to LOUIS XV
1715–1723

Marie = Louis, the dauphin
d. 1711

Marie = Louis, duke of   Philip, duke
Burgundy, d. 1712   of Anjou   = (1) Maria of = (2) Elizabeth Farnese
PHILIP V,   Savoy
king of Spain
1700–46

LOUIS XV = Marie Lesczyncki

FERDINAND VI
king of Spain
1746–59

Maria = Louis, the dauphin
d. 1765

LOUIS XVI = Marie Antoinette
1774–1793

CHARLES III = Maria of
king of Spain   Saxony
1759–88
king of Naples
1735–59

CHARLES IV
king of Spain
1788–1808

Stuarts

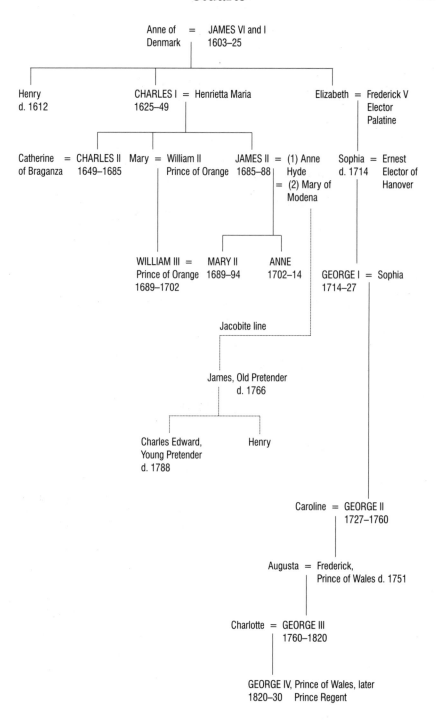

Hohenzollerns

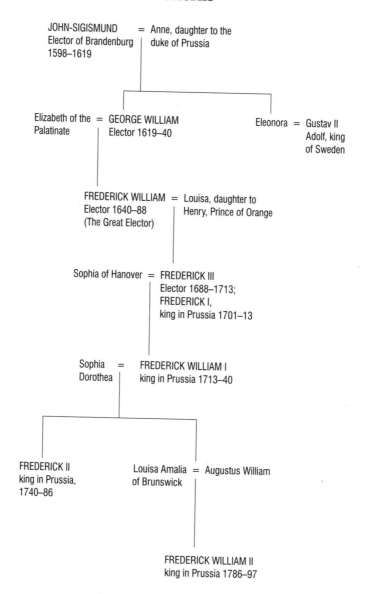

Romanovs

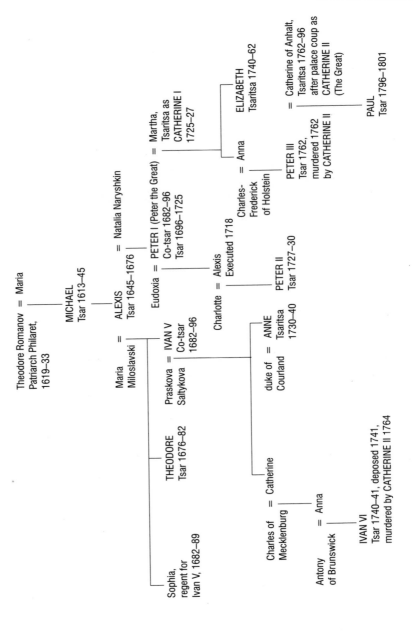

Theodore Romanov = Maria
Patriarch Philaret,
1619–33

MICHAEL
Tsar 1613–45

ALEXIS = Natalia Naryshkin
Tsar 1645–1676

Maria = IVAN V   Eudoxia = PETER I (Peter the Great) = Martha,
Miloslavski Co-tsar   Co-tsar 1682–96   Tsaritsa as
Praskova   1682–96   Tsar 1696–1725   CATHERINE I
Saltykova   1725–27

THEODORE
Tsar 1676–82

Charlotte = Alexis
            Executed 1718

Sophia,
regent for
Ivan V, 1682–89

duke of = ANNE   PETER II   Charles- = Anna   ELIZABETH
Courland Tsaritsa   Tsar 1727–30   Frederick   Tsaritsa 1740–62
          1730–40   of Holstein

Charles of = Catherine

Antony = Anna
of Brunswick

IVAN VI
Tsar 1740–41, deposed 1741,
murdered by CATHERINE II 1764

PETER III = Catherine of Anhalt,
Tsar 1762,   Tsaritsa 1762–96
murdered 1762 after palace coup as
by CATHERINE II CATHERINE II
              (The Great)

PAUL
Tsar 1796–1801

Bibliography

It has been decided to confine this bibliography to publications in the English language. This does not exclude non-anglophone scholarship: it includes some translations, most of the publications cited outside the field of British history do draw on the work of scholars working in other languages, and almost all the monographs cited have their own bibliographies which list such works. The starting point for any student is the general surveys of the period and the most extensive of these are the volumes of the *New Cambridge Modern History*. Since this is a work of collective scholarship, inevitably some sections have more to offer than others, but taken as a whole it is an indispensable guide to events and interpretations. The relevant volumes for this period are: J. P. Cooper, ed., vol. IV: *1609–1659* (1970); F. F. Carsten, ed., vol. V: *1648–1688* (1961); J. S. Bromley, ed., vol. VI: *1688–1725* (1970); J. O. Lindsay, ed., vol. VII: *1713–63* (1957); A. Goodwin, ed., vol. VIII: *1763–1793* (1968); P. Burke, ed., companion vol. XIII (1979), *The New Cambridge Modern History Atlas* (1970). The following are general surveys on a more modest scale. *The Macmillan History of Europe*: T. Munck, *Seventeenth Century Europe 1598–1700* (1990); J. Black, *Eighteenth Century Europe 1700–1789* (1990). *The Fontana History of Europe*: G. Parker, *Europe in Crisis 1598–1648* (1979); J. Stoye, *Europe Unfolding 1648–1688* (1969); W. Doyle, *The Old European Order 1660–1800* (1978). *The Longman History of Europe*: D. H. Pennington, *Europe in the Seventeenth Century* (1989); M. S. Anderson, *Europe in the Eighteenth Century 1713–1783* (1987).

1. The European World of the Seventeenth Century

A useful survey of economic developments is the *Fontana Economic History of Europe*: C. Cipolla, ed., vol. II: *16th and 17th centuries* (1974); vol. III, *The Industrial Revolution* (1973). A summary of the extended debates on demographic history is M. W. Flinn, *The European Demographic System 1500–1820* (1962); on climate history, H. H. Lambe, *Climate History and the Modern World* (1982); E. Le Roy Ladurie, *Times of Feast, Times of Famine: a History of Climate since the Year 1000* (1971). Contribution to the ongoing discussion on the economy and society can be found in I. Wallerstein, *The Modern World System*, vol. II (1980); L. P. Burke, ed., *Economy and Society in Early-Modern Europe* (1972); R. Davis, *The Rise of the Atlantic Economies* (1973); F. Braudel, *Structures of Everyday Life* (1981) and *Wheels of Commerce* (1982). Views on a possible general crisis of European society can be found in G. Parker and L. Smith, eds., *The General Crisis of the Seventeenth Century* (1978); K. Thomas, *Religion and the Rise of Magic* (1971); N. Cohn, *Europe's Inner Demons* (1975); C. Hill, *Religion and Politics in Seventeenth-Century England* (1986); C. Larner, *Enemies of God: The Witch Hunt in Scotland*

(1981); H. C. E. Midelfort, *Witch Hunting in South-West Germany 1564–1684* (1972). The debate on mercantilism is found in E. Hekscher, *Mercantilism* (1935); C. Wilson, *Mercantilism* (1958); D. C. Coleman, ed., *Revisions in Mercantilism* (1969). On agrarian history and society, see B. H. Schlicher van Bath, *The Agrarian History of Western Europe* (1963); R. Brenner, 'Agrarian class structure and economic development in pre-industrial Europe', *Past and Present*, 70 (1976); T. H. Aston and C. H. E. Philpin, eds., *The Brenner Debate* (1985); T. Scott, ed., *The Peasantries of Europe* (1995); P. Goubert, *The French Peasantry in the Seventeenth Century* (1986). On the landlords, see H. M. Scott, ed., *The European Nobilities*, 2 vols. (1995). On the urban sector, see J. de Vries, *European Urbanisation 1500–1800* (1984); C. R. Friedricks, *The Early-Modern City* (1995). On the development of a distinct popular culture, see P. Burke, *Popular Culture in Early-Modern Europe* (1978); R. Muchembled, *Popular Culture and Elite Culture in France 1400–1750* (1985); B. Capp, *Astrology and the Popular Press: English Almanacs 1550–1800* (1979); M. Spufford, *Small Books and Pleasant Histories: Popular Fiction and its Readership in Seventeenth-Century England* (1981). On the impact of print, see E. L. Eisenstein, *The Printing Revolution in Early-Modern Europe* (1983). On developments in religion, see J. Bossy, *Christianity in the West* (1986); J. Delumeau, *Catholicism between Luther and Voltaire* (1977). On the early scientific movement, see H. Kearney, *Science and Change 1500–1700* (1971); M. B. Hall, *The Scientific Renaissance 1450–1630* (1962); A. R. Hall, *From Galileo to Newton 1630–1720* (1962); A. Koestler, *The Sleepwalkers* (1959).

2. The First European War

Some general studies of the Thirty Years War are G. Pagès, *The Thirty Years War* (1970); C. V. Wedgwood, *The Thirty Years War* (1938); C. V. Polisensky, *The Thirty Years War* (1971); T. K. Rabb, ed., *The Thirty Years War* (1964); G. Parker, ed., *The Thirty Years War* (1984); S. H. Steinberg, 'The Thirty Years War, a new interpretation', *History*, 32 (1947). On the debate on the consequences, see R. Ergang, *The Myth of the All-Destructive Fury of the Thirty Years War* (1956); G. Benecke, *Germany in the Thirty Years War* (1978); H. Kamen, 'The economic and social consequences of the Thirty Years War in Germany', *Past and Present*, 39 (1968). On the Spanish involvement, see B. Chudoba, *Spain and the Empire* (1952); C. H. Carter, *The Secret Diplomacy of the Habsburgs 1598–1625* (1964); G. Parker, *The Army of Flanders and the Spanish Road* (1972); J. H. Elliott, *Richelieu and Olivares* (1984); J. T. Israel, *The Dutch Republic and the Hispanic World 1606–1661* (1982). On the Baltic and east European component of the wars, see D. Kirby, *Northern Europe in the Early-Modern Period: The Baltic World 1492–1772* (1982); M. Roberts, *Gustavus Adolphus: A History of Sweden 1611–1632*, 2 vols. (1953, 1958); M. Roberts, ed., *Essays in Swedish History* (1967); N. Davies, *God's Playground: A History of Poland*, vol. I (1981); S. P. Oakley, *The Story of Denmark* (1972).

3. The Origins of the Modern State: The Absolutist Route

There is an extensive literature on the history of France before Louis XIV. Basic reference books are: R. Mousnier, *The Institutions of France under the Absolute Monarchy*, 2 vols. (1979, 1980); R. Bonney, *Political Change in France under Richelieu and Mazarin 1624–1662* (1978); *Society and Government in France under Richelieu and Mazarin 1624–1662* (1988); M. Greengrass, *France in the*

Age of Henri IV (1984); V. L. Tapié, *France in the Age of Louis XIII and Richelieu* (1974). On the finances, see R. Bonney, *The King's Debts: Finance and Politics in France 1589–1661* (1981); J. Dent, *Crisis in Finance: Crown Financiers and Society in Seventeenth-Century France* (1973). On Richelieu, see R. J. Knecht, *Richelieu* (1991); J. Bergin and L. Brockliss, eds., *Richelieu and his Age* (1995); J. Bergin, *Cardinal Richelieu: Power and the Pursuit of Wealth* (1985); R. Bonney, 'The secret expenses of Richelieu and Mazarin', *English Historical Review*, 91 (19XX). On Mazarin, see G. R. R. Treasure, *Mazarin: the crisis of absolutism in France* (1995). On the resistance to absolutism, see J. H. Shennan, *The Parlement of Paris* (1968); R. J. Knecht, *The Fronde* (1975); R. Mousnier, *Peasant Uprisings in France, Russia and China* (1971); A. D. Lublinskaya, *French Absolutism – The Crucial Phase 1620–1629* (1968). On the military revolution, see M. Roberts, 'The military revolution' in his *Essays in Swedish History* (1967); G. N. Clark, *War and Society* (1958); G. Parker, 'The military revolution 1560–1660 – a myth?', *Journal of Modern History*, 48 (1976); and *The Military Revolution: Military Innovation and the Rise of the West 1500–1800* (1988); F. Tallett, *War and Society in Early-Modern Europe* (1992). There is also an extensive literature on Habsburg Spain: basic surveys are J. Lynch, *Spain under the Habsburgs*, 2 vols. (1981); J. H. Elliott *Imperial Spain 1469–1716* (1963); *The Count-duke of Olivares* (1986); *The Revolt of the Catalans* (1963). On the decline of Spain, see Elliott, 'The decline of Spain', *Past and Present*, 20 (1961); H. Kamen 'The decline of Spain', *ibid.*, 81 (1978); E. J. Hamilton, 'The decline of Spain', *Economic History Review*, 8 (1937); and *American Treasure and the Price Revolution in Spain 1501–1660* (1934); see also H. Kamen, *The Inquisition and Society in Spain* (1984); S. T. Perron, 'The Castilian Assembly of the Clergy', *Parliaments, Estates, Representation*, 18 (1998).

4. The Origins of the Modern State: Alternative Routes

The literature on early Stuart Britain is very extensive, but some basic contributions are: J. P. Kenyon, *Stuart England* (1978); R. Ashton, *The English Civil War 1603–1649* (1978); D. Hirst, *Authority and Conflict: England 1603–1658* (1986); D. C. Coleman, *The Economy of England 1450–1750* (1977). On the reign of Charles I before 1640, see C. V. Wedgwood, *The King's Peace* (1955); K. Sharpe, *The Personal Rule of Charles I* (1992). On the English revolution, see C. Russell, 'The British problem and the English civil war', *History*, 72 (1987); C. Russell, ed., *The Origins of the English Civil War* (1973); G. E. Aylmer, *Rebellion and Revolution: England 1640–1660* (1986); J. S. Morrill, *Cheshire 1630–1660* (1974); I. Roots, *The Great Rebellion 1642–1660* (1966); M. Kishlansky, *The Rise of the New Model Army* (1980); A. Woolrych, *Soldiers and Statesmen* (1987); B. Worden, *The Rump Parliament* (1974); C. Hill, *God's Englishman* (1970); J. Morrill, ed., *Oliver Cromwell and the English Revolution* (1990); B. Coward, *Cromwell* (1991); I. Roots, *Cromwell: A Profile* (1973). The Dutch republic is much more sparsely covered, but a sound introduction is C. Wilson, *The Dutch Republic* (1968); the most comprehensive account is in J. Israel, *The Dutch Republic* (1995). Aspects of internal politics are covered in M. C. t'Hart, *The Making of a Bourgeois State: War, Politics and Finance during the Dutch Revolt* (1992); J. L. Price, *Holland and the Dutch Republic in the Seventeenth Century: The Politics of Particularism* (1994). External policy is covered in C. R. Boxer, *The Dutch Seaborne Empire* (1965); C. Wilson, *Profit and Power: England and the Dutch Wars* (1957). The special characteristics of Dutch society in the seventeenth-century world are explored in S. Schama, *An Embarrassment of Riches: An Interpretation of Dutch Culture in the Golden Age* (1987).

5. Towards 'Absolutism': Variations round a Theme

The volume of writings about Louis XIV is formidable. General surveys of the reign after 1660 are: F. Goubert, *Louis XIV and Twenty Million Frenchmen* (1970); J. B. Wolf, *Louis XIV* (1968); R. M. Hatton, ed., *Louis XIV and Europe* (1976) and *Louis XIV and Absolutism* (1976); J. C. Rule, ed., *Louis XIV and the Craft of Kingship* (1969). There are also many detailed studies of aspects of the reign including R. Mettam, *Government and Society in Louis XIV's France* (1977) and *Power and Faction in Louis XIV's France* (1976); C. W. Cole, *Colbert and a Century of French Mercantilism*, 2 vols. (1939); E. Asher, *The Resistance to the Maritime Classes* (1960) on attempts to reform naval administration. A major new study of the army is J. A. Lynn, *The Giant of the Grand Siècle: The French Army, 1660–1799* (1997). P. Sonnino, *Louis XIV and the Origins of the Dutch War* (1988), examines a central policy decision of the reign; another strategic policy decision is analysed in W. C. Scoville, *The Persecution of the Huguenots and Economic Development 1680–1720* (1960). Coverage of attempts at state-building by the Vienna Habsburgs is patchy. Basic studies are R. J. Evans, *The Making of the Habsburg Monarchy* (1979); J. B. Spelman, *Leopold I* (1977); J. Bérenger, *A History of the Habsburg Empire* (1994); T. Barker, ed., *Army, Aristocracy, Monarchy: Essays on War, Society and Government in Austria, 1618–1780* (1982). Among the few monographs and articles in English are R. Wines, 'The imperial circles: princely diplomacy and imperial reform', *Journal of Modern History*, 39 (1967); J. Stoye, *The Siege of Vienna* (1964); H. F. Schwarz, *The Imperial Privy Council in the Seventeenth Century* (1943); C. W. Ingrao, *In Quest and Crisis: Emperor Joseph I and the Habsburg Monarchy* (1977). Two useful general works on Hungary are: D. Sinor, *A History of Hungary* (1989); C. A. Macartney, *Hungary: A Short History* (1962). The last phase of Habsburg Spain is surveyed in: J. Lynch, *Spain under the Habsburgs*, vol. II (1981); H. Kamen, *Spain in the Later Seventeenth Century, 1665–1700* (1980); R. A. Stradling, *Philip IV and the Government of Spain* (1988). Some useful periodical articles are: C. H. Jago, 'Habsburg absolutism and the Cortes of Castile', *American Historical Review*, 86 (1981); I. A. A. Thompson, 'Crown and Cortes in Castile, 1590–1663', *Parliaments, Estates, Representation*, 2 (1982); 'The end of the Cortes of Castile', *ibid.*, 4 (1984); C. Jago, 'The crisis of the aristocracy in seventeenth-century Castile', *Past and Present*, 84 (1979); L. P. Wright, 'The Military Orders in sixteenth- and seventeenth-century Spain', *ibid.*, 43 (1969); R. A. Stradling, 'A Spanish statesman of appeasement: Medina de las Torres', *Historical Journal*, 19 (1976).

6. The Evolution of the British State: A Different Model

There is a copious literature on later Stuart Britain, though most of it is focused on England and the Revolution of 1688. Some good general histories are J. R. Jones, *Country and Court. England 1688–1714* (1993); J. P. Kenyon, *Stuart England*, (1978); C. Hill, *The Century of Revolution* (1961); G. Holmes, *The Making of a Great Power: Late Stuart and Early Georgian Britain 1660–1792* (1993). The economic and social developments are surveyed in B. A. Holderness, *Pre-industrial Economy and Society 1500–1750* (1976); C. Wilson: *England's Apprenticeship 1603–1723* (1980); P. Earle, *The Making of the English Middle Class: Business, Society and Family Life, 1660–1730* (1969). A stimulating thesis on the politics of the period is J. Plumb, *The Growth of Political Stability in England* (1967). Other analyses of British politics are T. Harris, *Politics under the Later Stuarts: Party Conflict in a Divided Society* (1993); J. Miller, *Restoration England: The Reign of Charles II* (1985); *Popery and Politics in England* (1973); also his important article,

'The potential for absolutism in later Stuart England', *History*, 63 (1978); J. R. Western, *Monarchy and Revolution: The English State in the 1680s* (1972); J. R. Jones, *The Restored Monarchy, 1660–1688* (1979); G. Holmes, *British Politics in the Reign of Queen Anne* (1987); E. Gregg, *Queen Anne* (1980). The Revolution of 1688 is the subject of J. R. Jones, *The Revolution of 1688 in England* (1972); J. Miller, *James II: A Study in Kingship* (1989); W. A. Speck, *Reluctant Revolutionaries: Englishmen and the Revolution of 1688* (1988). On the developing British problem, see H. Kearney, *The British Isles. A State of four nations* (1989). On the emergence of political parties, see J. P. Kenyon, *Revolution Principles: The Politics of Party 1689–1720* (1977); W. A. Speck, *Whig and Tory: The Struggle in the Constituencies, 1701–1715* (1977); C. Jones, ed., *Britain in the First Age of Party* (1987). On the other major legacy of 1688, the transformation of British public finances, see P. G. M. Dickinson, *The Financial Revolution in England: A Study in the Development of Public Credit, 1688–1756* (1967); J. Brewer, *The Sinews of Power: War, Money and the English State* (1989).

7. Developments on the North-Eastern Periphery

A sound, modern account of the Baltic region is D. Kirby, *Northern Europe in the Early-Modern Period: The Baltic World 1492–1772* (1990); collected articles on this region are found in G. Rystad, ed., *Europe and Scandinavia: Aspects of the Process of Integration in the Seventeenth Century* (1983); A. Maczak, H. Samsonovicz and P. Burke, eds., *East-Central Europe in Transition* (1984); and two monographs: C. E. Hill, *The Danish Sound Dues and the Command of the Baltic* (1926); W. H. McNeill, *Europe's Steppe Frontier, 1500–1800* (1964). On Brandenburg–Prussia, see H. W. Koch, *A History of Prussia* (1978); F. L. Carsten, *The Origins of Prussia* (1954); F. Schevill, *The Great Elector* (1965); H. Rosenberg, *Bureaucracy, Aristocracy and Autocracy: The Prussian Experience, 1660–1815* (1958). Denmark is thinly covered in English. A basic history is S. P. Oakley, *The Story of Denmark* (1972); on the developing absolutism, see E. Ekman, 'The Danish Royal Law of 1665', *Journal of Modern History*, 31 (1959); E. L. Petersen, 'From domain state to tax state', *Scandinavian Economic History Review*, 23 (1975); L. Jespersen, 'The *Machstaat* in seventeenth-century Denmark', *Scandinavian Journal of History*, 10 (1985); T. Munck, *The Peasantry and Early Absolute Monarchy in Denmark, 1660–1708* (1979). Sweden is dominated by the works of M. Roberts, *Gustav Adolf: A History of Sweden 1611–1632*, 2 vols. (1953, 1958); *Essays in Swedish History* (1967); *Sweden as a Great Power* (1968); and, as editor, *Sweden's Age of Greatness, 1632–1718* (1979); finally *The Swedish Imperial Experience, 1560–1718* (1979). A recent monograph is A. F. Upton, *Charles XI and Swedish Absolutism* (1998). The basic history of Poland is N. Davis, *God's Playground: A History of Poland*, vol. 1 (1981). There is useful material in J. K. Fedorovicz, ed., *A Republic of Nobles: Studies in Polish History to 1864* (1982); and W. E. D. Allen, *The Ukraine: A History* (1940). The most useful general histories of Russia are P. Dukes, *The Making of Russian Absolutism 1613–1801* (1982); V. O. Kluchevsky, *A Course in Russian History* (1968); M. Raeff, *Imperial Russia 1682–1825* (1971); J. Blum, *Lord and Peasant in Russia* (1961); J. L. Keep, *Soldiers of the Tsar: Army and Society in Russia, 1462–1874* (1985). On the predecessors of Peter the Great, see R. O. Crumney, *Aristocrats and Servitors: The Boyar Elite in Russia 1613–1689* (1984); J. H. Keep, 'The regime of Filaret', *Slavonic and East European Review*, 38 (1959–60); L. R. Lewitter, 'Poland, the Ukraine and Russia in the seventeenth century', *ibid.*, 27 (1948–9); M. Cherniavsky, 'The Old Believers and the new religion', *Slavic Review*, 25 (1946–7); P. Longworth, *Alexis, Tsar of All the Russias* (1984); J. T. Fuhrmann, *Tsar Alexis* (1981). There is an extensive literature on Peter the Great. Good general surveys are M. S. Anderson, *Peter the Great* (1978); V. O. Kluchevsky, *Peter the Great* (1963); E. Anisimov, *The Reforms of Peter the Great – Progress through Coercion in Russia* (1993); see also J. Cracraft, *The Church Reforms of Peter the Great* (1971); W. M. Pintner and D. K. Rownery, *Russian Officialdom: The Bureaucratization of Russian Society from the Seventeenth to the Twentieth Century* (1980); C. Petersen, *Peter the Great's Administrative and Judicial Reforms* (1979); B. H. Sumner, *Peter the Great and the Ottoman Empire* (1949).

8. The Second European War, 1660–1721

Studies on war in general in this period are J. Childs, *Armies and Warfare in Europe, 1648–1789* (1982); M. S. Anderson, *War and Society in the Europe of the Old Regime* (1988); J. Black, *European Warfare, 1660–1815* (1994); C. Duffy, *The Fortress in the Age of Vauban and Frederick the Great, 1660–1789* (1985); F. Tullett, *War and Society in Early-Modern Europe* (1992). On war finance, see P. G. M. Dickson and J. Sperling, 'War finance 1685–1714', *Cambridge Modern History*, vol. IV (1970); and the J. Brewer study (see Chapter 6 above). J. A. Lynn has written *The Wars of Louis XIV, 1667–1714* (1999); more detailed studies of the war are in R. Hatton, ed., *Louis XIV and Europe* (1976); R. Hatton and J. S. Bromley, *William III and Louis XIV* (1967); Stoye, *Siege of Vienna* (Chapter 5 above). On Spain after 1700, see J. Lynch, *Bourbon Spain* (1989); A. D. Francis, *The First Peninsular War, 1702–1713* (1975); H. Kamen, *The War of the Spanish Succession in Spain* (1969); S. Conn, *Gibraltar in British Diplomacy* (1942). On the United Provinces, see A. C. Carter, *Neutrality or Commitment: The Evolution of Dutch Foreign Policy, 1667–1795* (1975). In addition to biographical studies of Louis XIV and Leopold I (Chapter 5 above), see R. Hatton, *George I, Elector and King* (1978); D. McKay, *Prince Eugene of Savoy* (1977). The Northern War is covered in Kirby, *Baltic World* (Chapter 7 above); R. Hatton, *Charles XII of Sweden* (1968); and *George I* (above). A general history of Poland is J. Lukowski, *Liberty's Folly: The Polish Lithuanian Commonwealth in the Eighteenth Century, 1697–1795* (1991); see also L. R. Lewitter, 'Russia, Poland and the Baltic 1697–1721', *Historical Journal*, 11 (1968); P. Englund, *The Battle of Poltava: The Birth of the Russian Empire* (1992).

9. Changing Mentalities

The best introduction to the concept of intellectual shift is P. Hazard, *The European Mind, 1680–1715* (1965). There are general surveys in R. Mandrou, *From Humanism to Science, 1480–1700* (1978); R. A. Nisbet, *The History of the Idea of Progress* (1980); see also H. Trevor-Roper, 'The Baroque Century', in H. Trevor-Roper, ed., *The Age of Expansion: Europe and the World 1559–1660* (1969). There is a very large literature on the scientific breakthrough. The best introduction is H. Butterfield, *The Origins of Modern Science, 1300–1800* (1957); see further R. Briggs, *The Scientific Revolution of the Seventeenth Century* (1969); H. Kearney, *Science and Change, 1500–1700* (1971); T. Kuhn, *The Copernican Revolution* (1957); A. Koestler, *The Sleepwalkers* (1959). On religion, see J. Delumeau, *Catholicism between Luther and Voltaire* (1977); on high culture, F. Haskell, *Patrons and Painters: A Study in the Relations between Italian Art and Society in the Age of the Baroque* (1980); H. Raynor, *A Social History of Music from the Middle Ages to Beethoven* (1978); on popular culture, see P. Burke, *Popular Culture in Early-Modern Europe* (1978); R. Muchembled, *Popular and Elite Culture in France, 1400–1800* (1985); B. Capp, *Astrology and the Popular Press: English Almanacs,*

1550–1800 (1979); M. Spufford, *Small Books and Pleasant Histories* (1981); and, on the root of cultural change, see R. A. Houston, *Literacy in Early-Modern Europe: Culture and Education, 1500–1800* (1988).

10. Change in the Economy and Society

There is a very extensive literature on most aspects of economic developments. A general survey is J. De Vries, *The Economy of Europe in an Age of Crisis, 1600–1750* (1976); F. Braudel, *The Wheels of Commerce* (1982); the controversial I. Wallerstein, *The Modern World System,* vol. II: *Mercantilism and the Consolidation of the European World Economy, 1600–1750* (1986); R. Davis, *The Rise of the Atlantic Economies* (1973); P. Earle, ed., *Essays in European Economic History* (1974); P. Burke, *Economy and Society in Early-Modern Europe: Essays from the 'Annales'* (1972). On demography, see M. W. Flinn, *The European Demographic System, 1500–1820* (1981); J. D. Post, *Food Shortage, Climatic Variability and Epidemic Disease in Pre-Industrial Europe* (1985); on agriculture, see J. Blum, *The End of the Old Order in Rural Europe* (1978); C. E. Mingay, *The Agricultural Revolution 1750–1815* (1966); J. Cooper, 'In search of agrarian capitalism', *Past and Present*, 80 (1978). For European expansion overseas, see H. Furber, *Rival Empires in the Orient, 1600–1800* (1976); G. S. Graham, *The Empire of the North Atlantic* (1950); J. H. Parry, *Trade and Dominion: The European Overseas Empires in the Eighteenth Century* (1971); R. Davies, *A Commercial Revolution: English Overseas Trade in the Seventeenth and Eighteenth Centuries* (1967). For the slave trade, see O. Rainsford, *The Slave Trade* (1971); D. B. Davies, *The Problem of Slavery in Western Culture* (1966); H. A. Wyndham, *The Atlantic and Slavery* (1935). At the heart of the European economy stood the United Provinces, a leading force for development through the period; some relevant studies are K. Glassman, *The Dutch Asiatic Trade, 1620–1740* (1958); V. Barbour, *Capitalism in Amsterdam in the Seventeenth Century* (1950); J. C. Riley, *International Government Finance and the Amsterdam Capital Market, 1740–1815* (1980); C. Wilson, *Anglo-Dutch Commerce and Finance in the Eighteenth Century* (1941); A. Attman, *Dutch enterprise in the World Bullion Trade, 1550–1800* (1983). On France, see R. Price, *The economic modernisation of France 1730–1800* (1975). On industrial development the focus is on Britain. See R. M. Hartwell, ed., *The Causes of the Industrial Revolution in England* (1967); T. S. Ashton, *The Industrial Revolution* (1965); P. Deane, *The First Industrial Revolution* (1965); E. Dawson, *The Early Industrial Revolution* (1966).

11. Social Change

The base on which all societies rested was the labour of the peasants and their families in agriculture. A general review of peasant societies is T. Scott, ed., *The Peasantries of Europe from the Fourteenth to the Eighteenth Centuries* (1995); see also R. J. Evans and W. R. Lee, eds., *The German Peasantry: Conflict and Community in Rural Society* (1980); this includes the article by W. Hagen, 'The Junkers' faithless servants: peasant insubordination and the breakdown of serfdom in Brandenburg-Prussia 1763–1811'. Also by Hagen is 'Seventeenth-century crisis in Brandenburg: the Thirty Years War, the destabilisation of serfdom and rise of absolutism', *American Historical Review*, 94 (1989). On the new serfdom, see L. Makkai, 'Neo-serfdom: its origins and nature in east-central Europe', *Slavic Review*, (1975); A. Kamminski, 'Neo-serfdom in Poland Lithuania', *ibid.*, 34 (1975). The peasant problems in Austria are studied in W. Wright, *Serf, Seigneur and Sovereign: Agrarian*

Reform in Eighteenth-Century Bohemia (1966); E. M. Link, *The Emancipation of the Austrian Peasantry, 1740–1789* (1949); a study of Spanish peasants is M. Weisser, *The Peasants of the Montes* (1977). On France the classic study is M. Bloch, *French Rural History* (1931); another major study is E. Le Roy Ladurie, *The Peasants of Languedoc* (1974). Their landlords are surveyed in H. M. Scott, ed., *The European Nobilities in the Seventeenth and Eighteenth Centuries,* 2 vols. (1995). On British landed society, see G. E. Mingay, *The Gentry: The Rise and Fall of a Ruling Class* (1978); J. Habbakuk, 'The rise and fall of English landed families', *Transactions of the Royal Historical Society* 29, 30, 31 (1979, 1980, 1981); L. Stone and J. C. F. Stone, *An Open Elite? England 1540–1880* (1984); J. A. Cannon, *Aristocratic Century: The Peerage of Eighteenth-Century England* (1984). Studies of French nobility include G. Chaussinard-Nogaret, *The French Nobility in the Eighteenth Century: From Feudalism to Enlightenment* (1985); J. Q. C. Mackrell, *The Attack on Feudalism in Eighteenth-Century France* (1973); C. B. A. Behrens, 'Nobles, privileges and taxes in France at the end of the ancien regime', *Economic History Review,* 15 (1962–3); F. Ford, *The Robe and the Sword: The Regrouping of the French Aristocracy after Louis XIV* (1953); D. D. Bien, 'Manufacturing nobles: the Chancellories in France to 1769', *Journal of Modern History,* 61 (1989); G. J. Cavanagh, 'Nobles, privileges and taxes in France', *French Historical Studies,* 8 (1973–4). On Germany, see O. Hintze, 'The Hohenzollerns and the nobility', in *The Historical Essays of O. Hintze* (1989); on Poland, see 'The szlachta of the Polish–Lithuanian Commonwealth and their government', in I. Banac and P. A. Buchteovitch, eds., *The Nobility of Russia and Eastern Europe* (1983). On Sweden there are two essays in Roberts, *Age of Greatness* (Chapter 7 above): S. Dahlgren, 'Estates and Classes', and K. Ågren, 'Reduktion'. In Rystad, *Europe and Scandinavia* (Chapter 7 above), there is his chapter 'The king, the nobility and the growth of bureaucracy in seventeenth-century Sweden'; see also K. Ågren, 'Rise and decline of an aristocracy: the Swedish social and political elite in the seventeenth century', *Scandinavian Journal of History,* 1 (1976). On Russia, see B. Meehan Waters, *Autocracy and Aristocracy: The Russian Service Elite of 1730* (1982); R. E. Jones, *The Emancipation of the Russian Nobility, 1762–1785* (1973); M. Raeff, *The Origins of the Russian Intelligentsia: The Eighteenth-Century Russian Nobility* (1966). On the urban sector, see Friedrichs, *The Early-Modern City* (Chapter 1 above); J. De Vries, *European Urbanisation, 1500–1800* (1984); for local studies, see P. Clark and P. Slack, *English Towns in Transition, 1500–1700* (1976); C. Corfield, *The Impact of English Towns, 1700–1800* (1982); N. McKendrick, J. Brewer and J. H. Plumb, *The Birth of a Consumer Society: The Commercialization of Eighteenth-Century England* (1982); L. Weatherill, *Consumer Behaviour and Material Culture in Britain 1660–1760* (1988). L. Bernard, *The Emerging City: Paris in the Age of Louis XIV* (1970); J. N. Hittle, *The Service City: Towns and Townsmen in Russia, 1600–1800* (1970). On the lower strata of society, see O. H. Hufton, *The Poor of Eighteenth-Century France* (1973); K. Snell, *Annals of the Labouring Poor: Social Change in Agrarian England, 1660–1900* (1980).

12. A New Search for Political Stability

General works on Hanoverian Britain include J. C. D. Clark, *English Society, 1683–1832* (1985); G. Holmes, *The Making of a Great Power: Late Stuart and Early Georgian Britain, 1660–1792* (1993); W. A. Speck, *Stability and Strife: England 1714–1760* (1977); L. Colley, *Britons: Forging a Nation 1707–1837* (1992); T. C. Smout, *History of the Scottish People, 1560–1830* (1970); T. W. Moody and W. E. Vaughan, *A New History of Ireland,* vol. IV (1986); G. Holmes and D. Szechi, *The Age of Oligarchy: Pre-industrial Britain, 1722–1783* (1993); F. O'Gorman, *The*

Long Eighteenth Century: British Political and Social History, 1688–1832 (1977). On party policies, see L. Colley, *In Defence of Oligarchy: The Tory Party 1714–1760* (1982); on the Jacobites, B. P. Lenman, *The Jacobite Risings in Britain 1689–1746* (1980). On Walpole's ascendancy, see Hatton, *George I* (Chapter 8 above); J. Black, *British Foreign Policy in the Age of Walpole* (1985); B. Hill, *Sir R. Walpole: Sole and Prime Minister* (1989); P. Langford, *The Excise Crisis: Society and Politics in the Age of Walpole* (1975). On France after Louis XIV, see J. H. Shennan, *Philippe, Duke of Orléans: Regent of France, 1715–1723* (1979); J. A Carey, *Judicial Reform in France before 1789* (1981); V. R. Crucher, *The Royal Provincial Intendants* (1968); C. T. Mathews, *The Royal General Farms in Eighteenth-Century France* (1958); A. Cobban, 'The *parlements* of France in the eighteenth century', *History,* 35 (1950); P. R. Campbell, *Power and Politics in Old Regime France, 1720–1745* (1996). On Prussia under Frederick William I, see R. A. Dorwart, *The Administrative Reforms of Frederick William I of Prussia* (1953). On Savoy, see G. Symcox, *Victor Amadeus II: Absolutism in the Savoyard State, 1675–1730* (1983); C. Storrs, *War, Diplomacy and the Rise of Savoy* (1999). On early Bourbon Spain, see J. Lynch, *Bourbon Spain* (Chapter 8 above); J. Herr, *The Eighteenth-Century Revolution in Spain* (1958).

13. The Stabilization of the North-Eastern Borderlands

On Poland, see J. F. Fedorowicz, ed., *A Republic of Nobles* (1982); Lukowski, *Liberty's Folly* (Chapter 8 above). On Sweden, see M. Roberts, *The Age of Liberty: Sweden 1719–1772* (1986); and *British Diplomacy and Swedish Politics, 1758–1773* (1980); M. Metcalf, 'The first modern party system', *Scandinavian Journal of History,* 2 (1977). On Russia after Peter the Great, see Raeff, *Imperial Russia* (Chapter 7 above); Dukes, *Russian Absolutism* (Chapter 7 above); M. Raeff. 'The domestic policies of Peter III and his overthrow', *American Historical Review,* 75 (1970).

14. The European Power Game, 1715–1740

On international relations in this period, general surveys are D. McKay and H. M. Scott, *The Rise of the Great Powers, 1648–1815* (1984); Black, *British Foreign Policy* (Chapter 12 above); A. M. Wilson, *French Foreign Policy during the Administration of Cardinal Fleury, 1726–1743* (1936). There are relevant chapters in P. Longford, *Great Britain in the Eighteenth Century, 1688–1815* (1976); P. Roberts, *The Quest for Security, 1715–1740* (1947); J. Black, *Natural and Necessary Enemies: Anglo-French Relations in the Eighteenth Century* (1986); see also Hatton, *George I* (Chapter 8 above). On Habsburg policy, see E. Wangermann, *The Austrian Achievement, 1700–1800* (1973); McKay, *Prince Eugene* (Chapter 8 above); K. A. Roider, *Austria's Eastern Question, 1700–1790* (1982); J. W. Stoye, 'The Emperor Charles VI; the early years of the reign', *Transactions of the Royal Historical Society,* 12 (1962). On Spain, see Lynch, *Bourbon Spain* (Chapter 8 above).

15. The Last European War of the *Ancien Régime*

The most useful general survey of these conflicts is in McKay and Scott, *Great Powers,* (Chapter 14 above). On British participation in the wars, see W. L. Dorn, *Competition for Empire* (1940). The Jacobite complication is studied in D. Szecki,

The Jacobites, Britain and Europe, (1994); the naval aspect is discussed in J. Black and P. Woodfine, eds., *The British Navy and the Use of Naval Power in the Eighteenth Century* (1988); the domestic input is discussed in J. O. McClachlan, *Trade and Peace with Old Spain 1667–1750* (1940); J. B. Owens, *The Rise of the Pelhams* (1956); J. C. D. Clark, *The Dynamic of Change: The Crisis of the 1750s and the English Party System* (1982). M. Peters, *Pitt and Popularity: The Patriotic Minister and Public Opinion during the Seven Years War* (1980); R. Middleton, *The Bells of Victory: The Pitt–Newcastle Ministry and the Conduct of the Seven Years War* (1985); R. Harris, *A Patriot Press: National Politics and the London Press in the 1740s* (1980). France is poorly served in English language publication, but see L. Kennett, *The French Armies in the Seven Years War* (1967); J. Pritchard, *Louis XV's Navy, 1748–1762* (1987); H. I. Priestly, *France Overseas through the Old Regime* (1939); D. Van Key, *The Damiens Affair and the Unravelling of the Ancien Regime: Church, State and Society in France 1750–1770* (1984); J. Rogister, *The Parlement of Paris, 1735–1755* (1995). On Frederick the Great, see the major scholarly biography of G. Ritter, *Frederick the Great* (1968); on Silesia, see P. Baumgart, 'The annexation and integration of Silesia', in M. Greengrass, ed., *Conquest and Coalescence* (1991); on the military aspect, see D. E. Showalter, *The Wars of Frederick the Great* (1985); C. Duffy, *The Army of Frederick the Great* (1974). On Austria, see R. Pick, *Empress Maria Theresa: The Earlier Years, 1717–1757* (1966); K. L. F. Szabo, *Kaunitz and Enlightened Absolutism* (1994); C. Duffy, *The Army of Maria Theresa, 1740–1780* (1977). On Russia, see C. Duffy, *Russia's Military Way to the West: Origins and Nature of Russian Military Power, 1700–1800* (1981); H. Kaplan, *Russia and the Outbreak of the Seven Years War* (1968). On the colonial struggle, see R. Pares, *War and Trade in the West Indies, 1739–1763* (1936); and 'American against continental warfare, 1739–1763', *English Historical Review,* 51 (1936). On the peace settlement, see Z. E. Rachel, *The Peace of Paris, 1763* (1952).

16. The Enlightenment

The literature on the Enlightenment is very extensive. Some general accounts are N. Hampson, *The Enlightenment* (1981); R. Porter, *The Enlightenment* (1990); J. H. Brumfitt, *The French Enlightenment* (1973); F. Venturi, *Italy and the Enlightenment* (1972); E. Cassirer, *The Philosophy of the Enlightenment* (1987); R. Porter and M. Teich, eds., *The Enlightenment in National Context* (1981); M. C. Jacob, *The Radical Enlightenment: Pantheists, Freemasons and Republicans* (1981); A. B. Cobban, *In Search of Humanity: The Role of the Enlightenment in Modern History* (1960); K. Epstein, *The Genesis of German Conservatism* (1966). On leading participants, see P. France, *Diderot* (1983); R. Scruton, *Kant* (1982); J. N. Sklar, *Montesquieu* (1987); P. Burke, *Vico* (1985); P. Gay, *Voltaire's Politics* (1959); K. M. Baker, *Condorcet* (1975); R. Grimsley, *Jean Jacques Rousseau; A Study in Self-Awareness* (1961); J. Moller, *Rousseau: Dreamer of Democracy* (1984). On the physiocrats, see E. Fox-Genovese, *The Origins of Physiocracy* (1976); R. L. Meek, *The Economics of Physiocracy* (1962). On the spread of ideas, see J. Lough, *The Encylopédie* (1971); M. Cranston, *Philosophes and Pamphleteers: Political Theorists of the Enlightenment* (1986). On the opponents of the Enlightenment, see R. J. White, *The Anti-Philosophes* (1970); D. D. Biens, *The Calas Affair* (1960); R. Darnton, *Mesmerism and the End of the Enlightenment in France* (1968); F. Manuel, *The Eighteenth Century Confronts the Gods* (1959). On the limitations of the Enlightenment, see H. Chisick, *The Limits of Reform in the Enlightenment: Attitudes to the Education of the Lower Classes in Eighteenth-Century France* (1981); S. Kaplan, *Bread, Politics and Political Economy in the Reign of Louis XV* (1971).

17. Enlightened Despotism: The Enlightenment in Action

A most useful collective work on enlightened absolutism is H. M. Scott, ed., *Enlightened Absolutism: Reform and Reformers in Later Eighteenth-Century Europe* (1990). On the history of Portugal and its empire, see D. Francis, *Portugal 1715–1808* (1985); C. R. Boxer, *The Portuguese Seaborne Empire* (1969); J. K. Lang, *Portugese Brazil: The King's Plantation* (1979); S. J. Miller, *Portugal and Rome c. 1748–1830: An Aspect of the Catholic Enlightenment* (1978). For Spain, see first Lynch, *Bourbon Spain* and Herr, *Eighteenth-Century Revolution* (Chapter 12 above). More detailed studies are G. J. Walker, *Spanish Politics and Imperial Trade, 1700–1789* (1979); W. S. Callahan, *Church, Politics and Society in Spain, 1750–1874* (1984); *Honor, Commerce and Industry in Eighteenth-Century Spain* (1972); R. Herr, *Rural Change and Royal Finances in Spain at the End of the Old Regime* (1985); R. S. Shafer, *The Economic Societies in the Spanish World, 1763–1821* (1958); G. M. Addy, *The Enlightenment in the University of Salamanca* (1966); L. Rodriguez, 'The Spanish riots of 1666', *Past and Present*, 53 (1971); C. C. Noel, 'Opposition to enlightened reform in Spain; Campomanes and the clergy', *Societas*, 3 (1973). For the Italian experience, see S. J. Woolf, *A History of Italy, 1700–1860* (1979); H. Acton, *The Bourbons of Naples, 1734–1825* (1956); D. Carpanetto and G. Ticuperati, *Italy in the Age of Reason, 1685–1789* (1987); Venturi, *Italy* (Chapter 16 above); D. Mack Smith, *A History of Sicily*, vol. II, *Modern Sicily after 1713* (1968); C. A. Bolton, *Church Reform in Eighteenth-Century Italy* (1969). On the *Aufklärung* in the Holy Roman Empire, see J. B. Kundsen, *Justin Möser and the German Enlightenment* (1986); K. Tribe, *Governing Economy: The Reformation of German Economic Discourse, 1750–1840* (1988); J. A. Vann, *The Making of a State: Württemberg, 1593–1793* (1984); C. W. Ingrao, *The Hessian Mercenary State under Frederick II, 1760–85* (1987); and 'The problem of enlightenment and absolutism in the German states', *Journal of Modern History*, 58 (1986); T. C. W. Blanning, *Reform and Revolution in Mainz, 1743–1803* (1974); G. Parry, 'Enlightened government and its critics in eighteenth-century Germany', *Historical Journal*, 6 (1963).

18. The Big Three and Scandinavia

A general view of problems of government is J. H. Shennan, *Liberty and Order in Early Modern Europe: The Subject and the State, 1650–1800* (1986); and M. Raeff, *Well-Ordered Police State* (1983); H. E. Strakosch, *State Absolutism and the Rule of Law* (1967); D. Beales and G. Best, eds., *History, Society and the Churches* (1985); J. Vann Horn Melton, *Absolutism and the Eighteenth-Century Origins of Compulsory Schooling in Prussia and Austria* (1988). On Frederick the Great, the model enlightened absolutist, see Ritter, *Frederick the Great* (Chapter 15 above); C. Duffy, *Frederick the Great, A Military Life* (1985); D. B. Horn, *Frederick the Great and the Rise of Prussia* (1964). More specialized studies are W. Hubatsch, *Frederick the Great: Absolutism and Administration* (1975); Duffy, *Army of Frederick* (Chapter 15 above); Rosenberg, *Bureaucracy* (Chapter 15 above); H. Weill, *Frederick the Great and S. Cocceji, 1745–1755* (1961); H. C. Johnson, *Frederick the Great and his Officials* (1975); W. L. Dorn, 'The Prussian bureaucracy in the eighteenth century', *Political Science Quarterly*, 46 and 47 (1931, 1932). On the reforms of the ruling trio in Austria, Maria Theresa, Joseph II and Kaunitz, see Wangermann, *Austrian Achievement* (Chapter 14 above); C. Ingrao, *The Hapsburg Monarchy 1618–1815*

(1994); Szabo, *Kaunitz* (Chapter 15 above); D. Beales, *Joseph II*, vol. I: *In the Shadow of Maria Teresa, 1741–1780* (1987); T. C. W. Blanning, *Joseph II and Enlightened Despotism* (1970); P. G. M. Dickson, *Finance and Government under Maria Theresa, 1740–1780* (1987); R. J. Kerner, *Bohemia in the Eighteenth Century* (1932); Link, *Austrian Peasantry* (Chapter 11 above): Duffy, *Army* (Chapter 14 above). The best survey of Russia under Catherine the Great is I. de Madariaga, *Russia in the Age of Catherine the Great* (1981). Specific studies are Duffy, *Russia's Military Way* (Chapter 15 above); P. Dukes, *Catherine the Great and the Russian Nobility* (1967); R. Jones, *The Emancipation of the Russian Nobility, 1762–1785* (1985) and *Provincial Development in Russia: Catherine II and Jacob Sievers* (1984); P. Ransel, *The Politics of Catherinian Russia: The Panin Party* (1975); J. T. Alexander, *Autocratic Politics in a National Crisis: The Imperial Russian Government and Pugachev's Revolt* (1963); articles by Madariaga are 'Catherine II and the serfs', *Slavonic and East European Review*, 52 (1974), and 'The foundation of the Russian educational system', *ibid.*, 57 (1979); G. Freeze, *The Russian Levites: Parish Clergy in the Eighteenth Century* (1977); J. P. Le Donne, *Ruling Russia: Politics and Administration in the Age of Absolutism* (1984). For the development of the eastern question and the partitions of Poland, see A. W. Fisher, *The Russian Annexation of the Crimea, 1772–1783* (1970); M. S. Anderson, 'The Great Powers and the Russian annexation of the Crimea', *Slavonic and East European Review*, 37 (1958–9); I. de Madariaga, 'The Secret Austro-Russian treaty of 1781', *ibid.*, 38 (1959–60); K. A. Roider, 'Kaunitz, Joseph II and the Turkish war, 1787–1792', *ibid.*, 54 (1976); P. P. Bernard, *Joseph II and Bavaria* (1985); A. Sorel, *The Eastern Question in the Eighteenth Century* (1898); D. Stone, *Polish Politics and National Reform* (1973); P. H. Lord, *The Second Partition of Poland* (1915). On the Baltic area, see C. Bjørn, 'The peasantry and agrarian reform in Denmark', *Scandinavian Economic Review*, 25 (1977); and Scott, *Enlightened Absolutism* (Chapter 17 above); T. Munck, 'The Danish Reformers'. On Sweden, see H.A. Barton, *Scandinavia in the Revolutionary Era, 1760–1815* (1986); and 'Gustav III and the Enlightenment', *Eighteenth-Century Studies*, 6 (1972–3); 'Gustav III of Sweden and the east Baltic question, 1771–1792', *Baltic Studies*, 7 (1976); R. J. Misunias, 'The Baltic question after Nystad', *Baltic History*, (1974).

19. Alternative Models

For the United Provinces, the basic survey is Israel, *Dutch Republic* (Chapter 4 above). Jacob and Mijnhardt, *The Dutch Republic in the Eighteenth Century*, includes the following: E. H. Kossman, 'The Dutch Republic in the eighteenth century'; J. A. F. de Jongste, 'The restoration of the Orangist regime in 1747'; W. P. de Brake, 'Provincial histories and national revolution'; N. C. F. van Sas, 'Patriot Revolution'; J. G. A. Pocock, 'The Dutch republican tradition'; W. W. Mijnhardt, 'The Dutch Enlightenment'; M. C. Jacob, 'Radicalism in the Dutch Enlightenment'. See also S. Schama, *Patriots and Liberators: Revolution in the Netherlands, 1780–1813* (1977); Wilson, *Anglo-Dutch Commerce* (Chapter 10 above). On Britain and America after 1763, see I. R. Christie, *Wars and Revolutions: Britain 1760–1815* (1982); and *The Crisis of Empire: Great Britain and the American Colonies, 1754–1783* (1984); M. Jensen, *The Founding of a Nation: A History of the American Revolution, 1763–1776* (1968); V. T. Harlow and F. Madden, *British Colonial Developments, 1774–1834* (1953); J. Derry, *British Politics and the American Revolution* (1976); P. Lawson, *George Grenville: A Political Life* (1984); D. M. Clark, *British Opinion and the American Revolution* (1930); P. Mackesy, *The War for America, 1775–1783* (1964); J. E. Bradley, *Popular Politics and the American Revolution in England* (1986); P. D. G. Thomas, 'George III and the

American Revolution', *History,* 70 (1985). For political change in Britain, see H. Butterfield, *George III and the Historians* (1957); L. B. Namier, *England in the Age of the American Revolution* (1961); and *The Structure of Politics at the Accession of George III* (1982); J. A. Cannon, *The Fox–North Coalition: The Crisis of the Constitution* (1969); L. G. Mitchell, *Charles James Fox and the Disintegration of the Whig Party, 1782–1794* (1971); F. O'Gorman, *Edmund Burke: His Political Philosophy* (1973); H. Bowen, *Revenge and Reform: The Indian Problem in British Politics, 1757–1773* (1991); J. Ehrman, *The Younger Pitt: The Years of Acclaim* (1969). For reform and radicalism, see G. Newman, *The Rise of English Nationalism: A Cultural History, 1740–1830* (1987); E. P. Thomson, *The Making of the English Working Class* (1968); G. Rudé, *Wilkes and Liberty* (1962); I. R. Christie, *Wilkes, Wyvill and Reform* (1962); and 'The Yorkshire Association', *Historical Journal,* 3 (1960); J. A. Cannon, *Parliamentary Reform, 1660–1832* (1972); J. Norris, *Shelburne and Reform* (1963); H. Dickinson, *Liberty and Property: Political Ideology in Eighteenth-Century Britain* (1979); D. Dickson, *New Foundations: Ireland, 1660–1800* (1987); R. B. McDowell, *Ireland in the Age of Imperialism and Revolution, 1760–1801* (1979); R. N. Sunter, *Patronage and Politics in Scotland* (1986).

20. The French Time Bomb

There is a stimulating and controversial discussion of the coming of revolution in R. R. Palmer, *The Age of Democratic Revolution* (1961). On the mounting political dysfunction in France after 1763, see P. M. Jones, *Reform and Revolution in France* (1995); J. Hardman, *French Politics, 1774–1789: From the Accession of Louis XVI to the Fall of the Bastille* (1995); Nogaret, *French Nobility* (Chapter 12 above); Carey, *Judicial Reform in France* (Chapter 12 above); J. F. Bosher, *French Finances, 1770–1795* (1970); Matthews, *Royal General Farms* (Chapter 12 above); W. Doyle, *The Origins of the French Revolution* (1980); also 'Was there an aristocratic reaction in pre-revolutionary France?' *Past and Present,* 26 (1963); 'The parlements of France and the breakdown of the old regime', *French Historical Studies,* 6 (1969–70); 'The price of offices in pre-revolutionary France', *Historical Journal,* 27 (1984); D. Echeverria, *The Maupeou Revolution* (1985); J. K. Godechot, *France and the Atlantic Revolution of the 18th Century* (1965); D. Dakin, *Turgot and the Ancien Regime in France* (1939); G. V. Taylor, 'Types of capitalism in eighteenth-century France', *English Historical Review,* 79 (1964); 'Non-capitalist wealth and the origins of the French Revolution', *American Historical Review,* 72 (1967); R. Forster, 'The provincial noble: a reappraisal', *ibid.,* 68 (1963); R. D. Harris, *Necker: Reform Statesman of the Ancien Regime* (1979). On the impact of ideas, see Chisick, *Limits of Reform* (Chapter 16 above); Darnton, *Mesmerism* (Chapter 16 above); N. Hampson, *Will and Circumstance: Montesquieu, Rousseau and the French Revolution* (1983); V. R. Gruder, 'A mutation in elite political culture: the French notables and the defence of property and participation', *Journal of Modern History,* 56 (1984); J. R. Censer and J. D. Popkin, eds., *Press and Politics in Pre-revolutionary France* (1987). On the American war, see J. R. Dull, *The Diplomatic History of the American Revolution* (1985); and *The French Navy and American Independence* (1975); T. 'The army in the French Enlightenment: reform, reaction and revolution', *Past and Present,* 85 (1975); R. B. Morris, *The Peacemakers: The Great Powers and the American Revolution* (1965); E. S. Cornin, 'The French objective in the American Revolution', *American Historical Review,* 21 (1916); I. de Madariaga, *Britain, Russia and the Armed Neutrality of 1780* (1962). On the final crisis in France, see M. Price, *Preserving the Monarchy: The Comte de Vergennes, 1774–1787* (1993); W. Doyle, *The Parlement of Bordeaux and the End of the Ancien Regime, 1771–1790* (1974);

G. Rudé, *Paris and London in the Eighteenth Century: Studies in Popular Protest* (1970); J. Egret, *The French Pre-revolution, 1787–1788* (1978); G. Taylor, 'Revolutionary and non-revolutionary material in the *cahiers* of 1789', *French Historical Studies,* 7 (1971–2); L. B. Stone, 'Robe against Sword: the *parlement* of Paris and the French aristocracy, 1774–1790', *ibid.,* 9 (1975–6); Behrens, 'Nobles, privileges and taxes' (Chapter 11 above); C. J. Cavanagh, 'Nobles, privileges and taxes in France: a revision reviewed', *French Historical Studies,* 8 (1973–4).

Index

England (from 1707 Great Britain, *see also*
England (from 1707 Great Britain, see also
    English Revolution), 26, 33, 40–1,
    91–109, 142–54, 193, 195–6, 197–202,
    204, 210–12, 215–21, 223–7, 231,
    232–39, 243, 244–6, 264–5, 267–74,
    278–86, 289, 318, 328, 334, 339,
    343–57, 364
  anti-popery in, 92–4, 107, 145–9, 243,
    289–90, 344, 355–6
  army in, 64–5, 108, 144–7, 148–9, 197,
    272–3, 350
  arts and culture in, 210, 211–12, 214–18
  central administration of, 95–6, 142–3,
    244–5, 278–9, 289–90, 343–6,
    348–9, 352–6
  economy of, 7–10, 97, 219–29, 223–4,
    226–7, 231, 282–3, 343–5, 353, 356
  foreign and imperial policy with, 65, 108,
    143, 151, 195–6, 200, 202, 223–4,
    226–7, 246, 267–8, 273–4, 278–80,
    282–6, 343–4, 348–9, 356
    American colonies, 224, 273, 278–80,
      282–3, 334, 341, 347, 348–53
    Austrian Habsburgs, 271–2, 279–80
    Brandenburg–Prussia, 281, 283, 356
    France, 145–7, 150, 154, 195–6,
      200–2, 226–7, 243–4, 264, 266,
      273–4, 279–80, 283–4, 348–9,
      351–2, 356–7
    Hanover, 151, 154–5, 202, 204, 215,
      227, 243–6, 265, 279–80, 283,
      345
    Russia, 204, 244, 265, 279–80, 356
    Spain, 91–4, 226–7, 246, 266–8, 273,
      283, 348, 356
    Sweden, 195, 204, 265
    United Provinces, 64, 92–3, 105, 144,
      195–7, 200–1, 279, 339–41, 356
  Jacobitism in, 152, 200, 244–5, 264,
    272–4, 345
  landownership in, 10–11, 26–7, 92, 107,
    143, 151–2, 220, 226, 231, 233,
    343–5
  legal system in, 92–3, 94, 96, 147–8,
    233–4, 356–7
  local administration of, 22, 26–7, 51,
    94–7, 100, 106, 143–4, 147–8,
    211–12, 233–4, 289–90, 355–6
  national identity in, 243, 344, 357
  navy of, 64–5, 96, 108, 143–4, 151,
    195–7, 201, 204, 225–7, 265–7,
    273–4, 279, 283–4, 350
  newspapers and press in, 218, 282–3, 344,
    357
  nobility and gentry of, 91, 97, 107, 142–3,
    149–51, 154, 216, 226–7, 234–6,
    245, 342–3, 345, 354–6

  oppositions in, 93–8, 108, 146–8, 149,
    151–2, 244–6, 273, 278–9, 344,
    346–7, 355–6
  overseas trade of 151–2, 199–202, 218,
    224, 226, 238, 245–6, 268, 275,
    282–4, 343–4, 348, 353–4, 355–6
  parliaments in, 22–3, 92–6, 98–106,
    142–6, 147, 153–5, 198, 200, 223–4,
    226, 233, 237, 243, 244–6, 268,
    273, 343–50, 352–6, 364
  political parties in, 146, 154–5, 243–4,
    345–6, 348, 352–4
    Tory party, 147, 151, 152–5, 244–6,
      283, 345–6
    Whig party, 146–8, 149, 151–5, 243–6,
      278, 283, 343, 344–8, 352–9, 356
  public finances of, 10, 11, 92–6, 101–2,
    143–4, 144, 147–8, 150–2, 198,
    204, 223, 227, 235, 244–6, 273,
    278, 283, 343, 347, 348–9, 355–6
  public opinion in, 265–6, 271–2,
    278–9, 282, 343–7, 351, 353–6
  religion in, 35–6, 107–8, 142–5, 147,
    150–2, 210–12, 217, 243, 245, 289,
    318–19, 355–6
    Church of England, 91, 94–7, 99, 101,
      103, 105, 107–8, 142–4, 146–8,
      150–1, 217, 234, 244, 245–6
    established clergy, 92, 143–4, 148–9,
      152–3, 211–12, 244–5
    dissenting religion in, 91–3, 96–7, 103,
      107–8, 143–8, 150–2, 217, 227,
      244, 246, 289–90, 347, 355–6
    Revolution of 1688 in, 147–50, 162, 197,
      243, 351, 354, 379
    royal Court in, 92–4, 151–2, 214–16, 244,
      283, 345–8, 354–5
    urban communities in, 91, 142, 147,
      237–8, 343–5, 352
      City of London in, 96, 99–100, 145–7,
        338–9, 343, 347
England English Revolution
  collapse of, 106–8
  first civil war, 100–3
  Ireland in, 100, 102, 105
  New Model Army in, 102–8
  Oliver Cromwell in, 65, 102–8
  origins of, 19–20, 64, 97–100
  radical movements in, 100, 103–6, 108
  regicide and republic in, 64, 104–6, 108,
    142
  religious issues in, 99, 101–3, 105–8
  Scotland in, 97–9, 102–4
Enlightened absolutism/despotism, 218, 241,
  282–306, 307–28, 334–8, 372
  and the churches, 295–7, 299, 301, 306,
    311–12, 322–3, 361